HERVÉ RYSSEN

HISTORY of ANTISEMITISM
set straight by a goy

Hervé Ryssen

Hervé Ryssen (France) is a historian and an exhaustive researcher of the Jewish intellectual world. He is the author of twelve books and several video documentaries on the Jewish question. In 2005, he published *Planetary Hopes*, a book in which he demonstrates the religious origins of the globalist project. *Psychoanalysis of Judaism*, published in 2006, shows how intellectual Judaism displays all the symptoms of hysterical pathology. There is no "divine choice", but the manifestation of a disorder that has its origins in the practice of incest. Freud had patiently studied this question on the basis of what he observed in his own community.

France is home to one of the largest Jewish communities in the Diaspora, with a very intense cultural and intellectual life. Hervé Ryssen has been able to develop his extensive work on the basis of numerous historical and contemporary sources, both international and French.

History of anti-Semitism
set straight by a goy

Histoire de l'antisémitisme : vue par un goy et remise à l'endroit,
Levallois-Perret, Baskerville, 2010.

Translated and Published by
Omnia Veritas Limited

www.omnia-veritas.com

© Omnia Veritas Limited - Hervé Ryssen - 2023

All rights reserved. No part of this work may be reproduced in any form without the prior written permission of the *copyright* holders. Infringement of these rights may constitute a copyright offence.

I. The Flight from Egypt 15

II. Amalek 17

III. The Philistines 18

IV. Nebuchadnezzar 19

V. The encounter with the Greeks 20

VI. Antiochus IV Epiphanes 24

VII. The Roman Conquest of Judea 28

VIII. Cicero 30

IX. Caesar, Cleopatra and Mark Antony 32

X. Herodo 34

XI. Tiberius, Sejanus and Pontius Pilate 35

XII. August '38: the Alexandria pogrom 38

XIII. Claudius 42

XIV. The revolt of 66 44

XV. Titus and the Destruction of the Temple 47

XVI. Domitian and the fiscus judaicus 52

XVII. Trajan 52

XVIII. Hadrian and the Siege of Betar 56

XIX. The Dynasty of the Severi 60

XX. The Christian Emperors 63

XXI. The Fathers of the Church 66

XXII. The End of the Western Roman Empire 70

XXIII. Emperor Peroz I 74

XXIV. The Weakness of Theodoric the Great 75

XXV. Zeno, the Byzantine Emperor 76

XXVI. Legislation and the Church 76

XXVII. The Justinian Code 82

XXVIII. Gregory I (590-604) 84

XXIX. Jerusalem, 614 86

XXX. Visigothic Spain I 88

XXXI. King Dagobert I 91

XXXII. Muhammad 92

XXXIII. Visigoth Spain II 95

XXXIV. Agobardo of Lyon and Amolon 101

XXXV. The trade kings in the East 107

XXXVI. Granada, 30 December 1066 109

XXXVII. Gregory VII 111

XXXVIII. The First Crusade 112

XXXIX. St Bernard 115

XL. The Second Crusade 117

XLI. The Almohads 122

Toledo, 1180 123

XLIII. Philip Augustus 125

XLIV. The Coronation of Richard the Lion-Hearted 129

XLV. In the East 132

XLVI. Innocent III 134

XLVII. Nicholas Donin and the Talmud 140

XLVIII. 1240: the expulsion from Brittany 148

XLIX. Louis IX, Saint Louis 150

L. St. Thomas Aquinas 155

LI. Pablo Christiani and the Barcelona dispute 157

LII. In Central Europe 160

LIII. Pointed Hats and Ritual Crimes 161

LIV. Nicholas IV, Turbato corde, 1288 163

LV. Edward I and the expulsion from England, 1290 164

LVI. In Persia, March 1291 167

LVII. Rindfleisch of Rættingen, 1298 168

LVIII. Philip IV the Fair 169

LIX. 1320: The Shepherds' Crusade 172

LX. 1328: The Navarrese revolt 176

LXI. Spain, prey to the Jews 176

LXII. The German Judenschlaeger, 1336-1338 181

LXIII. 1348. 1348: The Black Death 183

LXIV. The Late Awakening of John the Good 188

LXV. The Death of Blanca de Borbón 191

LXVI. Beltrán Duguesclín and the White Company 198

LXVII. May 1370: the wafers of Enghien 208

LXVIII. The funeral of Charles V of France 208

LXIX. The general uprising of 1391 in Spain 211

LXX. 1394: the expulsion from France 217

LXXII. Paul of St Mary 224

LXXIII. Vincent Ferrer 227

LXXIV. Hieronymus of Santa Fe and the dispute of Tortosa 229

LXXV. Martin V 233

LXXVI. The Hussites and the Council of Basle 234

LXXVII. 1449: The Statutes of Blood Cleansing in Spain 237

LXXVIII. John of Capistrano, the Scourge of the Hebrews 239

LXXIX. Alfonso de Espina 246

LXXX. Bernardino de Feltre 249

LXXXI. Torquemada against the Marranos 254

LXXXII. 1492: The Expulsion of the Jews from Spain 260

LXXXIII. 1497: the expulsion from Portugal 265

LXXXIV. Savonarola and the expulsion from Florence 267

LXXXV. The Sephardic Diaspora 267

LXXXVI. The Ashkenazi expelled from Germany 270

LXXXVII. 1501: The Expulsion from Provence 273

LXXXVIII. Lisbon, 1506 275

LXXXIX. Johannes Pfefferkorn vs Johannes Reuchlin 276

CX. Albert of Brandenburg 280

XCI. The Jewish origins of the Protestant Reformation 281

XCII. Martin Luther 286

XCIII. Julius III and the Talmud 290

XCIV. Paul IV, Cum nimis absurdum, 14 July 1555. 292

XCV. Ivan the Terrible 295

XCVI. St. Pius V 296

XCVII. The Synagogue, "blind and obstinate", 1593 299

XCVIII. The war of Vincent Fettmilch 302

XCIX. France, 1615-1617 304

C. Uriel and Vicente da Costa 308

CI. Back in liberated Spain 311

CII. Bogdán Jmelnitski, 1648 313

CIII. William Prynne, 1656 315

CIV. The expulsion of Austria, 1670 317

CV. Madrid, 30 June 1680 319

CVI. Johann Andreas Eisenmenger 321

CVII. The Jews of Rome under surveillance 324

CVIII. The Jew Süss, 4 February 1738 324

CIX. Frederick II and Empress Maria Theresa 326

CX. Benedict XIV, 1751 327

CXI. The Jews in the "Age of Enlightenment" 330

CXII. The Jews in France in the 18th century 331

CXIII. Louis XVI 333

CXIV. François Hell 334

CXV. The Revolution and the Empire (1789-1815) 336

CXVI. The Bourbon Restoration in France (1815-1830) 340

CXVII. Germany, 1814-1819 343

CXVIII. The Rothschild era 347

CXIX. France: the anti-Semitic scare 351

CXX. The policy of interference in Romania 355

CXXI. Jewish criminality in Germany 359

CXXII. Austria-Hungary under the Jewish Boot 369
CXXIII. La Civiltá Cattolica, 1870-1903 375
CXXIV. German Anti-Judaism in the 19th century 379
CXXV. The Anti-Jewish Counteroffensive in France 387
CXXVI. Austria-Hungary at the end of the 19th century 398
CXXVII. The Fall of Tsarist Russia 403
CXXVIII. Jewish Messianism 414
ANNEX I 427
Other titles 441

Translation Alejo Domínguez Rellán

The history of Judaism is that of a people—or a sect—at permanent war against the rest of humanity. At all times and in all places, Jews have given rise to anti-Semitism. The script always unfolds in the same way: after the violence and settling of scores, the *goyim* (non-Jews) legislate to try to curb the phenomenon and eventually expel the undesirables. But inevitably, after a certain period of time, the undesirables manage to re-enter the square, corrupt the kings and lords, and resume their trafficking and intrigues, without having learned anything from their past mistakes. This story has been repeating itself for nearly three thousand years.

The Jews, for their part, are constantly trying to give the world the image of a community persecuted for no reason. From the departure from Egypt to Auschwitz, from the destruction of the Temple to the Cossack pogroms, from the massacres committed by the Crusaders to the bonfires of the Inquisition, their history is a succession of dramas. To explain this phenomenon, Jewish intellectuals come up with all sorts of theories, more or less convoluted, and end up claiming that the history of the Jewish "people" is a "mystery", an extraordinary "enigma", a fabulous, even cosmic destiny. Most of the time they add or imply that they might be "God's chosen people". But when the matter is examined more closely, the problem is actually much simpler. In any case, after reading this book, we trust that no one will speak of "Judeo-Christian" civilisation any more.

I. Flight from Egypt

The first known manifestation of hostility towards the Jews was recounted in Exodus, the second book of the Torah (the Bible, the Old Testament). The Hebrews, we are told, rushed out of Egypt led by Moses and headed for the "Promised Land" where they arrived after wandering for forty years in the wilderness of Sinai.

Originally, a few centuries earlier, the Jews had been called to Egypt by Joseph (*Yosef*), the favourite son of Jacob (*Ya'akov*) who had been sold into slavery by his brothers. In Egypt (*Mitzrayim*), according to legend, Joseph had prospered, succeeded in gaining prominence and the trust of Pharaoh, and was eventually appointed viceroy. The country and the whole region went through a period of plenty and then a period of drought and famine, just as Joseph had foreseen. He hoarded the Egyptians' livestock: "Joseph said, 'Give me your livestock, and I will give you food in exchange for your livestock' (Genesis, XLVII, 16[1])" (Genesis, XLVII, 16). The following year, he acquired for Pharaoh all the land of Egypt: "So Yosef acquired all the land of Mitzrayim for Pharaoh, for the Mitzrayimim (the Egyptians) sold their land to Pharaoh, because the famine weighed upon them so severely. So the land became Pharaoh's property." Under Joseph's rule, the inhabitants were reduced to "slavery city by city, from one end of the land of Mitzrayim to the other" (Genesis, XLVII, 20).

In the meantime, Joseph had opened the gates of Egypt to his father and his Hebrew brothers, granting them the best lands: "Yosef found a place for his father and brothers, and gave them property in the land of Mitzrayim, in the best region of the country, in the land of Ramses" (Genesis, XLVII, 11). Within a few years, the Hebrews multiplied in the country and became considerably richer, as can be read in the Torah: "The sons of Yisra'el were fruitful, increased abundantly, multiplied and grew mightily; the land was filled with them" (Exodus I, 7). (Exodus I, 7).

The Egyptians were freed from their rule by a new Pharaoh who had never known Joseph (probably Seti I or Ramses II, in the 13th century BC). The Pharaoh ordered that newborn males be "thrown into the river". In addition, the Jews were forced to work with their hands: "They made them work relentlessly, making their lives bitter with burdensome labour— making clay, making bricks and all kinds of field work." (Exodus I, 13).

It was at that moment that the figure of Moses (*Moshe*) appeared. After his birth, his mother, fearing that the Egyptians would assassinate him, placed the newborn in a basket and abandoned him in the river. The child,

---

[1]Kadosh Israelite Messianic Bible; all translations at www.Bibliatodo.com. Translator's Note, NdT

according to Jewish legend, was picked up on the bank of the river by Pharaoh's daughter who was bathing there and decided to adopt him.

It was Moses who later negotiated the liberation of his "people". He forced Pharaoh to let the Hebrews out of Egypt by invoking a series of "plagues" that ravaged the country: bloody water, invasion of frogs, mosquitoes, horseflies, plague, rashes, locusts, etc. But each time the Pharaoh refused to let the Hebrews leave Egypt. The tenth "plague" was to exterminate all the firstborn of the Egyptians.

In the meantime, the Israelites stripped the natives of their most precious possessions. Moses thus followed Yahweh's will: "Now tell the people that every man shall ask his neighbour for jewels of gold and silver, and every woman her neighbour for jewels of gold and silver" (Exodus XI, 2). (Exodus XI, 2). "The sons of Yisra'el had done as Moshe had said—they had asked the Mitzrayimim to give them jewels of gold and silver; and Yahweh had turned the Mitzrayim so favourably disposed towards the sons of Yisra'el that they gave them what they had asked for. Thus they plundered the Mitzrayimim" (Exodus XII, 35).

In the middle of the night, there was a great outcry when the Egyptians realised the death of their sons. Pharaoh immediately went to Moses and authorised him to leave Egypt with the Hebrews, taking with them all the treasures stolen from the Egyptians. According to legend, the Jews' stay in Egypt would have lasted four hundred years.

The Hebrews set out for the land of Canaan, in order to take possession of it by virtue of the divine promise made to their ancestors. However, according to legend, Pharaoh changed his mind after their departure and sent his soldiers in pursuit to bring them back. The Israelites then fled across the Red Sea, which miraculously opened up before them and closed in on their pursuers.

However, the reality is probably very different. When we examine their history, we find in fact that the Jews were always expelled at one time or another from everywhere, from all countries without exception. If the soldiers supposedly pursued them, it was not to bring them back to Egypt, but rather to recover the riches that the Jews had stolen from the Egyptians. In fact, with all that wealth the Hebrews were going to be able to make their Golden Calf in the Sinai desert. As for the Egyptian texts of the time, they mention "the expulsion of a sick people, or of a people with a leprous king[2]". The Jews, indeed, "were regarded by the Egyptians with as much contempt as the Hyksos, their brethren, whom the hieroglyphic texts call the lepers and who are designated as plague and pestilence by some

---

[2] Jacques Attali, *Los judíos, el mundo y el dinero*, Fondo de cultura económica, 2005, Buenos Aires p. 29.

inscriptions³."

In short, all the ingredients that make up the long Jewish history were already present at that time⁴.

II. *Amalek*

In the wilderness of Sinai, the Jews had to fight the Amalekites, a nomadic people who lived between the Red Sea and the Dead Sea. The Israelites were barely out of the Red Sea when the Amalekites attacked them. Moses, standing on the top of the mountain, invoked Yahweh and raised his hands to heaven, while Joshua (*Yehoshua*) won the battle and triumphed for the first time over "Amalek", who would later generically symbolise the eternal hereditary enemy of the Jews, generation after generation.

We then see the Amalekites alongside the Moabites, fought by Ehud (*Ehud*) (Judges III, 13) and the Midianites, in turn fought by Gideon (*Gideon*) (Judges VI, 3).

Around 1050 BC, Saul (*Shaul*), the first king of the Israelites in the Land of Canaan, heard the prophet Samuel order him to wage a war of extermination against "Amalek". Saul then called all his soldiers to arms and began a dangerous war against King Agag. The Lord said to Samuel (*Shemuel*) (Samuel XV, 3–18): "Now go and attack Amalek, and utterly destroy all that they have. Do not spare them, but kill men and women, children and infants, cattle and sheep, camels and asses. Go and utterly destroy, you shall slay the sinners against me, even the Amalekites, and continue to make war against them until they are utterly exterminated." The prophet Samuel had given his instructions: there was to remain of Amalek "no vestige and no remembrance".

Saul then marched against the Amalekites, defeated them from Havilah, near the mouth of the Euphrates, as far south as the Red Sea, and then advanced towards his capital. This supposedly took place in 1053 BC. He took possession of the cities, killed men, women and children. He captured Agag, king of the Amalekites, cut the throats of all his people, but kept for

---

³Inscription of Aahmes, chief of the boatmen, quoted by Ledrain, *Histoire du peuple d'Israel*, I, p. 53, in Bernard Lazare, *L'Antisémitisme, sa histoire et ses causes*, (1894). Editions La Bastille, digital edition, 2011, p. 15. ["For their part, the Romans were not particularly eager to assimilate the Jews, whom some pamphlets described as "dirty", "savages", "cowards", "lepers", "child sacrificers"", in Jacques Attali, *Los judíos, el mundo y el dinero*, Fondo de cultura económica, 2005, Buenos Aires, p. 82].

⁴ "Is Moses the fruit of incest?" This is the question asked by a Jewish intellectual, Gilles Dorival, in an article in 2005 (Leuven University Press, p. 97–108). Read it in the last chapter of this book. And more in detail in *Psychoanalysis of Judaism*.

himself the best animals and possessions, in violation of Yahweh's express command.

At the news, Samuel was angered by Saul's disobedience and announced that a new king would be anointed to replace him. Samuel said to Saul, "I will not return with you, for you have rejected the word of Yahweh, and Yahweh will reject you as king over Yisra'el." Samuel asked for King Agag who lay in chains to be brought to him and ordered the king of Amalek to be quartered (Samuel XV, 26, 32–33). Samuel remained on the throne, despite being virtually deposed by Yahweh[5].

III. The Philistines

Around 1020 BC, King Saul marched to war against the Philistines. The Battle of Mount Gilboa took place in 1007 BC. The Philistines came into the plain with their cavalry and chariots, so the Israelites had to take refuge in the Gilboa Mountains where the Philistines chased them and tore them to pieces. Three of Saul's sons died, and Saul himself, finding himself suddenly cut off, killed himself with his own sword. The victory of the Philistines was complete. After resting for the night, the Philistines scoured the battlefield and stripped the dead of their clothes and weapons. In the midst of the corpses, they found the bodies of King Saul and his sons and sent their heads and weapons back to their country as trophies. They hung the decapitated bodies of Saul and his son Jonathan on the walls of Beit She'an. In memory of this victory, Saul's skull was preserved in a temple of the god Dagon, and his armour in a temple of the goddess Astarte (Ishtar-

---

[5]The God Yahweh is one of the gods, one god among many. The Hebrews have recorded a covenant between them and a God called Yahweh, first through Abraham and later confirmed by Moses (*Exodus III, 15*). Yahweh is an ethnic god. Nowhere is Yahweh presented as the only existing God. If the Hebrew people are faithful to the covenant with Yahweh, Yahweh will be faithful to his people and will favour them above all other peoples. To lead his people to victory, Yahweh leads the armies of his people and is merciless towards his enemies. In the Bible he is often referred to as "Yahweh of hosts". This form of religion, which belongs to polytheism, was very common in the Middle East. It can be called "*Monolatry*", i.e. the worship of a particular national god above all other gods, and has nothing to do with the dogma that there is only one God (*monotheism*). The wars of Yahweh and his people against the other peoples of the region (all Semites like the Hebrews, by the way) and their gods are notorious: war against the god Dagon (Amorites and Philistines), against the god Chemosh (Moabites and Ammonites), against the god Asshur (Assyrians), against the god Marduk (Babylonians), and so on. All these peoples and gods coexisted in the region, sometimes at war with each other, sometimes amicably establishing alliances, as with the god Baal of the Phoenicians. Yahweh is also often accompanied by a female deity, the famous Babylonian Ishtar who shared a marriage with many other gods. (NdT).

Astoreth). The Philistines then captured the cities in the valley of Jezreel and in the eastern Jordan region.

The Israelite state was later re-established by King David, Saul's successor. David had entered the court in Saul's service, marrying his daughter Michal. His fame as a hero grew with each battle he fought alongside his king, until Saul became jealous of his successes. The king went so far as to decree his death. David fled and went underground, gathering all the discontents around him. Saul's defeat at Gilboa enabled him to be crowned king in Hebron by the chiefs of the Judean clans. His numerous victories in the West against the Philistines, in the South against the Edomites, against the Moabites and Ammonites beyond the Jordan River, and in the North against the Arameans, made David the great king of Israel. According to legend, his son Solomon succeeded him, although King Solomon's name does not appear in any Middle Eastern archaeological document and the splendour of the kingdom must have been very relative[6]. After his death, the Jews were divided. Ten tribes founded the northern kingdom of Israel, which was destroyed and subdued in 722 by the Assyrians. In the south, the tribes of Benjamin and Juda formed the kingdom of Judah, with Jerusalem as its capital.

IV. Nebuchadnezzar

In September 605 BC, Nebuchadnezzar II was crowned king of Babylon. His main concern at the time was the struggle against the Egyptians who dominated the Middle East and threatened his western frontiers. A few months before his coronation, Nebuchadnezzar had defeated the Egyptians at the Euphrates and driven them out of Palestine and Syria. In the same year he entered Jerusalem, capital of the kingdom of Judah. But the kingdom proved to be insubordinate, the fate of the northern kingdom not having been chastened. The Babylonians occupied Jerusalem twice, in -597 and -586, after a long siege. In that fateful year the Jewish Temple was destroyed and part of the population deported to Mesopotamia.

The Judean Jews exiled in Babylon were nevertheless treated with great meekness by the Babylonian ruler. The celebrated Jewish historian

---

[6] The biblical Judaism (Torah) of Abraham, Isaac, Jacob, Moses, and the later kingdoms of Israel and Judah are legendary accounts largely refuted by modern historical criticism and research (see in Norman Finkielstein, Neil Asher Silberman, *The Bible Unearthed, A New Archaeological Vision of Ancient Israel and the Origins of its Sacred Texts* (2001), Siglo XXI, Madrid, 2003). (NdT).

Heinrich Graetz wrote in his monumental *History of the Jews*[7]: "The conquered people, forcibly removed from their own homes, were transplanted to this new city, while many Judean captives were given homes in the capital itself, those who had freely accepted Nebuchadnezzar's rule being particularly favoured. Indeed, so generous was his treatment that whole families and communities from the cities of Judah and Benjamin, with their relatives and their slaves, were privileged to remain together. They were free and their rights and customs were respected."

"Most likely, the exiles received land and housing in exchange for the land and housing they had lost in their own country. The land distributed among them was cultivated either by themselves or by their servants. They owned not only slaves, but also horses, mules, camels and donkeys. As long as they paid the tax on their land and perhaps also a suffrage tax, and obeyed the king's laws, they were allowed to enjoy their independence." After Nebuchadnezzar's death in 561, under the reign of his son, their condition was still more favourable. Among the young men employed at his court were Jews who served as eunuchs. Heinrich Graetz wrote: "Jewish youths from the royal house of David were at his court as eunuchs. How often these guardians of the harem, these servants of their lord's whims, became in turn masters of their lord[8]."

Around -550, the Persians took possession of the Babylonian Empire and in -536 their ruler Cyrus the Great authorised the exiled Jews to return to their homeland where they immediately began the reconstruction of the Temple which they completed in -515[9].

V. *The encounter with the Greeks*

From the 4th century BC onwards, the Persian empire was reeling under

---

[7] Heinrich Graetz, *Geschitchte der Juden* (*History of the Jews*), eleven volumes published in German between 1853 and 1875. Heinrich Graetz, *History of the Jews*, Philadelphia, The Jewish Publication Society of America, 1891. Heinrich Graetz, born Tzvi Hirsch Graetz (1817–1891), was a prominent Prussian Jewish historian and theologian. He was one of the first to write a comprehensive history of the Jewish people from a Jewish perspective. His magnum opus, *History of the Jews*, was translated into other languages and aroused interest in Jewish history throughout the world. In 1869, the University of Wroclaw awarded him the title of honorary professor and in 1888 he was made an honorary member of the Spanish Royal Academy of Sciences. (NdT).

[8] Heinrich Graetz, *History of the Jews I*, Philadelphia, The Jewish Publication Society of America, 1891, p. 330–331.

[9] The story of the Jewess Esther and King Ahasuerus (Xerxes I) is told in *The Mirror of Judaism*.

the thrust of Greek imperialism. In -338, a young, fair-haired European prince named Alexander defeated the Theban troops and began a prodigious career that would take him the following years to the ends of the known world in Asia.

The city of Alexandria, founded on the Egyptian coast in 332, had become the focus of Hellenic culture and a major centre of international trade. Alexander had encouraged the settlement of Jews there, as well as in other imperial cities, so that the city had become a cosmopolitan polis. By the 3rd century BC, a large Jewish community had settled in the city, provoking some defensive reactions from the rest of the inhabitants.

The earliest anti-Jewish writings that have come down to us are the work of Greek scholars from Alexandria. Hecataeus of Abdera, a Greek historian who lived in Egypt at the beginning of the third century BC, was the author of a *History of Egypt* which Diodorus of Sicily made extensive use of. Hecataeus of Abdera described Jewish customs as "inhospitable and anti-human". The Jews already seemed to live at that time in opposition to the rest of mankind, at least since Moses: "The sacrifices and customs which he established, wrote Hecataeus of Abdera, were entirely different from those of the other nations; in memory of the exile of his people, [Moses] instituted a way of life contrary to humanity and hospitality".

The Jews' aversion to sit at the table of non-Jews or to marry non-Jews was regarded by all as hostile and insulting behaviour. "They lived apart, in special quarters, withdrew into themselves, lived in isolation, and administered themselves by virtue of privileges of which they were jealous and which excited the envy of those around them," wrote the Jewish historian Bernard Lazare.[10].. "Their reserve in dealing with strangers was seen as hatred of mankind", wrote Heinrich Graetz.

Many were immensely rich: "Moreover, they had obtained a monopoly of navigation on the Nile, the wheat trade and the supply of Alexandria, and their traffic extended to all the provinces of the Mediterranean coast. They thus acquired great wealth," said Bernard Lazare, who also informed us that Jewish scholars were engaged in forging texts for their propaganda. Thus, verses by Aeschylus, Sophocles and Euripides celebrating the one God and the Sabbath were in circulation.

Historians were also falsified: "The most important of these inventions was that of the *Sibylline Oracles*, entirely fabricated by the Alexandrian Jews, and announcing the coming of the kingdom of the one God in future times[11]."

---

[10] Bernard Lazare, *Anti-Semitism, its history and causes*, *(1894)*. Editions La Bastille, digital edition, 2011, p. 16. The ghettos were desired and created by the Jews themselves, read in *The Jewish Mafia* and *The Mirror of Judaism*.

[11] Frag. Hist. Grac. Didot II, 391, according to Diodorus, XL, 3, in Georges Nataf, *Les*

The Jewish literature of that time, *Books I and II of Enoch, Jubilees, Testament of the Twelve Patriarchs, Sibylline Oracles* and others, were permeated with strong apocalyptic accents and full of imprecations against non-Jews: "Cursed be you, Gog, and all the peoples that follow after, and from you, Magog!" Several of these texts, such as the *Sibylline Oracles* or passages from *Enoch I*, were written in Greek and their effect on non-Jewish readers was catastrophic. For, indeed, we find in them the notion of an exclusively Jewish God who conspires with his people to exterminate all other peoples.

But the Greeks, at least the learned, did not really discover Judaism until the publication of the Greek translation of the Torah (Old Testament), known as the Septuagint Bible or Bible of the Seventy (abbreviated LXX), made in Alexandria in the third century BC during the reign of Ptolemy II. The text provoked outrage and angry protests among the learned. Israel's national God (Yahweh) ordered the destruction of the altars of the villages where they lived. And what about all the stories of treachery, rape, revenge, massacre and incest that appeared on page after page of this holy book?

Let us leave the floor on this point to Alphonse Toussenel, a 19th century socialist and disciple of the famous Fourier. His book, *The Jews as kings of the age, a history of financial feudalism,* published in 1845, is rather old, but we find in his introduction an interesting passage on the Old Testament. It reads: "I know not what great things the Jewish people have done, having read their history only in a book where nothing is spoken of but adultery and incest, butchery and savage wars; where every name that is venerated is sullied by infamy; where every great fortune invariably begins with fraud and treachery; where kings, who are called saints, have husbands murdered to steal their wives; where women, who are called saints, enter the beds of enemy generals to cut off their heads. I do not grant the title of a great people to a horde of usurers and lepers, who have been a burden to all mankind from the beginning of the centuries, and who drag their invincible hatred of other peoples and their incorrigible pride all over the globe[12]." The Greeks of Alexandria had been scandalised in the same

---

Sources païennes de l'antisémitisme, Berg International, 2001, p. 55.
[12]Alphonse Toussenel, *Les juifs rois de l'époque, histoire de la féodalité financière,* (1845), Gabriel de Gonet Edit, Paris, 1847, Introduction, p. I-II. [All "readers" of the Bible, whether they be called Jews or Genevans, Dutch, English or Americans, must have found written in their prayer books that God had granted to the servants of his law the monopoly of the exploitation of the globe, for all these mercantile peoples bring to the art of extorting money from mankind the same fervour of religious fanaticism. That is why I understand the persecutions which Romans, Christians and Mohammedans have inflicted on the Jews. The universal revulsion which the Jew inspired for so long was but the just punishment of his implacable pride, and our contempt the legitimate reprisals for the hatred which he seemed to profess for the rest of mankind."

way twenty centuries earlier.

Manetho, the high priest of the Sun god Ra at the temple of Heliopolis, was a Hellenised Egyptian of the 3rd century BC. He was the author of a *History of Egypt* of which only fragments have come down to us and which were quoted centuries later by the Jewish historian Flavius Josephus. Manetho claimed that the exodus of the Jews was not the heroic adventure narrated in the Pentateuch, but the expulsion of a colony of sick and lepers. He presented Moses as an apostate priest from Heliopolis named Osarsef who led a particularly cruel invading people. After arriving in the land of Canaan, "they besieged and burned the cities and villages, plundered the temples and defiled the statues of the gods[13]."

Hecataeus of Abdera had also claimed that the Exodus story was largely imaginary. The Jews had, in reality, been expelled from Egypt *manu militari*: "The natives therefore convinced themselves that if they did not expel the foreigners, they would never be rid of their evils. Immediately, the expulsion took place[14]."

Later, Lysimachus of Alexandria, a Greek scholar who lived at the end of the second century BC, disseminated this literature with perseverance. In his *History of Egypt*, he spoke of the Jews as a people afflicted with leprosy: "A great sterility followed in Egypt", he wrote. Lysimachus was quoted by Flavius Josephus: "When the lepers and the mangy ones had been drowned, the rest were gathered together and left in deserted places to die". Apparently, the Jews did not come to the desert by chance.

The laws they obeyed provoked great indignation. "A certain Moses advised them to take the risk of following a single path until they reached inhabited places; he ordered them to show no kindness to any man, never

---

A. Toussenel, *Les juifs rois de l'époque, histoire de la féodalité financière*. NdT].

[13]Georges Nataf, *Les Sources païennes de l'antisémitisme*, Berg International, 2001, p. 58. [In his work *Against Apion*, the first century historian Flavius Josephus discusses the synchronism between the biblical account of the Exodus of the Israelites from Egypt and two events mentioned by the Egyptian historian Manetho. It is difficult to distinguish between what Manetho actually told and what Josephus or Apion interprets. Josephus identifies the exodus of the Israelites with the first exodus mentioned by Manetho, when some 480,000 "Hyksos shepherd kings" (also designated as shepherds or as kings and as shepherd prisoners in his discussion) leave Egypt for Jerusalem. The mention of the Hyksos identifies this first exodus with the Hyksos period (16th century BC). Apion identifies a second exodus mentioned by Manetho when a renegade, whom the Egyptian priest called Osarsef, led 80,000 lepers in rebellion against Egypt. Manetho apparently combines the events of the Amarna period (in the 14th century BC) and the events of the end of the 19th dynasty (12th century BC). Apion further mixes it with the biblical Exodus and, contrary to Manetho, even alleges that this heretical priest changed the name of Moses. NdT.]

[14]Frag. Hist. Grac. Didot II, 391, according to Diodorus, XL, 3, in Georges Nataf, *Les Sources païennes de l'antisémitisme*, Berg International, 2001, p. 55.

to advise the best but the worst, and to destroy the temples and altars of the gods they found. The others agreed and complied with his advice. They crossed the desert and, after much suffering, came to an inhabited place. They ravaged the inhabitants, plundered and burned the temples, until they came to the country now called Judea, where they built a city and settled. This city was called Hierósila because of their nature. Later, when they were masters of the country, they changed its name to avoid shame and called the city Jerusalem, and themselves Jerusalemites[15]."

Democritus, a Greek historian contemporary of Lysimachus, made the oldest reference to the ritual crimes of the Jews: "Every seven years, they would capture a foreigner, take him to the temple and immolate him by tearing his flesh into small pieces[16]."

VI. Antiochus IV Epiphanes

After the death of Alexander the Great in -323, his generals divided his legacy, and the empire was finally divided. Ptolemy and Seleucus founded two ruling dynasties. The Ptolemies ruled Egypt, Judea and the borders of Syria, while the rest of the empire, including Persia, fell under the control of the Seleucids.

In -198, the Seleucid Antiochus III took control of Judea, but was defeated in -189 by the Roman Republic and its allies at the Battle of Magnesium (or 190 BC), having to pay a colossal indemnity after the Peace of Apamea (188 BC), which led to the progressive decline of the Seleucid Empire and to his successor Antiochus IV increasing the fiscal pressure on Judea.

Greek culture then permeated the entire Mediterranean and the Hellenisation of Judea continued with vigour. The Jews spoke and wrote in Greek. Philo of Alexandria wrote his philosophical treatises in Greek. Countless Greek words found their way into rabbinic literature, and great Jewish priests such as Menelaus and Aristobulus bore Greek names.

Increased taxation set off the Hebraic powder keg. In -169, Antiochus IV, returning from his Egyptian campaign to recruit new troops, decided to crush the Jewish revolt in Jerusalem. He entered the city, suppressed the uprising and desecrated the Temple, entering "by force into the Temple and even into the Holy of Holies, and as a mark of contempt for the God who

---

[15]Flavius Josephus, *Contra Apion*, Editorial Gredos, Madrid, 1994, p. 229-230, and in Georges Nataf, *Les Sources païennes de l'antisémitisme*, Berg International, 2001, p. 60. The account of Lysimachus is also reproduced in Tacitus, *Histories V* 3.
[16]Suidas, C. Müller, *Frag. Hist. Graec.* IV, 377, in Georges Nataf, *Les Sources païennes de l'antisémitisme*, Berg International, 2001, p. 61.

was worshipped there, he removed the golden altar, the candlestick, the table, the golden vessels, and all the treasures that still remained." The Temple was turned into a place of pagan worship. Menelaus, even more favourable to Hellenism than his predecessor, was elevated to the dignity of high priest. After defeating the Jews, Antiochus was nicknamed Epiphanes (the Illustrious).

Heinrich Graetz wrote: "A fable, half hallucination and half lie, inspired by his accomplice Menelaus", a story that was to ridicule Judaism in the eyes of civilised peoples for a long time:

"To palliate both the massacre of innocents and the desecration of the Temple, he invented a falsehood which long afterwards continued to give Judaism a bad name among all civilised nations. Antiochus declared that he had seen in the Holy of Holies the statue of a man with a long beard, riding on a donkey and holding a book. He believed it to be the statue of the lawgiver Moses, who had given the Jews inhuman and horrible laws to separate them from all other peoples. A rumour spread among the Greeks and Romans that Antiochus had found the head of a golden ass in the Temple, which the Judaeans worshipped, and that they therefore worshipped asses."

"Antiochus was probably the author of another infamous calumny invented to discredit the Jews: he was said to have discovered, lying on the bed of the Temple, a Greek, who begged to be released, for the Jews were in the habit of fattening and beheading a Greek every year and feeding on his entrails, swearing at the same time hatred against all Greeks, whom they were determined to destroy." Disgusted, the Jewish historian added: "Whether this vile slander came directly from Antiochus, or whether these fables were attributed to him alone, there can be no doubt that he blackened the reputation of the Jews by spreading the news that Judaism inculcated hatred for all other peoples[17]."

In June -168, Antiochus undertook a second expedition into Egypt, but the Hellenistic army was defeated and forced to beat a retreat back to its capital. Thus, wrote Graetz, "Antiochus, "the Illustrious", returned to his capital. Conscious of his tormenting humiliation... he vented his secret anger in unparalleled cruelties against the Jews. They, he said, had taken pleasure in his humiliation; they had loudly proclaimed that the God they worshipped humiliated the haughty, and had therefore prepared this mortification for him. Apollonius, one of their princely subjects, and former governor of Mysia, entered the Jewish capital, accompanied by fierce troops, apparently with peaceful intentions. Suddenly, however, one

---

[17] Heinrich Graetz, *History of the Jews I*, Philadelphia, The Jewish Publication Society of America, 1891, p. 451, 452.

Sabbath, when resistance was impossible, Greek and Macedonian mercenaries rushed upon the inhabitants, killed men and youths, took women and children prisoner and sent them to the slave markets. Apollonius also destroyed many houses in the capital and demolished the walls of Jerusalem, for he wished it to disappear from the list of important cities... The inhabitants who had not met death escaped, and only the most rabid Hellenists, Syrian soldiers and foreigners remained in the deserted places. Jerusalem became a stranger to her own children[18]."

Posidonius of Apamea, a Stoic philosopher born in Syria (-135 BC, -51 BC), reproached the Jews for their laws "contrary to the sacred laws of hospitality". Here is a passage from his account:

"The majority of Antiochus' friends were of the opinion that the city should be seized by force and the Jewish race annihilated completely, for of all nations it was the only one to refuse to live in society with other peoples, for they regarded them all as enemies. He was informed that the very ancestors of the Jews, ungodly men hated by the gods, had been driven out of all Egypt. Covered with leprosy and scabs, they had been rounded up as cursed beings and driven out of the borders to purify the land. Then, having been banished, they took possession of the territory of Jerusalem, formed the Jewish people and perpetuated among them the hatred of men. For this reason they had instituted special laws, such as never to sit at table with a stranger and never to show them any kindness[19]."

Since Judaism was opposed to the rest of mankind, it was therefore legitimate, for the good of mankind, to prevent and annihilate it. In -168, by an edict published throughout Judea—the so-called edict of Apostasy—Antiochus Epiphanes simply and plainly forbade the Mosaic law. Circumcision, the Sabbath and Jewish festivals were forbidden and severely punished; offenders were punished by death. Altars in honour of the Greek gods were erected everywhere and the temple in Jerusalem was consecrated to Zeus Olympias. On 6 July -168 (17 *tammuz* in the Jewish calendar), the high priest Menelaus sacrificed a pig on the altar and sprinkled the blood in the temple sanctuary. "A pig was slaughtered on the altar in the courtyard and its blood was sprinkled in the Holy of Holies, on the stone which Antiochus had imagined to be the statue of Moses; the flesh was boiled and its juice was poured over the leaves of the Holy Scriptures. The so-called high priest Menelaus and the other Hellenistic Jews were to consume the pork. The scroll of the Law, which was in the Temple, was not only sprinkled, but burned, because the Torah (that school of moral purity

---

[18] Heinrich Graetz, *History of the Jews I*, Philadelphia, The Jewish Publication Society of America, 1891, p. 453, 454.

[19] Quoted by Diodorus of Sicily, XXXIV, fr. 1, in Georges Nataf, *Les Sources païennes de l'antisémitisme*, Berg International, 2001, p. 66.

and universal love), Antiochus maintained, inculcated hatred of mankind. This was his first baptism of fire. The statue of Jupiter was placed on the altar, and to him sacrifices would henceforth be offered[20]," lamented Heinrich Graetz.

Antiochus Epiphanes issued decree after decree to punish recalcitrants with the utmost rigour. Anyone who openly professed Judaism was condemned to death by the executioner. Jews in the cities of Syria and Phoenicia who lived near the Greeks were forced to abandon Judaism. Wherever they found scrolls of the Law, the Greeks tore them up and burned them at the stake. All the prayer houses and Jewish schools that existed in the country were destroyed.

Some Jews voluntarily disowned the sect from which they came and denounced their former brethren to the Greeks: "Some reprobate Hellenists had probably betrayed the refuge of the Hasidians[21]", wrote Graetz. Immediately, the head of the garrison, the Phrygian Philip, set out with his soldiers and all perished in the fire or suffocated by the smoke.

The signal for the Jewish revolt was given by a priest named Mattathias Ben Johanan. After his death in -166, his third son Judas Maccabee ("The Hammer", *maccabi*) took over and led the resistance. These fanatical Jews organised guerrilla warfare against the Seleucid garrisons and against all Jewish supporters of the Hellenistic reformers. In that year, Judas Maccabeus won an important battle against the Greeks at Emmaus. Since then, this victory is celebrated every year all over the world by the Jews during eight days of celebration—Hanukkah, the Feast of Lights—on which they light a candle for each day. Between -166 and -164, the Greeks were even expelled from Jerusalem and its environs.

The Jewish victories only stirred up the hatred of the neighbouring peoples against them, Graetz wrote: "The victory of the heroes of Israel over the well-armed Syrian troops increased the burning hatred of the neighbouring nations against the Jews, and stirred them to cruel enmity against the members of the people who lived among them", as if there was already a special hatred against the Jews. "The Philistines, in the southwest;

---

[20] Heinrich Graetz, *History of the Jews I*, Philadelphia, The Jewish Publication Society of America, 1891, p. 455.
[21] The Hasidim (from the Aramaic hasí, plural hasídim: pious, holy) were a Jewish religious party, who claimed to be upholders of the Law of Moses against the encroachment of Greek customs. They were a pious movement with pretensions to renewal, emphasising radical observance of the Law of Moses. Their doctrine had a strong emphasis on the hope of the approaching Kingdom of God and the resurrection of the righteous. The movement was composed of priests, scribes and simple townspeople. They joined the cause of the Maccabees against the Hellenistic monarch. By 150 BC, according to Flavius Josephus, the Hasidim split into two distinct groups, the Pharisees and the Essenes.

the Phoenicians, in the northwest; the Ammonites, on the other side of Jordan; the Syrians and Macedonians, everywhere in the neighbourhood, and the Idumeans in the south, were imbued with hatred towards the Jews. Having been driven from their homes by the Nabataeans, the Idumeans had settled in the ancient territory of Judea, and had even taken possession of Hebron. In the time of Antiochus they were bitter enemies of the Jews, as they had been under the despotism of Nebuchadnezzar; they were always on the lookout for fugitives, whom they ill-treated and sometimes even killed. It was therefore very important to reduce them to submission. Judas Maccabee first undertook an expedition against the sons of Esau at Akkrabatha, defeated them and drove them from their dwellings. Then he crossed the Jordan with his army, fought against the Ammonites, who were led by a Syrian warrior, Timothy, a relentless and indefatigable enemy of the Jews. When Judas had defeated him and the Ammonites, he took possession of his capital Rabbath-Ammon (Philadelphia)[22]..."

Antiochus Epiphanes, who had just put down the Artaxias rebellion in Armenia, then launched an ill-fated expedition into Persia, where he fell ill and died in -164. His death marked the end of the persecution of the Jews and probably the most critical period in Jewish history[23]. The following year, in -163, the regent Lysias granted them freedom of worship and the high priest Menelaus was condemned to death and executed. However, a Seleucid garrison remained in the citadel of Jerusalem until -141 to protect the Hellenising Jews.

VII. The Roman Conquest of Judea

John Hyrcanus, the second son of Simon, the last of the Maccabees (dynasty of the Hasmoneans), set out to conquer Samaria and reduced the capital to ashes. He had concentrated in his hands the three powers: religious, civil and military. He devastated Scythopolis and massacred its population on the pretext that they spoke Greek. He was, according to Flavius Josephus, a bloodthirsty tyrant who believed himself to be

---

[22] Heinrich Graetz, *History of the Jews I*, Philadelphia, The Jewish Publication Society of America, 1891, p. 457, 474.

[23] This period of national liberation war was very important for Jewish history. With peace restored, a new independent state took hold with the Hasmonean dynasty, successors to the Maccabees, and several religious parties were formed: the Sadducees, the pro-dynastic priestly party, and the Pharisees and Essenes, both splinters of the Hasidim, who retained their original religious concerns and were increasingly critical of the Hellenizing evolution of the dynasty. Furthermore, it is known that the messianic-apocalyptic books of Daniel and Enoch were written by the Hasidim during this war. (NdT).

endowed with the gift of prophecy. When he conquered Edom, he put to the sword all those who would not convert to Judaism. The cruelty of the Jews towards the conquered populations spread beyond their borders.

In -134, in a last-ditch effort to try to recapture the lost provinces, the Seleucid king Antiochus VII laid siege to Jerusalem. His advisors recommended that he take the city and exterminate "the Jewish nation, since it was alone among all nations in avoiding intercourse with other peoples and regarded all men as its enemies", wrote Diodorus of Sicily in the 1st century BC, adding: "The ancestors of the Jews had been expelled from Egypt because they were an impious people and abhorred by the gods". The historian further wrote that the descendants of the Jews in Egypt had "raised their hatred of mankind to the level of a tradition[24]".

In the year -64, a part of Asia Minor and the Middle East was conquered by the Romans under the military tribune Marcus Emilius Scaurus who served under Pompey, the general of the Roman legions in the East. He summoned to appear before him the feuding brothers Aristobulus and Hyrcanus who were contesting for power in Judea. At Damascus, Pompey examined the reasons for their discord. Hyrcanus invoked his right of entailed estate, while Aristobulus claimed to be more worthy of power. Pompey was at first more favourable to the rich and fiery Aristobulus, but he later favoured Hyrcanus, who was more favourable to Rome. Aristobulus immediately organised resistance and barricaded himself and his men on the Temple Mount. Pompey ordered the invasion of Palestine with a large contingent of troops. The Roman legions joined the troops that had remained loyal to Hyrcanus, and Jerusalem endured another terrible siege that lasted three months. In June 1963, one of the temple towers was demolished and a breach was made through which the Romans penetrated. Pison, the lieutenant-general, took the temple on the official fast day. The legions and allied troops reached the court, slaughtered the Jews and beheaded the priests. The chronicles relate that Pompey first entered the Sanctum Sanctorum of the temple with sword in hand, where in principle no one except the high priest himself was allowed to enter.

This war cost the lives of 12,000 Jews. The title of king was withdrawn from Hyrcanus, who retained only the dignity of high priest and was placed under the guardianship of Antipater, who was appointed administrator of the country. The walls of Jerusalem were razed to the ground and Judea was treated as a conquered country. In addition, Judea was returned to its previous narrow borders to the Hasmoneans, successors of the Maccabees. The coastal cities were declared free, as were some inland cities.

---

[24] Diodorus Siculus, *Bibliotheca Historica*, XXXIV-XXXV, Loeb classical Library, 12 vol., Harvard University Press, in Gérald Messadié, *Histoire générale de l'antisémitisme*, Lattès, 1999, p. 42.

Having appointed Ahascurus governor of Judea, Lower Syria and the territories stretching from Egypt to the Euphrates, Pompey returned to Rome where he was greeted with a triumphant welcome. He had brought with him as prisoner Aristobulus, his daughters and two sons, Antigonus and Alexander, who despite close surveillance managed to escape during the journey.

The following year, Alexander led a new revolt. Aulus Gabinius, successor to Scaurus, raised an army of 10,000 men led by a young Mark Antony to defeat Alexander and joined by numerous soldiers from Antipater's army. The Roman legions won a decisive battle in which more than 6000 Jews were killed.

In Rome, Crassus, Pompey and Caesar shared power during a first triumvirate (-60). In -54 the consul Crassus, commander-in-chief of the armies of the East, appeared in Jerusalem and seized the treasure of the Temple (about 2000 talents of gold) which Pompey had left intact to finance the war in Persia against the Parthians. He collected a further 8000 talents from all over the country, already heavily controlled by the Romans, recovering in total some 10,000 talents equivalent to 34 tons of gold and silver (according to Flavius Josephus). Crassus plundered everything in the Temple, as well as all the gifts that the Diaspora Jews (the Jews of Asia and Europe) had sent to Jerusalem. In -53 he crossed the Euphrates to confront the Parthians, but was defeated at Carras. Retreating with the remnants of his army, Crassus was killed during an interview with the Parthian general Surena and his head sent to King Orodes II of Parthia. Cassius Longinus took command and retreated to Damascus where he held off the Parthian advance that threatened the whole of Syria. It was at this time that another revolt broke out in Judea against Roman suzerainty. In -53, Cassius Longinus invaded the country and crushed the revolt. About 30,000 Jewish men were taken prisoner and sold as slaves in the markets of the great cities of the Roman Republic.

VIII. Cicero

In Rome, the Jewish community already numbered 40–50,000 at the beginning of the 1st century. The Jews already had a certain influence on the course of affairs in Rome, Heinrich Graetz stated: "The Roman Jews influenced the course of Roman politics to a certain extent. Since the original emigrants, as well as the ransomed captives, enjoyed the power to vote in public assemblies, they could sometimes, by their combined action on a preconceived plan, by their assiduity, by their temperate and dispassionate analysis of the situation, and perhaps also by their keen intelligence, change the balance on some popular question[25]."

Here as elsewhere, the Jews were abhorred. A young writer, the Rector Apollonius Molon, who lived on the island of Rhodes—like Posidonius of Apamea—was the first to write a whole treatise against the Jews, enumerating various and numerous reproaches against them. His work is lost; we only know of it through the mentions made by Flavius Josephus in his treatise *Against Apion*. Apollonius depicted the Jews as "atheists and misanthropes", describing them as "most inept barbarians, and consequently the only ones who have contributed nothing useful to mankind[26]".

The illustrious lawyer and politician Cicero, who had been his pupil, had learned to know the Jews. In 59 BC, he had to defend the cause of his friend and client, the proconsul of Asia Lucius Flaccus, who was accused of embezzling funds intended for the fleet and of extorting money from several Greek cities during his rule in Asia Minor. His accusers also included a number of Jews who accused him of having appropriated the religious tax that the Jews of his province sent to the temple in Jerusalem each year. In his defence, Lucius Flaccus invoked a senatorial decree prohibiting gold shipments outside the Roman provinces.

The investigation was conducted by Decimus Lellius Balbus, a supporter of Caesar and Pompey, political enemies of Cicero and Flaccus. Caesar, and especially Pompey, promoted their investigation in Asia Minor, leading to a case of concussion and impeachment. The Jews, following their traditional desire to destroy the elites, had sided with Caesar, a leader of the people, against the aristocrats represented by Flaccus and Cicero.

In his plea, *Pro Lucius Flaccus Oratio,* Cicero devoted no more than two pages to the accusation of the Jews, but these became famous for their blatant anti-Judaism. The Roman Jews, who were keenly interested in the trial of Flaccus, had turned out en masse in the crowd. Cicero was afraid of openly revealing his hostile disposition towards them and attracting their resentment; so he spoke in a low voice. This is a passage of his plea which was not taken up by Heinrich Graetz, preferring to omit it from his history of the Jews. Cicero was here addressing the procurator Lelius Balbo:

"You know well what a compact group they form, what union there is among them, and what influence they have in the assemblies. So I am going to speak in a low voice so that only the judges may hear me; for there is no lack of those who incite these men against me and against all the best citizens; I am not going to give them any help by which their scheming might be easier for them. As every year gold used to be exported from Italy

---

[25] Heinrich Graetz, *History of the Jews II*, Philadelphia, The Jewish Publication Society of America, 1891, p. 68.
[26] Flavius Josephus, *Against Apion*, Editorial Gredos, Madrid, 1994, p. 260.

and from all our provinces to Jerusalem at the expense of the Jews, Flaccus forbade by an edict that it should be exported from Asia. Is there anyone, judges, who cannot rightly praise this measure? The senate, both on previous occasions and during my consulship, pronounced very severely against the export of gold. And it has been an act of severity to oppose this barbarous superstition, and an act of extraordinary firmness to belittle for the good of the republic that crowd of Jews sometimes inflamed in our assemblies[27]."

Graetz quoted instead this passage: "It requires great decision of character," he said, "to oppose the barbarous and superstitious Jews for the good of our country, and to show due contempt for these seditious ones, who invade our public assemblies. If Pompey did not avail himself of the rights of a conqueror, and leave the treasures of the Temple untouched, we may be sure that he held back not from reverence for the Hebrew sanctuary, but from cunning, to avoid giving the suspicious and slanderous Jewish nation an opportunity of accusing him[28]."

A year later, Cicero was condemned to exile, unable to go within 80 miles of the city. His house and property were completely destroyed.

IX. Caesar, Cleopatra and Mark Antony

In -48, Pompey, who had taken refuge in Greece, was defeated by Julius Caesar at Pharsalus. He then took refuge in Egypt where he was assassinated. In gratitude for their help, Caesar allowed the Jews to rebuild the walls of Jerusalem that Pompey had demolished during his siege of the city. He also ordered that all Jews who were still slaves in foreign countries, following the actions of Crassus and the orders of Cassius Longinus, should be freed.

Caesar showered the Jews with favours. He lowered their taxes considerably and exempted them from military service[29]. Here is an extract

---

[27] Marcus Tullius Cicero, *In Defence of Lucius Flaccus, XXVIII, Complaints of the Jews of Asia (66–69)*.

[28] Heinrich Graetz, *History of the Jews II*, Philadelphia, The Jewish Publication Society of America, 1891, p. 69.

[29] "But Julius Caesar not only favoured Antipater and his family, but all the Jews for their support and participation in the capture of Egypt, for without the support of supplies and extra military support the enterprise would have been almost impossible, so he also benefited Hyrcanus and his sons by appointing them allies of Rome and personal friends. He had also ratified the right to Jewish religious practices and in addition to the fact that any legal case against a Jew should be resolved by the Jews themselves through their high priest, he also exempted the Jews from the winter cantonment of troops, forbade extortion and ordered that the payment of taxes to Rome

from the edicts exhibited at the Capitol in Rome and in Alexandria:

"We, Caius Caesar, inform the magistrates of the Parianians that the Jews from various provinces came to see us at Delos to complain of your advocacy of their living according to your laws and of making their sacrifices, which is a severity against our friends and allies which we cannot suffer, since even in Rome they are permitted to practise these customs. While by this same edict we forbid public meetings in Rome, we exempt the Jews from this prohibition."

But Julius Caesar's rise to power destabilised the republican institutions and several conspirators, including Marcus Junius Brutus and Cassius Longinus, swore him to death and fomented a coup d'état.

On 15 March -44, Caesar was assassinated in Rome in the middle of the Senate, stabbed to death. The Jews, not forgetting that Caesar had allowed them to rebuild the walls of Jerusalem, gathered several nights in succession to watch and mourn at his tomb and kept his memory religiously. The Jews of Rome had good reason to be grief-stricken at the death of this great man, and they were fully justified in spending their sad night vigils at his ashes," wrote the Jewish historian Heinrich Graetz.[30] "The Jews of Rome had good reason to be grief-stricken at the death of this great man, and they were fully justified in spending their sad night vigils at his ashes," wrote the Jewish historian Heinrich Graetz.

Cassius moved to Syria where he seized power, his victory being

---

should take into account the particularities of Jewish law, excepting the sabbatical year of contributions since the land did not produce, He also returned to Jewish rule the maritime city of Jaffa which Pompey had liberated, and granted Hyrcanus and his family a place next to the senators in the Circus and the privilege of presenting requests directly to the Roman senate with the approval of the dictator or his deputy; the general population also received benefits, since they were exempted from the service of arms, respecting that the laws of Shabbat did not allow them to carry out activities on that day. Caesar knew how to reward his allies and the Jews were not badly placed with Rome, so that many Jews came to Rome itself and with the ease that characterises Judaism were able to adapt and become skilful merchants, occupying the other side of the Tiber to settle." Holtzmann & Oncken, 1918, pages 277, 286–290, quoted in Carlos Ruz Saldivar, *Outline of the History of Israel*) (NdT).

[30]Heinrich Graetz, *History of the Jews II*, Philadelphia, The Jewish Publication Society of America, 1891, p. 80. ["Caesar was entirely benevolent to the Jews and rewarded them for their loyalty. He granted the Alexandrian Jews many privileges, among others the right to equality with the Greeks and to be governed by a prince of their own (ethnarch). Again money was generously provided for the Temple. Caesar allowed the remittances to reach their destination; he prevented the Greek inhabitants of Asia Minor from molesting the Jews of those provinces, from summoning them before the courts of justice on the Sabbath, from interfering with the building of their synagogues, from disturbing them in their religious observances (47-44)." *History of the Jews II*, p 76–77. NdT.]

ratified by the Senate. At the beginning of 42 he joined Brutus' forces in Macedonia to face the decisive battle.

Facing these defenders of republican institutions were the "triumvirs" Lepidus, Mark Antony and Octavian, who fought against them on the plains of Philippi in October -42. Cassius, who led the left wing of the army, was defeated by Mark Antony. Believing that Brutus had also been defeated, he ordered his freedman to run him through with his sword. Three weeks later, Brutus was himself defeated by Octavian and committed suicide rather than be taken prisoner.

Octavian, Julius Caesar's great-nephew and adopted son, would now rule the western part of the empire while Mark Antony would rule the eastern part. Antony needed Egypt for the war he planned to wage against the Parthians. In -41, Cleopatra came to meet the one who had avenged Caesar so well against his assassins, her late lover who had restored her to the throne of queen of Egypt. Mark Antony's heart surrendered to the charm and beauty of the young Cleopatra.

Relations between Antony and Octavian quickly deteriorated and a confrontation became inevitable. Octavian singled out Cleopatra as responsible for the war, accusing her of wanting to reign in Rome. In September 31, at the naval battle of Actium on the west coast of Greece, the navy of Mark Antony and Cleopatra was defeated. The following year, Octavian landed at Alexandria with his army and Mark Antony, with no hope for his cause, ended his days. Cleopatra was brought before Octavian and allowed to retire with her court, but the queen preferred to receive the deadly bite of an Egyptian asp viper. Graetz wrote about her: "The Alexandrian Jews had suffered from her hatred... For, shortly before her death, this terrible woman had wished to murder with her own hands the Jews living in the capital of Egypt who were devoted to the cause of Octavian[31]."

X. *Herodo*

Because he had received hospitality from Antipater, Mark Antony had showered his son Antipater II with distinctions and honours. Antipater II (also called Herodotus) was twenty-five years old when he was appointed governor of Galilee.

The Parthians had entered Jerusalem, plundering Herodotus' palace and all that he had left behind him. These barbarians, as Flavius Josephus called them, had sacked Jerusalem and its environs before ravaging other cities

---

[31]Heinrich Graetz, *History of the Jews II*, Philadelphia, The Jewish Publication Society of America, 1891, p. 102.

and ruining the entire region. In -40, Herodotus took refuge in Rome where Mark Antony had him made king of Judea by the Senate.

The Romans and Herodotus' troops then reconquered the region, driving out their rival Antigonus who had allied himself with the Parthians. In 37, Herodotus besieged Jerusalem, and after five months of siege the city walls were demolished. This second Roman capture of Jerusalem came 27 years after Pompey's siege.

Herodotus then attested the whole of Judea with cities and monuments named after his Roman protectors, paying homage to Octavian, who in 27 BC had meanwhile become the first Roman emperor under the name Augustus. For more than a decade (from 23 to 12 BC), Herodotus had a first-rate maritime city, Caesarea, built, adorned with two colossi, one representing a deified Augustus in Jupiter Olympias, the other representing the city of Rome under the features of Juno. When the new city was inaugurated with sumptuous festivities, the Jews thought they saw a pagan city similar to Rome, so they nicknamed it *Little Rome*. Later, this city would become the seat of Roman government and a true rival to Jerusalem. "Whenever Caesarea rejoiced, Jerusalem wept."

Some Jews took a great dislike to this upstart who sought to destroy Jewish customs and traditions. Heinrich Graetz wrote of Herodotus, then called Herodotus the Great: "This prince was destined to become the evil genius of the Jewish nation; it was he who led it captive to Rome; it was he who triumphantly set his feet upon its neck[32]."

Meanwhile in Babylon, under Persian rule, Judaism was flourishing. Many Jews had resided there for centuries, even before the destruction of the first Temple in 586 BC. Their situation continued to improve. "They are prosperous and wealthy, wrote Elie Wiesel, they live in security and enjoy spiritual and even legal autonomy. Towns like Nehardea are entirely Jewish. No wonder that in the conflicts between Rome and Persia the Babylonian Jews support the latter. They contribute to the financing of their war effort[33]."

XI. Tiberius, Sejanus and Pontius Pilate

Wherever they were, the Jews nurtured the feverish hope of one day seeing a Messiah (a King of Israel sent by God at the End Times) and actively prepared for the coming of this great victor[34]. In a passage from

---

[32]Heinrich Graetz, *History of the Jews II*, Philadelphia, The Jewish Publication Society of America, 1891, p. 77–78.
[33]Elie Wiesel, *Célébration talmudique*, Seuil, 1991, p. 337.
[34]"The picture painted by the available sources of information about the situation in

his work, *The War of the Jews*, the writer Flavius Josephus himself confirmed the Jewish hopes and their will to dominate the world: "But what most impelled them to wage war was an ambiguous oracle, contained also in their sacred books, according to which at that time a personage from their country would rule the world. They believed that it was someone from their race[35]...".

The Roman historians Suetonius and Tacitus also echoed this idea deeply rooted in the Jewish soul. Tacitus mentioned in his *Histories* that "most were convinced that the ancient priestly texts pointed to precisely that time when the East would become strong and people from Judea would take over the world[36]."

Judaism had penetrated the entire eastern part of the Roman Empire. "They have invaded all the cities[37]", said the Greek geographer Strabon (58 BC - 21 AD), and it was not easy to name a place in the world which had not welcomed this tribe, or rather "which was not occupied by it[38]".

The Romans were suspicious of his intrigues, and some emperors took the necessary measures to contain his power. "Tiberius' antipathy to the Jews matched that of his predecessor and foster-father; it seemed as if the representative of imperialism in Rome foresaw the deathblow that Rome was destined to receive from Judaism," wrote Graetz.

To reward them for their support, Augustus, the first Roman emperor,

---

Palestine towards the end of the first century BC would have led us to believe, had a painter been able to paint it, that it was the work of a madman or a drug addict. A whole nation was in a state of delirium. The reigning ruler was a sick and melancholy tyrant. His embittered subjects had an almost cyclothymic fear and loathing of him. Religious fanatics fasted and prayed, preaching wrath and doomsday. The population, obsessed with the idea that the End Times had come, allowed terror and superstition to prevail over reason. Messianic fervour was accompanied by mortification. No wonder that at Herod's death the infernal powers were unleashed." Hugh Schonfield, *The Passover Plot* (1965); *Le Mystère Jésus*, Éditions Pygmalion, Paris, 1989, p. 33-34. [On this permanent state of mind of the Jews read *Psychoanalysis of Judaism*]. See translator's note in Appendix I: Messianism and politics in Judea at the time of the Roman rulers.

[35] Flavius Josephus, *La Guerra de los judíos, Libro VI*, Clásica Gredos 264, Madrid, 1999, p. 298. ["These are the well-known biblical prophecies about the coming of the Messiah, which in this case Flavius Josephus orients and manipulates in a Philo-Roman sense. Tacitus, *Histories* V 13, and Suetonius, *Vespasian* IV, confirm the existence of these predictions, which must be placed in the context of Jewish messianism, which by means of ambiguous prophecies advocated the advent of a new monarchy and a new kingdom. With the prophecies about the election of Vespasian, Flavius Josephus was trying to put an end to apocalyptic messianism by means of a real personage and a real empire, instead of waiting for the arrival of a golden age that was leading irremediably to the self-destruction of the Jewish people". Note 149 in Editorial Gredos].

[36] Cornelius Tacitus, *Histories*, Editorial Cátedra, Madrid, 2006, p. 309–310.

[37] Quoted by the Jewish historian Flavius Josephus in his *Jewish Antiquities*

[38] Ernest Renan, *L'Antéchrist*, 1873, chapitre 11.

had confirmed to the Jews of Egypt their political rights and privileges. But his successor Tiberius was more openly hostile to Judaism than his adoptive father had been. Following a scandal over a swindle in Rome, he expelled and deported several thousand Jews to Sardinia.

Flavius Josephus described in his *Jewish Antiquities* the case of four Jews who had persuaded an aristocratic convert, Fulvia, the wife of the senator Saturninus, to make a donation in gold to the Temple in Jerusalem. But instead of sending it to the Temple, the four Jews had kept the donation for themselves: "They persuaded Fulvia, a woman who frequented their circle and who, being one of the high-ranking Roman matrons, had converted to Judaism, to give them purple and gold to send to the Temple in Jerusalem. But they, having received these offerings, spent them on private uses, which was precisely the purpose for which the request had been made from the beginning. And Tiberius, to whom Saturninus, who was a friend of hers and husband of Fulvia, had communicated it to the matron, ordered that all the Jews should be expelled from Rome. And the consuls, after enlisting four thousand of them in the army, sent them to the island of Sardinia, and the vast majority of them were punished because of their refusal to join the army for the observance of the laws inherited from their Jewish ancestors[39]." The rest of the Jewish population was ordered to leave Italy by a stipulated date if they did not renounce their unfit rites, on pain of perpetual slavery.

A contemporary of Tacitus, Suetonius (69–125), in *his Lives of the Twelve Caesars*, stated that Tiberius "repressed foreign cults, Egyptian and Jewish rites...and under the pretext of military service, distributed the Jewish youth in provinces of very harsh climate, and the other individuals of this people or followers of similar cults he expelled them from Rome[40]".

Dion Cassius in turn recounted, years later, that "since many Jews had come to Rome and were converting many Romans to their beliefs, Tiberius expelled most of them[41]".

In accordance with this law—which would have been inspired by his all-powerful minister Sejanus—thousands of Jews were expelled to Sardinia and the Jews of all Italy were warned of expulsion. The young and able-bodied men were restricted to the service of arms every day, including the Sabbath; when they refused, they were severely punished. It was one

---

[39]Flavius Josephus, *Jewish Antiquities, Book XVIII, 81*, Akal Clásica, Madrid, 1997, p. 1092.
[40]Suetonius, *Lives of the Twelve Caesars I, Book III*, Editorial Gredos, Madrid, 1992, p. 333.
[41]Dion Cassius, *Historia Romana, Book LVII*, Editorial Gredos, Madrid, 2011, p 436–437.

of the first expulsions of Jews from the West[42].

Pontius Pilate, who had been given the government of Judea from 26 to 36, was a creature of Sejanus. Until then, the commanders of the Roman troops had respected the demands of the Jews. But Pontius Pilate, desirous of accustoming them to pay obeisance to the divine worship of the emperor, secretly transported the effigies of Caesar that adorned the legion's banners for public display in the cities of Judea. A violent uproar ensued and quickly spread throughout the country, so that Pilate had to have the images removed.

XII. August '38: the pogrom in Alexandria

The emperor Caligula did not appreciate them either. Under his reign a great revolt broke out against the Jews: "The favour shown by Caligula to Agrippa, which had naturally extended to the people of Judea, aroused the envy of the pagans and unleashed the hatred of the Greeks of Alexandria. In fact, the entire Roman Empire harboured secret and public enemies of the Jews. Hatred of their race and creed was intensified by the lurking fear that this despised but proud nation might one day attain supreme power. But hostile feeling against the Jews reached its peak among the restless, sarcastic and lustful Greek inhabitants of Alexandria[43]," Graetz explained.

---

[42]According to Valerius Maximus, a contemporary of the Emperor Augustus, Jews and astrologers had already been expelled from Rome in -139 BC by the praetor Cornelius Hispallus and sent back to their homeland because "they were trying to corrupt Roman customs with the cult of Jupiter Sabaeus". In some Greek intellectual circles of the Hellenistic age and the Second Sophistic, the belief spread that Sabatius (a deity of mystical character from Asia Minor or Phoenicia) could be identified with the god of the Jews, Yahweh. There are several reasons for this assimilation, which corresponds to an *interpretatio graeca*. Firstly, the phonetic similarity between the name Sabatius and the Hebrew invocation "Yahweh Sebaoth". It is also possible that the name of the Sabbath, sacred to the Jews, contributed to this identification. The context may have been the deportation of Jews in Asia Minor from 200 BC by Antiochus the Great. A testimony to this interpretation appears in a fragmentary text of Plutarch, one of the Moralia, where the question is posed: "Who is the god of the Jews", i.e. to which Greek god is he equivalent? In this regard, one of the interlocutors—the scene is in a *symposium*—claims that the Jews worship Dionysus because their Sabbath feast is a celebration of Sabaeus. In another summary of Valerius Maximus' words it is related that: "Hispalus himself expelled the Jews from Rome because they tried to transmit their sacred rites to the Romans and ordered their private altars raised in public places to be destroyed". [This reminds us of the Jewish menorahs currently displayed in public places in many European cities, ndt]. Read in Menahem Stern (dir), *Greek and Latin Authors*, Israel, 1980, in Shlomo Sand, *Comment le peuple juif fut inventé*, Fayard, 2008, p. 235–236.

[43]Heinrich Graetz, *History of the Jews II*, Philadelphia, The Jewish Publication Society

Nowhere else had malicious dispositions reached such a degree as among the Greek population of Alexandria, who saw the growing opulence of the Jews and endured their arrogance. Greek writers also opposed the Jews and their doctrines. We know nothing about Lysimachus at first hand; none of his writings have come down to us, but we know some of his texts from what Flavius Josephus reported about them.

Apion, a Greek intellectual from Alexandria who lived in Rome during the first century, was the author of several scholarly works. In his five-volume *History of Egypt*, he gave a version of the exodus of the Jews that corroborated that of his predecessors. Apion also wrote a *Treatise against the Jews* in which he claimed that the laws of Moses "are only evil and dangerous". He attacked with his sarcasm the members of this sect who held high office in Alexandria, recalling Cleopatra's animosity against the Jews when she saw that the Jews were hostile to the rest of humanity.

In his book *Against Apion*, Flavius Josephus repeated some of his accusations. The Jews, said Apion, used to "catch a Greek traveller and fatten him for a year. Then they would take him to a forest where they would kill him. They sacrificed his body according to their rites, ate his entrails and, during the immolation, swore to maintain their enmity against the Greeks; then they threw the remains of the victim into a pit".

Flavius Josephus was attempting to refute Apion's writings, but by insulting his adversary, thus inaugurating a long tradition among Jewish intellectuals: Apion, said Josephus, had "himself the heart of an ass and the shamelessness of a dog, animals which are usually worshipped by those of his race[44]."

These hostile dispositions of the Alexandrians were contained under Augustus and Tiberius, when the imperial governors of Egypt severely repressed violent demonstrations. But things changed under Caligula, as his governor Flaccus, who had been a friend of Tiberius, turned a blind eye to the violence committed by the exasperated Greek population. These anti-Judaic demonstrations were often instigated by certain scholars, including Denius, the amanuensis Lampon and the gymnast Isodorus.

Herodotus Agrippa I had been appointed king of Galilee by the emperor Caligula. In July 38, while on his way to Rome, he stopped in Alexandria where he was acclaimed by the Jews who saw in his rise hopes of national renewal. They decided to give a great feast in his honour, but his presence set off a powder keg. The Greeks petitioned the governor of Egypt, Flaccus, to issue an ordinance obliging the Jews to accept a statue of the emperor in their synagogues, which the Jews refused to do. In the face of popular

---

of America, 1891, p. 179.
[44] Flavius Josephus, *Against Apion*, Editorial Gredos, Madrid, 1994, p. 251, 249.

pressure, Flaccus withdrew the right of citizenship from the Jews of Alexandria, declaring them aliens and ordering the arrest of thirty-eight members of the Council of Elders and the confiscation of all their property. On 31 August 38, the leaders of the Jewish community were seized, chained and publicly flogged in a procession in the midst of the crowd, so that several died. Flaccus then ordered the army to search the houses of the Jews who were expelled by the people from the four quarters of Alexandria and rounded up in the Delta quarter near the harbour. The mob, which had been waiting for this moment for a long time, rushed into the abandoned houses, shops and workshops, looting and destroying everything. The Delta quarter was even besieged to prevent the Jews from leaving and succumbing to hunger and heat. Entire families died, old men, women and children of all ages and conditions. Four hundred Jewish houses were ransacked or destroyed, and places of worship desecrated and burned. As the emperor wished, statues in his effigy were finally installed in all the synagogues. These harassments lasted until mid-September without any intervention by the authorities. By then, an envoy of the emperor dismissed Flaccus and took him to Rome because of his personal disagreements with the emperor.

Philo of Alexandria, the famous Jewish philosopher, left a clear testimony of these events in a text entitled *On the Embassy to Gaius* (*Legatio ad Caium*), in which one can already perceive the propensity of Jewish intellectuals to ignore the real causes of anti-Semitism and to present Jews as innocent victims of religious persecutions organised by mindless fanatics.

Philo was speaking here of Caligula and his intention to place a statue of him (in the image of Jupiter) in all the temples of the Roman Empire, including the synagogues:

"And as for us, when the ruler became a despot, we were placed on the level, no longer of mere slaves, but of the most unworthy of slaves.

When the promiscuous and fickle Alexandrian plebs heard of this, they made us the target of their outrages, certain that a very advantageous opportunity had arrived, and brought out the hatred they had long kept latent, producing chaos and confusion in all orders.

As if they were, in effect, beings publicly condemned by the emperor to the most extreme misfortunes, or subjects of war, they brought ruin upon us with insane and bestial fits of rage, rushing upon the houses and evicting their owners with their wives and children until they left them empty of dwellers.

"They stole furniture and objects, no longer in the manner of thieves, who await the darkness of night for fear of being seized, but taking them out in broad daylight and showing them to those they met, as if they had received them as an inheritance or bought them from their owners. And in cases where those who had taken part in common plunderings were several in number, they divided the spoils in the middle of the square, often in full view of their owners, while they reviled and mocked them.

"Terrible things, then, are these in themselves; and how should they not be? To be suddenly turned from rich into poor, and from prosperous into needy, without having committed any fault; into homeless and drifting men, driven and banished from their own homes, to spend it in the open day and night, to meet their end by the scorching heat of the sun or the chill of the night.

"But these things are light compared to what remains to be mentioned. For, having rushed, as if they were herds or flocks, out of the whole city so many myriads of men, women, and children into a very small redoubt, a stable we might say, they expected to find in a few days heaps of accumulated corpses of dead, either from hunger in consequence of the scarcity of provisions, for they had not made a stock of the necessary things because they had had no forewarning of the sudden misfortunes; or else from crowding and drowning.

"There was, indeed, no ample room to add to what was available, and all the surrounding air was stale and empty of all that it contained that was life-giving for breathing, or, if truth be told, for the stifled breaths of the breathers. Inflamed by these breaths, and oppressed as if under the effects of a fever, it caused a hot and noxious vapour to penetrate through the nostrils, adding, as the proverb says, one fire to another fire...

"Unable to bear the lack of oxygen any longer, the Jews dispersed towards the deserted places, the seashores and the tombs, anxious to breathe pure and harmless air. As for those who were seized before they could escape in the other parts of the city, and those who, unaware of the misfortunes that would have befallen us, returned from the countryside, they suffered many misfortunes, being stoned or wounded with tiles or smashed to death with branches of holly or oak in the most vital parts of the body and especially in the head.

"Some of those who usually spent their time idle and idle, had stationed themselves around the enclosure of the Jews, who, as I have said, had gathered and concentrated themselves in a small section at one end of the city, coming to be as it were besieged; and they watched them lest any should escape unseen. Not a few, indeed, pressed for want of necessaries, were willing to leave for fear that their whole families might perish from hunger, forsaking their own safety. The stalkers watched their departures closely, and promptly put to death those who were seized, mistreating them with all sorts of tortures...

"Many, while still alive, they bound them with straps and ropes knotting their ankles, and dragged them through the square as they leaped upon them; and they spared not even the corpses. Even more brutal and ferocious than the wild beasts, cutting them limb from limb and part from part, they wiped every form from them, so that no remains were left to receive burial[45]."

In short, these events demonstrate the extent to which the Jews had exasperated the local population and aroused their hatred.

The Greek population of Alexandria had sent a delegation to Rome to prevent the Jews from regaining equal civic rights. This delegation was led by Apion, a sworn enemy of the Jews, whom Tiberius called *Cymbalum mundi*, the "carillon of the Universe". Isidore was also part of the retinue, while Philo represented the Jews. It is difficult to pronounce on the outcome of the dispute between the pagans and the Jews of Alexandria, but undoubtedly the emperor Caligula, the arbiter of this bitter controversy, hated the Jews, and was surrounded by his advisors Helicon the Egyptian and Apelles of Ascalon, also bitter enemies of the Jews.

Caligula had his statues erected in the synagogues of Judea and ordered all resistance to be suppressed with arms. In October 40, the governor of Syria Petronius was ordered to enter Judea with his legions and to transform the sanctuary in Jerusalem into a pagan temple. But in January 41, at the age of 28, and after only four years of reign, the emperor Caligula was assassinated by the soldiers of his guard, without it being known who the commander had been. His death came as a great relief to the Jews, and the rumour circulated in Alexandria that he had been murdered by the Jews of Rome. Like all princes who have resolutely opposed the rule of Israel, Caligula is regarded as a madman by Jewish historians and their followers.

XIII. *Claudio*

Caligula's successor on the Caesars' throne was the emperor Claudius, who reigned from 41 to 54. At first sight it seemed unlikely that Claudius would become emperor: he was a stammerer and his family had considered him unfit for public office. In reality, Claudius owed his crown to chance and the intervention of King Agrippa, the grandson of Herodotus the Great, who had received from Caligula the kingship over a third of the provinces of Palestine, including Galilee. Agrippa had curbed the unrest in Rome by manoeuvring to arrest the apostle Peter and behead James, the two disciples of Jesus of Nazareth. Agrippa had then persuaded Claudius to accept his election by the Praetorian guards and got the reluctant Senate to recognise him as emperor. Graetz wrote here: "Rome must have stooped low when an insignificant Jewish prince was allowed to speak in the Senate and, to some extent, to influence the choice of its ruler. Claudius was not

---

[45] Philo of Alexandria, *On the embassy to Gaius*, in Collected Works (José María Triviño, Universidad Nacional de La Plata, 1976).

ungrateful to his ally; he praised him before the assembled Senate, elevated him to the dignity of consul, and made him king of all Palestine, as Judea and Samaria were incorporated into the monarchy[46]." In Alexandria, Claudius re-established freedom of worship for the Jews and annulled the project of the imperial statues, although he recommended the Jews not to request further privileges and not to send embassies to Rome other than those of the Alexandrians. Finally, they were asked not to favour or help their fellow foreigners to enter the city. The edict of 41 also prohibited the Jews of Alexandria from participating in the athletic competitions presided over by the gymnasiarchs. The right to participate in these games was reserved for full citizens.

As if that were not enough, he sentenced Isidore and Lampon, the two leaders of the anti-Jewish insurrection, to death. The investigation of the case was carried out at a good pace, in just two days (between 30 April and 1 May 41), proof of the importance of the matter for the emperor. The execution of the sentence took place shortly afterwards. It must be said that Isidore had aggravated his case during his visit to Rome with Apion to accuse Agrippa. Isidore had support in the Senate, so he was probably too emboldened when he impudently blurted out to the emperor: "As for you, you are the despicable offspring of the Jewess Salome...".

Within the two great empires of the time, the Roman Empire and the Parthian Empire, Jews were everywhere, occupying all the important cities of the Mediterranean basin. Rejected from one country, they went to another. One can get an idea of the immense Jewish population at that time if one considers that in Egypt alone, from the Mediterranean to the borders of Ethiopia, there lived about 1 million Israelites. In Rome, the Jewish population, expelled by Tiberius, soon regrouped there and was so numerous and so noisy that the Emperor Claudius, although favourable to the Jews, had to deal with the problem by expelling them again. Suetonius briefly stated in his work: "He expelled the Jews from Rome, who were continually stirring up trouble at the instigation of Chrestus[47]". Indeed, at that early age, the distinction between Christianity and Judaism was not yet made[48].

---

[46]Heinrich Graetz, *History of the Jews II*, Philadelphia, The Jewish Publication Society of America, 1891, p. 191.

[47]Suetonius, *Lives of the Twelve Caesars II, Book V*, Editorial Gredos, Madrid, 1992, p. 102–103.

[48]Most scholars agree that the expulsion of some Jews mentioned by Suetonius took place around 49–50. Scholars are divided over the value of Suetonius' reference to a "Chrestus" (Christ= anointed to be king, the Jewish messiah); some see it as a reference to Jesus Christ, others see its historical value as a reference to disturbances by an unknown agitator. Jesus was crucified in 36, so we think it unlikely that only 13 years later, without the new testamentary canon yet in place (the Gospels and Pauline Epistles

Apparently, Claudius' intentions were not favourably perceived by the Jews. Indeed, the *Acts of the Apostles* informs us that Claudius issued an edict ordering the Jews to leave Rome. However, Dion Cassius wrote that Claudius did not banish them: "Although the Jews again became very numerous, he did not expel them because they could with difficulty have been removed from the city without causing disturbances because of their great numbers. On the other hand, he did forbid them to assemble as long as they continued to practise their ancient way of life[49]." This was probably what prompted Heinrich Graetz to write that Claudius was "a pedantic scholar and a fool." Or perhaps Graetz spoke thus of the Emperor Claudius because the latter had written in a letter dated 41 that the Jews were the "plague of the Universe[50]."

XIV. The revolt of 66

At the beginning of the Christian era, before 70 AD, there were, according to the most plausible estimates, six to seven million Jews in the empire, of whom two and a half million were in Judea and four and a half million in the Diaspora, i.e. 10% of the total population of the Roman Empire, when at that time Christians hardly numbered more than a hundred thousand or two hundred thousand souls at the end of the first century. Under the emperor Nero, we see that the Jews established in the empire were once again fully entitled to exercise their worship. Seneca (4 BC - 65 AD), the great philosopher and playwright of the Stoic school, already complained about their disproportionate influence[51]. Seneca had been an adviser at the imperial court of Caligula before he became Nero's preceptor. He played an important role with the latter before he was discredited and driven to suicide. Seneca abhorred the Jews: "The way of life of these perverse people was so powerful that they imposed themselves in all

---

are pre-Roman and anti-Jewish), Christians would have the power and interest to cause significant unrest in Rome, and without explicitly naming Jesus (Chrestos or Chrestos is a title, not a name). Instead, there were already numerous precedents for riots and altercations with the Jews because of his messianic ailments. This "Chrestos" would probably be an "enthusiast", another false self-proclaimed Jewish messiah. Read the final Annex (NdT).

[49] Dion Cassius, *Historia Romana, Libro LX*, Editorial Gredos, Madrid, 2011, p. 555.
[50] Marie-France Rouart, *L'Antisémitisme dans la littérature populaire*, Paris, Berg International, 2001.
[51] *Vistoribus victi legem dederunt*, Seneca, *De Superstitione*, in Georges-Bernard Depping, *Les Juifs dans le Moyen-Âge*, 1823, Paris, Imprimerie royale, Wouters, Bruxelles, 1844, p. 20.

regions: the vanquished gave laws to the victors[52]", he wrote. On the other hand, with regard to the Christians, who were very hostile to the Jews, but still few in number, Seneca spoke neither for good nor for bad.

In 66, Judea revolted against the Romans and the insurrection sowed even more confusion throughout the country[53]. The only available source for these events is the book of Flavius Josephus, *The Jewish War*. We read in it that the Zealots and the people of Jerusalem rose up, forcing the pre-Roman king Agrippa II to abandon the city: "Agrippa, who was equally concerned about the revolters and those against whom war was being prepared, who wanted to keep the Jews within the Empire of Rome, without losing his Temple and his metropolis, and who was aware that this revolt would bring him no benefit, sent to defend the people two thousand horsemen under the command of the cavalry chief Darius. The mutineers were superior because of their audacity, while the king's supporters were superior because of their experience. The latter fought, above all, to seize the Temple and drive out those who desecrated the sanctuary...For seven days a great slaughter took place between the two sides, without either of them yielding the part of the territory they had conquered[54]." The intervention of Florus, the Roman governor, was relentless and indiscriminate. "Florus stood as judge in front of Herod's palace, and brought before him the high priest and the men of highest rank, demanding that they deliver into his hands those who had dared to defy him. Trembling, they tried to make excuses for what had happened and begged for his mercy. But Florus ignored them and ordered the Roman soldiers to sack the market place, a neighbourhood inhabited by the rich. Like demons, the savage soldiers rushed into the market place and the adjacent streets, killed men,

---

[52] Sénèque, *De la Superstition (De Superstitione)*, Fragment XXXVI. XXXVI. Quoted in Geroges Nataf, *Les Sources païennes de l'antisémitisme*, Berg International, 2001, p. 77.

[53] "In addition to the spirit of lawlessness there was another source of discord and misery. As the present situation grew sadder and more desperate, the longing in the hearts of the faithful believers for the deliverance which was to bring peace to Judea grew more and more intense. Messianic hopes were now stronger among the people than they had been even during the time of the early Roman rulers, hopes which gave rise to enthusiasts who offered themselves as prophets and Messiahs, and made them find believers and followers. To throw off the yoke of Rome was the great aim of all these enthusiasts." Heinrich Graetz, *History of the Jews II*, p. 241.

[54] Flavius Josephus, *La Guerra de los judíos, Libro II*, Editorial Gredos, Madrid, 1999, p. 346, 347. ["The king's forces were overcome by the number and daring of the rebels and were forced to retreat from the Upper City. Then the others rushed upon the house of the high priest Ananias and the palace of Agrippa and Berenice and set fire to them. They then set fire to the archives in order to make the loan contracts disappear and thus prevent the debts from being collected. In this way the indebted people would join them and the poor would rise up against the rich with impunity", p. 348.]

women and children, ransacked the houses and carried off their contents. On that day (16th of the month *iyar*) more than three thousand six hundred men perished. The prisoners, by order of Florus, were scourged and crucified[55]."

"When news of the battle between the Zealots and the Roman cohorts in Jerusalem reached Caesarea, the Greeks and Syrians attacked the Jews who had returned there. The carnage that followed must have been appalling; more than twenty thousand Jews were slaughtered, and these, no doubt, did not succumb without causing other deaths in self-defence. Not a single Jew was left alive in Caesarea," wrote Graetz (following the version of Flavius Josephus), stating, moreover, without fear of exaggeration, that "on the same day and at the same hour, as if by divine Providence, the inhabitants of Caesarea murdered the Jews living in their city, so that in one hour they beheaded more than twenty thousand and the whole of Caesarea was emptied of Jews. For Florus also captured those who were fleeing and took them in chains to the dockyards[56]."

The Romans also suffered serious losses: "This unparalleled cruelty exasperated the whole population of Judea, and their hatred of the heathen broke out into a wild frenzy. Everywhere, as if by tacit agreement, bands of free troops were formed and attacked the heathen inhabitants of the country, burning, destroying, and killing. These barbarous attacks, of course, provoked the revenge of the heathen population of Judea and Syria. Many cities were divided into two hostile factions, which fought savagely together during the day and ambushed and wounded each other at night[57]."

The war between Jews and pagans spread to Alexandria. The Greeks of Alexandria thought of approaching Nero to have the Jews stripped of the rights which Claudius had solemnly confirmed to them. To this end, the Greeks, Macedonians, and probably many Egyptians, the eternal forgotten ones of Greek and Roman chroniclers, met in the amphitheatre to discuss the embassy they planned to send to Emperor Nero.

Heinrich Graetz wrote of this episode: "When some Judaisers were discovered in the crowd, they were fiercely attacked and insulted as spies. Three of them were dragged through the streets to be set on fire". In reality, the Jews had probably stormed the amphitheatre, but they had met their match. Indeed, other Jews had come "enraged at the savage treatment meted out to their brethren, the Jews armed themselves, took incendiary

---

[55] Heinrich Graetz, *History of the Jews II*, Philadelphia, The Jewish Publication Society of America, 1891, p. 255.
[56] Flavius Josephus, *La Guerra de los judíos, Libro II*, Editorial Gredos, Madrid, 1999, p. 354.
[57] Heinrich Graetz, *History of the Jews II*, Philadelphia, The Jewish Publication Society of America, 1891, p. 263.

stones and threatened to burn the amphitheatre where the Greeks were still assembled". The prefect Tiberius Alexander, nephew of the Jewish philosopher Philo, sent the legions to the Jewish quarter to restore order. Falvius Josephus noted in his account that the soldiers "had no pity for the little children, nor respect for the aged, but went about killing people of all ages, until the whole neighbourhood was flooded with blood and fifty thousand corpses were piled up. And no one would have survived, if they had not come to beg. Tiberius Alexander took pity on them and ordered the Romans to withdraw. The soldiers, accustomed to obey, abandoned the slaughter immediately, but it was difficult to calm the popular strata of Alexandria, because of their great hatred for the Jews, and they could hardly be kept away from the corpses[58]."

Heinrich Graetz took up these figures from Josephus: "Tiberius Alexander...ordered his legions into the Jewish quarter and unleashed the brutality he had worked so hard to contain. The soldiers, eager for blood and plunder, rushed into the beautiful Delta quarter of the city, slaughtering all in their path, setting fire to the houses and filling the streets with blood and corpses. Fifty thousand Judaisers lost their lives, and the man who ordered that dreadful butchery was the nephew of the Jewish philosopher Philo![59]" Tiberius Alexander was indeed of Jewish origin and hated by the Jews as an apostate.

Thus, between a quarter and a fifth of the Jewish inhabitants of Alexandria had perished, although it is also possible that Flavius Josephus exaggerated the figures. Naturally, wrote Graetz, "the Jews took revenge on their pagan neighbours. The savage enmity between the races rose still higher, overflowing the narrow borders of Palestine, and the hatred spread between the Jews on the one side and the Greeks and Romans on the other".

XV. Titus and the Destruction of the Temple

To tame Judea once and for all, a strong and vigorous arm was needed, so Emperor Nero chose to send General Vespasian. In the winter of 67 Vespasian left Greece for the theatre of operations. His son Titus brought from Alexandria the two legions whose ferocity the Jews had already suffered. In Ptolemais, above the Nile delta, the neighbouring princes, including King Agrippa and his sister Berenice, came before Vespasian to pay obeisance and offer their troops to the Roman general as a sign of

---

[58] Flavius Josephus, *La Guerra de los judíos, Libro II*, Editorial Gredos, Madrid, 1999, p. 362.
[59] Heinrich Graetz, *History of the Jews II*, Philadelphia, The Jewish Publication Society of America, 1891, p. 265, 271.

vassalage to Rome. It was there that Berenice met and entered into a love affair with Titus that was to last for several years, despite the fact that she was older than Vespasian's son.

The Romans entered the city of Gamala and massacred about 4000 men. Titus ordered the crucifixion of the prisoners, up to five hundred in a single day, to intimidate the most stubborn rebels. Sometimes he sent them back to Jerusalem with their hands cut off. When he had assembled an army of 80,000 men and a large number of siege machines, he marched on Jerusalem.

Three "Jewish traitors" (Graetz) helped Titus during this campaign. First, King Agrippa, by supplying him with troops and dissuading the inhabitants of Jerusalem from resisting the Romans by his speeches; Tiberius Alexander, who had already caused a massacre of his former fellow Jews in Alexandria and was about to reoccur in Judea. Titus, still inexperienced in warfare in this region, needed the advice of this apostate and appointed him general-in-chief of his guard (*præfectu prætario*). Finally, there was Yosef ben Matityahu ha-Cohen, better known as Flavius Josephus, a young general who had fought against the Romans and who, after being taken prisoner, served as a guide to Titus, whom he accompanied everywhere.

Flavius Josephus wrote two reference books already cited: *The Jewish War (*75–79), the only known account of the destruction of Jerusalem, and the *Jewish Antiquities* (93).

In the *Jewish Antiquities*, Flavius Josephus, regarded as a traitor by his peers, insisted, despite all the evidence, on proving that the Jews were well integrated into the empire, returning no less than eighteen times to this question. Nevertheless, he is one of the few ancient authors who can be considered a historian, given the precision and abundance of his information. Jewish by origin, he came from a priestly family on his father's side and from the Hasmonean kings on his mother's side. Like Philo, and like his nephew Tiberius Alexander, he belonged to a Hellenised aristocratic social class. For him, the inhabitants of Jerusalem were victims and prisoners of extremist and bloodthirsty "criminals" who were leading the town to ruin. In fact, he made no secret of his aversion to the Zealots, in his eyes a band of illuminati obsessed with the final catastrophe. Vespasian and Titus treated him with the utmost respect and consideration. During the Judean insurrection, Flavius Josephus was appointed commander-in-chief of the Roman troops on the northern front of the capital.

As for the Jews, the danger had brought about a certain understanding and compromise between all parties, and numerous volunteers had come from Judea and abroad to defend the city. The Zealots, the most radical of the Jewish resisters, did not hesitate to retaliate against the Jewish elite who preferred to collaborate with Roman power. When Titus arrived within the city walls in March 69, these "criminals" or "bandits", as Josephus put it, began to resort to looting and murder to liquidate the most eminent personalities and spread terror.

The zealots' side was itself divided into several rival factions. There was John bar Gischala, at the head of six thousand men; Shimon bar Giora, who had ten thousand men; and Eleazar bar Simon, who had behind him two thousand four hundred men. But soon they all began to kill each other, and—according to Josephus—the people came to pray for the speedy arrival of the Romans.

In May, Titus gave the order for the assault. The Roman troops conquered the third wall, then the second and the Upper City. Meanwhile, the Zealots, sensing their coming defeat, redoubled their cruelty. The Jewish warriors, exhausted by fighting and hunger, could no longer repel the Roman assaults. The Romans scaled the walls, seized the towers and rushed into the Upper City, slaughtering all the resistance.

Now only the Temple remained to be conquered. The last fanatical die-hard defenders had barricaded themselves inside, and the Romans wondered whether it should be destroyed. While many felt that the nest of revolts should be razed to the ground, Titus, on the other hand, was clearly in favour of preserving the building. This was probably due to the influence of Princess Bernice. It was therefore decided to take the Temple, but without destroying it. The next day, on the 9th of *April* (a fateful date in the Jewish calendar), the Jews attempted to leave, but had to retreat, overcome by Roman superiority in numbers.

On 29 August 70, after a last attempt to escape, the Temple was set on fire. A Roman took a burning blight and, climbing on the shoulders of his companions, threw it through a window into the building. The timbers of the galleries caught fire, and the fire spread rapidly throughout the building. Titus rushed in with his soldiers and ordered the fire to be put out, but was not heard. The Roman soldiers rushed furiously into the building, slaughtering those who had not been able to flee. Titus himself, moved by curiosity, entered the Sacrosanctus, until the smoke from the fire forced him to leave the place. The Temple burned to the ground, except for the foundations and a few remnants of the western wall. After the fire, Titus ordered all the houses still standing to be burned. The city walls were completely demolished, except for the three towers, Hippos, Mariamme and Fasael, which Titus preserved as monuments of his memorable victory. The last vestiges of Judean political independence were buried beneath the ruins of Jerusalem.

According to Josephus, 115,880 corpses were evacuated through the city gate guarded by Titus. In all, wrote the Jewish historian, 1,100,000 people had perished during the siege, but this figure is obviously excessive since it corresponded to half the population of Judea. The population of Jerusalem, augmented by the bands of Zealots, must have been about forty or fifty thousand souls, and the number of dead was probably twenty or twenty-five thousand[60].

Graetz wrote here: "More than a million lives had been lost during the siege. Counting those who had fallen in Galilee, Perea, and the provinces, it may be assumed that the Jews who inhabited their native land were almost entirely annihilated".

Judaism had lost its priestly institutions and its capital, its centre of gravity. Temple contributions would henceforth be paid into the Roman treasury. The annuity of two drachmas, which the Jews were accustomed to send to the Temple in Jerusalem, would go to the Temple of Jupiter Capitolinus, and ultimately this tax—the *fiscus judaicus*—would become the property of the emperor's personal treasury.

Thus began what the Jews call the *third captivity*, the period of *Roman exile* (*Galut Edom*). Most of the young men were scattered throughout the provinces to play for their lives in the circuses and arenas. The younger ones and the women were auctioned off and, given their large numbers, probably sold at knock-down prices to slave traders.

Titus celebrated his victory before his court at Caesarea, where King Agrippa resided. He organised fierce beast fights with the prisoners. Jewish prisoners were taken to the circus and forced to fight ferocious animals to the death. Sometimes the spectacle varied: the prisoners had to fight against each other. It was in this way, wrote Graetz, that 2500 young Jewish nobles perished, "to celebrate the birthday of Domitian, the emperor's brother".

Numerous victims perished before the eyes of Titus and Berenice. In Berite (present-day Beirut), on his father's birthday, 17 November, Titus displayed all his prodigality, once again offering Jews to the arena and to death. In all the cities of Syria, Titus provided the inhabitants of the empire with the joyful spectacle of the martyrdom of the Jews. All the Jews of the Roman Empire, especially in Syria, Asia Minor, Alexandria and Rome, came close to suffering the same fate as their Palestinian brethren. "For the war had aroused the hatred of the whole heathen world against the unfortunate children of Israel, a hatred that was fanatical in its intensity, its aim being the total destruction of the whole race[61]," Graetz lamented.

Again, Bernice must have inspired some clemency in Titus towards his fellows. As Titus' retinue approached Antioch, the people came out to meet him and begged him to expel the Jews from the city. But Titus did not consent and did not even withdraw their civil rights and privileges. The

---

[60] Gérard Messadié, *Histoire générale de l'antisémitisme*, JC Lattès, 1999, p. 98.
[61] Heinrich Graetz, *History of the Jews II*, Philadelphia, The Jewish Publication Society of America, 1891, p. 312–313, 316.

inhabitants of Alexandria also pleaded in vain with the emperor to annul the rights of the Jews in their city.

Meanwhile, in Rome, civil war raged. Nero had committed suicide in 69 and Emperor Galba would soon lie murdered in the middle of the Forum. Otho succeeded him in that "year of the four emperors", but had to go to war in Germany against the self-proclaimed Emperor Vitellius. He also committed suicide. His reign had only lasted a few months.

Titus' entry into Rome was accompanied by great triumphal honours, the most sumptuous that Rome had seen in many years, demonstrating, despite internal troubles, the great joy caused by Rome's victory over Judea. For several years gold, silver and copper medals were struck in remembrance of this glorious victory. The medals depicted Judea with the features of a woman sitting in grief under a palm tree, or standing with her hands chained and with a despairing countenance. *Judæa devicta* or *Judæa capta* were the legends on these medals. Later, a triumphal arch (Arco di Tito, next to the Colosseum) was built in honour of Titus, where the trophies of that victory can still be seen today carried on the shoulders of Roman soldiers. However, neither Vespasian nor Titus wanted to adopt the nickname *Judaicus*, as consuls and emperors were wont to do with other defeated peoples, as this name already had an infamous connotation.

Flavius Josephus had accompanied Titus during his triumph in Rome. Vespasian installed him in his own palace, conferring on him Roman citizenship and granting him rich estates in Judea. Josephus enjoyed the favours of the Flavian dynasty and so adopted the family name of his protectors: *Flavius Iosephus*. In 95, however, he published a work entitled *Against Apion in which he* refuted the accusations levelled against Judaism, thus earning the forgiveness and recognition of his co-religionists.

Flavius Josephus' political choices were not exceptional after all. When in 73, three years after the apocalyptic fall of Jerusalem, surviving Jewish hired assassins from Palestine entered Egypt and attempted to foment unrest, the Jewish gentry led the repression. Six hundred "criminals" were arrested; the others were chased into Upper Egypt and handed over to the Romans who tortured them to death.

In the same year, Jewish resistance was illustrated at Masada in Judea. Hundreds of zealots and their families had taken refuge in this fortress besieged by Roman troops. Their leader, Eleazar, urged them to put themselves to death rather than fall into the hands of their enemies. On the first day of Passover 73, encouraged by Eleazar's words, the Jews slit the throats of their wives and children before committing suicide. A deadly silence reigned in the square of Masada when the Romans entered it: only two women and five children were still alive (according to legend), amidst 960 victims.

Berenice lived in Rome with Titus in his palace as if she were already his official wife. In 75, he would have promised to marry her, as Titus seemed to really think about it. But the Romans hated the Jews too much to allow such a marriage. The scandal was immense and in 78 Titus had to resign himself and dismiss her.

It was not long before the Jewish princess became Roman empress. Berenice returned to Palestine, although she maintained some influence from a distance and intervened several times on behalf of her fellow Jews. In 79 Titus acceded to the throne, succeeding Vespasian, but died two years later, in September 81, without seeing his Jewish mistress again.

XVI. Domitian and the fiscus judaicus

Domitian, brother of Titus, reigned from 81 to 96 and was able to contain the power of the Jewish community. In his *Lives of the Twelve Caesars*, Suetonius described him as follows: "He was tall in stature; his face reflected modesty and was easily covered with blushes; his eyes were large, although he was rather short-sighted; he was also handsome and well proportioned, especially in his youth[62]".

Immediately after the destruction of Jerusalem, as we saw, Titus had forced the Jews to pay the didrachma they had previously paid to their temple. To avoid the *fiscus judaicus*, explained Heinrich Graetz, "many Jews denied their Hebrew origin".

But Domitian was clearly intent on enforcing the laws of Rome. "The cruel and greedy Domitian', as Graetz described him, had this tax levied even more rigorously, ordering the examination of those suspected of not belonging to the Jewish community. The historian Suetonius recounted how he had seen a nonagenarian old man undergo a public inspection to see if he was circumcised and therefore liable to the Jewish tax[63].

"Necessity made the Jews ingenious, and many of them employed a ruse to evade the Jewish tax, wrote Graetz. They managed to make the sign of the covenant unrecognisable on their bodies".

XVII. Trajan

The Roman Empire experienced its greatest glory and expansion during the reign of Trajan (98–117). Both Republican Rome and Imperial Rome

---

[62] Suetonius, *Lives of the Twelve Caesars II*, Book VIII, Editorial Gredos, Madrid, 1992, p. 342. 342
[63] *Life of Domitian*, XII, in Georges-Bernard Depping, *Les Juifs dans le Moyen-Âge*, (1823), Wouters, Brussels, 1844, p. 21, 22.

had not known such resounding victories as those of Trajan. The campaigns of this emperor of Hispanic origin were a succession of triumphs. When he took up his winter quarters at Antioch to receive the tributes of the vanquished (winter 115–116), Trajan might have considered the war in the East over, but in the following spring the emperor returned to break the last resistance of the Parthian enemy and turn Mesopotamia into the great avenue to India which he dreamed of conquering. The triumph was short-lived, however, as the subdued populations between the Tigris and Euphrates rebelled. This defection had been orchestrated by the Jews, who had organised a revolt throughout much of the Roman Empire. The Jews of Babylon, along with those of Egypt, Cyrenaica (the coast of Libya) and the island of Cyprus, had conceived the plan to throw off the Roman yoke by taking up arms again.

"Such unanimous action presupposed a concerted plan and a powerful leader. From Judea, the rebellion spread to the neighbouring countries as far as the Euphrates and Egypt (116–117)," wrote Heinrich Graetz. A pseudo-messiah named Andreas, or Luke, excited the fanaticism of the Jews. Judea revolted and organised insurrection in the neighbouring regions, from the banks of the Euphrates to Egypt (autumn 116 and winter 117). The slogan "soon the Temple will be rebuilt" had kept alive the love of freedom in the young Jews, who had not lost the custom of using weapons in their schools[64]." This prophetic faith animated their hearts, for it assured them of their future universal triumph.

In Egypt, this revolt, known as the war of Kitos, lasted three years, from 115 to 117. There is no record of the preparations and vicissitudes of this struggle; only the outcome is known to us. The leaders of the insurrection seem to have been Julian Alexander and Papo. The rebels first attacked the neighbours of their city, massacring Greeks and Romans. Emboldened by their early successes, they banded together and attacked the legions led by the general Marcus Rutilius Lupo. In the first confrontation, the Jews thwarted the strategic skill and discipline of the Romans, and Lupo was forced to retreat. This first battle was accompanied by appalling massacres; victors and vanquished engaged in atrocious acts of barbarism and savage cruelty, manifesting a long-contained, implacable racial hatred that could only be satiated by blood.

The pagans who had fled after the defeat entered Alexandria, whose Jewish inhabitants who were fit to bear arms had joined the rebel army. They arrested the Jews they found and executed them after terrible tortures. The Jewish army retaliated; the Jews invaded Egypt and conquered the

---

[64] Heinrich Graetz, *History of the Jews II*, Philadelphia, The Jewish Publication Society of America, 1891, p. 397, 398.

castle of Alexandria. They took the inhabitants prisoner and inflicted the same tortures on them. The pagan population of the city tried to save themselves by fleeing to the port. The Jews pursued them, catching up with them near the ships. A terrible struggle ensued. Apianus, then procurator in Egypt, told of having escaped the massacre by a miracle, stating that "the Jews ate the flesh of the Greek and Roman captives, smeared themselves with their blood and wrapped themselves in the skins torn from their enemies". Naturally, Graetz doubted this: "These horrors were totally foreign to the Jewish character and customs."

Alexandria suffered severe damage inflicted by the Jewish insurgents. Their fury had impelled them to destroy numerous monuments in the city, especially the temple of Nemesis, the Greek goddess of retributive justice and vengeance. There is evidence that the Jews forced the vanquished to go down to the arena to fight the ferocious beasts or to kill each other. Graetz mentioned this in his work: "The Jews made the Romans and Greeks fight with wild animals or in the arena. It was a sad retaliation for the horrible drama to which Vespasian and Titus had condemned the captive Jews".

The Jewish historian referred to other information, such as that "in Cyrenaica, 200,000 Greeks and Romans were killed by the Jews, and Libya, the strip of land east of Egypt, was so devastated that, a few years later, new colonies had to be sent there. On the island of Cyprus, which had always been inhabited by Jews, who owned synagogues there, one Artemion led the uprising against the Romans. The number of rebels was very large, and was probably reinforced by the discontented pagan inhabitants of the island. It is said that Cyprian's Jews destroyed Salamis, the island's capital, and killed 240,000 Greeks[65]."

Graetz thus relied on the account of Dion Cassius (150–235), the author of the monumental *Roman History* in eighty books, who recounted those events: "Meanwhile, the Jews in the region of Cyrene put a certain Andreas at their head and were killing both Romans and Greeks. They ate the flesh of their victims, made belts of their entrails, anointed themselves with their blood, and wore their skins for clothing; they sawed many in half from top to bottom; others they handed over to wild beasts, and still others they forced to fight as gladiators. In all, two hundred and twenty thousand persons perished. In Egypt, too, they perpetrated similar outrages; and in Cyprus, under the command of one Artemion. There, moreover, two hundred and forty thousand died[66]."

---

[65] Heinrich Graetz, *History of the Jews II*, Philadelphia, The Jewish Publication Society of America, 1891, p. 399, 400.
[66] Dion Cassius, *Roman History, book LXVIII*, 32, quoted in Georges Nataf, *Les Sources païennes de l'antisémitisme*, Berg International, 2001, p. 97.

In Alexandria, Marius Turbo devised the stratagem of endlessly harassing the Jews, by means of small skirmishes, and after a long and bitter struggle the Jews laid down their arms. The legions surrounded the prisoners and tore them to pieces, the women were raped and killed. The Jews who were left alive were for the first time assigned to enclosed places to live apart, in order to preserve the rest of the population from their contagious hysteria.

Turbo then set out with his forces to attack the island of Cyprus. The details of this military operation are not known, but there is no doubt that the Jews of the island were exterminated to the last. They were surely guilty of the worst atrocities, for from then on, wrote Graetz, "a deadly hatred against the Jews arose in Cyprus. This hatred was expressed in a barbarous law, according to which no Jew was to approach the island of Cyprus, even if he suffered shipwreck on that coast[67]."

Trajan had such a thirst for vengeance against the Jews that in Babylon he ordered Lusius Quietus to exterminate every last Jew. For "so great was the Emperor's fear and hatred of a nation whose power he did not seem to have rightly estimated in any way. For Trajan had to oppose the Jews on three sides, and if they had united and supported each other, the colossal Roman empire would perhaps have received a mortal blow,[68]" explained Graetz. The war of extermination waged by this general of Berber origin is not very well documented. All that is known is that thousands of Jews had their throats slit and that the cities of Nisibis and Edessa were completely destroyed. The houses, streets and roads were covered with corpses. Trajan, to reward Quietus for his great contribution to this war, appointed him governor of Palestine, giving him broad powers to quell any new seeds of revolt.

Convinced that the time had come when they would dominate all nations, Andreas and Artemion encouraged their co-religionists to perpetrate all these massacres [69]. Undoubtedly, "it is this spirit of domination that has always made them odious to all peoples[70]."

The famous historian Publius Cornelius Tacitus (55–120), born in Narbonne Gaul (perhaps in Vaison-la-Romaine), was close to the emperor Trajan at the beginning of his reign. Retired from political life, Tacitus devoted himself to his great literary work. His *Histories* were published

---

[67]Heinrich Graetz, *History of the Jews II*, Philadelphia, The Jewish Publication Society of America, 1891, p. 401. And in Dion Cassius, *Roman History, book LXVIII, 32*.
[68]Heinrich Graetz, *History of the Jews II*, Philadelphia, The Jewish Publication Society of America, 1891, p. 400.
[69]Augustin Lemann, *L'Avenir de Jérusalem, Éspérances et chimères*, 1901
[70]Mgr Henri Delassus, *La Conjuration antichrétienne II*, Desclée De Brouwer, Lille, 1910, p. 691.

between 104 and 109 and his *Annals* around 110 or 115. We can see quite well from his account that the Jews were not held in high esteem in Rome:

"Moses imposed on them a new religion, contrary to those of the rest of mankind: what we hold sacred is sacrilegious there, and, conversely, what is immoral for us is permitted to them... The rest of their practices, evil and sinister, were made to prosper by perversity, for the worst sort of people, after abjuring their ancestral faith, contributed taxes and donations which have increased the wealth of the Jews. Also because loyalty among them is stubborn and charity diligent, but against all others they harbour the hatred of enemies. They eat apart, they sleep apart. Although they are a very lewd people, they never have intercourse with foreign women. On the other hand, nothing is forbidden among them[71]." Tacitus further wrote: "No people have so hated others as the Jewish people, none in their turn so repulsed them, and none have so deservedly earned such implacable hatreds[72]."

XVIII. Hadrian and the siege of Betar

Hadrian succeeded Trajan. At the beginning of his reign, he wanted to establish cordial relations with the Jews in order to avoid a new war. He thought that the Jews could fight on his side in case the Parthians invaded Roman territory. Hadrian had therefore authorised the Jews to rebuild the Temple on its ancient site and to raise the ruins of Jerusalem. There was therefore great joy among the Jews of Judea, who for fifty years had been longing to have a religious centre once again. The work of rebuilding the Temple was progressing rapidly and the Senate decided to perpetuate the memory of this event by minting several medals, some depicting the emperor in his toga as he lifted up a humble Judea on his knees. But the good relations between Hadrian and the Hebrew nation did not last more than ten years. Hadrian had indeed conceived the plan to raise Jerusalem from its ruins, but to transform it into a pagan city, which provoked a new revolt.

The insurrection led by Simon Bar Kochba in 132 was the last great Jewish revolt during the empire. As usual, Bar Kohba, "the Son of the Star", presented himself as the Messiah and was recognised as such by the greatest rabbi of his time, Akiba ben Joseph[73]. The Romans first beat a

---

[71] Cornelius Tacitus, *Histories, Book V*, Cátedra, Madrid, 2006, p. 303–304.
[72] Beatus Rhenanus, in Léon Poliakov, *Histoire de l'antisémitisme, Tome I*, Point Seuil, 1981, p. 232, 361.
[73] Bar Kohba means "Son of the Star" in Aramaic. This nickname derives from an interpretation of the biblical verse *Num XXIV, 17* ("A star came down from Jacob") to which Jewish tradition gave a messianic meaning, the star of Jacob designating the Messiah. According to Jewish tradition, he was recognised as the Messiah by the

retreat, abandoning the rebels one fortress after another. After one year (132–133), 50 strongholds and 985 open towns and villages had fallen to the Jews, and the whole of Judea, as far as Samaria and Galilee, had been recaptured.

The new state reorganised by Bar Kohba had been in place for almost two years (summer 132–134). The Jews settled mainly on the Mediterranean coast, with the city of Betar occupying the centre of the defensive apparatus. Hadrian had to call from Brittany the most competent general of his time, Julius Severus (Julius *Severus*) to send against the Jewish rebels. Julius Severus attacked the various enemy corps one by one, crushing them with his cavalry. To intimidate the Jews, he systematically executed all the prisoners. The siege of Betar, which lasted about a year, was the last episode of this war which had lasted three and a half years.

The victors committed horrible massacres in Betar. "This was described in terrible detail. It is said that the horses waded with blood up to their muzzles, for the river ran full of blood to the distant sea carrying the corpses and great rocks[74]. Three hundred skulls of mangled infants were found on the rocks[75]." According to Jewish tradition, Bethar fell on the 9th day of the month of *Ab* in the year 135, a date that coincides once again—curiously enough—with those of the destruction of the two temples (486 BC and 70 AD) and also in the future, in the imagination of the Jews, with the date of the expulsion from Spain in 1492.

"One can hardly believe the number of dead that is said to have occurred, and yet Jewish and Greek historians confirm it. The authentic historian Dion Cassius relates that in addition to those who died of hunger and fire, half a million Jews fell," wrote Heinrich Graetz[76]. "The losses of the Romans were equally great, and Hadrian did not dare to use in his message

---

greatest sage of his time, Rabbi Akiba, one of the fathers of Rabbinic Judaism who took part in the revolt. This sage gave him his unconditional support. With the failure of Bar Kochba's revolt, the rabbis subsequently adopted an anti-Messianic orientation towards the aforementioned. They changed his name to Bar Kozeva, playing on the sound of the Hebrew word *kazav*, "lie". From saviour, he thus became the "Son of the Lie". In the Talmud he is referred to as the false Messiah.

[74] Heinrich Graetz, *History of the Jews II*, Philadelphia, The Jewish Publication Society of America, 1891, p. 422.

[75] Jews are manifestly obsessed with the skulls of mangled children. There are numerous "testimonies" from the Second World War accusing the SS of identical crimes, which obviously reflect nothing more than the guilt of the Jewish intellectuals themselves, who are accustomed to the procedure of accusatory inversion. In this regard, see *The Mirror of Judaism*.

[76] Heinrich Graetz, *History of the Jews II*, p. 422. Dion Cassius, *Roman History, IX, 43*. The population of Judea at that time must have been around two and a half million, in Gérard Messadié, *Histoire générale de l'antisémitisme*, JC Lattès, 1999, p. 103.

to the Senate the usual formula: "I and the army are well". The Senate did not decree the Emperor's triumph, but a medal was struck in commemoration of the services rendered by the army. This coin bore the inscription *"Exercitus Judaicus"*: "Thanks to the victorious army over the Jews". The honours were awarded to his general Julius Severus.

After the defeat of Bar Kohba, thousands of Jewish prisoners were sold into slavery in the markets of Hebron and Gaza. The Jews who still remained in their homeland hid in caves to escape the Roman soldiers. Hadrian thought that the Jews had not yet been sufficiently weakened and planned the final annihilation of their religion. He entrusted the execution of the plan to Quintus Tineius Rufus, while General Severus returned to Britain.

Titus had left some houses standing in Jerusalem, so some unfortunate people had built huts in between to live next to those precious ruins. But Rufus had the plough run over the whole city of Jerusalem and the site of the Temple. Jerusalem was thus completely razed to the ground. Hadrian was finally able to carry out his urban planning and transform the Jewish city into a pagan city. On the site of the old city now stood a beautiful Roman city, Aelia Capitolina, named after Aelius Hadrian and Jupiter Capitolinus. In all published acts, Jerusalem was now called Aelia, and the old name was forgotten. Judea was also renamed Palestine. Temples were erected to Bacchus, Venus and Serapis. The Temple of Jupiter Capitolinus, the patron god of Rome, stood on the site of the temple of the Jews. Statues of Roman, Greek and Phoenician divinities beautifully adorned the streets and squares. A theatre, public baths and various buildings were constructed. Hadrian established in the city colonies of veterans, mainly Phoenicians and Syrians. As for the Jews (but not Christians of Jewish origin), they were forbidden to set foot in the city on pain of death. They were only allowed to appear in the city once a year, on the day of the great fair, and they had to pay an entrance fee. The Romans carved a pig on the pediment of the main gate with the idea of scaring away the true Israelites before the emblem of the abhorred animal. The Jews tolerated in the neighbouring regions, in Tiberias, Capernaum and Nazareth, looked with envy and regret at the land now forbidden to them.

Hadrian thus followed the policy of Antiochus Epiphanes. He issued a decree in Palestine prohibiting, under severe penalties, circumcision, the celebration of the Sabbath and the study of the Mosaic Law. But, unlike the Hellenistic king, he did not force the Jews to worship Roman deities.

Observance of the least Mosaic practice was severely punished, so that Torah reading was done on the rooftops, away from the inquisitive eyes of the spies. Violators were skilfully tortured. Heinrich Graetz provided some details here: "A younger contemporary of this sad time described, almost dramatically, the cruelty of the Roman authorities who inflicted some cruel punishment for every religious ceremony. "Why are you to be scourged? Because I have brought a *lulab*. Why should you be crucified? Because I ate unleavened bread at Passover. Why should you be put to death by fire or by the sword? Because we read the Torah and allowed our sons to be circumcised". Even more terrible were the deaths inflicted on the accused by the Roman courts, which can only be compared to those inflicted by the Inquisition. Red-hot balls were placed in the armpits, or spiked reeds were passed under the fingernails, or wet wool was placed on the torso of one who was being burned to death to prolong the torture, or the skin was torn off, horrors that cause one to shudder just to enumerate them."

The Jews tried to evade the vigilance of the authorities and the informers. Some of these were former Jews who had chosen to leave the sect. The apostasy of Elisha ben Abuyah, a doctor of the faith, had dire consequences for the Jews. Elisha ben Abuyah, also nicknamed *Acher*[77] (*Ajer*), taught the authorities how to recognise Jewish practices, and the Roman spies were thus able to spy from afar that an illegal ceremony was taking place. The noise of a hand mill, for example, announced the preparation of the gunpowder needed for the healing of a newly circumcised child; illuminations indicated the celebration of a wedding. They were thus guided by these indications to discover the Jews and denounce them to the courts. Graetz evoked this treachery in his book: "Among them was *Acher*, who was imbued with great contempt for the Law. It is said that he gave information to the Roman authorities so that they could distinguish between religious ceremonies and those that were of no importance... Thus the Roman spies, who initiated the overseers into the various rites, were on the lookout for any attempt at religious observance. Hadrian or his representatives directed their strictest attention and inflicted the severest punishments in two special cases: the assembling of schools and the ordination of disciples...If the ordination of pupils as independent teachers could be prevented, then naturally there would be an obstruction in the vital current of Judaism. It must be confessed that the Roman policy was well judged on the part of their supporters, and they knew how to strike at the most vulnerable point in Judaism. Severe death penalties were inflicted on teachers who kept schools and those who ordained disciples; even the communities were held responsible. The city and its surroundings, where ordination took place, were condemned to destruction. It is possible that *Acher* instigated this persecution. In any case, it is said of him that he handed over the teachers of the Law to death and drove the disciples away from the study of the Law[78]."

---

[77] In Hebrew it means "it is another" (*A'her*). The Sages of the Talmud (*Chagigah, 15a*) called it A'her (*Ajer* in English).
[78] Heinrich Graetz, *History of the Jews II*, Philadelphia, The Jewish Publication Society

Elisha ben Ayubah was later renamed *Akher* (*Acher, Ajer*) by some Jews, as if his conversion had transformed him into a different man. The famous Jewish writer Elie Wiesel said of him in one of his books that he was "the symbol of abjuration and betrayal...He had pockets full of anti-Jewish pamphlets...Worse still: he began to militate in favour of forced assimilation...He sympathised with the occupier, became a collaborator and finally an accomplice of the Roman army". That Rabbi Elisha "was *Akher*—he represented the dark forces of the Jews, the forces of Evil present in man...At first he was called Rabbi Elisha, then Elisha ben Abuyah, then ben Abuyah, and finally *Akher*[79]."

Rabbi Akiva ben Yosef, the leader of the Jews, was treated with great severity by Rufus, the governor of the province. After keeping him in cages for a long time and inflicting atrocious tortures on him, Rufus finally handed him over to the executioner. Graetz recounted in his pages how his skin was torn off with iron hooks.

Hadrian's death three years after the fall of Bethar in the summer of 138 brought about a significant improvement in the situation of the Jews. This emperor, a lover of Greek culture, had become, like Antiochus Epiphanes, the personification of hatred against "the Jewish race" (Graetz). The Jews and Samaritans of the time never pronounced his name without adding this formula of curse: "May God reduce his remains to dust".

It was in the time of Hadrian that the final separation between Jews and Christians took place. By the year 70, the Christians had already shown themselves indifferent to the fate of the Jews. Under Hadrian, after the violent persecutions committed against them by the Jews, the Christians had decidedly sided with the Romans.

XIX. The dynasty of the Severi

Emperor Septimius Severus, who reigned from 193 to 211, ushered in a new era. Septimius Severus was born in Tripolitana, on the Libyan coast. On his mother's side, he was descended from Italic immigrants married to indigenous Libyans, probably Libyans. On his father's side, he was descended from a family of Punic-Berber origin and Punic culture. The

---

of America, 1891, p. 428–429. [However, the Jewish Encyclopedia (1901–1906) writes that "it is almost impossible to get a clear picture of this personality from rabbinical sources, and modern historians have differed widely in their assessment of his figure. For Graetz, he was a Gnostic; for Siegfried, a follower of Philo; for Dubsch, a Christian (of the Elcesaite type), for Smolenskin and Weiss, a victim of the inquisitor Akiva." Wikipedia. NdT]

[79] Elie Wiesel, *Célébration talmudique*, Éd. Seuil, 1991, p. 182-191. *Akher* is pronounced *Ajer*, with the English j.

historian Dion Cassius described him as a man of short stature, slender, very lively, but at the same time taciturn. He had a strong accent, which earned him the derision of his contemporaries. For the first time, the empire was in the hands of a provincial, certainly Romanised, but from a Berber family with strong African ties. The advent of this African prince led many to say that it was "Hannibal's revenge".

This greedy prince became completely corrupted by the gold of the Jews. Septimius Severus enacted laws that assimilated them to Roman citizens and they could be admitted to the highest public functions[80]. These were the first positive provisions made for them in the Roman Empire, and they were maintained throughout the pagan empire. From persecutors, the Jews became persecutors. In Palestine and elsewhere, they exercised vengeance against those of their countrymen who embraced Christianity[81].

His son Caracalla, who succeeded him between 211 and 217, had the same Berber and Syrian origins on his mother's side. He had begun his career by murdering his brother Geta, cutting his throat with a gladius when the latter had taken refuge in the arms of his own mother. He then went on to carry out a series of systematic assassinations (20,000 according to Dion Cassius) against Geta's friends, relations and supporters as well as possible rivals. Caracalla was evidently under the influence of the Jews when in 212 he granted citizenship rights to all inhabitants of the Roman Empire. This law, a real milestone in the history of Rome, contributed greatly to Roman decadence. Indeed, this kind of typically Jewish-inspired law always encourages systematic immigration and the dissolution of national identities[82]. Caracalla, hated by the Romans, was assassinated in April 217 during a military campaign in the East against the Parthians.

His nephew, Heliogabalus or Elegabalus, who reigned from 218 to 222, was born in Syria. Heliogabalus wished to follow faithfully the practices of El-Gabal/Baal, a Semitic sun god of Syria to whom he claimed to be a priest. He had himself circumcised and abstained from eating pork. He also wanted to publicly introduce Jewish, Samaritan and Christian cults in Rome by subordinating them to Baal: "The young emperor Elegabalus... living epitome of all vices, who disgraced the Roman world for four years

---

[80] *"Judæis privilegia reservavit. Lamprid.* in *Alex Sev. - Palæstinis plurima jura fundavit. Spart.,* in *Sev. — Eos qui judaicam superstitionem sequuntur, Severus et Antoninus honores adipisci permiserunt, sed et necessitates imposuerunt, quæ superstitionum eorum non lasderent. Digest.,* lib. 50, tit, 2; lib. 3, pars 3', in Georges-Bernard Depping, *Les Juifs dans le Moyen-Âge,* (1823), Wouters, Brussels, 1844, p. 23.
[81] Georges-Bernard Depping, *Les Juifs dans le Moyen-Âge,* (1823), Wouters, Brussels, 1844, p. 23. Georges-Bernard Depping (Munich, 1784—Paris, 1853) settled in France in 1803. He was naturalised in 1827. He was a serious and pro-Jewish historian. All his information comes with detailed references and footnotes.
[82] See Hervé Ryssen, *Planetary Hopes.*

(218–222), and who seems to have had no other vocation in history than to publicly degrade the pagan gods and Roman Caesarism, and to convince everyone of their worthlessness, seems to have tried and done many things in his methodical madness in imitation of Jewish practices. He offered himself for circumcision and refused to eat swine's flesh, though only in obedience to the commandments of his Sun-God. He proposed to introduce publicly in Rome the Jewish, Samaritan and Christian cults, but subordinating them to his Sun-god, Baal," Heinrich Graetz recounted. Indeed, there were many rumours circulating in Rome of his possible conversion to Judaism.

Heliogabalus left the reins of government to his Syrian grandmother and mother. This female control, the emperor's superstition, childish whims, irresponsible spending and homosexual marriages horrified the ancient Romans and precipitated his downfall. In July 221, his grandmother, sensing that her grandson's vices would destroy him and his family, persuaded him to adopt his cousin Alexianus Basanius under the name Alexander Severus, thus associating him with power under the title of Caesar. This serious, seasoned, virtuous, patient and wise young man had made himself popular with the only force that really mattered in the Empire: the army. When the officers and soldiers began to suspect that Heliogabalus was trying to get rid of his cousin, they immediately murmured against him. Heliogabalus wanted to arrest the ringleaders of the intrigues, but an angry mob invaded the imperial palace and massacred the emperor. His body was dragged through the streets of Rome and the mob tried to throw the corpse down the sewers. Finally, as the pipes were too narrow, the imperial corpse was thrown into the Tibre on 11 March 222.

The new emperor Alexander Severus (222–235) also held Judaism in high esteem. The Jews even saw in him a kind of new Messiah. According to Graetz, "he was well disposed towards Christians, although he seems to have had a greater predilection for Jews and Judaism. The inhabitants of Antioch and Alexandria, whose frivolous character made them more satisfied with immoral emperors than with an austere ruler of the nature of Alexander Severus, mocked him in epigrams, and gave him the nicknames 'Syrian Head of the Synagogue' (*Archisynagogus*, i.e. Rabbi), and 'High Priest'[83]."

In 234, the emperor went in person to Mainz to confront the Germans, especially the Alamanni, but hesitated to fight them head-on, preferring to buy peace. He was murdered in his tent and the legionaries proclaimed one of their own, Maximus, emperor. This assassination inaugurated a period

---

[83] Heinrich Graetz, *History of the Jews II*, Philadelphia, The Jewish Publication Society of America, 1891, p. 473, 485.

of fifty years of military anarchy, until the reigns of Aurelian (270–275) and especially Diocletian (284–305). The Severan dynasty had ended in the same way it had begun: with a coup d'état.

XX. The Christian emperors

Constantine, who reigned from 306 to 337, was the first Roman emperor to convert to Christianity. Through the Edict of Milan in 313, he ended an era of persecution and helped the Church to develop by establishing freedom of worship. He provided donations of money and land, helped finance the construction of large basilicas and frequently minted coins with Christian symbols. Constantine also took measures to protect Christians against the fury and intolerance of the Jews. On 18 October 315, he forbade Jews to persecute their co-religionists who had converted to Christianity, on pain of the stake. On March 7, 321, he decreed Sunday as an obligatory holiday, except for work in the fields. Constantine was not unaware that this measure took a day's work away from the Jews who already rested on the Sabbath. The emperor also forbade Jews to incite Christians to apostatise, and ordered the slaves of circumcised Jews to be freed[84].

His son Constantius II, who reigned until 361, had a law enacted according to which the circumcision of slaves by Jews not only implied their automatic release, but also entailed the confiscation of all the Jewish owner's property and the death penalty. On the other hand, it was decided that a Christian who married a Jewess would have all his property seized by the Imperial Treasury; a Christian in the Imperial factories who married a Jew would be dismissed and her Jewish husband executed.

In 355, from Constantinople, the new imperial capital, Constantius gave full powers to his cousin Julian to fight the Alamanni raids. In 361, upon his death, Julian took control of the entire empire. His reign lasted only two years and was a brief hiatus during which he attempted to restore paganism. Julian reopened the temples and forbade Christians to teach the Greco-Latin classics. He published an essay, *Against Galileans*, a neo-Platonic critique in which he described Christians as uneducated and uncouth.

But, on the other hand, the Jews did not have to suffer with him the slightest hostile legislation, quite the contrary: "For this reason he was all the more friendly to the Jews and was the only emperor, after Alexander Severus, to show a serious interest in Judaism. More than one reason led him to prefer Judaism. Educated in the Christian religion, he had come to

---

[84] Georges-Bernard Depping, *Les Juifs dans le Moyen-Âge*, (1823), Éd. Wouters, Brussels, 1844, p. 24.

know Judaism through the Holy Bible, and the more Judaism was hated and persecuted by Christianity, the greater was the reverence with which he regarded it...Julian's reign, which did not last two years (from November 361 to June 363), was a period of extreme happiness for the Jews of the Roman Empire. The emperor favoured them, relieving them of the oppression and disgrace that came with the mockery of blasphemy. He called the patriarch Hillel his venerable friend and honoured him with an autograph letter, in which he assured him of his goodwill and promised him that he would try to put an end to the evils of the Jews. He also addressed an epistle to all the Jewish communities of the empire, and made preparations to rebuild the Temple of Jerusalem, which had become a Christian city since the time of Constantine[85]." That letter signed in Antioch is dated autumn 362.

Indeed, Julian made no mere promises and set everything in motion to raise the temple from its ruins. The success of the enterprise was very important to him and he spared no expense. Numerous labourers were sent to Jerusalem to clear the land on which the ruined sanctuary had stood for three centuries, and building materials were transported in great quantities.

Julian "the Apostate" had in the Jews his best allies in the war he was waging against the Christians. The Jews, wrote Monsignor Henri Delassus[86], "were quick to take advantage of the emperor's dispositions to once again satisfy their traditional hatreds. They were seen in Egypt and Asia setting fire to Christian basilicas with impunity[87]."

Unfortunately for the Jews, Julian failed in his expedition against the Persians and was pierced by an arrow shot by a Christian in his army (according to legend). The Jews benefited for a long time from the positive effects of his reign, for the restrictive measures against them, which Julian had abolished, were no longer applied to them by Constantine and Constantius.

An assembly of high officials and officers then met and elected Valentinian I emperor, who reigned from 364. He was the son of an officer of Pannonian (now Croatian) origin. Valentinian I ruled over the western part of the empire and enforced respect for the religious beliefs of all his subjects. He rebuilt the fortifications on the Rhine, reorganised the army of Gaul and liberated it from the Alamanni. His great general Theodosius the

---

[85] Heinrich Graetz, *History of the Jews II*, Philadelphia, The Jewish Publication Society of America, 1891, p.603-605.
[86] Mgr Henri Delassus (1836–1921) was a French Catholic priest, doctor of theology, protonotary apostolic, honorary canon of the diocese of Cambrai and anti-Masonic essayist and critic of Judaism.
[87] Mgr Henri Delassus, *La Conjuration antichrétienne II*, Desclée De Brouwer, 1910, p. 683.

Great reconquered the province of Brittany, which had been overrun by the barbarians of Scotland and Ireland.

Valentinian handed over the East to his brother Valens, who reigned in Constantinople. Valens belonged to the Arian sect of Christianity (Arianism)—according to which the divinity of God (the Father) precedes and is superior to that of Jesus Christ (his Son incarnate as Man)[88]—and was therefore the target of Catholic attacks. So he protected the Jews and repeatedly showed his esteem for them. Under his reign the Synod of Laodicea (364) took place. Christians were commanded not to remain idle on the Sabbath (canon 29), not to accept the unleavened (unleavened) bread of the Jews, and not to participate in their feasts and sacrileges (canon 37 and 38)[89].

St. Athanasius, Bishop of Alexandria, an illustrious Church Father who lived at that time, did not confine himself to theological debates, but noted in practice that the customs of the Jews were quite peculiar, stating further that "the Jews were no longer the people of God, but the chiefs of Sodom and Gomorrah[90]."

In the Balkans, Valens had to face the Visigoths and Ostrogoths, dying according to the chronicle of Amianus Marcellinus in battle during the battle of Adrianople on 9 August 378, thus foreshadowing the future general invasion of the empire by the Germanic tribes.

In 367, in Amiens (Gaul), Valentinian became seriously ill and proclaimed his son Gratian, only 8 years old, emperor. Gratian reigned from 375 to 383, showing himself benevolent towards Pope Damasius I. He was the first emperor to refuse the ancient Roman cult title of *Pontifex maximus* (sovereign pontiff), later assumed by the bishop of Rome.

In January 379, Gratian proclaimed Theodosius, a native of Cauca (Coca, Segovia), son of the great general Theodosius the Great, as Augustus. Theodosius I received the eastern part of the empire. In 380, together with Gratian, he stopped the Goths in Epirus and Dalmatia. He installed part of the Ostrogoths in Pannonia, settling himself in Constantinople while the usurper Magnus Maximus seized power in the West.

---

[88] Arianism was a form of non-trinitarian Christianity. The Arians did not believe in the traditional doctrine of the Trinity, which holds that God the Father, Jesus and the Holy Spirit are one being. It holds that Jesus Christ is the Son of God, proceeding from the Father, but not eternal, but begotten in time. Arianism holds that the Son of God did not always exist, but was created by God the Father.

[89] Mgr Carl-Joseph Héfélé, *Histoire des Conciles, d'après les documents originaux*, 1870, Paris, 1914.

[90] *Traité de l'Incarnation*, 40, 7, in Maurice Pinay, *Complot against the Church*, Chapter XLI (1962), Transcription pdf from Ediciones Mundo Libre, Mexico, 1985, p. 362.

By the Edict of Thessalonica on 28 February 380, Emperor Theodosius (379–395) elevated Christianity to the status of the only official and obligatory religion. Christianity thus became the state religion. In 381, Arianism was condemned at the Second Ecumenical Council of Constantinople. Theodosius also enacted laws against the Jews, referring to them as a "bestial sect" (*feralis secta*). According to some sources, "Theodosius would go so far as to say that to be a Jew was a hopeless and incurable evil[91]".

Despite the exhortations of Ambrose of Milan and other members of the Catholic clergy, Theodosius the Great did not allow officials to interfere in the religious affairs of the Jews. He enacted severe penalties against Christians who disturbed their tranquillity. But imperial orders were useless in changing the spirit of the times. Moreover, before the reign of Theodosius, several restrictive laws against the Jews were already in existence and remained in force.

XXI. The Church Fathers

Saint Ambrose (340–394), bishop of Milan and famous Church Father, was a contemporary of Theodosius. On learning that the emperor had condemned a bishop of Callinicus in northern Mesopotamia to rebuild at his own expense a synagogue he had ordered burned down, Ambrose was outraged and wrote to the emperor. While acknowledging that the bishop had gone too far and should be reprimanded, he protested so strongly that the emperor was forced to rectify his decision[92].

St. Ambrose would declare that the Synagogue was "a house of impiety, a receptacle of wickedness which God Himself had condemned." When the Christian masses, in reaction to the actions of the Hebrews, could not suppress their anger and burned a synagogue in Rome, St. Ambrose not only backed them up, but said, "I declared that the synagogue should be burned, or at least I ordered it to be burned. And if it be objected to me that I did not personally set fire to the synagogue, I protest that it began to burn by the judgment of God[93]."

Heinrich Graetz wrote that "Ambrose of Milan surpassed Chrysostom in violence and hateful calumnies against the Jews. He called the usurper Maximus a *Jew*, because he had ordered the Roman senate that a

---

[91] Elie Wiesel, *Célébration talmudique*, Seuil, 1991, p. 336.
[92] Epist. 29. Sozomène hist. Trip. L.7, c.8 et L.9, c.30, in *Revue Catholique des Institutions et du Droit*, October 1893, article by Charles Auzias-Turenne.
[93] Maurice Pinay, *Complot against the Church, Chapter XLI* (1962), Transcription pdf from Ediciones Mundo Libre, Mexico, 1985, p. 361.

synagogue in Rome burned by the Christians should be rebuilt at the expense of the city.[94]."

Saint Ambrose of Milan is recognised by the Catholic Church as a model worthy of imitation for bishops and as one of the most illustrious examples of Christian charity. "This shows that charity should not be used to protect the forces of evil", Maurice Pinay wrote judiciously.

At that time, the Jews could no longer persecute Christians as they once did. The great theologian Tertullian, Father of the Church and prolific author, left his testimony about the Jewish persecutions against Christians in the previous centuries. He was born in Carthage between 150 and 160, the son of a centurion of the Roman legion. In the first half of the 3rd century, Tertullian inaugurated Christian literature in the Latin language. "In his treatise "*Adversus Judaeos*", he makes very harsh accusations against the Israelites; in "*Scorpiase*", he states that: "the Synagogues are the points from which the persecutions against the Christians come". And in "*Ad Nationem*"... he affirms: "It is from the Jews that the calumnies against the Christians come from[95]"."

According to St. Ambrose, the Jews reduced a large number of churches to ashes in the time of Julian the Apostate, including the Basilica of Alexandria, and no one demanded reparations or punishment for this.

Two hundred years later, St. Gregory of Nyssa, another illustrious Christian, theological head of the Council of Constantinople, also accused the Jews very harshly in his *Oration on the Resurrection of Christ*: "Murderers of the Lord, murderers of the prophets, enemies of God, men who hate God, men who despise the laws, adversaries of Grace, enemies of the faith of their fathers, advocates of the Devil, brood of vipers, slanderers, scoffers, men whose minds are in darkness, leaven of the Pharisees, assembly of demons, sinners, perverse men, stoners, enemies of honesty[96]."

The most vehement of the Christian anti-Jews was undoubtedly John Chrysostom (349–407), the most revered of the Eastern Church Fathers. He was born in Antioch and was bishop of Constantinople. His unparalleled eloquence was at the origin of his nickname Chrysostom, "golden mouth".

In Antioch, he denounced how the Jews occupied the first commercial

---

[94]Heinrich Graetz, *History of the Jews II*, Philadelphia, The Jewish Publication Society of America, 1891, p. 620–621.
[95]Maurice Pinay, *Complot against the Church, Chapter XLI* (1962), Transcription pdf from Ediciones Mundo Libre, Mexico, 1985, p. 370.
[96]Maurice Pinay, *Complot against the Church, Chapter XLI* (1962), Transcription pdf from Ediciones Mundo Libre, Mexico, 1985, p. 366. (And in Marcel Simon, *Verus Israel*, Paris, 1948, p. 255.)

positions in the city, paralysing business when they celebrated their feasts. He delivered no less than eight homilies to warn Christians against their tricks and seductions[97].

Chrysostom tirelessly denounced the Jews as a "nation of murderers, lustful, rapacious, voracious and perfidious thieves", predicting that "they will continue to be punished for their crimes until the end of the world". The Jews are "infanticides...guilty of a thousand horrors," Chrysostom asserted. He thundered against them, denouncing that "the Jews of today, gathering in effeminate troops, in bands with numerous and miserable courtesans, transform the synagogue into a theatre with histrionics on stage; for their synagogue is not very different from those public places! The synagogue is not only a theatre and a place of prostitution; it is also a den of thieves, a cavern of wild beasts[98]."

St. John Chrysostom had already noted in his time a certain inclination of some Jews towards procuring: "Their synagogues are only places of debauchery where they indulge in lewdness and dissoluteness[99]. Moreover, this first illustrious anti-Semite already suspected Judaism of constituting a kind of sickness of the soul. John Chrysostom warned Christians against them and their medical or theurgic-cabalistic practices: "Flee and reject the Jews; they claim to be the most skilful doctors in the world, but their medical science is only imposture, incantations, charms, amulets and practices borrowed from magic"!

Saint Jerome (340–420), born into an aristocratic Roman family in present-day Croatia, received a perfect education in Rome, where he converted to Christianity at the age of 25. He was secretary to Pope Damasus I and went down in history for his Latin translation of the Bible from Greek and Hebrew (the Vulgate). Naturally, he also professed a deep

---

[97]John Chrysostom, 1884, *Adversus Judæos homilia,* in Claude Jannet, *L'Église et la constitution sociale,* 1884. "In the fourth century," wrote Abraham Leon, "the Jews belonged to the wealthy and rich strata of the population. Chrysostom says of the Jews that they possessed large sums of money and that the patriarchs accumulated immense treasures. He speaks of the wealth of the Jews as if it were a fact well known to contemporaries". (Abraham Léon, *La Conception matérialiste de la question juive,* Études et Documentation internationales, 1942, Paris, 1968, p. 63). Abraham Léon quotes here Rabbi L. Lucas, *Zur Geschichte der Juden in vierten Jahrhundert,* Berlin, 1910.

[98]Gougenot des Mousseaux. *The Jew, Judaism and the Judaisation of Christian peoples,* pdf version. Translated into Spanish by Professor Noemí Coronel and the invaluable collaboration of the team of Nacionalismo Católico Argentina, 2013 p. 107

[99]John Chrysostom, pp. 358–362, 3,4, etc.,. Quoted in *Oeuvres completes* vol. II, ed. 1865. In Gougenot des Mousseaux. *The Jew, Judaism and the Judaisation of Christian peoples,* p. 555. On Jewish pimping and the White slave trade, see *The Jewish Mafia.* And on the clinical picture of Judaism, *Psychoanalysis of Judaism.*

hostility towards Judaism. The historian Heinrich Graetz had this to say about him: "As his enemies reproached him for his heresy because of his Jewish studies, he convinced them of his orthodoxy by asserting his hatred of the Jews: "If it is necessary to despise them as individuals and as a nation, so I abhor the Jews with an ineffable hatred[100]."

In his letter to the brothers Pamachius and Oceanus, St. Jerome wrote: "If there is interest in hating some men, in hating a race, I oppose the circumcised with extraordinary hatred. To this day they persecute Our Lord Jesus Christ in the synagogues of Satan". St. Jerome thus took up the words of Christ quoted by the Apostle John: "Ye are of your father the devil, and the lusts of your father ye will do." (John, VIII, 44. Reina Valera 1862).

In the Apocalypse (II, 9), St. John called to be wary of the slander of the Jews: "I know your works, and your tribulation, and your poverty—but you are rich—and I know the blasphemy of those who say they are Jews, and are not, but are the synagogue of Satan".

The Catholic writer Maurice Pinay confirmed St. Jerome's views in the 20th century: "St. Jerome said that, if it was necessary to abominate the Jews and Judaism in order to be a good Christian, he wanted to do it in an exemplary way". And he added: "There is nothing strange in this if one takes into account that the Jews are the capital enemies of Christianity and of the human race[101]."

Bishop Cyril of Alexandria, who was strongly opposed to the hysteria and aggressiveness of the Jews, succeeded in driving them out of the city in 415, which led to some disturbances. But despite the great energy deployed to defend the Jews, the prefect Oreste was unable to contain the disturbances and could only raise a complaint against Cyril. The court in Constantinople, however, upheld the bishop.

This staunch anti-Judaism of the Church Fathers had already been professed by the founders of Christianity. St. Paul claimed to be a Jew, "born in Tarsus in Cilicia", an ancient city on the southern coast of present-day Turkey. Paul (Saul) abandoned Judaism, turning against the sect. He would later apply three times for Roman citizenship, as we read in Luke's gospel.

In his epistles, he systematically denigrated the Jews and their teachings, describing them as enemies of all men: "For ye, brethren, have been imitators in Christ Jesus of the churches of God which are in Judaea: for ye also have suffered the same things of your own nation, as they also have suffered of the Jews: Who have killed both the Lord Jesus and his own

---

[100]Heinrich Graetz, *History of the Jews II*, Philadelphia, The Jewish Publication Society of America, 1891, p. 632–633.
[101]Maurice Pinay, *Complot against the Church, Chapter XIX* (1962), Transcription pdf from Ediciones Mundo Libre, Mexico, 1985, p. 235.

prophets, and have persecuted us; and are not acceptable to God, and are enemies to all men: Hindering us, that we should not speak to the Gentiles, that they might be saved; to fill up the measure of their sins for ever: for wrath hath overtaken them to the uttermost." (1 Thessalonians, II, 14–16, King James Version 1862). St. Paul was beheaded, probably in the year 67, after a trial that took place under the reign of the emperor Nero.

The figure and destiny of Jesus Christ, his exemplary character, his sacrifice for the salvation and rebirth of the world, corresponded profoundly to the outlines of the great Greco-Latin mythologies. Anthropomorphic divinisation was already a widespread belief in the pagan world. His figure was particularly close to that of the god Dionysus, son of Zeus, who according to Orphic tradition had been dismembered by the Titans before being resurrected by Zeus. Similarly, the acceptance of the Eucharist, involving the symbolic consumption of divine flesh and blood, was already present from ancient times in the Dionysian, Eleusinian and Orphic mysteries. Finally, by authorising and promoting sacred representations (sculptures, paintings, mosaics), Christianity succeeded in framing itself completely and harmoniously in Greco-Roman culture[102].

XXII. The End of the Roman Empire in the West

On the death of Theodosius the Great, the Roman Empire fell into the hands of his two sons and was officially divided into two, the Empire of the West, up to the borders of present-day Bosnia, and the Empire of the East.

In the East, Emperor Arcadius (395–408), or rather his all-powerful advisors Rufinus and Eutropius, reigned. Graetz described the situation as follows: "Rufinus and Eutropius were extremely favourable to the Jews. Rufinus loved money, and the Jews had already discovered the magical power of gold to soften stubborn hearts. So numerous laws were passed in their favour[103]."

---

[102] "Concerning the gods, the ancients have handed down to later generations two different conceptions. Some, they say, are eternal and immortal...each of these gods, indeed, has its origin in eternity and an existence for eternity. But the other gods, they assert, are earthly beings who, through their benefits to mankind, have attained immortal honours and fame, such as Herakles, Dionysus, Aristeus, and others like these." Diodorus Siculus, *Bibliotheca Historica, VI 1, 2*. "It was on account of the great magnitude of their services that these gods came to be established...The customs proper to community life consented that excellent men should be raised up to heaven, amidst fame and recognition, for their good deeds. Hence Hercules, Castor and Pollux, Aesculapius and also Dionysus". Cicero, *De Natura Deorum, II, 62*.

[103] Heinrich Graetz, *History of the Jews II*, Philadelphia, The Jewish Publication

Having defeated the Goths in 400, Arcadius reigned alone and, with the help of the patriarch of Constantinople John Chrysostom, initiated an iron religious policy. Since Jews manifested their tribal solidarity in court by giving false testimony in order to influence the decisions of the judges, they were forbidden to appear as witnesses in Christian courts[104].

In the West, Emperor Honorius forbade the Jews from any official function in the empire, although their worship was respected. They were free to practise their national customs and had judges of their own nation, except in capital cases. The first functions of the state were forbidden to them. But in addition to civil careers, they could engage in commerce, industry and literature. Judging by the numerous complaints of the Christians, they were already engaged in them with the ardour that always characterised them in all times.

Claudius Rutilius, an early 5th century pagan poet from Toulouse, "complains that the vanquished nation oppresses the conquerors, and Saint Augustine [the illustrious Church Father, Bishop of Hippo, in present-day Algeria] thought it necessary to lower the pride of the Jews by reminding them that they were excluded from the highest dignities of the State, that they were not admitted to the table of the great lords, and that they were subject to taxation[105]."

Theodosius II (408–450), the successor of Arcadius was "a good-natured but somewhat monkish emperor, whose weakness allowed the fanatical zeal of many bishops to go unpunished and encouraged cruelty. The edicts of this emperor forbade the Jews to build new synagogues, to exercise the office of judge between Jewish and Christian litigants, and to own Christian slaves...Under this emperor, the [Jewish] Patriarchate finally disappeared, though Gamaliel, the last of the Patriarchs, enjoyed great distinction at the imperial court, such as none of his predecessors had ever had[106]." Jewish aggressiveness had to be contained, and in 425 Theodosius II and Valentinian III (for the West) imposed new restrictions on Jews, especially on holding public office and litigating in the courts[107]. But the enforcement of these laws was very poor, as the wealth of the Jews

---

Society of America, 1891, p. 623.

[104]Codex Theodosianus, XVI, 8, 10, 11 and 15, quoted by James Parkes in *The Conflict of the Church and the Synagogue*, Hermon Press, New York, 1974, quoted by Gérald Messadié in *Histoire générale de l'antisémitisme*, JC Lattès, 1999, p. 155.

[105] Georges-Bernard Depping, *Les Juifs dans le Moyen-Âge*, (1823), Éd. Wouters, Brussels, 1844, p. 26.

[106]Heinrich Graetz, *History of the Jews II*, Philadelphia, The Jewish Publication Society of America, 1891, p. 624–625.

[107]Constitutions de Sirmond IV et VI et *Novelles* de Theodose II nov. III, in Claude Jannet, *L'Église et la constitution sociale*, 1884.

allowed them to circumvent them.[108]

Often, wealthy Jewish merchants abused their position to oppress or pervert Christians of lower status. In 430, for example, the Jews of Imnestar, a Syrian town between Aleppo and Antioch, had celebrated one of their feasts by crucifying a Christian[109]. In his *History of the Jews*, written at the end of the 19th century, Heinrich Graetz acknowledged that the Jews might have been the cause of some excesses, although he excused their co-religionists from any malicious acts:

"The Jews in Christian countries had no choice but to take up the weapons of mockery; consequently, they mocked their enemies behind their backs, which was always everywhere and at all times the way in which the weakest try to alleviate their grievances. Thus, they sometimes made use of coarse jokes to express their feelings about Christianity. Such jokes were made especially on the occasion of the feast of Purim[110], when the joy of the feast led to drunkenness, and drunkenness to irresponsible expressions and demonstrations. On this day, the Jews, in their jubilation, used to hang Haman, their arch-enemy[111], in effigy on a gallows, and this gallows, which was usually burned afterwards, took, accidentally or intentionally, the form of a cross. Naturally, the Christians complained of the desecration of their religion, and the Emperor Theodosius II ordered the ruler of the province to put an end to such misconduct by threat of severe punishment, without, however, being able to repress it. It is said that, on one occasion, this carnivalesque fun had horrible consequences. The Jews of Imnestar, a small Syrian town between Antioch and Chalcis, having erected one of these gallows of Haman, were accused by the Christians of having hung a Christian boy on a cross upon it, and of having scourged him to death. Accordingly, the emperor ordered the culprits to be punished[112]."

In Rome and Italy, since the advent of the Christian emperors, the Jews had progressively lost their power and were no longer the masters.

"It is likely, Graetz wrote, that they witnessed with hearts full of joy the invasion of the barbarians and the fall of Rome, once the mistress of the world. But it is more than likely that they were also the main catalysts of

---

[108] Claude Jannet, *L'Église et la constitution sociale*, 1884.
[109] Socrates *Hist. Ecclesiastica lib. VII c. 16*. Cf. Justinian Code *of Judaeis et Caelicolis*, laws 3, 11, 13 and 14 repressing similar cases, in Claudius Jannet, *L'Église et la constitution sociale*, 1884.
[110] On the festival of Purim, read *The Mirror of Judaism*.
[111] The book of Esther tells how the Jews managed to thwart the plan of the evil Haman, King Ahasuerus' prime minister, and how they managed to exterminate 75,000 of their enemies thanks to Esther, the king's mistress. (NdT)
[112] Heinrich Graetz, *History of the Jews II*, Philadelphia, The Jewish Publication Society of America, 1891, p. 627–628.

Roman decline[113]. Indeed, at that time "the hopes of the coming of the Messiah, which kept the minds of the Jews in greater suspense than ever in that age of migration of nations and universal revolution, just when Rome, burdened with sin, was suffering God's chastisement. An ancient sibylline saying, attributed to the prophet Elijah, was commonplace, according to which the Messiah would appear in the eighty-fifth Jubilee (between 440 and 470 CE). Such Messianic expectations always generated crowds of enthusiasts who sought to convert their silent belief into fact, and, without really intending to deceive, they sought to draw in those of the crowd who were of like opinion and excite them to such an extent that they would willingly sacrifice their lives[114]."

Rome had been besieged on all fronts by the Germans for decades. The capital of the empire had finally been sacked in August 410 by Alaric's Visigoths and in 439 Carthage was taken by Genseric's Vandals. The Jews may have thought that the messianic times were at last at hand, that the messiah would come and they could at last exercise their vengeance on the Goyim. The sages claimed, however, that it was not possible for the messiah to appear before the eighty-fifth Jubilee, "but after that period hope could be maintained, though not certainty." These Jewish hopes manifest themselves throughout history and usually end each time in bloodshed.

The invasion of the Huns in the middle of the fifth century further consolidated this idea in the Jews. The messianic times had finally arrived. Heinrich Graetz wrote here: "The rough Huns, the scourge of God, carried away horde after horde, tribe after tribe...The period of the migration of the nations confirmed almost literally the words of the prophet: '*The earth staggers like a drunkard, and her sins are heavy upon her; she falls and cannot rise, and the Lord Sebaoth[115] punishes the bands of heaven in the sky, and the kings of the earth on the earth*'". No wonder the Jews saw in the Goths—the first wave of the migration of tribes that flooded and devastated the Roman empire—Gog from the land of Magog, of whom a prophet had said: "*Thou shalt come like a storm, and shalt be as a cloud covering the earth—thou and all thy troops, and many other peoples with*

---

[113] In the Age of Enlightenment, Edward Gibbon, in his *History of the Decline and Fall of the Roman Empire (1766–1788)*, had put forward the idea that Christianity was at the origin of Roman decadence. Pagan authors of the 20th century have taken up this analysis again, while also vituperating against Christianity, concealing the dissolving role of Judaism which they can nevertheless verify on a daily basis in our time, especially through the media propaganda (apology for diversity, tolerance, miscegenation, immigration, homosexuality and world government, etc.). Cf: *Planetary Hopes*, 2005.
[114] Heinrich Graetz, *History of the Jews II*, Philadelphia, The Jewish Publication Society of America, 1891, p. 617.
[115] Yahweh of hosts.

thee" (Ezekiel XXXVIII, 9). In this remarkable alternation of disappearance and formation of nations, the conviction prevailed among Jewish thinkers that the Jewish people was eternal: "One nation arises, another disappears, but only Israel remains forever". The barbarian tribes, avengers of the long enslaved nations, settled on the ruined sites of the Roman empire[116]."

The entire Western empire was collapsing. Only Gaul was successfully defended by the Roman general Aetius. Roman troops, in coalition with Visigoths and Franks, defeated the Huns at the Battle of the Catalunian Fields in September 451, forcing them to retreat.

With the death of Attila in 453, the Hun empire disintegrated and the Asians returned to the lands from whence they had come. But the assassination of Aetius by Emperor Valentinian III in 454 dashed the empire's last hopes of recovery. In 455, Rome was again sacked, this time by Genseric's Vandals. Once the Western empire was destroyed, the anarchy into which society fell was eminently favourable to Judaism.

XXIII. Emperor Peroz I

In Babylonia and Persia, a bloody persecution was directed against the Jews under the reign of the Sassanid emperor Peroz I (457–484). The motive for the persecution was allegedly Peroz's revenge against the Jews of Ispahan, where some of them had reportedly murdered and skinned two priests (Zoroastrian Magi). "As punishment for this act, Peroz killed half the Jewish population of Ispahan and had the Jewish children forcibly educated in the temple of *Horvan* as fire-worshippers. The persecution also spread to the Babylonian communities and continued for several years, until the death of the tyrant."

"A few years later, the persecution spread still further; schools were closed, meetings for pedagogical purposes were forbidden, the jurisdiction of the Jews was abolished, and their children were forced to embrace the religion of the Magi (474). The city of Sora seems to have been destroyed in that period."

"For this reason, like Hadrian, Peroz was nicknamed by the Jews of later times "the Wicked" (*Piruz Reshia*). The immediate result of this persecution was the emigration of Jewish settlers, who settled as far south as Arabia, and as far east as India[117]."

---

[116] Heinrich Graetz, *History of the Jews II*, Philadelphia, The Jewish Publication Society of America, 1891, p. 612.
[117] Heinrich Graetz, *History of the Jews II*, Philadelphia, The Jewish Publication

Thus, in the year 4250 of the creation era (490), the Jews of Babylon migrated to these new regions where they resumed their multi-secular customs and activities...

XXIV. The Weakness of Theodoric the Great

Under their leader Theodoric, the Ostrogoths destroyed what was left of Roman power. Theodoric undertook the conquest of Italy in 488. The peninsula was then in the hands of a Herulus chieftain named Odoacer who had gone down in posterity for having deposed Romulus Augustus, the last Roman emperor of the West, in 476. In 493, Ravenna was taken and Odoacer was defeated and killed by Theodoric himself. Rome ceased to be the capital of Italy and Ravenna, alternately with Verona, became the political centre of the new Ostrogothic state.

At that time, by order of Theodoric, the minister and counsellor Cassiodorus wrote to the Jewish community of Milan: "You seek peace on earth, O Judah, when in your obstinacy you are unable to find peace in eternity". When the Jews of Genoa asked for permission to restore their synagogue, Theodoric sent them the following reply: "Why do you desire what you should avoid? While we grant you the permission you ask for, we reprove your erratic desire. However, we do not wish to impose religion or force heretics to believe against their conscience[118]." Theodoric did not permit the Jews to erect new synagogues, nor to beautify the old ones, but merely to repair the dilapidated ones. He granted the Jews only a rather restricted freedom, though at least he protected them against all aggression.

Theodoric's policy towards the Jews exasperated the people, who were oppressed by the economic and financial domination of the Jews. When, one day in the year 500, some slaves revolted in Rome against their Jewish masters, the sympathetic people set fire to the synagogues, mistreated the Jews and ransacked their houses. Informed of these disturbances, Theodoric ordered the Senate to punish the culprits and rebuild the synagogues at their own expense. Since the culprits were not found, the municipality had to pay for the reconstruction of the destroyed buildings. In spite of various harassments, the Italian Jews were happy under Theodoric. They prospered not only in Ravenna and Rome, but also in Milan and Naples[119]. It is often argued that the Ostrogoths' protection of the Jews was one of the reasons why the Italians preferred to be ruled by

---

Society of America, 1891, p. 636–637.
[118] Heinrich Graetz, *History of the Jews III*, London, Myers High Holborn, 1904, p. 31.
[119] Georges-Bernard Depping, *Les Juifs dans le Moyen-Âge*, (1823), Éd. Wouters, Brussels, 1844, p. 27.

the court of Constantinople, where Jews were subject to much stricter laws.

Theodoric died in Ravenna in 526. Cassiodorus became a monk, founded a monastery and composed, among other works, a commentary on the Psalms. In it he often rebuked the Jews, Graetz wrote, by dedicating to them opprobrious insults such as: "scorpions and lions", "wild asses", "dogs and unicorns[120]"."

XXV. Zeno, the Byzantine Emperor

The Roman Empire in the West had been submerged by the Germans; but in the East, the Byzantine Empire lasted a thousand years more until the capture of Constantinople by the Turks in 1453.

Emperor Zeno reigned from 474 to 491. In 466, while still a general, he managed to repel the Huns led by Attila's youngest son. Under his reign, ten years later in 476, the Western Roman Empire disappeared for good. That year, Odoacer, king of the Heruli, a Germanic tribe from Scandinavia, dethroned the last emperor Romulus Augustus and sent the imperial insignia to Zeno. Between 478 and 483, Zeno in turn had to fight against Theodoric's Ostrogoths, who finally gave up on taking Constantinople.

At that time, some public disturbances took place after a horse race. The city of Antioch, like most of the great cities of the Byzantine Empire, was divided into two factions, two sides: the blue and the green. One day the latter provoked a riot, attacking their opponents and killing, among others, many Jews. They threw their corpses into the fire and set fire to several synagogues. "When the Emperor Zeno was informed of this event, he exclaimed that the only fault of the Greens was that they had burned only the dead Jews, and not the living ones as well[121]."

The people of Antioch were especially hostile towards the Jews. One day, a famous chariot driver named Calliopas came from Constantinople to Antioch to line up under the green flag. On 9 July 507, further riots broke out in Daphne, near Antioch, where the supporters of Calliopas "without sufficient cause, destroyed the synagogue and its sanctuaries and savagely murdered the worshippers".

XXVI. Legislation and the Church

The Catholic Church never wavered on the Jewish question. It always wanted the Jews as persons to be respected, but, at the same time, it always

---

[120] Heinrich Graetz, *History of the Jews III*, London, Myers High Holborn, 1904, p. 32.
[121] Heinrich Graetz, *History of the Jews III*, London, Myers High Holborn, 1904, p. 11.

wanted them to be kept in a state of submission and isolation which would deprive them of the means of doing harm to others. The councils were chiefly concerned to isolate the Jews from society by forbidding all communication with them; but the continual renewals of the prohibitions show how difficult it was to enforce them.

In October 1893, the *Revue catholique des Institutions et du Droit* published an exhaustive and illustrated study on ecclesiastical law in relation to Jews. It contains, under the signature of the Catholic jurisconsult Charles Auzias Turenne, the prescriptions of the councils, as well as the advice given by the Popes or the dispositions dictated by them, the bulls, letters and other pontifical documents, as well as the doctrine of the doctors on this subject. We have drawn the following information from this detailed study[122].

In his *History of the Councils*, published in 1870, Mgr Carl-Joseph Héfélé, Bishop of Rottenburg, recalled that the first council where the Jewish question was raised was held in Spain, in Elvira (305–306). Elvira, in Latin *Illiberis*, was a town in Andalusia, near Granada. Canon 16 forbade giving daughters in marriage to Jews[123]. Bishop Osius of Cordoba, a member of the Council of Nicaea and organiser of the Council of Elvira, had a decision adopted whereby the penalty of excommunication was pronounced against Christians who had relations with Jews or contracted marriages with them. This prohibition was renewed by the Ecumenical Council of Chalcedon in 451.

Canon 50 of the Council of Elvira also forbade eating with them. This provision was taken up by the Council of Vannes in 465, the Council of Agde in 506 and the Council of Epaona in 517 (now in Yenne, in Savoy, in the diocese of Vienna).

Canon 34 of the Council of Agde stipulated that Jews who wanted to

---

[122] Charles Auzias-Turenne, *Revue Catholique des Institutions et du Droit*, October 1893. The councils are to be found in Labbe's compilation, in Mercator, Yves de Chartres, the Lacensis collection and in Monsignor Héfélé's *History of the Councils*; the bulls in the Bularium, the letters in Labbe, in the editions of the Benedictines of Saint-Maur, or in Migne's Patrology. The author specifies here: "It seemed useless to us to refer each time to the sources because we indicate the dates and because in the compilations which contain them, the councils and other documents are arranged in chronological order".

[123] Mgr Carl-Joseph Héfélé, *Histoire des Conciles*, 1870, Paris, 1914. [It was in Spain that the Christian clergy first aroused the fanaticism of the Christian population against the Jews. The same Bishop Osius (*Hosius*) of Cordoba, who had taken part in the Council of Nicaea and had convened a council in *Illiberis*, also succeeded in passing a resolution forbidding Christians, on pain of excommunication, to trade with Jews, to marry them or to have them bless the produce of their fields". Heinrich Graetz, *History of the Jews II*, Philadelphia, The Jewish Publication Society of America, 1891, p. 627].

become Catholics—and since they "tend to return easily to their vomit"—should spend at least eight months in the catechumenate before being baptised[124].

In the years 530, 533 and 541, three successive councils took place in Orleans. Marriages with Jews were again abolished and the ban on eating with them renewed; they were also forbidden to leave their homes for four days after Maundy Thursday and to attempt to convert anyone to Judaism, on pain of confiscation of all their slaves. The second Council of Orleans forbade marriages between Jews and Christians, a prohibition that was renewed in several councils. The Council of Clermont, in 535, excluded Jews from the magistracies; in 581, the Council of Mâcon deprived them of the office of tax collector[125].

The 517 Council of Epona, where important canons concerning the administration of the Church and the discipline of the clergy were adopted or updated, was presided over by Avito, a close relative of the Western Roman emperor Avito, who had reigned briefly in 455–456 and was a nobleman of Gallo-Roman origin, from Arvernia. A widower at the age of 40, Avito had distributed all his property to the poor and retired to a monastery. He had succeeded his father as bishop of Vienna in 490. A theologian and poet, he was deeply concerned for the poor and for the life of the whole Church. Becoming archbishop, metropolitan of a province in the kingdom of the Burgundians, Avitus' first objective was to combat Arianism. His letter congratulating Clovis on his conversion (496) has been preserved to this day. He also contributed to the conversion of King Sigismund, the king of the Burgundians, who abandoned the Arian heresy in 516 to embrace the Catholic religion. Avitus sanctioned the measures of the Council of Epona in 517.

Avito made inflammatory speeches against the Jews. According to Graetz, "in the Frankish empire, hatred of the Jews came from a man who could be considered its incarnation. This was Avitus, Bishop of Arverna, whose see was at Clermont[126]." Gregory of Tours, a pupil of his, left this historical testimony:In the year 516, Avitus had already "exhorted them several times to convert, without his words having produced the slightest effect. On Ascension Day, the people gathered, for what reason or pretext is not known, and destroyed the synagogue. The bishop, favouring the riot, which in his eyes was nothing more than a fervent zeal for religion, again urged the Jews to convert or leave the city, for at that time the civil power had largely passed into the hands of the clergy. He coolly offered them this

---

[124] Mgr Carl-Joseph Héfélé, *Histoire des Conciles*, 1870, Paris, 1914.
[125] Georges-Bernard Depping, *Les Juifs dans le Moyen-Âge*, (1823), Éd. Wouters, Brussels, 1844, p. 38.
[126] Heinrich Graetz, *History of the Jews III*, London, Myers High Holborn, 1904, p. 39.

alternative: "If you agree to have the same faith as the Christians, you will also have the same residence; if, on the other hand, you wish to maintain your errors, leave and evacuate the city. Besides, we do not want to convert you by force; decide freely". The Jews, outraged by this violence from the mouth of a shepherd of the people, who instead of appeasing the crowd was stirring it up, refused to give in to the popular clamour. For their safety, they withdrew to a common building. The people surrounded the house; their fury was growing every moment; they threatened to storm the building and massacre all the Hebrews. Seeing death near, and probably determined by the desperate cries of the women and children, the Jews sent a messenger to the bishop to beg him to rescue them from the hands of the maddened mob; they declared that they were ready to do whatever was asked of them. The bishop came, calmed the crowd; they rejoiced in the city that they had won so many souls for the Christian religion, without thinking how they had acquired them, and on the day of Pentecost, all the Jews were baptised in the presence of a great concourse of inhabitants of Clermont and the countryside: they numbered five hundred[127]." The Jews who refused to convert took refuge in Marseilles.

The poet Venantius Fortunatus (Venantius Fortunatus) was commissioned by Gregory of Tours to celebrate this triumph. When Vitus of Vienna died in 519, he was elevated to sainthood by the Catholic Church. His saint's day is celebrated on 5 February.

The bishops of Arles and Marseilles acted with the same zeal, and the pope had to write to them, following complaints from Jews trading in Marseilles, that the two prelates should be more moderate and practise conversion of the Jews by persuasion. Shortly afterwards, the bishop of Bourges expelled from his city the Jews who refused to abandon Judaism.

Childeric I, king of the Franks from 561 to 584, followed the example of Avitus and forced the Jews of his kingdom to be baptised. It is said that he himself deigned to hold the neophytes over the baptismal fonts. While it is true that "he contented himself with the mere appearance of conversion and did not oppose the Jews, and they continued to celebrate the Sabbath and observe the laws of Judaism[128]."

In his *History of the Franks*, Gregory of Tours (538–594), the French bishop and historian, described King Gontran's entry into Orleans to the cheers of the Jews and their discontent:

"Woe to this wicked and perfidious Jewish nation, always deceitful by nature! Today they praise me with flattery, proclaiming that all nations

---

[127]Grégoire de Tours, *Hist. Franc, lib. V*, chap. 11. —Venance Fortunat, in tome III of *Biblioth. Patrum*, in Georges-Bernard Depping, *Les Juifs dans le Moyen-Âge*, (1823), Éd. Wouters, Brussels, 1844, p. 39.
[128] Heinrich Graetz, *History of the Jews III*, London, Myers High Holborn, 1904, p. 41.

must worship me as their lord so that I may order their synagogues, recently demolished by the Christians, to be erected at public expense; which I will never do, for the Lord forbids it."

Gregory of Tours denounced the important role played by Jewish merchants in the slave trade, as well as in the receiving of stolen goods[129]. As part of their commercial activity with the East, the Jews were indeed engaged in the slave trade. Christians increasingly abhorred this ignoble trade, unlike the Jews who never had such scruples. In fact, they were protected at the time by the barbarian kings, who saw in them a way of profiting from the numerous captives they captured during their military campaigns.

Jews bought sacred vessels and urns from the frequent looting of churches at that time. At that time, an important part of the precious metals had taken this form[130]. Jews enriched themselves in this way and bought land. The letters of St. Gregory the Great and other documents present them as wealthy landowners throughout Italy. However, this did not mean that they were farmers. For as the Jewish historian Bernard Lazare wrote: "They had land, but they had it cultivated by slaves, for their tenacious patriotism forbade them to plough foreign soil[131]."

The Council of Mâcon in 581 dedicated canons 13 to 17 to the Jews, which have since been incorporated into the *Corpus Iuris* and regularly reproduced. The council forbade Jews to own Christian slaves and ordered that those they did own be freed in exchange for twelve solids (*solidus*) of gold. Jews could not exercise functions that would allow them to pronounce penalties against Christians. They were strictly forbidden to occupy the functions of judge or tax collector "so that the Christian population would not appear to be under their command."

Jewish insolence was also to be repressed: so they were obliged to show respect to the Christian priests, and could not sit in their presence without their prior authorisation. Finally, the Council of Mâcon reaffirmed the prohibition for Jews to go out on the streets during the Christian Passover.

Four councils, held successively at Toledo in 589, 633, 638 and 681 for Spain and Narbonne Gaul; another at Paris in 614, the most important of the Frankish councils where 79 bishops met, and another at Rheims (in 625, 40 bishops), renewed these provisions and added some more. All insisted, especially that of Paris, on the fact that no public civil or military office

---

[129] Readers of the *Jewish Mafia* know that these accusations are still valid today, in the 21st century.

[130] Gregor. Turon. *Historia Francor.* IV, 12, 35; VI, 5; VII, 23. S. Gregor. Magni Epistolae I. 68, in Claudius Jannet, *L'Église et la constitution sociale*, 1884.

[131] Bernard Lazare, *Anti-Semitism, its history and causes, (1894)*. Editions La Bastille, digital edition, 2011 p. 49.

should be conferred on them. The Council of Toledo in 633 extended this incapacity to the children of Jewish converts. In addition, Jews were insistently forbidden to work on Sunday.

Canon 11 of the Council of Constantinople (692) forbade Christians to accept or take their medicines, eat or bathe with them on pain of exclusion from the clergy and excommunication for the laity.

Various prohibitions already mentioned, such as that of eating with them, were reaffirmed at the Councils of Rome (743), Nicaea (787), Regiaticina (Pavia, 850) and Metz (888). Another prohibition, not only to have slaves but simply to have Christian servants or wet nurses, appeared in the Councils of Coyaca (near Oviedo, 1050), Szabole (1091) and Gran in Hungary (1114, canon 61)[132].

In his *History of the Councils*, Mgr Carl-Joseph Héfélé summarised the main ordinances of ecclesiastical legislation as follows:

1. Christians must never work for the Jews, nor accept paid employment with them.
2. Christians are forbidden to go to Jewish doctors, to receive their care or to use medicines prepared by them.
3. On pain of excommunication, it is forbidden to live in the same house and in the same family as Jews.
4. Christian women are formally forbidden to take a job as a wet nurse in a Jewish family.
5. Jews must not be allowed to exercise public functions that would give them any authority over Christians.
6. Christians should not attend Jewish weddings or accept Jewish invitations to dinner[133].

There are also a considerable number of pontifical acts concerning the Jews: counsels or reproaches to bishops and princes, reminders of the canons of the councils, bulls, constitutions for the Papal States, etc. Evidently, these documents present greater variety and differences than the conciliar decrees, which were general laws, since the Popes often pronounced on particular cases. Nevertheless, the policies pursued by the Popes present, on the whole, a remarkable unity and continuity over time which is not usually observed in those of princes or secular governments.

Some Jewish intellectuals sometimes boast of certain legislative

---

[132] Charles Auzias-Turenne, *Revue Catholique des Institutions et du Droit*, October 1893.
[133] Mgr Carl-Joseph Héfélé, *Histoire des Conciles*, 1870, Paris, 1914. Decretum, p. 2 to c. 28, quaest. 1 cap. 10 et s. Decretal. I. v, t. 6, in Charles Auzias-Turenne, *Revue Catholique des Institutions et du Droit*, October 1893.

provisions or doctrines of the Church that were favourable to them. They boastfully enumerate a long list of Popes who claim to have been very benevolent towards them. They cite certain facts, certain protective measures, even concessions of privileges in the Papal States; above all, they often reproduce certain favourable letters or bulls.

But the guiding principle of the Church never ceased to be that of the Lateran Council, stated in these terms in 1179: "*Iudeos subiacere christianis oportet et ab eis pro sola humanitate foveri*": that Jews should be treated humanely. If the Jews commit excesses that are liable to necessary repression, only the legitimate authorities should intervene. They should be treated as sparingly as possible and should never be allowed to leave their state of inferiority[134].

As soon as the vigilance of the goyim was relaxed, the Jews advanced their pawns and took control of the country, enriching themselves in such a way that gold and silver ended up in their hands and thousands of unfortunates who had gone astray by resorting to their services were thrown into misery.

"Often, wrote Charles Auzias-Turenne, the prescriptions of synods and councils were forgotten or openly trampled underfoot, with the result that the Jews soon became rich and monopolised the goods and all the money of the country; so that far from being dependent, it was they who imposed the yoke on the Christians. When this yoke became intolerable, if the princes did not intervene, the exasperated mobs sometimes resorted to the most deplorable forms of violence: Jews were attacked, massacred, burned or drowned by the thousands. Atrocious crimes that can be explained, but cannot be excused in the slightest. It is certainly understandable that the Popes and bishops intervened forcefully on their behalf, giving them asylum and drafting the strong letters or documents claimed by their modern defenders".

There were indeed popes who, inclined to indulgence and hoping to ingratiate and convert the Jews, began to soften the measures enacted against them. But almost always—if their reigns were of any length—these same pontiffs had to retrace their steps.

XXVII. *The Justinian Code*

Justinian came to power in Constantinople in 527, in his forty-fifth year. He was born into a modest family of Romanised Illyrians in present-day Croatia. He possessed undoubted qualities: a great sense of the state and of

---

[134] Charles Auzias-Turenne, *Revue Catholique des Institutions et du Droit*, October 1893.

the imperial idea, and great strength of character. He was a cultivated and sober man, which was quite rare for the time: he was a vegetarian and a teetotaler. His wife, Theodora, a former actress, was also of modest origin.

As lord and master of the Byzantine Empire, Justinian attempted to rebuild the Roman Empire. The emperor first attacked the Vandal kingdom in North Africa. On 15 September 533, his most famous general, Flavius Belisarius, took Carthage and buried the short-lived kingdom founded by Genseric. The Byzantine armies then seized Corsica, Sicily and Sardinia. In 535, two armies, one coming from Dalmatia and the other from Sicily, overran the Ostrogothic armies to enter Naples and then Rome on 10 December 536, and finally Ravenna in 540. Most of the Mediterranean was once again under "Roman" control.

But, above all, Justinian reorganised the administration and set in motion a major legislative reform. The *Corpus Iuris Civilis* (Body of Civil Law), which we call the Code of Justinian, was written in Latin, the vernacular language of the Roman Empire, even though it was not understood by most of the citizens of the Eastern Empire. The Code of Justinian is one of the great legacies of Roman antiquity. It is a synthesis of ancient jurisprudence embodied in a series of new laws: the *Novellae Constitiones, the* fourth part of the *Corpus,* which were written in Greek (534). Justinian's legislative work was of fundamental importance, because from the 12th century onwards the medieval West adopted Roman law on the basis of this source.

Justinian was also a great builder. He had the majestic Hagia Sophia in Constantinople built. Throughout the empire, he financed the building of cities, bridges, baths and roads. He was also the champion of religious orthodoxy, although in return for his protection and favours he sought to impose his will on the Church itself.

Justinian did everything possible to contain the power and influence of the Jews. The Justinian Code forbade Jews the right to hold public office and deprived them of all honours. Their testimonies in court against the Christians were declared null and void, because of the large number of false declarations which the Jews were accustomed to make in order to help their fellow Jews. Fathers and mothers were also forbidden to disinherit children who had converted to Christianity.

It is interesting to note that, already at that time, the authorities of the empire and the Church had agreed to exclude not only declared Jews but also baptised Jews from higher positions and military careers.

"The reason for such measures, wrote Maurice Pinay in *Complot against the Church (1962),* becomes clear if one takes into account that other authoritative Jewish historians, such as Heinrich Graetz and Cecil Roth, clearly confess that the conversions made by the Hebrews to Christianity were feigned, for although they practised this religion in public, in secret they remained as Hebrews as before; and that among such false Christians, the occult practice of Judaism was transmitted from father to son, although the latter were baptized and lived in public as Christians[135]."

These measures were the distant origin of Spain's 15th century statutes of limpieza de sangre, which excluded Catholics of Jewish descent from leading positions in the State and the Church in order to prevent infiltration and destruction from within.

In 553, Emperor Justinian forbade the dissemination of the Talmud throughout the Roman Empire, "the soul of the Jewish nation", as Heinrich Graetz wrote. Its elaboration had been completed by the end of the 5th century and the following generations made it their main, if not their only, intellectual nourishment[136]. For more than ten centuries, the Jews thus remained totally indifferent to the outside world, to nature, to men and world events. They knew the Bible (the Torah), the history of their forefathers and the eloquence of their prophets only through the Talmud.

Later, in the 13th century, Popes Gregory IX and Innocent IV condemned the Talmud themselves and ordered the burning of the book, which effectively contained all manner of blasphemies and advice to harm non-Jews by every conceivable means. Subsequently, other Roman pontiffs condemned the work: Julius III, Paul IV, Pius IV. Gregory XIII, Clement VIII, Alexander VII, Benedict XIV, among others, but Justinian the Great has the honour of having been the first to prohibit the dissemination of this dreadful book.

XXVIII. Gregory I (590–604)

After Justinian, much of Italy fell into the hands of the Lombards, a semi-pagan, semi-Arian people, who cared little for the Jews and let them grow and prosper as they pleased. In Western Europe, in Gaul and Hispania, where the Church found it difficult to establish its authority, the Jews were at first happier than in the Byzantine Empire and in Italy. The collapse of the Roman Empire had given way to anarchy that was highly favourable to Jewish interests, which were free to corrupt officials, judges and magistrates.

---

[135]Maurice Pinay, *Complot against the Church, Chapter IX* (1962), Transcription pdf from Ediciones Mundo Libre, Mexico, 1985, p. 44.
[136]The Talmud is a fundamental text. It is a sort of constitution or Magna Carta for the Jews. It is a work that mainly collects rabbinical discussions on Jewish law, traditions, customs, narratives and sayings, parables, stories and legends. It is not a book of thought or philosophy. It is an immense civil and religious code based on the Torah [the Old Testament], drawn up between the 3rd and 5th century by Hebrew scholars in Babylonia and Palestine. (NdT).

The Jews were then engaged in the large-scale slave trade. In this regard, the Jewish historian Heinrich Graetz acknowledged that "the repeated invasions of the barbarian tribes and the numerous wars had increased the number of prisoners, and the Jews carried on a vigorous slave trade... In the Frankish Empire, where fanaticism had not yet taken hold, the Jews were not forbidden to trade in slaves[137]."

Fortunately, at that time lived the great Pope Gregory I, who served his pontificate from 590 to 604. Gregory I did not want the Jews to be tolerated at all for having Christian slaves (*"omnino grave exsecrandumque est christianos in servitio esse Iudaerum"*). They were to be taken away immediately or their freedom bought if there was no other way. If the Jew converted to Christianity, the slaves were not returned[138].

In 593, he enacted measures against a Sicilian Jew named Nasas, who worshipped the prophet Elijah—into which many Christians had been duped—and traded in slaves. Gregory urged the prefect of Sicily to disband the sect and free the captives.

Gregory became even angrier when he learned that the Jews of Catania were buying pagan slaves in order to circumcise them and educate them in Judaism. He recalled the emperors' laws against this capital crime, forbidding the circumcision of slaves and ordering that circumcised slaves be freed immediately.

The ostentatious wealth and inordinate pride of the Jews multiplied the conflicts between them and the Christians. "On another occasion, a Christian, after having been the slave for eighteen years of a Jew, implored the protection of the pope against the son of his former master, who, having converted to Christianity, wished to return the former slave to servitude. The Pope declared that, since the first slavery had been illegal, the son, though a Christian, had no right to claim it[139]."

Gregory the Great once wrote a letter to Theodoric, king of the Burgundians, to Theodebert, king of Austrasia, as well as to his wife and queen Brunegild, the famous Visigothic princess, to exhort them "to remedy promptly this evil and to deliver the believers from the hands of their enemies". He took great care to enforce the imperial constitutions and the decisions of the councils, ordering the bishops to punish those who used their wealth to pervert the Christian people[140].

---

[137] Heinrich Graetz, *History of the Jews III*, London, Myers High Holborn, 1904, p. 30, 35.
[138] Charles Auzias-Turenne, *Revue Catholique des Institutions et du Droit*, October 1893.
[139] Georges-Bernard Depping, *Les Juifs dans le Moyen-Âge*, (1823), Éd. Wouters, Brussels, 1844, p. 29.
[140] Epistol. III. 38; VI. 33. 9 Epistol. IX. 36; IV. 21, VI. 7, IX. 109, IV, in Claude Jannet,

But, on the other hand, the pope did not allow violence to be used to convert them and even ordered that the confiscated synagogues be returned to them[141]. Gregory I established as a principle that the conversion of the Jews was to be sought, not by force, but by persuasion and gentleness.

So he wrote to Virgil and Theodore, bishops of Gaul, to forbid the forced baptism of the Jews. On another occasion, he went so far as to admonish the bishop of Terracina who had deprived the Jews of their synagogue, before demanding its return. In fact, the code of Theodosius (L. 83, *de his qui super.*), approved by the Popes and Fathers of the Church, had ruled that the Jews could keep and repair their old synagogues, but under no circumstances build new ones. Now, the synagogues in question, which the three bishops had allowed the people to close, were indeed attested ancient synagogues.

Gregory also promised to exempt part of the property tax for Jewish farmers or landowners who converted to Christianity. Certainly, Gregory had no illusions about the sincerity of such proselytes, but he predicted that "if we shall not win them to Christianity, we shall at least have their children".

XXIX Jerusalem, 614

In 608, in Antioch, a new edifying episode in the age-old confrontation between the Jews and the rest of humanity took place. The Jews pounced on their enemies, wrote Graetz, "all who fell into their hands they killed and threw into the fire...The Patriarch Anastasius, called the Sinaitic, the object of special hatred, was shamefully maltreated by them, and his body dragged through the streets before he was finally executed". The Jewish historian justified these bloody outrages: "the Jews took revenge on them in proportion to the injuries they had suffered", for this "event proves how much the Jews must have suffered from the arbitrariness of the officials and the arrogance of the clergy to be dragged into such a barbarous act of violence."

As soon as Emperor Phocas was informed of the serious disturbances, he appointed Bono as governor of the East and charged General Kotis with the punishment of the rebels. In September and October 608, many Jews were executed and others banished and condemned to exile.

The Jews quickly found a way to take revenge when the Persian king Cosroes II invaded Asia Minor and Syria. Under the command of General

---

L'Église et la constitution sociale, 1884.
[141] S. Gregor. Magn. Epistolae I. 25; III. 1; IX. 55, IX. 6; I. 47; IX. 56, in Claudius Jannet, *L'Église et la constitution sociale*, 1884.

Jarbarzar, a Persian army corps penetrated as far as the Lebanese highlands to invade Palestine. Once again, the Jews sided with the invaders.

But let Heinrich Graetz explain his side of the story:

"At the news of the weakness of the Christian arms and the advance of the Persian troops, a burning desire to fight was awakened in the hearts of the Jews of Palestine. It seemed to them that the hour had come at last to avenge themselves on their double enemy, Roman and Christian, for the humiliations they had endured for centuries. The origin of the warlike movement which thus animated the Jews was in the city of Tiberias. It came from a certain man named Benjamin, who possessed a prodigious fortune which he employed in enlisting and arming Jewish troops. A summons was issued to all the Jews of Palestine, inviting them to assemble and join the Persian army. To this summons the sturdy Jewish inhabitants of Tiberias, Nazareth and the hill towns of Galilee rallied to the Persian standard. In such spirit and fury, they did not spare the Christians and their churches in Tiberias, and probably destroyed the bishopric. With Jarbarzar's army, they marched on Jerusalem to wrest the holy city from the Christians. The Jews of southern Palestine joined their compatriots and, with the help of these troops and the support of a band of Saracens, the Persian general took Jerusalem by storm (July 614). It is said that ninety thousand Christians perished in Jerusalem, but the story that the Jews bought the Christian prisoners from the Persians and killed them in cold blood is pure invention. In their fury, however, the Jews ruthlessly destroyed the Christian sanctuaries. All the churches and monasteries were set on fire, and the Jews undoubtedly had a greater share in this than the Persians. Had not Jerusalem, the original possession of the Jews, been taken from them by violence and treachery? Were they not obliged to consider that the holy city had been vilely desecrated by the worship of the cross and the bones of the martyrs, as well as by the idolatries of Antiochus Epiphanes and Hadrian[142]?"

For fourteen years, the Jews were once again the masters of Palestine, until the Byzantines regained control under Emperor Heraclius after defeating the Persians. On his entry into Jerusalem in 630, Heraclius brought the Holy Cross with him, carrying it himself on his shoulders along the Via Dolorosa to the Church of the Holy Sepulchre, which had been rebuilt.

The Jews of Palestine had to pay for the atrocities they had committed. The Byzantine emperor "instituted a persecution of the Jews throughout Palestine and massacred those who could not take refuge in mountain

---

[142] Heinrich Graetz, *History of the Jews III*, London, Myers High Holborn, 1904, p. 19, 20–21.

hideaways or escape to Egypt," wrote Graetz. Of all the Palestinian Jews, Benjamin of Tiberias, the instigator of the revolt against Constantinople, was apparently the only one to be saved after converting to Christianity.

XXX. *Visigoth Spain I*

The Visigoths, converted to Arianism from 341 onwards, were probably the most prestigious and legendary Germanic people of antiquity. As long as they were Arian, the Visigoths subjugated the Catholics and had a free hand with the Jews, respecting their civic and political rights, even allowing them access to public functions and circumcising their pagan and Christian slaves. This situation led to great prosperity for the Jews of Spain for more than a century, until King Recaredo abjured his Arian faith in January 587 along with most of the Arian nobility and clergy.

The third Council of Toledo in May 589 consecrated the triumph of the Catholic Church in the peninsula. The pride and power of the Jews was at last to be reduced. They were forbidden to hold public office and to marry Christians. Children of mixed marriages were to be baptised by force. They were also forbidden to own slaves, a measure that greatly annoyed them. The Jews tried to bribe the king, as usual: "The rich Jews who owned slaves endeavoured to obtain the repeal of Recaredo's law, and to this end they offered a considerable sum of money to the king. Recaredo, however, refused their offer, and for this fact was praised beyond measure by Pope Gregory, whose heartfelt desire was fulfilled by this law (599)[143]."

The Jews were, however, able to easily circumvent the laws enacted by Recaredo, as the king had rather limited power at the time. In fact, the Visigothic lords, who elected their sovereign, were absolute lords and masters in their lands and still allowed the Jews to own slaves and appointed them to positions of responsibility in their fiefdoms. So much so that after twenty years, Recaredo's laws had been completely forgotten and fallen into disuse. His successors also disregarded them and were generally favourable to the Jews.

This situation changed radically in 612, when Sisebutus came to the throne. This contemporary of the Byzantine emperor Heraclius was, like the latter, a bitter enemy of the Jews, whom he persecuted relentlessly. King Sisebutus, Graetz wrote without irony, "acted in this way without the slightest hint of provocation on the part of the Jews, of his own free will and almost against the wishes of the Catholic clergy".

As soon as he was elected by the Visigothic chiefs, Sisebutus' first

---

[143] Heinrich Graetz, *History of the Jews III*, London, Myers High Holborn, 1904, p. 48, 49, 50.

measure was to put an end to the abuses of the Jews, bringing back on the agenda the canons of the third council of Toledo, which had largely ceased to be applied. He renewed the edicts of Recaredo and ordered ecclesiastics, judges and the people themselves to keep a close watch on their application. He went even further than Recaredo, forbidding Jews not only to buy new slaves, but to keep those they already owned. Only converted Jews were allowed to own slaves and with the added right to inherit those owned by their Jewish relatives. Sisebutus deputed his successors to enforce this edict, and solemnly declared: "May the king who dares to abolish this law incur the deepest disgrace of this world, the flames of purgatory in the world to come, and the eternal torments of hell".

Despite his forceful reprimands, the lords of the land often granted their protection to Jews who lent them money. Sisebutus then took a harsher measure, forcing all Jews in the country to accept baptism within a given period of time or leave Visigothic territory. Recalcitrant Jews were to be punished with the whip and their property confiscated. Some, about 90,000, submitted for fear of losing their property and accepted baptism; the remainder emigrated to France and Africa.

It was probably during the reign of Sisebuto that the Jews of Toledo, converted and then relapsed[144] and threatened with punishment, promised to live more Christianly in the future. In that singular act[145], the converts swore that henceforth they would have no more relations with Jews (those who had not accepted baptism); that they would cease to practise Hebraic customs and usages; that they would not celebrate the Sabbath; that they would not marry their former co-religionists; that, although they could not eat pork because it was contrary to their custom, at least food seasoned with it would not be repugnant to them; that they would faithfully believe in Jesus Christ and the Gospels; that they would do nothing contrary to the Christian religion, and that, if one of them violated this commitment, they would burn or stone him, or put that person and his property at the disposal of the king.

Sisebutus died in 620. The new king, Suintila, a weak and corrupt man, allowed himself to be bought and abrogated Sisebutus' laws, so that the Jews returned to the country and the converts returned to Judaism. "The laws were repealed by his successor, Suintila, a just and liberal monarch, whom the oppressed called "father of his country". The exiled Jews returned to their homeland and the proselytes returned to Judaism...However, the noble king Suintila was dethroned by a conspiracy of nobles and clerics," wrote a grateful Heinrich Gratez.

---

[144] Those who return to their former faith after having abjured it.
[145] The act was inserted in the *Fortalitium fidei, lib III* (Fuero juzgo, or Code of the Visigoths).

Thus, it is likely that under Suintila's protection the Jews regained great power and once again endangered the nation and its institutions, which explains and justifies the conspiracy of the Catholic clergy to depose the felon monarch.

The leader of this new episode of resistance to Judaism was Isidore of Seville, one of the most illustrious Fathers of the Church. Suintila was dethroned by Sisenando. The clergy regained their influence, and again the ecclesiastical assemblies had to curb Jewish power in order to protect the Christians.

In 633, the fourth council of Toledo met under the presidency of Isidore, archbishop of Hispalis (Seville). Isidore was a highly learned, intelligent and moderate prelate. Sisebuto's measures seemed so forceful that the council formally disapproved of them, declaring that those who did not have the faith were to be persuaded and not compelled. Canon 57 of the Council of Toledo thus forbade the use of force or coercion: "No Jew should in future be compelled by force to embrace Christianity". However, the council did not deem it appropriate to overturn what had been done to date and declared that Jews baptised by order of Sisebutus would remain Christians. "Great inconveniences arose from these forced conversions. As it was impossible to watch over so many neophytes or to isolate them, they relapsed in part into Judaism[146]." Canon 59 confirmed all suspicions, for these baptised Jews were often secretly Jews.

Strict measures were taken against these Jews who, baptised in the time of King Sisebutus, had returned to their old faith. We see in the acts of the councils, several provisions against these rebellious ones. To prevent apostasy, canon 62 forbade baptised Jews to associate with their former co-religionists[147]. They were to be forcibly prevented from observing the prescriptions of Judaism and their children were to be brought up in convents. Converts who observed the Sabbath and Jewish festivals, or married according to Jewish rites, or practised circumcision or abstained from food forbidden by Jewish law, would be enslaved. According to this canonical legislation, neither forcibly converted Jews nor their descendants were allowed to testify before a court of law. Thus, this ancient council already marked an essential difference between Jews and those who were Christians in appearance.

Protected by the Hispano-Visigoth nobility, the Jewish converts did not suffer much from these measures of the Fourth Council of Toledo that King Sisenando had taken against them. But a new king came to the throne in

---

[146] Georges-Bernard Depping, *Les Juifs dans le Moyen-Âge*, (1823), Éd. Wouters, Brussels, 1844, p. 32.

[147] Cardinal Ximenés, *Les affaires religieuses en Espagne*, Tournai, Casterman et fils éditeurs, 1856.

636 and this prince named Chintila hated the Jews deeply.

Chintila convened a new council in Toledo. It renewed all the old laws of exception concerning the Jews and decreed that no one could dwell in the Visigoth empire who did not profess the Catholic religion. The Jews were expelled and those who preferred to convert were forced to sign a declaration of commitment to practise the Catholic religion. "But the confession thus signed by men wounded to the soul, wrote Graetz, was not, and could not be, sincere. They firmly hoped for better times when they could remove their masks, and that the elective form of the Visigothic empire would place those times in the near future[148]."

Indeed, the frequent palace revolutions, the lack of stability in the authority of the kings, and the commotions that accompanied each event prevented the strict execution of the conciliar decrees. Thus, the condition of the Jews improved at the end of Chintila's brief reign.

XXI. *King Dagobert I*

The situation of the Jews had become much worse in France under the Merovingian kings. In 540, Childebert had forbidden them to have Christian slaves, "it not being just, said this king, that he who was redeemed by the precious blood of Jesus Christ should be subjected to the infidel who blasphemes his holy name".

In the following century, the situation of the Jews was continually bad. In 615, Clotius II, who had united the entire Frankish empire under his crown, enforced the decisions of the Council of Paris forbidding Jews to exercise higher functions or to serve in the army.

"His son Dagobert must be counted among the most anti-Jewish monarchs in the history of the world. Many thousands of Jewish fugitives, who had fled to the Frankish Empire to escape the fanaticism of Sisebutus, king of the Visigoths, aroused the jealousy of this sensual monarch who was ashamed of being inferior to his Visigothic contemporary and of displaying less religious zeal[149]", Graetz reported. In 633, he issued an edict ordering all those who did not profess the faith of Jesus Christ to leave his states[150]. It is likely that they then retreated towards southern France and the Rhineland.

In the midst of their internal dissensions, the Franks nevertheless had to ease the pressure, and the Israelites, always on the lookout to take

---

[148] Heinrich Graetz, *History of the Jews III*, London, Myers High Holborn, 1904, p. 51, 53.
[149] Heinrich Graetz, *History of the Jews III*, London, Myers High Holborn, 1904, p. 41.
[150] *Chronique de Frédégaire*, Aimoin, *Histoire de France*.

advantage of any weakness or favourable circumstance, gradually penetrated the kingdom to engage in their usual lucrative enterprises, especially the slave trade. "The Council of Châlons sur Saône, held around 630, had also forbidden the sale of slaves outside France, to prevent them from falling into the hands of Jewish merchants trading abroad[151]." King Clovis II, son of Dagobert, would also prohibit the transport of slaves in his kingdom, even going so far as to buy the freedom of those who had had the misfortune to fall into the hands of these ignoble human traffickers.

XXXII. Muhammad

When, in the year 622, a handful of Muhammad's followers left Mecca for Medina (year 0 of Hegira in the Islamic calendar), some Jews recognised in him the long-awaited prophet and embraced Islam. But the Jews of Medina were not convinced, and, as time went on, the Muslims realised that they would never be convinced and distanced themselves from the "people of the book".

Among Muhammad's opponents was a certain Abdullah, son of Saura, considered to be the wisest Jew in the Hijaz (western Arabia). He mocked Muhammad, "the one sent by God", treated him with contempt, ridiculing his revelations and his preaching. He was unaware that the poor fugitive from Mecca who was begging for help at the gates of Medina would soon subdue and exterminate the Jews of the Arabian Peninsula.

The war against the Mekki was dragging on and the Jews of Medina were increasingly unable to bear the Muslims' domination of the city. Some Jewish notables took advantage of a defeat of Muhammad to travel to Mecca and incited the Meccans to take advantage of the occasion and finish off the defeated. In order to finish them off, the Mekids formed a coalition of several Arab tribes, and in 627 an army of 10,000 men marched on Medina.

The siege of the city was interminable and the besiegers exhausted their forces to no avail. In the end, Muhammad succeeded in sowing discord among the Confederates, who decided to lift the siege.

After the coalition had left Medina, Muhammad immediately marched with three thousand men against the Jewish tribe of the Banu Qurayza. The latter, too weak to fight in the open, barricaded themselves in their castle. After a siege of 25 days (February-March 627), the besieged men ran out of food and thought of capitulating. They then asked the Prophet for permission to emigrate with their wives and children and part of their

---

[151] Georges-Bernard Depping, *Les Juifs dans le Moyen-Âge*, (1823), Éd. Wouters, Brussels, 1844, p. 45.

property, but Muhammad refused, and about 700 Jews, including the chiefs Ka'b ibn As'ad and Huyayy ibn Ajtab were beheaded in a public square in Medina; their corpses were thrown into the same pit. The place where this execution took place was called the *market of Banu Qurayza*.

Muhammad took two beautiful captives from this war: Safia, the daughter of his enemy Huyayy, and Zanaib. Zanaib tried to take revenge on Muhammad, whom she considered the murderer of her brother Marab and his co-religionists. Disguising her hatred, she feigned deep affection for Muhammad and gained his trust. But finally, one day, he served the prophet a dish of poisoned meat. Muhammad found his food tasteless and rejected it, but one of his guests died. After this incident, Zanaib was evidently executed and Muhammad ordered his soldiers to use the crockery taken from the Jews only after having washed it in boiled water.

Muhammad warned his followers against the Jews: *"The Hour of Judgement will not come until you fight with the Jews and the stone behind which a Jew hides will say: 'O Muslim! "O Muslim! There is a Jew hiding behind me, kill him*[152]*!"."*

But "the rest of the Jews...intrigued against him and made common cause with some disgruntled Arabs. The house of a Jew, Suyailim, in Medina, was the meeting place of the malcontents, whom Muhammad and his fanatical followers called "the hypocrites" (*Munafikun*). However, this plot was uncovered and the house of Suyailim burnt to the ground. The Jews of Arabia felt a real joy at the death of Muhammad (632), because they, and many others, believed that the Arabs would be cured of their false belief that he was a superior being endowed with immortality," Graetz recounted of these events. But the Koran had already acquired the force of law, and Muhammad's violent imprecations against the Jews were regarded by all Muslims as articles of faith.

By 640, the second Caliph, the mighty Omar, decided to expel the Jewish tribes that the prophet had tolerated in his lands. He did not want the sacred soil of Arabia to be sullied by their traffic. The Muslim warriors thus divided up the Jews' vast domains in the peninsula.

However, as the Jewish historian Heinrich Graetz wrote, "just as no evil in history is without good consequences, the dominance of Islam favoured the rise of Judaism from its deepest depression[153]."

---

[152] Hadith 2926, *L'Authentique d'Al Bukhârî*, Maison D'Ennour, Paris, 2007, tome 2, chapitre 94, p. 449.
And at https://sunnah.com/bukhari/56/139.
[153] Heinrich Graetz, *History of the Jews III*, London, Myers High Holborn, 1904, p. 85–86. ["A mystical Apocalypse makes a clear reference to the joy experienced at the victory of Islam. Shimon Bar Yochai, who was considered a mystic, predicted the rise of Islam, and lamented it in the prayer that went like this: 'Have we not suffered enough

After Muhammad's death, Muslims spread beyond the borders of Arabia, sword and Koran in hand, electrified by his rallying cry: "There is no God but Allah and Muhammad is his prophet[154]".

The ancient kingdom of Persia fell at the first onslaught. The Jews, there as elsewhere, had opted for those who would guarantee them the greatest freedom in their dealings. Since the Sassanid kings ruled the whole country and tended to check and control its financial power, they naturally sided with the invaders. "The Jews of the old Babylonian district (called Iraq by the Arabs) achieved great freedom through the victories of the Mohammedans," Gratez told us.

Byzantine provinces such as Palestine, Syria and Egypt also fell under Arab rule. "Jews and Samaritans helped the Arabs to conquer the land, in order to free themselves from the heavy yoke of the evil Byzantine domination. A Jew placed at the disposal of the Muslims the heavily fortified city of Caesarea, the political capital of the kingdom, which was said to contain 700,000 men to mobilise and among whom were 20,000 Jews. He showed them an underground passage that would lead the besiegers into the heart of the city. The Holy City, after a brief siege, also had to surrender to the Mohammedan arms".

Thus, in 638, Jerusalem fell to the second caliph Omar, who had a mosque built on the site of the ancient Temple. Omar forbade Jews to remain in Jerusalem and subjected them to a number of restrictive laws that also applied to Christians. They were not allowed to build new synagogues, nor were they allowed to embellish the old ones; they were not allowed to sing during the service except in a half voice; they had to recite the funeral prayers in a low voice; they could not hold any public office, nor could they judge Muslims, nor prevent their co-religionists from converting to Islam. Finally, they were required, like Christians, to wear clothes of a particular colour and were not allowed to ride horses.

While Muslims were exempt from all taxes or paid only a small tax to help the poor, Jews and Christians were subjected to a personal tax and a property tax. But despite all these restrictions, Heinrich Graetz insisted once again, "in spite of all this, the Jews felt freer under the new rule of

---

from the dominion of wicked Edom (the Roman-Christian dominion), that now the dominion of Ishmael should rise upon us? Metatron, one of the chief angels, replied, "Fear not, son of Man! God only establishes the kingdom of Ishmael to deliver you from the dominion of wicked Edom. He will raise up a prophet for them, he will conquer countries for them, and there will be great hatred between them and the children of Esau" (the Christians). Such were the sentiments of the Jews during the conquests of the Mohammedans." p. 89–90].

[154] šhādu anna lā ilāy illā [A]llâhu wa anna Muhammadan rasūlu l-lâh: "I bear witness that there is no divinity but God and Mohammad is the messenger of God". (NdT).

Islam than in the Christian lands. Omar's restrictive laws were not enforced even during Omar's lifetime, and while the Muslim fanatics rejected the Jews as co-religionists, they did not despise them as citizens, but showed great honour to worthy Jews. The early Mohammedans treated the Jews as their equals; they respected them as friends and allies, and cared for them even as enemies[155]."

XXXIII. Visigoth Spain II

The Jews of Spain, as we have seen, had to either emigrate or convert to Catholicism and promise in writing, at the express request of King Chintila, their sincere rejection of Judaism.

"But, though they had been forcibly converted, the Jews of Visigothic Spain nevertheless clung firmly to their forbidden religion. The independent Visigothic nobles protected them to some extent from the king's severity, and no sooner were the eyes of the fanatic Chintila closed when he died than the Jews openly returned to Judaism under Chindasvinto, his successor (642–652)."

Chindasvinto's son and successor, Recesvinto (652–672), was very hostile to the Jews. He strongly recommended to the ecclesiastics, gathered at the eighth council of Toledo, to take strong measures against the Jews, especially the Relapsed. The council voted no new measures and merely confirmed the provisions of the fourth council. Jews were allowed to remain in the country, but they had no right to own slaves, hold public office or testify against a Christian.

Knowing that the nobility of the country defended the Jews and allowed those who had been forced into baptism to live according to their customs, Recesvint issued an edict that no Christian should protect those who practised Judaism in secret, on pain of excommunication or exclusion from the Church. This law did not, however, produce the desired effects. The *Judaising Christians,* as those who remained attached to their old religion were called, "soon learned the art of remaining faithful in their inmost souls to their religion, and of wearying the suspicious vigilance of their enemies. They continued to celebrate the Jewish festivals in their homes, disregarding the festivals instituted by the Church[156]."

During the reign of King Wamba (672–680), Jews were still numerous in the peninsula. But since he owed his election to the clergy, the new king

---

[155] Heinrich Graetz, *History of the Jews III*, London, Myers High Holborn, 1904, p. 88, 89.
[156] Heinrich Graetz, *History of the Jews III*, London, Myers High Holborn, 1904, p. 103, 106.

had to take the oath prescribed by the Council of Toledo and order that all unconverted Jews be expelled from the kingdom.

This time, the decree was ruthlessly executed. The many Jews who refused to accept baptism crossed the Pyrenees and sought refuge in Septimania. The governor of this province, Count Hilderic, had refused to recognise the newly elected king and led the rebellion. In order to rally new supporters, he had offered Jewish converts refuge in his lands, guaranteeing them religious freedom, and many responded to his invitation. Hilderic's insurrection at Nîmes reached a major dimension, but the insurrectionists were eventually defeated. Wamba appeared with his army in front of Narbonne and expelled the Jews from the city.

False converts also tried to infiltrate the Catholic Church by buying the highest ecclesiastical magistracies. The problem was raised at Toledo in a new council. Canon 9 insisted on the repression of simony against those who "attempted to buy the dignity of bishop."

Wamba was dethroned by a lord of Byzantine origin named Ervigius. Before the council that was to crown him, in 681, Ervigius delivered a fanatical speech against the Jews that began as follows: "With tears streaming from my eyes, I implore this honourable assembly to manifest its zeal and purify the country of this leprosy of corruption. Rise up, I cry to you! Rise up, I cry to you; Exterminate these stinking Jews who never cease to harden themselves into new follies, put to the test the laws against the apostasy of the Jews which we have just enacted[157].""

Heinrich Graetz had distorted the text here in his own translation. Maurice Pinay, in *Plot against the Church*, presented the original text: ""Repair most reverend Fathers and honourable Priests of the heavenly Ministries...therefore I present myself with an outpouring of tears at the venerable meeting of Your Paternity, so that, with the zeal of your regime, the earth may be purged of the contagion of wickedness. Arise, I beseech you, arise, untie the bonds of the guilty, correct the dishonest customs of the transgressors, bring the discipline of your fervour against the perfidious, and extinguish the bitterness of the proud, relieve the burden of the oppressed, and what is more than all this, root out the Jewish pestilence, which is growing every day with greater fury (*et quod plus hic omnibus est, Iudaeorum pestem, quae in novam semper recrudescit insaniam, radicibus extirpate*). Examine also with the greatest attention the laws which our glory promulgated a short time ago against the perfidy of the Jews, add to them your sanction and gather them together in a single statute to restrain the excesses of the same perfidious[158] "."

---

[157] Heinrich Graetz, *Geschitchte der Juden; Histoire des juifs III*, Éd. Durlacher, Paris, 1888, p. 308-309.
[158] Maurice Pinay, *Complot contra la Iglesia*, Chapter XIV (1962), Transcription pdf

Of the twenty-seven paragraphs which King Ervigius submitted for the council's approval, only one concerned the Jews. All the others concerned those who had converted out of interest and who, despite their handwritten declarations, continued to Judaise in secret. In order to bring the Jews to Christianity, Ervigius proposed simply to compel them, their children and all their relatives to present themselves for baptism within a year, and, if they did not obey this order, to confiscate all their property, to punish them with a hundred lashes, to tear off the skin of their foreheads and heads, and to expel them from the country.

The council also passed a measure aimed at destroying the Jewish fifth column in the Church. Canon 18 established a real espionage in the domicile of Christians of Jewish descent, and obliged their Christian servants to denounce their Jewish practices, offering them as a premium for denunciation the release from their servitude. "The aforementioned law, referring to the aforementioned servants, orders:" ...that, at any time, whoever proclaims, acknowledges and says and swears that he is a Christian, or that he has become a Christian, and discovers the infidelity of his masters (masters), and he denies his error, shall at that time go free publicly, with all his peculium and have the possibility of bequeathing it (to his successors)[159] "."

Judaising Christians who travelled through the territory were also obliged to present themselves to the clergy of the localities where they were staying in order to prove that they were faithfully fulfilling their religious duties.

A new council, presided over by the Jewish metropolitan Julian of Toledo, approved all the measures proposed by Ervigius and decided that they could never be abolished. Two days after the closing of the assembly, on 25 January 681, the Jews were summoned to be informed of the new measures taken against them. For the third time, baptised Jews had to abjure Judaism and sign an act of faith. They were also ordered to bring with them the text of the laws concerning them, so that they would not be able to claim ignorance of them in case of non-compliance.

The power of the Jews in Spain was completely annihilated during the reign of Egica between 687 and 702.

In the year 694, a great conspiracy was uncovered. False Christians, in collusion with their brothers in Africa, conspired to foment a revolution. Felix, Archbishop of Toledo, reacted swiftly and convened a new council which dealt with and reported the evidence of the crypto-Jewish conspiracy.

---

from Ediciones Mundo Libre, Mexico, 1985, p. 202, citing source: Juan Tejada y Ramiro, Colección de cánones citada, tomo II, pp. 454, 455.

[159] Maurice Pinay, *Complot against the Church, Chapter XIV* (1962), Transcription pdf from Ediciones Mundo Libre, Mexico, 1985, p. 205.

The eighth canon of the 17th Council of Toledo, literally entitled "On the damnation of the Jews" (*Iudaeorum damnatione*) set out its forceful conclusions: ""It is known that the Jewish plebs are stained with a most ugly note of sacrilege and bloody effusion of the blood of Jesus Christ, and defiled moreover with the profanation of the oath (among other things because they had sworn to be faithful Christians and not to Judaise in secret), so that their wickednesses are without number; Therefore it is necessary that they should mourn for having incurred in so grave a sin of animosity, those who, on account of their wickedness, have not only wished to disturb the state of the Church, but with tyrannical boldness have attempted to ruin the country and the nation, so much so that, rejoicing in the belief that their time had already come, they have caused various havoc to the Catholics. For which reason the cruel and stupendous presumption must be extirpated with a crueler torture. So that the judgement against them must be all the more severe, because everywhere they punish what is known to have been wickedly defined".

King Egica expropriated them completely, forbade them to own houses and land, to trade and sail to Africa and, in general, to do business with the Christians. The Jews were forced to cede all their property to the treasury for a small compensation. They were also expelled from their place of residence.

All the Jews of Spain were placed under servitude and distributed among the great lords of the country, without ever being able to be freed: "And concerning their children of both sexes, we decree that as soon as they reach seven years of age, they shall be separated from the company of their parents, without allowing them any friction with them, their lords themselves having to hand them over to most faithful Christians, to be educated, so that the boys may marry Christian women and vice versa, neither the parents nor the children being allowed, as we have already said, to celebrate under any circumstances the ceremonies of the Judaic superstition, nor to return on any occasion to the path of infidelity[160]"."

The punishments approved by the council against the crypto-Jewish conspirators were applied in all the provinces of the Visigothic kingdom, except in Gallia Narbonensis (Septimania), then devastated by a deadly epidemic. This toleration was granted on condition that they became sincere Christians. Numerous Jews then emigrated there, but as the following centuries showed, these false Christians did not abandon Judaism and the South of France became a new Judea. In fact, the region was to become the headquarters and cradle of the most destructive

---

[160] Maurice Pinay, *Complot contra la Iglesia, Chapter XVI* (1962), Transcription pdf from Ediciones Mundo Libre, Mexico, 1985, p. 211-212, citing source: Juan Tejada y Ramiro, Colección de cánones citada, tomo II, pp. 602, 603.

revolutionary heresies in Europe, especially the Gnostic doctrines and the Hebrew Cabala[161].

Unfortunately, Egica's son Witiza was a disastrous prince whose policies ended the Visigothic empire in Spain. In April 711, Tarik, a daring and skilful Muslim general, crossed the Strait of Gibraltar and invaded the south of the peninsula with considerable forces. The Jews banished from Spain swelled the ranks of the Muslim armies, and the help of those who remained was invaluable. In July the armies of Rodrigo (Roderic), the last Visigothic king, were defeated and the Muslims quickly penetrated the interior of the country. Thanks to the Jews who were entrusted with guarding the conquered cities, the Muslim generals always had all their troops at their disposal to continue their conquest of the country.

In Toledo, on Palm Sunday 712, the Jews drove the Moors into the city. The aristocrats and clergy had fled, and while the Christians pleaded for divine protection in their churches, the Jews threw the doors of the temples wide open, joining the Muslims in massacring the Christians[162].

The testimonies of Christian historians are quite consistent with those collected by Heinrich Graetz, who also stated that "in each city they conquered, the Muslim generals could only leave a small garrison of their own troops, for they needed all the men to subdue the country; they therefore entrusted them to the custody of the Jews. Thus the Jews, who until recently had been serfs, became masters of the cities of Cordoba, Granada, Malaga and many others. When Tarik came to the capital, Toledo, he found it occupied by only a small garrison, the nobles and clergy having fled to safety. While the Christians were in church, praying for the safety of their country and their religion, the Jews threw open the gates to the victorious Arabs (Palm Sunday, 712), welcoming them with acclamations, and thus avenging the many miseries that had befallen them in the course of a century after the time of Recaredo and Sisebut[163]."

Another well-known Jewish intellectual in France, Jacques Attali, whose work we have examined extensively for our previous books, confirmed this: "With their help, the Muslim troops defeated King Roderic in July 711 and quickly conquered the entire peninsula". So the Jews were

---

[161] See *Psychoanalysis of Judaism* (N.T.).
[162] Chronicle of the Bishop of Tuy.
[163] Heinrich Graetz, *History of the Jews III*, London, Myers High Holborn, 1904, p. 111. By contrast, Cecil Roth is by far the most dishonest Jewish historian. In his *History of the Jewish People* (*Histoire du peuple juif*, 1936, Stock, 1980), he wrote: "Later, the ill-intentioned ecclesiastical chroniclers attributed the debacle of the Visigoths to the Jews who had supposedly invited and helped the invaders" (page 183). (page 183). Certainly, with Cecil Roth, nothing—not even the slightest error—ever makes it possible to understand why the Jews are the target of the hostility of the Goyim.

naturally exposed to further reprisals: "Thus, the Archbishop of Toledo accused the Jews of treason in favour of the Saracens, provoking an uprising; he also organised the sacking of the synagogues[164]".

Almost all of Spain became a Muslim province. In return for their support, the Moors treated the Jews with great benevolence, allowing them to practise their religion openly and to have their own courts. They thus regained all the power they had lost and were able to advise and guide the caliphs as they pleased.

Heinrich Graetz explained the advantages of the regime change for the Jews as follows: "The first caliphs of the house of Ommiyyah...had

---

[164]Jacques Attali, *Los judíos, el mundo y el dinero*, Fondo de cultura económica, 2005, Buenos Aires, p. 134, 204. ["It is known that the invasion of the Arabs was solely sponsored by the Jews living in Spain. They opened the gates of the main cities to them. For they were numerous and rich, and already in the time of Egica they had conspired, seriously endangering the security of the kingdom. The XVIIth Council punished them very severely, reducing them to slavery (Can. VIII); but Witiza favoured them again, and to such patronage they responded by conspiring with all the discontented. The indigenous population could have resisted the handful of Arabs who passed the Straits; but Witiza had disarmed them, the towers were on the ground, and the spears had become rakes. History remembers no quicker conquest than that. Goths and Jews, political discontent, personal vendettas and religious hatreds were all helping in the struggle". Marcelino Menendez Pelayo, *Historia de los Heterodoxos españoles*, Tomo I, Ed. F. Maroto, Madrid, 1880, p. 216. Menendez Pidal was very critical of the Visigoths and their historical legacy in Spain: "Witiza is for us the symbol of the Visigoth aristocracy, neither Arian nor Catholic, but sceptical, an enemy of the Church, because the latter moderated the royal power and opposed its excesses. The Gothic nobility was extremely relaxed in its customs: cruelty and lechery stain the pages of its history at every step...

"That same individualism or excess of personalism which the races of the North brought with them, induced them to frequent and scandalous rebellions, to internal discord, and what is worse, to treachery, to perjury against their people and race, because they did not cherish those great ideas of homeland and city, proper to Hellenes and Latins. That is why the Visigoth nobility, led by the sons of Witiza and by the archbishop D. Oppas, sells the land to the Romans. Oppas, sold the land to the Muslims, defected to the Guadalete, and Teodomiro, after a brief resistance, surrendered to Abdalassis in a dishonourable pact. The Visigothic race had great faults to purge. Not the least of these was its utter inability to form a stable regime or civilisation. And yet, what greatness in that period! But science and art, canons and laws, are the glory of the Church, the glory of Spain. The Visigoths have left nothing, not a stone, not a book, not a memento, if we exclude the letters of Sisebuto and Bulgoranos, perhaps written by Spanish bishops and placed in the name of those high personages. Let us be disillusioned: peninsular civilisation is Roman from head to toe, with some Semitism; we have nothing of Teutonic, thank God. What the Goths brought us was reduced to a few barbarous laws, which clash with the rest of our Codes, and to that indiscipline and disorder which ruined the empire they established". *Historia de los Heterodoxos españoles*, Volume I, Ed. F. Maroto, Madrid, 1880, p. 213–214, 215].

completely freed themselves from that narrow-mindedness and persecutory mania which characterised the founder and the first two caliphs...They were much more worldly than spiritual; their political horizon was broad and they confined themselves very little to the narrow precepts of the Koran and the traditions (Sunna)[165]."

Spain under Muslim rule remains in the Jewish imagination as a much longed-for golden age. The great Jewish historian Leon Poliakov wrote: "In 711, the Arab invasion catapulted them to the top of the social ladder, as advisors and allies of the conquerors[166]". Jacques Attali confirmed once again: "The Jews have never known a more beautiful place to stay than this European Islam of the 8th century". Jewish financiers triumphed[167].

XXXIV. Agobardo of Lyon and Amolon

The reigns of Charlemagne (768–814) and his son Louis I or Louis the Pious (814–840) were a happy period for the Jews. The latter "was extraordinarily favourable to the Jews," wrote Graetz, "...they could own land, exercise trades and become shipowners and did not have to suffer inconvenience or vexation".

For "the remarkable favour shown to the Jews by the pious emperor was mainly due to commercial motives. The international trade which Charlemagne established, and which Ludwig's advisers wished to develop, was for the most part in the hands of Jews. The latter could more easily enter into trade relations with their brethren in other countries[168]..."

At that time, Jews settled in various regions of Germany, extending from there to the Slavic-inhabited territories beyond the Oder River, as far as Bohemia and Poland. They dominated the great trade, they were "the principal agents of export and import trade, wrote Graetz, they bought and sold merchandise and slaves."

The activity of the Western Jews developed in all directions. Bernard Lazare described the situation as follows: "Protected in Spain by the Caliphs and supported by Charlemagne, who let the Merovingian laws fall

---

[165]Heinrich Graetz, *History of the Jews III*, London, Myers High Holborn, 1904, p. 112.
[166]Léon Poliakov, *Histoires des crises d'identité juives*, Austral, 1994, p. 22.
[167]Meanwhile, in the East, another new "Messiah" was appearing. In 723, a certain Zonaria manifested himself in Syria, and the Jews of Spain and elsewhere believed him to be the true Messiah. Their illusions did not last long: the vali of Cordoba Ambisa Ben Sohim seized the property of all those who had followed him. (Joseph Conde, *Histoire de la domination des Arabes et Maures en Espagne et en Portugal*, tome I. Alexis Eymery, Paris, 1825, p. 129).
[168] Heinrich Graetz, *History of the Jews III*, London, Myers High Holborn, 1904, p. 165.

into oblivion, they extended their trade which, until then, had consisted mainly in the sale of slaves. They were, moreover, in particularly favourable conditions for this. Their communities were in constant contact with each other[169]."

Charlemagne had, however, imposed on Jews who appeared in court, as witnesses or litigants against Christians, a special formula which distinguished them from other inhabitants: "They were required to surround themselves with thorns, to take the Torah in their right hand, and to invoke upon themselves the leprosy of Naaman and the punishment of the faction of Korah[170] in testimony to the truth of their statement." This is a proof of how much the Christians distrusted the Jews, always prone to systematically defend their fellows.

But the most gracious time for the Jews of France was undoubtedly during the reign of Louis the Pious (also nicknamed in France the Good-natured). The emperor "took them under his special protection, shielding them from injustice, both from the barons and the clergy. They enjoyed the right to settle anywhere in the kingdom. Despite numerous decrees to the contrary, they were not only allowed to employ Christian labourers, but could even import slaves. The clergy were forbidden to baptise the slaves of the Jews so that they could regain their freedom. Out of respect for them, the market day was changed from Saturday to Sunday. The Jews were freed from the punishment of flogging, and had jurisdiction over Jewish criminals in their own hands. Moreover, they were not subjected to the barbarous ordeals of fire and water. They were allowed to exercise their trades without hindrance or impediment, but they had to pay a tax to the treasury and make a periodic declaration of their income. The Jews also collected the taxes, and obtained through this privilege a certain power over the Christians, although this was contrary to what was expressly determined in the canon laws." For example, the merchant Abraham of Saragossa had full freedom to buy servants abroad—mostly Slavs still pagans—and resell them in the Empire or to the Saracens[171].

During the reigns of Charlemagne and his son, the Jews, thanks to their relations with their co-religionists abroad, concentrated in their hands all

---

[169] Bernard Lazare, *Anti-Semitism, its history and causes, (1894)*. Editions La Bastille, digital edition, 2011, p. 46.

[170] Korah ben Izhar (Korah, son of Izhar), is a biblical character who conspired against Moses and Aaron. Eventually, Yahweh punished the rebels and most of them were swallowed up by the earth. Instead, Korah and 250 other men who were at the entrance of the tabernacle were consumed by a fire of divine origin. (NdT).

[171] Heinrich Graetz, *History of the Jews III*, London, Myers High Holborn, 1904, p. 164–165, 147 and in Charta, Ludov., n. 32, 33, 34, in volume IV of *Historiens de France*.

the trade of the country, especially the export and import of goods[172]. The Jews were able to have their own courts and a special official, with the title of *lord of the Jews* (*magister Judærum*), was charged with ensuring that their rights were respected. Some were even appointed tax collectors. Ludwig I's favour was probably due to the influence of his second wife, Judith of Bavaria, who deeply revered Judaism.

Agobard, a prelate of Hispanic origin and archbishop of Lyon from 814 to 840, denounced the weakness of Louis the Good-natured with regard to the Jews and opposed their growing influence with all his might, displaying tireless ardour. He was "a bitter enemy of the Jews", wrote Graetz. But at court, the all-powerful Jewish financiers had corrupted the political staff and won to their cause the leading officials and lords. Proud of the imperial charters they triumphantly wielded, the Jews believed themselves unpunished and ignored the threats of the clergy and the statutes of the ancient church councils.

We have seen how, during the reigns of the Merovingian dynasty, a simple order from a bishop was enough to banish the Jews from a diocese. Agobard, the bishop of Lyon, and therefore one of the chief clergy of France, was not even remotely capable of enforcing the decrees of kings and councils against them.

Indeed, Agobardo suffered several setbacks in his fight against the Jews and went so far as to formally complain and expose their excesses in a letter to Emperor Louis in 822 entitled *Epistola de baptizandis Hebraeis*. Five other letters would follow[173]. In his treatise *De insolentia Judaeorum* (827), the emperor again warned against the Jews: they build synagogues, they extort money by all means, they do not tolerate public markets on Saturdays when it was the universal custom; finally, they even kidnap Christian children to take them to Spain and sell them to the Saracens as slaves.

Agobardo cited specific events, such as the arrival in his diocese of a Spaniard from Cordoba who, twenty-four years earlier, had been stolen by Jews from Lyon and sold into slavery while still a child. The Cordovan had managed to escape along with another victim, originally from Arles, who had been in the same situation for six years. Agobardo had requested an investigation into this shameful traffic, which had revealed that the abduction and sale of Christian children by Jews was nothing exceptional[174].

---

[172]Mas L. Margolis and Alexandre Marx, *Histoire du peuple juif*, Payot, Paris, 1930, p. 323, in Abbé Jules Minvielle, *De la Cabale au progresisme*, Éditions Saint-Rémi, p. 143.
[173]B. Blumenkranz, *Juifs et chrétiens dans le monde occidental*, Paris, 1960.
[174]Read *The Jewish Mafia*, Omnia Veritas. 2022.

Agobardo once baptised a slave girl who had run away from her master's house—a Jew from Lyon—in order to free her from her condition. Jewish officials had asked the imperial administration to return the runaway slave to her owner, but Agobardo had refused to obey, and was deposed. Despite having won the support of the ecclesiastical party at court, the Jews, for their part, had asserted their influence with the emperor. Louis the Pious then appointed a commission to examine the matter in dispute, which finally decided in favour of the Jews.

Retired to his diocese, Agobardo continued to fight his enemies. He addressed the issue in five epistles that followed the traditional doctrine of the Church: "Keep the Jews at a distance, do not let them dominate[175]", he warned his contemporaries. Following his orders, the priests attacked the Jews in their sermons, forbade their parishioners to have relations with them, to buy or sell anything to them, to have lunch or dinner with them or to work for them under any circumstances. The Jews of Lyon then obtained *Letters of Protection (Indiculi)* bearing the imperial seal, and Agobardo was ordered to put an end to their propaganda (around 828).

The bishop of Lyon was not discouraged. He organised a collective petition and wrote to all the bishops of France to put pressure on King Louis to lift the barrier that once protected Christians. They were probably informed that conspirators were ready to support the rebellion of the children of the emperor's first marriage against the empress and Archchancellor Bernhard, who had advised the monarch to redistribute the empire in favour of Judith's son. At the repeated urging of Agobard, numerous prelates met in Lyon in 829, and a missive was sent to Louis to expose the dangers resulting from the liberties granted to the Jews. He also wrote a letter to Nibridius, bishop of Narbonne, *De cavendo convictu et societate Iudaeorum*, and finally, in collaboration with Bernard, archbishop of Vienna, a short treatise entitled *de Iudaicis superstitionibus*. This treatise, *On the Superstition of the Jews*, was preceded by an introduction in which Agobardo justified the conduct he had hitherto maintained towards the Jews. Not only did he accuse the Jews, but he wrote a severe criticism against their protectors and those who had been corrupted by their gold.

But Louis the Kind did not take into account the act of accusation formulated by the synod of Lyon. In 830, Agobard, who had taken part in the conspiracy against the empress Judith and her friends, was deposed and forced to flee to Italy. He was later canonised by the Church.

In 840, on the death of Emperor Louis the Pious, war immediately broke out between his sons over the division of Charlemagne's great empire. The

---

[175] According to Monsignor Bressoles, honorary vice-president of the Catholic Institute in 1949. *Doctrine et action politique d'Agobard*, Paris, Librairie philosophique J. Vrin, 1949.

rights granted to Charles the Bald, son of Louis and Judith, to the detriment of his older half-brothers, were the cause of the troubles that plagued the end of the reign. In 843, Charlemagne's empire was divided into three parts.

Charles the Bald, who received western France, seemed to have inherited his mother's predilection for Judaism. He employed numerous Jews at his court, as did other Carolingians. An Israelite named Juda was his personal banker or treasurer. In a letter, Charles called him *Juda his loyal one*, mentioning the good services he rendered him[176]. His physician was another Jew named Sedecias. "Under Charles the Bald," wrote Graetz, "as under his predecessor, the Jews enjoyed equality with the Christians. They were allowed to exercise their trade without hindrance, and also to own real estate [177]". "The Hebrews had succeeded in establishing themselves in the offices of tax collectors, from which they had been excluded under the Merovingian kings. The Christians complained, as in the past, of the humiliating harshness with which this collection was carried out by the infidels[178]." Charles imposed only a slight restriction on Jewish merchants, obliging them to pay 11% of their revenues to the treasury, while other merchants paid one tenth (10%).

His bitter enemy at the time was Agobard's disciple and successor, Amolon, the new archbishop of Lyon. In his *Amulonis Epistola contra Judaeos*, Amolon wrote: "Cursing the infidelity of the Jews and always seeking to protect the Christian people from their contagion; I have thrice publicly ordered that the infidels be put away, that no Christian should be their servant in the cities or in the villages, leaving their heathen slaves to help them in their labours; I have forbidden to taste their food and drink. Moreover, I have issued several strict orders in order to root out the evil and imitate the example of our pious pastor, master and predecessor Agobardo."

Hinkmar, the bishop of Rheims and favourite of Emperor Charles, as well as the archbishop of Sens and Bourges and other ecclesiastics, supported him in his struggle. In 845, meeting in the council of the city of Meaux, these prelates decided to re-establish the old canon laws. They did not designate exactly what measures the king should apply to the Jews, but limited themselves to pointing out to him the edicts promulgated in the past against them since Constantine the Great, mentioning the prohibition of Theodose II to hold a job or any dignity, reminding him of the decisions of

---

[176] Letter of Charles the Bald in *L'Histoire des comtes de Barcelone*, by Diago, in Georges-Bernard Depping, *Les Juifs dans le Moyen-Âge*, (1823), Éd. Wouters, Brussels, 1844, p. 46.
[177] Heinrich Graetz, *History of the Jews III*, London, Myers High Holborn, 1904, p. 173.
[178] Georges-Bernard Depping, *Les Juifs dans le Moyen-Âge*, (1823), Éd. Wouters, Brussels, 1844, p. 46.

the councils, as well as the edict of the Merovingian king Childebert who had forbidden them to exercise the functions of judge or customs officer and to go out on the streets during the feast of Passover. They also invoked the synodal decisions promulgated outside France, especially the provisions adopted by the Visigoths in Spain against the rebellious Jews.

Charles the Bald decided to disregard the advice of the bishops and, despite the fact that his favourite Hinkmar was a member of the meeting, he dissolved the council. On 14 February 846, he ordered a new council to meet in Paris to examine the changes to be made to the organisation of the Church, but the king forbade the subject of the Jews to be discussed.

Amolon then advised the high clergy to address the princes and lords in order to exhort them to abolish the privileges of the Jews. In his letter to the prelates, he enumerated the same grievances that Agobardo had pointed out in his time. Little by little, anti-Judaism progressed. In Beziers, the bishop gave impassioned sermons every year, from the eve of Palm Sunday to the day after Easter, which then led to serious riots. For this one occasion only stones were allowed, and the people ran to stone the houses of the Jews. The Jews, following the same ancient custom, had the possibility of defending themselves with stones as well. The city was then in a state of anarchy and civil war until Passover. One chronicle even claimed that there were often many wounded on both sides[179]. "These misdeeds were repeated year after year for centuries. The Jews of Beziers defended themselves, and on these occasions physical injuries were inflicted on both sides," wrote Graetz. So these disturbances became a kind of tradition in this town and it was only by dint of money that the Jews of Beziers succeeded in 1160 in putting a stop to this custom. Viscount Raymond Trencavel, in a solemn act found in the archives of the cathedral of Beziers, undertook to forgive the Jews the usual humiliations and insults in exchange for the payment of two hundred sous[180] and a rent of four pounds payable on Palm Sunday for the ornamentation of the church[181].

Another curious tradition was the right of the Counts of Toulouse, on Good Friday, to slap the syndic of the city's Jewish community in front of the cathedral. This ceremony was known as the "*colaphisation*[182]". In 1018,

---

[179] Georges-Bernard Depping, *Les Juifs dans le Moyen-Âge*, (1823), Éd. Wouters, Brussels, 1844, p. 48.

[180] An ancient French coin derived from the Roman *solidus*. After Charlemagne's reform, the solidus was no longer 1/72 of the Roman gold pound but 1/20 of the Carolingian silver pound. The sou was divided into 12 *deniers*, which, with a few exceptions—such as the gros *tournoi* of Saint Louis—were the only ones in circulation in practice. The system of 1 pound = 20 sous of 12 deniers would remain unchanged until the French Revolution.

[181] Catel, *Histoire du Languedoc*.

[182] In French, from the disused verb *colaphiser* (Latin: *colaphizare*, noun *colaphizo*,

the chaplain of Count Aimeric de Rochechouart, called Hugo, requested authorisation to exercise this seignorial right, giving the syndic such a brutal slap that the Jew died[183]. This custom had been instituted after the treachery committed by the Jews at the time of the Muslim invasion.

We also have news of the Jews in the 10th century, in the time of Charles III the Simple: the Jews had been expelled from the county of Narbonne and the king had seized and donated to the archbishopric and the churches the lands, vineyards, houses and mills that had belonged to them[184]. But the kingdom of France was in those years ravaged by the Viking invasions and hardly anyone cared anymore about the fate of the Jews.[185]

XXXV. The kings of commerce in the East

In the East, the Jews did not suffer much under Harun al-Rashid and his sons who succeeded him in Baghdad. But they were distinguished from the other inhabitants: in 807, Harun al-Rashid forced them to wear a distinctive mark, a piece of yellow cloth on their dress. It is possible that this measure was the counterpart of the persecution directed against Christians, who were required to wear a blue piece of cloth.

In Palestine, the situation had worsened considerably. In 809, after the death of Harun and the division of the empire, war broke out between his two sons, Muhammad al-Amin and Abdallah al-Mamun. Graetz wrote of this episode: "The sufferings must have been so terrible that a preacher of the time declared them to be a sign of the coming of the Messiah[186]. "Israel can only be redeemed through penitence, and true penitence can only be evoked by suffering, affliction, wandering and need," this speaker declared for the consolation of his afflicted congregation. In the civil war between the two caliphs, he thought he saw the imminent destruction of Ismaili rule and the coming of the messianic empire. "Two brothers will finally rule over the Ishmaelites (Mohammedans); there will then arise a descendant of David, and in the days of this king the Lord of Heaven will establish a kingdom that will never perish". "God will exterminate the children of Esau (Byzantium), the enemies of Israel, and also the children of Ishmael, their

---

from Ancient Greek *Kolaphizo*: blow with a punch) (NdT).

[183]S. Schwarzfuchs, *The world History of the jewish people*, Massadah Publishing, Tel-Aviv, 1966.

[184]See the regulations of the years 899, 914, 928, in volume IX of the *Historiens de France*, in Georges-Bernard Depping, *Les Juifs dans le Moyen-Âge*, (1823), Éd. Wouters, Brussels, 1844, p. 49.

[185]In 848, the Jews of Bordeaux also betrayed the city during the Viking invasion.

[186]On the pains of the birth of the Messiah read the last chapter of this book, as well as *Psychoanalysis of Judaism, Jewish Fanaticism and The Mirror of Judaism*.

adversaries[187]."""

Indeed, we know that in Jewish eschatology Christians and Muslims will be definitively defeated and annihilated forever. "But these, as on many other occasions, were illusory hopes," acknowledged Heinrich Graetz. The caliphate faltered, but was not destroyed by civil war; al-Amin died and al-Mamun was declared head of the empire. After al-Mamun's death, Jews were gradually subjected to various restrictions, as in Christian countries. The caliph al-Mutawakkil, al-Mamun's third successor, renewed the laws of Omar against them, imposing on them, as on Christians, a particular form of dress and colour, transformed synagogues and churches into mosques, forbade them access to public functions and prohibited Muslims from instructing them (849–856). They had no right to ride horses and were only allowed to ride donkeys or mules (853–854). If they bought a house, they had to pay the caliph a tenth of its value.

Even so, the Jews exercised their dominance over trade and finance. By about the year 1000, they were the masters of money, as the Jewish historian Leon Poliakov wrote: "Kings of the finances of Baghdad and bankers to the caliphs for a quarter of a century, although ben-Pichas and ben-Amram were the first, they were not the only ones. Another chronicle informs us that most of the merchants of Tustar in Persia were Jews. In Ispahan, known for its flourishing trade as "the second Baghdad", the Yahudia quarter was the centre of business[188]."

Very few sources exist on the Radhanites, those Jewish traders of the early Middle Ages who dominated trade between the Christian and Muslim worlds. From the Rhone valley, they travelled down to North Africa, via Spain or Italy, progressed to the Middle East, and then to India and China, crossing the Asian continent. Ibn Khordadhbeh, director of the postal service and police in the province of Jibal, wrote around 870 in his *Book of Routes and Kingdoms*: "These traders speak Arabic, Persian, Greek, Frankish, Spanish and Slavic. They travel from east to west, by land and by sea. They carry from the west eunuchs, women slaves, children, silk, swords, beavers, sables and other furs".

The merchants could take another route—from the Rhône via Germany and the Balkan countries, or from the north via Russia. Historians Cecil Roth and Claude Cahen placed the centre of Radhanite activity in the Rhône valley, whose Latin name was Rhodanus. But other scholars claim that the name comes from Persian, from *rah* ("road") and *dan* ("he knows").

The Radhanites played an essential role in the slave trade that was widespread in the 9th and 10th centuries. Verdun was then an important

---

[187]Heinrich Graetz, *History of the Jews III*, London, Myers High Holborn, 1904, p. 148.
[188] Léon Poliakov, *Les Juifs et notre histoire*, Science Flammarion, 1973, p. 48.

trading centre and one of the first slave markets. Slaves were captured from the Slavic and pagan tribes in the eastern markets of the Carolingian Empire and resold throughout the Muslim world. The trade was controlled by Jewish merchants: "The trade must have been important because the word *servus* disappeared in favour of the word *slavus* from which "slave" was formed. However, we know that the Jewish community of Verdun, known for running this trade, had only a few dozen members[189]."

Verdun was also an important place for the castration of slaves. Indeed, the Jews of Verdun were in the habit of castrating their Christian slaves to make them eunuchs destined for the harems of the Saracen princes[190]. The letters of Emperor Louis the Pious have left us the names of two merchants from Lyon, David and Joseph, who benefited from the privilege of this lucrative trade. From Lyon, the merchants transported human livestock to Arles, home to a large Jewish community, then on to Narbonne, then home to the largest Jewish community in Europe, before crossing the Pyrenees[191]. The European slave trade gradually declined in the following centuries as Muslims began to replace them with Blacks from sub-Saharan Africa.

Granada, 30 December 1066.

The whole of southern Spain was in the hands of the Muslims. Since Tarik's invasion in 711, the Jews experienced a true golden age. They were the main traders and facilitators of goods. The medieval historian Jacques Heers wrote: "Authors, Muslim and Christian, insist particularly on the role of the Jews, who, in Muslim Spain, constituted the majority of the population of the great cities, especially in Granada, commonly called in the 8th century the "city of the Jews". Traders in luxury goods, metals, jewellery, silk and moneylenders used to group together in small societies of relatives and friends (…)".

The white slave trade was their monopoly. Roberta Strauss-Feuerlicht, a Jewish historian, confirmed this: "The golden age of Jewry in Spain owed much of its fortune to the existence of an international network of Jewish merchants… Jews from Bohemia bought Slavs and resold them to Spanish Jews, who in turn resold them to the Moors[192]."

---

[189] André Cheville, *La France au Moyen Âge*, Presses Universitaires de France, 1965, p. 28.
[190] Read the testimony of Luitprand of Cremona (died around 972), a historian and diplomat who made several embassies to the Eastern Roman Empire. On slavery, see *The Jewish Mafia*.
[191] S. Schwarzfuchs, *The world History of the jewish people*, Massadah Publishing, Tel-Aviv, 1966.
[192] Roberta Strauss-Feuerlicht, *The Fate of the Jews*, New York, Time Books, 1983, p.

In the 10th century, Muslim traders were reluctant to travel to Gaul, "where they found only hostile populations. They were not seen to frequent the slave markets, while the Jews were commonly designated as the masters of that infamous trade, wrote Jacques Heers. It was also said that since the Muslims refused to do so, these Israelite traffickers ensured the smooth running of the slave castration centres[193]."

However, here as everywhere and at all times, their prosperity, their arrogance, their immorality, their constant mockery of the customs of others and their desire to establish their absolute domination earned them the hostility of the people.

At the head of Andalusian Judaism was a certain Semuel Ibn Nagrella. By 1025, he had become a personal adviser to King Badis ben Habus, who consulted him on all important matters. In 1027, on the death of his vizier, the Berber king Habus elevated Semuel to the rank of secretary of state (*Katib*), entrusting him with the direction of diplomatic and military affairs. The old Semuel ibn Nagrella died in 1055 and was buried in Granada, near the Elvira Gate. His son, Abu Hussein Yosef ibn Nagrella (born in 1031) erected a magnificent mausoleum and succeeded his father in all his functions and dignities. Unfortunately for him, the people were at that time fed up with Jewish domination.

The nineteenth-century writer Eduard Drumont recounted this episode in his famous book *Jewish France (1886)*: "He turned everyone against him with his insolence (*insolentia Judeorum*), grossly insulted the religion of the country, and soon everyone wished to get rid of him and the clique that followed in his footsteps. The kingdom," said an Arab historian, "was then worth less than a night-lamp after daybreak". A religious poet, the glorious Abu Ishaq Al Elbiri (of Elvira), went from town to town, censuring faults, preaching dedication and sacrifice, reconciling between them the Cindajites and the Berbers long at enmity, reciting everywhere his famous Kacida rhymed in *nun* to excite courage. Everywhere people everywhere repeated with him the refrain of his song: "The Jews have become great lords...They reign throughout the capital and the provinces; they have marble palaces, beautiful fountains and gardens. They dress beautifully and dine sumptuously, while you are poor and ill-fed".

The Jewish historian Leon Poliakov presented in one of his books the words of the same Muslim poet Abu Ishaq of Elvira:

"The chief of these apes has adorned his residence with precious inlays of marble; he has ordered fountains to be built from which the purest water flows, and while he makes us wait before his door, he mocks at us and our

---

39.
[193] Jacques Heers, *Les Négriers en terre d'Islam*, Perrin, 2003, Poche, 2007, p. 17.

religion. If I were to say that he is as rich as you, my King, I would speak the truth; hasten to slit his throat and offer him as a burnt offering, sacrifice him! He is a fat ram! Nor spare his kinsmen and allies; they too have amassed immense treasures...[194]" It is one of the rare examples, under the pen of a Jewish author, where the anti-Semitism of the population is more or less explained.

The murder of the Jew was carried out by a small number of conspirators. The occasion was presented by the incursion of soldiers of Almotacén, prince of Almería, who had invaded Granada. The Berbers besieged the palace of Yosef Nagrella one Saturday night, broke down the entrance gate and killed the Jew. His corpse was crucified at the gate of Granada on 30 December 1066.

The death of the minister further aroused the people, who were determined to wipe out the Jews of the kingdom once and for all. More than four thousand Jews were liquidated. The cleansing of Granada deeply shook Jewish Spain, leaving a deep mark on its memory.

Eduard Drumont recounted the end of the episode: "Legend has preserved the memory of the superb gesture of selflessness shown by Abu Ishaq. When, in the gardens of the persecutor, the crowd came to carry the poet, before whom the military chiefs had respectfully lowered their bloody scimitars, the piles of gold, the sparkling gems, the precious necklaces, the glittering fabrics and the objects of art that covered the ground by the thousands, Abu Ishaq picked up a pomegranate hanging from a fruit tree, opened it slowly, moistened his lips with it and said: "The heat is pressing today, I was thirsty; share these treasures among yourselves, my sons, but do not forget to say your prayers tonight, for God alone is great[195]!""

XXXVII. Gregory VII

The situation of the Jews did not begin to darken in Europe until the end of the 11th century. In 1012, the Germanic Emperor Henry II had already expelled the Jews from Mainz. To save their lives and property, many Jews had embraced Christianity. But the wealthy Jews had lobbied the prince through one of their most notable congeners: "Simon ben Isaac, by bribing the officials with large sums of money, and after showing great commitment, succeeded in stopping the persecution, and even obtained permission for the Jews to settle again in Mainz," Graetz recounted.

But in 1078, at the Council of Rome, Pope Hildebrand, known as

---

[194]Léon Poliakov, *Histoire de l'antisémitisme, tome I*, 1981, Points Seuil, 1990, p. 104.
[195]Edouard Drumont, *La France juive*, 1886, tome I, p. 153, 154.

Gregory VII, the son of a modest carpenter, decided to undermine Jewish power. He forbade the admission of Jews to public employment or any office that would place them above Christians in authority. Heinrich Graetz wrote here somewhat comically: "He, the mightiest of the mighty... also wished to humiliate the defenceless Jews and rob them of the respect and honours they had acquired through their own merits[196]."

In the Holy Empire, despite the prohibitions of canon law and the express will of the Pope, Jews could still buy slaves and hire Christian wet nurses and servants. Emperor Henry IV himself offered them his protection. On 6 February 1095, he issued an edict forbidding the forcible baptism of Jews or their slaves, and ordering that trials between Jews and Christians be governed by Hebrew law.

In a document from the year 1090, the Jews of Prague—at that time a city of the Empire—were described as merchants and money changers who possessed large sums of money; they were the richest merchants of all peoples. The Jewish author Julius Brutzkus wrote: "In the 10th century, Jews already owned salt mines in Nuremberg. They dealt in weapons and exploited the treasures of the churches. But their great speciality was slavery".

In fact, there is mention in documents from 1124 and 1222 of Jews trading in slaves from the Far East, crossing the borders in their caravans. The interest rate demanded by the Prague Jews, whose business was booming, varied between 108% and 180%.

In Poland, too, some Jewish merchants thrived on slavery. The chronicler Gallus claimed in 1085 that Judith, the wife of the Polish prince Ladislas Herman, endeavoured to buy the freedom of Christian slaves from Jewish merchants[197].

XXXVIII. The First Crusade

At the end of the eleventh century, the umpteenth enlightened Jew who believed himself to be a prophet or messiah had reawakened messianic hopes in the hearts of the Jews of Germany and northern France. He had calculated that, towards the end of the 256th lunar cycle, between 1096 and 1104, the Messiah would at last come to gather the scattered children of Israel to bring them to Jerusalem and offer them empire over the world. But instead, the Jews saw the crusaders embark for the Holy Land.

---

[196]Heinrich Graetz, *History of the Jews III*, London, Myers High Holborn, 1904, p. 252, 300.
[197] Abraham Léon, *La Conception matérialiste de la question juive*, Études et Documentation internationales, 1942, Paris, 1968, p. 113.

On 27 November 1095, at the Council of Clermont, Pope Urban II launched an appeal for a crusade to help the Byzantine emperor threatened by the Turks and to liberate the Holy Land. The first two Crusader armies, led by Peter the Hermit and Gualterius (Walter the Indigent), did not particularly mistreat the Jews; but other groups from France, England, Lorraine and Flanders prepared for war against the Muslims by massacring all Jews in their path. They are "proud", "wicked" and "insolent" wrote the Cluny monk Raul Glaber. Even in France, from where the crusade had set out, massacres were very rare. Only in Rouen, a city under English rule, did the Crusaders attack Jews, forcing them to convert or be beheaded if they resisted. As it was said in old French: *"Et cel qui ne voudrent croire furent occis et commandez as doubles[198]."* Neither the excommunications launched by the priests, nor the threats and prohibitions of the princes could stop these violent outrages.[199]

Guibert de Nogent (1055–1125), abbot of Nogent-sous-Coucy, born in the district of Beauvaisis, was one of the main chroniclers of the first crusade who recounted some episodes in his *Gesta Dei per Francos*: "We wish to go and fight the enemies of God in the East, but we have our eyes on the Jews, a race more hostile to God than any other[200]", wrote this chronicler and crusader.

Peter of Cluny, who was then the most important figure in Christendom after the Pope, took up Guibert de Nogent's reflection and put this question to Philip I: "Why should we look for the enemies of Christ in distant countries, when blaspheming Jews, worse than the Saracens, live in our midst and outrage Christ and the sanctuaries of the Church with impunity?" In 1096, Philip I followed the advice of Peter of Cluny and expelled the Jews from his lands.

But it was especially in Germany that Christian vengeance was satiated with the most violence and bloodshed. The bands that entered that country were led by a French knight named Guillaume le Charpentier (William the Carpenter). When the arrival of the Crusaders was announced, the Jews of Trier fled in terror. Meeting to deliberate what action to take, they decided, on the advice of one of their leaders named Micah, to "adopt Christianity in appearance" (Heinrich Graetz). Bishop Egibert read aloud the Christian Creed, the Jews repeated it and were then baptised.

From Trier the Crusaders went to Speyer. The Jews of this city had been declared inviolable by the bishop and the emperor, but the crusaders did

---

[198] Giberti abbat. Monodiarum lib I, et Chron, Richardi Pictav. Ad ann. 1096, in volume XII of the *Historiens de France*.
[199] Georges-Bernard Depping, *Les Juifs dans le Moyen-Âge*, (1823), Éd. Wouters, Brussels, 1844, p. 87.
[200] Quoted by V. Duruy, *Histoire de l'Europe et de la France au Moyen Age*, 1875.

not take this into account, and on 3 May 1096, the Christians took revenge for all the humiliations they had suffered. The Jews who escaped the massacre sought refuge in the palace of Bishop Johansen, who granted them protection and asylum, as well as in the imperial castle. The bishop ordered the arrest and hanging of several crusaders, enough to stop the disorder.

The bands waited for new pilgrims, and, with these reinforcements, marched on the city of Worms. Bishop Allebrand refused to defend the Jews in the city, but he did offer asylum in his palace to some of them. On Sunday, 16 May, the Crusaders ransacked and destroyed Jewish houses, smashed synagogues and burned Torah scrolls. Eight hundred Jews perished that day.

In Mainz, the crusaders were led by a count named Emich of Leiningen (in the Rhineland), who was a close relative of Archbishop Ruthard. More than thirteen hundred Jews were encamped in the courtyard of the archbishop's mansion when, at dawn on Tuesday, May 27, Emich broke in with his bands and invaded the archbishop's residence. None of the Jews imprisoned in the archbishop's palace got out alive. The only one who could have interceded on behalf of the Jews, Emperor Henry IV, was then in Italy busy defending himself.

After Mainz, Cologne was next. Under the leadership of William the Carpenter, the crusaders gathered around the city on the eve of Pentecost. On St. John's Day, they invaded Neus, one of the villages where the Jews had been hiding, and massacred them. From there, they followed the trail and killed other Jews in the surrounding villages.

The number of Jews from the Rhine communities killed from May to July 1096 is estimated at twelve thousand. The survivors, who had temporarily embraced the Christian faith, hoped that the emperor would return from Italy and take them back under his protection and allow them to return to their former faith.

Indeed, on his return from Italy in 1097, Emperor Henry IV publicly expressed his compassion for the Jews and, at the request of the head of the community of Speyer, Moses ben Guthiel, authorised all Jews who had been forcibly baptised to return to Judaism. "This was an outburst of joy for the Jews of Germany. The converts did not hesitate to make use of their freedom to throw off the mask of Christianity". In 1103, the emperor also made the princes and burghers swear an oath not to mistreat the Jewish population and to let them live in peace.

Following this news, the Jews of Bohemia also returned to their old religion. However, fearing further persecution, they decided to emigrate with their wealth to Poland and Hungary. Upon hearing of the Jews' decision, the Duke of Bohemia, Wratislaw, returning to his own land, ordered the occupation of all the houses by soldiers and gathered the heads of the Jews, informing them that all their property would be seized: "You did not bring any of the treasures of Jerusalem to Bohemia. Conquered by Vespasian and sold for nothing, you have been scattered throughout the world. Naked you have entered this land and naked you may come out." The Jews of Bohemia were thus stripped of all their wealth which they had amassed at the expense of the Christians.

When, after a long siege and great efforts, Godfrey of Bouillon finally succeeded in taking Jerusalem, the Jews and Saracens were badly beaten. "If you want to know what happened to the enemy in Jerusalem, know that in the Portico and in the Temple of Solomon our people had the vile blood of the Saracens up to the knees of their horses". The Crusaders perpetrated a great "massacre of the Mahometans, drove the Jews, Rabbanites and Karaites together, into a synagogue, set fire to it, and cruelly burnt all within its walls (July 15, 1099)[201]."

XXXIX. St Bernard

The audacity of the Jews went so far as to claim the throne of St. Peter. But the supporters of Cardinal Pierleoni were met with vigorous resistance.

In early 1130, as Pope Honorius II lay on his deathbed, Cardinal Aimericus persuaded the dying pope to set up a commission of eight cardinals to elect his successor. The Sacred College of Cardinals would only have to ratify the choice. Pierleoni's supporters, a majority in the Sacred College but a minority in the commission, would thus be defeated. When Honorius II died on the night of 13–14 February, Aimerico assembled the members of the commission present and the virtuous Papareschi, Cardinal of St. Angelo, of Judaeo-sceptic tendency, was thus elected with six votes to one, taking for his reign the name of Innocent II. The vote was confirmed by ten cardinals of the same faction, most of them French. But a few hours later, three-quarters of the cardinals elected Pietro Pierleoni, a false Christian who took for himself the name of Anacletus II. Thus a schism broke out in Rome.

Anacletus II was supported by the Jews of Rome and the Normans of King Roger II of Sicily, so Innocent II was forced to leave Rome. He went into exile first in Tuscany, then in Liguria and finally in Provence.

When St. Bernard, Doctor of the Church and Abbot of Clairvaux, heard of these unfortunate events, he resolved to abandon his peaceful and quiet life in the monastery and throw himself into battle, even though the cause seemed lost, for the crypto-Jewish pope was in complete control of the

---

[201]Heinrich Graetz, *History of the Jews III*, London, Myers High Holborn, 1904, p. 313, 315.

situation thanks to the gold and support he had garnered. For his part, Innocent II had been abandoned and excommunicated by Anacletus. In a letter to Emperor Lotarius, Bernard wrote that "it was an affront to Jesus Christ that a descendant of a Jew should occupy the throne of St. Peter".

Emperor Lotary II was in no hurry to make up his mind, but the French King Louis VI was more reactive, no doubt thanks to the good advice of his minister Suger de Saint-Denis. He summoned to Etampes the archbishops of Sens, Rheims and Bourges, as well as the bishops and abbots, including Saint Bernard. In October 1130, Innocent II in turn convened a synod at Clermont-Ferrand to excommunicate Anacletus. After the Council of Rheims in October 1131, Pierleoni only had the support of Italy (for the most part) thanks to the support of his brother-in-law, Duke Roger II of Sicily, who dominated the situation on the Italian peninsula. The strategic marriage of the Jewish convert Pierleoni, the sister of the antipope, to the duke had strengthened his position in Italy. Married to Pierleoni's sister, Roger II supported the Jewish antipope with all his might, while opening his court to Jews and Muslims.

To defeat the crypto-Jewish occupation of Rome, a military invasion was necessary. St Bernard and St Norbert of Xanten, founder of the Norbertine order and archbishop of Magdeburg, succeeded in convincing the German Emperor Liberius II to undertake one. With a small army, he joined Innocent in northern Italy and together they marched on Rome, which they took without resistance, as many nobles had betrayed Anacletus at the last moment. Lotario installed Innocent at the Lateran, while Pierleoni took refuge in the castle of Sant Angelo. But Roger II counterattacked with his powerful army, forcing Lotario to retreat, and once again the Jewish antipope took control of the situation in the Vatican. The position of the "Jewish Pontiff" was maintained until his death on 25 January 1138.

Innocent had to take refuge in France. There, this combative monk turned pope obtained the support of King Louis VII and raised an army at the head of which he once again entered Italy. At the gates of Rome, he received unexpected support this time from Roger II of Sicily. Over the years, in fact, this Norman prince had changed considerably and realised that he had been deceived. He had enacted laws in his states that forced Jews to convert to Christianity. When he offered his assistance to Innocent, Roger of Sicily had therefore made a 180-degree turn from his previous policy. The Pope accepted his help and, on 28 November 1149, Innocent II entered Rome accompanied by Norman troops. Innocent II died in 1153, the same year that St Bernard died. Thanks to "the crusade organised at the behest of St. Bernard... it was possible, with God's help, to save the Holy Church from the clutches of Judaism, while St. Bernard achieved his well-deserved canonisation[202]."

XL. The Second Crusade

Under the reigns of the two Capet kings Louis VI and Louis VII, during the first half of the twelfth century, the Jewish communities of France enjoyed a prosperous situation. "The congregations of northern France lived in comfort and prosperity, which easily aroused envy against them. Their granaries were full of corn, their cellars of wine, their storehouses of goods, and their coffers of gold and silver. They owned no property, but had fields and vineyards, which they cultivated themselves or Christian serfs. It was said that half the population of the city of Paris, which had not yet attained great importance, was composed of Jews[203]", wrote Heinrich Graetz.

Jewish financiers dominated the economic situation of the kingdom. "A Jew from Dijon, called Salamine, was a creditor of some of the largest abbeys in Burgundy, such as Sainte-Benigne and Sainte-Seine. It was the Duchess Alix of Burgundy who, in 1122, settled the debts owed to the banker for these two abbeys, as can be seen from two letters from this duchess".

The Count of Montpellier, for example, owed a Jew named Bendet a sum of 50,000 sous. In a letter to the King of France, Pope Innocent III expressed his indignation at the fact that Jews were appropriating Church property and taking over land and vineyards[204].

"Now, if the powerful lords and the great religious communities were indebted to the Jews, we may suppose how many private individuals were dependent on these money merchants whose capital grew daily by enormous usury and skilful speculation. Soon the French found themselves so indebted that they despaired of ever being able to pay their debts, and the position of the debtors became more and more critical and embarrassing to the authorities, the Jews being unwilling to slacken for a moment in their usurious pretensions[205]."

The slave trade was still one of the favourite activities of Jewish merchants. In 1105, Count Bernard III granted a monopoly on the import of Sicilian slaves to three Jewish merchants and shipowners from

---

[202] Maurice Pinay, *Complot against the Church*, Volume II, Chapter I (1962), Transcription pdf from Ediciones Mundo Libre, Mexico, 1985, p. 136.
[203] Heinrich Graetz, *History of the Jews III*, London, Myers High Holborn, 1904, p. 350.
[204] Abraham Léon, *La Conception matérialiste de la question juive*, Études et Documentation internationales, 1942, Paris, 1968, p. 83.
[205] Georges-Bernard Depping, *Les Juifs dans le Moyen-Âge*, (1823), Éd. Wouters, Brussels, 1844, p. 115.

Barcelona[206]. In Germany, the slave trade was flourishing at that time. In the list of customs duties in Wallenstadt and Koblenz, it can be seen that Jewish merchants had to pay four dinars for each slave. A document from 1213 explained that the Jews of Laubach "are extraordinarily wealthy and that they trade extensively with the Venetians, Hungarians and Croats[207]."

The spirits of the time were also very concerned about the reconquest of Jerusalem, then in the hands of the Saracens. On 31 March 1146, in Vézelay, in the presence of King Louis VII and a large crowd, Bernard of Clairvaux preached the crusade, promising absolution for all sins to those who took up the cross. The following year, Louis VII set out on the crusade accompanied by Queen Eleanor.

St Bernard is often cited by defenders of the Jews because of two letters of 1146 in which he railed against those who slaughtered them without mercy. In the first, addressed to the bishops and the Frankish people, he did indeed remind them that it was not permitted to kill, mistreat or despoil the Jews. But in his sermons, he repeatedly insisted on the provisions of Pope Eugene III's bull which, in order to strengthen the Crusader armies, had exempted all the Crusaders from paying interest on their debts to the Jews.

A contemporary of St Bernard, Peter de Montboissier, abbot of Cluny, known as Peter the Venerable (1092–1156), was the author of a *treatise against the inveterate harshness of the Jews (Tractatus adversus Iudeorum inveteratam duritiem)*. He seems to have been the first in the Christian West to have based himself directly on the original texts of the Talmud. He wrote to Louis VII in 1146: "What is the use of going to distant countries in search of the enemies of Christianity, when we allow the Jews, who are worse than the Saracens, to be at peace among us and to outrage our most sacred practices? For the Saracen, while denying the incarnation, at least admits that Jesus was born of a virgin, while the accursed Jew rejects all our beliefs. True to the law that forbids murder, I do not ask you to order the killing of these blasphemers: God does not want them to be exterminated; they must wander through the world like Cain, burdened with shame and disgrace, and lead a life a thousand times worse than death. Their existence is vile, miserable and troubled by continual fear. Therefore, they should not be killed, but inflicted with a punishment commensurate with their condition."

Peter the Venerable ended his letter by advising the king to strip the Jews of all their goods: "It is time that justice should be done, and far be it from me, however, to think that they should be put to death; but what I ask is that they should be punished in proportion to their perfidy. And what

---

[206] Abraham Léon, p. 84. A. Léon was referring here to Henri Pirenne's book, *Les Villes au Moyen Age*.
[207] Abraham Léon, p. 84. On the slave trade and the White slave trade, see *The Jewish Mafia*.

kind of punishment more fitting than that which is at once a condemnation of iniquity and a satisfaction given to charity? What more just than to strip them of what they have accumulated by fraud? They have cheated and plundered like thieves; and, what is worse, like thieves secured to this day with impunity! What I say is widely and publicly known. It is neither by the simple labours of agriculture, nor by regular service in armies, nor by the exercise of honest and useful functions, that they fill their shops with grain, their taverns with wine, their coffers with gold and silver. What have they not amassed with all that cunning enabled them to wrest from Christians and to buy stealthily and at a vile price from robbers[208]!"

The abbot also denounced the Jews as the main receivers, especially of sacred objects stolen from churches: "When a thief takes sacred vessels, chalices and censers by night, he takes refuge in the lair of the Jews and sells the objects of his theft. An ancient but detestable law, enacted however by Christian princes, seems to protect them in this scandalous trade. According to this law, a Jew who finds sacred ornaments in his house, even if they have been stolen in sacrilege, is not obliged to return them, nor to denounce the thief. Thus his crime goes unpunished, and what would bring the ultimate torment to a Christian enriches the Jew and makes him swim in plenty[209]." Then he continued, "Let this overabundance (*pinguedo*) of ill-gotten riches be taken from them, or at least greatly reduced, and let the Christian army, which for the love of Christ spares neither its gold nor its goods to be in a position to triumph over the Saracens, spare neither these treasures of the Jews, so criminally acquired. Let them live, then, but let their money be taken from them. *Reservetur eis vita, auferatur ab eis pecunia*[210]."

Louis VII was not prepared to repress them with the same forcefulness. While he had to allow the papal bull exempting the crusaders from paying their debts to the Jews to be enforced, there were no legal measures of retaliation against the Jews under his reign. "Pope Alexander III wrote to the Archbishop of Bourges to complain of the king's excessive tolerance and
to remind him of the severe measures recently prescribed by the Lateran

---

[208]Patrologie de Migne (T. 189, 1. IV, epist. 36). See also in *L'Église et la Synagogue* (Paris, 1859). The letter is reproduced in part by Roger Gougenot des Mousseaux in *El Judío, el Judaísmo y la judaización de los pueblos cristianos (1869)*, pdf version, translated into English by Professor Noemí Coronel and the invaluable collaboration of the team of Nacionalismo Católico Argentina, 2013, p. 168.

[209]Epist. Petri Venerab. ad. Ludovicum, regem Francor. *Sutirn Bernardi Epist.*, in volume XV of the *Historiens de France*. In Georges-Bernard Depping, *Les Juifs dans le Moyen-Âge*, (1823), Éd. Wouters, Brussels, 1844, p. 90.

[210]Charles Auzias-Turenne, *Revue Catholique des Institutions et du Droit*, October 1893.

Council[211]." The king simply ordered that converts who returned to Judaism could not remain in the kingdom, on pain of being condemned to capital punishment.

Thanks to the benevolence of the king and his ministers, and also to the intervention of Abbot Suger of Saint-Denis and Saint Bernard, the Jews were spared the fury of the crusaders.

It was different in Germany, especially in the Rhine communities that had already suffered the ravages of the First Crusade. It was a French monk, Rudolph, a former Cistercian from Clairvaux, who with his inflammatory speeches provoked a wave of violence against the Jews. He led the revolt, going from town to town, from village to village, preaching everywhere the extermination of the Israelites. The popular revolt would have been even bloodier than the first if Emperor Conrad III had not provided the Jews with effective protection.

In his own domains, in Nuremberg and other strongholds, Conrad offered them asylum and asked lay and ecclesiastical princes to defend them in cities or regions where he had no direct authority.

There were, however, victims. The Jews on the Rhine bought from the princes the right to take refuge in their castles. Cardinal Arnold of Cologne provided them with the castle of Wolkenburg near Kœnigswinter, as well as weapons to defend themselves, but as soon as they left the square, the Crusaders pounced on them and decimated them.

The archbishop of Mainz, Henry I, chancellor of the empire, had also offered asylum in his palace to some Jews persecuted by the vengeful people, but some locals managed to enter the archbishop's mansion and massacred the Jews before the prelate's eyes. The archbishop reported this event to St. Bernard, begging him to try to suppress this violence. The Abbot of Clairvaux then published a pastoral letter in which he branded the monk Rudolph as "an unworthy son of the Church, a rebel before the superior of his convent, disobedient to the bishops, a preacher of murder in opposition to the laws of his religion". He further stressed that it was indispensable not to mistreat the Jews, since the Church prays for their conversion in a special prayer on Good Friday. "Now," he said, "it is impossible to convert them if they are killed." This pastoral was sent to the ecclesiastics and Christians of France and Bavaria.

He wrote to the clergy: "The Jews are not to be persecuted; they are not to be slaughtered or hunted like wild animals. See what the Scriptures say about them. I know what is prophesied about the Jews in the Psalm: "The Lord," says the Church, "has revealed to me His will concerning My

---

[211] Pope's letter of 1179, inserted in volume XV of the *Historiens de France*, page 769, in Georges-Bernard Depping, *Les Juifs dans le Moyen-Âge*, (1823), Éd. Wouters, Brussels, 1844, p. 91.

enemies: Do not kill them, lest My people become forgetful. They are, indeed, the living signs that remind us of the Passion of the Saviour. Moreover, they have been scattered throughout the world, so that while they pay the guilt of so great a crime, they may be witnesses of our Redemption[212]."

Again, in his letter 365, addressed to Henry, Archbishop of Mainz, he wrote: "Does not the Church triumph every day over the Jews in a nobler way by making them see their errors or by converting them, than by killing them? It is not in vain that the Universal Church has established throughout the world the recitation of the prayer for the obstinately unbelieving Jews, that God may lift the veil that covers their hearts and lead them out of their darkness into the light of truth. For if She did not hope that those who do not believe might believe, it would seem simple and purposeless to pray for them[213]."

St Bernard did not hesitate to preach in front of burnt synagogues. But the rioters in the Rhine valley understood neither his Latin nor his French. Nevertheless, he succeeded in stopping the persecutions. The monk Rudolph, for his part, disregarded the orders of St. Bernard and continued his work of radical liberation of the people.

One day, the body of a Christian was found near Würzburg. Immediately the Jewish community of Wurzburg was attacked and twenty Jews were executed, including Rabbi Isaac ben Eliakim. Others were mistreated and tortured until they were left for dead. The bishop of the city had the corpses transported to his palace and buried them in the garden. This happened on 24 February 1147.

When Emperor Conrad took the cross with his knights and most of his army and left Germany, revolts against the Jews multiplied. In May 1147, the people massacred the Jews in various parts of the territory.

The insurrection spread to France, although there were only a few local disturbances. At Carentan in Normandy, in a courtyard where many Jews were gathered, there was a real pitched battle with the crusaders. The Jews all succumbed, as none of them were spared.

In England, where numerous Jews from France had settled since the time of William the Conqueror, they did not suffer any notable persecution either, for King Stephen of England did not tolerate these outrages.

The second crusade was therefore less painful for the Jews than the first; on the one hand, because the princes and high dignitaries of the Church protected them more effectively, and also because the Emperor of Germany and the King of France, who had led the crusaders, had not this time

---

[212] St. Bernard, Epist. 363 and 365. Migne 182.
[213] Julio Meinvielle, *El judío en el misterio de la historia*, Cruz y Fierro Editores, Buenos Aires, 1982 p. 120-121. 120-121

accepted in their armies bands such as those of William the Carpenter and Emich of Leiningen.

Even so, the Jews of Germany paid dearly for the protection granted by the authorities: the emperor was henceforth regarded as the protector of the Jews, and the Jews, hitherto free and independent like the Germans and Romans, became "servants of the imperial chamber". They were inviolable as servants of the emperor, but in return they had to pay an annual tribute to the imperial treasury.

XLI. The Almohads

In North Africa, a reformer named Abu Abdalah Muhammad ibn Tumart, a former pupil in Baghdad of the mystic philosopher Al-Ghazali[214], had founded the sect of the Almohads, i.e. the "supporters of unity". Ibn Tumart spread his doctrine with the sword in the Almoravid empire, and after him, his disciple Abd al-Mu'min continued his work. From victory to victory, he overthrew the Almoravid dynasty and seized power throughout North Africa.

In 1146, after seizing the city of Marrakesh which had endured a long siege, 'Abd al-Mu'min summoned all the Jewish inhabitants and presented them with a choice: convert to Islam or death. Abd al-Mu'min allowed them to emigrate and even gave them time to sell their real estate and other property that they could not take with them. Those who remained had to become Muslims or die. Throughout the Almohad empire, which stretched from the Atlas Mountains to Egypt, synagogues were destroyed. Many Jews then left the Maghreb to settle mainly in Spain or Italy, but most of them temporarily submitted to the edict of 'Abd al-Mu'minn and accepted the religion of the Prophet Muhammad. "Most of them, for the time being, willingly obeyed the edict and adopted the guise of Islam in the expectation of more favourable times (1146)... for, although many North African Jews had ostensibly accepted Islam, only a few actually did so. In fact, they were required to do no more than profess their faith in Muhammad's prophetic mission and occasionally attend mosques. Privately, however, they practised the Jewish rites in every detail, for the Almohads did not employ police spies to observe the actions of converts," Graetz explained.

---

[214] Ab Hamid Muḥammad ibn Muḥammad al-Ghazali (1057–1111) was a Persian-born polymath, Sufi theologian, jurist, philosopher and mystic, considered one of the most important thinkers in Islamic philosophy, representing the deepest mysticism. A member of the *Shafi'i school*, his works enabled Sufism to be accepted as orthodox in Sunnism for the first time. He is also credited with introducing Aristotelian logic and syllogistics into Islamic jurisprudence and theology. He wrote *The Revival of the Religious Sciences*, possibly his most important apologetic work.

Many pious rabbis did not hesitate to become Muslims because it was enough to declare Muhammad a prophet without having to explicitly disavow their religion. "They were not required to deny Judaism. They were simply required to pronounce the formula of believing that Muhammad was a prophet, which was in fact far from idol worship. Some consoled themselves with the hope that they would not long remain in this situation, for they hoped that the Messiah would soon appear and deliver them from their misery."

Abd al-Mu'minn passed through the straits and marched on Andalusia. Torn by internal divisions, Muslim Spain was quickly conquered. Cordoba fell to the Almohads in June 1148, and within a year most of Andalusia suffered the same fate. Wherever the conquerors passed, Jews were condemned to choose between apostasy, emigration or death, and synagogues were razed to the ground. The Jewish schools of Seville were closed and many Jews left the city. "The others followed the example of the African Jews, yielded for the time being to coercion, pretended to recognise Islam, and privately observed their old faith, until they found the opportunity to return openly to Judaism[215]."

Toledo, 1180

With the conquest of Muslim Andalusia by the Almohads, the Jews disappeared from the map, at least in appearance. Many of them had migrated north in the time of Alfonso VII of León, to the land of those they had betrayed centuries before, in the five Christian kingdoms of Castile, León, Aragon, Portugal and Navarre.

Toledo, the capital of Castile, at that time had more than 12,000 Jews and several synagogues. The country was ruled by King Alfonso VII, who was easily corrupted and took as his advisor a Jew named Judah ibn Ezra[216].

---

[215] Heinrich Graetz, *History of the Jews III,* London, Myers High Holborn, 1904, p. 368, 369, 370.
[216] Judah ben Yosef ibn Ezra was a notable 12th-century Jew of Spain. He was elevated by Alfonso VII of Castile and León to the dignity of steward of the royal household. Judah used his position and wealth for the benefit of his co-religionists, who were persecuted by the Almohads. With Alfonso's permission, Judah fought vigorously against Karaism, a Jewish movement based solely on the written Hebrew Bible (the Torah) that was taking root in Castile and a staunch adversary of traditional rabbinical Judaism, as it did not recognise the authority of the Talmud (the oral tradition). Judah ibn Ezra wrote several refutations of their arguments in the form of literary and poetic exegesis, but he also fought them by other means: "Judah ibn Ezra resorted to the aid of secular arms and begged the kind permission of Emperor Alfonso VII to allow him to pursue the Karaites... Judah ibn Ezra humiliated the Karaites so severely that they were never able to raise their heads again. They were probably banished from the cities

After having reconquered the fortress of Calatrava, located in the south between Toledo and Cordoba, Alfonso handed over the government of the town to Juda ibn Ezra, even granting him the title of prince.

In Christian Spain, Jews exercised, among others, the prominent professions of bankers, tax collectors and suppliers to the king. The royalty protected them because they represented a great economic and political support. In Aragon, a certain Judah de la Cavalleria was one of these great Jewish "capitalists" of the 13th century. He leased the salt mines, minted money, supplied the army and owned large tracts of land and a multitude of flocks[217]. Israel Abrahams noted in turn in an article in the *Jewish Encyclopedia* (volume II, page 402), that, in the 12th century, "the Spanish Jews owed their great fortune to the slave trade".

King Alfonso VIII of Castile (grandson of Alfonso VII of León) also surrounded himself with imminent Hebraic characters. "Under Alfonso VIII, called the Noble (1166–1214), many talented Jews obtained high offices, were appointed state officials and, for their part, worked for the greatness of their beloved homeland [Israel]. Joseph ben Solomon Ibn Shoshan, called "the Prince", was a distinguished figure at the court of Alphonso. (He was born around 1135 and died in 1204-5.) Erudite, pious, wealthy and charitable, Ibn Shoshan enjoyed the king's favour and was probably active in the affairs of state. "The king and the great ones granted him favours and showed him goodwill. With his usual liberality, he encouraged the study of the Talmud and erected, with princely magnificence, a new synagogue in Toledo. His son Solomon equalled him in many virtues[218]." Alfonso VIII, married to the English-born princess Eleanor Plantagenet (daughter of the famous Eleanor of Aquitaine), also had a Jewish favourite for seven years named Rachel, daughter of his finance minister. These legendary love affairs between Raquel "la Fermosa" and King Alfonso VIII would inspire Lope de Vega, four centuries later, in his play *Las Paces de los Reyes and Judía de Toledo*. The Spanish playwright's work would be taken up again in the 19th century by Franz Grillparzer, in his tragedy *Die Juden von Toledo*. This love affair had aroused the jealousy and hatred of Queen Leonor.

In 1180, a conspiracy was hatched to eliminate the one who had bewitched the monarch's heart. The conspirators broke into the palace and murdered Rachel and her friends before the eyes of the king himself. This bloody attack was followed by a direct attack on the Jews. Alphonse, seeing

---

where the Rabbanites lived (1150-57)." Heinrich Graetz, *History of the Jews III*, p. 372.
[217] Abraham Léon, *La Conception matérialiste de la question juive*, Études et Documentation internationales, 1942, Paris, 1968, p. 84.
[218] Heinrich Graetz, *History of the Jews III*, London, Myers High Holborn, 1904, p. 395–396.

the fury of his subjects, from the Great Ones to the common people, dared not punish any of the murderers for fear of suffering the same fate as his mistress. It was a terrible warning to him.

Having encouraged by all means the Muslim invasion of the peninsula in the 7th century, it was now in the interest of the Jews to fight the Muslims. As usual, the Jews outsourced the task and, thanks to their gold, entrusted the Christians with the difficult enterprise. The Jews of Toledo, who prospered in the Christian kingdoms, seconded King Alfonso in his fight against the Moors, providing him with money and considerable loans[219]. At the battle of Alarcos on 19 July 1195, Alfonso was badly defeated and lost the elite of his knights. But on 16 July 1212, he took his revenge and crushed the Saracens at Las Navas de Tolosa.

XLIII. *Philip Augustus*

Some of the Jews who had left Muslim Spain, conquered by the Almohads, took refuge in the south of France. At the end of the 12th century, the Jews of Languedoc and Provence were quite numerous. Heinrich Graetz wrote, without irony, that "the Jews of this country, so highly blessed by Nature, felt themselves also favoured, carried their heads high, took a lively interest in the welfare of the country and strove in spiritual matters with untiring zeal". He added: "The [Jewish] congregations loyally supported one another and were interested in each other's innermost affairs. If danger threatened any particular congregation, the others immediately took steps to help and avert the impending danger. Its general prosperity was attained partly by agriculture and partly by the trade which was then carried on with Spain, Italy, England, Egypt and the East, and was at its most flourishing[220]."

In northern France, their situation remained prosperous until the last two decades of the 12th century. King Louis VII, as we have seen, protected the Jews. He did not even want to enforce against them the Lateran Council's decision forbidding them to have Christian wet nurses or servants, and, despite the Pope's prohibition, he allowed them to build new synagogues. In the population, on the other hand, the Jews were the object of a very special hatred.

It was from this time onwards that accusations of ritual crimes and

---

[219] Alfonso VIII owed the Jewish moneylenders an enormous amount of maravedis - 18,000 maravedis, they say—with which he paid for the war enterprises of the reconquest of Cuenca and the war against the Almohads. (NdT)

[220] Heinrich Graetz, *History of the Jews III*, London, Myers High Holborn, 1904, p. 402, 403.

desecrations of sacred hosts appeared against them. From the 12th century onwards, more than one hundred cases of desecration of hosts and more than one hundred and fifty trials for ritual crimes can be recorded, but these figures are probably lower than the reality[221].

In 1144, the body of an apprentice was discovered in a forest near Norwich in England. Three years later, in Würzburg, the body of a Christian discovered in the river Main had led to the massacre of twenty Jews.

In 1171, in Blois, all Jews (men, women and children) were burned alive after being condemned by a court. For the first time, Jews were accused of using Christian blood for their Passover celebration. One evening, near twilight, a lord's servant saw a Jew throw the corpse of a child into the river Loire, which had frightened his horse and prevented him from fording the river. Count Theobald (Thibaut) of Chartres then ordered the imprisonment of all the Jews of Blois (about fifty). The Jews then tried to buy their lives by offering him one hundred pounds of silver and the remission of one hundred and eighty pounds owed, but Theobald refused to be corrupted and condemned them all to be burnt alive. Thirty-four men and seventeen women perished in the flames. This took place on the 20th day of the month of *Sivan* (26 May 1171)[222].

In 1180, Philip Augustus succeeded his father Louis VII. According to the historian Rigord, the Jews had acquired ownership of almost half of the city of Paris[223]. Served by Christian servants, they were the creditors of the bourgeoisie, soldiers and peasants. In the towns, villages and suburbs, the network of their credits extended. A large number of Christians had been expropriated by them because of their debts.

On this subject it is necessary to read the text of Abbot Claude Fleury (1640–1723). A native of Rouen, Abbot Claude Fleury was the author of an *Ecclesiastical History,* a true monument of erudition. He was elected to the French academy and appointed religious instructor to the future Louis XV. What he wrote about Philip Augustus gives us an idea of the grievances of the time against the Jews:

"King Philip was still animated against the Jews, because the antiquity of their establishment in Paris and the reputation of their doctors had so enriched them that they possessed nearly half the city, that in defiance of

---

[221] See, for example, *Le Diable pour père,* an article in the magazine *Sodalitium* which lists some sixty cases.
[222] These are the figures given by Heinrich Graetz. According to the chronicle of Robert de Torigny, abbot of Mont St Michel, 21 men and 17 women were burnt at the stake for the crime. This figure was taken up by the historian Jean Delumeau: 38 in all. That year, the Jews were expelled from the city of Bologna because of their usurious abuses.
[223] Rigord, *Gestis Philippi Aug.*, in volume XVII of the *Historiens de France.*

the laws and canons (that is to say, the rules of ecclesiastical law) they kept in their houses Christian slaves of both sexes, Judaising them, and practising usury without limit on Christians, nobles, burghers and peasants, many of whom were forced to sell their inheritances, others to remain in the houses of the Jews as prisoners, being bound to them by oath[224]."

"They live only by traffic, and of the most sordid kind; they are dealers, brokers, and usurers. Many of them were engaged in medicine, giving themselves to it from the time of which I speak here... A woman is mentioned in the Gospel who had suffered from many physicians, who had consumed her whole fortune in medicines[225]."

One of Philip's first decisions was to solve the problems linked to the presence of Jews in his territory. On 19 January 1180, a Sabbath day, he had all the Jews in the royal domain[226] arrested, without making any precise accusations against them, caged them and did not release them until he received a ransom of 1500 silver marks.

In the same year, he cancelled all Christian debts to the Jews, but obliged the debtors to pay one-fifth of their debts to the treasury.

On 10 March 1182, a king's edict stripped them of all their property and expelled them from the royal domain. The Jews were to leave the royal territory between April and St. John's Day (24 June). As usual, they offered large sums of money, but the king remained intractable. Despite all his gold, Philip Augustus remained firm in his resolve.

Only their movable property could be taken; the remaining assets were distributed to the corporations. The fields, vineyards, farms and other real estate were to revert to the king. King Philip could almost be considered a moderate, for he only demanded to collect one-fifth of all debts from the Jews and forgave the rest to their debtors.

This measure applied mainly to Jews from the region of Ile-de-France, who later emigrated to the South, Burgundy, Champagne, Alsace and Lorraine.

Rigord elaborated further on this episode: "That year, Rigord explained, deserved to be called a jubilee year, because thanks to the king's action the Christians regained forever their freedom, compromised by debts to the Jews".

The following year, the king transformed all the synagogues into

---

[224] Abbé Claude Fleury, *Histoire ecclésiastique*, tome quatrième, livre soixante-treizième, paragraphe 41, édition de 1856, p. 769.

[225] Abbé Claude Fleury, *Mœurs des Israélites et des Chrétiens*, Tours, 1867, troisième partie, chapitre 33, *Les Mœurs des Juifs des Derniers Temps*, p. 109.

[226] Crown lands, crown estates, *domaine royal de France* (from *demesne*, royal domain, royale) refer to the lands, fiefs and rights directly held by the kings of France.

churches, thus gaining the blessing of all his people[227]. Only a few Jews who had accepted baptism retained their property and freedom.

In October 1187, the capture of Jerusalem by Saladin made a great impression on Christendom, and the event prompted Philip Augustus and King Richard the Lionheart of England to take up the cross together in the Third Crusade. King Richard was particularly prominent, saving the Latin states of the East. Philip, for his part, had to return hastily to France and settle the Flemish succession.

Having just returned from the Holy Land, he also had to deal with a very unpleasant matter. In 1192, while in Saint-Germain-en-Laye, he learned that in Braisne (now Bray-sur-Seine, upstream from Paris), in the domain of a vassal of the Count of Champagne, the local lady called Agnès, Countess of Dreux, had abandoned to the vindictiveness of the Jews a man accused by them of robbery and murder. He had been bound by the hands, crowned with thorns and scourged by the village, and finally crucified.

The king was informed that the man was innocent and that the Jews had mocked him like Jesus Christ. The indignation was general. On hearing of this, the king immediately went in person to Braisne, surrounded the square, seized all the Jews and ordered them to be burned on the spot in his presence[228]. Twenty-four Jews perished in the flames that day.[229]

A few years later, in 1198, the energetic Pope Innocent III launched the Fourth Crusade. The preacher Fulk of Neuilly went through towns and villages to encourage Christians to take part. Like the monk Rudolph, Fulk encouraged them to plunder the houses of the Jews to recover what they had stolen from the Christians. Overexcited by his fiery speeches, many barons let the exasperated people take the law into their own hands and expel the Jews from their lands.

In July 1198, Philip Augustus allowed the Jews to return to his dominions, but as serfs attached to the glebe and without the right to own anything, which did not discourage them in the least. "The fortune of the Jews belongs to the baron" was then a principle accepted throughout northern France, where the Jew was accepted in proportion to his income. So, for example, a nobleman had sold his property and his Jews to the

---

[227] Abbé Claude Fleury, *Histoire ecclésiastique*, tome quatrième, livre soixante-treizième, paragraphe 41, édition de 1856, p. 769.

[228] Vincent de Beauvais, *Spec. Histor.*, lib. XXX, cap. VIII

[229] *Histoire des ducs et comtes de Champagne*, t. IV, 1st part, p. 72; Paris, 1865; by M. d'Arbois de Jubainville, written according to the Lettres and awarded the grand prix Gobert of the Académie des Inscriptions, in Roger Gougenot des Mousseaux, *The Jew, Judaism and the Judaisation of the Christian peoples (1869)*. Pdf version. Translated into English by Professor Noemí Coronel and the invaluable collaboration of the team of Nacionalismo Católico Argentina, 2013, p. 195.

Duchess of Champagne.

However, it remains true that the Jews continued to prosper, for after the Fourth Crusade, "King Philip Augustus had to issue the famous ordinance of September 1206 which stated among other things: 'No Jew may take more interest than two denarii per pound per week [the maximum rate of usury was set at 43% interest. This means that in the past usurers used to charge more]. At the time of the loan, the Jew and the debtor shall be obliged to declare: first the debtor; that he has received all the contents of the obligation and that nothing has been given or promised to the Jew, and second the Jew; that nothing has been received and nothing has been promised to him. And if they are afterwards convinced to the contrary, the Jew shall lose his right, and the debtor shall be at the mercy of the king. There shall be in every city "two men of probity" who shall keep the seal of the Jews, and shall take an oath on the Gospel that they shall not seal any pledge, unless they have knowledge from themselves or others that the sum contained therein was rightfully due[230] "."

The ordinance further forbade Jews to receive sacred vessels and bloody garments as pledges, which was clearly another of their customs.

XLIV. *The coronation of Richard the Lionheart*

William the Conqueror, who had victoriously invaded England in 1066, had forbidden Jews to have Christian servants and to employ Christian wet nurses. In England and in the French territories dependent on the crown of England, Jews nevertheless lived in relative safety. "They inhabited the great cities, and in London many of them became so wealthy that their houses had the appearance of royal palaces," Graetz told us.

At the time of King Henry II, in the second half of the 12th century, the Jews were already practising usury on a large scale. They are generally very rich," wrote Abraham Leon, "and their clientele is composed of large landowners. The most famous of these bankers was a certain Aaron of Lincoln, who was very active at the end of the 12th century. King Henry II alone owed him 100,000 pounds, a sum equivalent to the annual budget of the kingdom of England at the time. Thanks to extremely high interest rates—these ranged from 43 to 86%—a huge mass of land of the nobility passed into the hands of Jewish usurers[231]."

---

[230] Mgr Henri Delassus, *La Conjuration antichrétienne III*, Desclée De Brouwer, 1910, p. 1154.
[231] Abraham Léon, *La Conception matérialiste de la question juive*, Études et Documentation internationales, 1942, Paris, 1968, p. 81, 82. Abraham Leon was a Marxist of Trotskyist tendency.

His troubles began on 3 September 1189, the day of Richard's coronation. On his return from the cathedral, where he had been crowned by the Archbishop of Canterbury, Richard received several delegations, including one from the Jews. At the sight of the magnificent gifts the Jews offered him, Baldwin, the Archbishop of Canterbury, advised the king that it was his duty to refuse the gifts and expel the Jews from the room. Richard nodded, and rumour spread throughout the city of London that the king had expelled the Jewish delegates from the palace. It was the signal for a general insurrection.

The people and the crusaders immediately agreed to plunder the Jews, and the insurgents set fire to their mansions. Houses and synagogues were burned and numerous Jews were massacred in London, Lincoln and Stamford[232].

The next day, King Richard ordered the arrest and execution of the main ringleaders and declared the Jews inviolable. But as soon as he left England, to lead the crusade with Philip Augustus, the London massacres were imitated in several English towns. Bloody scenes were repeated in Lynn and Norwich, where Jews were murdered and their homes ransacked.

The chronicler Richard of Devizes, a monk of the convent of Swithun, Winchester, wrote: "On the very day of the coronation, at the solemn hour when the Son was immolated to the Father, they began in the city of London to immolate the Jews to their father the devil. And so much time was spent in celebrating so great a sacrifice that the holocaust was scarcely completed the next day. Other cities, other towns in the country, imitated the act of faith of the Londoners, and sent with the same devotion to hell all those leeches and the blood with which they had gorged themselves. On this occasion, and throughout the kingdom, but with unequal fervour, similar actions were taken against the reprobate. Only the town of Winchester spared the vermin it fed: the inhabitants of that town are wise and prudent, and have always shown restraint[233]."

A year later, tragedy befell the northern city of York: "But most tragic of all was the fate of the Jews of York, for among them were two men who enjoyed princely fortunes, had built magnificent palaces, and had consequently aroused the envy of the Christian inhabitants. One of them was Joseph, the other Benedict, who had been so brutally maltreated at Richard's coronation. The latter, who had returned to Judaism after his

---

[232]Guill. Neubrigensis, de Rebus anglicis, lib. IV.; Radulphi Coggeshale Chron. Anglic.; Annal. Waverley; Chronicon anonymi Laudun. Canonici, in volume XVIII of the *Historiens de France*.

[233] In Michèle Brossard-Dandre and Gisèle Besson, *Richard Coeur de Lion, Histoire et légende*, Christian Bourgeois, 1989, quoted by Gérald Messadié, *Histoire générale de l'antisémitisme*, Lattès, 1999, p. 197.

forced baptism, died of wounds inflicted on him in London. Crusaders who wanted wealth, citizens who frowned on the prosperity of the Jews, nobles who owed them money, and priests animated by bloodthirsty fanaticism, all conspired to destroy the Jews of York[234]," wrote Heinrich Graetz.

Under the leadership of a certain Mallebidde (or Malebydde), the gentlemen debtors attacked the Jewish creditors, who were joined by all the Christians. It was not so much envy and fanaticism that animated the Christians, but exasperation. Everyone, peasants, artisans, bourgeois, nobles and monks, wanted to confront and put to the sword these ignoble usurers who did not cease, to top it all, to mock the Christian religion, to receive stolen goods, and to indulge in disgusting customs.

"In the city of York the people ransacked and burned the house of Benedict, a wealthy Israelite who had been slain in the London riot. All the other Jews of the city then fled with their families and valuables to the castle, where they maintained a siege against the insurgent people. After vain attempts to appease the animosity of the people, desperation drove them to commit atrocities similar to those that the persecutions had provoked in Germany. The besieged buried their gold and silver, burned their other belongings, slit the throats of their wives and children, and committed suicide. The ruins of the old Clifford's Tower, which, according to tradition, was the scene of these horrors, can still be seen near York." Legend, fuelled by Jewish historians, claims that not a single member of the York community survived; the number of Jews killed would have been approximately five hundred.

"The people, whose anger had not yet been satisfied with the death of the Jews, went to the cathedral and, after making the public officials return the contracts of the Jewish debts, handed over all these deeds to the flames in the nave of the church.

"The government, however, did not remain an idle spectator of this popular insurrection. The chief culprits were prosecuted, the sheriff and the governor of the town were deposed, and the burgesses were summoned before the court to answer for their conduct[235]."

On Palm Sunday, there was a settling of scores in every town in England where Jews lived.

At St Edmond's, seventy-five Jews were massacred. King Richard instructed his chancellor to prosecute and execute the culprits, but the crusaders had disappeared and the nobles and burgesses who had taken part in the riots had fled to Scotland. The Jews, however, were able to remain

---

[234] Heinrich Graetz, *History of the Jews III*, London, Myers High Holborn, 1904, p. 422, 425–426.
[235] Mathieu. Paris, Hist. Angl. — Tovey, Anglia judaica. in Georges-Bernard Depping, *Les Juifs dans le Moyen-Âge*, (1823), Éd. Wouters, Brussels, 1844, p. 99–100.

and continue trading in England. Richard simply subjected their money lending to more legal formalities, in order to avoid the numerous frauds.

John Without Land, who succeeded his elder brother Richard, was perhaps a little less sentimental and more pragmatic. Because a Jewish financier, Abraham of Bristol, refused to pay the contribution demanded of him, the king ordered that all his teeth be pulled out, one tooth a day. Tradition has it that on the seventh extraction Abraham finally submitted to the monarch's will.

XLV. in the East

The Byzantines had always barred Jews from public employment, and they were subject to heavy taxation. In the Christian cities, there were hardly any small groups of Jews. All of Christian-held Palestine had no more than a thousand Jews. Benjamin of Tudela, a Jew of Navarre, who travelled in the twelfth century to the Holy Land to all the places where he thought there would be synagogues, in order to inquire into the state of the sect, reported that he had found no more than two hundred Jews in Jerusalem. They were almost all woollen dyers, clustered in a secluded quarter below the Tower of David[236]. His account was confirmed by that of Rabbi Petaiah of Regensburg, who also visited his Judean brethren in the same century[237].

Both Jerusalem and the Holy Land were depopulated by Jews. Even Tiberias was no exception. Benjamin of Tudela found no more than fifty people of his sect, only one synagogue and a few graves.

In the cities of Asia Minor where Islam dominated, on the contrary, the Jews were very numerous. The largest communities were then to be found in the region between the Tigris and Euphrates rivers. The community of Mosul was at least as important as that of Baghdad.

In the Maghreb and Andalusia, the Almohads kept Judaism firmly in line to prevent it from being harmful. But in Egypt, Jewish bankers were king. The Jewish community "had flourished there under the reign of the Arabs", wrote historian Cecil Roth. "Although the mad Hakim (996-1021) had exercised the most fanatical repression against the followers of dissenting religions, his successors treated Jews kindly, employing them even in public administration: from 1044 until his assassination in 1047,

---

[236] *Itinerarium D. Benjaminis cum versions et notis*, Constant. L'Empereur; Lugd. Batavorum, 1733, p. 41.

[237] *Tour du monde, ou Voyage du rabin Péthachia, de Ratisbonne, dans le douzième siècle,* par Carmoly; Paris, 1831, p. 98. In Augustin Lemann, *L'Avenir de Jérusalem, Éspérance et chimères*, 1901, première partie, chapitre III

the banker and court steward, Abraham (Abu Said) ben Sahl, vizier to the Sultan's mother, ruled the country effectively[238]."

It was in Egypt that the greatest Jewish intellectual of the Middle Ages, the celebrated Moses ben Maimon, Maimonides, born in Cordoba in 1135, found refuge with his family. From all parts of the Jewish world, men appealed to his judgement and judgement. "When a false Messiah appeared in Yemen, or an epidemic of persecution arose in the Maghreb, or a philosophical doubt troubled the rabbis of Marseilles, the great Egyptian scholar wrote to indicate in the clearest terms what attitude should be adopted in order to be in accord with the principles of Judaism[239]."

Moses Maimonides had also used his science to justify the conduct of Jews who pretended to practice Islam in order to more effectively undermine the enemy from within. An author already quoted and rather pro-Jewish Georges-Bernard Depping wrote: "It is annoying to find in the works of Maimonides the hatred of the Jews towards those who practise another religion. Not only does he allow them to be deceived, but he forgets himself to the point of expressing his conviction that traitors, Epicureans and heretics must be exterminated, on the banal pretext of all persecutors, that the danger threatening the true religion must be averted[240]."

Sheikh Abd al Qadir al Khilani (1083–1166), an Iranian saint of Ali's lineage, was probably right when he wrote: "The Jews, who live scattered all over the world and yet are firmly united, are cunning and enemies of men; they are dangerous creatures to be compared to the poisonous snake: as soon as it approaches, crush its head, for if you let it raise its head, even for a moment, it will bite you and its bite is deadly[241]."

In Baghdad, Benjamin of Tudela, on his visit to the city, counted twenty-eight synagogues and ten yeshivas (Jewish universities). Some 40,000 Jews lived in the city. The Almohads had imposed a yellow garment on them and the Mamluks of Egypt a turban of the same colour (blue for the Christians). But the Islamic *dhimmituda* (*dhimmi* status: legal status of protection and submission for Jews, Christians and Zoroastrians, ndt) was a mild regime compared to what the Jews endured in the Christian world.

In the Ottoman Empire in the 16th century, some Jews held the highest positions in the state apparatus. We also know that they played a leading

---

[238] Cecil Roth, *Histoire du peuple juif*, 1936, Stock, 1980, p. 204. All those who oppose its influence are systematically treated as "madmen" by Jewish intellectuals, to this day.
[239] Cecil Roth, *Histoire du peuple juif*, 1936, Stock, 1980, p. 205.
[240] See his treatise *Hilkolh avarlah sarah*, chapter X. In Georges-Bernard Depping, *Les Juifs dans le Moyen-Âge*, (1823), Wouters, Bruxelles, 1844, p. 63. Wouters, Bruxelles, 1844, p. 63. And also in Israel Shahak, *Historia judía, Religión judía, El peso de tres mil años*, Ediciones A.Machado, 2016, Madrid.
[241] Abd al-Qadir al-Khilani, in al-Fath ar Rab-bani wal-Faid ar-Rahmani, Mag. 37.

role during the Kemalist revolution of 1922 in Turkey[242]. In the Muslim world in general, the situation did not deteriorate for them until after the Second World War, following the creation of the State of Israel in Palestine.

XLVI. Innocent III

The Papacy, like most of the authorities of the time, was until the 13th century relatively tolerant towards the Jews. Pope Alexander III (1159–1181) was quite favourable to them. In fact, his treasurer was the Jew Yehiel ben Abraham.

But with Innocent III (1198–1216), the Jews encountered an opponent who put up real resistance. Innocent III, "the most thoughtless and arbitrary of all the princes of the church" was undoubtedly, wrote Graetz, "a bitter enemy of the Jews and Judaism, and struck harder blows against them than any of his predecessors[243]." The great papal bulls concerning the Jews therefore appeared from the year 1200 onwards.

Although at the beginning of his magisterium Innocent III had shown himself to be quite even-handed towards the Jews, intervening against the violence of the crusading soldiers, prohibiting the forced baptisms of Jews, the spoliation of their property without legal authorisation, attacks with scourges or stoning them during their feasts or desecrating their cemeteries, he abhorred them no less.

One of Innocent III's main letters was addressed to the archbishop of Sens and the bishop of Paris in 1205. In the same year, he reproached King Philip Augustus for his lack of vigilance after he had readmitted them to his kingdom and recommended more severity: "I learned that in France the Jews have appropriated the goods of the Church and of Christians by usury; that, contrary to the decision of the Lateran Council held under Alexander III, they employ Christian wet nurses and servants; that the courts do not accept the testimony of Christians against Jews; that the community of Sens has built a new synagogue which surpasses in height the neighbouring church, and where prayers are recited, not in a low voice, as before the expulsion, but in such a loud voice as to disturb the worship of the Christians; and, lastly, that Jews are allowed to show themselves in public during Holy Week, in towns and villages, and that they even divert the faithful from their faith[244]."

---

[242] On the role of the Dunmehs (crypto-Jews) in Turkey, see *Psychoanalysis of Judaism* and *The Mirror of Judaism*.
[243] Heinrich Graetz, *History of the Jews III*, London, Myers High Holborn, 1904, p. 417, 512.
[244] Regesta L. VIII, 121, insérée aux Décrétales (L. V t. 6 *De Iudaeis*, ch. 3)

He also mentioned that "the houses of the Jews remained open till the middle of the night, and were used to hide stolen goods; even murders took place, as was witnessed by a poor schoolboy who had recently been found dead in a Jewish house. The Pope advised that some examples of severity should be given to inspire a salutary fear[245]."

In May, the pope wrote a harsh letter to Alfonso VIII of Castile, because the prince did not allow the clergy to take Muslim slaves from the Jews in order to baptise them, nor did he oblige Jews and Muslims to pay the due tithe to the clergy.

He then wrote another letter for the attention of the Count of Nevers, dated January 1208. The Pope said: "The Jews should wander, like Cain, through the world, and bear the mark of their abjection on their faces. Instead of humiliating and enslaving them, Christian princes protect them, harbour them in cities and towns, and use them as bankers to extort money from Christians. On top of that, they put the Christian debtors of the Jews in prison and allow Christian castles and villages to be pawned to them, whose tithes are no longer paid to the Church. And is it not scandalous that the Christians have their animals slaughtered and their grapes pressed for the Jews, so that the Jews take what they want and leave the leftovers to the Christians?"

However, Innocent III did not preach a war of extermination as he did against the Albigensians, the Gnostic sect of the Cathars in Languedoc. The doctrine of the Church was that the Jews should be the people who witnessed the victory of Christianity.

Innocent III had summarised the doctrine and jurisprudence concerning the Jews as follows (Constitution *Licet perfidia Iudaeorum* of 15 September 1199): "No Christian should be allowed to harm them, to seize their goods or to change their customs without legal judgement. Let no one molest them on their feast days, either by beating them, or by stoning them, and let no one impose on them on those days deeds which they may do at other times. Moreover, in order to oppose with all our might the wickedness and covetousness of men, we forbid anyone to violate their cemeteries, to dig up their corpses and to take money from them. Those who contravene these provisions shall be excommunicated[246]." The number of pontifical documents of this kind—constitutions, bulls, letters, epistles, etc.—is truly considerable.

Whenever exasperated peoples committed massacres or plunder, the

---

[245] Letter of Innocent III, 1205, in volume II of *Diplomata*, de Brequigny et Dutheil ; Letter 186 and letter of 1208, in Georges-Bernard Depping, *Les Juifs dans le Moyen-Âge*, (1823), Éd. Wouters, Brussels, 1844, p. 121.

[246] Julio Meinvielle, *El judío en el misterio de la historia*, Cruz y Fierro Editores, Buenos Aires, 1982 p. 62. 62.

popes had raised their voices, condemning the crimes and demanding that bishops intercede and protect the victims, congratulating those who had done so of their own accord. The popes had always allowed Jewish fugitives to settle in their states, whether in the county of Venesino or in Italy. Likewise, popes had repeatedly forbidden Christians to force Jews to be baptised, to dispossess them of their property and to violate their cemeteries[247].

All these documented facts did not prevent the Jewish historian Heinrich Graetz—like all his colleagues—from twisting history as he pleased: "Innocent III was the first pope to treat the Jews with inhuman harshness[248]", he wrote proudly.

The heretical sect of the Albigensians had had some success in Languedoc, in the south of France, where it was protected by some of the local nobility. The heresy—and this is no coincidence—had taken root in a land where the Jewish population was very large and prosperous. Raymond V of Toulouse exercised a benevolent sovereignty over them, and his successor, "Raymond VI of Toulouse favoured the Jews perhaps even more than his father, and promoted them to official positions (1194–1222)," confirmed Graetz.

Talmudic Judaism was evidently the main source from which the Albigensians drew in their hatred of the Catholic Church. Indeed, Heinrich Graetz explicitly acknowledged this: "The Albigensians of southern France, whom they branded as heretics and who were the most resolute opponents of the papacy, had been imbued with hostility through their relations with educated Jews. Among the Albigensians there was even a sect which declared without hesitation that Jewish law was preferable to that of the Christians. Innocent's gaze was therefore directed at the Jews of southern France, as well as at the Albigensians, in order to curb their influence on Christian spirits[249]."

So it was not without reason that Pope Innocent III kept a close eye on the Albigensians and the Jews in the south of France. Raymond VI was the target of many attacks and suffered many displeasures, both for his friendship with the Jews and for protecting the Albigensians. In 1209, he was humiliated by Milon, the pope's legate: the Count of Toulouse was seized, scourged and led naked into the church with a rope around his neck. He had to confess his sins in public and swear, among other things, that he would dismiss all his Jewish officials. Thirteen barons, accused like him of being favourable to the Albigensians and the Jews, were in turn forced to

---

[247] Charles Auzias-Turenne *Revue Catholique des Institutions et du Droit*, October 1893.
[248] Heinrich Graetz, *Geschitchte der Juden; Histoire des juifs IV*, Éd. Durlacher, Paris, 1888, p. 163.
[249] Heinrich Graetz, *History of the Jews III*, London, Myers High Holborn, 1904, p. 517.

swear that they would expel their Jewish officials and never appoint any more.

The pope finally decided to organise an expedition against the Cathars, promising the combatants the same indulgences and favours as the crusaders going to the Holy Land. He first asked King Philip Augustus to take the lead in this expedition, but the latter, still at war with the English King John of England, did not want to open another front and refused the task. At first, the King of France even forbade the barons of the kingdom to take part in the Albigensian crusade, before changing his mind and giving his authorisation. The pope also obtained from the king that the Christian debtors of the Jews who marched to fight the Albigensians would be declared free of all interest on arrears, and that the payment of the capital would be deferred[250].

The crusaders, led by Count Simon IV de Montfort and Arnold Amalric, Abbot of Poblet, inquisitor and legate of the Pope, met in Lyon before heading south. To preserve their states from threat and destruction, Raymond VI of Toulouse agreed to make peace (18 June 1209).

Arnold Amalric then decided to attack without further delay the fiefs of Raymond Roger Trencavel, Viscount of Beziers and Carcassonne, villas that were home to a multitude of Cathars and Jews. On 22 July 1209, the Crusaders stormed Beziers, taking the town and subduing it with blood and fire. They asked Arnold how to distinguish the heretics from the faithful, to which he reportedly replied: "Kill them all, God will recognise his own" (*"Caedite eos. Novit enim Dominus qui sunt eius"*).

After the capture of the city, the legate wrote to the pope: "We have not taken into account either sex or age: about twenty thousand people have fallen under our blows. After the massacre, we have plundered and burned the city". Two hundred Jews had perished in the slaughter and many had been taken prisoner.

In September, the Council of Avignon, presided over by Milon—the pope's legate—decided that the barons and all free cities should promise on oath that they would no longer employ Jews and that they would not allow Jews to employ Christian servants. This same council forbade Jews to work on Sundays and Christian holidays and to eat meat on Christian fast days. The fourth canon forbade Christians to do pecuniary business with the Jews, and the Jews were condemned to repay all that they had extorted by usury[251].

Arnold Amalric's soldiers then went to Spain, where the Christians

---

[250] Letter of 1208, *Epistol. Innocent. III*, lib. XI, in Georges-Bernard Depping, *Les Juifs dans le Moyen-Âge*, (1823), Éd. Wouters, Brussels, 1844, p. 121.
[251] Charles Auzias-Turenne *Revue Catholique des Institutions et du Droit*, October 1893.

were fighting against the Muslims. In those years, an Almohad chieftain from the Maghreb, Muhammad Alnassir, had brought about half a million of his Muslim co-religionists across the Strait of Gibraltar. Faced with imminent danger, the Christian kings of Spain had united and asked Pope Innocent III to preach a crusade against the Muslims. Numerous European warriors travelled beyond the Pyrenees to fight the crescent, including the Abbot of Cîteaux, Arnold Amalric, and his soldiers, the "Ultramontanes". In 1212, they pounced on the Jews of Toledo and would probably have massacred the entire community without the intervention of King Alfonso VIII, Archbishop Giménez de Rada and the Christian burghers of the city who came to the defence of the Jews.

The Twelfth Ecumenical Council, the Fourth Lateran Council, which met in Rome in November 1215 in the Lateran Basilica, confirmed the ancient injunctions against the Jews and added additional ones. The lack of obedience on the part of princes and peoples made these frequent reminders necessary.

Canons 67, 68 and 69 forbade Jews to demand exorbitant interest, on pain of "ostracism". Christians, for their part, were not to have continued relations with them on pain of excommunication. It was not permitted to give them public jobs; failing that, the offender was to be punished and the Jew, after being disgracefully revoked, was also to hand over to the bishop all the salary he had received. The confiscated money was to be distributed to the poor.

We see, moreover, the obligation for Jews to wear a mark in order to distinguish them from Christians, and this from the early age of twelve years. This custom was already ancient, but it was the first time that a council had expressly imposed it: since then the order to conform to it was frequently repeated in Christendom.

The mark imposed was usually a yellow circular cloth insignia, called a *rodella (*from *rotella (Latin), rouelle* in French*)*. The Jews always tried to diminish it by wearing it down, to make it invisible until it almost disappeared, or to conceal it in the form of a subtle ornament.

Women were also required to wear the *buckler*, or, as prescribed by certain councils, notably the Council of Avignon in 1326, *cornelias*, a kind of spiky hairstyle. In Italy, on the other hand, it was the men who had to distinguish themselves with a headdress, namely a yellow cap, the *birettum glaucum*.

The *buckler*, as it was called, was not really a novelty. The pope seems to have been inspired by the legislation of Muslim countries. Indeed, it was the Almohad prince Abu Yusuf Ya'aqoub al-Mansur who first forced the Jews, who had been forced to embrace Islam in his lands, to wear a special garment, a coarse dress with long sleeves and, in place of the noble turban, a ridiculously shaped veil.

If I were sure," said this shrewd prince, "that the Jews were sincere converts, I would allow them to marry Muslims. If, on the other hand, I knew that they persisted in their old faith, I would put them to the sword, enslave their children and confiscate their property. But I have my doubts, so I want them to wear clothes that ridicule them."

It was this law that Innocent III introduced in Christian countries on 30 November 1215. Following the pope's decision, provincial councils, states and princes deliberated on the buckler to determine precisely its colour, shape, length and width. But whether it was round or square, yellow or red, on the hat or on the chest, the result was in fact the same: the buckler enabled Christians to protect themselves against the wiles of the Jews, who were always ready to pass themselves off as natives in order to better deceive the unwary.

The councils of Narbonne (1227), Rouen (1231), Tarragona (1239) and Beziers (1246) renewed all or part of the above prescriptions and added some more. All insisted on the kneel, as did the Teutonic councils of Fritzlar (1259) and Aschaffenburg (1292), near Mainz, which also forbade Jews, under a fine of a silver mark, to go out (the first council) and to look out of windows (the second council) on Good Friday[252].

Innocent III's successor, Honorius III (1216–1227) insisted with the utmost clarity and severity that the Jews of England be compelled to wear the buckler. In 1222, the Council of Oxford renewed the measures dictated by the Fourth Lateran Council seven years earlier. In this country, the buckler took the form of two white squares, evoking the tablets of the Law, which the Jews were required to sew on their coats and cloaks. For the rest, from the death of John the Landless and during Henry III's minority, the real ruler of the realm was Stephen Langton, Archbishop of Canterbury, "an implacable enemy of the Jews", according to Graetz.

In the Holy Empire, Emperor Frederick II, who reigned until 1250, was a "liberal and enlightened" prince. At his court, Jewish scholars translated philosophical works from Arabic into Latin, altering the meaning of the texts according to their interests: "He loved the sciences and supported geniuses with princely generosity. He was keen to have writings on philosophy and astronomy translated from Arabic, and for this purpose he employed many skilled Jews… Yet, despite all this, Emperor Frederick was no less an enemy of the Jews than his opponent, the intolerant Louis the Saint of France[253]". Although he was a staunch adversary of the papacy, he enforced in his states the bull which removed Jews from public employment and imposed on them the decisions of the Lateran Council

---

[252]Charles Auzias-Turenne *Revue Catholique des Institutions et du Droit*, October 1893.
[253]Heinrich Graetz, *History of the Jews III*, London, Myers High Holborn, 1904, p. 583, 585.

even more harshly than the kings of Spain. Although he allowed the Jews from Africa, who were fleeing from the Almohads, to settle in Sicily, they had to pay heavy taxes, while the rest of the immigrants were exempted from them.

XLVII. Nicholas Donin and the Talmud

During the reign of Louis VIII, the son and successor of Philip Augustus, the complaints of debtors and the lawsuits brought by usurers caused new disturbances. By an ordinance of 1223, the new king cancelled at a stroke the interest obligations contracted with the Jews that year since All Saints' Day. He declared titles dated five years earlier null and void and gave debtors three years to pay off their debts in nine equal instalments. This measure had no other purpose than to rid the government of incessant demands, but the Jews continued to practice usury[254]. "You shall not lend at interest (usury) to your brother; it does not matter whether the loan is money, food, or anything else that can accrue interest. To a foreigner you may lend at interest, but to your brother you shall not lend at interest, so that Yahweh your Elohim may prosper you in whatever you undertake to do in the Land you are entering to take possession of," the Torah clearly states (Deuteronomy XXIII, 19–20).[255]

Queen Blanche of Castile—mother of Saint Louis—who ruled the kingdom of France during her son's minority, tried to put an end to the scourge of Jewish usury. In December 1230, the ordinance of Melun established that the sums owed to the Jews would be paid in three years and the final payment would be made on All Saints' Day. Jews were to present their bills or obligations to their lords before All Saints' Day. In 1234, a new ordinance made it easier for Christians to pay their debts to Jewish usurers.

The poet Gautier de Coincy (1178–1236), a monk and troubadour born in Picardy, was one of the greatest French poets of the Middle Ages. He knew how to express clearly the contempt of the common people for the members of this sect:[256]

Plus bestial que bestes nues
Sont les Juyfs, ce n'est pas doute (...)

---

[254]Charter of the year 1223, in Brussel, *Usage général des fiefs*, tome I, liv. II chap. XXXIX, in Georges-Bernard Depping, *Les Juifs dans le Moyen-Âge*, (1823), Éd. Wouters, Brussels, 1844, p. 122.
[255]Messianic Israelite Kadosh Version, at www.bibliatodo.com. (NdT).
[256]Gilbert Dahan, *Les Juifs dans les miracles de Gautier de Coincy*, Archives juives, N°16, 1980. See also the studies on the work of Gautier de Coincy available on Gallica.bnf.fr.

> *Moult les haïr, et je les haiz,*
> *Et Dieu les het, et je si faiz.*
> *Et tout li monde les doilt haïr*[257].

During the summer of 1236, the Crusaders leaving for Palestine exposed the violent resentments of the Christians against the Jews. In Anjou and Poitou, in Bordeaux and Angoulême, great massacres took place: "The Crusaders acted with unprecedented cruelty towards them, and trampled many of them under the hooves of their horses. They spared neither children nor pregnant women, and left the corpses unburied, prey to wild beasts and birds. They destroyed the holy books, burnt the houses of the Jews and seized their property. On this occasion more than three thousand perished, while more than five hundred embraced Christianity. Once again, the surviving Jews complained to the Pope about this unbearable cruelty. The Pope felt compelled to send a letter on this matter to the Church prelates of Bordeaux, Angoulême and other bishoprics, and also to King Louis IX of France (September 1236), in which he deplored the events that had taken place, and pointed out that the Church was opposed to the total annihilation of the Jews, as well as to their forced baptism[258]."

In 1249, the Count of Poitou, Alphonse, brother of Saint Louis and lord of La Rochelle, ordered the expulsion of the Jews from his estates. In 1291, public aversion towards the Jews grew so virulent in La Rochelle that the town council, in line with the general animosity, decided to expel them all from the town.

The popular revolt of 1236 had been encouraged by a certain Nicolas Donin. He stirred up the mob against the Jews, going through the region, from town to town and village to village. Nicolas Donin was a former Jew who had abandoned Judaism and turned against the sect. Knowledgeable in the Hebrew language, he had been excommunicated by the rabbis after having expressed doubts about the value of the Talmud and the authenticity of the Oral Law. He had then completely disassociated himself from Judaism and accepted baptism under the baptismal name of Nicholas. In 1238, he went to Rome to denounce to Pope Gregory IX the horrors contained in the Talmud.

Let us recall that the Talmud, the holy book of the Jews, contains the teachings of the rabbis of the first centuries after Jesus Christ (medieval

---

[257] More beastly than naked beasts.
It is the Jews, no doubt (...)
Many hate them, and I hate them,
And God hates them, so I hate them.
Everyone must hate them.
[258] Heinrich Graetz, *History of the Jews III*, London, Myers High Holborn, 1904, p. 588.

rabbinism is the direct successor of Pharisaism, ndt). It transcribes or summarises the stormy discussions that took place in the various academies of Palestine and Babylonia. A master would state a problem, his disciple would propose a solution to which the disciple's disciple would reply in turn, until it was solved by the next generation. Several generations of teachers and pupils had thus continued the same debate, which the Talmud summarised in a short passage or a simple paragraph[259].

The simplest and most unremarkable questions were the subject of endless chicanery. The rabbis thus sought mysteries in the plainest or most insignificant phrases of the Torah, indulged in extravagant conjectures and extrapolations. They went so far as to maintain that every passage of the Torah was susceptible of seventy, or even six hundred thousand, different explanations.

It can be shown from the Talmud that the rabbis preach one thing and its opposite, praise and condemn tolerance, approve and reject usury, value and despise women, etc. But it is no less true that the work contains a great many passages outrageous to non-Jews[260].

It is beyond doubt," wrote Graetz, "that the Talmud, composed without any spirit of scientific or historical criticism, contains all sorts of assertions". The Jewish historian acknowledged that some statements by rabbis could offend Christians, although he defended himself: "In order to harm the Jews, it was intended to give equal value to everything contained in the Talmud and to put simple jokes and important prescriptions on the same level[261]."

"The apostate had extracted several passages from the Talmud and formulated thirty-five articles on which he based his accusations. In some of them it was stated that the Talmud contained many gross errors and absurdities, as well as blasphemies against God; in others it was asserted that it sustained the practice of infamy and deceit against all mankind; in

---

[259] Elie Wiesel, *Célébration talmudique*, Seuil, 1991, p. 275.
[260] The Talmud collects the Mishnah (the written collection of the oral laws, according to Exodus 24, 12) and the Gemara (the Rabbis' commentaries on the Mishnah). The Rabbis' Gemara explains the Mishnah. The Talmud is divided into 63 tractates in six main orders. The central orders are *Zeraim* (the Seedings: agricultural treatises), *Moed* (Seasons and holidays, containing the fundamental treatise on the Sabbath), *Nashim* (devoted entirely to women, sexuality and reproduction, and consisting of numerous rather lurid treatises), and the properly legal order called *Nezikin* (on damages. Civil and criminal law). Exclusivism and the notion of racial and sexual purity are omnipresent in the Talmud. In fact, an entire tractate, called *Niddah*, deals with women's blood and menstruation. Basically, the Talmud deals with questions of money, sex, purity and messianism, as well as a number of very tedious and twisted contingencies and issues. The Talmud is also fiercely supremacist and anti-gentile.
[261] Heinrich Graetz, *Histoire des juifs III*, Éd. Durlacher, Paris, 1888, p. 195.

others it was again asserted that the Talmud insulted and blasphemed against Jesus, the Virgin and the Church... However, among his accusations against the Talmud, Nicholas Donin had distorted the truth. He claimed that the Talmudic writings taught that it was a meritorious deed to kill the best man among Christians; that a Christian who rested on the Sabbath or studied the Law should be punished by death; that it was lawful to deceive a Christian without any scruple; that it was permissible for Jews to break a promise made on oath; and many other mendacious assertions[262]."

The accusations that Nicholas Donin first made against the Talmud had painful consequences for "the chosen people". Subsequently, the Christian Hebraising scholars went on to study the Talmud and confirmed what everyone suspected. Here are some precepts taken from this "holy book" written by the "wise men" of Israel:

Christians are idolaters, do not associate with them (*Hilkhoth Maakhaloth*); Christians are impure because they eat impure food (*Shabbath, 145b*[263]); Jewish women are defiled by the mere encounter with Christians (*Yore Dea, 198*); Jews are human, Christians are not, they are beasts (*Keritot, 6b*[264]); Christians are created to serve Jews (*Midrash Talpioth, 225*[265]); Christians are no more to be pitied than pigs when they are sick to their guts (*Orach Chayim, 57, 6a*); the soul of non-Jews comes

---

[262] Heinrich Graetz, *History of the Jews III*, London, Myers High Holborn, 1904, p. 595-593.

[263] "(...)For what reason are the Gentiles morally defiled? He answered: Because they eat abominable creatures and things that creep, and that cause bad character traits". *Shabbath, 145b.* (sepharia.org) (NdT).

[264] "The Mishnah includes in its list of people susceptible to *Karet* [punishment]: One who applies anointing oil to his skin. The Sages taught in a *Baraita* [tradition, teaching, but outside of the Mishnah]: One who applies the anointing oil to animals or vessels is exempt, and one who applies it to gentiles or corpses is exempt. The Gemara objects: It is true that one is exempt in the case of animals and vessels, since it is written, "On the flesh of a person it shall not be applied" (*Exodus 30:32*), and animals and vessels are not the flesh of a person. It is also clear why one is exempt if one applies it to a corpse, since once someone has died, the body is called a corpse and not a person. But if one applies anointing oil to gentiles, why is he exempt—are they not included in the meaning of the term person [Adam]? The Gemara explains: Indeed, they are not. As it is written, 'And you, My sheep, the sheep of My pasture, are people [Adam]' (*Ezekiel 34:31*), from which it follows that you, the Jewish people, are called Adam, but the gentiles are not called Adam." *Keritot, 6b.* (sepharia.org) (NdT).

[265] Ovadia Yosef, the leading rabbi of Israel's Shas party, had declared at a public event: "The Goyim were born only to serve us. Other than that, they have no purpose in the world; only to serve the People of Israel." In *JTA, Jewish Telegraphic Agency*, October 18, 2010: *Sephardi Leader Yosef: Non-Jews exist to serve Jews*. In 2013, his funeral was the largest in Israel's history, gathering nearly 800,000 attendees during the last procession. "Public figures sent their condolences, remembering a giant of Jewish thought", in *The Times of Israel*, October 7, 2013. (NdT).

from death and the shadow of death (*Emek Haschanach, 17a*[266]); the seed of the goyim is like that of the beasts (*Yevamot, 98a*[267]); dead Christian slaves are to be replaced like cattle (*Yore Dea, 377*[268]); Jews are to be called men, not Christians (*Yevamot, 61a*[269]); striking a Jew is like slapping God in the face (*Sanhedrin, 58b* [270]); a pious Jew is always considered intrinsically good, despite the sins he may commit. Only his shell is defiled, never his insides (*Chagigah, 15b*[271]); a Jew should not enter a gentile's house on a feast day and greet him, as it would appear that he is blessing him in honour of his feast day *(Gittin 62a);* Avoid eating with Christians, it breeds familiarity *(Iore Dea 112, 1);* do not drink milk milked by a

---

[266] Common belief of Chabad Lubavitch Hasidic Jews. Read about it in *Psychoanalysis of Judaism*.

[267] "Learn from this, that the Merciful One strips the male gentile of his offspring, as it is written concerning the Egyptians: "Whose flesh is the flesh of asses, and whose semen is the semen of horses" (*Ezekiel 23:20*), i.e. the offspring of a male gentile is considered no more related to him than the offspring of asses and horses". *Yevamot, 98a.* (sepharia.org) (NdT).

[268] "Concerning male and female slaves, no consolation is offered to their master, but they say to him, "May the Lord replace your loss", just as they say to a man concerning his ox and his donkey, "May the Lord replace your loss"." *Yoreh De'ah, 377.* (sepharia.org) (NdT).

[269] "The graves of the gentiles do not become unclean through a tent, as it is stated: "And you My sheep, the sheep of My pasture, are men [Adam]" (*Ezekiel 34:31*), from which it follows that you, the Jewish people, are called men [Adam] but the gentiles are not called men [Adam]. Since the Torah introduces the halachah of the ritual impurity of a tent with the words, "When a man [Adam] dies in a tent"(*Numbers 19:14*), this halachah only applies to the corpses of Jews, but not to the corpses of gentiles." *Yevamot 61a.* (sepharia.org) (NdT).

[270] "Rabbi Ḥanina says: A gentile who strikes a Jew is liable to receive the death penalty, as stated when Moses saw an Egyptian strike a Hebrew: 'He saw a Mitzrayimi [Egyptian] strike a Hebrew, one of his brothers. He looked this way and that; and when he saw that there was no one around, he killed the Mitzrayimi and hid his body in the sand' (*Exodus 2:11–12*) And Rabbi Ḥanina says: Whoever slaps the cheek of a Jew is considered as having slapped the cheek of the Divine Presence; as it is stated: 'It is a snare to dedicate to Elohim offering lightly and reflect on the vows afterwards. "(*Proverbs 20:25*). The verse is interpreted homiletically in the sense of: Whoever strikes [*nokesh*] a Jew is considered as if he wounded the cheek [*lo'a*] of the Holy One." *Sanhedrin, 58b.* (sepharia.org) (NdT).

[271]"The Gemara asks: (…) one source states that one may only learn from a scholar who is blameless in his ways, while another indicates that it is permissible even to learn from one whose character is not blameless (…) Rava taught: What is the meaning of what is written: "I went down to the orchard of the walnut trees to see the greenness of the valley" (*Song of Songs 6:11*)? Why are Torah scholars compared to walnuts? Just as this nut, even though it is stained with mud and excrement, its contents do not become repulsive, for only its shell is stained; so too a Torah scholar, even though he has sinned, his Torah does not become repulsive." *Chagigah, 15b.* (sepharia.org) (NdT).

Christian (*Avodah Zarah, 35b*); wine should be thrown away if it has been touched by a Christian (*Avodah Zarah, 72a, b*); the vessel bought from a Christian should be thrown away or purified (Iore *Dea. 120, 1*[272]); any contact with Christians must be stopped three days before the beginning of one of their feasts (*Avodah Zarah, 2a*[273]); a Jewish child must not be breastfed by a Christian wet nurse, because her milk will give it an evil nature (*Iore Dea, 81*[274]); Christian wet nurses lead Jewish children into heresy (*Iore Dea, 153*); one may feign joy with Christians during their festivals if we can thus conceal our hatred (*Iore Dea, 148*); the property of a Christian or a Gentile is for nothing, it belongs to the first Jew who claims it (*Baba Batra, 54b*[275]); if a Christian mistakenly returns too much money, it must be kept (*Choschen Ham, 183, 7*); Jews can keep a Christian's belongings without worrying about it (*Choschen Ham, 226*); it is permitted to perjure and cheat Christians in court (*Baba Kamma, 113a, b*[276]); Jews

---

[272] "(...) When you serve wine, do not let a gentile come near to help you, lest you let your guard down and rest the vessel in the hands of the gentile, and the wine comes out due to its strength and it becomes forbidden..." *Avodah Zarah (72a and b)*; "Whoever acquires from an idol worshipper a metal or glass food vessel or vessels or lead-covered inside—even if they are new—must immerse them in a *mikveh* [purification bath] or in a stream that has forty *se'ot.*" *Yoreh De'ah (120, 1)* (sepharia.org) (NdT).

[273] "Mishnah: On the three days before the feasts of the gentiles the following actions are forbidden, as they would make the gentile, who would subsequently give thanks to the object of his idol worship on his feast, happy: It is forbidden to do business with them; to lend them objects or borrow objects from them; to lend them money or borrow money from them; and to pay debts owed to them or collect payment of debts from them. Rabbi Yehuda says: One may collect payment of debts from them because this causes distress to the gentile. The Rabbis said to Rabbi Yehuda: Even if he is distressed now, when he pays back the money, he will rejoice after he has been released from the debt, and therefore there is concern that he will give thanks to his object of idol worship on his feast." *Avodah Zarah, 2nd* (sepharia.org) (NdT).

[274]*Iore Dea 81* (=Yoreh *De'ah, 81*) is not translated into English on sepharia.org, only the Hebrew text appears. Only verse 4 is translated, which reads: "It is permitted to eat the placenta of a donkey, because it is only considered a secretion". Lol.

[275] "(...)The Gemara relates: Rav Huna bought land from a gentile. Another Jew came and ploughed it lightly. Rav Huna and that Jew came before Rav Naḥman, who established the property in possession for the latter. Rav Huna said to Rav Naḥman: What are you considering in making this ruling? It is because Shmuel says that the property of a gentile is like a desert, and anyone who takes possession of it has acquired it" *Bava Batra, 54b.* (sepharia.org). (NdT).

[276] "Rav Ashi said: The Mishnah issues its ruling regarding a gentile customs collector, who can be deceived, as taught in a *baraita* [tradition, teaching, but outside of the Mishnah]: In the case of a Jew and a gentile coming to court to be tried in a legal dispute, if you can defend the Jew under Jewish law, defend him, and say to the gentile: This is our law. If he can be defended under Gentile law, defend him, and say to the Gentile: This is your law. And if it is not possible to defend him under either system of law, approach the case indirectly, seeking a justification to defend the Jew. This is Rabbi

who cheat a Christian must share the benefit equally (*Choschen Ham, 183, 7*); usury is permitted with Christians and apostates (*Iore Dea, 159*[277]). Furthermore, Jews may lie, if it is in the interest of one of their own and the community, or to condemn a Christian (*Baba Kamma, 113a*). Jews may swear falsely by using double meaning phrases, or by any subterfuge (*Schabbouth Hag., 6d* and *Kol Nidré*[278]). It is permitted to indirectly kill a Christian, e.g. if someone who does not believe in the Torah falls into a well, one must quickly remove the ladder (*Choschen Ham, 425*); We do not help a non-Jewish woman to give birth on Shabbat, not even by doing something that does not involve desecration of Shabbat (*Orach Chayim*

Yishmael's statement. Rabbi Akiva disagrees and says: One does not approach the case in a circuitous manner to defend the Jew due to the sanctification of God's name, for God's name will be profaned if the Jewish judge employs dishonest means. The Gemara infers from this *baraita*: And even according to Rabbi Akiva, the reason why the court does not employ devious means to defend the Jew is only because there is the consideration of the sanctification of God's name. Consequently, if there is no consideration of the sanctification of God's name, the court approaches the case in a devious manner. Apparently, it is permitted to deceive a gentile. The Gemara answers that Rav Yosef said: It is not difficult, since this ruling that permits the court to deceive a gentile is issued with regard to a normal gentile, whereas that verse, which teaches that it is forbidden to deceive a gentile, is stated with regard to a gentile who resides in Eretz Yisrael and observes the seven noachic mitzvot [*ger toshav*]." *Baba Kamma, 113a, b.* (sepharia.org) (NdT).

[277]"That it is permitted to lend to gentiles and apostates with usury, in three parts: The Law declared that it is permitted to lend to gentiles with usury (...) Usury to apostates is permitted, but to borrow from them usuriously is proscribed." *Yoreh De'ah, 159.* ["For Yahweh, your God, will bless you, as he has spoken to you, and you shall lend to many peoples, and you shall not have to borrow from anyone; you shall rule over many nations, and they shall not rule over you.'" (*Deuteronomy 15:6-8*); "As we learned in a mishnah: Rabbi Yishmael says: He who seeks to be wise should devote himself to the monetary laws, for there is no greater discipline in the Torah, for they are like a flowing well from which innovations are constantly gushing forth." *Berakhot, 63b.*] (sepharia.org).

[278]"Jews may swear falsely by using double-meaning phrases, or any subterfuge." (Talmud, *Schabbouth Hag., 6d*). Moreover, on the eve of Yom Kippur, the feast of atonement for sins, the most solemn of Jewish holidays, the religious celebration begins with the recitation of *Kol Nidré*: "All pledges, restrictions, oaths, oaths, excommunications, renunciations, and any synonyms, by which we have pledged, sworn, or by which we have excommunicated or restricted ourselves; from the present Yom Kippurim until the following Yom Kippurim, which is for our benefit, (as to all of them), we repudiate them. They are all undone, abandoned, cancelled, annulled and invalidated, of no force and effect. Our promises are no longer promises, and our prohibitions are no longer prohibitions, and our oaths are no longer oaths." The content of the *Kol Nidré* prayer appears in the Talmud in the Book of *Nedarim 23a-23b*. Vows and promises are not valid, as long as one remembers them at the time of their pronouncement.

330, 2); one must never heal a Christian, unless he thereby becomes an enemy of Israel (*Yore Dea, 158*); regarding Christians who are not enemies, a Jew must not however intervene or warn them in the face of a mortal threat (*Yore Dea, 158, 1*); one must not save Christians in the face of mortal danger (*Hilkhot Akum, 10, 1*); Anyone who confesses Israel's secrets to non-Jews must be killed before he reveals anything to them (*Choschen Hamm, 386, 10*); heretics, informers and apostates are to be lowered into a pit and forgotten there (*Avodah Zarah, 26b*[279]); those who give Jewish money to Christians are to be killed (*Choschen Hamm, 388, 15*); goyim who attempt to discover the secrets of Israel's Law commit a crime punishable by death (*Sanhedrin, 59a*); baptised Jews must be punished by death (*Hilkhot Akum, X, 2*); even the best of the goyim must be put to death (*Avodah Zarah, 26b*); if a Jew kills a Christian, it is not a sin (*Sepher Or Israel, 177b*); shedding the blood of the wicked is a sacrifice pleasing to God (*Yalkut Simoni, 245c*[280]), etc. And many more quotations that might not seem credible to neophytes, as they are really very insulting to the goyim[281].

Nicolas Donin had collected several extracts from the Talmud, followed by thirty-five charges as the basis of the accusation. As a result of his work, on 9 June 1239, Pope Gregory IX sent a letter to all the bishops of France, England, Castile, Aragon and Portugal ordering them to confiscate all copies of the Talmud and hand them over to the Dominican and Franciscan monks. The sovereigns of these countries were to assist the bishops, while the priors of the Dominicans and Franciscans were charged with opening proceedings against the Talmud and burning all confiscated copies.

When the vigilance was relaxed, the Jews hastened to reproduce new copies of their "holy book". So the orders of popes and bishops were frequently renewed. After Gregory IX, popes Innocent IV (1244), Clement IV (1267), Honorius IV (1286), John XXII (1320), Benedict XIV (1415), Julius III, Paul IV, etc. warned Christians again and again against the barbarities contained in the pages of the Talmud.

---

[279] On sepharia.org (NdT).

[280] Not translated into English on sepharia.org.

[281] The parts or tractates of the Talmud called *Choschen Ham* and *Schabbouth Hag* (as well as some parts of *Iore Dea*) mentioned in the text are untraceable on the internet (sepharia.org and halakha.com). Some claim that these aggressive passages do not exist and were purposely invented by the author of the well-known "anti-Semitic" book, *Le Talmud démasqué—Les Enseignements rabbiniques secrets concernant les chrétiens* (Latin: *Christianus in Talmude Iudaeorum- sive Rabbinicae doctrinae de christianis secreta*)—*The Talmud unmasked—The Secret Rabbinical Teachings on Christians,* by Justinas Bonaventura Pranaitis (1861–1917). Others claim that some of the most offensive tractates of the Talmud were expurgated and concealed over time by the rabbis themselves. (NdT).

XLVIII. 1240: the expulsion from Brittany

The main occupation of the Jews in Brittany, as elsewhere, was lending at interest. But Brittany was the province of France that showed the most tenacity in combating Jewish usury. In 1239, the states (the parliament) of the duchy decided that the debtors would be declared free of their debts to the Jews, and that the Jews would be banished from the country and that all property, movable and immovable, which they held in pledge would be returned to the borrowers. The assembly even obliged the Duke of Brittany to promise on oath, in his name and on behalf of his descendants, and on pain of excommunication in case of contravention, to no longer admit Jews into the duchy and not to tolerate any of his barons harbouring them on his lands. The aversion to Jews had reached such an extent that the murders of Jews, which had taken place a few years earlier on the occasion of the Crusades, were exonerated and it was forbidden to prosecute anyone for those massacres[282].

Bertrand d'Argenté presented in 1588 the Latin text of the document reproduced below: "At that time the country was much ravaged by the Jews dwelling in the country of Brittany, who by the inclemency and cruelty of their usury, which they were allowed, consumed nobles and merchants, and above all the common people, which shocked the country and led to the assembling of the Estates, the Clergy, the Nobles and the Third Estate, and made immediate injunction to the Duke to expel them, which was finally resolved, that the Jews should be banished according to patent and which reads as follows, extracted from the letters of Brittany found in the correspondences of St. Melanius, of the Abbey of Kemperlé[283]."

In 1716, Dom Pierre Morice summarised this document as follows: "The usuries were so outrageous, that the Prelates and the Barons begged the Duke to expel them [the Jews] completely from the lands of their obedience. To satisfy them, the Duke, being in Ploërmel on the 20th of April 1240, issued an Edict in which he declared: 1st. that he expelled the Jews from all Brittany and that he would no longer tolerate them in his lands, nor in those of his subjects; 2nd. that he abolished all debts contracted with the Jews, of whatever nature; 3rd. that the movable or immovable property, pawned to the Jews, would be extinguished. That

---

[282]Proclamation of Duke Jean de Bretagne, dated Ploërmel and inserted among the documents in volume II of *L'Histoire de Bretagne,* by D. Pierre H. Morice, and volume I of *Mémoires pour servir de preuves à l'histoire de Bretagne,* par D. Pierre H. Morice, in Georges-Bernard Depping, *Les Juifs dans le Moyen-Âge,* (1823), Éd. Wouters, Brussels, 1844, p. 130.

[283]Bertrand d'Argenté, *Histoire de Bretagne — des roys, comtes et princes dicelle,* Paris, 1588, p. 245.

movable or immovable property, pledged as security for those debts, shall revert to the debtors or their heirs, except such as were legally sold to Christians; 4th. That no one shall be investigated for the death of Jews hitherto deceased; 5th. That he will prevent debts contracted with Jews in his father's lands from being paid; and, finally, that he will have his Edict confirmed by the King of France. The Duke undertook under oath to keep this Ordinance in force all his life, and submitted himself in case of contravention to the censure of the Church. He subjected all his successors to the same oath, and forbade them to give allegiance before they had fulfilled this duty and obligation. The Prelates and Barons also swore on their part that they would no longer tolerate the Jews in their lands[284]."

We reproduce below the edict of 20 April 1240 by which the Duke of Brittany Jean I le Roux (John I the Red-headed), on the proposal of the parliament of Brittany, expelled the Jews from their lands:

"To all who read these letters, I, John, Duke of Brittany, Count of Richemont, Greetings.

"Know that we, at the request of the bishops, abbots, barons and vassals of Brittany, having carefully weighed the interest of the country, expelled from Brittany all Jews. Neither we, nor our heirs will ever tolerate any in our lands of Brittany, and we will not allow any of our subjects to have any in theirs.

"All debts contracted with Jews settled in Britain, in whatever form and for whatever reason, we repay them in full and give receipt for them.

"All lands mortgaged to Jews, all movable or immovable securities held by them shall be returned to the debtors or their heirs, except lands and other pledges which were sold to Christians by judicial decision of our court.

"No one shall be charged or prosecuted for killing a Jew.

"We will beg and request in good faith and with all our power our lord the king of France to confirm by his letters the present decision or ordinance, and we answer for our father and ourselves that the debts contracted in Brittany with the Jews will never be paid in the land of our father.

"This decision, as written, we have sworn in good faith to observe in perpetuity; if by any means we should contravene this, all the bishops of Brittany, together or separately, may excommunicate us and banish us from our lands situated in their dioceses, notwithstanding any privilege obtained or to be obtained by us.

"Moreover, we desire and agree that our heirs, who in times to come

---

[284]Dom Pierre-Hyacinthe Morice, *Histoire ecclésiastique et civile de Bretagne*, Paris, 1716, ed. 1974, t. I, p. 174, quoted by Alain Guionnet.

will succeed us when they reach the legitimate age, undertake under oath to faithfully respect this decision as described here. The barons, the vassals and all those who are obliged to swear allegiance to the Count of Brittany shall not swear it, nor shall they pay obeisance to our heirs until they, duly requested by two bishops or two barons at least in the name of the others, have sworn to faithfully keep this decision. But this oath having been sworn, the barons and all those who owe allegiance to the Duke of Brittany shall immediately swear allegiance and pay obeisance to our heirs.

"Given at Ploërmel, the Tuesday before the Resurrection of Our Lord, year MCCXXXIX[285]."

The edict was strictly upheld and for centuries there were no more Jews in Britain.

Meanwhile, on the other side of Europe, the Mongols and Genghis Khan's Tartars were ravaging Russia and Poland and attempting raids deep into Germany. Once again, the Jews played the invader's card. Heinrich Gratez wrote: "A story circulated in Germany that the Jews had offered to supply the Mongols with poisoned provisions. Under this pretext they had tried to provide them with weapons of all kinds locked in barrels. A daring customs officer at the border, his suspicions aroused, insisted that the barrels be opened, and the plot was discovered. This story was greeted with general credulity and was the cause of much suffering for the German Jews[286]."

XLIX. Louis IX, Saint Louis

Saint Louis reigned in France from 1226. This king, popularised by history for his justice and goodness, was naturally horrified by Judaism[287].

---

[285] Arthur le Moyne de La Borderie, *Histoire de Bretagne*, Rennes, t. 3, 1899, p. 337; quoted by Alain Guionnet. La Borderie specifies after this dating: "20 April 1240 new style". In 1240, Easter fell on 15 April, the previous Tuesday was 13 April (La Broderie's note, p. 339).

[286] Heinrich Graetz, *History of the Jews III*, London, Myers High Holborn, 1904, p. 599–600.

[287] "The once noble and well-disposed monarch, Louis IX, was so dominated by this feeling of aversion, that he could not bear to look upon a Jew. He encouraged by all means the conversion of the Jews, and allowed the children of converted fathers, who had again adhered to Judaism, to be torn from their mothers' wombs. The Jews had only one means left with which to appease the wrath that had been kindled against them, and that was money... But this means proved to be a double-edged instrument which turned against the very people it was intended to benefit. In order to obtain large sums of money, the Jews were forced to charge exorbitant interest and even to resort to fraud. In this way they earned the hatred of the population and were subjected to further outrages. Repeated complaints about their usury necessitated the law of Louis IX, which

We know the famous anecdote told by Saint Louis himself, as told by John (Lord) of Joinville:

"The king told me that there was a great dispute between clergy and Jews in the monastery of Cluny. There was a knight there, to whom the Abbot gave the opportunity to intervene. The knight asked the Abbot to let him have the first word, although he was granted it with difficulty. So he rose, leaning on the cross of his sword, and said that the greatest clergy and the greatest master of the Jews should be brought to him. They did so. Then he asked a question like this:

Master," said the gentleman, "I ask you this question: Do you believe that the Virgin Mary, whom God carried in her womb and in her arms, gave birth as a virgin, and is she the mother of God?

"(original text: *Et li juii respondi que de tout ce en creoit il riens*).

"The knight replied that many were mad and foolish, who neither believed in her nor loved her and entered her monastery and abode:

And truly," said the gentleman, "you will pay for it!

"Then he raised his pitchfork, struck the Jew on the ear and threw him to the ground. The Jews turned and fled, and took their badly wounded master with them. Thus ended the quarrel.

"The Abbot then came to the knight and told him that he had committed great folly. To which the knight replied that it was he, the Abbot, who had committed even greater folly in making such a dispute. For, the layman, when he hears evil spoken of the Christian faith, must not defend the Christian faith except by the sword, from which he must give between belly in, as much as he can enter[288]."

---

limited it appropriately and in many cases condoned a part of the debts contracted with the Jews." Heinrich Graetz, *History of the Jews III*, London, Myers High Holborn, 1904 p. 589

[288]Jean de Joinville, by R. P. Bruckberger, in *Tableau de la littérature française*, tome I, Gallimard, 1962, p. 125-127. [The text in old French is also found in www.archives.org, Sire de Joinville, *Histoire de Saint-Louis, Roi de France*, Chez l'éditeur rue Grange-aux-Belles, Paris, 1822, p. 16–17:

"Il me conta que il ot une grande desputaison de clers et de juis ou moustier de Clygni. Là ot un Chevalier à qui l'Abbé avait donné le pain léens pour Dieu, et requist à l'abbé que il li lessast dire la première parole et en li otria à peinne.

Et lors il se leva et s'apuia sus sa croce, et dit que l'en li feist venir le plus grant clerc et le plus grant mestre des juis, et si firent il; et li fist une demande qui fu tele: — 'Mestre, fist le Chevalier, je vous demande se vous vous créez que la Vierge Marie qui Dieu porta en ses flans et en ses bras, enfantast vierge, et que elle soit mere 'de Dieu'. —'Et li juis respondi que de tout ce en creoit il riens. —'Et le Chevalier li respondi, que moult avait fait que fol, quant il ne la créoit, en ne l'amoit, et estoit entré en son moustier et en sa mesori, Et vraiement, fist le Chevalier, vous le comparrez, et lors il liauça sa potence et feri le juif lés l'oye et le porta par terre. 'Et les juis tournèrent en fuie, et enporterent leur mestre tout blecié; et ainsi demoura la desputaison.

This story of the knight of Cluny was told by King Saint Louis himself, who wanted it to be an example for all Christians: unless you are a learned man, a "very good clergyman", you do not argue with the Jew, but you pierce his body with your sword.

So as the great king said it in old French: "*Aussi vous di je, fist li Roys, que nulz, se il n'est très bon clerc, ne doit desputer à eulz; mès l'omme lay, quant il ot mesdire de la loy crestienne, ne doit pas deffendre la loy crestienne; ne mais de l'espée de quoy il doit donner parmi le ventre dedens, tant comme elle y puet entrer.*"

Louis IX, Saint Louis, gave the order to organise a public controversy between Nicolas Donin and four rabbis, in order to expose the Jews. The four defenders of the Talmud were Yehiel of Paris, Moses of Coucy, Juda ben David of Melun and Samuel ben Solomon of Château-Thierry. The controversy took place on 25 June 1240 at the king's court, in the presence of several bishops and Dominicans, and before the queen mother, Blanca of Castile, daughter of Alfonso VIII of Castile.

The debate revolved around these two questions: Does the Talmud contain blasphemies against God and anti-moral statements? Does it contain blasphemies against Jesus Christ? Graetz wrote about this: "Yehiel refuted the accusations that were made concerning the alleged blasphemous and immoral expressions. With regard to the second of these accusations, he stated that there was no doubt that in the Talmud many hateful facts were related concerning one Jesus, son of Pantheras; however, these did not refer to Jesus of Nazareth, but to one of a similar name who had lived long before him. He made this statement in all seriousness, almost as an oath, because tradition and Talmudic chronology had led him to believe erroneously that the Jesus whose name appeared in the Talmud was not identical with the founder of Christianity."

Obviously the Talmud was condemned, and on 6 June 1242 twenty-four carts full of copies of this nauseating book were burned in a public square in Paris.

"The pain of the French Jews at these events was heart-rending. They felt as if their hearts had been torn out. The most pious men among them celebrated the anniversary of the burning of the Talmud with a day of

---

Lors vint l'Abbé au Chevalier, et li dist que il avait fait grant folie. Et le Chevalier dit que encore avoit il fait greingneur folie, d'assembler tele desputaison; car avant que la desputaison feust menée à fin, avoit il séans grant foison de bons crestiens, qui s'en feussent parti touz mescréanz, parce que il n'eussent mie bien entendu les juis. —'Aussi vous di je, fist li Roys, que nulz, se il n'est très bon clerc, ne doit desputer à eulz; mès l'omme lay, quant il ot mesdire de la loy crestienne, ne doit pas deffendre la loy crestienne; ne mais de l'espée de quoy il doit donner parmi le ventre dedens, tant comme elle y puet entrer.' (NdT)]

fasting[289]."

This was the first time since the time of Emperor Justinian that legislation had been passed against the Talmud. In 1244, when Pope Innocent IV was informed that the Jews had managed to save a large number of copies of the Talmud from the flames, he encouraged the King of France to carry out further searches and seizures.

Since the Talmud and other clandestine books of the Hebrews incited them to commit all sorts of misdeeds, the pope ordered in the same Bull that all these works be publicly burned "to confound the perfidy of the Jews". The important Bull of 9 May 1244, *Impia judaeorum perfidia,* read: "The impious perfidy of the Jews, from whose hearts, because of the immensity of their crimes, our Redeemer did not tear the veil, but let them remain still in blindness... that, out of mercy alone, Christian compassion receives them and patiently tolerates their coexistence; they commit such enormities that they cause astonishment to those who hear them, and horror to those who are told of them[290]."

Jews, as mentioned above, were obliged to wear a distinctive sign. St. Louis wanted at all costs that the Jews should be easily recognisable to the Christians, so he had imposed a heavy fine of ten pounds on Jews who omitted to wear their buckler. This mark did not, by any means, prevent the Jews from continuing to practice usury and ruin the Christians by all means.

Moreover, the king had urged the Jews of Languedoc to engage in honourable trades and legal commerce, but they clearly preferred to engage in interest-bearing loans and other more lucrative trades. The borrowers, unable to free themselves from their debts, were forced to sell their property and became prisoners of their ruthless creditors.

Most of the French councils that took place at that time cursed and condemned usury: the Council of Château-Gontier in 1231, the two councils of Lyon in 1245 and 1247, those of Albi in 1254, Montpellier in 1258, Sens in 1269, Arles and Poitiers in 1273, Avignon in 1282, etc.[291]

---

[289]Heinrich Graetz, *History of the Jews III*, London, Myers High Holborn, 1904, p. 595–596, 598.

[290]Maurice Pinay, *Complot against the Church, Chapter XLI* (1962), Transcription pdf from Ediciones Mundo Libre, Mexico, 1985, p. 371.

[291]"Throughout history, we have seen popes who have served as protectors of this oppressed people, and other popes who have approved or supported the rigours of kings and the hatred of the people. I feel I must throw more light on this variable conduct of the Church. In 1213, a council met in Paris; Robert de Courzon attended as legate. This council ordered Christians to declare to the priests all they knew about usurious transactions, and usurers to give an account of their loans, to return usurious profits or to compromise with the borrowers, on pain of excommunication and confiscation of usuriously acquired goods. Impenitent usurers were to be abandoned by their own families and their bodies thrown into the street: "As usurers and extortioners have

The Councils of Béziers in 1246 and Albi in 1254 forbade Christians to go to a Jewish doctor. The Council of Vienna in 1267 ordered that a Jew who had fornicated with a Christian woman should be sentenced to a fine of 10 marks of silver, and that the woman should be publicly flogged and banished from the city in perpetuity.

In 1254, in the General Ordinance for the reform of customs, St. Louis ratified what had been previously ordered by his mother. He added the order to burn the Talmud, in accordance with the prescriptions of Innocent IV. But Jewish usury resisted all the king's efforts. One third of all usurious debts were abolished, two instalments were provided for the payment of the rest, and the merinos of the kingdom were forbidden to arrest Christians on account of debt to the Jews or to force them to sell their patrimony.

"The Ordinance of the Jews, which we wish to see respected, is: namely, that the Jews cease their usuries, blasphemies, spells and sorceries, and that their Talmud and other books wherein blasphemies are found be burnt, and that the Jews who do not abide by this be expelled and the transgressors be lawfully punished; and so let all Jews live by the labours of their hands and other tasks without usuries[292]."

This ordinance was strictly enforced with extreme rigour. The authors relate how the Jews complained of suffering such unprecedented persecution. In 1257 or 1258, St. Louis decreed that the usury exacted by the Jews would be returned to those who had paid it or to their heirs.

But these orders were not enough, and again an act of authority had to be resorted to. Thus we see, in an act of Theobald I, King of Navarre and Count of Champagne, that King Louis and his son had secretly planned to

---

established and rooted themselves too solidly, continued the Council, in almost all the cities, towns and villages of the kingdom of France, synagogues which are vulgarly called *communes*, for the subversion of all ecclesiastical jurisdiction, We order, under pain of liability at the Last Judgment, that no one shall submit to the punishments which the said synagogues have decreed against all those who secretly denounce to the bishops the exactions and other crimes of usurers. We decree, under pain of suspension and excommunication, that no lawyer may plead the cause of these synagogues or *communes* against the churches and bishops". And further on the council fathers said: "Since usurers and persecutors of the Church everywhere form synagogues or assemblies of wicked men, armed against God and the Church; who have recently founded new schools and new sciences, opposed to the true sciences taught in the schools, and since they instruct their children only to keep account of the debts acquired by their parents by usury, the council enjoins the youth to abandon this kind of studies, to learn only useful sciences, since it is unlawful to enrich themselves at the expense of others."" In Georges-Bernard Depping, *Les Juifs dans le Moyen-Âge*, (1823), Éd. Wouters, Brussels, 1844, p. 277–278. (NdT).

[292]Auguste-Arthur Beugnot, *Les Juifs d'Occident*, 1824, p. 94. Beugnot was a Catholic scholar, originally from Picardy, a philo-semite and member of the Académie des Inscriptions et Belles Lettres.

arrest all the Jews in their domains on the same day in 1268[293].

L. St. Thomas Aquinas

The Neapolitan theologian Thomas Aquinas (1225–1274) had formally established this in his *Summa Theologica* (II-II. c. 10, art. 8): "Among the infidels there are those who have never accepted the faith, such as the Gentiles and the Jews. These, certainly, should by no means be forced to believe, since believing is an act of the will. Nevertheless, if the means are available, they should be forced by the faithful not to put obstacles to the faith, either by blasphemy, or by crooked incitement, or even by open persecution... Jews should not be forced to embrace the faith if they have by no means accepted it".

On the other hand, St Thomas was well aware of the danger posed by the Jews to Christian society, which is why he maintained that they must imperatively be subjected to the authority of the Church: "There is no alternative but either to expel them from the country, or to let them live, but subject to a harsh servitude that binds their hands and prevents them from causing so much harm". Now, for St. Thomas the words *servis, servitus*, did not have the exclusive meaning they have today. It is not slavery as such, but a state of inferiority which deprives Jews of various rights enjoyed by other citizens and subjects them to various burdens from which others are free, in order to prevent them from doing harm to society[294].

St. Thomas clearly warned the Christian faithful: "If, indeed, they are Christians firm in the faith, so much so that from their communication with the infidels the conversion of the latter may be expected rather than the alienation of the former from the faith, they should not be forbidden to communicate with infidels who have never received the faith, that is, with pagans and Jews, especially when the need is urgent. If, on the other hand, they are simple and weak in the faith, whose perversion may be feared as probable, they should be forbidden to have intercourse with the infidels; above all, they should be forbidden to have excessive familiarity and unnecessary communication with them." (*Summa Theologica*, II-II a, c. 10, art. 9).

---

[293]Public act of Theobald, King of Navarre, from the year 1268. Treasury of Letters, cardboard J, 613. Letters patent of the year 1268. Brussel, *Usage général des fiefs*, tome I, liv. II, chap. XXXIX, in Georges-Bernard Depping, *Les Juifs dans le Moyen-Âge*, (1823), Éd. Wouters, Brussels, 1844, p. 127.
[294]Charles Auzias-Turenne, *Revue Catholique des Institutions et du Droit*, October 1893.

Another of his writings entitled *De regimine Iudaeorum* was not presented as a treatise on the subject, as one might expect, but in the form of a short reply to the Duchess of Brabant, Alix of Burgundy, who had consulted St Thomas on various subjects in 1261 to assist her in her government after the death of her husband. To reaffirm her faith and conscience, Alix had consulted the great doctor of the Church.

St. Thomas replied: "Your Excellency," wrote the Dominican to the Duchess Alix, "asked first of all whether it was lawful, and on what occasion, to impose taxes, contributions and confiscations on the Jews. To this question, formulated in an absolute manner, he would reply that the Jews, as is said in law, are by virtue of their guilt condemned to perpetual servitude, and that therefore the masters of the land may use the goods of these men as their own. However, they must do so sparingly, so that in no case what is necessary for their subsistence is taken from them..." (*Necessarium vitae subsidia eis nullatenus substraantur*). He recommended a certain clemency and not to practice abusive reprisals and specified that the word "necessary" should be understood in a broad sense.

Further on, St. Thomas asserted that princes should compel the Jews to earn their living by honest labour, rather than let them enrich themselves by usury: "Your bewilderment in this respect seems to me, so far as I can conjecture it, to be increased by the consequences of your first question. You tell me that the Jews in your States possess only what they have acquired by their detestable usury; you are therefore ignorant whether it is permissible to demand anything from them, since they ought to return what they have extorted in this way. On this point my reply is this: it is evident that the Jews cannot lawfully retain the proceeds of their usury; therefore, if you take it from them, you cannot lawfully retain it, unless it comes from extortions of which you or your predecessors have been the victims. If, on the contrary, it comes from the extortion of others, and you have seized it, you must restore it to those to whom the Jews themselves ought to have restored it: Thus, if there are persons from whom the Jews have extorted usurious sums, these must be restored to the persons concerned; if there are none, they shall be applied to pious works on the advice of the diocesan bishop and of men of recognised probity, or to objects of public utility, provided the necessity is pressing and the general good commands it. And it would even be permitted to demand this restitution a second time from the Jews, in conformity with the customs observed by your predecessors and with the intention of making the use indicated above[295]."

He concluded by recommending to the Duchess to apply in her

---

[295] Georges-Bernard Depping, *Les Juifs dans le Moyen-Âge*, (1823), Éd. Wouters, Brussels, 1844, p. 140, 141.

dominions the provision of the councils concerning the yellow kneel: "In every Christian kingdom and at all times, Jews of both sexes must be distinguished from nationals by an external sign". This was a wise piece of advice that made it possible to identify at a glance the fox entering the henhouse.

LI. Pablo Christiani and the Barcelona dispute

King Alfonso X the Wise of Castile, who reigned from 1252 to 1284, issued several edicts against the Jews based on Visigothic legislation: "Out of love for the Church, or also because of its intolerance, he imposed many restrictions on the Jews by various laws, and reduced them to a degraded condition. It is uncertain whether the collection of Western Gothic laws (called *Forum Judicum*, Fuero juzgo) was translated into Castilian by Alfonso or by his father. From this collection the Spaniards derived an indelible spirit of hatred against the Jews. Whether Alfonso is responsible for this or not, it is certain that he intended to reduce the Jews to a miserable state by means of a series of ordinances promulgated by himself[296]", wrote Heinrich Graetz. The Visigothic code had probably been translated into Castilian by order of Alfonso in the years 1257 to 1266. A chapter was added to it stating that "no Jew may hold a public office or be granted a dignity in Spain".

Alfonso X integrated into his code all the laws of exception that the Byzantines and the Visigoths had enacted against the Jews, and added other restrictions. He ordered Jews and Jewesses to wear a distinctive sign in their hairstyle, under penalty of fine or flogging for offenders. Jews and Christians could not eat together, nor could they bathe.

Alfonso X the Wise also attested that the Jews crucified a Christian child every year and reaffirmed the prohibition against them going out on Good Friday. On the other hand, he did not allow Christians to attack or desecrate their synagogues, to impose forced baptism on the Jews, or to make them appear in court during their festivals. Alfonso X did not put all these laws into effect, but they were later applied and helped to contain the aggressiveness of the Jews in Spain.

According to a census of the time, there were around 850,000 Jews in Castile, who made up more than eighty communities in the country, the most important being that of Toledo[297].

---

[296] Heinrich Graetz, *History of the Jews III*, London, Myers High Holborn, 1904, p. 614.
[297] "The Jews of the kingdom of Castile, whose population amounted to almost 850,000 souls, contributed 2,780,000 maravedis in taxes... In these territories there were more

Aragon formed an independent kingdom, with Majorca and Sicily. Jews were less free than in Castile. The King of Aragon, James I, who owned property in southern France and was in frequent contact with St Louis (his nephew) and his advisers, tightened Jewish legislation.

His confessor, Raymond of Peñafort, the master general of the Dominican order had probably played an important role in these decisions. In the hope of converting the Jews, Peñafort had organised schools where preaching monks studied Arabic and Hebrew in order to prepare them to fight the learned Jews more successfully. He thus created a tradition of apologists who no longer confined themselves to tracing and compiling Old Testament passages prefiguring the Holy Trinity or prophesying the coming of the Messiah, but sought to refute rabbinical books and Talmudic assertions.

A Dominican named Paul Christiani—a former Jew originally from Montpellier—challenged and provoked the Jews in public controversies in southern France and other regions to demonstrate that their own holy books had already announced the divinity of Jesus.

His superior, Raymond of Peñafort, decided to organise a controversy at court between Paul and one of the most famous rabbis of the time, Nachmanides, master of the Kabbalist school of Gerona. In 1263, King James, bowing to the wishes of the Dominicans, invited Nachmanides (also known as Bonastruc ça Porta in Catalan) and several rabbis to take part in a public colloquy in Barcelona.

For four days, beginning on 20 July, Nachmanides and Paulus Christiani disputed over the divinity of Jesus. The famous "disputation" (*disputatio*) took place in the palace of the sovereign, in the presence of the entire court, the high dignitaries of the Church, the nobility and the assembled people[298].

---

than eighty Jewish communities, the most famous being the capital of Toledo, which, together with the adjacent smaller towns, had 72,000 Jews. There were also very large communities in Burgos, with almost 29,000 souls, in Carrión, with 24,000, and the same in Cuenca, Valladolid and Ávila. More than 3,000 Jews lived in Madrid, which at this time had not yet attained any degree of importance." Heinrich Graetz, *History of the Jews III*, London, Myers High Holborn, 1904, p. 638.

[298]Diago, *Histor. Provin. Aragoniae*, lib. I, cap. XV."[The debate revolved around the following questions:
1. whether the Messiah had appeared or not. 2. whether, according to the Scriptures, the Messiah was a divine or a human being 3. whether the Messiah was destined to suffer and die. 4. whether with the advent of the Messiah, the Jewish law and rituals had lost their force, and consequently whether Jews or Christians had the true faith.
Faced with the accusation of concealing the arrival of the Messiah, the rabbi replied that for Judaism such an arrival had not taken place because the parameters indicated

The advocate of Judaism was finally banished and Paul Christiani sent to preach to the Jews in the principal cities of the kingdom, with the special power to gather the Jews wherever he deemed necessary and with the right to seize all their books. Assisted by several clerics, Father Christiani carried out his mission with great zeal.

These books were used by the Dominican Raymond Martin to compose the treatises *Capistrum Judeorum* (*Gag on the Jews*) and above all the *Pugio fidei* (*The Dagger of Faith*). The latter work, published in 1278, was the most successful. It was widely consulted, studied and plagiarised. The author was a man versed in Hebrew, Arabic, Chaldean and Syriac (a language derived from Aramaic), and of great erudition. Martin had a better command of Hebrew than St. Geronimo and was well versed in biblical and rabbinic literature. He had studied the Talmudic Haggadah, the writings of Rachi, Ibn Ezra, Maimonides and Kimhi. He fought the Jews with their own weapons, namely the Mosaic law and the Talmud. His enormous infolium was strewn with Hebraic quotations, as well as diffuse quibbles which showed that the author had been a pupil of the rabbinical school before he became a violent antagonist of the rabbis. He reproached the rabbis for teaching—among other doctrines—that it was permissible for Jews to kill goyim. Indeed, tractate *Avodah Zarah (26b)* recommends abandoning goyim in wells when they fall into them, as well as throwing *minims* (heretical Jews), traitors and apostates into them[299].

"Another convert, Geronimo of Santa Fe, made the same reproach to the Jews and quoted for it a passage from Rabbi Simeon, son of Rabbi Joanhia, who states that the best of Christians must be killed, just as the head of the best of snakes must be crushed[300]."

While the situation of the Jews was still "quite good" in Castile at the time, Graetz told us, it was "very satisfactory" in the young kingdom of Portugal, under the reign of Kings Alfonso III (1248–1279) and Dionisio (1279–1325). "Not only were they exempt from the canonical decrees requiring them to wear a distinctive sign and to pay tithes to the Church,

---

in the prophecies for the arrival of the Messiah had not been fulfilled: Universal Peace had not been achieved, the Jews had not been called to the Promised Land and Solomon's Temple had not been rebuilt". (at https://www.jewishvirtuallibrary.org/disputation-of-barcelona). Read Hervé Ryssen, *Planetary Hopes* and *Psychoanalysis of Judaism*].

[299] Raymundi Martini, *Pugio fidei adversus Mauros et Judæos*, cunt observationibus Jos. De Voisin, et introductione J.B. Carpzovii. Lipsiæ, 1687. See in this work Wolf, *Bibliotheca hebræ*, volume I. Basnage, *Histoire des juifs*, tome IX, part. 3. Chiarini, *Théorie du Judaism*, tome I, page 96.

[300] Alfonso de Spina, *Fortalilium fidei*, lib. III, ch. 16. *Crudelitas Judoeorum*, in Georges-Bernard Depping, *Les Juifs dans le Moyen-Âge*, (1823), Ed. Wouters, Brussels, 1844, p. 233.

but also prominent persons among them were elected to very important positions. King Dionysius had a Jewish finance minister named Judah. The Chief Rabbi of Portugal, Rabbi Mor, was so wealthy that he was able to advance large sums of money for the purchase of a city. Jews and Mohammedans were commissioned to obtain redress from the rebellious clergy, who, constantly instigated by the Papacy, were endeavouring to modify the national laws in accordance with canonical decisions; this attempt ignited a fierce struggle between the monarchy and the Church... Dionysius finally gave in and introduced the canon laws in his country, although he did not actually put them into practice[301]."

LII. In Central Europe

By the end of the 13th century, Jews in Poland enjoyed sufficient freedoms to exercise their dominion over Christians. The Charter of Boleslas, signed in Kalisz in 1264 (confirmed in 1343 in Kraków by King Casimir), had granted them complete freedom to act as they pleased. The Jews were rich, powerful, masters and lords of almost all trade.

Similar provisions existed in some neighbouring regions. In Silesia, the Duke of Breslau, Henry IV, who had been totally corrupted by Jewish financiers, had also guaranteed the protection of his government to the Jews, their property, their religion and schools, as well as all their business, traffic and speculations. It was even forbidden to bring against them the common accusation of infanticide, unless the accusation was supported by the testimony of three Christians and as many Jews. If the accuser could not prove it, he faced the punishment that would have befallen the guilty Jew.

In Moravia, Jews were protected by special laws, as in Silesia and Poland. Otakar II, King of Bohemia, had enacted them in 1254. The Jews became rich and, as everywhere else, the money of the burghers gradually passed into their hands. But when the miter of the Abbot of Trebish came to be pawned to a Jewish establishment, the exasperated burghers, people and clergy of that town reacted by expelling the Jews[302].

In 1267, after the Council of Vienna, Otakar finally took protective measures, restoring all the old restrictions to the Lower Austrian states. They were obliged to wear a special costume, with a high, wide headdress and probably a pointed hat. They were forbidden to build new synagogues or to enlarge and beautify old ones, to employ Christian workers or servants,

---

[301]Heinrich Graetz, *History of the Jews III*, London, Myers High Holborn, 1904, p. 638–639.
[302] Georges-Bernard Depping, *Les Juifs dans le Moyen-Âge*, (1823), Éd. Wouters, Brussels, 1844, p. 153, 154.

to hold public office, to practice medicine, and to sell food or drink. Christians and Jews were not allowed to have lunch together, to meet in markets, at baths or weddings. The priests ruled in cases of complaints of excessive usury and were in charge of collecting a tax that Jews had to pay to Christians as compensation in the places where they settled. Finally, if one of them had carnal relations with a Christian, he would be punished with imprisonment and a fine of at least ten marks, while the Christian would be flogged and expelled from the city[303].

Jews held numerous public jobs in Hungary. They owned salt mines, collected taxes and were often landowners. The Hungarian King Bela IV (1235–1270) kept them in their jobs and even introduced the rule of Frederick II in his country, which protected Jews against the people and granted them special jurisdiction.

After the intervention of the Papacy, this situation changed abruptly. Legions of Dominicans and Franciscans invaded the Carpathian regions, partly to preach a crusade against the Mongols, partly also to bring back the authority of the pope to the schismatics of the Greek Church.

Under his impetus, the prelates of Hungary and southern Poland met at the synod of Ofen (Budapest, formerly Ofen-Pesth) in September 1279, presided over by the pope's legate, and enacted restrictive laws against the Jews of Hungary, Poland, Dalmatia, Croatia, Slovenia and Galicia.

It was forbidden to lease anything to Jews or to give them public functions. The Synod of Ofen also obliged the Jews of Hungary to wear a red cloth insignia in the form of a buckler on their chest. But these measures were not enforced very seriously. Nearly fifty years passed before the last king of the Arpad house, Ladislaus IV, gave these synodal rules the force of law.

LIII. *Pointy Hats and Ritual Crimes*

In Germany, after the death of Emperor Frederick II in 1250, a struggle broke out between the Guelphs, supporters of the pope, and the Ghibellines, supporters of the emperor. During the power vacuum, until the election of Emperor Rudolf of Habsburg in 1273, the Jews no longer benefited from the security guaranteed by the authority of the prince. The common people took revenge for all the humiliations to which they had been subjected and

---

[303] Charles Auzias-Turenne, *Revue Catholique des Institutions et du Droit*, October 1893. The Jews, for their part, also applied very severe rules: "Blasphemers had their tongues cut out. Jewish women who had relations with Christians were condemned to disfigurement: they had their noses cut off", Bernard Lazare, *Anti-Semitism, its history and causes*, *(1894)*. Editions La Bastille, digital edition, 2011, p. 51.

thousands of Jews had their throats slit.

Every year, new massacres took place in Wisssembourg, Arnstadt, Koblenz, Sinzig, Erfurth and many other cities in Germany. The anti-Semites then proudly called themselves the *Judenbreter, the Jew-slayers*.

The Council of Vienna in 1267, presided over by a papal legate, decided that, instead of the buckler, Jews would wear a pointed hat or a horn-shaped hairstyle, the *Judenhut*. The council recalled all previous measures and ordered Christians to conform strictly to them. It also added the prohibition to attend Jewish games and to buy meat from the Jews.

Ritual crimes regularly triggered popular revolts. One day in 1234, the body of a Christian was discovered in the Bade country between Lauda and Bischofsheim. Eight members of the Jewish community were put on trial and executed on 2 and 3 January 1235.

In 1283, around Easter, the body of a Christian child was found on the banks of the Rhine near Mainz. The archbishop of the city, Werner, Archchancellor of the Empire, tried in vain to calm the crowd by proposing to open proceedings and bring the accused before an ordinary court. But the Christians, out of their minds, pounced on the Jews on the second day of Passover, murdered a dozen of them and plundered several of their houses. The intervention of the archbishop restored order. On the same day, in the neighbouring town of Bacharach, twenty-six Jews had their throats slit.

Two years later, in 1285, the body of another Christian child was found in Munich. The people once again avenged the crime. The Jews who managed to escape tried to escape the fury of the mob by taking refuge in the synagogue. The assailants piled wood and flammable materials around it and set it on fire. One hundred and eighty-eight Jews died in the fire.

The revenge of the Goyim was also unleashed in 1286 in Boppard and in Oberwesel near Bacharach, where forty Jews were executed after the body of a man the local people called *good Werner* was discovered.

The Jews proposed to Rudolph of Habsburg to pay him 20,000 silver marks if he would agree to punish the rioters in Oberwesel and Boppard and to protect the Jews against the violence of the people. Rudolf, who was quite tolerant and favourable to the Jews, accepted the conditions, but his protection was not enough to stop the popular anger and the Jews of several communities in Germany decided to emigrate in the spring of 1286. In Mainz, Worms, Spire, Oppenheim and other towns, numerous Jewish families abandoned all their goods and possessions to emigrate to Palestine. Indeed, the rumour was circulating that the Messiah had finally appeared in that country and that he would liberate the "people of Israel". Although, "these unfortunates had probably learned that their brethren were living happily in Syria, under the rule of a Mongol ruler, who showed even more consideration for Jews than for Muslims and entrusted them with high functions[304]", wrote Graetz.

The collusion between Jews and Mongols was then of public notoriety since even in England, in the 17th century, William Pryne, a prolific author, still recounted how in Germany in 1241 Jews had been discovered conspiring with the enemy to supply the Tartar invader with weapons and destroy the Christians[305].

In France, during Passover 1288, the corpse of a Christian was found in the house of one of the important personalities of the Jewish community of Troyes, named Isaac Châtelain. The investigation was carried out by the Franciscan and Dominican friars, and, on 24 April, thirteen Jews, mostly members of the Châtelain family, were burned at the stake.

LIV. Nicholas IV, Turbato corde, 1288

Faced with this harsh repression, some Jews had falsely converted to Christianity in order to continue from within their slow work of destroying Christianity. One of the Popes who fought most energetically against crypto-Judaism was Nicholas IV. In his Bull of 5 September 1288, *Turbato corde*, he charged the inquisitors, clerics and secular authorities to prosecute the Marranos with firmness, as well as those who sheltered and protected them: *"We hear and relate that not only some converts from the error of Judaic blindness, in the light of the Christian faith, have returned to their former perfidy, but also very many Christians, renouncing the Catholic faith, have exchanged it for the Judaic rite, which is worthy of condemnation.Against all those who have committed this, as against heretics, and also against their supporters, abettors and defenders, you must proceed with zeal. As for those Jews who have induced Christians of both sexes to their execrable rite, or have induced them to it, punish them with a deserved penalty[306] "*, the Holy Father expressly said.

This Bull was one of the most solid foundations of the Church's fight against the Jewish fifth column infiltrated into Christianity and against the inducers of heresy or their protectors. Indeed, it was enough to defend or cover up a crypto-Jew or a heretic to fall under the jurisdiction of the pontifical Inquisition[307].

---

[304]Heinrich Graetz, *Geschitchte der Juden; Histoire des juifs III*, Éd. Durlacher, Paris, 1888, p. 221.
[305]Daniel Tollet, *Les Textes judéophobes et judéophiles dans l'Europe chrétienne à l'époque moderne*, Presses universitaires de France, 2000, p. 156.
[306]Maurice Pinay, *Complot against the Church, Chapter XLI* (1962), Transcription pdf from Ediciones Mundo Libre, Mexico, 1985, p. 372.
[307]"That is why, from the time of the crypto-Jewish heretical movements of the first millennium, and especially those of the Middle Ages, there was a tendency to transform

As long as the popes firmly supported the provisions of this Bull and the canons of the Lateran Councils, it was very difficult for the Jews to penetrate the Christian citadel. This did not happen until Martin V (1417–1431) and Leo X (1513–1521) disregarded what their predecessors had ordered. Only then could the Synagogue begin to patiently demolish Christianity.

LV. Edward I and the expulsion from England, 1290

In England, King Henry III Plantagenet (1227–1272), son of John the Landless and Isabella of Angoulême, favoured Jewish immigration and protected them from the wrath of the people.

In 1255, a general outcry arose throughout the kingdom: in Lincoln, a ten-year-old boy, who had disappeared several days earlier, was found in a shallow grave. According to the chronicler of the time, Matthew Paris, numerous Jews were massacred by the mob and, on 25 August 1255, the Jew found guilty by the court of justice was tortured and hanged[308]. His Jewish neighbours had been arrested on the same charge and taken to London. Eighteen of them were hanged and the others acquitted. The child they had murdered was known as St. Hugh of Lincoln.[309]

In 1263 and 1264 there was a revolt of the barons against royal power, led by Simon V de Montfort, Earl of Leicester. The Jews were accused of being the instruments of royal oppression, and the communities of London, Cambridge, Canterbury and Lincoln were the scene of serious riots. In Worcester, Simon de Montfort expelled the Jews from their lands after abolishing debts. In London in 1264, more than 500 Jews were massacred, their homes ransacked and synagogues destroyed.

Jews had been expelled from several cities during the reign of Henry III: the citizens of Newcastle in 1234 and those of Derby in 1260–1261 had even bought the right to veto Jews from residing among them[310].

---

the mentality of Christians and of the leaders of the Church and of the State by trying to change their anti-Judaism into a philo-Judaism, a plan which gave rise to these constant pro-Jewish movements organised by the Hebrew fifth column introduced into Christian society and into the clergy of the Church". Maurice Pinay, *Plot against the Church*, chapter XXVIII, p. 294.

[308]Mathieu Paris, *Histor. Angl.*, ad ann. 1255. Alph. De Spina, *Fortalitium Fidei*, cap. Tertia expulsio Judæorum.

[309]See the Anglo-Norman ballad on the assassination of the Lincoln child published with notes by Franc. Michel, in volume X of the *Mémoires de la Société royale des antiquaires de France*, in Georges-Bernard Depping, *Les Juifs dans le Moyen-Âge*, (1823), Éd. Wouters, Brussels, 1844, p. 134.

[310]Cecil Roth, *A History of the Jews in England*, Oxford, 1964, p. 82.

In the early years of the reign of Edward (1272–1307), son of Henry III and Eleanor of Provence, the king forbade them to build synagogues and to own fiefs and land. The *Statutum de Judaism* of 1275 forbade them to borrow money at interest, but some tried to circumvent this prohibition. Bad idea: 293 were hanged for violating the royal decree.

It was soon discovered that counterfeit currency was circulating in England and that the country's silver denarii were often minted. King Edward I's reaction was exemplary. On Friday 17 November 1278, all the Jews in the country, men, women and children, were imprisoned and enquiries were launched. About three hundred Jews were found guilty of having altered the coinage. Most were hanged, others were sentenced to life imprisonment and the rest were expelled from the country and deprived of their property.

The ignominies committed by the Jews multiplied. After the murder of a Christian boy in Northampton, the culprits were arrested in London. On 2 April 1279, they were hacked to pieces and their bodies hung on a gibbet.

One of the leading minds of the time, the theologian John Duns Scot (1266–1308), then a professor at Oxford, distinguished himself by taking a stand for the best way to annihilate Judaism. Duns Scot represented the pride of the Franciscan order and profoundly influenced William of Ockham. The "subtle doctor" (*doctor subtilis*) went further than St. Thomas, for he proposed a radical solution to the Jewish problem consisting in the complete destruction of the sect.

To the question, "Should Jewish children be baptised against the will of their parents?", the doctoral canons and theologians of the 13th century, with St Thomas at their head, answered in the negative. Duns Scot, on the contrary, thought it was the king's duty to take Jewish children from their parents and baptise them[311].

Against the argument of the necessary preservation of the Jewish people, pending their conversion at the end of time, the Franciscan considered that for this purpose "it is sufficient to keep a small number of them apart on an island".

In November 1286, the new Pope Honorius IV, in a letter to his legate and the Archbishop of York, demanded urgent action. On 16 April 1287, the clergy of England met in a synod in Exeter and decided to update and enact all the measures decreed by the councils against the Jews. A fortnight later, King Edward decreed that all Jews in England would again be imprisoned, but this time the Jews were quickly released in exchange for the payment of a large sum of money, some twelve thousand pounds

---

[311] Readers of our previous books know that this salutary measure would break the chain of incestuous generations and end the transmission of trauma in the Jewish community.

sterling.

The year 1290 should have been a happy one for the Jews. Abraham Abulafia, an enlightened kabbalist from Spain, a self-proclaimed prophet of Israel, had a decade earlier conceived the strange plan to convert the pope to Judaism: "In 1280 he undertook a journey to Rome to appear before the pope and argue with him "on behalf of the Jews" and convert him to his messianic doctrine and bring about the work of the Messiah who was to unify the three Abrahamic branches to fulfil the prophecies of the End Times. In this endeavour he was undoubtedly influenced by the writings of Nachmanides of Gerona: "When the time of the end comes, the Messiah, by God's command, will go to the Pope and ask him for the deliverance of his people; only then will it be considered that the Messiah has really come, but not before". On learning of Abulafia's plan, Pope Nicholas III gave orders to arrest Abulafia and execute him. But the pope's sudden disappearance saved his life[312]." Abulafia then travelled to Sicily, where he directly declared himself the Messiah in person: God had revealed his secrets to him and announced the beginning of the messianic liberation. This blessed period would begin, according to him, in 1290.

But the year 1290 was not a good one. That year, in Prague, an insurrection against the Jews spread rapidly throughout Bohemia, Moravia and Germany, and multiple massacres took place without the authorities being able to stop them. There was talk of 10,000 deaths. In any case, it was one of the bloodiest reactions the Jews had suffered since their entry into Europe.

In England, at last, by the decree of 18 July 1290, Edward I expelled all the Jews from the kingdom, on his own authority and without having consulted parliament. The date, according to Heinrich Graetz, coincided that year with the 9th of the month of *Av* (again), the date on which the Jews commemorate the destruction of the Temple in Jerusalem. They were allowed to convert their property into cash until November, after which time those still in the territory were to be hanged. They also had to return to their owners all the pledges that Christian debtors had deposited.

King Edward forbade his officials to mistreat them on their departure and to extort money from them at the ports of embarkation. Finally, on 9 October, sixteen thousand five hundred and eleven Jews left England. The goods they had failed to sell were confiscated and handed over to the Royal Treasury.

Graetz recounted how, despite a royal order, a ship's captain had played a trick on a group of Jews: "The captain of a ship, charged with transporting several families across the Thames to the sea, crashed the ship against a

---

[312] https://www.kabbale.eu/abraham-aboulafia/

sandbank and made them disembark until the tide came in. When the tide began to return, he re-embarked in his ship with his sailors, set sail and scornfully shouted to the desperate Jews: "Let them cry out to Moses, who led their forefathers safely through the Red Sea, to bring them to dry land". These poor people perished in the waves[313]."

The Jews of Guiana, then an English duchy in the south-west of France, were included in the general proscription. They emigrated to the lands of the French king, where Philip the Fair initially allowed them to settle. But soon, in 1291, King Philip changed his mind and, with the agreement of Parliament, decreed that the exiled Jews of England and Guiana should all leave France at Mid-Lent (*Mi-carême*[314].).

LVI - In Persia, March 1291

Persia had fallen under the yoke of the Mongols, led by Arghun Khan. Their physician, a Jew named Sa'ad al-Dawla, had drawn the attention of his sovereign to the embezzlement of some officials, thus gaining the confidence of the prince. At the beginning of 1288, Sa'ad al-Dawla was sent to Baghdad to audit the city's accounts and on his return in the summer he was elevated to the rank of finance minister. Since the khan did not hold Muslims in high esteem, Sa'ad al-Dawla gave the most important posts to Christians and Jews. Thus, "it was natural that Sa'ad al-Dawla now favoured his relatives in particular, for they had helped him with great zeal in his difficult office. Thanks to the fidelity with which Sa'ad-al-Dawla served his lord, he gained so much confidence that almost all affairs of state passed through his hands, and he even had the power to make decisions without referring all the details to the great Khan. Probably thanks to his help and advice, Arghun established diplomatic relations with Europe and even with the Pope. With the help of the Europeans, the Mohammedans could be expelled from the Middle East and, in particular, from Palestine. The Pope, however, was under the illusion that Arghun would become a member of the Catholic Church," Graetz recounted.

The Muslims, who were banned from all important public posts, had an invincible hatred for the Jewish minister. A sect of criminals, the *assassins*, founded especially to kill the enemies of Islam, decided to kill his entire family, but the plot failed.

Sa'ad-al-Dawla had earned much hatred because of his arrogance, even

---

[313]Heinrich Graetz, *History of the Jews III*, London, Myers High Holborn, 1904, p. 668.
[314]The *Mi-Carême* (half Lent) was a traditional carnival festival of French origin. It was celebrated on the day that falls in the middle of Lent, which, according to Christian tradition, is the twentieth day of the forty days of fasting prior to Easter.

among the Mongols. So when Arghun fell ill in November 1290, all the malcontents united against the minister. In March 1291, when all saw that the Khan was definitely doomed by illness, they hastened to assassinate the Jewish minister and his favourites, sending messengers to the various provinces to seize all Sa'ad-al-Dawla's relatives, confiscate his property and reduce his wives and children to servitude.

"The Mohammedan population also rushed upon the Jews in all the cities of the empire to take revenge on them for the degradation they had suffered under Mongol rule. In Baghdad there were veritable pitched battles between the Mohammedans and the Jews, and many were killed and wounded on both sides[315]."

In the following generation, the theologian Ibn Qaim Al-Jawziah (1292–1350), author of more than sixty works, wrote: "As for the nation that arouses divine wrath, these are the Jews, the nation of lies and perfidy, of swindling, deceit and subterfuge".

LVII. Rindfleisch of Rættingen, 1298

In 1294, in Bern, a new case of ritual crime led to the expulsion of the Jews, after which the municipality built a monument with a significant name: *Kinderfressenbrunnen,* the fountain of the child-eater.

In the same year, Jews fled Zurich after having to pay a fine of fifteen hundred guilders. Thirty-eight Jews were burned at the stake in Schaffhouse and Vinterthur, and those who escaped the flames sought refuge outside Switzerland[316].

During the civil war in Germany between Adolf of Nasau and Albert of Austria, a nobleman named Rindfleisch, originally from a small town in Franconia called Rœttingen, decided to set aside the impositions of church doctrine and began directly to exterminate the Jews. A story of a desecrated host had set off a powder keg.

On 20 April 1298, Rindfleisch ordered all the Jews in the area to be thrown into the flames. Under his leadership, Christians fed up with the Jews went from town to town, recruiting new followers along the way and killing all Jews who fell into their hands.

On 24 July, the Würzburg community was completely massacred. In

---

[315]Heinrich Graetz, *History of the Jews III*, London, Myers High Holborn, 1904, p. 669–670, 672.
[316]Letter of the dance Jacques de Kienburg, from the year 1294. *Pro impetitione de occisione Beati Radolfi quem dicti Judoei ut dicitur occiderunt, 500 marcas roibi expedierunt in meara utilitatem.* Jean de Millier, Geschichten schweiz. Eidgenossenschaft, liv. II, chap. 7, in Georges-Bernard Depping, *Les Juifs dans le Moyen-Âge*, (1823), Éd. Wouters, Brussels, 1844, p. 142.

Nuremberg, the Jews, sheltered in the city's castle, bravely defended themselves. But on 1 August, the castle was taken over and all the Jews were ruthlessly annihilated. In Bavaria, only two communities were spared the vengeance of the Christians: Regensburg and Augsburg.

"This bloody persecution stretched from Franconia and Bavaria to Austria, wiped out more than one hundred and forty communities and more than 100,000 Jews, and lasted almost half a year. All the Jews of Germany trembled and prepared for destruction. This would have happened if the civil war in Germany had not ended with the death of Emperor Adolf and the election of Albert. The second Habsburg vigorously restored peace in the country, prosecuted the perpetrators of the maltreatment of the Jews and imposed fines on the cities that had taken part in it, claiming that he had suffered losses[317]."

LVIII. Philip IV the Fair

The King of France, Philip the Fair, was particularly illustrious for the firmness of his policy towards the Jews. Here is one of his edicts of July 1291, concerning the situation in Poitou:

"I, Philip, King of the Franks, by the grace of God, to all who read this letter, greetings.

Having learned from the reports of a great number of men very worthy of faith, that the territory of Poitou is inhumanly exploited and absolutely crushed by a considerable number of Jews who indulge there in criminal usury and in all kinds of illicit trade; Desiring to watch over the happiness of the inhabitants of this territory and to yield to the will which they have come to express in various ways; We grant to all, prelates, chapters, abbots, priors, colleges, cities, communes, barons and other temporal lords of the seneschalty of Poitiers, to all who govern men and to all who also depend on them, that the Jews be expelled in perpetuity and irrevocably from the said seneschalty. We do not at any time permit them to take up residence there; we order them to be expelled and banished by our seneschal before the Nativity of the Blessed Virgin Mary[318]."

In 1299, he renewed the ordinance of Saint Louis which provided for the restitution of usury extorted by the Jews. In 1304, through a convention agreed with the Duke of Burgundy, Philip forbade his officials to deal with complaints from Jewish usurers in the duchy and to pursue the Burgundians

---

[317] Heinrich Graetz, *History of the Jews IV*, Philadelphia, The Jewish Publication Society of America, 1894, p. 36.

[318] Henri Delassus, *La Conjuration antichrétienne III*, Desclée De Brouwer, 1910, p. 1155-1156.

whom the duke himself had excused from repaying their debts[319].

But Philip soon decided to apply a definitive solution and root out factional powers capable of directly threatening royal power. He began first with the Jews, before turning his attention to the Knights Templar. In the summer of 1306, he secretly ordered all officials, great and small, to imprison all the Jews of France. On the morning of 22 July, all the Jews were arrested by the king's officials and imprisoned. The order was executed on the day after the anniversary day of the destruction of the Temple in Jerusalem (9 *Av*, in the Jewish calendar); the Jews had not yet recovered from the fast they had observed in commemoration of that event when they were informed that they had one month to prepare to leave the kingdom. After that date, those who had not left France would be executed.

Heinrich Gratez commented in his work: "Their ruthless plunder showed that their aim was the possessions of the Jews. The officials left the unhappy Jews nothing but the clothes they wore, and each of them no more than enough to live on for a day. Carts full of the Jews' goods, gold, silver and precious stones were transported to the royal treasury; and less valuable objects were sold at a ridiculously low price[320]."

"The king showed such contempt for the exiles that he gave his coachman the synagogue that the Jews of Paris had owned in the Rue de la Tacherie. Several years earlier, he had fined the Jews of Paris three hundred pounds for singing too loudly in their synagogue[321]."

"At first, a period of twenty years was granted to their former debtors. The commissioners had great difficulty in finding their way through the maze of obligations, agreements and contracts, most of them clandestine, which had been concluded between Jews and Christians; facilities were granted to debtors who denounced themselves; but few of them were naïve enough to reveal the obligations they had secretly contracted.

"The Jews offered to make known the exact state of their debts if they were allowed to return. In fact, a number of them were allowed to return, who, while working out the state of their assets, knew how to take such good advantage of their return that they corrupted the royal commissioners and returned to lend at usury. In the list of debtors they presented there were so many widows, orphans and paupers—who also denied their obligations—that the king, not daring to dispossess these poor wretches,

---

[319] Georges-Bernard Depping, *Les Juifs dans le Moyen-Âge*, (1823), Éd. Wouters, Brussels, 1844, p. 146.
[320] Heinrich Graetz, *History of the Jews IV*, Philadelphia, The Jewish Publication Society of America, 1894, p. 47–48.
[321] Auto of the year 1288, quoted by Brussel, *Usage des fiefs*, tome I, in Georges-Bernard Depping, *Les Juifs dans le Moyen-Âge*, (1823), Éd. Wouters, Brussels, 1844, p. 147.

rejected the Jews' declarations as false and slanderous, ordered them to leave the kingdom immediately, dismissed the commissioners of the provinces and ordered them to come to Paris to give an account of their conduct. At the same time, he forbade the authorities to investigate further the debts of the Jews and to collect them unless they were obvious and of little value[322]."

In the month of September, nearly one hundred thousand Jews had to leave France. In Troyes, Paris, Sens, Chinon, Orléans, and many other cities, the royal commissars were responsible for selling the houses, synagogues and schools of the Jews; sales that generated considerable profits.

Most of them settled in the border regions of France, in Lorraine, Alsace, Savoy, in the Dauphinate, in Provence—part of which was under the authority of the Holy Roman Empire—and also in Roussillon.

Emperor Albert protected the Jews who sought refuge in the Germanies; and when popular revolts broke out again in Franconia, Swabia and Bavaria, he guaranteed them asylum and had the insurgents prosecuted and punished[323]. It should be noted that the Jews were for the emperors a property from which they made a substantial usufruct, as if they were real estate. In fact, they refer to them in this sense in their public acts and express themselves in a very imperious way to refer to their rights of possession over all the Jews of the Empire.

In Gascony, the King of England, Edward II, overwhelmed by complaints about the abuses of usurers, ordered all Jews to leave his estates in 1314. The order was probably not carried out to the letter as he renewed it more than thirty years later, stating that it was his express wish that the Jews be banished[324].

Nevertheless, there remained in France a very particular class of Jews, the converts. Most of them were very dubious Christians, and as soon as they entered into relations with their former co-religionists, they returned to the faith and customs of their fathers. But the Inquisition was there to watch over the flock of the Church... Apostasy was a crime on a par with heresy, and those who sought to return to Judaism were mercilessly

---

[322]Ordinance of Saint-Ouen of the year 1311, volume I of *Ordonnances des rois de France*, in Georges-Bernard Depping, *Les Juifs dans le Moyen-Âge*, (1823), Éd. Wouters, Brussels, 1844, p. 156.

[323] Chronicle of Otakar, quoted by Menzel, *Geschichte der Deutsehen*, volume IV, in Georges-Bernard Depping, *Les Juifs dans le Moyen-Âge*, (1823), Éd. Wouters, Brussels, 1844, p. 148.

[324]Letter of Edward to the Seneschal of Gascony, 1314, to the Tower of London, in Georges-Bernard Depping, *Les Juifs dans le Moyen-Âge*, (1823), Éd. Wouters, Brussels, 1844, p. 130.

persecuted.

LIX. 1320: *The Shepherds' Crusade*

The banishment of the Jews did not last long. Indeed, in 1315, Philip the Fair's successor Louis X the Self-willed (i.e. the *quarrelsome*), who reigned for no more than two years, readmitted all Jews to the kingdom to finance the war in Flanders[325] for a period of twelve years, with the promise that, if the king decided to expel them after that time, he would give them a year's notice. Despite protests from all regions of the kingdom, the Jews were readmitted. Jewish commissioners, appointed by the king, took it upon themselves to give all those who wished to return letters indicating where they could settle.

When a year later, after the death of Louis X, he was succeeded by his brother Philip V, known as the Long, he confirmed and even extended the privileges of the Jews, protecting them especially against attacks by the clergy and decreeing that only royal officials would have the right to confiscate their goods and books. A public act fixed their rights and duties and assured them a tolerable existence. Here are the provisions of the principal articles: they shall live by the work of their hands or by the sale of goods; they may lend in pledge, but without incurring usury. They will be paid their old debts; they will receive one third and the king the remaining two thirds (probably this article was one of the main reasons for their return); they cannot be sued for what happened before their return. No lord may retain Jews other than his own on his lands. Their former privileges will be restored to them and they will be able to buy back their synagogues and cemeteries at the sale price. Those of their books which had not been sold will be restored to them, except the Talmud, condemned by the Church[326].

Still quite frequent in the 13th century, theological debates before large audiences disappeared in the course of the 14th century. The Talmud was no longer discussed, but burned. In Delamarre's monumental *Traité de la police*, published four centuries later, in 1705, we read that the treaty of June 1315 agreed "that all the books of the law be returned to them, except the Talmud, for that book is abominable (...) Made of innumerable indignities, this enormous work contains, besides multitudes of abominations, the curses and frightful imprecations which the perfidious

---

[325]This is the interpretation of Robert Fawtier, *L'Europe Occidentale de 1270 à 1380*, Paris, Presses Universitaires de France, 1940, p. 429.
[326]Read the text of the ordinance in Auguste-Arthur Beugnot, *Les Juifs d'Occident*, 1824, p. 107–109.

and ungrateful Jews utter every day against Christians in their prayers and exercises of devotion. We will therefore take that impious book worthy of all anathemas[327]."

"The Jews, therefore, might have occupied an honest position in society, engaging in handicrafts and trade, and even in legal lending, in accordance with the privileges they had just obtained. The terrible lessons they had received should have inspired them with an extreme circumspection which unfortunately seems to have been unknown to them. At least the cries against usury did not cease: in the same year that Philip the Long confirmed their privileges, the usury of the Jews of Montpellier had to be repressed and they were forced to bear the mark. The king's parliament went so far as to impose on the entire Jewish nation of the kingdom, as a fine, a contribution of fifteen hundred pounds, an enormous sum for the time[328]."

On their return to France, the Jews had not yet learned their lesson. In 1317, in Chinon, another case of ritual murder took place. Another case of murder also took place in Saint Quentin. The Jews of Lunel, in Languedoc, were incriminated in 1319 for having parodied the Passion of Christ and desecrated a cross.

In 1319, at the instigation of the inquisitor Bernard Gui, ecclesiastics burned two carts full of copies of the Talmud in Toulouse. The following year, Pope John XXII, originally from a well-to-do bourgeois family in Cahors and pope since 1316, promulgated a bull, *Cum sit absurdum*, condemning the Talmud once again. A revolt broke out in Le Puy in 1320, following another accusation of ritual murder[329]. That year the revolt of the Shepherds broke out.

After a pilgrimage to Mont Saint-Michel in Normandy, groups of *Miquelots*, mainly young peasants from the north of France, spontaneously organised themselves into a crusade. This popular movement was encouraged by the passionate preaching of an apostate Benedict and a priest. In large bands, these shepherds converged on Paris, where they entered on 3 May 1320. Five days later, informed of this uncontrolled and subversive movement, Pope John XXII declared excommunication against all those who crossed without pontifical authorisation.

---

[327] *Traité de la police* de Delamarre, 4 vol. in-fol., t.1, pp. 282–284, 1705, in Roger Gougenot des Mousseaux, *The Jew, Judaism and the Judaisation of Christian peoples (1869)*, p. 87. The four volumes of this *Traité de la police* were published in 1705, 1710, 1719 and 1738. Gougenot invited the reader to read "the monumental work of Baronius", *Annales ecclesiasticæ*, etc. *In Angliam Judæi...ut ob graviora scelera...*, 1286.

[328] Georges-Bernard Depping, *Les Juifs dans le Moyen-Âge*, (1823), Éd. Wouters, Brussels, 1844, p. 160.

[329] R. Anchel, *Les Juifs de France*, Paris, J.B. Janin, 1946, p. 82-83.

After perpetrating several pogroms, the Shepherds were persuaded to leave Paris. A troop of forty thousand Shepherds marched from village to village, banners unfurled. This unique union of shepherds and peasants spread like a torrent through France, devastating everything in its path. Far from shrinking from the obstacles it encountered, the movement saw its ranks swell steadily.

At the beginning of June, they crossed the Saintonge and Perigord, which they devastated and plundered, recruiting new followers along the way. More and more numerous, they penetrated into Guiana. More than five hundred Jews had taken refuge in the fortress of Verdun (near the River Garonne), initially managing to repel the attackers' repeated assaults. All the Jewish children, whose parents dared not sacrifice, were baptised.

Arriving in the Agen region, the Shepherds split into two groups. The first crossed the Pyrenees on the road to Santiago to continue their massacres in Spain. These Shepherds entered Jaca, savagely slaughtered the Jews of Montclús before heading for Pamplona, the capital of Navarre. James III of Aragon put an end to their exploits by sending his son Alfonso who annihilated them by force of arms.

The second group followed the valley of the Garonne River, massacring Jews along the way. These settlements of accounts spread throughout the region, from Bordeaux to Albi, Foix and other towns in the south of France. More than 120 Jewish communities were thus destroyed in Gascony.

John Raymond of Comminges, whom Pope John XXII had appointed Archbishop of Toulouse, wrote to the pope for help and advice. "The pope then accused the king of France of irresponsibility and was surprised before his legate Gaucelme that the royal foresight had neglected to repress the excesses and the pernicious example of the Shepherds, who should rather be called rapacious and homicidal wolves, for their actions gravely offend the Divine Majesty, dishonour the royal power and prepare ineffable dangers for the whole kingdom if they are not curbed."

On 25 June, the Shepherds were on the attack against the Jews of Albi and Toulouse. The government of Toulouse ordered its knights to arrest them. Numerous shepherds were seized and imprisoned in that city, but the rioting mob freed them and again pounced on the Jews, who were massacred. Certainly, the Shepherds were everywhere with the help and complicity of the common people.

Four days later, they were at the gates of Carcassonne where the royal army awaited them. Under the command of Aimeric de Cros, seneschal of Languedoc, the army was supported by the troops of the young Gascon II of Foix-Bearn. The Shepherds were finally crushed.

The survivors escaped towards Narbonne. The consuls, informed by the Seneschal, then put their city in a state of alarm and prepared to defend it. The Pope wrote to Archbishop Bernard de Fargues to do the same. The roads and mountain passes were cut off and the fugitives, or anyone resembling them, were systematically hanged. By the autumn of 1320 there was not a single Pastor left in the region.

However, the Jews did not seem to have understood the lesson. In 1321, the seneschal communities of Carcassonne officially asked King Philip the Long to expel the Jews because of their usury and outrages. They were also accused of pimping and blasphemy: "They corrupt Christian women, abuse their insolvent female debtors and insult the Christian religion[330]."

That year, Edward II, King of England and Duke of Aquitaine, hastened to write to the seneschal of Gascony to claim the property of the slaughtered Jews: "This property," said the monarch coldly, "belongs to us, and to no other person[331]."

The Jews took revenge for the persecutions by poisoning the wells. In July 1321, many were arrested for this crime, tortured and burned at the stake. In Chinon, one hundred and sixty Jews were burned in two days. They dug a pit, set a great fire and threw them in, both men and women.

In Vitry-le-François, forty imprisoned Jews were executed. It is estimated that after these accusations of poisoning, about five thousand Jews paid for this crime with their lives (Heinrich Graetz). For the Jewish historian Leon Poliakov, this was evidently a "new myth" that created the "legend of the poisoning Jews[332]." Be that as it may, the truth is that the Jews of France were sentenced to pay a fine of 150,000 pounds for poisoning the water wells.

In Brabant, anti-Semitic insurgents laid siege to Genappe, home to a large Jewish community. Duke John II vigorously repulsed the rebels, with the support of the pontifical court of Avignon, which approved of the Duke of Brabant's harshness.

In the same region, in Mons, in 1326, a Jewish convert was accused of having defiled an image of the Virgin painted on the wall of an abbey in Cambron. The Jew was arrested and subjected to a harsh interrogation. However, since in the midst of the pains the Jew continued to protest and claim his innocence, he was released. But at that moment, a blacksmith broke through, claiming to have received in a dream the mission to avenge the Virgin, and offered to fight in ordeal against the Jew. An enclosed field

---

[330] Devic-Vaissete, *Histoire générale du Languedoc*, t. IX, Toulouse, 1885, p. 411.
[331] Letter of Edward II, in the archives of the Tower of London, in Georges-Bernard Depping, *Les Juifs dans le Moyen-Âge*, (1823), Éd. Wouters, Brussels, 1844, p. 165.
[332] Léon Poliakov, *Histoire de l'antisémitisme*, Tome I, Point Seuil, 1981, p. 288, 289. Let us recall that, in 1945, Jewish commandos had poisoned the bread in German prison camps. In May 2006, a report by Amnesty International accused Jews of poisoning water tanks in Palestine. But all this is probably nothing more than "legend". On these exactions, read *The Jewish Fanaticism*.

was set up at the gate of Mons and a crowd came to watch the spectacle. The two champions entered the arena, both armed with sticks. The farrier prevailed and the Jew succumbed. They hung his corpse by the feet and lit a fire under him to burn slowly[333].

LX. 1328: The Navarrese Revolt

Navarre had been integrated into the kingdom of France in 1285 through the marriage of Joan of Navarre to Philip the Fair. "In Navarre, which for half a century had belonged to the crown of France, hatred against the Jews burned with a frenzy that had hitherto only been seen in Germany", acknowledged Heinrich Gratez.

The death of Charles IV in February and the consequent power vacuum favoured instability. On 5 March 1328, a Sabbath day, the inhabitants of Estella gave the signal for an attack. The inhabitants of the town, encouraged by the Franciscan Pedro de Oligoyen and seconded by bands of "Jew-killers" from outside, stormed the Jewish quarter, whose inhabitants were massacred. Throughout Navarre, the mob pounced on the Jews and perpetrated a veritable massacre. According to the sources, more than 6,000 Jews were killed. Only the community of Pamplona, the capital of Navarre, seems to have escaped the Christian attacks[334].

Philip VI marked the beginning of the reign of the Valois dynasty in France. As soon as he came to the throne, this new king imposed fines on all the towns and cities involved in these events amounting to 200 pounds in Viana and up to 10,000 pounds for some towns such as Estella. Brother Pedro de Oligoyen was imprisoned under the custody of the bishop.

LXI. Spain, prey to the Jews

The centre of Jewish activity in Europe was at that time in Spain. "The brilliant business which the Jews carried on in the administration of the

---

[333] *Mathœi Analecta*, tome II.

[334] "The repercussions of this fanaticism were felt in Navarre, where the people, following the example of the frenzied French, wanted to take revenge on the usurious Jews, and plundered and massacred them first in Estella, then in Viana, Marcilla and other towns. According to history, ten thousand Hebrews were immolated by this barbarous fury. However, it is doubtful that there were so many Israelites in Navarre. In Aragon the same fury was unleashed, but the king quickly dispersed the rebels and punished some of them. In Tudela, charitable Christians opened their granaries to the persecuted." Georges-Bernard Depping, *Les Juifs dans le Moyen-Âge*, (1823), Éd. Wouters, Brussels, 1844, p. 164.

kingdom's finances, the harshness with which they treated the Christians, and probably also their arrogance, soon attracted the hatred of the grandees, the prelates and the people. A league was formed against these rich and powerful financiers, and they only waited for a favourable opportunity to break out. It was at the Cortes of Madrid in 1309 that this league was formed. They complained about the Hebrew treasurers and spoke of the desirability and even the necessity of removing them from the management of monetary affairs.

"At the Cortes of Burgos in 1315, it was decided, among other rules, that the collectors of the king's taxes and duties should be chosen from among the notable burghers of the various places, and that they could not be nobles, priests or Israelites. The clergy supported the states of the kingdom and decided at the Council of Valladolid in 1322 to enforce the old canons of the Church that excluded Jews from public employment[335]."

But the decisions of the Church councils had little effect. Under the reign of Alfonso XI (1325–1350), "the Jews were in such a prosperous situation that, in comparison with other countries in Europe, this period could be called the Golden Age. Several intelligent Jews, under the modest title of finance ministers, successively exercised their influence on the course of politics. Not only the court, but also the great nobles, surrounded themselves with Jewish advisers and officials. Instead of the humble and servile bearing, and the degrading insignia which the Church decreed for the Jews, the Spanish Jews still wore their heads erect and dressed in gold and silk. Dazzled by the brightness of this favourable state of things, some recognised the fulfilment of the ancient prophecy, "The sceptre shall not depart from Judah," which the Christians had so often employed in their attacks on Judaism."

"It is not surprising that the Spanish Jews rejoiced unduly at the promotion of some of their number to state office. Such prominent public men were, for the most part, a protective shield for the communities against the avaricious and turbulent orders of the nobility, against the stupid credulity and envy of the populace, and the serpentine cunning of the clergy, hidden but always ready to attack the Jews. The Jewish ministers and counsellors in the king's service, dressed in court dress, and bearing at their side the knight's sword, by these very circumstances, without special intercession, disarmed the enemies of their brethren in faith and race. The impoverished nobles, who possessed nothing but their swords, were filled with envy of the rich and learned Jews of the court; but they were obliged to repress their feelings. The masses, guided by appearances, did not dare,

---

[335] Georges-Bernard Depping, *Les Juifs dans le Moyen-Âge*, (1823), Éd. Wouters, Brussels, 1844, p. 222.

as they did in Germany, to maltreat or murder any Jew they came across, as an outcast or a pariah, because they knew that Jews enjoyed great favour at court,[336]", Graetz recounted with satisfaction.

When he came of age, Alfonso XI took the reins of government himself, choosing two Jewish favourites, Don José de Écija and Samuel Ibn Wakar, to advise him.

The full royal name of Don Joseph of Ecija was Yosef ben Ephraim Benevist Halevi. Recommended by his uncle, the king had appointed him treasurer and personal adviser. José de Ecija went out only in his official carriage accompanied by knights, and the great men of Spain often sat at his table to dine.

Don Samuel Ibn Wakar (Samuel Abenhuacar), the other Jewish favourite, was the sovereign's physician, astronomer and astrologer. Although he did not have a political function, he enjoyed great credit at court. Don José and Don Samuel were suspicious of each other, and their rivalry was to have serious consequences for each other.

"Some wealthy Jews, probably relying on the favourable position of their friends at court, engaged in unscrupulous monetary transactions. They extorted at a high rate of interest and mercilessly pursued their dilatory Christian debtors. The king himself encouraged the usury of Jews and Moors, because he profited from it. The complaints of the people against the Jewish usurers became very numerous. The courts of Madrid, Valladolid, and other cities made this point the subject of petitions presented to the king, demanding the abolition of these abuses, and the king was obliged to yield to their entreaties. The spirits of the people, however, were still inflamed against the Jews. The Madrid courts then requested the enforcement of several restrictive laws against the Jews, such as that they should not be allowed to acquire property and that they should not be appointed royal treasurer or tax collectors (1329). This time Alfonso replied that, in general, things should continue as before. Don Samuel Ibn Wakar rose even higher in royal favour. Don Alfonso entrusted him with the exploitation of the revenues derived from the importation of goods from the kingdom of Granada. In addition, he obtained the privilege empowering him to issue the coinage of the kingdom only below the legal title. José de Écija became jealous and offered a higher sum for the right to collect the import taxes of Granada. Just when he thought he had supplanted his rival, the latter dealt him a severe blow. Ibn Wakar succeeded in persuading the king that it would be more advantageous for the people of Castile to take the system of protection to its ultimate

---

[336] Heinrich Graetz, *History of the Jews IV*, Philadelphia, The Jewish Publication Society of America, 1894, p. 75–76.

consequences and ban all imports from the neighbouring Moorish kingdom (1330–1331)".

With the rapid and steady rise of trade, numerous Jews had been attracted to Aragon and prospered there through usury. By royal ordinance, Jews who lent at interest were forbidden to charge more than twenty percent and to accumulate interest and capital. "But a simple prohibition was not enough to prevent the abuses of Jewish speculation. A few years later it was necessary to draw up more detailed statutes *against the avarice of the Jews and the harshness of usury* (this was the statement of the contents of the statutes). From the many wise precautions prescribed therein, in order to prevent the various frauds of usurers, we see that in Aragon their inventive spirit had found, as elsewhere, a way to circumvent the laws. It was said in the preamble that the Christians had almost completely renounced usury, but that the insatiable greed of the Israelite usurers had reached the point of upsetting fortunes, and no longer knew any restraint, especially through the accumulation of interest with capital. It is not the intention of the government to prevent Jews from lending money, especially as these transactions are useful and convenient to Christians; but in order to put a stop to abuses, it is ordered that all Jews who wish to lend money at interest in the cities or in the country shall first swear before a tabelion [notary] that they will conform to the laws[337]."

Throughout the country, the exasperation of the Christians reached paroxysm. "Their champion was a Jew who, as soon as converted to Christianity, became a fanatical persecutor of his brethren. This was the infamous Abner of Burgos, or as he was later called, Alfonso of Valladolid. He was well acquainted with biblical and Talmudic writings, devoted himself to science and practised medicine. His knowledge had destroyed his religious beliefs and had turned him not only against Judaism, but against all religions... Abner decided, when he was almost sixty years old, to adopt Christianity, even if this religion was not able to bring him inner satisfaction, like the one he had abandoned...He became a sacristan of a large church in Valladolid[338]." He was the author of several writings of religious controversy and above all of the great *Libro mostrador de justicia*, an anti-Jewish sum that denounced the daily prayers of the Jews and the curses professed against Christians. "He showed towards his former co-religionists a violent hatred. Familiar with Jewish literature, he pointed out all the passages that could be misleading and multiplied his accusations

---

[337] Georges-Bernard Depping, *Les Juifs dans le Moyen-Âge*, (1823), Éd. Wouters, Brussels, 1844, p. 228–229.
[338] Heinrich Graetz, *History of the Jews IV*, Philadelphia, The Jewish Publication Society of America, 1894, p. 80, 81, 82.

against the Jews and Judaism[339]."

He wrote many writings in which he harshly attacked the religion of his ancestors or defended Christianity against the objections of the Jews. Since he was less fluent in Spanish than in Hebrew, Abner denounced in Hebrew the writings of the Talmud that contained insulting passages against Jesus Christ.

At Abner's request, the king of Castile invited the delegates of the Valladolid community to come and publicly discuss the matter with their enemy. When asked to justify themselves, the representatives of the Valladolid Jews claimed that these imprecations were in no way directed against the founder of Christianity and his followers; but they failed to deceive anyone. On 25 February 1336, as a result of this controversy, King Alfonso decreed that Jews would henceforth be forbidden to recite the incriminated passages.

King Alfonso took as his favourite another man named Gonzalo Martínez (Núñez) de Oviedo, originally a poor knight of Asturias who had been promoted through the patronage of the king's Jewish favourite, Don José de Écija. But far from being grateful to his benefactor, he felt a deep hatred against the one who had thus elevated him, and his hostile feeling extended to all Jews. When he ascended to the position of minister of the royal palace, and later to that of Grand Master of the Order of Alcántara (1337), he revealed his plan to annihilate the Jews. He formally accused Don José and Don Samuel Ibn Wakar of having illicitly enriched themselves in the service of the king. He obtained the king's permission to deal with them as he wished, in order to extort money from them. Gonzalo then ordered both of them, along with two of Ibn Wakar's brothers and eight relatives and their families, to be imprisoned and confiscated their property. Don José de Ecija died in prison and Don Samuel died as a result of the torture to which he was subjected. After this first success he tried to destroy two other Jews who held high positions in the court, Moses Abudiel and Sulaiman Ibn Yaish. He implicated them in an accusation, but all the while pretending to be friendly with them. With their falls from grace, Gonzalo Martinez thought he could carry out his plan against the Castilian Jews without difficulty. Before a campaign against the kingdom of Granada, in which he participated as a general, Gonzalo encouraged the king to imitate Philip the Handsome and deprive the Jews of their wealth and expel them from Castile. In this way, large sums of money would enter the royal treasury. But his advice was refuted by the royal council and even by the most prominent prelates.

---

[339] Heinrich Graetz, *Geschitchte der Juden; Histoire des juifs IV*, Éd. Durlacher, Paris, 1893, p. 267.

Finally, Gonzalo marched to the border against the Moorish army and won a brilliant victory. The Moorish general Abumelik was pierced by an arrow and his defeated army fled in disarray. The glory of the Grand Master of Alcántara then reached its climax.

"He then thought to obtain such a preponderance in Spanish affairs that the king would be obliged to approve all the measures proposed by him. He was, indeed, full of that pride which precedes a fall. But the weak hand of a woman was the cause of his downfall. The beautiful and sprightly Leonora de Guzman, who had so captivated the king with her charms that she was more faithful to him than to his wife, hated the favourite Gonzalo Martinez, and succeeded in making the king believe that she spoke ill of him. Alfonso, anxious to know the truth of the matter, commanded Gonzalo to appear before him in Madrid; the latter, however, disobeyed the royal order. In order to defy the king's wrath, he incited the knights of the Order of Alcántara and the citizens of the towns assigned to his rule to rebel against their sovereign, entered into treacherous negotiations with the king of Portugal and with the enemies of the Crown[340]." Thus, the intervention of a court lady saved the Jews at the last moment and precipitated the fall of Gonzalo Martínez.

In 1339, Alfonso XI summoned all his knights and marched against the rebel. Frightened by the consequences of a civil war, several knights of Alcántara abandoned the cause of their Grand Master and surrendered the towers under his command and custody to the king. Finding himself powerless to continue the fight, Gonzalo begged the king's pardon, but was condemned to death as a traitor and burned alive. The Jewish communities of Castile then celebrated the day of his death as a day of liberation. King Alfonso again treated the Jews with benevolence and gave Moisés Abudiel a high position at court.

LXII. The German Judenschlaeger, 1336–1338

A new revolt against the Jewish oppressor broke out in Germany. Emperor Ludwig of Bavaria was rather pro-Jewish, while his rival, the Austrian Frederick the Fair, was much more hostile, ordering his states to search for and destroy copies of the Talmud and insisting, along with other princes, that the pope bring the Jews to heel.

Faced with the imminent danger, the Jews of Rome sent a delegate to the court of the pope in Avignon to defend their cause and another to King Robert of Naples, the feudal lord of Rome who protected the Jews. The

---

[340] Heinrich Graetz, *History of the Jews IV*, Philadelphia, The Jewish Publication Society of America, 1894, p. 82–85.

Jewish delegate managed to calm the anger of the pope and his sister "thanks to a gift of 20,000 ducats", wrote Gratez. The danger was thus averted.

From 1236, the Jews of the empire were no longer free men but "servants of the imperial chamber". Ludwig of Bavaria imposed a new tax on them: the gold denarius. Every Jew or Jewess in the Germanic Empire over the age of twelve, who had twenty guilders at his or her disposal, had to pay an annual tax of one guilder. In his opinion, this tax was justified by the fact that the Jews had been paying since the time of Vespasian and Titus an annual tax to the Roman emperors of whom the Germanic Caesars claimed to be the legitimate and direct heirs.

Under the reign of Emperor Ludwig, the Jews suffered the consequences of the unrest of the civil war then raging in Germany. For two consecutive years (1336–1338), bands of peasants and bandits, calling themselves "Jew-killers", devastated the communities of southern Germany.

At the head of these *Judenschlaeger* were two members of the nobility and an Alsatian innkeeper called Cimberlin, the "king of the poor". These ringleaders called themselves *Armleder*, "leather arm", because of the leather bandages they wore wrapped around their arms. For more than two years, they roamed the territories between Alsace and Austria, killing Jews and destroying all their property. Armed with pitchforks, pikes and flails, some five thousand peasants took revenge for all the humiliations they had suffered.

In Alsace, the first places they entered, Roufiach and Ensisheim, they felt the pent-up rage of the common people who had been despised for too long. Nearly 1,500 Jews were massacred. The surviving Jews took refuge in the walled city of Colmar. The troops of the rebels soon arrived under the walls and demanded the surrender of their victims. When the magistrates refused, the insurgent peasants scattered throughout the country and committed all sorts of disorders.

The emperor's protection was either ineffective or came too late. The *Judenschlaeger* dispersed, or at least were contained by the arrival of Emperor Ludwig, but after his departure, the Judenschlaeger regrouped and resumed their activities. The bishop tried to form a league of lords and magistrates to break the resistance. In the end, the armed force succeeded in capturing one of the *Armleder* and the emperor ordered his beheading.

Several similar massacres took place at that time in Bavaria after a new case of desecration of hosts. The town councillors of Deckendorf themselves had set the date for the insurrection. On 30 September 1337, when the church bell gave the signal, the knight Hartmann von Deggenburg, followed by several horsemen, rode into Deckendorf and overwhelmed the Jews by surprise. The Jews were plundered, massacred and their corpses burned. The inhabitants built a church on the site dedicated to the Holy Sepulchre, which became a place of pilgrimage. From Deckendorf, unrest spread throughout Bavaria and into Bohemia, Moravia and Austria. Thousands of Jews succumbed irretrievably.

The emperor, who at the time was at great odds with the pope and the king of France, had turned a blind eye. His relative Henry, Duke of Bavaria and the Palatinate, even congratulated the inhabitants of Deckendorf for liquidating the Jews and allowed them to publicly enjoy all that had been taken from them.

The Jews, protected by the popes, had always had the possibility of taking refuge in their States. If they were never persecuted in Rome or Avignon, it was because they were never allowed to oppress the people, engage in illicit trafficking, mock religion and foment heresy, as was often the case in the dominions of the temporal lords.

In the same year, a council meeting at Avignon adopted this resolution, among many others: "Every Christian must reject and despise the fetid services of the Jews. The Jews elevate themselves too far above the servile condition which is their due".

LXIII. 1348: The Black Death

The Black Death arrived from the East in the port of Marseilles on ships of international Jewish merchants[341]. From 1348 to 1352, the disease decimated the population for four years with unprecedented virulence, killing a quarter of Europe's population, some twenty-five million individuals. The plague also affected the Jews, although apparently, as Graetz wrote, "they died in smaller numbers", which gave rise to a legitimate distrust among the population. Moreover, the Jews had already poisoned the water wells twenty years earlier to take revenge on the crusader Shepherds.

The people, persuaded that the Jews had caused the plague out of hatred for the Christians, went on a campaign of massacres which the authorities were barely able to suppress.

In mid-May, some Jews were lynched. After this, the movement spread to Catalonia and Aragon. In Barcelona, the people had killed twenty Jews and ransacked several houses. A few days later, the same scenes were repeated in Cervera. Eighteen Jews died, the rest fled. Throughout northern Spain, Jewish communities took cover in their neighbourhoods.

At the beginning of July, Pope Clement VI promulgated a bull

---

[341]Durante, *Histoire de Nice*, III, page 3, in Jacques Decourcelles, *La Condition des Juifs de Nice aux XVII et XVIII siècles*, Paris, 1923, p. 12.

forbidding, on pain of excommunication, the killing of Jews without a condemnation by ordinary justice, and also forbidding them to be baptised by force or to have their goods and property stolen. This bull may have had some effect in southern France near the pope's residence in Avignon, but it had none in the rest of Christendom.

The area around Lake Geneva also became the scene of bloody riots. On the orders of Duke Amadeus of Savoy, several Jews, accused of poisoning, were imprisoned in Chillon, Thonon and Chatel. In Chillon, the accused were subjected to torture. One of these Jews, surnamed Aquet, declared that he had poisoned several wells in Venice, Apulia, Calabria and Toulouse. These statements were recorded by the clerks in their minutes and countersigned by the judges. After these confessions, they proceeded to burn not only the accused but also all the Jews in the city. Pope Clement VI issued a new bull, but it was no longer obeyed.

The massacres took on a savage character, especially in the Holy Roman Empire. In vain, the new Emperor Charles IV tried to intervene.

Graetz wrote here: "The Germans did not commit their terrible atrocities against the Jews merely for the sake of plunder... Sheer stupidity led them to believe that the Jews had poisoned the wells and rivers. The councils of several cities ordered that springs and wells be stopped up, so that the citizens would not be poisoned, and had to drink rainwater or melted snow[342]."

Towards the end of 1348, Jews were expelled from all towns on the upper Rhine. They were considered outside the law and were either expelled or driven straight to the stake. Once expelled from the towns, they were rounded up and beaten to a pulp in the countryside by the peasants.

In Basel they suffered the ordeal. Crammed onto an island in the Rhine, they were locked up in a specially built house and burned alive. After this summary expulsion, the council decided that for two centuries no Jews would be allowed to settle in the city. A few days later, it was the turn of the Jews of Freiburg.

The verses of William of Machaut (1310–1377), the most famous French poet of that century, probably reflect quite well the feelings of the French people at that time. Here is a passage from his *Judgement of the King of Navarre*[343] (1349):

Then came a patulea

---

[342] Heinrich Graetz, *History of the Jews IV*, Philadelphia, The Jewish Publication Society of America, 1894, p. 106. It is known, however, that in 1945 groups of Jewish "Avengers" had planned to poison the water of several cities such as Munich, Nuremberg and Hamburg (see *Jewish Fanaticism*, 2007).

[343] *Jugement du roi de Navarre*, in Marie-France Rouart, *L'Antisémitisme dans la littérature populaire*, Berg International, p. 63.

> *False, treacherous and renegade*
> *It was Judea the infamous*
> *The evil one, the disloyal one*
> *How well he hates and loves everything bad,*
> *Who donated so much gold and silver*
> *And he promised Christian people*
> *What wells, rivers and springs*
> *Clear and serene*
> *In so many places they poisoned*

In the Delphinate, the sovereign was also an accomplice of the anti-Jewish insurgents: while the people rushed upon the Israelites and massacred them, the lord arrested the others in order to condemn them and seize their property[344]. "The Delphic archives contain accounts of the cost of executing those whom the Delphic judges had found guilty. The proceedings against the Jews of Vizille lasted ten days and cost twenty-seven francs seventeen centimes and one denarius. Mention is made in these accounts of a master Girard who was cut in two and tied to the gallows after being accused of stealing a Christian child and handing it over to the Jews. At Yeynes, in the country of Gap, thirteen individuals of this nation were massacred; those of Sam Saturninus met the same fate a few days later[345]."

In Rouffach, a large number of Jews were burned in a valley that has since retained the name "valley of the Jews". In Strasbourg, pots full of poison were found in the wells. The magistrates of the city persisted in their benevolent sentiments towards the Jews, but the burgomaster had to yield quickly to the demands of the mob. The labouring corporations assembled in the cathedral square, banners raised at their heads, and did not separate until they had compelled Wintertur and his colleagues to resign their offices. Then the scenes of revenge began. On 14 February 1349, two thousand Jews were taken to prison and then dragged to their cemetery where several hundred were burned in a large barrack[346]. On the site of the cemetery the prefecture house was built and the synagogue was demolished and replaced by a chapel. The new council forbade Jews to reside in Strasbourg for a century and the immense wealth of the Jews was confiscated. The only ones who managed to save themselves were those who converted to Christianity.

In many towns and cities, magistrates seized treasures and stones from

---

[344] Valbonais, *Histoire du Dauphiné*, tome II
[345] Fragment of *Memorabilia Humberti*, in Georges-Bernard Depping, *Les Juifs dans le Moyen-Âge*, (1823), Éd. Wouters, Brussels, 1844, p. 170.
[346] Chronicle of Koenigshoven, in Georges-Bernard Depping, *Les Juifs dans le Moyen-Âge*, (1823), Éd. Wouters, Brussels, 1844, p. 168.

Jewish houses to embellish their own cities[347].

"In Mulhouse, in Alsace, where already in 1290 the German emperor had acquitted the inhabitants guilty of violence and condoned them two hundred pounds of silver owed to the Jews, an imperial charter again acquitted the burghers after the massacres of 1348 and granted them the houses and property of the victims[348]."

"Equally cruel scenes took place in Spire, Worms, Oppenheim and Mainz, where many Jews committed suicide after burying their treasures in order to leave nothing to their persecutors. Their corpses were placed in barrels and rolled down the Rhine. The magistrates forbade the search of the victims' treasures, probably to prevent the sight of gold and silver from rekindling the murderous ardor in people's hearts. Some imperial officials in Alsace dared to defy the fanaticism of the mob: Count Palatine Rupert, disregarding the clamour of the wild crowd, took in and protected the Jews who had escaped from Spire and Worms. In Frankfurt, where the authorities were not so firm, the looting of Jewish houses resulted in a fire that destroyed a quarter of the city. In Germany, other exalts appeared: the flagellants, who went in groups from town to town crying penance and frightening the people, inspiring a new terror in the Jews. Thus, in Mainz, a troop of flagellants stirred up the populace, who then attacked the Jews of the city and chased them into their homes, where the unfortunate ones were all burned[349]."

The persecution following the Black Death epidemic reached Cologne, where Jews were particularly numerous after the expulsions of Jews from neighbouring regions. They were attacked by the Christians on the same day that their co-religionists in Mainz succumbed. They were all massacred.

These massacres spread from town to town throughout Germany, from the Alps to the North Sea. The contagion reached Bavaria and Swabia, where the inhabitants of Memmingen obtained letters from the emperor absolving them of any responsibility for the massacres they had committed on the Jews[350]. A few years earlier, in 1344, the Jews of Memmingen had been powerful enough to get the bishop to censure the burghers, probably because of their debts. They paid dearly for this imprudence when the general riot against the Israelite nation broke out[351].

---

[347] Alberti Argent. Chronicle. P. 149, in Georges-Bernard Depping, *Les Juifs dans le Moyen-Âge*, (1823), Éd. Wouters, Brussels, 1844, p. 169.

[348] Graf, *Histoire de Mulhouse*, tome I, chap. VII, in Georges-Bernard Depping, *Les Juifs dans le Moyen-Âge*, (1823), Éd. Wouters, Brussels, 1844, p. 170.

[349] Georges-Bernard Depping, *Les Juifs dans le Moyen-Âge*, (1823), Éd. Wouters, Brussels, 1844, p. 169.

[350] Schelhorn, *Beytræge zur Erlœuterung der Geschichte*. Memmingen, 1774.

[351] Georges-Bernard Depping, *Les Juifs dans le Moyen-Âge*, (1823), Éd. Wouters,

Augsburg, Würzburg and Munich also killed their Jews. "The Jews of Nuremberg, thanks to their extensive trade, possessed great wealth and houses, and were therefore particularly hated by the Christians," reported Heinrich Graetz. Emperor Charles IV then warned the city council that they would be held responsible for any ill-treatment inflicted on them. Eventually, their fate was fulfilled. At a place later called *Judenbühle* (Jews' Hill), the Christians erected a mound, and all those who had not been able to flee were burned on a large bonfire.

In Regensburg, too, where the oldest community in southern Germany was located, the common people demanded the death or at least the expulsion of the Jews. They were saved by the Council and the gentry, who solemnly begged the burgomaster Bertold Egoltspecht to defend them against all aggression.

In Brussels, all the Jews of the city, at least five hundred, were massacred by the mob. In Brabant it was not a sudden and anecdotal accession of fury: during the whole epidemic, that is to say for about two years, Jews and lepers were continuously executed. When the popular fury was subsiding, the flagellants appeared again to revive it.

There were, however, several countries where the Jews did not suffer too much. Louis, the king of Hungary, had expelled them from his states, accused of being impious, but not of being poisoners.

In Poland, where the plague also ravaged the country, the Jews were not mistreated thanks to the protection of King Casimir the Great, who was always friendly to the Jews. It must be said that this king had fallen for the charms of a Jewess named Esterka, his mistress. In 1354, at the request of some influential Jews, Casimir confirmed the charter of Kalisz, enacted in the previous century, which granted the Jews exorbitant privileges. The Jews took refuge en masse in the Polish kingdom, which then began a long decline until its dismemberment by its neighbours at the end of the 18th century.

In November 1355, a sort of constitution of the Germanic Empire was promulgated at the Diet of Nuremberg under the name of the Golden Bull. The monarch granted the seven great Electors of the Empire certain state powers, such as the right to acquire metal mines and salt mines, as well as the right to own freehold Jews, i.e. to have an additional source of income. In practice, therefore, the Jews were at once rejected and desired, despised and desired by the princes and nobility.

"Thus the Jews were at once repelled and attracted, shunned and courted, outlawed and flattered. They knew very well that they were not tolerated for their own sake, but only for the advantages they offered to the

---

Brussels, 1844, p. 171.

authorities. How could they not be expected to devote themselves to making money, the only means by which they could prolong their miserable existence[352]?"

LXIV. *The late awakening of John the Good*

King John II, known as John the Good, was King of France from 1350 to 1364. He had been taken prisoner by the English in 1356 at the Battle of Poitiers. During his captivity, the Jews had skilfully negotiated their readmission to the kingdom with his dauphin, the future Charles V, obtaining privileges that were confirmed after King John's return.

By the edict of March 1360, the Jews were allowed to return to France on payment of an annuity and for a limited period of twenty years. They then obtained considerable commercial privileges: "Their trade enjoyed maximum protection. They were allowed to charge 80% interest (4 denarii per pound) on loans[353]".

The Jewish banker Manassé de Vesoul had conducted this negotiation with zeal and great skill. He was entrusted with the collection of the annual taxes imposed on his co-religionists. To defend them against the arbitrariness of judges and officials, a Jewish court was authorised to exercise civil and criminal jurisdiction over them. These privileges attracted many Jews to France.

"They probably owed these advantages to a Jewish banker of the court, Manassé de Vesoul, who was appointed their commissioner, and to whom the government repaid by this condescension to his nation the services he rendered during the treasury shortage.

"Here are the articles of the treaty concluded between the Israelite banker and the royal government[354]: "The king allows the Jews to enter the kingdom, to remain in it for twenty years, to acquire houses, to trade and to intermediate, to practice the liberal and mechanical arts, to lend money at interest, all this without hindrance from the authorities of the kingdom and from the lords, to be under royal protection and to have no other judges than the royal commissioner, the count of Étampes. Each Jew shall pay upon entering the kingdom fourteen guilders for himself and his wife, and one guilder two *gros tournois*[355] for each of his children and his people. In

---

[352] Heinrich Graetz, *History of the Jews IV*, Philadelphia, The Jewish Publication Society of America, 1894, p. 128.

[353] Heinrich Graetz, *History of the Jews IV*, Philadelphia, The Jewish Publication Society of America, 1894, p. 130.

[354] See the various Ordinances in volume III of the Ordinances of the Kings of France, and volume V of the Compilation of Ancient French Laws, Paris, 1824.

[355] After the fall of the Roman Empire, the various kingdoms that were established more

addition, each Jew shall pay seven guilders of capitation per year for himself and his wife, and one guilder for each of his sons and his people. In return for this payment, they shall be free from all other taxes of any kind, and shall not be subject to any servitude or manorial levy. They shall have a protector or guardian, to whom the king appoints the Count of Etampes, prince of the blood; they shall be answerable only to him or to the king, and no other judge in the kingdom may prosecute them in case of crime; even so, the king's procurators shall not try them until the cases against them have been thoroughly investigated. In case of simple offences, they shall be released on bail provided by Jews or Christians. No Jew may be prosecuted for any offence or crime committed before his return to the kingdom.

"Should any of them become unworthy to remain in the community, two rabbis, assisted by four other Jews appointed for the purpose, may banish him from the kingdom; but in this case the king shall confiscate his property and receive from the two rabbis the sum of one hundred florins. Those who lend money to Christians in exchange for a pledge may only charge four denarii a week interest on each pound. Whatever they have overcharged will be returned to the debtors. The authorities shall assist them in collecting their debts; they may lend on all kinds of bonds and pledges, except church vessels and farm implements...They may not be compelled to attend the sermons of the Christians, nor to fight in an enclosed field; their books may not be seized. All ordinances contrary to these liberties are abolished; the old privileges will be confirmed whenever they wish".

"It is evident that the drafting of this treaty had been recommended by the Jews themselves, for no doubt the king's government would not have put together by itself and with such care all the guarantees likely to prevent past injustices...

"The privileges granted were exorbitant and heralded new violence. Philip Augustus had fixed an interest rate of two denarii per week, which was already excessive. The rate they were now allowed was twice as high.

"It is clear that under King John it was the Jews who raised the rate to four denarii, that is, almost eighty per cent per annum... But whatever the scarcity of money, it must be admitted that the legal rate fixed by the

---

or less adopted the *denarius/solidus/librae* system. In the Middle Ages, the denarius was equivalent to 1/240 of a pound. However, this rate underwent numerous modifications under the action of the various royal monetary reforms. In France, the *tournois pound* was the ancient coin of account from the reign of Saint Louis until 1795. Six *double tournois* formed a *gros tournois*. Twenty *gros tournois* made a *livre tournois*. In the time of Saint Louis the *livre tournois* contained 80.88 grams of fine silver. The Florentine florin was the gold coin of reference until the 15th century.

ordinance of 1361 was intolerable, and that the king was either very unfortunate or very short-sighted in allowing himself to be surprised in this way by the greed of the Jewish usurers who were quite sure of being able to compensate in a short time at the expense of the king's subjects for the capitation they had undertaken to pay to the Treasury. If what they contributed in capital to the kingdom was to be so profitable as to repay them eighty per cent in the first year, what abundant harvest could they expect during the twenty years they were to remain in France?"

This is the main reason why the Jews were always so insistent on remaining among the Christians, despite all the setbacks and punishments they regularly suffered over time.

"All the money of the French was to be gobbled up in the Jews' safes, and their stay was to cost the kingdom far more than the captivity of the king[356]."

The Jews also stipulated in the treaty the right to own houses, but without ever mentioning farmland. This is because for them the essential point was the right to lend money, not to work the land. Jewish historians or philo-Semitic historians who defend the idea that Jews in the Middle Ages practised usury because they were forced to do so are either ignorant or dishonest. Readers of our previous books know perfectly well where they stand on this subject.

And what was bound to happen happened once again: complaints against the usurers were raised from all parts of the kingdom. The king, alerted by the notables of the great cities, "declared by an ordinance issued at Rheims, in October 1363, that the great abuses committed by the Jews in respect of the privileges they had obtained obliged him to abolish them; he accordingly compelled them to wear on their robes a red and white buckler the size of the royal seal and, notwithstanding all the prerogatives previously granted, he subjected them to the authority of the ordinary courts of the territories where they lived. He also declared null and void the obligations for which the Christians had pawned their bodies to the Jews[357]." This clearly shows that after stripping their debtors of the property they owned, the Jewish usurers used to demand physical servitude from the people who owed them money. For "it is certain that the favourable

---

[356] Georges-Bernard Depping, *Les Juifs dans le Moyen-Âge*, (1823), Éd. Wouters, Brussels, 1844, p. 176–178. G. B. Depping expresses several times in his work his compassion towards the Jews, but acknowledges in this case that the interest rates demanded were excessive.

[357] Edict of the kings, October 1363, in volume IV of the Ordinances of the kings of France, and in volume V of the General Compilation of Ancient French Laws, in Georges-Bernard Depping, *Les Juifs dans le Moyen-Âge*, (1823), Éd. Wouters, Brussels, 1844, p. 179–180.

auspices under which they had entered France and the extraordinary privileges granted to them must have led them to believe that everything was permitted to them and that nothing would prevent their greedy speculation. The obligation to wear the buckler on their clothing was renewed shortly afterwards at the assembly of the States General held at Amiens[358]." From 1215 to 1370, twelve councils and nine royal ordinances prescribed Jews to wear the buckler, proof that they were continually trying to avoid it.

LXV. The death of Blanca de Borbón

Alfonso XI of Castile was married to Maria of Portugal, who had borne him a son named Pedro. But the king had neglected his wife and legitimate son in favour of his mistress, the beautiful Leonora de Guzmán. This situation aroused a deep resentment in Pedro I and his mother, who, after the king's death in 1350 (from the Black Death during the siege of Algeciras), wanted to take revenge on the late king's bastards, so that Pedro soon came to be nicknamed "the Cruel".

Don Pedro, son and successor of Alfonso XI, ascended the throne at the age of 15. During his reign, the Jews enjoyed a very great influence in the affairs of Castile. So much so that "for prominent Jews the king's favour was unlimited. Don Juan Alfonso de Alburquerque, their guardian and all-powerful minister, recommended for the post of finance minister a Jew who had rendered him great services, and the king appointed Don Samuel ben Meir Allavi (or Ha-Levi), a member of Toledo's leading family, the Abulafia-Halevis, to a government post of trust, thus defying the decision of the courts that Jews were no longer eligible for such functions. Samuel Abulafia became not only chief treasurer (Tesorero Mayor), but also personal (private) adviser to the king, who had a voice in all important consultations and decisions...Another prominent Jew who figured in Don Pedro's court was Abraham Ibn-Zarzal, the king's physician and astrologer. Don Pedro was, in fact, so surrounded by Jews that his enemies reproached his court for being Jewish. It is not known whether his protection of his Jewish subjects was due to the influence of these Jewish favourites or to his own impulses[359]", Heinrich Graetz recounted. In fact, the court of Peter

---

[358]Edict or Ordinance of 5 December 1363, in Volume III of the Ordinances of the Kings of France, and Volume V of the Compilation of Ancient French Laws, in Georges-Bernard Depping, *Les Juifs dans le Moyen-Âge*, (1823), Éd. Wouters, Brussels, 1844, p. 180.
[359] Heinrich Graetz, *History of the Jews IV*, Philadelphia, The Jewish Publication Society of America, 1894, p. 115–116.

I was contemptuously called a Jewish court by the Spaniards.

In 1352, in order to seal a strategic alliance, Peter decided to take as his wife Blanche de Bourbon, sister of Jeanne de Bourbon, the queen consort of France (wife of Charles V).

There were then great and lively dissensions among the courtiers, some declaring themselves in favour of the princess of Bourbon and others in favour of the king's mistress, Maria de Padilla. Samuel, and with him all the Jews of Spain, had sided with Maria de Padilla. They had learned that Blanca took a dim view of the high position of the Jews at court and had publicly declared her intention to expel them.

In July 1353, Peter the Cruel married Blanche of Bourbon, but on the pretext of delaying payment of the dowry, he abandoned his young wife shortly afterwards, imprisoning her to join her lover, who had already given him a daughter. The failure of this marriage immediately led to the break-up of the alliance with the King of France. Don Pedro then emancipated himself from his mother's guardianship by sending his mother into exile, to Evora in his native Portugal, before ordering her poisoning. Then, in 1358–1359, he got rid of all his enemies, starting with his three half-brothers. He then instigated the assassination of his aunt Leonor of Castile and his sister-in-law Juana Nuñez de Lara (wife of another of his half-brothers). Castile was then bloodied by civil war. Enrique de Trastámara, another of Don Pedro's half-brothers, took the lead in the revolt.

At the court of Don Pedro, Samuel Ha-Levi now enjoyed considerable power. His wealth was immense and he favoured the building of many synagogues, wrote Graetz, so that "many Jews, unwavering in their hopes, saw the high status of Samuel and other Jewish favourites as clear evidence that the Messianic times were at hand[360]."

Don Pedro was offended and had the entire fortune of Samuel and his family confiscated. The royal treasury thus recovered 230,900 doubloons[361], 4,000 silver marks, 125 boxes of precious fabrics and 180 slaves. "According to some authors, an extraordinary amount of gold and silver was found buried under Samuel's house. Don Pedro ordered his former favourite to be imprisoned in Toledo and tortured to force him to reveal the whereabouts of his treasures. But Samuel stood firm, revealed nothing and succumbed under torture…Samuel's death did not affect the friendly relations between the king and the Jews. The Jews remained loyal to him and he continued to confer important distinctions on members of the

---

[360]Heinrich Graetz, *Geschitchte der Juden; Histoire des juifs IV,* Éd. Durlacher, Paris, 1893, p. 293.
[361]Before 1350, Alfonso XI of Castile minted the first gold coins imitating the Almohad gold dinars, known locally as *doubloons* or *doubloons,* and in French as *"alfonsinos".* They weighed each 4.6 g of 23¾ carat gold (NdT).

community[362]," Graetz acknowledged. It is therefore not without reason that Henry of Trastamara continually referred to Peter as "the king of the Jews".

In 1361, Pedro had his first wife Blanca de Borbón, whom he had previously imprisoned, murdered. According to Graetz, "a story was concocted that a Jew had administered poison to the queen on the king's orders, because she had insisted on the expulsion of the Jews from Spain. A French romance perpetuated this legend[363]."

This legend was, however, a proven historical fact that decided the King of France to send the famous Constable Beltrán Duguesclín (Bertrand Du Guesclin) and his great companies to Spain to lend a hand to Henry of Trastámara. The year was 1365. The detailed account can be found in the *"Collection complète des Mémoires relatifs à l'Histoire de France"* (Complete *Collection of Memoirs on the History of France*)[364]. Volume IV, published in 1819 by Jean Petitot, is devoted to the memoirs of the Constable of France and Castile Beltran Duguesclin. It is a reprint of a text by Jacques Le Febvre, "provost and theologian of Arras, former chaplain and preacher to the Queen", published in 1692 in Douai and entitled: *"Anciens Memoires du quatorzième siècle, depuis peu découverts, où l'on apprendra les aventures les plus surprenantes et les circonstances les plus curieuses de la vie du fameux Bertrand Du Guesclin, connétable de France."*(*"Ancient Memoirs of the fourteenth century, recently discovered, in which we will learn the most surprising adventures and the most curious circumstances of the life of the famous Beltran Duguesclin, Constable of France"*).

In this edition, Jean Petitot set out in detail the historiography concerning Beltran Duguesclin, and explained his preference for the work of Le Febvre, which was an imitation of the old medieval chronicles. Le Febvre had preserved the old language of Duguesclin's time. "I thought," he wrote, "that the grace of fourteenth-century patois, which I use in some parts of my book, but with great reserve and discretion, would serve to entertain my reader, and even delight his spirit, thus showing him the lively and ingenuous features conveyed by its energy."

Jean Petitot added: "We have therefore decided to reproduce the

---

[362] Heinrich Graetz, *History of the Jews IV*, Philadelphia, The Jewish Publication Society of America, 1894, p. 121.
[363] Heinrich Graetz, *History of the Jews IV*, Philadelphia, The Jewish Publication Society of America, 1894, p. 122, andHistoire *des juifs IV*, Éd. Durlacher, Paris, 1893, p. 295.
[364]*Collection complète des Mémoires relatifs à l'Histoire de France depuis le règne de Philippe-Auguste jusqu'au commencement du XVIIe siècle*, tome IV, Paris, Foucault, librairie, 1819.

original text by Le Febvre, whose own carelessness is rather reminiscent of the tone and manners of fourteenth-century authors".

Chapter XIV was entitled *"De l'origine de la guerre qui se fit en Espagne entre le roi Pierre, dit le Cruel, et son frère naturel Henry, comte de Tristemarre"* (*"On the origin of the war that took place in Spain between King Peter, called the Cruel, and his natural brother Henry, Count of Trastamara"*).

"Beltran was always looking for new opportunities to demonstrate his courage and bravery, and he found a place to satisfy his warlike inclination in Spain, where the people were divided, some on the side of King Peter and others on the side of Henry, Count of Trastamara. Beltran supported the latter's quarrel, as we shall see below. The cause of this dispute was the misconduct and cruelty of Pedro, accused of two enormous injustices. The first was his mistreatment of Queen Blanche of Bourbon, his wife and sister of the Queen of France. The indignities he inflicted on this princess scandalised all his subjects, who could not but be indignant at all the cruelties he inflicted on her, for a lady whose sweetness, birth and beauty should have been the three ties most capable of binding him closely to her. But the ardent love he felt for Maria de Padilla, who had charmed him with a philter she had made him take, smothered in his heart all the tenderness he should naturally feel for so accomplished a Queen. This concubine had acquired such ascendancy over his spirit that she dominated him absolutely and made him commit a thousand affronts to his own wife, whom he considered his rival.

"The other injustice of which this King was accused was that he had no dealings with the Christians, whose customs and religion he greatly disliked. The Jews were the only confidants of all his secrets; he lent them his whole ear, and told them all that was most hidden in his heart. With regard to all others, he kept a profound dissimulation, making himself not only impenetrable to all the lords of his Court, to whom he could not deny access, but also impracticable in matters which could not be prevented from being communicated to him by the eminence of his character and the royal authority he held in his hands. Even his closest relatives could not have the key to his heart, so secretive and mysterious was he in everything. This astonishing behaviour alienated all spirits, and earned him the dislike of all his subjects, who only wished for a revolution, in the hope of seeing matters turned round.

"This prince, who was rightly called Peter the Cruel, carried so far the inhumanity he felt for his wife, that he not only deprived her of her liberty, confining her in prison, but also made an attempt on her life, by a poison which he had her administer, but from which she was able to prevent herself by vomiting, because, knowing the evil nature of this prince and the jealousy of his concubine, she was always on her guard. All these outrages

did not make her lose the respect and consideration she should have for him, promising herself that God would touch his heart and disabuse his eyes to bring him out of his blindness.

"As Pierre made himself odious, so Henry, his supposed natural brother, made himself loved. It seemed that the Crown owed more to him than to this barbarous king, for he had found the secret of winning all hearts with his alluring airs, and no one left his presence but was well satisfied with the welcome he had received, for such was his gift for pleasing everybody. All hearts turned towards him. The pride of the former made people adore the gentleness of the latter, and the Catholic religion, of which he made a high and sincere profession, made Peter's inclination for the superstition of the Jews odious. They wished therefore to see him on the throne in place of the latter, whose conduct they could no longer endure.

"Henry spoke to King Peter of his conduct, hoping to amend it, which only made him still more sour...The departure of this prince was very unadvisedly seconded by a Jew named James, who happened to be there at the time; wishing to flatter Peter and woo him at Henry's expense, he had the audacity to tell the latter that it was very bold to pretend to lecture the wisest king in the land, and that the best thing he could do in future would be never to appear before him again; But Henry soon made him swallow these words at the cost of his own life; for after reproaching him for the pernicious counsels he lavished on Peter, and the infamy of his nation, he thrust his dagger through his heart, and cast him dead to the ground. The King, much surprised and indignant at this attack committed in his presence, wished to avenge the Jew's death on his brother by another murder, drawing a knife from its sheath to kill him; but he was prevented by a knight who seized him by the arm as he was about to strike the blow.

"Henry escaped at the same instant, and no sooner had he descended the steps than he told his men to saddle their horses, that he might unceasingly save his life by running away. Peter had four men holding him, cursing those who held him a thousand times, and reproaching them for being accomplices of that bastard, whom he would never forgive for the blood he had just shed. No matter how much he was told that it was only the death of a Jew, whose race had attracted upon itself the curse of God, being a nation that had become the horror and execration of men, for the deicide it had committed in the person of the Saviour: but all this oil that was thrown on the fire rekindled it with such force, that Peter had this poor gentleman hanged at once, who had prevented him from killing Henry."

Chapter XV of the account by the good Jacques Le Febvre was entitled *"De la mort tragique de la reine Blanche de Bourbon, commandée par Pierre le Cruel, son propre mari"* ("Of the *tragic death of Queen Blanche de Bourbon, ordered by Peter the Cruel, her own husband"*).

"This barbarous king had conceived such a deadly aversion to Blanca de Bourbon, his wife, that he had arranged everything to undertake it against her life. The poison he used to get rid of her had no effect on her, because, knowing the design to put her to death, she took all the necessary precautions to protect herself from such poisoning. Maria de Padilla, Pedro's mistress, put it in the prince's mind to remove her entirely from the Court, and to settle her in some province, so that she might never be seen, and that this absence, without hope of return, might have the same effect as her death. Peter, madly in love with this concubine, followed her advice. He confined this princess in the province farthest from the Court, and gave her some lands to maintain her status as Queen, not daring to anger his people further against him if he dared to reduce her publicly to a destitute condition. This dominion, which Blanca had received, earned her the due homage of all the vassals who depended on her lordship.

"A wealthy Jew had land within the Queen's domain. He came to her Court to perform, like the rest, his duty as a subject to her, and as at that time it was customary to kiss the cheek of the sovereign out of respect, to mark the zeal and affection that one would have all one's life in his service, this Jew approached the Queen to salute her as his mistress and mistress; she could not resist receiving from him this token of servitude as her subject; but after he had left her chamber, she showed her horror at this ridiculous ceremony, reproaching her servants for the little care they had taken to prevent this villain from approaching her, and immediately caused hot water to be brought to wash her mouth and face, and cleanse, as it were, the stains which the Jew's kiss had left upon them. Her indignation did not stop there, for as she was sovereign, she wished to punish with the ultimate torture the temerity he had shown in thus emancipating himself; and in her first angry reaction she wanted him to be hanged. When the Jew was told that he had been condemned by the Queen, and that he was wanted to be tied to the gallows by her order, he immediately fled, and hastened to complain to King Peter of Blanche's purpose to have him put to death, making it a capital offence for him to perform a ceremonial duty which he had taken the liberty of performing. The King took him under his protection, beseeching him to fear nothing in this respect, and telling him that he was well aware that this princess, who had a hatred and aversion for all persons whom he considered, would not hesitate to make an attempt on his own life also when she found occasion; that she should therefore be warned; though he would be only too glad to get rid of her by secret means, to keep up appearances, and without giving her advantage over him.

"The Jew, burning with a desire for revenge, assured him that nothing could be easier than to dispatch her without a single blow or wound appearing on her body. Peter greatly appreciated this solution and declared that whoever could pull out this thorn would do him a great favour. He therefore allowed the Jew to carry out the matter as he had planned, *without making any fuss. This vindictive man, who was dying to satisfy his resentment against this princess, was delighted to have received this barbarous order from Peter. He assembled many of his nation to assist him in carrying out the coup, and, walking through the night, went with them all to the Queen's apartments. He penetrated to her chamber, and knocking at the door at such an unseasonable hour, one of her Majesty's wives refused to open, and, astonished at the noise, said through the keyhole that it was not the right time to speak to her mistress, and asked what was the object of a visit made so late and so unseasonably. To make himself open, the Jew replied that he had very pleasant news to give the Queen, for her husband, to show that he wished to be completely reconciled to her, was coming to lie with her Majesty. The maid ran at once with joy to announce to her mistress this unexpected adventure, which was to please her very much, congratulating her beforehand that the King was returning her heart and wished to do her more justice in future than he had done her. The Queen, who saw the danger that threatened her, immediately began to weep, knowing that she had yet but few hours to live, for she foresaw that the Jews, who hated her mortally, would not have come to her chamber in such numbers and at such an improper hour without having some bloody order against her which they were ready to execute. When the maid became aware of her mistress's sorrows and misfortunes, she began to cry aloud, and, shedding torrents of tears, said she would not open the door unless Her Majesty absolutely commanded her to do so. The Queen beckoned her not to struggle any longer with the Jews for the entrance to her chamber, and at the same time raised her eyes to heaven to commend the salvation of her soul, protesting that she did not repent of dying innocent after the example of her Saviour, and praying God to lavish his blessings on the Duke of Bourbon, her brother, on the Queen of France, her sister, on Charles the Wise, and on all her royal family. As soon as she had finished these words, the Jews rushed into her room. They found this holy princess lying on her bed, with a psaltery in one hand and a candle in the other to read in her hours; and turning her eyes towards those who had just entered she asked them what they wanted of her and who had sent them so late to speak to her. They replied that they were in despair at being obliged to announce to her the stern order they had received from the King to put her to death, and that she must prepare herself beforehand for this last hour.*

"*This speech was interrupted by the cries of her maidservants, who tore out their hair, and made the whole room resound with their sobs and sighs, telling each other that the best princess in the world was to be unjustly put to death, and praying Heaven to avenge this inhumanity on the authors of it. The poor Queen begged them to restrain their complaints, adding that they should not pity her with so much grief, as she was to die innocent, and that it was rather the conduct of her husband Peter that should make them* pity him, committing this barbarity by the evil counsels of his concubine, long since altered in his blood.

"The Jews, fearing that the screams and uproar which the Queen's wives were about to make would prevent the execution of their mistress and reveal the murder they wished to conceal, dragged them out of the bedroom and dragged them into a cellar, where they strangled them and then killed the White Queen with greater secrecy and freedom. These rabid men were not long in dispatching her, by piercing her belly with the fall of a great beam, which they dropped upon her to suffocate her, without a drop of blood appearing on her face or body: and when they had performed this detestable deed, they immediately retired to a castle situated on a high rock, which the King had indicated to them as a safe asylum.

This inhuman prince, not wishing to be reproached for the murder he had ordered, kept up all the pretence he could dare, by publishing a manifesto in which he exculpated himself as best he could of this action; but his subsequent conduct too well justified that he was the author; for instead of besieging this castle, in which these wretches were cantoned, to take justice into their own hands, they left the square six months afterwards with an impunity which horrified every one, and it was clear that they had been only the ministers of Peter's cruelty. They all uttered imprecations against this wicked prince who had not been ashamed to commit so execrable an outrage against a princess whom he should have adored for her innocent morals and the nobility of her extraction. Even most of the Jews, who had hitherto been her most outspoken supporters, could not keep quiet about it. Peter, for his part, took precautions against any action Henry might take in his States. He collected strong troops, won over the principal lords of Castile with gifts and favours, and went to such lengths to win the people to his side that poor Henry was abandoned by all, and compelled to seek asylum in foreign countries. This unfortunate prince threw himself into the arms of the King of Aragon, who took him into his court with great honesty[365]."

LXVI. Beltrán Duguesclín and the White Company

Peter the Cruel then ordered the King of Aragon to stop protecting his enemy, under threat of declaring war on him. In order to avoid armed conflict, the King of Aragon was forced to separate from his friend.

---

[365] Jacques Le Febvre, " *Anciens Memoires du quatrozième siècle...* in *Collection complète des Mémoires relatifs à l'Histoire de France depuis le règne de Philippe-Auguste jusqu'au commencement du XVIIe siècle*, tome IV, Paris, Foucault, librairie, 1819, p. 306-320.

Chapter XVI was entitled *"De l'adresse dont Bertrand se servit pour faire un corps d'armée de tous les vagabonds de France et les mener en Espagne contre Pierre le Cruel, pour venger la mort de la reine Blanche et faire monter en sa place Henry sur le trône"* (*"Of the skill that Beltrand made use of to form an army corps of all the vagabonds of France and lead them to Spain against Peter the Cruel, to avenge the death of Queen Blanche and put Henry on the throne"*).

"*All France learned with grief of the inhumanity that Pierre had committed against Queen Blanche, his own wife, by having her die unjustly and abandoning her to the will of the Jews, who had struck her down in her bed after entering her bedroom at night and finding her praying with a candle in her hand. All these circumstances aggravated Pierre's crime and made the fate of this princess even more pitiful. The Queen of France, her sister, and the Duke of Bourbon, her brother, strongly condemned such a vile action, which deserved exemplary revenge. King Charles the Wise sympathised strongly with their resentment, and was only looking for an opportunity to make it known as soon as possible. The one which presented itself to him was the most favourable in the world. The kingdom of France was overrun with scoundrels and vagabonds, who desolated it with their brigandage and pillaging. This disorder could not be prevented, for the multitude of these robbers grew daily, owing to a million foreigners who had penetrated into the kingdom to join them, taking advantage of the licence and impunity. Numerous Germans, English, Navarrese and Flemish were infesting the whole countryside, burning castles after plundering them and extorting all the nobility. The prince's edicts were scorned. Their force and violence made sovereign law in the state, to the point that it seemed that France had become the prey of these enraged men.*

"*King Charles, desirous of arresting the course of so many evils, called together the wisest heads of state, so that together they might devise the means of putting an early remedy to so many misfortunes, without resorting to open war against all these bandits. Beltran brought him out of his embarrassment by suggesting to him the specious pretext of avenging in Spain the cruel death of Queen Blanche, his sister-in-law, and assuring him that, if he succeeded in making terms with these bands of vagabonds, he would so well cajole them, as to win them to his sentiments, and inspire them with a desire to turn their arms against King Peter, in the hope of enriching themselves by the spoils of all Spain, which would be opened to them by the war that would be declared against this prince. He even offered to place himself at their head and command them, to secure the success of so just an expedition, representing to the King that by this artifice he would save France from all these foreigners, and employ them usefully elsewhere against the enemies of the Crown. Charles at once accepted Beltran's judicious proposal, and immediately dispatched a herald to the chiefs and commanders of all these people to obtain from them a safe-conduct, so that he could then send them some one to take charge of the expedition."*

Beltran Duguesclin then went to Chalon-sur-Saône, where the "Grande Compagnie", an amalgam of undisciplined soldiers who ravaged the kingdom of France after the war against the English, were stationed.

"Beltran told them the reason why he had come to them, telling them that the King of France, being enraged against Peter, intended to make him repent of the cruel death he had caused to Queen Blanche, his sister-in-law, and that, to punish this cruel prince for so black an outrage, he had resolved to carry the war into his States; That the King, his lord, had charged him to tell them in his name, that if they would accept so just a resentment, and lend him their troops and aid, he would not only make them pay the sum of two hundred thousand pounds in cash, but would also intercede with the Holy Father for absolution for all the sins they had committed; that he advised them to take sides, the more so as they would go into a very fat country, the spoils of which might make them very rich."

Hugues de Caurelay gathered all the chiefs, *"Gascons, English, Bretons, Navarrese, who gave him their word to march under the banners of Beltran... Duguesclin returned with the greatest satisfaction, and hastened to Paris to assure the King that he would rid the kingdom of all the brigands and knaves who had hitherto plundered it with their pillages".*

These leaders were invited to the Temple in Paris, where King Charles had taken up residence.

"The prince caressed them in a thousand ways, treated them as well as he could, and made them rich entertainments to commit them still more to his interests. The principal lords of the Court were not content to make their acquaintance, but wished to enter into a closer friendship with these generals with whom they were to spend more than a day. The Comte de la Marche, the Besque de Vilaines, the Marshal d'Andreghem, Olivier de la Mauny, Guillaume Boitel and Guillaume de Launoy approached them and declared that they would be delighted to share with them the dangers of the war they were about to undertake. These chiefs were delighted to learn of their resolution, assuring them that such noble and generous company would give them all the more fervour to fight well. Beltran gathered them all together at Chalons-sur-Saône and marched them to Avignon."

In the autumn of 1365, Beltran Duguesclin set out for Spain. At Avignon, in the Pope's city, he made a cardinal understand that it was in the Pope's interest to pay them *"if they would restrain the licence of all those vagabonds, whose hands were accustomed to rapine, and who cared less for the absolution they promised them than for the denarii they asked for, being all ready, in case of refusal, to make horrible depredations in the Pope's States."*

The cardinal took notice, and immediately went to inform the pope of what had happened. The pope, hearing of the situation, gathered the bourgeois of the city and put them to contribution. Soldiers, vagabonds and rascals left the square with their pockets well filled and with the Pope's absolution. They then made their way to Toulouse, and finally to Aragon to assist Henry against Peter the Cruel, *"who had no good feelings towards the Christian religion, but whose whole inclination was towards Judaism, of which he made a secret profession, and which, moreover, had become the horror and execration of all Europe"*.

Henry came to meet Beltran. *"Duguesclin embraced him tenderly, and made him a very sincere proclamation that he would not set foot in France again before he had raised him to the throne of Spain."*

"It should be noted," wrote Le Febvre, *"that the troops led by Duguesclin called themselves the White Company, because they all wore a white cross on their shoulders, as if to testify that they had taken up arms only to abolish Judaism in Spain, and to combat the ill-fated prince who protected it to the detriment of the cross."*

The army left Aragon *"to go deeper into Spain, in search of Pedro, and to give him neither rest nor respite"*. They were to reach the town of Magallón. *"From there, they could easily cross Spain."*

The city was taken and sacked, *"after the victorious soldiers had put to the ground a great number of Spaniards and Jews who pretended to resist. The spoils were great, for the Jews who surrendered at discretion, to save their lives, sacrificed all their wealth to redeem themselves and pay their ransom. Never did an army make a more agreeable booty. Beltran had promised it; so it was necessary to satisfy the greediness of so many Bretons, French, Normans, Liègeans, Walloons, Flemings, Brabants, and Gascons, of whom his troops were composed, and who had only embarked on this expedition to enrich themselves by the ruin of Spain. Marshal d'Andreghem, Hugues de Caurelay, Gautier Hüet and his brother, Guillaume Boitel and Monsieur de Beaujeu seconded Beltran with admirable bravery, placing themselves at the head of those who commanded and leading them in the assault by giving them an example of how to do it well."*

Heinrich Graetz wrote: "Duguesclin was even harsher towards the Jews, whom he treated not as soldiers fighting for their king, but as slaves in rebellion against their master[366]."

---

[366] Heinrich Graetz, *History of the Jews IV*, Philadelphia, The Jewish Publication Society of America, 1894, p. 126. "At the head of these French and English bandits was the most outstanding warrior of his time, the hero and knight-errant Bertrand du Guesclin, celebrated for his exploits, his ugliness and his eccentricity, who, like the Cid, was glorified by legend. The Jews joined their fortune to that of Don Pedro's party and supported him with their money and blood. They flocked to his standard on the

The capture of Magallón spread terror throughout Spain. Beltran left a garrison in the town and continued on his way to Borja[367]. Archers and crossbowmen fired on the besieged who came to the walls to defend them, while *"servants and footmen"* filled the pits. The walls were opened *"by force of pikes and crowbars"* and rope ladders allowed the most intrepid to penetrate the fortress, *"even though the Jews and Saracens, of whom the city was full, threw boiling water on them"*. Quickly the soldiers of the White Company took over the square.

"One Norman was bold enough to be the first to plant Beltran's banner on the wall and shout to the others that the city had been taken and to bravely climb up in turn. He was soon followed by a crowd of determined men who clung to the steps and joined him in great numbers. Thence, streaming into the city, they went to seize the gates, and opened them to their companions, who rushed headlong upon them, all the burghers crying for mercy, who, kneeling with their wives and children, begged for quarter, declaring that they surrendered to Prince Henry, whom they wished to acknowledge in future as their master and sovereign."

Henry, *"who wished to make merit of his clemency in order to attract others to his side, yielded to their entreaties, and promised them that he would not only spare their lives, but also the enjoyment of their goods, which he forbade to be touched. He was willing to show this leniency only to Christians, but to the Jews and Saracens, whom he knew to be wholly devoted to Peter, he showed no mercy...*

"After the White Company had spent some time in this country to rest and recover from all the fatigues of these two sieges, and after the wounded had been cared for, these victorious troops proceeded to Bervesque, a fortress where Pedro had brought a large garrison of Spaniards who were completely devoted to his cause."

Duguesclin immediately ordered the siege of the city, and placed himself at the head of the bravest to undertake the attack. *"The besieged came to the walls determined to defend themselves well. While Beltran entertained them with the marksmen who threw their darts and arrows at them, Hugues de Caurelay chose some of the most battle-hardened troops with whom he approached the Jewish quarter, where he made the wall open with great blows of the steel hammer and opened wide gaps in it: the Jews, all fearing that great carnage would be made of them if they persisted in putting up stubborn resistance, facilitated the entrance to the city through their quarter to save their lives. A Breton from Caurelay immediately went*

---

battlefield and garrisoned the cities against the attacks of Don Enrique and Du Guesclin. The savage mercenaries whom they opposed took revenge not only on the Jewish soldiers, but also on those who had not borne arms." *History of the Jews IV*, p. 123.

[367] Villas of Magallón and Borja, between Zaragoza and Soria (NdT).

to the ramparts and raised the standard of Beltran, shouting Duguesclin. This signal encouraged the others to make a last effort to climb up several rope ladders of which there was a good supply. This assault was somewhat deadly on both sides: while the French climbed up the ramparts and pulled each other to the top of the wall, the Spaniards threw buckets full of boiling water over their heads and made them fall into the moat. This misfortune did not dampen the ardour of the besiegers, who rose up with greater rage and fury, and resumed the assault with renewed obstinacy. The besieged threw barrels full of stones and large beams at them, so that this vigorous resistance caused the French to doubt the success of the siege. They thought they were losing too much time, and that they might be forced to picket the square without having done anything. Henry, fearing that the siege would be abandoned, was also making the last efforts in person with his people, when Beltran, who was never disturbed, and whose intrepidity increased in the presence of danger, came to the gates with an axe, and discharged blows so heavy that he broke them down. All the bravest, encouraged by his example, rushed forward in a mob and made so great a raid that they rushed into the city with the enemy on all sides and made a horrible slaughter of them. Those who were able to avoid the fury of the soldiers by fleeing hid in their houses, thinking that they would be safe from all danger, but at the last they were no safer either. Women knelt before the victors to save the lives of their husbands, and children prostrated themselves at the feet of the soldiers to beg them not to put their parents to death: but all these submissions were powerless to stop their violence and slaughter. There remained to be taken an old tower where some Jews had taken refuge. Beltran set fire to the gates with a firework, which soon brought them down. No quarter was given to the most obstinate of those inside, but some leniency was shown to the others, who surrendered at discretion in good faith."

Peter the Cruel, who was in Burgos with his court, was informed of the capture of Bervesque by two burghers who had managed to escape:

"They told him that the enemies had climbed like monkeys over its walls with rope ladders, and that they had opened the passage in spite of all the efforts they had made to dispute it; that at last the city was all flooded with the blood of the Jews, Saracens, and Spaniards they had shed to seize it. This prince at first found it hard to believe this astonishing conquest, and imagining that these two burghers had sold the city for money, he threatened to have them put to death. One of them, to exculpate himself, told him that those who had taken the city were not men, but demons against whom it was impossible to stand; that they were people who feared neither darts nor arrows, neither death nor wounds; that they made their way through all dangers, always advancing without ever retreating, and that he did not believe there was in all their States a single fortress which could withstand for a whole fortnight such determined troops, who seemed to have come out of hell..."

"Peter did not return from the distress that troubled him, so he sent for three Jews in whom he had singular confidence. The first was named James, the second Jude, and the third Abraham, and he asked them to share with him their knowledge and advice in the deplorable state to which his ill fortune had reduced his condition. These three men were themselves rather uneasy, not knowing what course the prince should take to extricate himself from such a perilous situation. A fourth counsellor of this nation, named Manases, came forward, and took the liberty of telling him that he did not think he was safe in Burgos, and that he would do better to settle in Toledo, whose walls were secure and citadel well fortified...Pedro thought he had put his affairs in very good order, and discounting the loyalty of those of Burgos, thought of nothing else but to set out for Toledo, accompanied by the Count de Castro and his four Jews, his most intimate confidants. He was received in this great city with extraordinary acclamations... No sooner had Pedro left Burgos than a spy left the city to come and bring the news to Henry, telling him that he had taken the road to Toledo, where it was believed his design was to shut himself up. Bertrand, who was present at the report made by this spy, was of the opinion that Burgos should be taken, promising Henry that there he would be crowned King of Spain...

"The army's march began at dawn the next day. The advance guard was led by Marshal d'Endreghem, seconded by Olivier de Mauny, Hugues le Caurelay, Nicolas Strambourc, Jean d'Evreux, Gautier Huët, and many English gentlemen, all of whom were of good and ready composure. The rearguard was commanded by Beltran, whose name alone was so fearsome that all were persuaded that he alone was worth a whole army. The Count de la Marche, Monsieur de Beaujeu, Guillaume Boitel, Guillaume de Launoy, Henry de Saint Omer, all were honoured to accompany so great a captain and to share with him the danger and the glory they were to encounter on this excursion; but, above all, Prince Henry convinced himself that this would be advantageous to him, under the banner of a general whose arms had always been victorious, hoping moreover that God, knowing the justice of the cause which impelled them all to act, would shower his blessing on their enterprise, since the enemy against whom they had to fight was a reprobate prince, who had not only publicly disowned the Christian religion by his infamous dealings with the Jews, to the great scandal of all his subjects, but had also sullied his hands in the innocent blood of the holiest and most accomplished princess in all the land, whom he ought to have cared for all the more as she was his own wife, and who was likewise descended from St. Louis."

Chapter XVIII was entitled *"De la reddition volontaire que ceux de Burgos et de Tolede firent de leurs villes, aussitôt qu ils apprirent que*

Bertrand et la Compagnie blanche étaient en marche pour les assierger" *("On the voluntary surrender that those of Burgos and Toledo made of their cities, as soon as they knew that Beltran and the White Company were on the march to besiege them").* Where we are told that the *"three sects"*, Christians, Saracens and Jews, *"had all had the same feeling and recognised Henry as their King...provided he promised not to undermine their customs and privileges".*

The coronation of King Henry and the Queen took place in Burgos in April 1366, on Easter Day.

"Beltran and all his white Company, having gloriously executed what they had undertaken in favour of Henry, held council, with the idea of turning their arms towards Granada, against the Saracens who had taken possession of it. But Henry, seeing that this purpose would be very injurious to their interests, that they would be left imperfect, and might fall into decay if abandoned by them, urged them to follow their first courses, and brandish their points against the States of Peter, as they had so well begun, representing to them that if it was a motive of religion which made them turn their thoughts against the kingdom of Granada, because it was full of Jews and Saracens, that there were no less in the lands of obedience to Peter, which could serve them as an object for the accomplishment of their pious designs; That he would also leave them the spoils of all the conquests they made, from which they might greatly enrich themselves."

On hearing this news, Pedro the Cruel left Toledo to take refuge in Cardona and hide in a forest, *"so terrified was he of the danger that threatened him".* The bourgeoisie of Toledo, terrified, did not fight. Henry approached the city with his army and received the keys of the city from the bishop. Fleeing from his enemy, Pedro made his way to Seville, the only city of any importance left to him. From there he learned that Cardona had also surrendered.

He then lashed out at his two Jewish advisers, Danius and Turcan, *"whose pernicious counsels had entangled him in all the unpleasant affairs he had to endure. He reproached them with being the cause of all his misfortune, since they had maliciously advised him to have the White Queen killed, having themselves become the ministers and instruments of this cruelty, to satiate their particular vengeance; that from this detestable crime they had aroused the indignation of all his subjects, and the revolt of his own brother, who had been defeating him everywhere, that they deserved to be punished with the supreme torture, but that he was content to banish them for ever from his Court, which he forbade them to approach on pain of death. These two Jews obeyed without reply, and without attempting to exculpate themselves before this wrathful prince whose wrath they feared, they took the road to Lisbon to take cover from the storm that threatened them. But unfortunately they were met one morning by Matthew of Gournay, an English knight, who surprised them coming out of a valley on his way to forage. As soon as he saw them, he approached them with sword in hand, ordering them to surrender or risk their lives. These two wretches, trembling with fear, cried out for mercy: he asked them whether they were Jews or Saracens; Turcan replied that they were indeed Jews, but that if he would be good enough not to put them to death, they would promise to surrender the city of Seville to him the next day. The knight assured them that their lives would not only be spared, but that they would be rewarded in proportion to so essential a service, if they had fortune and skill enough to perform the deed. Turcan again took the floor, revealing the means he would use to defeat them. He told him that, as the Jews had a separate quarter in Seville, which they could open and shut when they pleased, it would be easy for him to enter the place they occupied, and win over the most notable, with whom he had secret intelligences; that they would so well turn their heads in their favour that he would make them condescend to what he pleased, provided they were promised that, in assisting Henry's troops to take the city, their property, and still less their lives, would not be touched."*

Indeed, Turcan succeeded in convincing the leaders of the Jewish community in Seville. Peter, informed in time of this treachery by a Jewish spy, left Seville in haste. *"Enrique, Beltran and the whole White Company took advantage of this favourable occasion to present themselves before the city walls. The intelligence they already had in the square with the Jews greatly facilitated their surrender"*, and Henry entered Seville at the head of his army.

Chapter XIX recounted the subsequent events: Pedro set out for Lisbon to meet the King of Portugal to ask for help, but the latter made him realise that he did not have the means to fight the French. On the other hand, the Prince of Wales, the first-born son of the King of England, who controlled Guiana, would undoubtedly be more willing to support him. *"These reasons encouraged Pierre to travel to Bordeaux to speak to the Prince of Wales, who had his court there. So he had a ship prepared and loaded with his richest and most precious possessions, not forgetting his gold table, and then embarked on it, followed by twenty-five knights, fifty Spanish squires and a large number of Jews, who formed a very loyal company."*

In February 1367, the Prince of Wales, whose distinctive black armour had earned him his nickname the Black Prince, crossed the Pyrenees. His vanguard suffered a defeat at the hands of the French, but in April, against Duguesclin's advice, Henry fought a battle at Najera, drawn by the impetuosity of some young Spanish lords. The battle was lost and Duguesclín was taken prisoner, while Henry of Trastámara took refuge on the other side of the Pyrenees, where he immediately reorganised his army.

Peter the Cruel, who no longer needed the Prince of Wales, perfidiously invited him to station his troops on the side of Navarre, making him believe that there would be abundant supplies and that he himself would come forward to pay him all the sums he had promised him. But once in Navarre with his troops, the Black Prince did not find sufficient provisions, *"the whole harvest having been consumed...and Peter, who was to bring him so much money, so much wealth and so much treasure, left him to languish with all his people"*.

Duguesclin set his ransom himself at 100,000 guilders. The Princess of Wales offered him some 30,000 guilders and 4,000 French knights and squires who had followed him in Spain paid the rest. The Black Prince gladly released him, as it was also rumoured that he was being held prisoner because he feared him. Duguesclin returned to Castile with Henry and they quickly reconquered the country. The siege of Toledo lasted nine months. The city was bravely defended by Don Pedro's supporters, "especially by the Jews", wrote Graetz: "The community of Toledo suffered the most. Emulating the Christian followers of Don Pedro, they made the greatest sacrifices for the defence of the city, and endured a long and dreadful siege. The famine during the siege was so great that the wretches consumed, not only the scroll of the Law, but even the flesh of their own children. Because of famine and war most of the Toledo community perished, according to some authors 8,000 people, according to others more than 10,000".

Peter the Cruel had come to the aid of Toledo with an army composed mainly of Moors and Jews. On 14 March 1369, he suffered a heavy defeat at the Battle of Montiel and was taken prisoner. When Duguesclin went to visit him with Henry, the two half-brothers fought each other: "When the brothers met, it is said that Henry hurled these insulting words in his face: 'Where is the Jew, son of a harlot, who calls himself king of Castile? They then engaged in a fight. Don Pedro was defeated and beheaded by his brother's general, Du Guesclin", Heinrich Gratez recounted in his pages. Thus, the death of Peter the Cruel pacified Spain, and Du Guesclin was able to return to France with the feeling of having accomplished his mission, having increased his fame and gained great wealth. When Pope Urban V heard the news "he could not contain his joy at the news of Don Pedro's death. "The Church must rejoice," he wrote, "at the death of such a tyrant, a rebel against the Church and a partisan of Jews and Saracens. The righteous exult at such retribution". The humiliation of the Spanish Jews, which the Papacy had so long failed to achieve, was unexpectedly obtained by the civil war in Castile[368]."

---

[368] Heinrich Graetz, *History of the Jews IV*, Philadelphia, The Jewish Publication Society of America, 1894, p. 126.

LXVII. May 1370: the hosts of Enghien.

Rumour spread in Brabant that Jews from the town of Enghien had stolen sixteen consecrated hosts from the church in Brussels to pierce them in their synagogues with daggers and knives. An elderly Jewish woman had denounced the culprits to the priest, after which the outcry of indignation was unanimous. "The elders of the synagogue of Enghien were tortured; three of these unfortunates were tied up and burned alive on 22 May 1370 near the Namur Gate in Brussels; one of them, Jonathas, had acquired great wealth through his speculations. All the other Jews were banished from Brabant and their property confiscated... It was decided to perpetuate the memory as a glorious event for Brabant. Eighteen pictures were painted for the church of St. Gudula in Brussels, with all the details of the event, including the gruesome execution of the three elders of the synagogue. A secular feast was instituted, the ephemeris of which was later fixed at half a century[369]."

"In July 1820, the story of the Enghien hosts and consequent persecution was still being celebrated for eight days. Religious ceremonies were combined with worldly amusements... the Blessed Sacrament, containing the sixteen desecrated hosts, was carried in procession, adorned with rhinestones, while the streets were planted with cornflowers and flowers, and tapestries were hung in the houses; there were banquets, concerts, shootings, fireworks and illuminations[370]."

LXVIII. The funeral of Charles V of France

When Charles V ascended the throne of France in 1364, in a devastated country partly occupied by the English, he hastened to abolish the restrictions ordered by his father on the privileges of the Jews and authorised them to prolong their stay in France. The privileges of the Jews were reinstated for another six years. With their gold, the Jews "obtained at the court of this weak prince all they wanted. Manasseh of Vesoul, their agent, very skilfully used his credit in their favour.

Despite the express prohibition against taking more than four denarii of interest per pound each week, the Jews, incorrigible, went far beyond this rate, which was already too high. As usual, complaints reached the King,

---

[369]Sander, Chorograph. sacra Brabant. — Calfmcier, *Vénérable histoire du tréssaint Sacrement*, etc., in Georges-Bernard Depping, *Les Juifs dans le Moyen-Âge*, (1823), Éd. Wouters, Brussels, 1844, p. 174.

[370]*Unterhaltungsbloetter fur Welt und Menschenkunde*, 1082, n° 8, in Georges-Bernard Depping, *Les Juifs dans le Moyen-Âge*, (1823), Éd. Wouters, Brussels, 1844, p. 174.

who must have been rightly indignant that people who had just returned to the kingdom thanks to a special pardon were incorrigible in their vicious habits and retained such greed for the nation that had taken them in. The Provost of Paris instituted proceedings against them and condemned them to heavy fines; there was even talk in the King's Council of expelling this race of dishonest usurers from the kingdom once more; but Manasseh of Vesou, for fifteen hundred gold francs, obtained a royal order to hush up the matter and silence the King's prosecutor; then, for three thousand gold francs, the Jews obtained a ten years' extension of their stay in France, which had already been prolonged to twenty-six[371]."

If they frequented the fairs of Champagne and Brie, it was not so much to exhibit goods as to speculate on other merchants' need for money. They also mortgaged the property of borrowers, driving them to ruin.

Charles Evrart of Tremagon, a Breton jurist who lived at the time, was the author of the *Dream of the Vergel (Songe du Verger)*, completed in 1376, one of the most penetrating books of the 14th century and also an indictment of Judaism. In this dialogue between a clergyman and a knight we read statements such as these:

"And, indeed," said one, "I know a so-and-so who borrowed X francs[372] from a Jew, for which he paid XIII hundred francs both for the lot [capital] and for the usury [interest], and he is not yet at peace. And whoever would make a diligent enquiry would find fifty thousand persons in the kingdom of France disinherited and impoverished by these Jews."

And the other replied, "Christian women, because of their great poverty, in order to recover their garments, lie with them reproachfully." And both agreed on "the evils and horrors that are happening every day to Christendom as a result of conversing [frequenting] with the Jews[373]."

Jews were still subject to a fee at some tolls. In Saint-Symphorien d'Oson, a Jew on foot had to pay four denarii, a Jew on horseback and a pregnant Jewess paid double.

A more insulting humiliation was practised in Le Puy. When a Jew dared to show himself in the city, he was liable to be executed by the altar boys of the cathedral. In a sentence of 1373, these children condemned to

---

[371] Privileges agreed by Charles V, Vincennes, 1373; charter of the same, of the year 1374, in volume V of the Compilation of Ordinances, in Georges-Bernard Depping, *Les Juifs dans le Moyen-Âge*, (1823), Éd. Wouters, Brussels, 1844, p. 183.

[372] This is the *"Franc à Cheval 1360"* (*"Franc à Cheval 1360"*), the first gold coin to introduce the historical currency: the Franc. Created on 5 December 1360, this coin was issued to pay the ransom of King John II the Good, who was held prisoner by the English. Equivalent to a pound tournois, this coin spread the use of the word *"Franc"* to designate the French national currency throughout the country. (NdT)

[373] *Livre du Verger*, 1376, livre premier (*Book of the Vergel*, 1376, first book).

a fine of three hundred pounds a Jew who had been caught inside the city[374].

In the county of Lesmont, in Champagne, every Jew who passed by was obliged to kneel down in front of the door of the lord or his tenant to receive a slap in the face[375]. Georges-Bernard Depping, who referred to these events in the middle of the 19th century, was indignant afterwards and wrote: "These were the affronts to which the people of Moses and Solomon were inhumanely exposed[376]!"

Charles V died in September 1380. The Parisian common people seized the occasion and revolted against the Jews. The capital's Jewish quarter was razed to the ground and some Jews were killed. The powerful provost of Paris, Hugues Aubriot, known to be the defender and protector of the Jews, could not prevent the riots[377].

Aubriot had long used an iron fist, so his enemies were countless. On 24 September, during the king's funeral, an incident occurred. When the rector of the University of Paris, followed by the teachers and students, wanted to join the funeral procession, Hugues Aubriot forbade them to pass, and a fierce brawl ensued. The next day, as Charles V's coffin was being carried from Notre-Dame Cathedral to Saint-Denis, the same incidents were repeated. To take revenge, the university students met with the provost's detractors and launched an assault. The ecclesiastics then accused Aubriot of heresy and an inquisition trial came to support the civil proceedings of which the rector managed to take the lead. The accused was spared the stake, but had to make amends: he was stripped of his functions and imprisoned.

In the *Chronicle of the Four first Valois (Chronique des Quatre premiers Valois) we* can read that Aubriot was accused of being a "backslider of heresy, a sodomite and false Christian", and of "having done many horrible and abominable things, such as possessing women bestially against nature, of having carnal company with Jewish women, as well as returning children of Jews who had been Christians to Jews, as well as having corrupted women, and then having hanged their husbands, for being a sodomite and not keeping the Christian law[378]."

---

[374] Archives of the Church of Puy, cited in volume IV of the *General History of Languedoc.*

[375] Lesmont County toll right banner, inserted in volume I of Grosley's Ephemerides, p. 162, 1811 edition.

[376] Georges-Bernard Depping, *Les Juifs dans le Moyen-Âge*, (1823), Éd. Wouters, Brussels, 1844, p. 163.

[377] Chronicle of Charles VI. Sauval, *Antiquités de Paris*, tome II, liv. X, in Georges-Bernard Depping, *Les Juifs dans le Moyen-Âge*, (1823), Éd. Wouters, Brussels, 1844, p. 185.

[378] *Chronique des Quatre premiers Valois*, p. 294-295 — Année 1381. "Soon he himself was the target of the blackest accusations. The university denounced him to the Bishop

In the neighbouring duchy of Burgundy, the Jews did not fare so badly. Philip the Bold (1363–1404) had maintained the prohibition imposed on Jews to wear coloured garments, to bathe in the same places as Christians, to touch the food displayed in the markets to be sold, as well as the obligation to have only one cemetery and synagogue per diocese. He also ordered them to abstain from eating meat during Lent like the Christians. But during his reign there was no bloody persecution.

In Strasbourg, the imperial city, the Jews were readmitted to the city in 1383, by a public act that initially limited their stay to a small number of years; but once they were reinstated in the square, the Jews had no difficulty in remaining and gaining respect.

Here is a story that happened in Alsace at that time: "A nobleman of Mulhouse, instead of going to the Pope, took a shorter and more violent way to get rid of his Jewish creditor. On being sued for his debt, the interest on which already exceeded the capital, he invited the Jew to come to his house, after having secretly removed all his belongings; then, on the creditor's appearance, he had four stout servants put him into a boot and transported him to Burgundy, whence the prisoner only returned at the end of four weeks, and after having paid four hundred florins for his ransom. The case was brought before the magistrate, and the gentleman, known as de Neuenstein, was banished for life, and his house confiscated for the benefit of the city, which converted it into a tile factory[379]."

LXIX. *The general uprising of 1391 in Spain*

Henry of Trastámara, who ascended the throne of Castile in 1369, was not malicious towards the Jews of his kingdom. His struggle with Don Pedro had absorbed huge sums and he owed a lot of money to his allies. He therefore needed skilled financiers to find the necessary money and collect taxes regularly. To this end, he called in two Jews from Seville, Don José Pichon (or *Picho*), whom he appointed Minister of Finance, and Don Samuel Abrabanel.

From the first meeting of the Cortes of Toro in 1371, feelings of hostility towards the Jews grew. "The Cortes expressed to the king their displeasure

---

of Paris as a secret devotee of Judaism. It was claimed that Jewish women exercised the greatest influence over the man who ruled the court and the city; there was talk of heresy and impiety. Aubriot, the magistrate to whom the city owed its improvements and good order, was condemned to spend the rest of his life in a dungeon. This fall of their protector exposed the Jews to new calamities". In Georges-Bernard Depping, *Les Juifs dans le Moyen-Âge*, (1823), Éd. Wouters, Brussels, 1844, p. 185.

[379] Georges-Bernard Depping, *Les Juifs dans le Moyen-Âge*, (1823), Éd. Wouters, Brussels, 1844, p. 173.

that this "wicked and audacious race", these enemies of God and Christianity, were employed in "high offices" at court and by the grandees of Spain, and that they were entrusted with the collection of taxes, by means of which the weak Christians were subdued and terrorised", wrote Heinrich Graetz.

Henry must have taken these recriminations into account and issued two edicts against the Jews. He ordered them to wear the buckler, like their fellow Jews in the rest of Europe, and to change their Castilian surnames and take their real Jewish surnames.

There were about 200,000 Jews in Castile in 1370, or three to five percent of the total population. In the kingdom of Aragon, with 60,000 Jews, the proportion was six to seven percent.[380]

The richest and most influential Jews had entered the entire state apparatus, enriched themselves with usury, and strutted in public in gold and silk dresses. They were also pimps: in 1387, in Barcelona, a Jewish pimp was punished with a heavy fine[381]. Graetz wrote that some "Jews complained that their moral sense was deeply wounded by the selfishness and greed of their rich brothers. "For these troubles," said one, "the rich and titled Jews are most responsible; their only consideration is their position and their money... In fact, the union, which had once been the main source of strength among the Spanish Jews, broke down. Jealousy and envy among the great Jews had undermined the fraternal feeling which had formerly induced each to unite his interests with those of the community at large, and to unite all for the defence of each other. "Most of the rich Jews," said Solomon Alami in his *"Mirror of Morals,"* who are admitted to the royal courts, and to whom are given the keys of the public treasuries, are proud of their dignities and riches, but think nothing of the poor. They build palaces for themselves, ride in splendid carriages or ride on richly harnessed mules, dress in magnificent robes and adorn their wives and daughters like princesses with gold, pearls and precious stones[382]".

More and more, denunciations were occurring among Jews. "Even rabbis were denounced", Graetz noted. The Jewish minister Joseph Pichon was accused of embezzlement by several Jewish court favourites and was subsequently imprisoned and sentenced to a fine of 40,000 doubloons. After paying this sum, he was released. To take revenge, or perhaps simply to justify himself, Pichon implicated his accusers in a "very serious

---

[380] Yod, *Revue des études modernes et contemporaines hébraïques et juives*, issue 35, 1992.
[381] M. Kriegel, *Les Juifs à la fin du moyen âge*, p. 249, in Georges Valensin, *La Vie sexuelle juive*, p. 65, 66
[382] Heinrich Graetz, *History of the Jews IV*, Philadelphia, The Jewish Publication Society of America, 1894, p. 138, 154.

accusation", Graetz wrote without elaborating on the matter.

King Enrique died in 1379. During the coronation festivities of his son Don Juan I in Burgos, a court of rabbis condemned Pichon as a denouncer without even hearing his defence. Some Jews of the court then asked the young king for authorisation to execute a dangerous co-religionist whose name was kept secret. Armed with the letter stamped by the king and the arrest warrant, Pichon's enemies went to the chief of police—the bailiff—and asked for his assistance in carrying out the sentence of the rabbis.

Early in the morning on 21 August 1379, Jews accompanied by the constable entered Pichon's house, woke him up and dragged him out of the house under some pretext. When they reached the threshold of the door, the former minister was shot down.

This execution caused a deep commotion. The young King Juan I sentenced the Jewish murderers, a member of the rabbinical court of Burgos and the bailiff Fernán Martín, to death. In addition, the king withdrew criminal jurisdiction from the Jewish courts: henceforth, the Jews were to choose Christians to conduct their criminal trials. John I also ordered them, on pain of severe punishment, to refrain from proselytising and to remove insulting passages from their prayers.

Thereafter, the situation of the Jews of Spain worsened markedly. At the behest of the Cortes of Valladolid in 1385, John I converted into state law the canonical provisions that forbade Jews to stay in the same house as Christians or to employ Christian wet nurses and maids. He also decided that neither Jews nor Muslims could serve as royal treasurers, whether for the king, queen or princes.

It was the archdeacon[383] of Ecija, Ferrán (or Fernando) Martínez, who raised the Spanish people against their oppressors. From 1378, Martinez, former confessor to Queen Eleanor of Aragon, thundered against their wiles, denouncing in his sermons "their wealth and their indomitable pride". "One day, on 15 March 1391—a memorable day, not only for the Jews and for Spain, but for the history of the world, for on that day the first germ of

---

[383] The archdeacon (from the Greek ἀρχι: the first and διάκονος: servant, minister) or archdeacon was the chief deacon of a cathedral. They were mainly concerned with charitable works on behalf of the bishop, with administering the dioceses and finally with running certain areas (especially rural areas) called archdeaconries or archdeaconries. By the 12th century, the figure of the archdeacon had spread throughout Christendom and new functions had been entrusted to him, such as those of judge in ecclesiastical cases, always with the delegated authority of the bishop; He appeared in cathedral councils to preside over them, as the bishop's natural vicar, as judge or provisor, administrator of goods and visitator of the diocese; he had power over rural archpriests, parish priests and other priests, summoned the diocesan synod, united and dismembered benefices and imposed censures. Although his authority emanated from the bishop, he came to emancipate himself from him.

the Inquisition was created—Martinez, preaching as usual against the Jews, deliberately incited the crowd to riot in the hope that many Jews would abjure their religion. The passions of the crowd were inflamed and broke out into wild riots." The authorities, under the baton of the bailiff of Seville, punished two of the ringleaders of the mob, but this intervention only fanned the anger of the people. "Some of the leading Jews of Seville, seeing that the local authorities were not strong enough to deal with the uprising, hastened to the court of the young king and appealed to the council of regency to stop the slaughter of their brethren. Their protests were favourably received. Immediately messengers were sent to Seville with instructions to the populace to refrain from further atrocities. The local nobility seconded the king's action and, siding with the Jews, succeeded in subduing the rioters[384]", Graetz recounted in his work. Popular resistance had thus been crushed by the elites.

Nevertheless, Fernando Martínez continued with his preaching. Three months later, on 6 June 1391, the people of Seville again descended on the Jewish quarter and set it on fire. The mob massacred the population so that the Jewish community of Seville almost completely disappeared: "The result was that, of the important and wealthy community of Seville, which had numbered 7,000 families, or 30,000 souls, only a few remained. The murders counted no more than 4,000 victims, but to escape death most of them accepted baptism by force. Women and children were sold as slaves to the Mohammedans. Of the three synagogues in Seville, two were transformed into churches". From Seville the insurrection spread throughout Spain.

After Seville, Cordoba, the cradle of Spanish Judaism, joined the movement. One part of the community was massacred, the other accepted baptism. In Toledo, part of the community also converted to Christianity. About seventy Jewish communities in Castile suffered the revolts of Christians who had had enough of Jewish domination.

In Saragossa, the main agitator was the archdeacon's nephew. People broke into the aljamas (Jewish quarters) as if they were engaged in a holy war.

In the kingdom of Aragon too, despite their differences with Castile, the Christians took up arms. Three weeks after the massacres in Toledo, the same scenes were repeated in Valencia: "Of the five thousand souls who constituted the Jewish community in the city of Valencia, not one was left. Some two hundred and fifty were killed, a few were saved by fleeing, and the rest embraced Christianity". It is estimated that some 7,000 Jews

---

[384] Heinrich Graetz, *History of the Jews IV*, Philadelphia, The Jewish Publication Society of America, 1894, p. 167, 168.

converted to escape death.

In Palma de Mallorca, a group of vagrants and sailors raised a cross and crossed the Jewish street of Montesión shouting: *Death to the Jews!* Three hundred Jews were killed that day, and many abjured their faith. Sicily, an Aragonese land at the time, was also the scene of violence against the Jews.

Three days later, the massacre began in Barcelona, the capital of Catalonia. The Jews of the Call neighbourhood were to experience four days of terror[385]. On Saturday 5 August 1391, at about half past one in the afternoon, a small troop of sailors from Castile crowded into the port and began to burn the gates of the Jewish quarter, penetrating and massacring hundreds of Jews. The mob joined in the looting, which continued throughout the night, while the surviving Jews took refuge in the royal castle. By Sunday, 6 August, calm had returned to the city. Attempts were even made to launch a counter-attack, and some of the culprits were arrested and imprisoned. Royal officials, councillors and city leaders stood guard around the Jewish quarter and the castle to protect them.

On Monday 7 August, dozens of men-at-arms gathered under the orders of the councillors, and ten Castilian sailors were condemned to be hanged. At one o'clock in the afternoon, when Guillén de San Clemente, *ciutadan honrat* of the urban oligarchy and delegate of the king, was about to carry out the sentence, an uprising of the common and humble people broke out again. The rebels went to the prison and freed the prisoners. On Tuesday 8 August, hungry and thirsty, the Jews in the castle surrendered. A procession left the cathedral to approach them and most of the Jews immediately accepted baptism in the cathedral and churches. The rest were executed. Shortly afterwards, Lérida, Gerona and other cities experienced similar episodes. On the other hand, Saragossa was not affected, as its lordship was more powerful and able to maintain order.

On 14 December 1391, eleven leaders of the Barcelona insurrection were hanged. On 22 December, another ten met the same fate, and two were dismembered, including a tailor named Armentora. The total number of those condemned rose to 25 people.

These disturbances, which lasted more than two months, from 6 June to

---

[385]In its golden age, in the 13th century, the Call de Barcelona was the largest aljama in Catalonia. Medieval Barcelona had approximately 15% Jews during its golden age, and most of them made their living from the 4000 Jews who lived in the Jewish quarter. Barcelona gained a reputation as a 'city of scholars' among Jews. Jews worked as doctors, scientists, merchants and moneylenders for the Catalan aristocracy. Jews became the official financiers of the sovereigns of Catalonia. Jews were officially the property of the crown, and at the Fourth Lateran Council in 1215, papal instructions required Jews to wear hoods and a red button sewn on their clothing to identify them. By 1268, King James I removed the requirement that Jews in aljama must wear the insignia. Source Wikipedia, NdT.

13 August 1391, had resulted in hundreds of deaths. The highest estimates seem doubtful: 4,000 dead in Seville, more than 2,000 in Córdoba. Other estimates are more limited: between 100 and 250 in Valencia, 250 and 400 in Barcelona, 78 in Lérida[386].

Heinrich Graetz wrote here: "For three months fire and sword raged irresistibly through most of the Spanish juderias. When the storm subsided, the Jews who remained were so broken in spirit that they did not venture out of the places where they had taken refuge... The consequences of the persecution were even more terrible than the persecution itself. Their pride was utterly crushed, and their spirit permanently darkened. They, who had once held their heads so proudly high, now slunk timidly away, eagerly avoiding every Christian as a possible murderer. If a hundred Jews were gathered together, a mere incident was enough to send them fleeing like a flock of frightened birds. This persecution gave them their first experience of the bitterness of exile, for, despite many adverse circumstances, they had always imagined themselves safe and at home in Spain [387]." These violences and adversities undoubtedly indicated the approaching arrival of the messianic times and augured their early liberation[388].

---

[386] Yod, *Revue des études modernes et contemporaines hébraïques et juives*, number 35, 1992, p. 15-22. [The lesser intensity of the revolts has been noted in their spread to other places once they reached Ciudad Real, Toledo and Madrid. Illescas, Ocaña and Torrijos suffered less serious damage. Other towns in the central area with notable Jewish quarters do not seem to have suffered riots, such as Maqueda, Talavera de la Reina, Alcalá de Henares, Guadalajara, Hita, Uceda, Buitrago, Mondéjar, Pastrana, Almoguera, Zorita, Tendilla, Cogolludo, El Puente del Arzobispo, Cobeña or Torija. This has been attributed to the subjection of these Jewish quarters to powerful lords, such as the Archbishopric of Toledo, the Order of Calatrava and the House of Infantado. As for the Crown of Aragon, while the Jewish communities of Barcelona, Valencia and Mallorca were severely affected (it is even said that they "disappeared"), that of Saragossa even prospered, growing from 300 families in 1369 to 350 at the beginning of the 15th century. Source Wikipedia, NdT].

[387] Heinrich Graetz, *History of the Jews IV*, Philadelphia, The Jewish Publication Society of America, 1894, p. 169, 170–171, 172–173.

[388] "The difficult times, casting shadows of an even more unhappy future, produced the melancholy phenomenon of another messianic frenzy. This again arose in the minds of the mystics. The *Zohar* had been skilfully elevated to the dignity of approved authority, and the Qabalah was acquiring more and more influence every day, though it was not studied in proportion to the zeal with which its authority was defended. Three cabalists were particularly active in exciting the emotions and turning the heads of the Jewish people: Abraham of Granada, Shem Tob ben Yosef, and Moses Botarel. The first composed (between 1391 and 1409) a Kabbalistic work, a farrago of strange names of the Deity and angels, of transposed letters and juggling with vowels and accents. Abraham of Granada had the audacity to teach that those who could not apprehend God by cabalistic methods belonged to the weak in faith, were ignorant sinners, and, like the depraved and the apostate, were disregarded by God and not considered worthy of His

Some Spanish Jews crossed the Mediterranean to settle in Algiers or Fez. Others went to Portugal, which became an asylum for Jews who had not renounced their messianic faith. King Joao I vigorously maintained order and ruthlessly punished agitators.

Pope Boniface IX once again forbade Christians to use violence to baptise Jews. His bull was published in every town in Portugal and elevated to state law. On 17 July 1392, King Joao I issued an edict punishing rebellious Jews (those who had returned to their religion of origin).

Meanwhile, at the other end of Europe, in the Holy Empire, more than three thousand Jews were massacred in Prague during a popular uprising, and the synagogues were burned and destroyed (Easter 1389). The following year, Emperor Wenceslas issued an edict that "all counts, barons, lords, knights, servants and footmen, burghers and other subjects living in the Frankish country were released and absolved of all Jewish debts in principal and interest".

LXX. 1394: the expulsion from France

In 1380, "on Charles VI's accession to the throne, barely out of infancy, the government was given over to the intrigues of the courtiers; the dukes of Berri, Burgundy, and Orleans had their supporters and their factions; whoever had the most credit at the time obtained the royal orders he desired, or stopped proceedings in Parliament. The Jews were too skilful not to win friends and protectors in this struggle of parties; undoubtedly they had also more than one important debtor."

As we have seen, anti-Jewish riots took place in Paris and other provincial towns in these circumstances. The people, angered by the impunity of usury, had plundered the Jewish quarters and injured or killed many members of the Jewish community. But the Jewish community was able to assert itself and received large compensation payments. The Jews claimed that they had been robbed of the valuable goods they had taken as collateral—gold, silver, stones, jewellery, etc.—and therefore could not return them to their owners. So they were exempted without the government thinking of compensating the borrowers.

---

special Providence. He thought that the renunciation of their religion by the educated Jews was explained by their dismal devotion to scientific study and their contempt for the Kabbalah. On the other hand, he professed to see in the persecutions of 1391, and in the conversion of so many prominent Jews to Christianity, the signs of the Messianic age, the suffering that was to precede it, and the coming of the Redemption." Heinrich Graetz, *History of the Jews IV*, Philadelphia, The Jewish Publication Society of America, 1894, p. 196–197. Read about the process of Israel's (and the world's!) Redemption and messianic liberation in *Psychoanalysis of Judaism*.

"We see from the public records of the time that, while they complained of their poverty, they did not fail to provide the king with funds, both for his wars and for his other expenses. In 1388, as the price of these cleverly offered advances, they wrested from him an act of concession which was at once a misjudgment on the part of Charles VI. and a display of the audacity of the Jews of France. They had long enjoyed the right to charge four denarii per pound as interest, an exorbitant rate, as already noted above. In granting them this wide concession, the kings had always prohibited the accumulation of annuities with the capital, and the charging of interest on interest, which in the language of the time was called *making montes de montas*.... The Jews had never been allowed to carry usury to this extent; but under Charles VI., trusting to the ascendancy they had attained, and probably also to the money they distributed at court, they practised usury in this ruinous manner. In accordance with the laws in force, the king's prosecutor and other court officials instituted proceedings against the guilty usurers. Fearing that they would eventually discover transactions that would have unleashed a new storm against them, the Jews hastened to advance a large sum to the king; then they came to complain that the officers of the law were persecuting them, out of hatred or for other reasons, and begged the king to protect them from this persecution. The monarch had the incredible weakness to impose perpetual silence on his prosecutor and to protect them from any persecution for ten years[389]."

"The unfortunate borrowers had to pay perhaps ten times what it had cost the Jews to obtain this concession. The king was so condescending that he forbade the prosecutor to accuse them of any abuse during this period, to trouble or hinder them in any way, in order to allow them to make full use of their privileges; as a result, the wealth of private individuals was left at the discretion of the usurers for ten years. Never since the reign of Ludovico Pio (9th century) had they obtained so much. Under an insane king and a faction-ridden government, the Jews could easily have avoided public scrutiny and been no more than honest, hard-working citizens; instead, they preferred to speculate on public misery and get rich quick as moneylenders…Believing they had nothing to hide, they naively admitted in one of their petitions that almost all their assets consisted of debts that the Christians had contracted with them. They demanded that the king should no longer grant to debtors those letters of deferment which were

---

[389]"*… Let us remember that until the age of ten years, some priests, procurators and officials will not be allowed to approach the Jews, nor will they be allowed to bring them to trial or to bring them to trial for abuse of mountains or for making or having made mountains in other abuses, so that they will not be accused of anything else, etc. "*", in Georges-Bernard Depping, *Les Juifs dans le Moyen-Âge*, (1823), Éd. Wouters, Brussels, 1844, p. 187.

obtained against the persecution of creditors, when one had credit at court; and the king, who had signed these letters, declared that they would be of no value; but it cost them ten thousand francs to obtain the seal for this grant. All the rest of the same reign was a succession of concessions made to the Jews[390]."

Fortunately, some upright judges reacted against these parasites. "Despite the formal orders of an insane king, the Jews guilty of having exceeded the legal rate of interest and of having made *mounts of mounts*, were seized, locked up in *La Conciergerie*, and there was talk of putting them on trial and confiscating their property. The Israelitish nation prevented this affront, or rather this just punishment; with money in hand they went to court to plead that the prisoners were innocent, that they had merely made use of their privileges, and that, notwithstanding all the persecutions hanging over their heads, the community was willing to pay any sum of money which the king might wish to impose upon them. By the payment of six thousand francs, in cash, they obtained the release of the guilty and letters of abolition again imposing silence on the king's prosecutor."

"In 1388, the guards of the Montpellier mint arrested a Jew convicted of issuing counterfeit coinage; the defender of the Jewish privileges of the city claimed the prisoner, alleging that he alone had the right to judge him; but when the case was brought before the king's council, it was decided that the sentence belonged to the general masters of the mint[391]." What the sentence was is unknown.

The Jews lost their credibility after the Denis Machault case. He was a very rich Jew from the Villa-Parisis who had converted to Catholicism. One day he simply disappeared. There was a great uproar in the village, and the case was brought before the provost of Paris. Seven Jews were arrested who admitted having urged Denis Machault to return to Judaism. Apostasy was a crime so little tolerated at the time that a Christian was even burned at the stake in Paris for having had children with a Jewish woman who practised her mother's religion[392]. Assisted by lawyers and theologians, the provost condemned the Jews to the stake. But the case was referred to Parliament, which commuted the sentence to banishment and confiscation, and decided that the culprits should be flogged in three public squares in Paris, that they should pay a fine of ten thousand pounds for the construction of the *Hôtel-Dieu* bridge, and that they should remain in prison until they had brought back Denis Machault.

---

[390] Sauval, *Antiquités de Paris*, tome II, liv. X.
[391] Georges-Bernard Depping, *Les Juifs dans le Moyen-Âge*, (1823), Éd. Wouters, Brussels, 1844, p. 185, 186–188, 191.
[392] Jean Gullas, quoted by Sauval, *Antiquités de Paris*, tome II, liv. X.

The poet Eustace Deschamps, in his *Complainte de l'Église* (1393) (*Lamentation of the Church*), directly advocated the expulsion of the Jews.

The opponents of the Jews took advantage of the Denis Machault case to obtain the revocation of all privileges granted to the Jews and their expulsion from the kingdom. We do not know the details of the intrigues at court that finally led to this expulsion. The period of twenty-eight years that King John had allowed them to remain in France in 1360, plus the sixteen years' extension that Charles V had granted them, expired in 1404. But the crimes and abominations they committed on a daily basis forced King Charles VI to bring the deadline forward. The exasperation of the people was so great that it could no longer be contained.

"The Jew who charged very high interest rates and had debtors imprisoned if they did not want to pay" earned all the enmity. "The people hated the Jew", wrote Graetz. The incessant mockery of the Catholic religion, the taking of stolen goods, the vile usury, pederasty, pimping, ritual crimes, all kinds of trafficking and swindling had aroused the weariness and hatred of the Christians towards the members of the sect. On 17 September 1394, the Day of Atonement, the king finally took the decision to expel the Jews from the kingdom:

"For a long time and on several occasions we have been informed by trustworthy persons, our procurators and officers of several great complaints and clamours which reached them every day of the excesses and offences which the Jews commit every day against the Christians, and for this reason, our procurators have made several investigations by which it appears that the Jews have offended in many ways, especially against our faith and the contents of our letters... By mature deliberation of our council, we desire by way of irrevocable establishment or constitution that henceforth no Jew shall live, reside or convert in our kingdom, etc.[393]".

The debts of the Jews were cancelled and their debtors released from payment. This memorable edict put an end to the legal existence of the Jews in France.

The following text is by Michel Pintoin, a religious of Saint Denis and historian of the king: "The usuries of the Jews were becoming more and more odious and were spreading throughout the kingdom. Numerous families had been thrown into the most dreadful misery. These enemies of Jesus Christ had thus earned the hatred of all the French. The king, informed of these disorders and yielding to the wise advice of the queen, his beloved wife, resolved, in spite of the enormous sums extracted each year from the Jews who increased his treasury, to separate the wheat from

---

[393] Royal Ordinance of 17 September 1394, in volume VIII of the Ordinances, in Georges-Bernard Depping, *Les Juifs dans le Moyen-Âge*, (1823), Éd. Wouters, Brussels, 1844, p. 193 (note 3).

the chaff and to protect the believers from the infidels. An ordinance, published in all the cities of the kingdom, ordered the Jews to leave France before Christmas and to seek asylum abroad, on pain of being found guilty of lèse-majesté and having all their property confiscated[394]."

Heinrich Graetz suggested that this edict would have been knowingly promulgated on the Day of Atonement (Yom Kippur) while the Jews were gathered in their temples. However, the Jewish historian did not provide many explanations for this, but rather vague and exculpatory ones: "The royal decree could not impute specific crimes or offences to the Jews and was therefore limited to vague generalities. His Majesty had been informed by trusted persons, including many of his lieutenants and other officials, that complaints had been made about offences committed by the Jews against the Christian religion and the special laws drawn up for their control[395]."

Charles VI nevertheless treated them less harshly than his ancestor Philip the Fair. He granted them time to collect their legitimate debts and ordered the provost of Paris and the governors of the provinces to protect them and guard them by officers up to the border to prevent any attack on them. The Jews did not leave France until late 1394 and early 1395. They went to Provence, which was not yet French, Italy and the Germanic Empire. Some were able to remain in the Pope's territories: in the Venesine County, Avignon and Carpentras.

Some Jews had given large sums of money to the famous Nicolas Flamel, a writer sworn in at the University of Paris, who had a reputation as a sorcerer and alchemist, capable of transforming mercury into gold, and who frequented the cabalists of his time. It was said that Flamel never returned his money to the Jews and that he would have used these sums to enlarge the church of *Saint-Jacques-de-la-Boucherie*, of which today only the bell tower remains, near the Town Hall[396].

When the expulsion of the Jews was decreed, the great theologian John Gerson praised Charles VI for this decision[397].

In 1398, the Provençal prior Honorius Bonet, who was then living in

---

[394] *Chronique du Religieux de Saint-Denis*, tome second, Paris, 1839, p. 118-123, translated from Latin.
[395] Heinrich Graetz, *History of the Jews IV*, Philadelphia, The Jewish Publication Society of America, 1894, p. 175–176.
[396] The Tower of Saint Jacques is the only remnant of the church of *Saint Jacques de la Boucherie*, founded in the 12th century, enlarged in the following centuries and destroyed in 1797 during the French Revolution. This sanctuary was the meeting and departure point for pilgrims taking the *Via Turonensis*, the route to Santiago de Compostela via Tours. The pilgrims set off southwards, crossing the Île *de la Cité* and arriving via the *Petit Pont* at the *Rue de Saint-Jacques*, where they left the city. (NdT).
[397] *Archives juives*, numéro 1, 1973

Paris, published a text entitled *L'Apparition de maistre Jehan de Meun (The Apparition of Maistre Jehan de Meun)*. The great writer appeared to him in a dream, charging him with reproaches for the evils that were ravaging France and against which he had sworn to rise up. It was through the mouth of Jean Meun, the author of the poem *Le Roman de la Rose,* that Honorius expressed his recriminations against the Jews:

"You were expelled from the kingdom because of your great iniquities, your usury and your sins. Moreover, so many reproaches will be found against you that you should all have been burned, because you exercise no good trade and no profit or usefulness arises where you live. You do not plough the land or exploit the sea. Ye shall have no part in Paradise."

Some Jews were left behind within the kingdom, probably involuntarily, or because they had outstanding claims from Christian creditors. In 1395, seven of these Jews appealed to the provost marshal of Paris against the king's prosecutor who had tried and "tormented" them. They remained in prison until at least 1397. Two of them died in prison, and eight more joined them. They had to pay 4,000 escudos of gold[398] to the queen to be released, and were then taken to the bridge of Lyon or Mâcon to be expelled from the kingdom, along with other Jews.

On 30 January 1398, an ordinance of Charles VI stipulated that all obligations contracted by Christians in favour of the Jews would be "cancelled, destroyed and burnt[399]."

This time, the country had become *judenrein,* purified of Jews. For the next four centuries, at least until 1789, France experienced a magnificent era of plenty and splendour in every respect.

After their departure, such a bad memory of their presence survived that for many years hatred and contempt for these "ferocious usurers" was still expressed. In *The Mystery of the Passion* (1452), Arnoul Gréban had his theatrical characters say that the Jews were *"more cruel than wolves", "more ruthless than the scorpion", "prouder than an old lion", "more rabid than false dogs"*. *"Evil and felonious", "lustful", "whore and perverse offspring", "devils from hell*[400]*"* were some of the expressions to refer to them.

---

[398] The escutcheon was a French coin of the Middle Ages. It was created around 1263 and could be made of gold or silver. The coin lasted until 1878, when production ceased. The value of the shield varied considerably over time. After the issue of gold shields, silver shields, known as silver escudos, were introduced. The value of the silver shield was usually worth between a quarter and a half of the value of the gold shield. The majority of the population did not have gold shields in their possession.

[399] *Archives juives*, numéro 1, 1973

[400] *Mystère de la Passion*, in H. Pflaum, *Les Scènes de juifs dans la littérature dramatique du Moyen Âge*, Revue des études juives, 1930, p. 111-134, in Jean Delumeau, *La Peur en Occident*.

HISTORY OF ANTI-SEMITISM

The "Jew-free", Jew-absent anti-Semitism that Jewish intellectuals pretend not to understand is explained by this, and not otherwise.

LXXI. 1397: The expulsion from Venice

Since Italy was divided into a large number of states, there could never be general measures against the Jews throughout the peninsula and the islands. If one state restricted their liberties, another prince benefited by protecting them.

The obligation to wear the buckler was as difficult to implement in Italy as it was in France, and had to be repeatedly renewed. The synod of Ravenna, in 1311, obliged them once again to wear the mark on their garments, and also ordered that Jews could not stay for more than a month in places where there were no synagogues[401].

"In Malta, the bishop was the keeper of the red buckler, i.e. he saw to it that Jews wore under their beards a red mark the size of the royal seal[402]...Pope Paul II obliged them to wear red *tabards* (a kind of short cloak), except for Jews who practised or studied medicine. Later yellow ribbons were imposed on them in Rome, but the ribbons were as difficult to introduce as the *tabars*[403]."

"As early as 1298, in Venice, the Grand Council found it necessary to appoint five magistrates to supervise the Jews and to fine those who engaged in usurious practices. At first, they were only granted permission to stay and open banks in Venice for five years, obliging them to renew this licence called *condotta* [conduct]. This licence was renewed in 1373 and 1381, and then they were granted a ten-year *condotta on the* condition that they pay four thousand ducats to the Treasury each year[404]... The legal interest rate on loans could not exceed ten percent if there was no contract; if there was a contract, the interest rate could rise to twelve percent. With this distinction, the Senate probably wanted to force the Jews to always draw up written contracts, in order to avoid the constant disputes between Jews and Christians over the interest on loans.

"In 1385, the Grand Council issued an ordinance stating that the special reason why the Jews had been welcomed in Venice was that they could help

---

[401]Muraotori, *Judæis Dissert.*
[402]*Rocchi Pirri Sicil. Sacra*, tom. II, p. 907. Act of Catana, of the year 1395
[403] Georges-Bernard Depping, *Les Juifs dans le Moyen-Âge*, (1823), Éd. Wouters, Brussels, 1844, p. 281.
[404]The ducat was a gold coin used in Europe since the Middle Ages. It remained in circulation in Austria and Hungary until 1914. First minted in silver by Roger II of Sicily (1140) for his duchy, it was adopted by Florence (gold florin, 1252) and Venice (gold cequí, 1283). (NdT).

to meet the pecuniary needs of the poor by giving them money in exchange for pledges; but that the Jews were committing serious abuses, either by refusing to lend or by demanding usurious interest, so that they were making considerable profits at the expense of the poor. Accordingly, they were ordered never to refuse to lend when the borrower pledged a pledge of the value of the loan. It was also denounced that they received all kinds of sacred vessels and ecclesiastical ornaments as collateral from the priests, and even displayed them for sale in their shops in the Rialto. They were forbidden to have intimate relations with Christian women, including prostitutes, on pain of a fine and six months to a year's imprisonment[405]."

However, these regulations did not put an end to the disorders. In 1388, the Senate began to complain that the Jews refused to lend 8% of sums of less than 30 ducats to the poor of Venice. The Senate again ordered them to grant these loans under threat of fine and forbade the pledging of objects of worship.

On 27 August 1394, two and a half years before the end of the ten-year term, the Senate almost unanimously decided that all Jews should be expelled from the city. In fact, one could read in the Senate's report that "all the movable wealth of the Venetians was in danger of falling into their hands". The *Judeorum expulsio* was to take effect from 21 February 1397. From that date, Jews could only enter the city with the proper fifteen-day permits and were obliged to wear the yellow kneel on their lapels. Lending usury in Venice, "publicly or secretly", was now punishable by a fine of 1000 ducats. It was not until the early 16th century that Jewish moneylenders from the neighbouring city of Mestre were allowed to do business in Venice, under certain conditions.

LXXII. Pablo de Santa María

While many Jews had fled Spain after the revolts of 1391, most had remained in the country, having had to convert to Catholicism. These new Christians were called marranos, or conversos. But, as Gratez wrote, "most of them, unable to leave Spanish territory but reluctant to abandon their old faith completely, participated in Jewish ceremonies and celebrations while pretending to be Christians. The kings of Castile and Aragon, who had disapproved of popular violence and forced conversions, allowed the Jews to do as they pleased. The authorities did not see or did not want to see their relapse into Judaism". The Inquisition did not yet exist, but the common

---

[405] Georges-Bernard Depping, *Les Juifs dans le Moyen-Âge*, (1823), Éd. Wouters, Brussels, 1844, p. 307–308.

people were not mistaken about the inner feelings of these false Christians. The Spanish people "who nicknamed them *Marranos* or *"Los Malditos"*, regarded them with more distrust and hatred than the openly Jewish, not because of their secret fidelity to Judaism, but because of their ancestry and their innate intelligence, energy and ability[406]", Graetz wrote proudly.

However, some Jews were indeed sincere converts. In fact, they were the first to call for the establishment of the Inquisition. Wherever they settled, the Marranos were targeted and persecuted, often by those sincere converts "who had no scruples and found special pleasure in the persecution of their old religion and its followers". Indeed, that was the way to test the sincerity of these new Christians: by the force of their anti-Judaism. And it still is.

Don Pero Ferrús, a baptised Jew and poet, launched countless tirades against the rabbi and the community of Alcalá. The monk Diego de Valencia was also a former Jew. He mixed Hebrew and Castilian words in his satires against the sect. The poet Alfonso Álvarez de Villasandino also embellished his poems with Jewish terms. The apostate physician Astruc Raimoc de Fraga, formerly one of the staunchest bastions of Judaism, distinguished himself by his active Christian propaganda under the name of Francisco Dios Carne.

But none of these Jews did so much harm to their former co-religionists as Solomon Levi of Burgos, known by his Christian name of Pablo de Santa Maria. Before his baptism, he was a rabbi, a bustling and busy man with the lifestyle of a great lord, going out in luxurious carriages and accompanied by a large retinue. In 1391, at the age of forty, he was baptised with his brother and four children. Paul of St Mary travelled to the University of Paris to study Christian theology and was ordained a priest after a few years. He then travelled to Avignon, where Cardinal Peter de Luna had just been elected antipope under the name of Benedict XIII. Thanks to his ability, zeal and gift of the gab, Paul won the pope's favours. He was appointed archdeacon and canon, and later bishop of Cartagena, thanks to the pope's recommendation. King Henry III of Castile in turn showered him with numerous favours. He also published the *Scrutinium Scripturarum contra perfidia iudaeorum*, a text in which he accused the Jews of murder, adultery, thievery and mendacity, and rejoiced at the massacres of 1391. Paul of St. Mary instigated new persecutions against the Jews, advising King Henry III to ban Jews and new Christians from public employment. "In his writings, Paul of St. Mary showed as much hatred for Judaism as for the Jews," wrote Graetz. "The shrewdest Jews

---

[406] Heinrich Graetz, *History of the Jews IV*, Philadelphia, The Jewish Publication Society of America, 1894, p.180.

soon recognised in this new Christian their bitterest enemy and prepared for a fierce struggle with him[407]."

Nevertheless, King Henry "the Suffering" kept his two Jewish physicians at his side, in whom he had absolute confidence. The reign of Henry III was for the Jews like the calm between two storms.

The situation deteriorated considerably after the death of the monarch in 1406. The heir to the throne, John II, was then two years old and the queen mother Catherine of Lancaster assumed the regency until her death in 1418. At her side, the infante Don Fernando, who would later become King of Aragon, held the co-regency. Among the councillors of the kingdom was Pablo de Santa María, the young prince's tutor, who enjoyed great influence in the regency council.

In 1408, an edict was promulgated in the name of the young king, reinstating all the paragraphs of Alfonso X the Wise's compendium of laws that were hostile to the Jews. Public jobs were forbidden to them. Any Jew who accepted an office from a nobleman or a town was liable to a sanction, usually a fine of double the amount earned in that office. If his fortune was not sufficient to pay the fine, all his property was seized and, in addition, he was condemned to receive fifty strokes of the belt.

On 2 January 1412, the regent Doña Catalina, in agreement with the Infante Don Fernando and Pablo de Santa María, promulgated an edict in the name of Juan II, consisting of twenty-four articles aimed at protecting the Christian population from the Jews, who were henceforth to remain in their special quarters (juderias), which could only have one door to enter and leave. The Jews were henceforth to remain in their special quarters (juderias), which could only have one door to enter and leave, were forbidden to practise medicine, to have commercial relations with Christians, to hire Christians, even on the Sabbath, and to occupy any public function. Their private jurisdiction was taken away. Some articles of the edict regulated the manner of dress: they could not wear the dress of the country, nor display rich fabrics, on pain of a heavy fine; in case of recidivism, they were liable to corporal punishment and even confiscation of their property. They were not allowed to carry arms. In addition, they were strictly required to wear the red buckler. A Jew was also forbidden to shave his beard or cut his hair too short, or he was punished with a hundred strokes of the belt. Finally, they could not be given in writing or verbally the title of Don, and were attached to live in a town, unable to change their place of residence or leave the territory without permission. All those who were arrested for emigrating lost all their property and were reduced to the

---

[407] Heinrich Graetz, *History of the Jews IV*, Philadelphia, The Jewish Publication Society of America, 1894, p. 185–186.

status of serfs of the king. The nobility and clergy were also severely punished if they protected the Jews.

This edict, in which the intervention of Paul of St. Mary was transparent, was strictly enforced. A contemporary Jewish writer, Salomon Alami, quoted by Graetz, described the effects of the edict on their situation as follows: "The rich palace dwellers were forced to live in miserable corners, in dark huts. In place of our elegant and sumptuous robes, we were obliged to wear miserable clothes, which drew contempt upon us. Forbidden to shave our beards, we had to look like mourners. The rich tax collectors were sinking into misery, for they knew no trade by which to earn a living, and the artisans could find no customers. Hunger was stalking everyone[408].""

LXXIII. Vincent Ferrer

Such was the plight of the Jews when Vicente Ferrer arrived at the court of Castile. Vincent Ferrer was a Dominican monk from Valencia who had turned down a high position at the court of Avignon to travel Europe barefoot, as a simple flagellant monk. For twenty years, from 1399 until his death, he travelled through Spain, Italy, Switzerland and even as far as Scotland. He was known for the great austerity of his habits, his contempt for riches and his sincere humility. He was often accompanied by an impressive crowd of disciples, so much so that he had to preach in large outdoor spaces in order to be heard by all. Full of verve and eloquence, his warm and vibrant voice was able to stir the masses. Whether he was narrating the Passion of Christ while sobbing, or announcing the coming destruction of the universe, Vincent Ferrer brought tears to the eyes of all present and exercised absolute dominion over them. Wherever he appeared, he was acclaimed as a saint. A multitude of disciples accompanied him. On his arrival in a town, the whole population would leave their work and come to meet him. When he commanded the crowd to uncover their shoulders and scourge their flesh as Jesus Christ had been, thousands of listeners would shed tears with him. The rich abandoned their possessions to live in austerity, the women of the great families withdrew to the cloisters. The confessors were not enough to cope with all the requests for confession: criminals, scoundrels and courtesans were seen loudly accusing each other of the scandal of their past lives. Notaries accompanying the Dominican drew up deeds of restitution of unjustly acquired property. Families, parties and cities were reconciled.

---

[408] Heinrich Graetz, *History of the Jews IV*, Philadelphia, The Jewish Publication Society of America, 1894, p. 204.

This missionary, revered as a saint by Christians, was greatly feared by the Jews. Vincent Ferrer enjoyed great influence with the kings of Spain, as he had more than once managed to appease popular revolts thanks to the authority he exercised over the masses. So it was easy for him to obtain permission from the royal family to preach in synagogues and mosques, and to force Jews and Muslims to listen to his preaching.

Vincent Ferrer was against physical violence against Jews and forcing them to be baptised. But with the support of the civil authorities, he forced the Jews to come and listen to his sermons. Cross in hand and a scroll of the Law in his arm, amidst an escort of flagellants and men with swords, he invited the Jews to accept baptism.

With pen and word, he waged a relentless crusade that lasted for many years. At first, he directed his attacks against the new Christians, whom he accused of not being fervent enough. Fearful of receiving the terrible punishment reserved for the relapsed, and perhaps also thanks to the fiery eloquence of the Dominican, many Marranos did penance publicly.

In 1412, in collaboration with Pablo de Santa Maria, Ferrer induced the government to promulgate the edict of the statutes of Valladolid, which forbade Jews, among other things, to sell or offer food to Christians, to have their lands ploughed for them, or to shave their beards. Jews were obliged to wear a distinctive sign and to submit to numerous other rules.

"In the midst of these tribulations, the Dominican Ferrer burst into the synagogues, crucifix in hand, preaching Christianity with a voice of thunder, offering his hearers the enjoyment of life and opportunities for advancement, or threatening damnation here and hereafter. The Christian people, inflamed by the passionate eloquence of the preacher, emphasised his teachings with violent attacks on the Jews...Flight was out of the question, for the law forbade it on pain of terrible punishment. No wonder, then, that the weakest and most lukewarm among them, the lovers of comfort and words, succumbed to temptation and were saved by baptism. Many Jews from the communities of Valladolid, Zamora, Salamanca, Toro, Segovia, Avila, Benavente, Leon, Valencia, Burgos, Astorga and other small towns where Vicente Ferrer preached, converted to Christianity. Ferrer transformed several synagogues into churches. During his four-month stay (from December 1412 to March 1413) in the kingdom of Castile, this disastrous proselyte inflicted such deep wounds on the Jews that the communities bled to death[409]", Heinrich Graetz reproached the Valencian missionary.

Called upon by the kingdom of Aragon, where several pretenders were

---

[409] Heinrich Graetz, *History of the Jews IV*, Philadelphia, The Jewish Publication Society of America, 1894, p. 204–205.

vying for the crown, Ferrer succeeded in June 1414 in crowning the infant Don Fernando king of that country, being immediately appointed, in reward for his services, confessor and director of conscience of the monarch.

Like his co-religionists in Castile, the Jews were forced to listen to the Dominican monk's sermons, and in many communities, in Zaragoza, Tortosa, Valencia and Mallorca, there were numerous abjurations, and it is estimated that around twenty thousand Jews in Castile and Aragon accepted baptism after his preaching. Vicente Ferrer died in 1419 and was canonised in 1455. He is celebrated on 5 April.

LXXIV. *Hieronymus of Santa Fe and the Tortosa Dispute*

The great Western schism[410], which saw two popes in two sees for forty years, one in Rome and the other in Avignon, came to an end in 1417 after the Council of Constance.

A few years earlier, in 1409, a council meeting in Pisa had tried to agree on a solution. The five hundred representatives had decided to depose the two popes and elect a new one. In June, the council pronounced the condemnation of the two rival popes and the cardinals elected Alexander V. These cardinals were in turn elected as the new popes. These cardinals were in turn excommunicated by the two rival popes, and the situation became even worse, for there were then three popes, two of whom were anti-popes.

In May 1410, Alexander V died and was replaced by John XXXIII. Enguerrand de Monstrelet described in his *Chronicles* the coronation of Pope (Antipope) John XXIII in Bologna, how on that day of celebration the Jews cheered the procession as it passed through their street, and how they presented the pope with a Torah scroll, as was their custom. The pope threw it behind him and said, "Your law is good, but ours here is better." The Jews followed the procession and tried to approach the pope, for they were also throwing coins. But the two hundred armed men at the head and tail of the procession each had "a leather mace with which they beat the Jews, so joyful was it to see him[411]."

---

[410]The Western Schism, also known as the Great Western Schism (as distinct from the Great Schism of East and West), and often called the Schism of Avignon, refers to the split that occurred in the Catholic Church in the period between 1378 and 1417, when two bishops, and from 1410 onwards even three, disputed papal authority. (NdT).

[411]Enguerrand de Monstrelet, *Choix de chroniques*, éd. Buchon, Panthéon litté., 1836, p. 170 in Archives juives, 1973, numéro 1. Also quoted by Jules Michelet in his *Histoire de France*, volume III.

The antipope of Avignon, Benedict XIII (Pedro Luna), was then trying to win supporters by encouraging mass conversions of Jews in Spain. To this end, and in agreement with King Ferdinand, he summoned the most learned rabbis and Jewish writers of Aragon to participate in a religious colloquium in Tortosa at the end of 1412. At this meeting, Jerome of Santa Fe was to demonstrate to them with the Talmud in hand that the Messiah had already arrived, incarnated in the person of Jesus. The papal court wanted above all to convert the eminent Jews of Aragon to Christianity, convinced that if the chiefs converted, the Jewish people would follow them.

Jerome of Santa Fe was at that time one of Israel's most implacable enemies. Like Paul of St. Mary, he was also a former Jew. Before his conversion, his name was Yosua Lorqui Alcañiz and he was the physician to the pope of Avignon. It was Jerome who drew up the list of people to be summoned to the debate.

The Jews knew from experience that these lectures were a trap for them, but they were in no position to refuse the invitation of the Christians. They had no choice but to be represented by their most skilled doctors in order to defend themselves. Twenty-two of the most important Jews of Aragon therefore turned up for the colloquium, headed by the poet and physician Vidal Benveniste Ibn Labi, from Saragossa, who came from a large Jewish family. All the representatives of Aragonese Judaism were well educated, but, wrote Graetz, "the succession of humiliations and persecutions had broken the manhood of even the proudest Jews, and had transformed them all into faint-hearted fuddy-duddies. They were not equal to these perilous times. When Benedict's summons reached them, they trembled. They agreed to act circumspectly and calmly, not to interrupt their opponent, and, above all, to be united and harmonious, but they disregarded these resolutions, exposed their weakness, and finally split into factions, each of which took its own course." In the course of the discussions, "the notables took courage and asked the Pope to release them from the controversy, adducing as a reason that their opponents employed scholastic methods of reasoning in which it was impossible for them to follow them, since their faith was not based on syllogisms, but on tradition[412]."

---

[412] Heinrich Graetz, *History of the Jews IV*, Philadelphia, The Jewish Publication Society of America, 1894, p. 208, 211 (cf. Salomon Ben-Virga, *Schevet Jehttda, chap. 40*). [The light that had formed in the great cities of Andalusia seemed to have flashed in the fifteenth century on all the cities of Spain where there were Hebrew communities; everywhere there were Talmudic scholars, physicians, mathematicians, poets and philosophers; they wrote Arabic alongside Hebrew, and composed a multitude of works on all kinds of subjects, copies of which are still preserved in manuscript in the library of the Escorial. But, surprisingly, in this quantity of writings there is none that can

This controversy lasted, with many interruptions, for twenty-one months (from February 1413 to 12 November 1414), spread over sixty-eight sessions, sometimes in front of two thousand spectators. On the sixty-third day, Jerome of Santa Fe virulently attacked the Talmud, as Nicolas Donin had done earlier, accusing it of containing all sorts of horrors, blasphemies and heresies, calling for the book to be condemned and censored. To achieve his goal, Jerome compiled and listed all these abominations. Heinrich Graetz noted here that "he had collected all the extravagances accidentally uttered by one or two of the hundreds of *aggadists* listed in the Talmud[413]."

Jerome then repeated the accusations made by his predecessor Alphonse of Valladolid. The Jews were then divided into two groups. In agreement with the majority of his colleagues, Astruc Levi declared in writing that the incriminated Talmudic *aggadahs* had no authority and represented no religious obligation. But Joseph Albo and Don Vidal protested and asserted that they submitted to the authority of the *aggadahs*, albeit with some reservation since, according to them, the passages quoted by Jerome were not to be taken literally.

The papal court had also demanded the presence in Tortosa of those thousands of Jews who had listened to Vicente Ferrer and had accepted baptism. They presented themselves in groups in the audience hall and publicly professed their Christian faith. Three thousand neophytes were thus paraded in the baptisteries of Tortosa, and the year 1414 was remembered by the Jews as "the year of apostasy". At the last session of the colloquy, the pope bade a cold farewell to the Jewish notables and announced that new restrictive measures would be taken against his co-

---

compare with the good taste of the classical models of antiquity. The Greek and Roman masterpieces were still almost totally unknown to the Hebrews, and the Jews of Spain could only imitate the Arabs, to whom they were perfectly suited in the exuberance of their words, the grandiloquence of their style, the exaggeration and disorder of their thoughts, and their busy imagination. One of their writers, Solomon Ben Virga, naively admitted this state of affairs through one of the interlocutors in his book *The Sceptre of Judah*: "In the old days," he said, "the Jews looked like men whose torch had been lit in a fire that glowed in the distance; they had the gift of divination and possessed precious traditions. The Hebrews of our century, alas! seem to draw with difficulty a few sparks from a pebble; their great efforts have little result: even what they produce is reduced to almost nothing.'" In Georges-Bernard Depping, *Les Juifs dans le Moyen-Âge*, (1823), Éd. Wouters, Bruxelles, 1844, p. 248. (The Jewish rabbis and sages do not practice Aristotelian logic, but commentary and timeless interpolation, their "tradition". See note 111 on the *Midrash* in *Psychoanalysis of Judaism*).

[413] Heinrich Graetz, *History of the Jews IV*, Philadelphia, The Jewish Publication Society of America, 1894, p. 213. [The *Aggadah* is a mixture of narratives and anecdotes about rabbis, biblical figures, angels, demons, sorceries and miracles. See note 106 on the *Aggadah* in *Psychoanalysis of Judaism*].

religionists. All but two of the rabbis declared, on behalf of the multitude of Jews who had attended the debates, that they acknowledged and abjured their errors and requested baptism[414].

"On May 11, 1415, the Pope sent from Valencia the bull which was to determine the fate of the unconverted Jews and to put a new seal of condemnation on this nation. The bull contained almost an entire code, each article of which was in some way a punishment for the Jews. They were ordered to deliver all copies, commentaries and abstracts of the Talmud to the churches and cathedrals of the various dioceses within a month; they were forbidden to read or teach this book, as well as the *Marmar Yeschu*, or any other book contrary to the dogmas of the Church, on pain of being treated as blasphemers. It was declared that no Jew could in future exercise the functions of judge, even for the trials of his nation, nor those of physician, surgeon, pharmacist, innkeeper, nor in short any public office which placed in his hands the affairs of Christians; they were forbidden even to trade and make contracts with Christians, to eat, to bathe with them, to be their stewards or agents, and to have Christian servants or nurses. It was further ordered that all newly built or repaired synagogues should be closed; that where there were two or more, only the smallest should be left open; that henceforth Jews should occupy separate quarters from Christians in towns and villages; that Jewish parents could not disinherit their converted children on any pretext; and that, lastly, wherever Jews remained, they were to be given three public sermons a year, which they were to be compelled to attend[415]."

The son of the apostate Paul, Gonzalo de Santa Maria, baptised at the same time as his father, was charged with overseeing the strict execution of this papal edict. Undoubtedly, this bull was merely a restatement of the dispositions taken by Queen Catherine. But with the difference that Benedict XIII's bull applied to Jews in all Christian countries and not only in Castile.

If Benedict XIII's bull had been applied, it would have meant the end of the Jews' political existence. In effect, the civil rights of the sect would have disappeared and the Jews would have been excluded from Christian society. But Antipope Pedro Luna, recognised only in Aragon, did not have sufficient authority over Christendom. Even Castile did not abide by his bull.

Benedict XIII, dismissed by the Council of Constance and abandoned by his friends, quickly saw his magnificence reduced to his small fortress at Peniscola. The fate of Jerome of Santa Fe after the fall of his protector

---

[414] See in Rodrigo de Castro, *Biblioth. Espan.*, vol.
[415] Georges-Bernard Depping, *Les Juifs dans le Moyen-Âge*, (1823), Éd. Wouters, Brussels, 1844, p. 238–239.

is unknown. In Jewish circles, this feared convert was nicknamed *Megaddéf* (the Blasphemer). King Ferdinand of Aragon, the regent Catherine and Vincent Ferrer disappeared from the scene at about the same time, between 1417 and 1419.

In Castile, Catherine's restrictive laws continued to apply, and Benedict XIII's bull remained in force in Aragon. "Ferrer's proselytising had seriously damaged the Spanish Jewish communities, and even abroad," wrote Graetz. In many other places in Europe, Ferrer, either by his preaching or by the fame of his exploits, had caused "considerable harm to the Jews."

LXXV. Martin V

After the end of the great schism in the West, a synod organised by the Jewish communities of Italy, held in Bologna and Forli (1416 and 1418), had raised the necessary funds to buy the protection of the Pope and the College of Cardinals. Pope Martin V allowed himself to be corrupted, and on 31 January 1419, he promulgated a bull which began as follows: ""Considering that the Jews are made in the image of God, and that the remnant of their nation will one day be saved, we decree, following in the footsteps of our predecessors, that they shall not be molested in their synagogues; that their laws, rights and customs shall not be attacked; that they shall not be forcibly baptised, compelled to observe Christian festivals, nor to wear new distinctive insignia, and that they shall not be hindered in their commercial relations with Christians.""

"What could have induced Pope Martin to show such a friendly countenance towards the Jews? The chief consideration was probably the rich gifts with which the Jewish representatives approached him. At the Council of Constance no cardinal was poorer than Martin, and his election to the throne of St. Peter's was largely due to this fact that he showed no aversion to money. On the contrary, everything could be obtained from him if money was paid; without it, nothing[416]", explained Gratez in his pages.

Afterwards, however, Martin V had to crack down on the crimes committed by the Jews. It is a well-known fact that the merchants of the sect never had any scruples when it came to trafficking in human flesh. On the shores of the Black Sea, some of them did not hesitate to sell young Christians to Muslims. The city of Cafa in the Crimea was a flourishing colony, an emporium of Genoese trade on the Black Sea. Many foreigners had settled there to take advantage of the activity of this Italian colony, and

---

[416] Heinrich Graetz, *History of the Jews IV*, Philadelphia, The Jewish Publication Society of America, 1894, p. 220.

the Jews were not left behind. We do not have much information about the business they conducted there, but we do know that several of them, although they did not worship publicly and were careful not to show any outward religious signs, were engaged in the slave trade. They bought young adolescent boys and girls from the Tartars, the Russians and in the Caucasus, and resold them to the Saracens at a handsome profit. Young Christian slaves, male and female, ended up in Muslim harems. The Dominicans of Cafa alerted the Pope to this abominable traffic, and Martin V, indignant, ordered in a bull that Jews should always wear the distinctive mark on their clothes; he then authorised the bishop of Cafa and the other Genoese emporiums to seize the goods of the Jews who had sold slaves and to use the money collected to ransom the young men sold. The recalcitrant ones were to be expelled from the colonies[417].

A 15th century Italian author, Giovani Fiorentino, had perfectly understood the nature of the Jews. In one of his stories, he showed a Jew from Mestre willing to cut a pound of flesh from the body of his Venetian debtor, simply for the joy of seeing a Christian die.

A text by an anonymous author entitled *Gernutus, the Jew of Venice*, had been published at the end of the 14th century. Sung to the tune of *Black and Yellow*, the ballad had been revived in 1765 by an English folklorist named Thomas Percy, Canon of Dromore: "In the city of Venice/ Not long ago/ Lived a cruel Jew/ Who lived by usury/ According to Italian writers[418]...". Between 1553 and 1640, the English theatre counted no less than sixty plays with a Jewish usurer among the main characters. William Shakespeare had taken up this well-worn theme in 1600 in his famous play *The Merchant of Venice*, whose horrible usurer Shylock still personifies today that implacable hatred of the Jew towards Christians[419].

LXXVI. The Hussites and the Council of Basle

On the other side of Europe, the population distrusted the Jews as much or even more than on the Iberian peninsula. The buckler, imposed since the Fourth Lateran Council in 1215, was useful to know who one was dealing

---

[417] Georges-Bernard Depping, *Les Juifs dans le Moyen-Âge*, (1823), Éd. Wouters, Brussels, 1844, p. 311–312. Let us recall that in the 1990s, after the collapse of the Soviet bloc, tens of thousands of young Russian, Moldovan and Ukrainian women were literally kidnapped through false advertisements and forced into prostitution in the brothels of Israel. Read about the White Slave Trade in the *Jewish Mafia* (2008).

[418] Marie-France Rouart, *L'antisémitisme dans la littérature populaire*, Berg International, p. 87.

[419] See the film *The Merchant of Venice* (2003), by Michael Radford, with Al Pacino. At least the trial scene.

with. Canon 33 of the Salzburg Council of 1418 contained a specific provision to warn off overly naive goyim: while Jewish men were ordered to wear the yellow cap, Jewish women were required to hang a small bell on their dress[420].

Unrest began in Austria in 1420 for the usual reasons. On 23 May, Archduke Albert (Albrecht) had the Jews of the kingdom arrested and imprisoned. In the prisons, women were separated from their husbands and children from their parents. Those who refused to abjure were led to the stake. More than a hundred victims perished in Vienna on 12 March 1421, burned in a meadow on the banks of the Danube. On the same day, the synagogue in Vienna was destroyed. In addition, an edict of the Archduke henceforth forbade all Jews to stay in Vienna.

The new converts took refuge in Poland, Italy and Bohemia. But the latter country became less and less safe for them. After the death of John Hus in July 1415, the religious struggle between Catholics and Hussites had become a national struggle between Czechs and Germans[421]. The Jews, who systematically favoured everything that contributed to weakening the Catholic Church, naturally supported the Hussite movement by providing them with money and weapons. So the Hussites did not show any hatred towards the Jews. Only on one occasion, when they plundered Catholic houses, they also plundered some Jewish houses.

"Whenever a constituted party within Christendom opposed the ruling

---

[420] Charles Auzias-Turenne, *Revue Catholique des Institutions et du Droit*, October 1893.

[421] The term Hussite refers to the reform and revolutionary movement that arose in Bohemia at the beginning of the 15th century. The name comes from the theologian John Hus (1369–1415), who was condemned and executed at the Council of Constance for taking a highly critical stance towards ecclesiastical power. His terrible death aggravated religious, social and national tensions, leading to the revolutionary outbreak of July 1419, when the mob stormed Prague's town hall, defenestrated the municipal authorities, freed several prisoners accused of being Hussites, and seized power in the city. The death of King Wenceslas in August of the same year and his brother Sigismund's claim to the Czech throne further complicated the political scene, as the high nobility supported him while the petty nobility, the bourgeoisie and the underprivileged social classes opposed his claims. John Hus, who had studied the ideas of the English theologian and reformer John Wyclif, did not confine himself to speaking on matters of faith, but added his own comments on the situation of the Church and his political views, particularly on the rights of the kingdom of Bohemia, which endeared him to his listeners. Through Hus, the scholarly reform movement began to connect with the emerging popular opposition to the abuses of the Church. From then on, the message of religious reform associated with the need for social and political change and the national question began to spread. Within a few years, almost all of Bohemia was following Hus's lead, and he was seen as a danger by a Church that was then coming to terms with the crisis of the Schism.

church, it assumed an Old Testament, not to say Jewish, character. The Hussites regarded Catholicism as paganism, and themselves as Israelites, who were to wage a holy war against Philistines, Moabites and Ammonites. Churches and monasteries were for them the shrines of a dissolute idolatry, temples of Baal and Moloch… to be consumed with fire and sword[422]", Graetz noted.

Emperor Sigismund then gathered considerable forces of his own, hiring German Lansquenets and mercenaries from Brabant and Holland. Armed bands came from all sides and marched on Prague, where the Hussite leader Ziska organised the defence of the country. German soldiers systematically attacked Jews as they passed through. In the Rhine provinces, in Thuringia and Bavaria, they killed every Jew they came across. Sigismund did not want to allow them to be mistreated, but he was not their fervent defender either. It was at this time that the Jewish community in Cologne was completely expelled (1426). In Ravensburg, Ueberlingen and Lindau, Jews accused of ritual murder were imprisoned and burned (1430).

The Council of Basel (June 1431—May 1443), deliberated on all major European issues. The council renewed all the old restrictive measures against Jews. Canonical rules were reinstated forbidding Jews to have relations with Christians, to employ them as servants, to be their physicians, and to hold public office. Jews were required to wear distinctive clothing and to remain in their special quarters. To these old prohibitions, the council added several new prohibitions: Jews were not to hold any university degrees and were to be forced, even by force, to listen to the preaching of missionaries. It was also decided to introduce the study of Hebrew, Chaldean and Arabic in the higher schools in order to facilitate conversions. This council also dealt with the problem of Jewish converts. It recommended to be kind to them, but to keep a close watch on them.

It is very likely that the apostates Gonzalo and Alfonso de Cartagena, sent as delegates to this assembly by King John II of Castile, played an important role. Indeed, the influence of the two brothers can be seen in several resolutions passed at the council, which were only justified because they were against the Jews of Spain. Certainly, at that time in Germany it was not yet possible to consider prohibiting Jews from holding a chair in a school, because German Jews did not yet dare to enter universities as professors.

Emperor Sigismund died in 1437. His successor Albert of Austria was an implacable enemy of the Jews and heretics, of whom Graetz wrote: "He

---

[422] Heinrich Graetz, *History of the Jews IV*, Philadelphia, The Jewish Publication Society of America, 1894, p. 222.

could not exterminate either, for the Hussites had courage and arms, and the Jews were an inexhaustible source of money; but he always tried to collaborate with those who wished to harm them. When the Augsburg city council decided to expel the Jewish community (1439), the emperor cheerfully gave his consent. They were given two years to sell their houses and real estate; at the end of that time they were all banished and the gravestones from the Jewish cemetery were used to repair the city walls. Fortunately for the Jews, Albert reigned for only two years, and the government of the Holy Roman Empire... fell to the kindly, weak, indolent and docile Frederick III [423]." Indeed, this monarch would be more favourable to the Jews.

LXXVII (1449): the Statutes of blood cleansing in Spain

The Spanish reaction against the Jews continued with greater force. In 1434, at the age of 82, Pablo de Santa María had written a new libel against the Jews and Judaism, *Examen de la santa Escritura*, which took the form of a dialogue between the unbelieving Saul and the convert Pablo.

A former rabbi named Juan de España, whom the preaching of Vincent Ferrer had led to Catholicism in his old age, had also denounced the crimes of Judaism. He justified his abjuration and encouraged his former co-religionists to imitate him. Jerome of Santa Fe's criticism of the Talmud during the Tortosa dispute had spread throughout the country. Following that great controversy, one of the baptised Jews, the jurist Pedro de la Caballería, wrote a treatise entitled *Zelus Christi contra Judeos, Saracenos et infideles* in 1450. During those decades, many Jews in Spain had definitively abandoned Judaism.

At the beginning of his pontificate, Eugenius IV was benevolent towards the Jews, confirming the privileges granted to them by his predecessor Martin V. He forbade forced baptisms or mistreatment of the Jews. But he quickly changed his policy, probably influenced by Alfonso de Cartagena, Bishop of Burgos, who at the Council of Basel had strongly defended the cause of Pope Eugenius. This bishop of Jewish origin was dubbed by the pope *the joy of Spain and the honour of the clergy*. On 10 August 1442, Eugene IV wrote a missive to the bishops of Castile and Leon to tell them that the Jews were abusing the prerogatives granted by previous popes. He reinstated all the restrictive measures enacted against the Jews

---

[423] Heinrich Graetz, *History of the Jews IV*, Philadelphia, The Jewish Publication Society of America, 1894, p. 249.

by Pope Benedict XIII that had never really been taken into consideration by King John II.

The "New Christians" had acquired a lot of influence in Spain, and not all of them were sincere converts, far from it. Heinrich Graetz wrote here: "Intoxicated by their brilliant position and riches, many of them showed the pride of upstarts, attracting with their presumptuous arrogance the envy and hatred of the old Christians[424]."

In 1449, in Toledo, the Constable of Castile Álvaro de Luna ordered a loan to be issued. The measure aroused the population's revulsion and resistance to the Marrano tax collectors. The insurrection, led by the mayor of the city, Pedro Sarmiento, managed to push back the royal army. For the first time clashes broke out during which several of the most notable New Christians were captured and hanged. This was the first anti-converso uprising in Spain. Pedro Sarmiento, who owned the place, expelled by decree (*Sentencia estatutos*) all the conversos from the important posts in the city of Toledo (councillors, judges, etc.). Given the duplicity of the Marranos, who pretended to be good Catholics, the concept of *limpieza de sangre* seemed legitimate.

On 2 May, a *Supplication* was sent to King John II and a court met to discuss the right of the conversos to hold public office. On 5 June, the court ruled, despite the opposition of the clergy: converts were declared unfit to hold public office in Toledo and to testify against Christians.

Pope Nicholas V condemned the Toledo *Sentence* in a bull of 24 September 1449, recommending "severe measures against the tormentors of *converts*" and ordering, by the bull *Humani generis inimicus,* that "all converts, present or future, Gentile or Jew, who led a good Christian life, should be admitted to all ministries and dignities, to witness and exercise all burdens on an equal footing with the old Christians".

This decision did not prevent Álvaro de Luna from taking the decision to remove the conversos who held positions in the administration. In 1451, King John II of Castile wrote to the new Pope Nicholas V to inform him that many new Christians, lay and ecclesiastical, monks and religious, were secretly practising Jewish rites and mocking the Church. Nicholas V then ordered, in a letter addressed to the Bishop of Osma and the Dominicans of the University of Salamanca, that the Marranos suspected of Judaising should be brought before a special tribunal. The accused, even if they were bishops, had to appear before this tribunal, justify themselves, and, if they were found guilty, be stripped of their property and dismissed from their functions and handed over to the secular arm to be executed (Relaxation).

---

[424]Heinrich Graetz, *Geschitchte der Juden; Histoire des juifs IV,* Éd. Durlacher, Paris, 1893, p. 359.

This court thus prefigured the Holy Inquisition.

LXXVIII. John of Capistrano, the Scourge of the Hebrews

From the 15th century onwards, Jews began to be frequently expelled from the most important cities in Germany: they were first expelled from Strasbourg in 1388, then from the Palatinate in 1394, from Austria in 1420, from Freiburg and Zurich in 1424, Cologne in 1426, Augsburg in 1439, Bavaria in 1442, Nuremberg in 1448, Würzburg in 1453 and Erfurt in 1458. A snowball effect ensued: Ulm in 1499, Regensburg in 1519, and so on. The Jews of Mainz had been expelled four times in fifty years, from 1420 to 1471. Many took refuge in Poland. Others camped at the gates of the cities. Those from Nuremberg, for example, were able to take refuge in Furth.

In 1450, in order to free the many debtors trapped in the nets of the usurers, the Bavarian Duke of Landshut, Louis IX The Rich, had all the Jews in his territory arrested in one day. The men were imprisoned and the women locked up in the synagogues. Christian debtors were authorised to pay their Jewish creditors only the capital owed, minus the interest already paid. As for the Jews, after a month's detention, they had to buy their freedom for 30,000 guilders and go into exile. Duke Ludwig would gladly have inflicted the same treatment on the wealthy and important Regensburg community under his jurisdiction, albeit only partially, but they, as burghers of the city, were entitled to protection by the city council. He therefore had to confine himself to imposing a tax on them.

At the provincial council of Bamberg in May 1451, a cardinal named Nicholas of Cusa (originally from Cues in the Moselle), who was also a papal legate, had succeeded in decreeing the obligation for Jews to wear a piece of red cloth on their bust and for Jewish women to wear a blue ribbon in their hair.

In Italy, the most prominent anti-Jewish figures were two Franciscans, John of Capistrano and Bernardino de Feltro. In Rome, Pope Nicholas V "deeply hated the Jews", wrote Graetz. He began by stripping the Italian Jews of their former privileges, after which he issued a new bull subjecting them to all the restrictive laws that his predecessor had enacted against the Jews of Castile. John of Capistrano, "sworn enemy of the Jews", was charged with overseeing their strict execution and "carried out his task with unprecedented ferocity".

Capistrano was a monk with a haggard face. He slept and ate little, was charitable to his fellow man, and his austere life earned him the admiration and respect of the people. John was born on 24 June 1386 in the town of

Capistrano, in the Abruzzo region, near Naples. According to Maurice Pinay, author of *Complot against the Church* (1962), he was descended from a noble lord, probably Angevin or Savoyard, who had followed Louis I of Anjou in his conquest of the kingdom of Naples. He was orphaned at an early age and was sent to Perugia where he studied civil and canon law for ten years. He was so brilliant that his teachers used to call on his judgement to answer thorny questions.

Appointed governor of Perugia by King Ladislaus (1412), John of Capistrano was a judge of integrity and incorruptibility. A lord had once tried to bribe him to obtain a death sentence against an enemy, but John, who had carefully investigated the case, recognised the innocence of the accused and released him despite the accuser's threats. Capistrano also had authority to punish Jews who transgressed canonical prescriptions or failed to wear the proper distinguishing mark imposed on them.

In 1415, he sold his possessions, distributed the rest of his belongings to the poor and, in October 1416, was admitted to the Franciscan order in Perugia, where he showed zeal and charity towards his sick brothers. He studied theology and had Bernardine of Siena as his first teacher, who was quick to note his pupil's astonishing progress. One day Bernardine said of him: "John learns by sleeping what others learn by working day and night".

A profound theologian and learned canonist, Capistrano was also the greatest missionary of his time. Around 1420, he was a deacon when Saint Bernardine sent him to preach in Siena and Tuscany. After his ordination to the priesthood around 1425, John travelled around Italy relentlessly to combat all errors, attacking all sects. His seductive voice and energetic will dazzled the masses. All over the peninsula, thousands of inhabitants flocked to listen to him. He denounced the usury of the Jews and their incessant intrigues to dissolve Christian society. Thousands of listeners gathered around him and vibrated with enthusiasm as they listened to him.

He was legate of Eugene IV in Milan (1432) and in Burgundy. After the Council of Florence, he was appointed apostolic nuncio in Sicily, then legate in France. He was then sent to Germany, where Emperor Frederick III and his brother Albert, Duke of Austria, asked for his help in fighting the Hussites and restoring concord among the German princes. John of Capistrano, apostolic nuncio and inquisitor, chose twelve companions and they set out on foot for Germany. Their passage through Lombardy was a triumphal march, for wherever John went he was received as God's envoy.

Pius II portrayed him thus: "He was small in stature, of advanced age (65 years), withered, emaciated, exhausted, with only skin and bones, and yet always cheerful and untiring in work. He preached every day, dealing with the deepest questions, pleasing both the simple people and the learned; he had from twenty to thirty thousand listeners every day; he preached in Latin, and an interpreter translated his discourse."

He expounded his teachings in the public squares, where many people could listen to him. John was quickly nicknamed the "holy preacher", or the *"Scourge of the Hebrews"* because he raised up the poor against the usury of the Jews. For Maurice Pinay, "St. John of Capistrano was the most energetic and effective anti-Jewish Christian leader to emerge after Christ our Lord and the apostles. The destruction he wrought in the Synagogue of Satan is considered by some Hebrews to be most catastrophic[425]". Heinrich Gratez confirmed: "When this enraged Franciscan visited Germany, he spread terror and consternation among the Jews. They trembled at the very mention of his name[426]."

John was an impressive missionary, preaching in Carinthia, Styria, Austria, Bohemia, Moravia, Silesia, Bavaria, Thuringia, Saxony, Franconia, Poland, Transylvania, Moldavia, Wallachia, and other provinces, performing wonders and healings, and even, according to legend, resurrections. He sent several of his religious to Prussia and other provinces, because everywhere they demanded his presence, they required his advice.

Bishop Godfrey of Würzburg, who was also Duke of Franconia, had at first granted numerous privileges to the Jews in his territory. But a few years later, after listening to Capistrano's preaching, his mentality changed completely. Thus, in 1453, he ordered the Jews to sell all their possessions before January of the following year and to emigrate fifteen days later, so that not a single Jew would be left in his bishopric. In turn, he had passed on the order to the cities, counts, lords and judges to carry out this expulsion of the Jews.

Capistrano proved himself worthy of his title of *"Scourge of the Hebrews"* in Silesia. At the invitation of Bishop Peter Nowak of Wroclaw, John went to Wroclaw and gathered the clergy in the church. When the doors were closed, John raised his voice with his usual eloquence against the Hussites and the Jews. His speech did not fall on deaf ears, for many nobles and burghers were in debt and threatened with ruin by the usurers. The Jewish historian Heinrich Graetz recounted the events as follows:

"After summoning the clergy to his presence, the Franciscan preacher rebuked them for their sinful, immoral and sensual life...But what interested him most, besides the recovery of the clergy, was the extermination of the Hussites, of whom there were many in Silesia, and the persecution of the Jews. The frenzied fanaticism with which Capistrano's harangues inspired the people of Breslau was directed mainly against the Jews. News spread that a Jew named Meyer, one of the richest Israelites in

---

[425] Maurice Pinay, *Complot against the Church*, Chapter XLI (1962), Transcription pdf from Ediciones Mundo Libre, Mexico, 1985, p. 369.
[426] Heinrich Graetz, *History of the Jews IV*, Philadelphia, The Jewish Publication Society of America, 1894, p. 258.

Breslau, in whose custody were many of the debts of the bourgeois and nobles, had bought a host from a peasant, desecrated it, and blasphemed it...".

"A wicked, baptised Jewess declared that the Jews of Wroclaw had once burnt a host and that, on another occasion, they had kidnapped a Christian child, fattened him and put him in a barrel with sharp nails which they rolled until the victim expired. His blood was distributed among the communities in Silesia. It was even said that the bones of the murdered child were found. The guilt of the Jews seemed to be proven in all these cases, and a large number of them, 318 persons in all, were arrested in different localities and brought to Breslau. Capistrano tried them and hastened to execute them[427]." On 2 June 1453, forty-one of these accused were burned on the *Salzring*, today's *Blücherplatz*, and the entire Jewish population was expelled from Wroclaw. Children under the age of seven were separated from their parents, baptised and given to Christian parents to be raised in the Catholic religion. The proceeds from the sale of Jewish property were used to build the Bernardine Church. In the other cities of Silesia, Jews met the same fate as in Wroclaw: some were burned at the stake, others were expelled.

The young King Ladislaus, solicited by the council of the city's bourgeoisie, was not content with forbidding the return of the Jews. As a worthy successor of his father Albert II, who had expelled the Jews from Austria, he approved of the torture inflicted on the Silesian Jews, considering "that they had been treated as they deserved". Probably at the instigation of Capistrano, who stayed for some time in Olomouc, Ladislaus again expelled the Jews from this city, as well as from neighbouring Brno.

The Jews of Poland enjoyed an incomparably better situation than their co-religionists in the other countries of Europe. They had long enjoyed the equal rights that had assured them preponderance over the Christians. Poland had thus become a paradise for the "persecuted" Jews of Germany, Austria and Hungary. Expelled from the Adriatic coast, the first Jewish

---

[427] Heinrich Graetz, *History of the Jews IV*, Philadelphia, The Jewish Publication Society of America, 1894, p. 260–262. ["Immediately, all the Jews of Breslau, men, women and children were imprisoned, all their property in the "*Judengasse*" was confiscated, and, what was most important for the perpetrators of the catastrophe, the bonds of their debtors to the value of about 25,000 Hungarian gold florins were confiscated (2 May 1453). The guilt of the Jews was made more credible by the flight of some of them, who, however, were soon apprehended. Capistrano took over the direction of the investigation of this important matter. As inquisitor, he was rightfully entitled to take the lead in the prosecution of the blasphemers of the consecrated host. He ordered some Jews to be laid on the rack, and personally instructed the torturers in their task, for he was experienced in such work. The tortured Israelites confessed." *History of the Jews IV*, p. 261].

families had arrived in the country around 1264, although the great wave of emigration did not begin until seventy years later, under King Casimir. Indeed, the charter of Kalisz granted them freedoms and great privileges that were the basis of their religious, national and economic existence for three centuries[428]. In order to intensify trade and industry, Casimir "The Great" (1333–1370) enacted laws favourable to the Jews when they were persecuted in Germany for their crimes and usury. Under his reign, masses of Jewish emigrants poured in. This king, who unified the Polish state, was largely responsible for Poland's future decline, until the final partition of the country in the 18th century and its complete disappearance.

The kings of Poland were heavily indebted to Jewish financiers. Casimir, for example, had borrowed an enormous sum of 15,000 marks from Jewish bankers. King Ludwig of Hungary, for his part, owed the usurer Levko of Kraków more than 30,000 Gulden. King Vladislav II Jagiellon and Queen Hedwig also owed him very large sums. Lithuanian chancellery records indicate that during the period from 1463 to 1494, the Jews leased almost all the customs in the Lithuanian duchy[429].

Important Jewish communities were established in the capital of the kingdom, in Kraków, in Lemberg and other large towns[430]. It is said that Casimir's benevolence was due to his romance with a Jewess named Esther, the daughter of a tailor. The common people, on the other hand, viewed the presence of the Jews with hostility. In Poznan in 1399, a rabbi and thirteen notables of the community were arrested and burned at the stake. In Krakow, a massacre of Jews took place in 1406. But Poland's misfortune was that its princes were easily bought by financiers. Casimir IV, King of Poland and Prince of Lithuania (1447–1492), also protected the Jews as best he could.

The powerful bishop of Kraków, Cardinal Zbigniew Olesnizki, the head of the Polish clergy, invited Capistrano to come and preach in his diocese. In Kraków, the Franciscan monk was triumphantly received and during his entire stay in Kraków (1453–1454) he and the bishop did not cease to exhort the king to fight the Hussites and the Jews, publicly rebuking King Casimir and predicting that he would finally be defeated in his war against the Teutonic knights of Prussia if he did not decide to abolish the privileges of the Jews and separate from the Hussites. In September 1454, the

---

[428] The committed writer Manes Sperber (1905–1984) did not hesitate to write these words about his Polish-Jewish ancestors: "Among backward peoples, they set out to create a civilisation exemplary for its humanitarian and religious values", *Être Juif*, Odile Jacob, 1994, p. 115, 116.

[429] Abraham Léon, *La Conception matérialiste de la question juive*, Études et Documentation internationales, 1942, Paris, 1968, p. 114-117.

[430] Simon Doubnov, in *Précis d'histoire juive, des origines à 1934*.

Teutonic knights defeated the Polish army and forced Casimir to flee the battlefield in disgrace. The king then took action against the Jews. Throughout the country, public criers announced that all Jewish privileges were abolished.[431]

It was at this time that a crucial historical event took place that shook the whole of Christendom and had very favourable consequences for the Jews: on 29 May 1453, Constantinople was taken by the Turkish conqueror Mehmed II, finalising the destruction of the Byzantine Empire. The victor inflicted all sorts of humiliations and tortures on the vanquished. The historian Herinrich Graetz did not conceal a certain satisfaction and revanchism: "From Constantine, the founder of the Byzantine empire, who put a bloodstained sword into the hands of the church, to the last of the emperors, Constantine Dragases, of the dynasty of the Palaeologians, all in the long series of rulers (with the exception of the apostate Julian) were more or less inspired by falsehood and treachery, and by an arrogant, hypocritical spirit and an excessive ardour of persecution. And the people, as well as the servants of the state and of the church, were worthy of their rulers. From them, the German, Latin and Slavic peoples had derived the principle that the Jews were to be degraded by exceptional laws, or even exterminated. Now, however, Byzantium itself lay shattered in the dust, and savage barbarians were raising the new Turkish empire in its place. A great revenge had been exacted."

Mehmed II allowed Jews to settle freely in Constantinople and other cities of the Ottoman Empire. He allowed them to build synagogues and schools, guaranteeing them complete commercial freedom. Everyone was free to dispose of his property as he pleased, to dress freely, to cover himself with silk and gold. "In short, Graetz wrote, Turkey was aptly described by one Jewish enthusiast as a land "in which nothing, absolutely nothing, was lacking". Two young immigrants, Kalman and David, thought that if German Jews knew one tenth of the happiness that could be found in Turkey, they would defy any difficulty to get there[432]." Indeed, this would come to pass a few decades later with the mass expulsion of the Jews from Spain in 1492.

After the fall of Constantinople, the Turks threatened Hungary. Mehmed II prepared the invasion with an army of 100,000 men. The Christians, for their part, prepared for war. At the Diet of Neustadt on 2 February 1455, John of Capistran succeeded in proclaiming the crusade.

---

[431]The Jews of Poland were briefly expelled by Grand Duke Alexander in 1495, but reintroduced a few years later by the new king of Poland, Alexander I, in 1501. Thus, in Europe, only the Netherlands never expelled Jews.
[432] Heinrich Graetz, *History of the Jews IV*, Philadelphia, The Jewish Publication Society of America, 1894, p. 267, 271.

He triumphantly entered Hungary, and, at the Diet of Bude, he dispelled all hesitation and stirred all hearts and minds. He preached throughout the country in favour of the crusade and was finally appointed generalissimo of the crusade by John Hunyadi.

John Hunyadi first supplied and fortified the city of Belgrade at his own expense. He then built up a supporting army and a fleet of two hundred corvettes. The Hungarian overlords, wary of his growing power, once again let him finance the entire operation. Hunyadi had gathered about 15,000 mercenaries, and Capistrano brought with him an army of 35,000 peasants, artisans and students, most armed only with slings and scythes. The two marched at the head of their soldiers towards Turkish-held Belgrade. On 14 July 1456, John Hunyadi arrived near Belgrade and managed to break the Turkish naval blockade. During the eleven days that followed the naval victory, Capistrano remained day and night in the midst of the crusaders, never faltering, encouraging them to resist.

On 21 July, Mehmed II, eager to take advantage of the damage done to the fortress, ordered the final all-night assault. The attackers entered the lower town and began attacking the fortress. Hunyadi then ordered the defenders of Belgrade to throw flammable materials at the Ottomans. In fact, the janissaries were separated from the rest of the army by flames. They were surrounded and the battle turned in favour of the Christians who repulsed the assailants outside the city walls. On 22 July 1456, the Crusader peasants took spontaneous action. Despite Hunyadi's orders, they broke out of the almost ruined walls of Belgrade and attacked the Ottoman soldiers. Immediately, other Christians joined the offensive, and the unexpected movement turned into a truly decisive battle. John of Capistrano then decided to lead some 2,000 crusaders against the Turkish lines, shouting *"The God who started it will see it through!"* At the same time, Hunyadi took advantage of the situation to charge from the fort to seize the Turkish guns. The 5000 janissaries tried in vain to restore order and stop the panic in the ranks of the Turkish army. The sultan himself had to intervene in the battle, but an arrow in the thigh knocked him down, causing the Turkish troops and their wounded to retreat.

After this great victory, an outbreak of plague appeared in the Hungarian army. John Hunyadi fell ill and died on 11 August 1456 in the arms of John of Capistrano. John of Capistrano, exhausted by years and fatigue, devoured from within by a constant fever, also saw the hour of death approaching. On 23 October 1456, he received the last sacraments in the convent of Vilak and died peacefully at the age of seventy. John Capistran's body was buried in the Vilak convent church. He was canonised in October 1690, and his feast day has been celebrated on 23 October ever since.

The Christian victory at Belgrade halted the Ottoman advance in central

Europe for a few decades, but in 1521 the Turks took the city and Vilak Castle, razing the Franciscan convent to the ground. By 1527, they were at the gates of Vienna.

LXXIX. *Alfonso de Espina*

The situation of the Jews in Spain still seemed quite satisfactory during the reigns of Henry IV (1457–1474), the King of Castile, and John II (1450–1479), the King of Aragon. Henry IV, perhaps even more indolent than his father John II of Castile, was not too concerned with whether the canon laws concerning the Jews were actually enforced. But the anger of the people was growing everywhere.

Alfonso de Espina, a Franciscan monk who was rector of the University of Salamanca, thundered against them from the top of his chair, attacking the Jews and their protectors with word and pen. Around 1460, he wrote in Latin a libel against heretics, Jews and Muslims, under the title *Fortalitium fidei,* the *Strength of the Faith,* in which he expressed the usual recriminations: "Spirit of treason, ritual crimes, poisoning doctors, destruction of Christians with the outrageous practice of usury, false Jews and sodomites, etc.".

The greed of the Israelites already made them particularly odious. Alfonso de Espina cited the case of a usurer from Zamora, who for ten thousand silver coins lent had received sixty thousand in interest. Others had demanded one hundred percent interest; squires and noblemen were in fact his prisoners. The peasants, in order to get rid of their debts, were obliged to give them the fruits of their crops. At the Cortes of Valladolid in 1385, many complained that the nobles were getting along with them to dispossess the municipalities of their goods[433].

The Franciscan also presented an enumerated and chronological catalogue of ritual crimes perpetrated by the Jews. Murders and acts of witchcraft were the main infamies of this long black series.

"Alfonso de Espina accused the Jews of the greatest crimes and the most odious vices. He maintained that in Spain they indulged in shameless sodomy, that they subtly mixed poisons, and that every year they agreed to slit the throat of a Christian child in one city or another. He cited one such example, according to an eye-witness, who told him more or less in these terms of the dreadful scene he was obliged to witness. His name was Manuel, and he was the son of a skilful physician of Genoa named Solomon; in 1450 he made his confession before the bishop who was to baptise him,

---

[433] Georges-Bernard Depping, *Les Juifs dans le Moyen-Âge,* (1823), Éd. Wouters, Brussels, 1844, p. 255.

as well as before the dean of the church of Compostella and before other notable men, ecclesiastical and lay, and the notary of the royal audience made a record of the deposition to be preserved in the archives of the convent where the deed was signed[434]: When I was in Savona, a city dependent on Genoa," he said, "my father took me to the house of a Jew, where seven or eight men of his religion were secretly gathered to sacrifice a Christian child. After locking the doors with great care, they all solemnly swore never to reveal anything of what they were about to do, and to die and take their lives rather than reveal the least thing to any mortal. This oath having been taken, they brought in a boy of about two years of age and placed him on a vase in which the blood of the circumcised was usually collected. Two Jews stretched out his arms in the form of a cross; a third held his head up; a fourth, who was in charge of the execution, put steaming oakum in his mouth to prevent him from screaming; then he took long iron spikes and stuck them into various parts of the boy's body, so that his entrails were pierced and the blood flowed abundantly into the vase. I was deeply horrified by this cruel spectacle; I could no longer watch and had to leave. My father followed me and implored me never to reveal to anyone what I had just seen, and that I would rather die by my own hand than admit it. Then he took me back to the room: the boy had already expired. His body was thrown into a deep latrine. Then they cut into pieces various fruits, such as apples, pears, walnuts, hazelnuts, etc., and threw them into the blood-filled vase. I was obliged to do the same as the others, but as soon as I tasted it I nearly fell ill, and for two days my guts seemed to churn with horror every time I wanted to eat anything[435]"."

Alfonso de Espina also recounted the case of a Jewish doctor who had provided a poison to a nobleman called Juan de Vega, who wanted to get rid of his older brother in order to receive his inheritance. The crime was discovered. The nobleman escaped prosecution by taking monastic vows and the Jew committed suicide[436].

The eschatological perspective was also present in the *Fortalitium fidei*: when the Antichrist appears, the Jews will gather around him and worship him as a god. Following the example of Duns Scot and John of Capistrano, Alphonsus de Spina advocated the separation of young Jewish children

---

[434]Certissime enim çompertum est quod omni anno in qualibet provincia sortes mittunt quæ civitas vel oppidum christiani sanguinem aliis civitatibus tradat. *Fortalitium fidei*, lib. III, cap. Quinta crudelitas Judoeorum.

[435] Georges-Bernard Depping, *Les Juifs dans le Moyen-Âge*, (1823), Éd. Wouters, Brussels, 1844, p. 246–247.

[436] Georges-Bernard Depping, *Les Juifs dans le Moyen-Âge*, (1823), Éd. Wouters, Brussels, 1844, p. 255.

from their parents in order to bring them up in the Catholic faith[437]. Moreover, he agreed with all the persecutions of the past, including massacres. The *Fortalitium fidei* had at least eight reprints in fifty-eight years (1471–1529), including three in the city of Lyon in France.

In Spain, the Christian people were especially suspicious of the Marranos, for these new Christians had reached the highest political and ecclesiastical echelons and played a leading role in the Cortes and the Council of State, even occupying episcopal seats[438]. The Franciscans were the first to sound the alarm against these false converts in the religious orders and the secular clergy. In 1461, they begged the General of the Order of St. Geronimo, Brother Alonso de Oropesa, for help in extirpating the evil. The Order of St. Geronimo had many new Christians in its midst and the General was caught in the crossfire. He proposed, however, that the bishops should be in charge of judging the Marranos and instituted an Inquisition to judge the cases. He wrote a treatise entitled *Lumen ad revelationem gentium et gloriam Israel* (1465), in which he denounced both Jews and Marranos.

The *Book of Alboraique*, published in 1488 by an anonymous author, "took up again in about ten pages the popular accusations addressed this time to both New-Christians and Jews: liars, vain, cowards, blasphemers, sacrilegious and sodomites[439]." The author wrote in the introduction that

---

[437] It would indeed be the best way to break the trauma and the chain of "incestuous generations". Read *Psychoanalysis of Judaism* and *The Mirror of Judaism*.

[438] "But after 1391, when the pressure on the Jews became more violent, whole communities embraced the Christian faith. Most of the neophytes eagerly took advantage of their new position. They thronged in their hundreds and thousands to places from which they had previously been excluded by their faith. They entered forbidden professions and the quiet cloisters of universities. They conquered important positions in the State and even penetrated the sanctum sanctorum of the Church. Their power increased with their wealth, and many could aspire to be admitted to the oldest and most aristocratic families in Spain...An Italian near contemporary observed that Jewish converts practically ruled Spain, while their secret adherence to Judaism was ruining the Christian faith. A wedge of hatred inevitably drove the relations of old and new Christians apart. The neophytes were known as marranos (probably "the reprobate" or "the swine"). They were despised for their triumphs, for their pride, for their cynical adherence to Catholic practices. While the masses viewed the triumphs of the new Christians with grim bitterness, the clergy denounced their disloyalty and insincerity. They suspected the truth that most of the converts were still Jews at heart, that forced conversion had not extirpated the heritage of centuries. Tens of thousands of the new Christians outwardly submitted, mechanically went to church, mumbled prayers, performed rites and observed customs. But the spirit had not been converted. In Abram Leon Sachar, *History of the Jews*, Ch. XVI (*The Marranos and the Inquisition*), trans. from the 2nd American ed. revised to 1940, Ediciones Ercilla, Santiago de Chile, 1945, p. 276, 277.

[439] Daniel Tollet, *Les Textes judéophobes et judéophiles dans l'Europe chrétienne à*

he wished to provide his readers with "weapons against the enemies of Christ."

Alfonso de Espina's preaching against the Marranos sparked popular unrest in Madrid. In Toledo, altercations took place in 1467, repeating the scenes of 1449; but this time it was the conversos who started the fight by storming the cathedral. They then took possession of the bridges and city gates. This momentary success lasted until their return to the cathedral, for inside the temple the besieged Old Catholics managed to ring the bells and reinforcements arrived. The counter-offensive of the Old Christians completely disrupted the Marranos, who were totally defeated. The mob massacred one hundred and thirty Marranos. Those who defended themselves were hanged from the gallows and six hundred houses of the Marranos were burnt down.

In 1469, the marriage of the Infanta Isabella, later dubbed *the Catholic*, to the Infante Ferdinand of Aragon finally ushered in the era of Spanish preponderance. At the beginning of Ferdinand and Isabella's reign, there were new popular revolts against the Jews. In 1471, the inhabitants of Sepúlveda, a small town near Segovia, took revenge on the local Jews after the death of a Christian child during Holy Week. By order of the bishop, Juan Arias Dávila, son of the Marrano minister Diego Arias Dávila, eight of the accused considered guilty were taken to Segovia and condemned. Some were burned at the stake, others were hanged or seized. Apparently, this execution was not a sufficient punishment for the people of Sepúlveda, who preferred to finish off the Jews directly, massacring almost all of them mercilessly.

In Cordoba, the Marranos were pilloried. In 1473, a religious confraternity consecrated to the Virgin Mary was formed in this city, from which converts were excluded. During the procession organised by this confraternity on Easter Eve, the houses and streets of Cordoba were decorated with flowers and tapestries. But during the procession, a young Marrano girl threw dirty water on the image of the Virgin. The houses of the marranos were all set on fire and most of them were killed while the rest fled the city.

LXXX. *Bernardino de Feltre*

---

l'époque moderne, Presses Universitaires de France, 2000, p. 30, 34. *Et quod vereor calamo scribere... ceciderunt in passiones ignominiæ... laudantes se per vicos et plateas crimen pessimum commississe. Fortalitiumfidei*, lib. III, cap. *De statu Judoeorum in regno Castellœ*, in Georges-Bernard Depping, *Les Juifs dans le Moyen-Âge*, (1823), Éd. Wouters, Brussels, 1844, p. 246.

In Italy, as elsewhere, Jewish usurers had reduced many Christians to abject poverty. Of course, Heinrich Graetz had a more nuanced view of the situation: "The Jews, as capitalists and skilled diplomats, were therefore well received in Italy. Proof of this was the fact that when the city of Ravenna wanted to join Venice, it included among the conditions of the union the demand that rich Jews be sent to it to open credit banks and thus alleviate the poverty of the population. In many Italian cities, Jewish capitalists received from the reigning princes or senates extensive privileges that allowed them to open banks, establish themselves as brokers and even charge a high rate of interest (20%)...A Jew from Pisa, named Yechiel, controlled the money market in Tuscany. He was by no means a mere heartless miser, as the Christians used to call him, but rather a man of noble mind and tender heart, always ready to help the poor with his gold and to comfort the unfortunate in word and deed[440]."

To counteract this situation, Franciscan monks decided to combat Jewish usury by creating credit institutions—the montes de piedad—which were to compete with the Jews on their own turf. These pawnshops lent at a very low interest rate[441]. The tireless preaching of the Franciscan monks led to the creation of about thirty such institutions throughout the country between 1462 (Monte di Pietà of Perugia) and 1496 (those of Treviso, Udine, Pisa and Florence).

In 1462, in Perugia, a Franciscan monk named Barnaba had managed to raise a large amount of capital to make available to borrowers. The poor could deposit some garments as collateral and take small sums of money in exchange for a small interest to cover the pawnshop's maintenance costs.

Imitating the example of Perugia, the inhabitants of Savona, who also suffered from Jewish usurers, created the same credit institution and obtained confirmation from the Holy See in 1479. A few days later, the city of Mantua founded another similar institution which was to be governed by twelve directors, four of whom would be religious, two nobles, two jurists or doctors, two merchants and two bourgeois. The religious were to be members in perpetuity and the eight laymen were to occupy their posts for two years, with half of them being renewed each year.

---

[440] Heinrich Graetz, *History of the Jews IV*, Philadelphia, The Jewish Publication Society of America, 1894, p. 286. ["The Jews of Italy were desirable citizens, not only for their financial ability, but also for their skill as physicians. In his letter to Yechiel, Abravanel asked whether there were Jewish physicians in the Italian states, and whether the princes of the church employed them. The physicians, he said, hold the key to the hearts of the great, on whom the fate of the Jews depends'", in *History of the Jews* IVp. 287.]

[441] The French (and Spanish) term comes from a mistranslation of the Italian "*monte di pietà*"; from *monte* (value, amount, sum) and *pietà* (piety, charity). It should have been translated as "*crédito de caridad*" or "*crédito de piedad*".

Bernardino de Feltre, a native of Veneto, was the most diligent promoter of these mountains of piety, and one of the staunchest enemies of the Jewish bankers and usurers. He was the most implacable enemy of the Jews of his time and a worthy successor of Capistrano. An outstanding orator of great popularity, Bernardino preached in Italy against luxury and raised the masses against usurers.

"Because some Jewish capitalists had been successful, he branded all Jews as vampires and extortionist parasites, arousing the ill-will of the people against them," wrote Gratez.

For him, Capistrano was the model of a true Christian. While "admitting that Christianity enjoined being just and humane towards the Jews, he took more into consideration the provisions of canon law which forbade any trade with them, such as sharing food with them or consulting their doctors... "I, said Bernardinus, who live on alms and live on the bread given me by the poor, cannot remain like a silent dog, without barking, when I see the Jews devour Christians to the marrow. Why would I not bark in honour of Jesus Christ[442]?"

Tireless in his zeal, Bernardino succeeded in establishing monasteries of piety in Assisi, Parma, Cesena, Chieti, Rieti, Narni and Lucca. In Camposampiero, a small town in Padua, he expelled the Jewish owner of a pawnshop in order to found a pious monastery. All Jewish enterprises were subject to the attacks of this impetuous monk.

In Plasencia, usurers charged interest that could reach up to one hundred percent, so it was not difficult to introduce the idea of creating a new pawnshop. The same happened in Padua, where the monte de piedad lent free of charge for sums of less than thirty sous. For larger sums, the interest rate did not exceed 5%.

"Ravenna, Cremona, Vicenza, Bologna and even Florence, as well as many other Italian cities, had their pawnshops in the late 15th or early 16th century... Rome and Naples did not have them until 1539 and 1540. In the latter of these cities, two charitable citizens released all the effects pawned by Jews and returned them without interest, and as soon as the pawnshop was founded, the viceroy of Toledo expelled the Jews from the kingdom of Naples[443]."

Bernardino de Feltre made the local authorities very uncomfortable because of the revolts he fomented. Some high-ranking figures, corrupted by the gold of the Jews, contributed to the failure of his projects. In Florence, and in general throughout Tuscany, the prince and the council

---

[442]Heinrich Graetz, *Geschitchte der Juden; Histoire des juifs IV*, Éd. Durlacher, Paris, 1893, p. 385; and in *History of the Jews IV*, p. 296.
[443] Georges-Bernard Depping, *Les Juifs dans le Moyen-Âge*, (1823), Éd. Wouters, Brussels, 1844, p. 287.

vigorously defended the usurers[444]. Bernardino de Feltre accused them of having allowed themselves to be bought by Yechiel of Pisa and other rich Jews in the country. When he came to Bergamo to preach against the Jews, he was gagged by Galeazzo, the Duke of Milan. Likewise, the magistrates of Venice forbade him to preach against the Jews. The Jews, who had bribed the magistrates, were allowed to return to the city since Bernardino himself had been expelled.

Finally, in Florence, since "Bernardino was inciting the youth of the city against the Jews, and a popular uprising was imminent, the authorities ordered him to leave Florence and the country immediately, and he was forced to submit.

Gradually, however, by tirelessly repeating the same accusations, he succeeded in so inflaming public opinion against the Jews that not even the Venetian senate was able to protect them. Finally, he succeeded in bringing about a bloody persecution of the Jews, but not in Italy, but in the Tyrol, from where it spread to Germany."

His imprecations against the Jewish usurers rang out in all the churches of Trent. Then a new case of ritual crime broke out. On Holy Tuesday 1475, in the middle of Easter week, a two-and-a-half-year-old boy from a poor family, named Simon, disappeared and was later found drowned in the Adige. His body washed up in the water and ran aground in a dam. The bishop of Hinderbach, accompanied by two notables, went to the site and had the body transported to the church. Bernardino de Feltre and the other priests publicly exposed the body of the child and then "the bishop had all the Jews of Trent imprisoned... He initiated proceedings against them and called a physician, Matthias Tiberinus, to testify to the violent death of the child. A baptised Jew, Wolfkan, from Regensburg, an engraver, came forward with the most fearful accusations against his former co-religionists. His accusations found more credibility when the imprisoned Jews confessed under torture that they had killed Simon and drank his blood on Passover night. They said that the Jewess Bruneta had provided the needles to prick the body. It was also said that a letter was found in the possession of a rabbi, Moses, which had been sent from Saxony, asking for Christian blood for the coming Passover... All the Jews of Trent were burned and it

---

[444] "Florence was one of the richest and most commercial cities in Italy; the Florentines had been the greatest speculators and ruthless usurers. Muratori admitted that it was to this usury that Florence owed much of its splendour; this usurious and commercial republic thus owed a certain indulgence to an unfortunate people who had this speculative and usurious spirit in common with itself, but who, instead of the splendour of the Florentine people, had received only exile and opprobrium in Europe." In Georges-Bernard Depping, *Les Juifs dans le Moyen-Âge*, (1823), Éd. Wouters, Brussels, 1844, p. 288.

was resolved that no Jew should henceforth settle in the city. Only four Jews accepted baptism and were pardoned[445]."

In every country where the news of this event reached, the Jews were exposed to the greatest dangers. In Italy itself, they could no longer leave the cities without risking attack by Christians. Anti-Jewish riots broke out in Brescia, Pavia, Mantua and Florence, some provoked by Bernardino de Feltre. The clergy organised pilgrimages to visit the remains of the martyr, the innocent Simon of Trent, who was to be beatified in 1582.

In Germany, hatred of Jews increased even more. A few years earlier, in Endigen in the Bade country, parishioners had discovered the bodies of a man and a woman, as well as the remains of two decapitated children, in the midst of work on the church ossuary. This was in 1470. They had been identified with a poor family who had disappeared eight years earlier after being last seen entering the house of a Jew. A ritual crime trial took place and four Jews from the city were convicted and executed. The case later became the subject of a famous play of the time, *L'Endinger Judenspiel*.

After the murder of Simon of Trent, the bourgeoisie of Frankfurt am Main erected a statue near the bridge leading to Saxenhausen depicting the child martyred by horrible Jewish characters in conversation with the devil. On the pedestal were engraved these two verses: *So lan Trient und das kind wird gennant/ Der Juden Schelmstück bleibt bekannt.* Which meant: *As long as there is talk of Trent and the child, the malice of the Jews will be remembered*[446].

In Regensburg, the new bishop Henry and Duke Ludwig, a resolute enemy of the Jews, joined forces to secure the support of the pope and some of the most influential members of the Council of the bourgeoisie, and to enlist the services of two Jewish renegades. One of them, Peter Schwarz, "wrote defamatory and libellous pamphlets against his former co-religionists. The other, a certain Hans Vayol, poured the vilest calumnies on the elderly Rabbi Israel Bruna, accusing him, among other things, of having bought a seven-year-old Christian boy from him and of having sacrificed him[447]...", according to Graetz.

---

[445] Heinrich Graetz, *History of the Jews IV*, Philadelphia, The Jewish Publication Society of America, 1894, p. 297, 298.

[446] Heinrich Graetz, *Geschitchte der Juden; Histoire des juifs IV,* Éd. Durlacher, Paris, 1893, p. 388. In February 2007, a very delicate case broke out in Italy and caused a great stir. Professor Areil Toaff, son of the former Chief Rabbi of Rome, had just published a 400-page book entitled *Pasque di sangue (Passover of Blood, the Jews of Europe and the Accusations of Ritual Murder)*. Professor Toaff, a professor at Bar-Ilan University in Jerusalem, acknowledged that ritual murder had been practised by some Ashkenazi Jews in northern Italy. Read in *Jewish Fanaticism*.

[447] Heinrich Graetz, *History of the Jews IV*, Philadelphia, The Jewish Publication Society of America, 1894, p. 301–302.

In any case, news of the murder of the boy from Trent reached Regensburg at that time. Bishop Henry then immediately asked the Regensburg Council to initiate criminal proceedings against several of the city's Jews. Guards blocked the four gates of the Jewish quarter, preventing everyone from entering or leaving. The property of the Jewish community was seized.

In the spring of 1478, the Jews of Passau, who had bought and desecrated hosts, were executed by order of the bishop. Some were condemned to death by the sword, others were burned alive at the stake, and some even had their flesh torn off with red-hot tongs. Emperor Frederick, however, forbade the torture or killing of Jews for desecration of hosts. All Jews in Swabia were expelled at that time. Many ritual crimes were recorded between 1478 and 1492, in Mantua, Arena, Portobuffolé (near Trevisa), Verona, Viadana (near Mantua), Vicenza and Fano, and all carried death sentences. In 1490, the city of Nuremberg expelled the Jews after opening a mount of piety.

Bernardino de Feltre had returned to Italy, for we see him in 1488 in Ravenna founding another mount of piety and convincing the authorities to expel the Jewish usurers from the city. Bernardino died in Pavia on 28 September 1494, the date on which he has been celebrated ever since. His tomb remains in that city, in the Church of Santa Maria del Carmine.

LXXXI. Torquemada against the Marranos

In Spain, the Marranos, or New Christians, "who numbered in the hundreds and thousands in the kingdoms of Aragon and Castile... held high offices of state and, thanks to their wealth, wielded great influence. They were also related to many of the old nobles; in fact, there were few families of importance who did not have Jewish blood in their veins. They formed about a third of the population of the towns... These Marranos, for the most part, had retained the love of Judaism and of their race deep in their hearts[448]." For the great majority of the Spanish population, this situation was unbearable; "It seemed to them that the whole court was of Jewish origin[449]."

The marriage between Isabella of Castile and Ferdinand of Aragon in 1469 was to radically change the situation on the peninsula. In 1478, at the initiative of Ferdinand and Isabella, Pope Sixtus IV issued a bull

---

[448] Heinrich Graetz, *History of the Jews IV*, Philadelphia, The Jewish Publication Society of America, 1894, p. 308.
[449] Heinrich Graetz, *Geschitchte der Juden; Histoire des juifs IV*, Éd. Durlacher, Paris, 1893, p. 393. See again note 438.

authorising the royal couple to appoint ecclesiastics as inquisitors with powers to judge heretics and rebellious people, as well as their protectors. It is likely that the monarchs' reaction was prompted by a Dominican named Alfonso de Ojeda, prior of the convent of San Pablo in Seville and with privileged access to the queen. A commission set up by the "Catholic kings" was charged with drafting the tribunal's regulations, and in 1480, the tribunal of the Inquisition began to function. It was composed of two Dominican monks, Miguel Morillo and Juan de San Martino, and lay assessors. The tribunal had its first seat in Seville, to supervise this region directly governed by the sovereigns—without the intermediary of the Cortes—and which had had a large number of marranos for a century. By royal ordinance, all officials were invited to collaborate fully with the inquisitors.

"If the demons of the deepest hell had conspired to torment innocent men to the last limit of endurance and to make their lives a ceaseless martyrdom, they could not have devised more perfect means than those which these three monks employed against their victims," complained Heinrich Graetz, who added: "As soon as the New Christians of Seville and vicinity received the news of the establishment of the Inquisition, they held a meeting to consider means of deflecting the blow directed against them. Several wealthy and respected men from Seville, Carmona and Utrera, among them Abulafia, the royal couple's financial agent, prepared to give battle to their persecutors".

However, "a few days later the conspirators of Carmona, Seville and other cities, and three of the richest and most respected Marranos, among them Diego de Susón, possessor of ten million, and Abulafia, a former Talmudist and rabbi, were burnt to death. On 26 March, seventeen victims died at the stake of the *Quemadero*[450]."

The plot had been denounced by Suson's daughter, who was secretly having an affair with a Christian knight. Several conspirators were imprisoned. Other arrests followed and soon so many marranos were imprisoned that the dungeons of the San Pablo convent were overflowing.

Many new Christians from this city took refuge in the south, in the region of Medina Sidonia and Cadiz, to escape persecution. But on 2 January 1481, an edict of the tribunal of the Inquisition prescribed to all officials the capture and surrender of all fugitive Marranos and the seizure of all their goods, threatening anyone who contravened these orders with excommunication and the punishments reserved for heretics. The arrests were so numerous that the court decided to establish itself in a larger place

---

[450] Heinrich Graetz, *History of the Jews IV*, Philadelphia, The Jewish Publication Society of America, 1894, p. 312, 313, 317.

to judge all the accused. The tribunal was then established in a castle on the outskirts of Seville called La Tablada.

The tribunal was then able to open its first session. Six rebellious marranos, who proclaimed before their judges their loyalty to Judaism, were condemned to death by the prior Alfonso de Ojeda and burnt at the stake. The conspirators, led by the very rich Diego de Susón, were then brought before the court. In the following days, there were so many daily victims that the city of Seville had to make one of its squares available to the court to keep a bonfire burning permanently. This square was given the name of *Quemadero*.

In addition to clearly marranos individuals, the inquisitors encouraged all Spanish Christians to strengthen their vigilance and denounce all heretical Judaisers they knew of. To facilitate these denunciations, the Inquisition listed all the facts constituting the crime of heresy or apostasy: a converted Jew was relapsed if he celebrated the Sabbath or any other Jewish feast, if he circumcised his children, if he observed the dietary laws, if on Sabbath he wore a white shirt or more beautiful clothes than usual, or if he failed to light the fire. They were also accused of apostasy if they were seen to go out in the street barefoot or to ask forgiveness of a friend on the Day of Atonement (*Yom Kippur*), or if they blessed their children by placing their hands on their heads without making the sign of the cross, or if they recited a blessing formula with a cup of wine before making the guests drink. One was really suspect when one refrained from following Christian customs, such as finishing a psalm without adding "Glory be to the Father, the Son and the Holy Spirit", or eating meat during Lent. If someone sent to or received gifts from a Jew during the Feast of Booths (*Sukkot*) he was also accused of Judaising. So the prisons of the Inquisition quickly filled up. From the first day, some fifteen thousand arrests were made.

In the first auto de fe—act of faith—the priests inaugurated the stake with a solemn procession: dressed in sackcloth—the sambenito—with a red cross painted on it, the condemned men advanced towards the place of execution accompanied by ecclesiastics and nobles dressed in black, amidst the chants of the assembled people. On arrival at the stake, the inquisitors read out the condemnations before proceeding with the executions. The impenitent heretics were thrown into the flames without further delay, unless they repented at the last moment, and were then strangled beforehand. On 26 March 1481, seventeen victims were burnt at the *Quemadero*. From that day until November, nearly three hundred people perished at the stake in Seville. The persecution reached the point where, if it was discovered that deceased Marranos had Judaised during their lifetime, their bones were dug up and burned, and the property of their heirs confiscated.

Note that only Marranos could be the subject of an inquisitorial process and not Jews per se. Unbaptised Jews could not be summoned before the tribunal of the Inquisition, nor could unbaptised Moors. Only the relapsed of these two nations were summoned. But the Jews were the most stubborn, for they were determined to attract converts to them and were tireless in their proselytising.

From all sides, opinions and demands arose for the complete isolation of the Marranos from the Jews. In 1482, the royal couple ordered the Jews to be expelled from Andalusia, especially from the dioceses of Seville and Cordoba, where the new Christians were very numerous. More than 4,000 Jewish-owned houses were left uninhabited. Outside Andalusia, in the cities where they were allowed to settle, they were subject to laws that totally restricted trade with Christians and forced to wear distinctive signs. "Gone were the days, wrote Graetz, when influential Jews could get the court to intervene on behalf of their co-religionists and soften the effect of restrictive laws[451]."

During the first years of the Inquisition, several thousand Marranos had disappeared from Spain, some burned at the stake, most of them forgotten in prisons. Until then, the Inquisition's action had been limited to southern Spain, mainly in the provinces of Seville and Cadiz. Due to the opposition of the Cortes, it had not been possible to extend it to the rest of the Spanish provinces.

Despite the complaints of the Jews to the Holy See, Pope Calixtus IV allowed the Spanish monarchs to introduce the Inquisition in the Aragonese provinces and to appoint a supreme judge. The kings thus appointed in 1943 an inquisitor general to set up tribunals wherever he considered it necessary, and to direct and supervise them. The post fell to the Dominican monk Tomás de Torquemada.

Immediately after his nomination, Torquemada established three new tribunals in the cities of Cordoba, Jaen and Villareal. He drew up a sort of code to serve as a regulation for heresy trials. A period of grace was granted to those who spontaneously denounced themselves as Judaisers, but they had to put their confessions in writing, answer questions honestly, indicate the names of their accomplices and even those who seemed suspicious. The names of the guilty would be revealed after the period of grace and they would lose their property. They would be acquitted, but forever tainted, unable to hold any public office, nor would their descendants.

The tribunal of the Inquisition in Toledo was inaugurated in May 1485. In the kingdoms of Aragon and Valencia, the Inquisition was set up in the

---

[451] Heinrich Graetz, *Geschitchte der Juden; Histoire des juifs IV,* Éd. Durlacher, Paris, 1893, p. 398.

same year. The influential Marranos then used all their power, getting the Cortes of Saragossa to protest vigorously to the pope and the king against the establishment of these courts. In Rome, the success of the demand was almost certain, since "by putting up the price", wrote Graetz, it was possible to obtain the favourable intervention of the pontifical court. But it proved more difficult to bend Ferdinand's will. In fact, Ferdinand categorically refused to abolish these tribunals.

The Jews then decided to hatch a conspiracy to make Canon Pedro de Arbués, whom Torquemada had appointed Grand Inquisitor in the kingdom of Aragon, disappear. At the head of the plot were Juan Pedro Sánchez, an influential figure at the royal court, a jurisconsult called Jaime de Montesa, and two Marranos. The conspirators had the full support of the notables of Jewish origin.

On 15 September 1485, before dawn, Arbués was stabbed while praying on his knees in the cathedral of Saragossa. The news of this murder caused deep emotion and all the Marranos would have been massacred without the intervention of Archbishop Alfonso of Aragon, who rode through the city on horseback to calm the population, promising that the culprits would be severely punished.

The Dominicans knew how to exploit the murder of Arbués to avenge it. Thanks to the public confessions of one of the conspirators, a certain Vidal de Uranso, the inquisitors learned the names of all those who had taken part in the conspiracy and persecuted them with double cruelty: as heretics and as enemies of the Holy Office. Once arrested, the main culprits were dragged through the streets of Saragossa, their hands cut off and hanged. More than three hundred Marranos were condemned to the stake, among them about thirty men and women from the best families of the city.

Gaspar de Santa Cruz, one of the conspirators, managed to escape and take refuge in Toulouse, where he died undisturbed. After having burnt his effigy, the inquisitors imprisoned his son, who they accused of having helped his father to flee, forcing him to travel to Toulouse to dig up and burn his father's remains with the help of the Dominicans of that city.

In 1486, the inquisitors of Toledo, having forced the rabbis of the synagogue to denounce the converts who had returned to Judaism, condemned seven hundred and fifty Marranos to make amends by parading barefoot, wearing the sambenito and holding a candle in their hands in the middle of the crowd. Another seventeen hundred received the same punishment and twenty-seven were burned alive.

The will of King Ferdinand and the tenacity of Torquemada put an end to all resistance. The year after the death of Arbués, the inquisitors began to investigate in Barcelona and on the island of Mallorca, consigning two hundred sows to the flames: "A Jew of the time, Isaac Arama, wrote of these events as follows: "In these days the smoke from the stake of the martyrs rose unceasingly to heaven in all the Spanish kingdoms and on the islands. One third of the Marranos had perished in the flames, another third wandered homeless over the land seeking where to hide, and the rest lived in perpetual terror of the trial of the Inquisition."

Under the impetus of the eleven tribunals that functioned in Spain, the number of Marranos discovered grew year by year. During the thirteen years of Torquemada's rule (1485–1498) more than two thousand Marranos died at the stake and an estimated seventeen thousand were banished after having made an act of contrition. From 1480 to 1487, in Seville, 5,000 conversos were accused of Judaising, and 700 relapsos were burned. In Toledo, in four years, there were 4850 "reconciliations" and 200 executions.

In 1490, six Jews and five converts from La Guardia, near Toledo, were accused of black magic and of having crucified a Christian child. The Spaniards punished the criminals and have since venerated the "Holy Child of La Guardia", just as the Italians and Germans had organised the cult of Simon of Trent.

Torquemada was not unaware that his energetic action had attracted the eternal hatred of the Jews, and he continually feared for his life. On his table was always a statuette of a unicorn, which, according to the superstitions of the time, was believed to have the power of nullifying the effects of poisons. When he went out, he was always escorted by a guard of fifty horsemen and up to two hundred infantrymen. After attacking the Marranos, the Inquisition was naturally supposed to break the Jewish power. Graetz described the situation as follows: "The relationship between the Jews and the Marranos was too close for the former not to share in the misfortunes of the latter. They had intimate relations with each other, they were bound together by close fraternal ties. The Jews sympathised heartily with their unfortunate brethren, who so reluctantly wore the mask of Christianity, and endeavoured to keep them in touch with the Jewish community. They instructed the Christian-born Marranos in the rites of Judaism, held secret meetings with them for prayer, provided them with religious books and writings, kept them informed of the observance of fasts and festivals, supplied them at Passover with unleavened bread, and throughout the year with meat prepared according to their own ritual, and circumcised their new-born sons[452]."

Ferdinand and Isabella then decided to strictly prohibit all trade with the Jews, although this prohibition had no effect. "The strictly enforced law of separation could not sever the affectionate relations existing between

---

[452] Heinrich Graetz, *History of the Jews IV*, Philadelphia, The Jewish Publication Society of America, 1894, p. 332, 334, 335.

Jews and Marranos. Nevertheless, the closest communion was maintained between them, only more secret, more circumspect. The greater the danger of discovery, the greater the attraction of meeting together, to comfort and support each other, in spite of the watchful eyes of the priestly spies and their henchmen".

Once the Inquisition was convinced that the Jews would never denounce the Marranos, but would continue to maintain secret relations with them, it asked the Catholic kings to expel all Jews from Spain. The Jews could not have imagined the catastrophe so close at hand. They had, wrote Graetz, "unbounded confidence in the influence of Jewish favourites at court". In addition to Abraham Senior, who was held in high esteem, another Jewish personality occupied a very high position at the court of Castile at that time: the famous Isaac Abravanel. But with Isaac Abravanel the long series of Jewish statesmen who had had such a disastrous influence on the history of Spain came to an end.

LXXXII. 1492: The expulsion of the Jews from Spain

Alfonso V, King of Portugal, had enlisted the services of Abravanel to manage the finances of his kingdom. Admitted to the court, he had gained the absolute confidence of his sovereign, who consulted him on all important matters. Abravanel enjoyed at the court of Portugal the full life of a minister and, thanks to his credit, the Jews established in the kingdom and the refugees from Castile lived in peace and free to continue their traffics. Most of the country's tax landlords (*Rendeiros*) were Jews. In Portugal, the Jews bore no distinctive signs and had an autonomous legal organisation.

But when Alfonso V died, everything changed. His successor, his younger and more energetic son Joao II (1481–1495), wanted to imitate his French contemporary Louis XI and tried to establish an absolute monarchy by reducing the power of the great lords. In June 1483, the Duke of Bragança was imprisoned, tried as a traitor and executed, and his possessions passed into the royal domain. As a friend of the Duke and his brothers, Isaac Abravanel was also implicated in the charge of treason. Thus Abravanel arrived in Spain. The Portuguese sovereign dismissed all the protests of the Jewish financier and confiscated all his property[453].

---

[453] "Alfonso's reign was the end of the golden age for the Jews of the Iberian Peninsula. Although in his time the Portuguese code of laws (*Ordenaçoens* de Alfonso V), which contained Byzantine elements and canonical restrictions for the Jews, was completed, it must be remembered that, on the one hand, the king, who was a minor, had not participated in its elaboration and, on the other hand, the odious laws were not carried

In Castile, Abravanel began a new career. He founded a bank and became rich again, being quickly introduced to Ferdinand's court and gaining the king's confidence. Ferdinand and Isabella then handed over the administration of Spanish finances to him, despite the repeated prohibition of the Cortes to employ Jews. "Abravanel himself recounts that he enriched himself in the service of the king, and bought lands and estates, and that he received great consideration and honour from the court and the greatest lords. It must have been indispensable, seeing that the Catholic sovereigns, under the very eyes of the malignant Torquemada, and in spite of the canonical decrees and all the resolutions repeatedly established by the Cortes forbidding Jews to hold office in the government, were obliged to entrust to this Jewish minister of finance the mainspring of political life. How many services Abravanel did his own during his term of office! The grateful memory could not preserve them because of the storm of misfortunes that later befell the Jews; but in Castile, as he had been in Portugal, he was for them like a wall of protection", Graetz recounted admiringly.

The kingdom of Granada was still under Muslim rule, and it was also home to many Jews, who had been joined by many Marranos after the first trials of the Inquisition. The Jews were free to practise their religion and trade freely. There, too, some of them were very influential at the prince's court, such as a certain Isaac Hamon, who was the physician to one of the last sultans of Granada. But here too, they became unbearable. The anger of the people manifested itself violently: "One day a quarrel broke out in the streets of Granada, and the passers-by implored the disputants in vain to cease in the name of the prophet. But when they were asked to surrender in the name of the Sultan's physician, they yielded. This event, which

---

out. In his time, the Jews of Portugal did not wear insignia, but rode on richly harnessed horses and mules, wore the costume of the country, long coats, fine hoods and silk waistcoats, and carried golden swords, so that they could not be distinguished from the Christians. Most of the tax collectors (*Rendeiros*) in Portugal were Jews. Church princes went so far as to appoint Jews as recipients of ecclesiastical taxes, and the Lisbon courts complained. The independence of the Jewish population under the chief rabbi and the seven provincial rabbis was protected during Alfonso's reign, and included in the code. This code granted Jews the right to print their public documents in Hebrew, instead of in Portuguese as had been ordered until then. Abravanel was not the only favourite Jew at Alfonso's court. Two Black Ibn-Yachya brothers also frequented the Lisbon court. They were sons of a certain Don David, who had advised them not to invest their rich inheritance in real estate, as he saw that Portuguese Jews were destined for exile. As long as Isaac Abravanel enjoyed the king's favour, he was like a "shield and a wall for his race, and protected the suffering from their oppressors, healed the differences and kept the fierce lions at bay", as his poetic son, Judah Leon, wrote." Heinrich Graetz, *History of the Jews IV*, p. 338–339.

proved that Isaac Hamon was more respected by the people than the Prophet Muhammad, incited some intransigent Mohammedans to fall upon the Jews of Granada and massacre them. Only those who took refuge in the castle escaped. The Jewish doctors of Granada then decided to stop wearing silk and riding horses so as not to provoke the envy of the Mohammedans".

The kingdom of Granada finally fell into Christian hands: on 2 January 1492, Ferdinand and Isabella solemnly entered the city with their troops to the sound of bells. Muslim power disappeared from the Iberian Peninsula after eight centuries of presence. As in the time of the Visigoths, the whole of Spain was once again Christian.

On 31 March 1492, in an edict signed in the palace of the Alhambra, the Catholic Monarchs ordered the expulsion of all Jews from Spain. They were ordered to leave the territories of Castile and Leon, Aragon, Sicily and Sardinia within four months on pain of death. They would be allowed to take their belongings with them, except for precious metals and money. They were ordered to leave their gold and silver in Spain, and to take only their bills of exchange and merchandise. After the expiry of the four-month period, the property of any Christian who sheltered or took in a Jew was to be seized.

This was for the Jews a "terrible catastrophe", "they were stunned by the blow they had received", wrote Graetz. Abravanel approached King Ferdinand and Queen Isabella, and three times offered them considerable sums to have the expulsion edict revoked. But as soon as Torquemada learned of the Jewish minister's intentions, he appeared before the kings with a crucifix in hand and addressed them with these words: "Judas Iscariot sold Christ for thirty pieces of silver; your highnesses are about to sell him for 300,000 ducats. Here it is, take it and sell it". Then he left the room leaving the crucifix behind[454]." This scene made a great impression on Queen Isabella, who managed to impose her judgement on her husband and keep the edict of expulsion intact.

Don Abraham Senior, a great favourite of the queen, also tried to interfere on behalf of his co-religionists, but in vain. At the end of April 1492, it was proclaimed throughout the country, to the sound of a trumpet, that Jews were no longer tolerated in Spain and that at the end of July those who prolonged their stay beyond the agreed period would be liable to the death penalty.

The Jews of England, expelled in 1290, and the Jews of France, expelled a century later, had been able to go into exile with their wealth. The Jews of Spain, on the other hand, were forced to sell everything and

---

[454] Heinrich Graetz, *History of the Jews IV*, Philadelphia, The Jewish Publication Society of America, 1894, p. 343, 344, 348.

transform their money into bills of exchange, as they were forbidden to take it with them. But they were unable to procure enough bills of exchange: "In Spain, due to the dominant chivalric and ecclesiastical sector, there were no places of exchange as in Italy, where commercial effects had value. Large-scale business was in the hands, for the most part, of Jews and Marranos, and the latter, out of fear, had to keep away from their brothers of race. The Jews who owned land were obliged to part with it at absurd prices, because there were no buyers, and they were obliged to beg from the Christians even the most trifling thing in return." With this Jewish monopoly on economic activity and in the absence of buyers, the real estate of the outlaws was sold at derisory prices. According to the testimony of a contemporary named Andrés Bernáldez, priest of Los Palacios, a house was exchanged for a donkey and a vineyard for a piece of savannah or cloth. And to make it even more difficult for the Jews to sell their property, Torquemada forbade Christians to trade with them. "And so it was, how the considerable wealth of the Spanish Jews vanished into thin air[455]."

About 50,000 Jews chose baptism, and two hundred thousand preferred to go into exile, as they no longer considered the possibility of embracing Christianity and Judaising in secret since they had realised that the Inquisition would be implacable. A year before the promulgation of the edict of expulsion, in the city of Seville alone, thirty-two new Christians had been burned alive and sixteen others only in effigy; six hundred and twenty-four had been condemned to humiliating penance. For his part, Graetz estimated the number of Jewish exiles at three hundred thousand. They went to the neighbouring kingdoms of Navarre and Portugal, as well as to Italy, Turkey and Africa.

The converts helped their exiled brothers as best they could, accepting deposits of gold and silver, and then sending them these precious metals through trustworthy persons, or compensating them with bills of exchange in foreign places. When the king was informed of the manoeuvre, he ordered the search and seizure of these riches.

Despite the prohibition, numerous outlaws had tried to take their gold and silver with them, literally (physically) swallowing not inconsiderable amounts. The rumour spread and some Spaniards did not hesitate to

---

[455]Heinrich Graetz, *Geschitchte der Juden; Histoire des juifs IV,* Éd. Durlacher, Paris, 1893, p. 418. Heinrich Graetz intended to make the expulsion of the Jews from Spain (31 July 1492, i.e. 7 Av, in the Jewish calendar) coincide with the anniversary date of the destruction of the Temple, 9 Av: "Instead of expelling the Jews on 31 July, as they had originally decided, Ferdinand and Isabella authorised them to remain until two days later. By an astonishing coincidence, their final exodus from Spain took place on the 9th of Av, the most painful date of all in Jewish history, as it reminded Israel of the destruction of the Temple in Jerusalem".

disembowel them to search for these treasures in their entrails. Genoese ship captains and crews treated them "with savage ferocity". "For greed, or for sheer pleasure in the agony of the Jews, they threw many of them into the sea. "The descriptions by contemporaries of the sufferings of the Jews make one's hair stand on end. They were persecuted wherever they went. Those who had been spared from plague and famine fell into the hands of brutalised men," claimed a chagrined Graetz (the author went into considerable detail about the tribulations of the Sephardic Jews [456]). Undoubtedly, the Spaniards must have long harboured feelings of revenge against the Jews and did not let this opportunity pass them by.

About 95,000 of them crossed the Portuguese border and went to live in the towns that the sovereign had assigned them for their provisional stay. Another twelve thousand settled in Navarre, but Ferdinand, the king of Navarre, forced them to choose between emigration and baptism. Most of them converted, as the time to decide was very short.

Several thousand Jews from Aragon, Catalonia and Valencia settled in the kingdom of Naples. Among these outlaws was the prominent Abravanel and his family. In the early days of his stay, he lived in seclusion, on the fringes, occupied only with commenting on the historical books of the Bible, work he had had to interrupt in Spain[457]. But Ferdinand I, the king of Naples, discovered his presence and summoned him to offer him the post of finance minister of his kingdom.

Some Jews nevertheless remained in Spain, risking their lives to continue meeting in secret, practising their cult and cursing Christians while pretending in public to be good Catholics. "There were still Jews left in Spain, but they wore the mask of Christianity and hid under the name of New Christians... In order not to betray their secret attachment to Judaism, they were obliged to show greater zeal for the Christian religion, to make at all times the signs of the cross, to recite the rosary and to mumble the Our Fathers[458]."

"Some Jews, at the risk of their lives, continued to meet in secret to practise the worship of their fathers, while pretending in public to be Christians. In 1501 a clandestine synagogue was discovered in Valencia.

---

[456] Heinrich Graetz, *History of the Jews IV*, Philadelphia, The Jewish Publication Society of America, 1894, p. 362. ["Forcibly baptized, exiled, decimated by death in all its horrible forms; by despair, famine, pestilence, fire, shipwreck, all the united torments had reduced their number from hundreds of thousands to scarcely a tenth of that number. Those who were left wandered like spectres, hunted from country to country..." Heinrich Graetz, *History of the Jews IV*, p. 383].

[457] Read in *Psychoanalysis of Judaism* about Abravanel's exegetical ruminations, i.e. his vengeful prophecies to the gentile nations.

[458] Heinrich Graetz, *Geschitchte der Juden; Histoire des juifs IV*, Éd. Durlacher, Paris, 1893, p. 421, 422

The owner was arrested and forced to do penance in an auto de fe; his house was razed to the ground and the Inquisition erected a chapel in the square, which is still known as the Cruz Nueva (New Cross)[459]."

Many years later, the hatred of the population towards the Jews was still perceptible, which showed that they had left a very bad memory in the population. In Seville, there was a Jewish cemetery near the Minjoar Gate[460], named after a very wealthy Jew who had lived there. In 1580, the beautiful funerary monuments and tombs that remained there were systematically looted and demolished, as if to exorcise the presence of demons. Even at that time, the chimneys of the houses inhabited by the former converts were still being watched on the Sabbath, in order to check that no smoke was coming out of them during the Sabbath.

As for Torquemada, he never personally enriched himself with the great wealth and goods seized from the Marranos. The money had been used for the administration of the Inquisition tribunals and to open monasteries of the Dominican order. Once his mission was accomplished, Torquemada returned to the simple and austere life of a simple brother in the convent of Santo Tomás de Ávila, where he died a Christian death on 16 September 1498.

LXXXIII. 1497: the expulsion from Portugal

At the instigation of Pope Innocent VIII, King Joao II (John II) had appointed an inquisitorial commission to arrest all the rebellious Marranos from Castile and condemn them. He sent his youngest children (from three to ten years of age) to distant, newly discovered lands, such as the islands of St. Thomas, the Lost Islands or the Island of the Serpents, in order to uproot them from the tyranny of Judaism and raise them free of the sect.

On the death of Joao II in 1495, the young Manuel, his cousin, inherited the crown. The Catholic kings, anxious to forge an alliance with him, granted him the hand of their daughter Isabella, on condition that they allied themselves against the French King Charles VIII and expelled all Jews, native and immigrant, without exception, from their country.

Isabella, Queen of Portugal, was to be the instigator of the measures taken against the Jews, especially the expulsion of the Jews from Portugal. The marriage contract was signed on 30 November 1496. On 5 December 1496, the king promulgated a law ordering Jews and Muslims to become Christians or leave Portugal within a stipulated period, on pain of death.

---

[459]Llorente, *Histoire de l'Inquisition d'Espagne*, tome I, chap.10, in Georges-Bernard Depping, *Les Juifs dans le Moyen-Âge*, (1823), Éd. Wouters, Brussels, 1844, p. 260.
[460]The Meat Gate was the old entrance to the Jewish quarter.

They were given almost a year, until October, to make their preparations.

A former Jew, Levi ben Schem Tob, whose Christian name was Antony, had published a pamphlet against his former co-religionists. Thanks to his advice, King Manuel had all synagogues and Jewish schools closed, and Jews were forbidden to meet on the Sabbath. Since the Jews gathered in their homes, the king, again at Antony's instigation, secretly ordered that on Easter Sunday all Jewish children under the age of fourteen should be baptised. About 20,000 Jews were thus baptised at the beginning of April 1497.

In October, most of the Jews were still in Portuguese territory. King Manuel informed them, under the terms stipulated by law, that they would henceforth be slaves subject to his will alone, and proceeded to baptise them all. On this point, the historian Heinrich Graetz carefully nurtured the myth of the Jew preferring death to baptism and claimed that many Jews committed suicide: "But this did not succeed with most of them: they preferred to starve to death rather than belong to a religion that had followers like their persecutors. Faced with this, Manuel proceeded to take extreme measures. With ropes, pulled by their hair and beards, they were dragged from their homes to the churches. To escape, some jumped from windows and their limbs were crushed. Others broke free and jumped into wells. Some committed suicide in the churches. One father spread his *tallith* (prayer shawl) over his children and killed them and himself[461]." There is probably a good deal of legend in these repeated statements.

Those who had converted continued to practise Judaism in secret. Among the thousands of Portuguese Jews who had resigned themselves to baptism, "most were only waiting for a favourable occasion to emigrate to a country where they would be free to return to Judaism".

The Jews who remained in Portugal, submitting to baptism in order not to be separated from their children, sent a delegation to Pope Alexander VI with a large sum of money with which they wanted him to declare null and void the baptism imposed on them. On 30 May 1497, King Manuel finally promulgated an edict of toleration, which only applied to Portuguese Marranos, to protect all baptised Jews for twenty years: no investigation would be carried out into their private lives. Thus, throughout the reign of Manuel I, those who wanted to could continue to practise their ancient cult clandestinely without being disturbed by the authorities. On the other hand, and respecting the clauses of his marriage, according to which all Jews condemned by the Spanish Inquisition and taking refuge in Portugal were to be expelled within a month, King Manuel ordered the expulsion of all

---

[461] Heinrich Graetz, *History of the Jews IV*, Philadelphia, The Jewish Publication Society of America, 1894, p. 377.

Spanish Marranos. In Lisbon, the people ransacked their homes and massacred those who fell into their hands.

LXXXIV. Savonarola and the Expulsion from Florence[462]

In Florence, the Dominican Girolamo Savonarola preached fervently against luxury, greed for profit and the depravity of the powerful and the Church[463]. When the Médeci were overthrown by the French in 1494, he negotiated peace terms and avoided the sack of the city. The King of France authorised the Florentines to choose their own form of government, and Savonarola became the ruler of the city. From 1494 to 1497, the preacher instituted a theocratic dictatorship which he called a *Christian and religious republic*. He modified the tax system, enacted new laws against usury, established a court of appeal and a system of aid to the poor, and organised the famous *Bonfire of the Vanities*, where Florentines were invited to throw away their luxury objects and cosmetics, as well as books considered licentious. Savonarola also accused the Jews of having, in sixty years, accumulated profits of fifty million florins, so he decided to expel them from Florence. But these excesses in the repression of luxury, the pleasures of life and the arts cost him his life, and the Jews returned in Medici vans. Indeed, in Florence, compulsory virtue did not take root, for the powerful and the common people soon became nostalgic for pleasure.

LXXXV. The Sephardic diaspora

The expulsion of the Jews from Spain—the aristocracy of Israel, the "noblest of all, some direct descendants of King David", Graetz wrote—was a real "catastrophe". "They, princes among the Jews, were forced to knock like beggars at the doors of their brothers." Graetz specified the scale

---

[462] See translator's note in Annex II: Florence: Humanism and the Renaissance.
[463] Girolamo Savonarola (1452–1498) was a Dominican monk who dared to criticise the customs of Florence under the reign of Lorenzo the Magnificent. Witness to the Medici policy against the Church and France, he predicted the invasion of French troops in Italy. A critic of the Renaissance, he warned the Church of coming catastrophes if it did not reform first. Savonarole wanted to fight the Medici and restore morality by preaching a democratic and Christian government. But his politics became extremist and puritanical, and he became a kind of tyrant. The Church itself, after calling for moderation, could not accept his intolerance and condemned his rebellious attitude by excommunicating him. Savonarole finally lost power in 1498 and was hanged and his body burned at the stake. (NdT)

of the drama: "The thirty million ducats which, at the lowest estimate, the Spanish Jews possessed at the time of their expulsion, had melted in their hands, and thus they were stripped of everything in a hostile world, which valued the Jews only for their monetary value." The Jewish historian went on to point out a very peculiar and remarkable aspect of Jewish psychology: "The enormous misfortunes they endured raised the dignity of the Sephardic Jews even higher, to a level approaching pride. For they, whom the hand of God had struck so hard, so persistently, and who had suffered such unspeakable pain, must occupy a peculiar position and belong to the specially chosen. This was the thought or feeling that existed more or less clearly in the hearts of the survivors. They regarded their banishment from Spain as a third exile, and themselves as favourites of God, whom, because of His greater love for them, He had punished more severely[464]."

Almost all those who were expelled from Spain, Portugal or Germany went first to Italy to live under the protection of a tolerant prince, or to Greece, Turkey or Palestine. Of all the Italian rulers, the popes were undoubtedly the most benevolent. Alexander VI, Julius II, Leo X and Clement VII, more concerned with entrenching their temporal power in their states than with enforcing restrictive laws against the Jews, even hired Jewish doctors, as did the cardinals themselves, in direct contravention of the decisions of the Council of Basel. Thus Alexander VI had as his physician the Jew Bonet de Lates, originally from Provence, and Julius II hired the services of Simeon Sarfati.

Among the most notable fugitives, the family of Isaac Abravanel suffered the most hardships during his exile. "It was in Naples that, together with other Jews exiled from Spain, the famous Abravanel, once in charge of the finances of the Peninsula, took refuge. He was well received by Ferdinand I, who appreciated his great financial talents". But they had to flee before the invasion of the Italian peninsula by the French, led by their king Charles VIII.

During their visit to Rome in 1494, some of the French and Scottish guards attacked the Jews and decided to destroy the synagogue. The French King Charles VIII then ordered the arrest of the culprits and six of them were hanged in a public square[465]. Abravanel took refuge with his sovereign in Sicily, then on the island of Corfu. He later settled in Monopoli, in the region of Apulia. "Those who remained, panic-stricken, were ready to embrace Christianity, just to preserve their property and their freedom.

---

[464] Heinrich Graetz, *History of the Jews IV*, Philadelphia, The Jewish Publication Society of America, 1894, p. 383, 386–387. [Read about the peculiar Jewish psychology in *Psychoanalysis of Judaism*. NdT.]

[465] André de la Vigne, *Histoire du voyage de Naples du Roy Charles VIII*, éditions Godefroy, Paris, 1684, p. 124; in *Archives juives*, number 1, 1973.

But as soon as the danger passed, they forgot their profession of faith and baptism, and returned to Judaism, or at least stopped practising Catholicism. There was little concern to keep these Christians. So when Gonzalo de Córdoba took Naples for the king of Spain, there was talk of expelling all the Jews as at least seeming consistent, since they had been expelled from the Spanish states. But the king's captain, called the great Captain by his countrymen, considered that they would retire to Venice to the great detriment of the state, and that there were few true Jews since most of them passed themselves off as baptised Christians; he thought it would be better to persecute them as bad Christians than to expel them as Jews. Consequently, instead of promulgating the edict of expulsion, he wanted to establish the Inquisition. This happened in 1504...Protests rose from all sides, and, in 1510, the Jews were all expelled from the kingdom...Such was the end of the Israelite settlements in the south of the peninsula. Abravanel went to die in Venice, where he had gained the confidence of the government, as everywhere he had stayed. The Venetians had even commissioned him to negotiate a commercial treaty with Portugal on behalf of their republic...Charles Quintus, an enemy of Protestants, was even more an enemy of Jewish law. He expelled all the Jews from his states in Italy. These were finally dispersed in Turkey, in the Papal States and elsewhere[466]."

The Sephardic Jews transplanted the Spanish language and manners wherever they settled; in Africa, Turkey, Syria, Palestine, as well as in Italy and Flanders. The *Sephardim* contrasted sharply with the German Jews or *Ashkenazim*, who spoke German slang and lived separately from the Christians. The latter recognised the superiority of their Sephardic co-religionists, whose influence soon prevailed, even though they were a minority. Placed between these two groups, the Jews of Italy were of little importance and were often forced to learn German or Spanish.

In the end, most of the exiles ended their journey in Turkey. The Jewish community in Constantinople, which had grown considerably with the influx of fugitives from the Iberian peninsula, numbered about 30,000 souls and had forty-four synagogues. Thessaloniki also had a sizeable and very enterprising Jewish population. After the expulsion of the Jews from Spain, Sultan Bajazet had this naive goy phrase: "You call Ferdinand, who impoverished his country and enriched ours, a wise king!

The Jews, Graetz wrote, "were not only in charge of wholesale and retail trade by land and sea, but were also the manufacturers and craftsmen. Especially the Marranos fled from Spain and Portugal who manufactured

---

[466] Georges-Bernard Depping, *Les Juifs dans le Moyen-Âge*, (1823), Éd. Wouters, Brussels, 1844, p. 291–293.

for the warlike Turks new armour and firearms, cannons and gunpowder, and taught the Turks how to use them. In this way, persecuting Christianity itself provided its main enemies, the Turks, with weapons that enabled them to crush them with defeat after defeat, humiliation after humiliation[467]." Thus, we have no doubt that the Jews encouraged the Turks to war against the Christians, thus quenching their thirst for revenge.

LXXXVI. The Askenazis expelled from Germany

The Jews of Germany and central Europe then lived in isolation, enclosed within their own community and carefully avoiding mixing with Christians. The well-known Jewish historian Leon Poliakov recalled in his work the primacy accorded to study and scholarship in these 15th century Ashkenazi Jews: 'All aspects of Jewish community life reflected this climate of penitence and austerity. Only once a year, on Purim, was it permitted and even recommended to indulge openly in carnival merriment, to dress up and get drunk, and finally to take revenge on the guilty by burning in the public square the wooden dummy of Haman[468], the prototype of all anti-Semites... On other days, distractions were rare and, above all, strictly regulated. Profane theatre, equated with depravity, was strictly forbidden, as was dancing between men and women, even at weddings. Card games were permitted only in exceptional circumstances, so that in the end only chess and board games, such as charades on biblical themes, were the only forms of entertainment that never aroused the censure of the rabbis. All ornamentation and fancy dress was outlawed; men and women wore black or grey, at a time when colour and variegation reigned supreme[469]."

But apparently, these austere customs were not incompatible with greed, illicit trafficking and the desire to harm the goyim. In Germany, as we have already seen, the expulsions of the Jews went back to the 15th century and intensified from 1450 onwards. By the end of the century, there were only residual pockets of the Jewish population.

---

[467] Heinrich Graetz, *History of the Jews IV*, Philadelphia, The Jewish Publication Society of America, 1894, p. 356, 401. [Read in *Psychoanalysis of Judaism* about the Jewish thirst for revenge, especially the *Jaram* against Spain, the Jewish curse pronounced against Spain mentioned by Joseph Roth in his book *Wandering Jews*].

[468] Haman, according to the biblical account of Esther, was the vizier of the Persian Empire under the reign of Ahasuerus (Xerxes I of Persia). For Jews, Haman is the archetype of evil and anti-Semitism. Read in *The Mirror of Judaism*.

[469] Léon Poliakov, *Histoire de l'antisémitisme*, tome I, Point Seuil, 1981, p. 327. The Jewish historian Bernard Lazare did not hesitate to speak of "Talmudic tyranny" and "abominable oppression". (*L'Antisémitisme*, 1894, chapitre VI).

"In Villach, Carinthia, the Israelite families lived under the protection of the Bishop of Bamberg, whom they often helped out of their financial difficulties, and he in turn sometimes helped them with his excommunications to obtain payment from their creditors; but popular fanaticism eventually got the better of the bishop's indulgence. In 1421, public opinion accused the rabbis of having desecrated hosts. The authorities believed them, arrested these leaders, tortured them and condemned them to death. In 1454 and 1455, Ladislaus, King of Hungary and Bohemia and Duke of Austria, allowed the burghers of Znaym, Brunn and Vienna to expel the Israelites from their towns, to take possession of the houses, synagogues and lands belonging to these people, in exchange for the tax they were accustomed to pay, and to extinguish the debts the Jews still owed to the burghers[470]."

The people of Prague had repeatedly revolted against the Jews, and the bourgeoisie regularly called for their expulsion. The nobility, on the other hand, corrupted by the gold of the usurers, were often in their favour. In the mid-15th century, King Ladislaus finally authorised the expulsion of the Jews and even threatened to banish the Christians who supported them. But despite the monarch's decision—it is not known under what circumstances—the Jews remained in the city.

Emperor Maximilian had watched impassively as the Jews were expelled from the cities and states of the Empire. Under his reign, the Jews were accused of immolating Christian children, counterfeiting currency, imitating the seals on letters, and of having perpetrated enormous usury. The emperor, yielding to the cries of indignation of the people, decided to ban them from his states; the bishop of Bamberg did not dare to protect them in Villach. They dispersed to Gorice, Udine, Venice. A village near Villach still bears the name *Judendorf,* i.e. Jewish village.

"At the same time they were banished from Styria, where they had rich houses, especially at Gralz, Marburg and Judenburg... The emperor derived a good income from them, so when there was talk of banishing them, the Styrian states thought that they should compensate Maximilian for what he would lose by their departure in exchange for a sum of thirty-eight thousand guilders. They thought they would gain from this sacrifice, such was the hatred of the Jews at the time. The inhabitants of the country even included the expulsion of the Israelites among their rights, which they made the Archdukes of Austria swear to defend[471]."

They were expelled from Nuremberg in 1499. The emperor had been

---

[470] Charles of Ladislas in Prague, 23 and 27 July 1454, and in Tiena, 22 March 1435, in *Archiv fur Geschiehte, elc.,* year 1820.
[471] Georges-Bernard Depping, *Les Juifs dans le Moyen-Âge,* (1823), Éd. Wouters, Brussels, 1844, p. 317.

requested by the bourgeoisie to expel the Jews from this city because of their licentious behaviour: They were accused, wrote Graetz, of receiving too many "foreign co-religionists, so that the statutory number of Jews had increased excessively in the city; the practice of excessive usury; fraud in the collection of debts, so that honest merchants had been impoverished, and, finally, of harbouring rogues and vagabonds". Jews had already been expelled once during the Black Death, but had returned after the epidemic. In 1490, "a wealthy citizen named Antonio Koberger had the anti-Jewish libel *Fortalitium Fidei* by the Spanish Franciscan Alfonso de Spina reprinted at his own expense. After long deliberations, Emperor Maximilian finally acceded to Nuremberg's plea, "because of the fidelity with which the city had always served the imperial house", abrogated the privileges enjoyed by the Jews and allowed the city council to set a deadline for their expulsion, stipulating however that the Jewish houses, lands, synagogues and even the Jewish cemetery should pass into the imperial treasury[472]." The decision was taken on 5 July 1498. Initially, the Council only wanted to grant a period of four months for his travel preparations, but eventually three months were added. On 10 March 1499, the Jews of Nuremberg were finally expelled.

Other imperial cities expelled Jews at this time: Ulm, Nordlingen, Colmar and Magdeburg. The Jewish community of Regensburg was expelled a few years later. Only two large Jewish communities remained in Germany, in Frankfurt am Main and Worms, although they were also threatened with proscription.

At the beginning of the 16th century, the members of the sect also lost their settlements in Brandenburg: in addition to being expelled, they were forced to swear an oath that they would never return and that they would prevent their co-religionists from settling in the region again[473]. This oath was apparently only obligatory for the expelled individuals, as their descendants would soon return.

Expelled from their homeland, the German Talmudists settled further east, in Poland, Lithuania, Ruthenia and Volhynia. The German Jews transplanted their language there, and it was adopted by the native Jews of those regions. Poland was at that time the only country where the princes tolerated them and no apparent sign distinguished them from Christians, for they were even allowed to wear the sword. They had prospered greatly: "The leased tolls and distilleries were mostly in the hands of Jews. It goes without saying that they also owned land [which they leased] and traded. Compared to 500 Christians, there were in Poland 3,200 Jewish wholesale

---

[472] Heinrich Graetz, *History of the Jews IV*, Philadelphia, The Jewish Publication Society of America, 1894, p. 415.
[473] Gerken, *Codex diplomatie. Brandenburg.* Stendal, 1775, tome V.

merchants and three times as many craftsmen, including gold and silver workers, blacksmiths and weavers,[474]", wrote Graetz.

However, John Albert and Alexander, sons and successors of Casimir IV, abolished their privileges and confined them in their special quarters, and even expelled them from some cities (1496–1505). But as soon as Sigismund I (1506–1548) came to the throne, the Jews regained all their privileges. They also enjoyed effective support from the Polish nobility, who protected them out of self-interest. Moreover, since the Polish high officials came from the nobility, the restrictive laws enacted against the Jews remained a dead letter, much to the scandal of the clergy and peasantry.

LXXXVII. 1501: The Expulsion from Provence

Numerous Jews from France had settled in outlying regions such as Provence. There, as elsewhere, the inhabitants were as suspicious of them as of the plague. The Avignon statutes forbade Jews to touch bread or fruit on display in the markets. If they did, they had to pay for the goods. Leprosy and other contagious diseases were feared at the time, especially certain skin diseases that Jews tended to carry[475]. Jewish doctors were also distrusted. According to the rules of the town of Frejus, Christians could not consult a Jewish doctor or take medicine prescribed by him.[476]

In 1343, the Jewish community of Carpentras in the County of Venesino numbered about four hundred individuals. In 1359, ten years after the great massacres perpetrated against them, the Jewish fathers of families numbered 210, which amounted to a thousand Jews. This means that the

---

[474] Heinrich Graetz, *History of the Jews IV*, Philadelphia, The Jewish Publication Society of America, 1894, p. 419.

[475] There are numerous diseases and genetic defects that particularly affect Jews because of their long-standing extreme inbreeding and incestuous relationships practised for centuries. Skin diseases are common in the Jewish community. In addition, it is known that matchmaking was a speciality of the sect. "No one knew how to praise the advantages and qualities of a young man or woman for marriage like they did. A Provençal preacher of the time, Marini, as mischievous as many preachers of the time, told from his pulpit that a Jew, in charge of proposing a marriage to a young woman, would bid in favour of his client above all that the girl's father said was advantageous about her. In the end, however, the father ventured to say that his daughter was suffering from an unattractive skin disease, and the Jewish matchmaker, accustomed to bidding on everything, exclaimed: "Oh, my young man has scabs even on his ears and is covered with leprosy!". Georges-Bernard Depping, *Les Juifs dans le Moyen-Âge*, (1823), Éd. Wouters, Bruxelles, 1844, p. 198. On the matchmakers (*shadkhen*) and genetic defects in the community, see *Psychoanalysis of Judaism*.

[476] *Nulius in infirmitate vocare debeat medicum judaeum*, etc. *Statuta Bajuliæ Forojuliensis*, from the year 1235, manuscript of the King's Library, no. 4768.

Jews, despite regular beatings, were keen to remain in the midst of the Christians whom they exploited to the point of bloodshed.

In 1261, the inhabitants of Manosque had denounced usurers. They charged ten denarii a month interest per pound borrowed, i.e. 30% per annum. The Jews had taken over more than half of the entire territory of this town[477].

Whenever the States of Provence met, the privileges of the Jews and their usury were the subject of complaints to the lord. The records that have come down to us are full of them. It was then required that the Jews should wear the buckler, that they could not demand more than five denarii a month interest per pound, and also that they should be obliged to live in separate quarters. In 1421, the states, or rather the lords, even asked for amnesty for crimes committed against the Jews. But some lords had greater interests at stake. In 1448, the Jew Bonnefoy de Châlons received the monopoly of the bank of Nice for currency trading, exchange and pawnshops[478].

The region experienced major anti-Jewish riots in 1475. Between 1484 and 1486, several attacks against Jews took place in Aix, Marseille and Arles. After the annexation of Provence to the kingdom of France in 1481, the inhabitants of Provençal towns demanded their expulsion.

In 1484, farmers from Provence, the Dauphinate and Auvergne caused great disturbances in the city of Arles and destroyed the synagogue[479]. In 1487, Marseilles sent a deputy to ask for their expulsion because of the usury that ruined the people. "Finally, in 1498, in response to further complaints from the Christians, the Jews were ordered to leave the kingdom; however, the edict was not strictly enforced and Louis XII, in a new edict promulgated in 1501, ordered their final expulsion and confiscated the property of those who did not wish to become Christians. Some went to the Levant, others to the Venesine County. They also found sanctuary in the principality of Orange, but four years later Prince Philip of Châlons banished them from this small state[480]". Only the pope preserved them in the Venesino. The Jews were always able to remain there and maintain their synagogues in Avignon, Carpentras and Cavaillon.

---

[477] Columby, *De Manuasca urbe*, lib. III.
[478] Jacques Decourcelles, *La Condition des Juifs de Nice aux XVII et XVIII siècles*, Paris, 1923.
[479] Valbelle, *Journal manuscrit*, quoted by P. Bougerel.
[480] Gaufredy, *Histoire de Provence*. — Bouche, *Histoire de Provence* — Columby, *De manuasca urbe*, lib. iii.

LXXXVIII. Lisbon, 1506

Spanish conversos were closely watched by the Inquisition despite their conversion to Christianity, probably because they were hated for their duplicity and incessant crimes. The new inquisitor general who succeeded Torquemada was the Dominican Diego Deza, who treated the Marranos even more rigorously. Aided by Diego Rodríguez Lucero, Deza caused hundreds of marranos to perish. The third Inquisitor General, Giménez de Cisneros, treated the new Christians of Jewish origin with the same inexorable severity as his predecessors. When Charles Quintus had the idea of authorising the Marranos of Spain to freely practise the Jewish religion in exchange for a sum of 800,000 gold crowns, Gimenez de Cisneros did not hesitate to answer him with threatening language.

In Portugal, a revolt broke out in Lisbon on 19 April 1506 during Easter week. The Dominicans had revolted the town, and German, Dutch and French sailors joined the local population. About ten thousand people marched through the town killing all the marranos that fell into their hands, men, women and children. The massacre lasted three days and resulted in 2,300 dead. King Manuel I reacted firmly, had several dozen culprits executed and closed the Dominican convent. On 1 March 1507, he abolished the legal differences between the old and the new Christians, who thus obtained the right to leave the country, which they did en masse.

In 1536, under the pretext of persecuting the followers of the new Protestant doctrine, the Inquisition was finally introduced in Portugal following an agreement signed between the Pope and King John III. The Judaisers were not forgotten. King John had managed to infiltrate some spies among the Marranos, the most prominent being a new Spanish Christian named Henry Nunez. Trained in the school of the inquisitor Lucero, he wished to see Portugal imitate the neighbouring kingdom. He introduced himself as a friend into the houses of his former co-religionists to spy on them and communicate their secret thoughts, conspiracies and swindles to the king.

Under Inquisitor John Soares, the prisons were filled with swine and numerous bonfires were lit, much to the relief and satisfaction of the Christians. The Jewish poet Samuel Usque, who witnessed these scenes in his youth, left this dramatic description: "The Inquisition deprived the Jews of peace of mind, filled their souls with pain and sorrow, and drove them from the comforts of home into gloomy dungeons where they lived amid torments and sighs of anguish. She hung her halter round their necks and dragged them into the flames; by her decrees they must see their children slain, their husbands burnt to death, and their brethren robbed of life; they must see their children made orphans, the number of widows increased, the rich impoverished, the mighty cast down, the nobly born transformed into criminals, the chaste and modest women lodged in lewd and ignominious dwellings.He has burned many, not one at a time, but thirty by thirty, fifty by fifty. Not content with burning and annihilating, he leads Christians to boast of such exploits, to rejoice when their eyes behold the limbs of my body (the sons of Jacob) burning to death in the flames, kindled with logs dragged from afar on the shoulders of men[481]."

Between 1538 and 1609, there were 105 autos de fe in Portugal. The bonfires of the Inquisition, although less frequent than in Spain, sowed such terror among the Portuguese Marranos that what remained of Judaism gradually disappeared.

LXXXIX. Johannes Pfefferkorn v Johannes Reuchlin

German intellectual reaction to the aggressiveness of Judaism was quite vigorous in the early 16th century. Ortuin de Graes, known as Gratius, "hated the Jews with a passion", wrote Graetz. Born in 1491 in Holtwick, Westphalia, the son of a clergyman, he was a leading figure of the Cologne Dominican order who wrote a work entitled *De Vita et Moribus Judærum* (1504), which he later translated into German. Ortuin also translated Pfefferkorn's books into Latin.

Johannes Pfefferkorn was a famous and much talked-about polemicist. He had been baptised at the age of thirty-six with his wife and children, abandoning Judaism for good, as can be seen from the degree of anti-Semitism he later manifested. After his conversion, he became the protégé and favourite of the Dominicans in Cologne. He was also in contact with Cunegunda, Emperor Maximilian's sister, who was married to the Bavarian Duke Albert of Munich. When the latter died at a young age in 1508, Cunegunda retired to a convent and became abbess of the Poor Clares. Together with Pfefferkorn, the two of them undertook an intellectual and spiritual crusade against Judaism, agreeing that the nauseating spirit contained in the Talmud should first and foremost be extirpated. Cunegunda gave a letter to Pfefferkorn for his brother Maximilian, in which she assured him that she would welcome the Dominican's request. With this letter, Pfefferkorn went to the Emperor and, on 10 August 1509, succeeded in obtaining from him a general commission authorising him to confiscate and examine Jewish books throughout the Empire and to destroy those containing statements hostile to Christianity. Under the same decree, Jews were strictly forbidden to oppose the searches or to conceal the books in question.

---

[481] Heinrich Graetz, *History of the Jews IV*, Philadelphia, The Jewish Publication Society of America, 1894, p. 522.

Pfefferkorn began his public health work in the large community of Frankfurt, where at that time many Talmudists lived, "as well as numerous well-to-do Jews," wrote Graetz, and where there were many new copies of the Talmud and other Hebrew works. At Pfefferkorn's request, the Frankfurt Senate summoned all the Jews to the synagogue and informed them of the imperial order. On Friday 28 September 1509, in the presence of churchmen and several members of the Senate, all the prayer books in the synagogue were confiscated. It was the eve of the Feast of Booths (*Sukkot*). Pfefferkorn went further and forbade the Jews to go to the synagogue because he wanted to take advantage of the holidays to conduct house searches, but the clergymen present did not want to prevent the Jews from celebrating their holiday and postponed the searches until the following Monday.

In the meantime, the Jewish community of Frankfurt sent a delegate to Uriel of Gemmingen, the prince-elector and archbishop of Mainz, on whom the clergy of Frankfurt depended, to beg him to prevent the ecclesiastics from carrying out their project. The prelate agreed to their request and vigorously defended them. When the Frankfurt Senate was informed of the decision of the Archbishop of Mainz, it withdrew its support for Pfefferkorn. The Jews also delegated Jonathan Cion to plead their cause before Emperor Maximilian and invited all German Jewish communities to a meeting the following month.

Pfefferkorn visited the emperor again with a new and more pressing letter from his sister Cunegunda, and on 10 November 1509 Maximilian granted him a new mandate allowing him to seize the incriminated works. Archbishop Uriel of Gemmingen had the task of examining them, but in consultation with the theological faculties of Cologne, Mainz, Erfurt and Heidelberg, as well as with scholars such as Johannes Reuchlin, Victor of Karben and the Dominican Inquisitor Jacob van Hochstraten[482].

Pfefferkorn returned to Frankfurt where he seized fifteen hundred manuscript works and deposited them in the city hall, repeating the same operation with the same diligence in various places. The Jews, however, had once again put pressure on the emperor, and on 23 May 1510 Maximilian partially reversed his earlier orders and invited the Frankfurt Senate to return the books.

It was at this time that an incident occurred which the Dominicans were able to take advantage of. A ciborium with a golden monstrance had been stolen from a church in the Brandenburg Mark. The culprit arrested claimed to have sold the hosts to local Jews. Elector Joachim I arrested the accused

---

[482]Victor of Karben was the author of three treatises against the Jews: *Judeorum erroris et moris* (Cologne, 1509), *Propagnaculum fidei christiana* (1510), *De vita et moribus Judœrum* (with Ortuin de Graes).

and took them to Berlin, where they were charged with both the desecration of the hosts and the murder of a child. On 19 July 1510, on Joachim's orders, thirty-eight Jews were tortured on a burning gridiron. Two of them accepted baptism and were simply beheaded. The affair had caused a great commotion in Germany.

Cunegunda tried once more to convince her brother Maximilian. During a meeting with him in Munich, she begged him to stop favouring the Jews with his protection. On 6 July 1510, for the fourth time, Maximilian issued an order concerning the confiscation of Hebrew books: Archbishop Uriel was to request thesis reports on the matter from several German universities, as well as from the scholars Johannes Reuchlin, Victor de Karben and Jacob van Hochstraten, and Pfefferkorn was to transmit the conclusions to the emperor.

The "humanist" scholar John (Johannes) Reuchlin from Pforzheim played an important role in this whole dispute[483]. At the court of the old Emperor Frederick III in Linz, Reuchlin came into contact with the Jewish physician Jacob Loans, with whom he perfected his mastery of Hebrew. Reuchlin tried to show that Jewish works, far from being harmful to Christianity, could, on the contrary, serve to demonstrate its divine character, and he spoke out against the suppression of the Talmud. Pfefferkorn published a pamphlet against it in German entitled *The Handspiegel* (*Handspiegel*, Mainz, 1509) which was distributed by the thousands throughout the country. But in September 1511, Reuchlin responded to Pfefferkorn's pamphlet with another pamphlet written in German, *The Mirror of the Eyes*.

In Rome and Paris, the controversy between Reuchlin and the Dominicans gave rise to heated discussions. The Dominican Jacob van Hochstraten, professor of theology and inquisitor in Cologne, held the

---

[483] Johannes Reuchlin (1455–1522) was a German humanist. He studied at several universities in Europe before attending Hebrew classes at the Academy of Florence with Pico della Mirandola (see Appendix II). There he became familiar with Hebrew texts, such as the Kabbalah. As a result of these early readings, Reuchlin wrote *De Verbo mirifico*, his first Kabbalistic research. From Latinist and Hellenist, Reuchlin became a Hebraist and director of the Heidelberg library. In 1506, he published *De Rudimentis hebraïcis*, a remarkable work that provided a Hebrew dictionary and grammar and contributed decisively to the powerful influence of the Hebrew scriptures on Protestant thought. A defender of the Talmud against those who sought to destroy it, Reuchlin defended the usefulness of the Talmud and the Kabbalah for understanding Christianity (in his treatise *Augenspiel*). German scholars were then divided between kabbalists and scholastics. Finally, in 1517, Reuchlin wrote *De arte cabbalistica* (The Art of *the Kabbalah*), a treatise in which he proved himself to be the worthy successor of Pico della Mirandola, who subjected Christianity and the Bible to the Kabbalah, and a clear continuator of the Kabbalah of the *Zohar*. (NdT).

opinion of the masters of the University of Paris in high esteem, so he tried by all means to ingratiate himself with them. In Rome, too, he used all his influence.

A trial was to settle the dispute, the instruction of which was entrusted by Pope Leo X to Cardinal Dominic Grimani. This prince of the Church was known to be a connoisseur of rabbinical literature and the Kabbalah. Moreover, as superior of the Franciscans, he detested the monks of the order of St. Dominic. The Jews had been kept in the background, but their role was nevertheless evident: "No doubt prominent Jews worked in Rome for Reuchlin, but, like the German Jews, they had the good sense to remain in the background, so as not to endanger the cause by branding it as Jewish,[484]", Graetz acknowledged.

In June 1514, Cardinal Grimani sent a summons to both parties, but in consideration of Reuchlin's advanced age he allowed him to send a representative, while Jacob van Hochstraten had to appear in person, seconded by Arnold of Tongres, professor of theology.

But it was above all in Paris that all the efforts and hopes of the Dominicans were concentrated. The University of Paris was the oldest of all European universities and had great authority in theological matters. If it came to condemn Reuchlin's book, the pope himself would not dare to oppose its judgement. The French King Louis XII in turn exerted strong pressure on the University of Paris in favour of the Dominicans. It is true that France and Germany did not have very good relations, and since Maximilian had spoken out in favour of Reuchlin, Louis XII declared himself against it.

The university hesitated for a long time before taking a decision. The discussions lasted until August 1514. The vote of many French theologians was finally determined by the events of three centuries earlier: in 1242, it should be remembered, at the request of the apostate Nicolas Donin and by order of Pope Gregory IX, Saint Louis had ordered all copies of the Talmud to be burned. The *Mirror* of Reuchlin, which defended the Talmud, was therefore declared to contain heresy and had to be burned. "If it is Christian to hate the Jews," said Erasmus at the time, "then we are all excellent Christians." In Germany, the Dominicans hastened to publish a new pamphlet to publicise the Sorbonne's verdict.

Maximilian and several German princes pressured Pope Leo X to finally exonerate Reuchlin, while the King of France and the young Charles, the future Charles the Fifth, then Duke of Burgundy and later Emperor of Germany, King of Spain and ruler of America, demanded that *El Espejo be*

---

[484] Heinrich Graetz, *History of the Jews IV*, Philadelphia, The Jewish Publication Society of America, 1894, p. 458.

condemned.

The Pope then took the opportunity to disassociate himself from responsibility for the affair. He chose a commission from among the members of the Great Lateran Council, then in session, to re-examine the case and pronounce the verdict. This commission ruled against Hochstraten, but he did not give up. By dint of negotiations and appeals, he persuaded Leo X to suspend indefinitely the pronouncement of the verdict. Nevertheless, the Dominicans had suffered a setback and Jacob van Hochstraten left Rome confused and irritated. Yet his energy had not flagged and he did not despair of being able to resume the struggle in more favourable circumstances.

By not declaring himself openly in favour of one side or the other, Leo X had wanted to avoid upsetting both humanists and Dominicans. But this long struggle had overheated tempers, and both parties wanted to settle the dispute at all costs. When Hochstraten returned from Rome, his life was in danger and the Dominican was the target of several assassination attempts.

Some time later, Leo X, corrupted by Jewish gold, finally authorised the printing of the Talmud. In 1519, a wealthy and generous Christian printer in Venice, Daniel Bomberg (van Bomberghen), published a complete edition of the Babylonian Talmud in twelve volumes infolio which would also serve for later editions [485]. The pope even granted privileges to the printer to protect him against forgeries.

But then a movement arose in Germany that quickly put all the problems that had arisen from the conflict between the Dominicans and Reuchlin to one side: the Protestant Reformation, which would shake the papacy and shake the Catholic Church on its foundations and shake the whole of Europe.

CX. Albert of Brandenburg

At this time there were only three major Jewish communities in Germany, those of Regensburg, Frankfurt and Worms. The Margrave

---

[485] Until then, only printed texts in Hebrew language and characters were available to Jews: the first, in 1475 in Reggio Calabria, was a commentary by Rabbi Rashi on the Pentateuch; around the same time, Abraham Conat founded his printing press in Mantua; in 1480, in Soncino, Rabbis Joshua and Moses set up the printing press from which came the first *Tanakh* (books that make up the canon of the Jewish Bible) printed in 1488; in 1487, a Hebrew commentary on the Pentateuch was the first book printed in Lisbon; a Hebrew grammar was printed in Naples in 1488; in 1493, the printing of a commentary by Isaac Abravanel on biblical texts by Jews from Thessalonica was the first in the Ottoman Empire; in 1505, a Pentateuch with commentaries was printed by Jews from Constantinople, a first in that city. (NdT)

Albert of Brandenburg, first bishop of Magdeburg and then of Mainz, became a new adversary of Israel. He invited the clergy, the laity and the city councils, especially those of Frankfurt and Worms, to meet in order to decide on the final expulsion of the Jews from Germany. Numerous delegates responded to his call and met in Frankfurt in January 1516. On 8 March, the resolution to veto the Jews in perpetuity was adopted; but this resolution had to be submitted to the emperor for ratification.

Naturally, the Jews sent a mission to Maximilian to try to corrupt him. Although they were subjects of numerous princes and lords, the Jews of Germany, as we know, were dependent on the emperor only as servants of the imperial chamber. Corrupted by the Jews' money, Maximilian sent a harsh missive to Albert of Brandenburg, as well as to all those who had participated in the Frankfurt diet.

But Maximilian died in February 1519 and a revolt immediately broke out against the Jews led by the fiery preacher Balthazar Hubmayer. The Jewish community of Regensburg was eventually condemned to exile.

In 1529 another case of ritual crime took place in the Empire. In the Jewish community of Bösing, near Pressburg (Bratislava), the body of a Christian child was found mutilated. Thirty-six Jews were condemned and burned at the stake, and almost all the Jews of Moravia were imprisoned. It should be noted here that, two years earlier, Jews had served as spies for the Turks who had besieged Vienna, helping them as best they could.

XCI. The Jewish origins of the Protestant Reformation

The Catholic authors of the 19th century, who wondered about the origins of the French Revolution and who analysed the ferments of destruction of traditional Europe, had no difficulty in tracing it back to the Jewish source. A Jewish intellectual like Bernard Lazare, in his famous *Anti-Semitism, its history and causes* (1894), corroborated the idea of the Jewish origin of medieval heresies, Protestantism, rationalism and finally the philosophy of the Enlightenment (*Les Lumières*). The aim was always the same: to destroy the Catholic Church. "It was these rationalists and these philosophers who, from the 10th to the 15th century, up to the Renaissance, became the auxiliaries of what could be called the general revolution in humanity". During the 13th century, "the Israelites were in the front rank of the exegetes and rationalists...The Averroist Jews were the direct ancestors of the men of the Renaissance. It was thanks to them that the spirit of doubt was born, and also the spirit of enquiry. The [neo]Platonists of Florence, the Aristotelians of Italy and the humanists of Germany came from them. It was thanks to them that Pomponazzo composed treatises against the immortality of the soul and it was also thanks to them that in the thinkers of the 16th century the theism was born which corresponded to a decline in Catholicism...The Averroist Jews, unbelieving, sceptical and blasphemous, who undermined Christianity by spreading materialism and rationalism, also generated this other enemy of Catholic dogmas: pantheism[486]."

The Argentinean Thomist priest and philosopher Julio Meinvielle, author of several books on the subject, quoted in 1936 another passage from Bernard Lazare in his book *The Jew in the Mystery of the World*: "During the years leading up to the Reformation, the Jew became an educator and taught Hebrew to the wise men. He initiated them into the mysteries of the Kabbalah after having opened the doors of Arabic philosophy to them. He provided them, against Catholicism, with the fearsome exegesis that the rabbis, for centuries, had cultivated and strengthened: this exegesis that Protestantism and, later on, rationalism, will know how to use[487]."

The Jewish linguist James Darmesteter, who wrote several works at the end of the 19th century, confirmed this idea and said of "the Jew": "The Jew is concerned with discovering the vulnerable points of the Church and has at his service to discover them, in addition to his intelligence of the holy books, the terrible sagacity of the oppressed. He is the doctor of the unbeliever. All the revolted of the spirit come to him in the shadows or in the open. He is at work in the immense workshop of the blasphemous great Emperor Frederick and of the Princes of Swabia or Aragon; It is he who forges all that criminal arsenal of reasoning and irony which he will bequeath to the sceptics of the Renaissance, to the libertines of the great century, and Voltaire's sarcasm is but his last and resounding echo of a word muttered six centuries before in the shadow of the ghetto and still earlier in the time of Celsus and Origen, in the very cradle of the religion of Christ[488]."

For Jules Meinvielle there was no doubt about it: all the sects and secret societies, occultists and cabalists that swarmed everywhere at the end of

---

[486] Bernard Lazare, *Anti-Semitism, its history and causes*, (1894). Editions La Bastille, digital edition, 2011, p. 140, 141, 60, 142. Quoted by Monsignor Henri Delassus, *La Conjuration antichrétienne*, Desclée de Brouwer, 1910, p. 684 (See more in detail in the translator's note in Annex II).

[487] Bernard Lazare, *El Antisemitismo, su historia y sus causas*, (1894). Ediciones La Bastilla, Ed. digital, 2011, p. 61, quoted in Julio Meinvieille, *El Judío en el misterio del mundo (1937)*, Cruz y Fierro Editores, Buenos Aires, 1982, p. 72.

[488] James Darmesteter, *Coup d'œil sur l'histoire du peuple juif*, Paris, 1881, in Julio Meinvieille, *El Judío en el misterio del mundo (1937)*, Cruz y Fierro Editores, Buenos Aires, 1982, p. 72. The quotation was already in the book by Monsignor Henri Delassus, *L'Américanisme et la conjuration antichrétienne*, Société de Saint-Augustin, D. de Brouwer et Cie, Paris 1899, p. 48.

the Middle Ages in a more or less disguised form, "were strongholds of conspiracy against the Church and the Christian States, skilfully managed by the satanic Judaic hand[489]."

Meinvielle furthermore cited in support of his argument the famous German historian Werner Sombart, who was "neither Catholic nor anti-Semitic" and demonstrated in his book *Jews and Economic Life* (1911) that the Protestant sects, especially Puritanism, were of Jewish inspiration.

The fact is that during the Protestant Reformation close links were established between Judaism and certain Christian sects. The Gospels were abandoned in favour of the Bible (the Old Testament, the Torah of the Jews) and the enormous influence of this book on Lutherans and, above all, on Calvinists and Anglo-Saxon Puritans is well known. His great interest in Hebrew language and Hebrew studies is also well known. In 16th century England, the Puritans surrounded Jews with an almost fanatical cult. The *Levellers*, calling themselves Jews, demanded the enactment of a law making the Torah of the Jews the English Code. Cromwell's officials had proposed to him to constitute his Council of State with 70 members, after the manner of the Sanhedrin of the Jews. In 1629, there was even a proposal in Parliament to replace the Sunday holiday with the Sabbath[490].

---

[489]Julio Meinvieille, *El Judío en el misterio del mundo (1937)*, Cruz y Fierro Editores, Buenos Aires, 1982, p. 72. At the end of the second century, the philosopher Celsus, known for his contempt for Christians, showed greater indulgence towards the Jews. [Julio Meinvielle is also the author of *La Cabala al Progresismo*, an extremely interesting theological historical study that traces the ancient pagan and Jewish gnosis in all its forms up to the appearance of medieval and modern Kabbalah, and into contemporary philosophical, ideological and political doctrines. The political and economic elites of our time are imbued, at least diffusely, with all these esoteric and initiatory doctrines. It can be said, without fear of exaggeration, that Kabbalistic gnosis, through Freemasonry, is the secularised religion of the contemporary age that shapes the ideological and political principles of Western society. NdT.]

[490]Werner Sombart, *Les juifs et la vie économique*, 1911, Payot, 1923, p. 320-322. [The feelings of the Puritans towards the Jews were expressed in the following remark of Oliver Cromwell: "Great is my sympathy with this poor people, whom God chose and to whom He gave His law; they rejected Jesus, because they did not recognise Him as the Messiah. Cromwell dreamed of a reconciliation of Old and New Testament, of an intimate connection between God's Jewish people and the English Puritan theocracy. Other Puritans were so absorbed in the study of the Old Testament that the New Testament no longer mattered to them. Especially the visionaries in Cromwell's army and many members of Parliament, who looked forward to the Fifth Monarchy or the reign of the Saints, assigned to the Jewish people a glorious position in the expected millennium. A Puritan preacher, Nathaniel Holmes (Holmesius), desired, according to the letter of many prophetic verses, to become the servant of Israel and serve it on his knees"; "The Christian Bible [New Testament, ndt], with its monastic figures, its exorcists, its praying brethren and its pietistic saints, provided no models for warriors fighting against an unfaithful king, a false aristocracy and ungodly priests. Only the

Monsignor Henri Delassus, in his magnum opus *The Anti-Christian Conjuring*, published in three volumes in 1910, identified Judaism as the source of the evils undermining the Catholic Church and European society:

"For eighteen hundred years, it is hatred that has inspired and dominated this people, the most tenacious, the most incomprehensible of peoples. Its hatred has taken all forms, it has concealed and infiltrated, with a skill equal to its constancy, all the revolts of the human spirit against God, His Christ and His Church. From the beginning, Judaism infiltrated the Church itself, causing disorders, divisions and heresies. This was the work of Simon Magus of the Gnostics, Manes and his followers or emulators. Later, the Jew encouraged, if not inspired, all heresies; the more we study his action, the more we see him implicated in all resistance to the Spirit of God.In the Middle Ages, the Jew betrayed the Christians in favour of the Mohammedans, who despised and maltreated him in Spain as in the East; he was with the Albigensians against the Catholics, as he would be with the Protestants, as he is with the Freethinkers, the Jacobins, the Socialists and the Freemasons; as he is today with the nihilists in Russia. Like the vulture, it is on every battlefield, not to fight, but to feed on the remains of the massacre[491]."

"Since the beginning of the Christian era, the Jew has been, and still is, the great revolutionary and heresiarch in every respect. He destroys for the sake of destroying, out of hatred of the existing, but also in the hope of building on these ruins the Temple we have described: the Jerusalem of a new order, seated between East and West to replace the double city of the Caesars and the Popes, that is, the universal Republic and the humanitarian Religion of which he wants to be pontiff and sovereign[492]."

Protestantism was therefore nothing more than a new avatar of the

---

great heroes of the Old Testament, with the fear of God in their hearts and the sword in their hands, religious and national champions at once, could serve as models for the Puritans: the Judges, who freed the oppressed people from the yoke of foreign domination; Saul, David and Joab, who defeated the enemies of their country; and Jehu, who overthrew an idolatrous and blasphemous royal house: these were the favourite characters of the Puritan warriors. In every verse of the books of Joshua, Judges, Samuel, and Kings, they saw their own condition reflected; every psalm seemed composed for them, to teach them that, though surrounded on every side by ungodly foes, they need not fear so long as they trusted in God. Oliver Cromwell compared himself to the judge Gideon, who first obeyed the voice of God hesitatingly, but then bravely scattered the attacking heathen; or to Judas Maccabeus, who from a handful of martyrs formed an army of victorious warriors." Heinrich Graetz, *History of the Jews V*, Philadelphia, The Jewish Publication Society of America, 1895, p. 26, 27.

[491] Mgr Henri Delassus, *La Conjuration antichrétienne III*, Desclée De Brouwer, 1910, p. 1118-1119.

[492] Mgr Henri Delassus, *La Conjuration antichrétienne II*, Desclée De Brouwer, 1910, p. 688.

Jewish poison: "A Protestant, said the young Jewish poet Heinrich Heine, is a Catholic who abandons Trinitarian idolatry in favour of Jewish monotheism".

The Franciscan Nicolas de Lira had studied the rabbinic literature at length and was the forerunner of modern exegesis, which is, as the Jewish historian Bernard Lazare wrote, "the offspring of Jewish thought and whose rationalism is purely Jewish". For Nicolas de Lira, the literal explanation of the text of Scripture was to be the foundation of ecclesiastical science. He took many of his arguments from the Jewish Rashi, and Martin Luther in turn took them from him.

Bernard Lazare had explicitly stated: "Exegesis and free examination are fatally destructive, and it was the Jews who created biblical exegesis; it was they who first criticised Christian symbols and beliefs...The Reformation, in Germany as in England, was one of those moments when Christianity returned to Jewish sources. It was the Jewish spirit which triumphed with Protestantism[493]."

The Renaissance and Protestantism effectively breached the solid edifice of Christianity. From then on, the Jew would set about destroying Christianity and attempting to establish the universal empire of his dreams. In the 16th century, however, the Jews were still far from triumphant, for other Christian peoples were still watching.

Thus, while the northern Protestants were returning to the Jewish Bible, the Spaniards were moving away from it. The Bible had become an object of aversion. A Spanish inquisitor named Villanueva wrote in 1791: "It is well known how zealously the Holy Office has sought to keep the Bible out of the hands of the vulgar; with the result that the same people who once sought it, now look upon it with horror and detest it; many do not care for it; the majority do not know it[494]."

At that time, Russia had also experienced a Judaising heresy. At that time there were no Jews in Russia, for the Muscovite grand dukes distrusted them like the plague. But in 1480, a Kievan Jew named Zacharias, accompanied by several Lithuanian co-religionists, had come to Novgorod and corrupted several Christian priests. They went to Moscow, where they proselytised and founded the sect of the "Judaising Christians". The Grand Duke Ivan III reacted and, in 1504, immediately ordered all the leaders arrested and thrown alive at the stake. The problem was thus quickly solved.

---

[493] Bernard Lazare, *Anti-Semitism, its history and causes, (1894)*. Editions La Bastille, digital edition, 2011, p. 72, 141, 62.
[494] Leon Poliakov, *Histoire de l'antisémitisme*, tome I, Points Seuil, 1981, p. 182.

XCII. Martin Luther

By claiming that the Bible was the only legitimate source of religious authority, Luther, the father of Protestantism, challenged the authority of the Pope. In early 1521, after much debate, he was finally excommunicated, although his influence grew steadily thereafter. Wars of religion spread across Europe, lasting into the next century.

His position on Judaism had changed. At first, Luther tried to attract Jews to Christianity by being benevolent towards them. But as soon as he realised that the Jews were in fact completely rebellious to conversion and rejected the teachings of the Reformed religion, he declared merciless war on them.

In 1537 he succeeded in driving them out of Saxony, then in 1540 from several other German cities. In 1543 he tried unsuccessfully to drive them out of Brandenburg.

That year, three years before his death, he published a 200-page pamphlet, *On the Jews and their Lies* (*Von Juden und ihren Lügen*), in which he raged against the incestuous sect. Luther wrote, for example:

"Pay attention to how they lie when they say that we hold them captive, when we Christians have been harassed and persecuted by the Jews around the world for approximately three hundred years. We might as well claim that during that time they held us captive and killed us, which is the truth. Moreover, we do not know today what demon brought them to our country. For sure, it was not us who brought them from Jerusalem. Besides, no one is holding them here now."

And also: "Oh, what fanatics they are of the book of Esther, which is so perfectly in tune with their thirst for blood, vengeance and death. The sun has never shone on a more bloodthirsty and vengeful people than this, who imagine themselves to be God's people commissioned and sent to murder and kill the Gentiles. In fact, what they chiefly expect of their Messiah is that he should slay and murder with his sword the whole world...Their breath reeks with greed for the gold and silver of the Gentiles; for there is no nation under the sun more greedy than they were, still are, and ever will be, as is evidenced by their cursed usury. Then they comfort themselves because when Messiah comes, He will take the gold and silver of the whole world and divide it among them."

Luther reminded his readers that the Jews had been violently expelled from France and, "recently, our dear Emperor Charles has banished them from Spain, the best of all nests which they called '*Sepharad*' (also on the basis of Obadiah). This year they were expelled from Bohemia, where they have one of their best nests, in Prague. In the same way, during my lifetime they have been driven out of Regensburg, Magdeburg, and other places."

The preacher did not hesitate to encourage robbers and highway robbers against them. Having heard that a rich Jew was passing through Germany with twelve horses, he recommended the robbers to be less tolerant than the princes and to kidnap the Jewish travellers and their wealth. He referred to the Jews in these harsh terms: "Sons of the devil", "spawn of vipers (Matthew 12:34)", "wretched, blind and stupid", "thieves and scoundrels", "perverse and blasphemers", "scum-like", etc.

"So even we do wrong if we do not avenge all this innocent blood of our Lord and of the Christians, shed for three hundred years before the destruction of Jerusalem, and the blood of the children which they have shed since then (which still makes their eyes and their skin shine). We do wrong by not taking their lives. Instead, we allow them to live freely among us even though they murder us, curse us, blaspheme and lie against us, and defame us; we protect their synagogues, their houses, their lives and their property. Thus we make them idle and secure, and encourage them to shamelessly rob us of our money and our goods, as well as to mock us, to finally overcome us, to kill us all for this unpardonable sin, and to rob us of all our goods (as they pray and pray daily). Now, tell me if they have not every reason to be our enemies, to curse us and to fight for our final, complete and eternal ruin[495]", Luther warned.

Certainly, the popes used to recommend preserving synagogues from destruction, but Luther advised destroying them. So with Luther the Jews had not gained from the change, far from it:

"In the first place, we must set fire to their synagogues or schools and bury and cover with dirt all that we do not set on fire, so that no man will ever see stone or ashes of them again... **In the** second place, I also advise that their houses be razed and destroyed... Thirdly, I advise that their prayer books and Talmudic writings, by means of which they teach idolatry, lies, curses and blasphemies, be taken away from them... **Fourthly, I** advise that henceforth the rabbis be forbidden to teach, on pain of loss of life...Fifthly, that protection on the highways be abolished completely for the Jews. They have nothing to do on the outskirts of the cities... Sixthly, I advise that usury be forbidden to them, and that all money and all wealth in silver and gold be taken from them, and then all this be kept in a safe place. The reason for such a measure as this, as already stated, is that they have no other means of earning their living than by usury, by means of which they have robbed and stolen from us all that they possess...Seventhly, I recommend to put a flail or an axe or a hoe or a spade or a spindle or a distaff or a spindle into the hands of young and strong Jews and Jewesses and let them earn and eat bread by the sweat of their face, as was enjoined on the

---

[495] Martin Luther, *Von den Jüden iren Lügen*, translated by Martin H. Bertram, in *Oeuvres de Luther*, Philadelphia, Fortress Press, 1971. [Martin Luther, *On the Jews and their Lies*, Pdf, NdT.]

children of Adam (Genesis, 3:19). For it is not fitting that we cursed [goyim] should toil without rest in the sweat of our brows while they, the "holy people," spend their hours idling by the hearth, feasting and expelling their wind, and, as if that were not enough, boasting with blasphemies of their lordship over the Christians by means of our sweat. No; we must get rid of these lazy offenders by the seat of their trousers." Probably labour is for the Jews a worse punishment than death.

Luther also evoked their criminal instincts: "They are nothing but thieves and robbers, who daily do not eat a morsel, and wear clothes which they have robbed and stolen from us by their accursed usury. Thus they live day by day, together with wife and child, in robbery and theft, as arch thieves and robbers, in total impenitent security...I have read and heard many stories about the Jews which agree with this assessment of Christ, namely, how they have poisoned wells, murdered, kidnapped children, as has already been related. I heard that a Jew sent to another Jew, and this through a Christian, a vessel full of blood, together with a cask of wine, in which, after drinking it, a dead Jew was found. There are more such stories. Because of the abduction of children they have often been burnt at the stake or banished (as we have already heard)...This is what I was thinking of when I said above that the Christian has no more bitter and mortifying enemy than the Jew. To no one do we concede so much of ourselves and for no one do we suffer so much as we suffer for these infamous sons of the devil, these spawn of vipers[496]."

"We must prevent them from feeling their lies, slanders, curses and shameless defamations confirmed. Nor dare we be partakers of their demoniacal sermon by protecting them, giving them food and drink, offering them a roof, and other kindnesses, especially as when we help and serve them, they vilely and proudly boast that God ordained them lords and us servants. For instance, when a Christian kindles a fire for them on a Sabbath, or cooks for them in a tavern, they revile, curse, and defame us, supposing this to be a meritorious thing, and so they all live upon our wealth, which they have robbed from us. How desperate, how utterly wicked, venomous, and devilish these Jews are, who for these fourteen hundred years have been and still are our plague, our pestilence, and our woe!... If the authorities are reluctant to use force and restrain the diabolical indecency of the Jews, the latter should be driven out of the country and sent to their land and possessions in Jerusalem; there they can lie, curse, blaspheme, defame, murder, steal, rob, usurp, mock, and indulge in all those infamous abominations which they practise among us. Let them

---

[496] Martin Luther, *Les Juifs et leurs mensonges*, 1543, quoted by Joseph Lémann, *L'entrée des Israélites dans la société françaises*, 1886, book two, chapter IV.

leave us our government, our country, our life and our property, but above all our Lord, the Messiah, our faith and our church as yet undefiled and uncorrupted by their diabolical tyranny and malice...We shall have to drive them out like rabid dogs lest we become accomplices in their abominable blasphemy and all their other vices and thereby deserve the wrath of God and end up cursed along with them."

Several months after the publication of *On the Jews and Their Lies*, Luther wrote another pamphlet, *Vom Schem Hamphoras und das Geschlecht Christi* (Of *the Name of Hamphoras and the Lineage of Christ*): "Here in Wittenberg, in our church, a sow was hewn out of the stone: piglets and Jews suckle her, while behind her stands a rabbi lifting her right leg and with his left hand pulling her tail, bending down and diligently contemplating behind the tail the Talmud, as if he wanted to learn something very subtle and very special; no doubt, they received their *Schem Hamphoras* in that place[497]."

"When Judas hanged himself and his bowels gushed out and, as happens in such circumstances, his bladder also burst, the Jews were ready to receive the water and other precious things, and then they swelled with it and drank greedily among themselves, being then endowed with such fineness of spirit that they were able to perceive comments in the Holy Scriptures which neither Matthew nor Isaiah himself...would have been able to see, or perhaps they were looking into the very ass of their God "*Shed*," and found these things written in that steaming orifice."

Finally, Luther concluded that the Jews were the devil's people: "The Devil, with his angelic mug, devours what the oral and anal orifices of the Jews secrete; this is, indeed, his favourite dish, on which he gorges himself like a sow behind the bard[498]."

Emperor Charles Quintus had expelled the Jews from the kingdom of Naples in 1541. Under Luther's influence, other rulers reacted. In 1543, Elector John Frederick of Saxony revoked certain concessions. Johann of Kustrin, Margrave of Neumark, cancelled the safe conduct of Jews in his territories. Philip of Hesse added further restrictions to his ordinance on Jews.

The Jewish communities plotted their intrigues through one of their lawyers, a certain Yosef de Rossheim, who used to go to the emperor and princes to plead on behalf of his sect. Yosef de Rossheim regularly entered the court of Emperor Charles the Fifth and saved the Jews from great evils on many occasions in the years 1520–1550.

---

[497] *Vom Schem Hamphoras und das Geschlecht Christi*, quoted in Léon Poliakov, *Histoire de l'antisémitisme, Tome I*, Point Seuil, 1981, p. 311.

[498] Luther had also translated into German the *Toledot Jeschu*, a second-century pamphlet insulting Jesus Christ that had been republished by Raymond Martin.

Around 1570, the pastor Georg Nigrimus published *The Jewish Enemy*, which took up Luther's programme. Nikolaus Selnecker, one of the authors of the *Konkordienformel* (Latin: *Formula concordiae*), reprinted Luther's books. In 1573, Jews were expelled from all of Brandenburg. Luther's anti-Jewish tracts were reprinted at the beginning of the 17th century in Dortmund, where they were seized by Emperor Rudolf II. In 1613 and 1617, they were republished in Frankfurt am Main after the expulsion of the Jews. These editions were the last popular publications before those of the 20th century.

Johann Eck was Luther's great Catholic adversary in Germany. He too seemed to have understood the deep nature of Judaism, the essence of which is to destroy everything that is not Jewish[499]. He denounced the Hebrew religion, the project and behaviour of the Jews with the same zeal as Luther. In 1541, he published a pamphlet in which he demonstrated that "these Jewish scoundrels have done much harm to Germany and other countries", while denouncing the bloodthirsty character of Jews who desecrated holy hosts and used the blood of Christian children during their Passover.

XCIII. Julius III and the Talmud

The advance of the Protestant Reformation had provoked an energetic reaction in the Catholic world against the relaxation of discipline and customs. Two men, above all, had taken to heart the strengthening of Catholicism and the consolidation of the papacy: the Neapolitan Pietro Caraffa, later Pope under the name of Paul IV, and the Spaniard Ignatius of Loyola, founder of the Jesuit order.

The Catholic reaction against Protestantism affected the Jewish population of Italy, which until then had enjoyed a relatively peaceful life compared to that of Jews in the rest of Europe. In a bull of 1542, *Cupientes judeos,* Pope Paul III (1534–1549) ordered the surveillance of converts, their complete separation from Jews, their marriage to Christian women and the prosecution before the Inquisition of those who continued to practise Jewish rites.

The opponents of the Jews raised the question of the Talmud again. Forty years earlier, attempts by the Dominicans to burn this work had failed. But the situation had changed. As always, the main accusers were Jewish converts. Elia Levita, the famous Jewish grammarian, had had two grandsons: Elianus and Solomon Romanus. Eliano, the eldest, knew

---

[499]See our previous books: *Planetary Hopes (2005), Psychoanalysis of Judaism (2006), Jewish Fanaticism (2007), The Jewish Mafia (2008) and The Mirror of Judaism (2009).*

Hebrew and was a proofreader and scribe in several Italian cities. He had converted to Christianity under the name of Vittorio Eliano, and after entering the orders he was promoted to the rank of canon. When Romano learned of his brother's apostasy, he went to Venice to make him return to Judaism, although he was eventually persuaded to accept baptism in 1551 under the name of John the Baptist. Romano became a Jesuit and published several ecclesiastical works. The descendants of Elia Levita, along with two other apostates, Ananel di Fogio and Joseph More, revived Nicolas Donin's old accusations against the Talmud.

Pope Julius III (1550–1555) was not hostile to the Jews, but it was not for him to pronounce on the question. The matter was to be settled by the Inquisition, i.e. by Pietro Caraffa and his acolytes. He naturally ruled against the Talmud, and in August 1553 Julius III had to ratify his verdict. By the bull *Cum sicut nuper*, Julius III ordered the Talmud to be destroyed by flames. Emissaries of the Inquisition then entered all the Jewish houses in Rome, confiscated all the copies, and on 9 September 1553, Jewish New Year's Day, the Hebrew books were thrown into the fire.

From Rome, the records spread throughout Romagna, Ferrara, Mantua, Venice and even to the islands of Candia and Crete, the latter under Venetian rule. Thousands of copies of the Talmud were thus destroyed. Soon the confiscations were no longer confined to the Talmud but covered all Hebrew books indiscriminately. The Jews then applied pressure and appealed to the pope who, on 29 May 1554, issued a bull forbidding the delegates of the Inquisition to seize Jewish works other than the Talmud.

By the beginning of the 16th century, thanks to the newly invented printing press, the Talmud had been widely disseminated. The first complete edition of the Talmud, with all its blasphemies against the Christian religion, had been published in Venice in 1519. The Amsterdam edition of 1600 was still intact, as were virtually all Jewish books published in the 16th century. But towards the end of the century and the beginning of the 17th century, when many scholars began to study these works seriously, Jews, fearing for their safety, began to expurgate some chapters of the Talmud. Thus, for example, the Talmud published in Basel in 1578 had censored numerous passages attacking Jesus Christ and declaring "that the precepts of justice, equity and charity towards one's neighbour are not only impracticable, but also a crime[500]". It was left to the discretion of the teachers to explain these omitted passages orally to the pupils.

A few years later, the Jews thought they could restore them in a new comprehensive Kraków edition. But these reintegrated passages had raised

---

[500] Gougenot des Mousseaux. *The Jew, Judaism and the Judaisation of Christian peoples*, p. 102.

the hackles and indignation of Hebraising Christians, so that a Jewish synod meeting in 1631 in Poland prescribed their removal from future editions. The rabbis' slogan read as follows: "We therefore urge, on pain of major excommunication, not to print in future editions of the Mishchna or the Gemara, anything that has any connection, good or bad, with the acts of Jesus the Nazarene. We urge, accordingly, to leave blank the spaces that speak of Jesus the Nazarene. A circle like this one: **Or**, put in place, will caution rabbis and schoolmasters about *teaching* youth those passages viva voce only. By this precaution, the wise men living among the Nazarenes (Christians) will have no pretext to attack us on that subject[501]."

The famous rabbi convert, David-Paul Drach, who wrote in the early 19th century *"De l'harmonie entre l'Église et la Synagogue"* (On the harmony between the Church and the Synagogue) declared that the book contained "strange aberrations, cynical vileness, atrocious and senseless calumnies about all the objects of veneration of the Church[502]."

However, some Jewish books were later published with very few excisions, especially in the Calvinist Netherlands, where the Jews expelled from Spain were well received. The Talmud published there in 1644–1648 was almost identical to the Venice version.

The last subterfuge invented to deceive the censors was the introduction of the word *haiah (was)* in some places in the text, in order to indicate where the censored passages were to be found. In many passages, the rabbis could not help but show what they wanted to hide, using words such as *gam attah* (*even now*), to indicate that this law was still in force; and *aphilu bazzeman hazzeh* (*to this day*), thus underlining the validity of this law, and other subterfuges of the same kind[503].

XCIV. Paul IV, Cum nimis absurdum, 14 July 1555.

Pietro Caraffa, who had led the inquisitorial offensive against the Talmud, became Pope in 1555 as Paul IV (May 1555—August 1559). He belonged to a family of Neapolitan nobility. From the time of his accession, he imposed a tax of 10 ducats on every synagogue in his states to pay for the establishment of catechumenates where Jews were initiated into Catholicism.

---

[501] Gougenot des Mousseaux. *The Jew, Judaism and the Judaisation of Christian peoples*, p. 102, Drach, *Harmonie*, tome 1, p. 167–168.
[502] Charles Auzias-Turenne, *Revue Catholique des Institutions et du Droit*, October 1893. See also: *La Question juive*, by A. Béchaux, Correspondence August 1893, Rorhbacher, volume XV, p. 481.
[503] Justin Bonaventura Pranaitis, *Le Talmud démasqué*, 1892; *The Talmud unmasked*.

On 14 July 1555, less than two months after his election, the pope promulgated his famous bull *Cum nimis absurdum,* titled after the first words of the bull (like all papal bulls): *"It is too absurd and unseemly that the Jews, condemned by God to eternal slavery on account of their sins, under the pretext that they are treated with love by Christians and allowed to live among them, should be so ungrateful as to insult them instead of thanking them, and so bold as to set themselves up as masters where they ought to be subjects. We are informed that, in Rome and elsewhere, they are so impudent as to live among Christians in the vicinity of churches without wearing any distinguishing sign, that they rent the most elegant houses and around the squares of the cities, towns, and villages where they live, acquire and possess property, keep Christian maids and nursemaids and other paid servants, and commit various other misdeeds to their shame and contempt of the Christian name..."*

For the most part, the provisions adopted were only a summary of the canon law of past centuries, but unlike his predecessors, the uncompromising Paul IV applied them to the letter. In Rome and other cities of the pontifical state, the Jews were henceforth to live in a separate quarter from the Christians, which was to have a single entrance and exit. There was to be no more than one synagogue per city. Nor could they own real estate outside the ghetto, and they would have to sell the property they owned outside the city. They were given six months to sell their real estate and had to give up their property for one-fifth of its value. Jews would have to wear yellow hats and could not employ Christian servants. They would not work on Christian holidays. In addition, they were obliged to use Italian and Latin to keep their trade books, thus making it impossible to use Hebrew, which allowed them to trade accounts without the controllers being able to verify them. They were also forbidden to trade in wheat, or products necessary for human consumption, and to sell pledged goods within a year and a half. Let us note here that this prohibition implicitly revealed that many Jewish merchants were to speculate in grain in order to enrich themselves at the expense of the misery of the people. Officially, they could only practice the rag trade and money lending, their oldest speciality. But Jews could also continue their clandestine trade, for example as receivers or pimps.

These laws were rigorously enforced and many Jews emigrated from Rome. Those who remained were subjected to hard labour to help repair the city walls, then besieged by the Spaniards. Around the same time, twenty-four Marranos from Portugal were burned in Ancona. It was the only time in Italian history that such a condemnation took place.

Ghettos were officially established in the Republic of Venice, in Padua, Tuscany, Florence, Siena, Genoa and Turin. But we must remember that, in fact, Jews have preferred to live apart in ghettos since time immemorial.

The Jews, wrote Bernard Lazare, "separated themselves from the inhabitants by their rites and customs. They considered the soil of foreign peoples to be impure and sought in each town to constitute a sort of sacred territory. They lived apart, in special quarters, closed in on themselves, lived in isolation and administered themselves by virtue of privileges of which they were jealous... These ghettos were often accepted and even sought out by the Jews in their desire to separate themselves from the world and to live apart, without mixing with the nations, in order to preserve the integrity of their beliefs and of their race. While it is true that in many places the edicts ordered the Jews to remain confined in special quarters, they only consecrated an already existing state of affairs[504]."

Simon Dubnow, a famous 20th century Jewish historian, also recognised this: "It was not only by order of the powerful that Jews lived in separate streets. Often they themselves wanted it that way. Men of one nation, surrounded by hostile foreigners, felt the need to live together, close to their schools and synagogues, close to their rabbis and community leaders. Often, the Jewish quarter of the city was separated from the Christian quarter by a wall, or the streets ended in gates that could be closed to defend against the attacks of the hostile mob. More than once, this measure saved Jews from massacre. At the papal residence in Rome, the police locked the gates of the ghetto at night; no one could enter or leave."

Emperor Ferdinand I, who succeeded his brother Charles the Fifth in 1556, was also hostile and unforgiving towards Jews. Every Jew who travelled to Vienna on business had to report to the governor upon arrival and declare the reason for his visit and the length of his stay in the city. After taking other restrictive measures against the Jews, Ferdinand I decreed their expulsion from Lower Austria, giving them until St. John's Day to leave the country. However, they were granted further time limits for two years, but after two years they had to resign themselves to the path of exile.

In Prague in 1559, a Jewish renegade named Ascher of Udine encouraged the confiscation of Talmudic works and all prayer books. The books were sent to Vienna, while a fire reduced a large part of the city's Jewish quarter to ashes. Instead of helping to fight the flames, the Christian common people rushed to plunder Jewish property.

The same year in Cremona, the great library of the Jews was destroyed by order of a fiery Dominican, Sixtus of Siena. The monk coolly recounted in his writings that he had thrown more than twelve thousand volumes into the flames and that he regretted that the weakness and greed of the princes

---

[504]Bernard Lazare, *Anti-Semitism, its history and causes, (1894)*. Editions La Bastille, digital edition, 2011, p. 16, 55.

had allowed the Jews to still possess so many Talmudic books[505].

That year they were also expelled from the Papal States, except for the ghettos of Rome and Ancona.

On the death of Paul IV, the Jews of Rome crowned his statue with a yellow hat before dragging it through the mire of the ghetto. The Jews would succeed in corrupting his successor Pius IV into annulling most of the bull of 1555. Pius IV absolved them of any crimes they might have committed against the constitution of Paul IV and ordered the restitution of all the account books confiscated from them.

XCV. Ivan the Terrible

In Russia, Jewish merchants were known to be the main slavers and pimps. In the 13th century, they had been invited to settle in Kiev by the Tatars, where their supreme authority resided, earning the hatred of the other inhabitants. The great 20th century Russian writer Aleksandr Solzhenitsyn quoted the writer Nikolai Karamzine: "These people bought the right to collect tribute from the Tatars and practised exorbitant usury on the poor, and, in case of non-payment, declared them slaves and took them captive. The inhabitants of Vladimir, Suzdal, and Rostov lost patience and rose up unanimously, ringing their bells, against these wicked usurers: some were killed, the rest expelled."

Jewish merchants enjoyed immense fortunes. Solzhenitsyn cited another source: *The Little Jewish Encyclopedia*, published in Jerusalem in 1976: "The archives of the 15th century mention Jews from Kiev, tax collectors, who enjoyed substantial fortunes[506]."

In the mid-16th century, Tsar Ivan IV the Terrible solved the problem in his own way. At that time there were no Jews in Moscow. Previously, Jewish merchants from the Polish state used to travel freely to Moscow, but under his reign they had been barred from entering Russia. When in 1550, the Polish King Sigismund-Augustus requested that free access to Russia be allowed again, Tsar Ivan objected in these terms:

"Concerning what you write to us that we should allow your Jews to enter our lands, we have already written to you several times telling you of the evil deeds of the Jews, who turn our people away from Christ, bring poisoned drugs into our state and cause much harm to our people. You should be ashamed, brother, to write to us about them knowing of their

---

[505] *Sixti Sænensis, ord. prædic., Bibliotheca sancta*, 3rd edition. Cologne, 1586, in-fol., p. 125, in Georges-Bernard Depping, *Les Juifs dans le Moyen-Âge*, 1823, Paris, Imprimerie royale, Wouters, Bruxelles, 1844, p. 313.
[506] Aleksandr Solzhenitsyn, *Deux Siècles ensemble*, Tome I, Fayard, 2002, p. 21.

misdeeds. In the other States also they did much evil, and for this they have been expelled or sentenced to death. We cannot allow the Jews to enter our State, for we do not want to see evil in it; we only want God to allow the people of our country to live in peace, without any disturbance. And you, brother, should not, henceforth, write to us any more about the Jews[507]."

In 1563, the Russians seized the city of Polotzk from the Poles. As there were a large number of Jews there, Ivan IV ordered them all to be drowned in the Dviná River, men, women and children alike.

The Dane Peter of Arelsund left a testimony of his time at the Tsar's court: "Cruel and intolerant as he was, Ivan the Terrible never persecuted anyone on religious grounds, except the Jews. He made no attempt to instruct them in the Christian faith or to baptise them; he burnt them alive, hanged them and drowned them; he used to say that no prince should believe his words or have pity on them[508]." Undoubtedly, Ivan was a clear-thinking ruler.

XCVI. St. Pius V

Pope Pius V (1566–1572) was born into a peasant family. He had entered the Dominican order at the age of 14 and went on to teach philosophy and theology within the order. In 1546, he joined the Holy Office. Paul IV had appointed him commissary general of the Inquisition in Rome in 1551 and then in Milan and Lombardy in 1556. The following year, he was made a cardinal and elevated to the rank of grand inquisitor in 1558. He vigorously opposed Pius IV, whom he finally succeeded in January 1566.

In the face of the extreme aggressiveness of Judaism, Pius V was firm and determined. Alarmed by the constant subversive action of the Jews, he renewed their obligation to wear a distinctive sign, in order to protect Christians from their deceitful company and their fallacious speeches. On 19 April 1566, three months after his election, he promulgated the bull *Romanus Pontifex*, which reinstated all the restrictive laws issued by Paul IV against the Jews in the Papal States and extended their application to all Jews in Catholic countries. The bull confirmed the obligation for all Jews to wear a distinctive sign.

The pope not only denounced their usury, but also pointed out their larceny, deceit and "shameful flattery". Indeed, the Jews were the greatest

---

[507]Léon Poliakov, *Histoire de l'antisémitisme*, Tome I, Point Seuil, 1981, p. 419. These words are also quoted by Aleksandr Solzhenitsyn, in *Deux Siècles ensemble*, Tome I, Fayard, 2002, p. 26, 27.
[508]Léon Poliakov, *Les Juifs et notre histoire*, Science Flammarion, 1973, p. 84.

receivers of stolen goods and objects and engaged in pimping, the latter being one of their favourite activities[509]: *"Their impiety imbued with all sorts of execrable arts has reached such a degree that it is necessary, in view of the health of Our people, to restrain by force a disease of such a nature with a speedy remedy. For, omitting the numerous forms of usury by which the Hebrews have everywhere consumed the assets of needy Christians, we judge it to be quite evident that they are concealers and even accomplices of thieves and robbers who seek to transfer to another the things stolen and embezzled or to conceal them up to the present time, not only those of profane use, but also those of divine worship. And many under the pretext of dealing with matters proper to their trade, coveting the houses of honest women, lose them with very shameful flatteries; and what is most pernicious of all, given to sorceries and magic incantations, superstitions and evil spells, they induce many unwary and sick people into the deceptions of Satan, boasting of predicting the future, treasures and hidden things… Lastly, we have well known and inquired into the unworthy manner in which this execrable race uses the name of Christ, and to what degree it is injurious to those who are to be judged by that name, and whose lives are therefore threatened by their deceptions. Moved indeed by these and other most serious things, and moved moreover by the magnitude of the crimes which are daily increasing to the disgrace of our cities, thinking moreover that the said race, with the exception of insignificant groups in the East, is of no use whatever to our Republic[510]."*

The priest Jules Meinvielle, who referred to these words of the Bull of Pius V in his book *The Jew in the Mystery of History*, nevertheless explained that "Catholic theology did not fail to recognise that, although this danger was very real, this people nevertheless deserved a very special consideration. Indeed, the Jew may be very wicked, but he is a holy people, for whom the Church must have the highest regard, since in a certain sense he is the Father of the Church". Thus the conversion of the Jews, foreseen at the end of time, forbids any form of radical measures against them, no matter how heinous their crimes. The Church, conqueror of the Jews, has always sheltered the serpent in her bosom instead of "crushing its head".

Pius V accused and had imprisoned many Jews of his States who transgressed the canon laws: "Under the pretext that the Jews of the Papal States had infringed his canon laws, he had some of them imprisoned and

---

[509] See the chapter on this in *The Jewish Mafia* (2008).

[510] Julio Meinvielle, *El judío en el misterio de la historia*, Cruz y Fierro Editores, Buenos Aires, 1982, p. 61 and Maurice Pinay, *Complot contra la Iglesia*, Chapter XLI (1962), Transcription pdf from Ediciones Mundo Libre, Mexico, 1985, p. 365. (Pope St. Pius V, *Romanus Pontifex*, 19 April 1566, compiled in the *Bularium diplomarum e privilegiorum Sanctorum Romanorum Pontificum*. Turin, 1862. Volume VII, p. 439.)

their books seized and burned. The prosperous community of Bologna was investigated with particular severity, for the blow was directed against their wealth and property. In order to have a legal reason, confusing questions about Christianity were submitted to a formal hearing before the tribunal of the Inquisition; for example, it was asked whether the Jews regarded Catholics as idolaters; or whether the curse forms against the Mineos and the "Kingdom of Sin" in the prayers referred to Christians and the Papacy, and, especially, whether the story in a little-read work about a "Bastard Son of an Outcast" referred to Jesus[511]", Heinrich Graetz recounted in this connection.

These various accusations had been gathered by a Jewish apostate named Alessandro Franceschi, who had become a Jesuit missionary. The Curia forbade the wealthier Jews to leave Bologna, but they managed to corrupt a guard and a large part of the community took refuge in Ferrara. Pius V then announced to the College of Cardinals his intention to expel all Jews from his states.

On 19 January 1567, the Pope promulgated the Bull *Cum nos super,* "confirming those of many previous Popes, by forbidding the Israelites to acquire real estate, obliging them to sell it within a peremptory period, under penalty that further contempt of the Papal Bulls would directly trigger the confiscation of the said real estate".

On 26 February 1569, Pius V finally promulgated the bull *Hebraeorums gens sola*, which obliged all Jews in the Papal States, except those of Rome and Ancona, to emigrate within three months; beyond this period, they would be sold into slavery or condemned to even harsher penalties. Some Jews then accepted baptism, but most resigned themselves to emigrate. Given very little time, the exiles left in ruins. They sought asylum in the small neighbouring states of Pesaro, Urbin, Ferrara, Mantua and Milan.

In his *Complot against the Church* (1962), Maurice Pinay noted that this bull was novel on one important point: "This holy bull brings an important innovation compared to the expulsions of Jews carried out in Christian states in previous centuries. As we will recall, the Israelites were put in the dilemma of being expelled or of converting, with the result that the majority, in order to evade expulsion, pretended to convert to Christianity, thus constituting a greater danger to the Church and to the Christian states. St. Pius V, no doubt aware of this, decreed the expulsion from the Papal States, leaving them no recourse to the conversion with which they had always evaded the expulsion. It can be seen that this most holy Pope knew the Jewish problem better than many of the civil and

---

[511] Heinrich Graetz, *History of the Jews IV*, Philadelphia, The Jewish Publication Society of America, 1894, p. 590.

religious hierarchs who preceded him[512]."

The Jews of Avignon and the Venesine County, who had been able to remain in this part of France after the expulsion executed two centuries earlier, were also invited to leave the country.

All of these expellees sought asylum in the Ottoman Empire where they were usually given an excellent welcome if on the way they managed to avoid being seized by the Knights of the Order of Malta.

"At the end of the 13th century, the Angevins, who reigned in Naples, caused a general conversion of the Jews in their dominions, located in the vicinity of the city of Trani. Under the name of *"neophytes"*, the converts continued to live as crypto-Jews for more than three centuries. Their secret fidelity to Judaism was one of the reasons why the Inquisition became active in Naples in the 16th century. Many of them died at the stake in Rome in February 1572... Some managed to escape to the Balkans, where they joined the existing Jewish communities[513]."

Pius V also strove to unite Christendom against the Turkish danger. In 1566, Emperor Maximilian II had failed in his attempt to reconquer Hungary. Sultan Suleiman, seeking to seize the island of Malta, had been met with the stubborn resistance of the Knights of Malta and the population, supported by the Pope and the King of Spain. In 1570, his successor Selim II conquered the island of Cyprus, decimating the population mercilessly. It was imperative to halt the Ottoman advance, so Pius V urged the Christian princes to unite, again stirring up great momentum in Christendom.

On 7 October 1571, the 200 ships of the Holy League, mainly Spanish and Venetian, defeated the Ottoman fleet and its allies in the Gulf of Lepanto. By the end of the battle, forty thousand Turks had perished. The magnificent victory at Lepanto put a stop to Muslim expansion. Pius V died on 1 May 1572, a few months after the victory of the Catholic fleet. He was beatified one hundred years later and canonised in 1712. He remains to this day one of the most illustrious popes in the history of the Church.

XCVII. The Synagogue, "blind and obstinate", 1593

The Jews, who clearly bore no grudge against their persecutors, were readmitted by Pope Gregory XIII, at least in some cities of the Church

---

[512] Maurice Pinay, *Complot against the Church*, Chapter XLI (1962), Transcription pdf from Ediciones Mundo Libre, Mexico, 1985, p. 366, published by Omnia Veritas Ltd, www.omnia-veritas.com.
[513] Maurice Pinay, *Complot against the Church*, Chapter II (1962), Transcription pdf from Ediciones Mundo Libre, Mexico, 1985, p. 139.

States such as Ravenna. This was obviously because it was in their interest to live among Christians.

In his bull of 1581, Pope Gregory XIII (1572–1585) informed us that the Jews used to hang a lamb from a cross on Good Friday to mock Christ. Gregory XIII forbade the granting of the last sacraments to any dying Christian who had called a Jewish doctor to his bedside. The offender would then be buried in an unconsecrated place. This prescription was valid for all, without distinction of rank, class or privilege.

Pope Sixtus V (1585–1590), bribed by the Jews, had allowed many of them to return to Rome, and by 1599 there were again about 200 families in the city. Sixtus V also forbade the Knights of Malta to continue enslaving the Jews they captured at sea when they travelled to the Levant.

The Jews were still banished from the kingdom of Naples, but in Venice there lived a large community with a certain splendour. Unlike other Jews, the Israelites of Venice wore scarlet hats with black linings.

Pope Clement VIII (1592–1605) followed the example of Paul IV, Pius V and Gregory XIII in respecting the Jews. He too confirmed the expulsion measures, allowing them only partial residence in Rome, Ancona and Avignon, where they were in fact subject to numerous restrictions. The bull *Cum hebraeorum malitia* of 25 February 1593 forbade them to read the Talmud, to encourage prostitution, gambling, receiving money, pederasty and denounced the usury of the "blind and obstinate" synagogue (*Cœca et obdurata*): "*Cœca et obdurata... pietati christianae pro gratia injuriam reddens, non cessat quotidie tot committere enormes excessus, tot detestanda patrare flagitia in prejudicium ipsorum Christi fidelium...*" ("The whole world suffers from the usury of the Jews, from their monopolies, from their deceit. They have reduced many unfortunate people to poverty, especially farmers, artisans and the poorest and most hardworking..."). When the Holy See later acquired the duchies of Urbin and Ferrara, the Jews residing there were tolerated. But by a new encyclical, Clement VIII ordered that the Talmud and the books of the Kabbalah be searched for and destroyed everywhere[514].

In 1597, Philip II of Spain expelled them from the Duchy of Milan. "In Genoa, around the middle of the 16th century, they obtained permission to live in the places assigned to them, to have banks and pawnshops there. Doctors were allowed to practice medicine. They must have raised serious complaints, for in 1598 an ordinance banished them from the republic. They later returned, but lived with many limitations and little protection from public insults[515]."

---

[514] Charles Auzias-Turenne, *Revue Catholique des Institutions et du Droit*, October 1893 [On Kabbalah read *Psychoanalysis of Judaism*].
[515] Georges-Bernard Depping, *Les Juifs dans le Moyen-Âge*, (1823), Éd. Wouters,

The bishop of Volturara, near Naples, Simone Maioli, had published in 1615 a treatise entitled *Dierum canicularium (The Canicular Days)*. In the chapter entitled *De perfidia Judaeorum*, he explicitly accused Jews of being spies and traitors, as well as being the first receivers of stolen goods, pimps and traffickers in human flesh:

"These traitors, the most wicked of men, hand over our homeland to the Turk, our resources, our forces, and we tolerate them and feed them! It is like putting fire in our bosom, like harbouring the serpent there". Distrust, and more distrust! for "experience never fails to show that, from first to last, the Jews persecute the Christians with the most implacable hatred; and that, if the occasion promises them impunity, they assemble and rush upon them in close battalion, resembling troops of harpies who cannot satiate themselves with the blood they suck." Ah, distrust even their attentions, even their obsequious submission; for they have much more to fear when perfidy creeps under their attentions. Look at the thousand fraudulent forms in which they conceal usury! Carried away by them, usury lends itself to unimaginable ambushes to devour them; and look even: if thieves, rogues, prostitute women are found, the house of the Jew opens for them and recognises them as guests (*promptum proebent hospitium*). That these people of robbery come to offer the Jew the products of robbery, and that he buys them at a vile price; he encourages these wretches, stimulates them and helps them in their misdeeds. True fruits of the gallows (*furciferi*), scourges of the honest, devoid of the right to any toleration, the Jews are, in a word, the inciters and helpers of the son against the father of the family, of the daughter against her mother, and of the servant against his master. And what minion of magic is not to be found among their ranks[516]!"

The popes had tolerated the Jews in the Papal States and in the Venesine County, but applied the Church's regulations to them, updating them severely when the administrators and lords relaxed or allowed themselves to be corrupted. The Jews should have preferred to settle en masse in these territories where they had no need to fear persecution or plunder. In fact, when there was a bloody reaction anywhere, they came to take refuge under the protection of the papacy; but they did not stay for long. The reason was very simple: while they were protected in the Papal States, they were also closely guarded and kept apart. In other countries, on the contrary, they

---

Brussels, 1844, p. 311.
[516] Simone Maioli, in Gougenot des Mousseaux. *The Jew, Judaism and the Judaisation of Christian peoples*, p. 109–110. (*Nec libertatem hereditario acquisitam, ita temere prostituere velint.* T. III, p. 920, col. 2; Moguntiae, 1615: *Hodie etiam apud Judaeos, praesertim in Oriente, quid magia frequentis...Tradunt ipsi Judaici scriptores septuaginta seniores suos, seu Sanhedrin, magiam apprime calluisse, idque, inquit, R. Semoloh, tu praestigiatores eo facilius convincerent!*)

enjoyed a certain freedom of manoeuvre and were able to exploit Christians as they pleased, despite the angry reactions they provoked[517]. This explains why, once the storm was over, they were always ready to pay the price to be accepted again among the Goyim they despised.

XCVIII. *The war of Vincent Fettmilch*

In Frankfurt am Main, the craftsmen's guilds angrily called for the expulsion of the Jews. The leading confectioner, Vincent Fettmilch, openly described himself as the new Haman, after the name of the minister of the Persian king Ahasuerus who had been hanged at the beginning of the 5th century BC. According to legend, a Jewish woman named Esther had seduced the king and intrigued against the "anti-Semitic" minister. The whole affair had finally ended with the massacre of 75,000 Persians at the hands of the Jews, as recounted in the Torah in the *Book of Esther*[518].

Once again, the exasperation reached its peak. On 1 September 1614, the Jews, gathered in their houses of prayer, heard the clamouring and knocking at the gates of their neighbourhood. There were several dead and wounded on both sides, but the supporters of Vincent Fettmilch triumphed and throughout the night they ransacked the Jewish quarter, raiding and destroying all the houses. The Jews who had not managed to hide took refuge in the cemetery, fearing that they would be massacred there. The insurgents left them in uncertainty throughout the day. In the afternoon, the Jews were finally ordered to leave Frankfurt through the Sinners' Gate, stripped of all their goods and belongings. Almost 1,400 Jews were thus expelled from the city.

Similar disturbances took place in Worms at the instigation of a lawyer surnamed Chemnitz. In April 1615, despite the Magistrate's protests, the city corporations, led by Chemnitz, notified the Jews to leave Worms before the last day of Easter. The Archbishop of Mainz and the *Landgrave* [519] Ludwig of Darmstadt authorised the Jews to settle temporarily in the small towns and villages of their domains. At the news

---

[517] Charles Auzias-Turenne, *Revue Catholique des Institutions et du Droit*, October 1893.

[518] Read it in *The Mirror of Judaism*. The authenticity of this story is doubtful, but Jews celebrate this massacre every year during the *Purim* festival.

[519] Landgrave was a noble title commonly used in the Holy Roman Empire and later in the territories derived from it, comparable to that of sovereign prince, although etymologically meaning count of a country, having a feudal duty directly to the emperor. His jurisdiction sometimes extended over considerable areas, without being subject to an intermediate office, such as duke, bishop or count palatine. The landgrave exercised sovereign rights; his power of decision was comparable to that of a prince.

of the events in Worms, the Elector Frederick, a friend of the Jewish physician Zacuto Lusitanianus, sent infantry, cavalry and artillery to suppress the unrest. Chemnitz, along with several of his lieutenants, was imprisoned, and in January 1616, by order of Emperor Matthias, the Jews of Worms were able to regain their homes.

Two months later, the Jews of Frankfurt were also reintegrated into their estates. They returned almost triumphant, preceded by numerous imperial commissars and to the sound of music. Since Frankfurt had endured scenes of looting and crime, the perpetrators of these disorders were more severely punished than the agitators of Worms. Vincent Fettmilch was hanged, his house razed to the ground and his family banished. To compensate the Jews for their losses, the city had to pay them 175,919 guilders.

After these violent events, the Jewish community in Frankfurt decided to celebrate the day of the punishment of the "German Haman" every year on 20 Adar. This holiday became known as "Purim-Vicent" (from the name Fettmilch). Two centuries later, the Germans of the region remembered the arrogance of the incestuous sect.

It is well known that many of the Marranos from Spain and Portugal had gone into exile in Northern Europe, especially in Amsterdam, London and Hamburg. The community of Portuguese Jews in Hamburg grew rapidly in wealth and influence[520]. The Teixeira family, in particular, attracted attention with its luxurious lifestyle. The founder of this financial house, Diego Teixeira de Matos, was nicknamed in Hamburg—like Joseph of Naxos in Constantinople—*the rich Jew*. Originally from Portugal, this Marrano had fled the Iberian peninsula to return to Judaism after landing in Flanders. "Over seventy years old, he underwent the circumcision operation to become a real Jew. Thanks to his wealth and his connections with the nobility and capitalists, Diego Teixeira could pass for an aristocrat. He drove a satin-lined carriage and owned freed servants."

Alongside the Portuguese community, there was a small German community in Hamburg. The Lutheran pastors then attacked the Jews with renewed vigour. Prominent among them was a certain Johannes Müller, who was to become one of their bitterest enemies. The dean of St. Peter's

---

[520] "The more the Portuguese Jews, by their capital and their commercial connections, gained weight among the business men of the senate, the more they broke the bounds drawn by obtuse legislation. When the bank of Hamburg, to which this city owed its commercial prosperity (1619–1623), was founded, no less than twelve Jewish capitalists supported it with their funds and efforts, as the Portuguese of Amsterdam had done in the formation of the Dutch companies that traded across the seas. The Portuguese Jewish settlers alone founded Hamburg's important trade with Spain and Portugal. Hence they could assume that the senate, which held the reins of government, acquiesced in these violations of the law." Heinrich Graetz, *History of the Jews IV*, Philadelphia, The Jewish Publication Society of America, 1894, p. 688–689.

Church, between 1631 and 1644, he was unceasing in his demands for the closure of all synagogues. He was supported in his campaign by the three theological faculties of Wittemberg, Strasbourg and Rostock. Johannes Müller denounced the wealth and arrogance of the Jews: "They strut about adorned with gold and silver, costly pearls and precious stones. At their weddings they eat and drink on silverware, drive carriages befitting persons of high rank and, in addition, have horsemen and many followers[521]." The Germans had only to keep quiet, put up with their innumerable swindles and endure their incessant taunts.

XCIX. France, 1615–1617

The one hundred and fifty years that followed the expulsion of the Jews from the kingdom of France in 1394 were a liberation. In our country, the whole of the Renaissance was singularly free of Jews. If, by any chance, a few wandering Jews entered the territory, they always had to pay the due taxes at the bridges and at the entrance to the villages. These were the old taxes of yesteryear, established especially for them, *"the cloven-footed tax"* (*"l'impôt du pied fourchu"*), of which we have at least two examples to report.

Lucien Rebatet[522], in the weekly *Je Suis Partout* of 17 February 1939 devoted to the Jewish question, dusted off the following document. It was the regulation of the Châteauneuf-sur-Loire toll, "by virtue of an order of the Court of 15 March 1558". After the list of animals for which a fee was to be paid, one could read:

"For each ox, pig and Jew: one sou. A Jew shall be twelve denarii. A fat bean: nine denarii. A single bean: six denarii. One dead bean: five sous. A dead Jewess: thirty denarii." Rebatet added: "I confess that the meaning of this last rate escapes me. Is it a copying error which all the historians

---

[521] Heinrich Graetz, *History of the Jews IV*, Philadelphia, The Jewish Publication Society of America, 1894, p. 690–691.
[522] Lucien Rebatet (1903–1972) was a French writer, music and film critic who was a member of *Action française*. In 1932 he joined the fascist newspaper *Je suis partout*, which from 1941 onwards was the main French collaborationist and anti-Semitic newspaper during the German Occupation. It enthusiastically welcomed the publication of Céline's openly anti-Semitic pamphlet *Bagatelles pour un massacre*. Rebatet turned out to be a virulent anti-Semite. In addition to attacking Jews, he also attacked communism, democracy and the Church, openly declaring himself a fascist. In 1942 he published *Les Décombres*, a fierce anti-Semitic pamphlet. Condemned to death during the liberation, but later pardoned, he abandoned polemics and devoted himself to film criticism and his writing career, publishing his masterpiece *Les Deux Étendards* in 1951. Critics generally regard this book as a masterpiece of 20th-century French literature.

overlooked without batting an eyelid? Or perhaps it is a macabre joke which we of course disapprove of?"

On the river Seine, on the Saône, in Lyon and Trévoux, border countries, Jews were also taxed like pigs. At the Montlhéry toll, a Jewish traveller paid more if he carried with him a seven-branched candelabrum and his Hebrew books. These tolls remained in force until 1784.

Some Marranos had come to France seeking asylum and refuge. At first they could only live disguised as Christians. In 1550, King Henry II had authorised them to stay in Bordeaux and to go about their business. There was also a small Marrano community in Bayonne and elsewhere. "Outwardly", wrote Graetz, they behaved like Christians, baptised their children, married with the help of Christian priests and bore Christian names, but secretly practised Judaism[523]." In 1636, Bordeaux counted two hundred and sixty Marranos, and many of them had risen to high positions as doctors, jurisconsults or writers.

King Louis XIII was informed of the presence of Jews in the territory and decided to put an end to the situation: by a declaration of 23 April 1615, "all Jews are ordered to leave the Kingdom, countries, lands and seigneuries under the obedience of the King, within one month, under penalty of death and confiscation of their property". His Majesty the King of France banished all Jews from his kingdom and forbade them to remain there. The Jews were given one month to leave the country. The following is a brief excerpt from this text:

"I, Louis, by the grace of God, King of France and Navarre: To all who read these letters, greetings.
"The Kings, our predecessors, having always preserved this beautiful title of Most Christian which we now possess, have consequently abhorred all the enemy Nations of this name, and especially that of the Jews, whom they have never wished to suffer in their Kingdoms, countries, lands, and lordships under their obedience; even since the time of King St. Louis of most praiseworthy and happy memory, who completely expelled from the whole State those whom he had before suffered, in which we are resolved to imitate them as much as we can, as in all other excellent qualities which have made them admirable among foreign Nations. In order that we may omit nothing which may serve the reputation of this State, and the preservation of the blessings which God has been pleased to bestow upon it, and especially as we have been warned that, contrary to the Edicts and Ordinances of our predecessors, the so-called Jews have for some years disguised themselves in various places in our Kingdom; not being able to suffer the impiety of this nation without committing a very great fault

---

[523] Heinrich Graetz, *Histoire des juifs V*, Éd. Durlacher, Paris, 1897, p. 148.

against the Divine Goodness, offended by their ordinary and recidivist blasphemies: We are advised to provide and remedy it as soon as possible. For these reasons: we have said and declared, willed and commanded, and presently say, declare, will, will and are pleased and order that all Jews found in our Kingdom, Countries, Lands and Lordships of our obedience, be required, under capital punishment and confiscation of their goods, to vacate and remove from here incontinently, and this in the time and term of one month after the publication of the present[524]..."

It should be told here how the young King Louis XIII had seized power. Since their expulsion on 17 September 1394, there were no more Jews in France until the conquest of Alsace by Louis XIV in 1678. Neither the Sun King nor any other European sovereign ever granted them the right of citizenship, which they only obtained as a result of the general chaos generated by the French Revolution.

After the assassination of King Henry IV[525], however, some Jews managed to infiltrate the country again under the regency of Queen Maria de Medecis. She had been literally subjugated by the Italian Concini and his unbalanced wife, the pietra and hysterical Leonora Dori "Galigai", a capricious and greedy woman who suffered from epilepsy and practised exorcisms and undoing spells. For seven years, from 1610 to 1617, this foreign-born couple, surrounded by Jews, amassed a colossal fortune and de facto reigned over France through terror. Leonora Dori's fortune was estimated at 15 million pounds, or the equivalent of three quarters of the

---

[524] *Causes célèbres et intéressantes, avec les jugements qui les ont décidées*, recueillis par Mr. François Gayot de Pitaval, avocat au Parlement de Paris, tome dix-neuvième, 1750. Cf: on the Internet.

[525] Henry IV of Bourbon (1553–1610), born in Pau, in a small Pyrenean province, was the first king of France of the House of Bourbon, which would later reign in Spain. He was King of Navarre and a prince of Huguenot blood, a belligerent in the French Wars of Religion, after which he abjured his Protestant faith. A victor over the Catholic League and Spain who refused to recognise his legitimacy to the throne of France, he finally converted to Catholicism to consolidate his reign, signing the Edict of Nantes which authorised Protestant worship in France. His is the famous and cynical expression: "Paris is worth a mass" (Catholic). At the age of 19, the young Henri had already changed his religion three times. He was assassinated by an extremist Catholic, François Ravaillac, in 1610, when he was preparing a new war against Spain. Henry IV is a very controversial figure in French history, being hated during his lifetime by both religious camps because of his conversions and worshipped after his death. He also owes his nickname "Gaunt-Green" to his ardor towards his 73 official mistresses, who bore him 22 legitimate or unacknowledged children who lived at court. On the episode of the St Bartholomew's Day Massacre, after which Henry survived, and the French religious political context of the time, the reader can watch the excellent French film *La Reine Margot* (1994). Miguel Bosé plays a formidable Henry of Lorraine, Duke of Guise, historic and ill-fated head of the Catholic League and ally of Spain. (NdT).

annual budget of France, not counting approximately one million pounds in jewels and silverware. Ungodliness and corruption had blighted the whole country. "Such great power, exercised for so many years with such lack of scruples, had never before been seen in this country," wrote Michel Carmona in his biography of Marie de Medecis.

The French reaction was energetic. The Paris Parliament solemnly issued the edict of expulsion of the Jews by letters patent on 12 May 1615. A climate of civil war was in the air. To intimidate the Parisians, Concini had fifty gallows erected in various parts of the capital; the French guards had been replaced by Swiss-Germans, who were reluctant to fraternise with the population, as well as by Italians who were totally loyal and committed to their compatriot.

It was finally the Baron de Vitry, captain of the king's guard, who took it upon himself to settle this disastrous affair with the approval of the young Louis XIII, who was only 15 years old. On 24 April 1617, in the great courtyard of the Louvre, Vitry and his guards approached Concini, while his escort lagged behind.

"In the name of the King, you are under arrest!" he said in a loud voice. The French readied their pistols and *Signor* Concini received three well-aimed bullets: one between the eyes, one in the throat and a third in the eye. To make sure of the job, the body was stabbed before being completely stripped—jewellery, papers, clothes. The corpse was left completely naked.

From the guards' room the words of Louis XIII were heard: *"Merci! Grand merci à vous! Á cette heure, je suis Roi."* After lunch, Louis mounted his horse and rode around Paris, where he was acclaimed by an appreciative crowd. The next day, Concini's corpse, which had been hastily buried in the church of Saint Germain l'Auxerrois, was dug up by the Parisians, beaten to a pulp and dragged through the streets of the capital. The mutilated body was then hung by the feet on one of the gallows that Concini himself had had erected, and again beaten and outraged. Some pieces of his corpse were cooked and his remains were finally burnt and scattered to the four winds.

While the king received an uninterrupted parade of courtiers and notables who had come to congratulate him, Leonara Galigai was arrested and imprisoned. "She buried her gold, jewels and silverware in her straw mattress, lying on it like an animal protects its litter," wrote Philippe Erlanger in his biography of Louis XIII. She degraded herself to the point of claiming that her husband "had deserved it", but this last baseness did not save her life. Galigai was accused of witchcraft, and the presence of Jewish doctors at her side, such as Philoteo Montalto, did not help her defence either. At that time, kabbalah, magic and witchcraft were considered equivalent by everyone. On 8 July 1617, she was condemned to be beheaded on the scaffold erected on the Place de Grève, a decision that was carried out on the same day. Her body and head were reduced to ashes.

C. *Uriel and Vicente da Costa*

With the deployment of the Holy Inquisition throughout the Iberian Peninsula, some Marranos preferred to seek their fortune in America, specifically in Brazil, Mexico and Peru, where some became rich in the sugar cane plantations, the slave trade and by exploiting some of the famous silver mines of Potosí[526]. Many others had settled in northern Europe, mainly in Hamburg, London and Amsterdam. We know that the Calvinists of Flanders and Holland, in their war against Spain, had been financially supported by the Jews, always ready to weaken the Church and the Catholic monarchies. "In 1566, among the instigators of the Flemish resistance were the influential Marranos Marcos Perez, Martin Lopez and Fernando Bernuy[527]."

As a republic, the Netherlands was to become the main asylum for Jews and all Protestant sects in Europe. The Protestant religion, especially the Calvinist branch, was perfectly in tune with the mercantilist spirit and exalted enrichment almost theologically. The Netherlands became for a time the leading trading and piratical nation in Europe, before being overtaken by England. Materialistic Jewish values seemed to have triumphed with Calvinism and Anglo-Saxon Puritanism.

In 1593, a Jewish community was established in Amsterdam. It progressed rapidly, thanks in part to tolerant legislation that limited itself to prohibiting Jews from intermarriage and access to public employment. The Jews soon spread throughout the Netherlands. They were essentially involved in overseas banking and trade. Thanks to their relations with the Marranos of Spanish America and the Caribbean, they built up immense fortunes through the slave trade and the triangular trade with Africa. Amsterdam was rightly called the New Jerusalem[528].

---

[526] *"In the first half of the 16th century, all the large sugar plantations were in the hands of the Jews of Brazil"*, Abraham Léon, *La Conception matérialiste de la question juive*, Études et Documentation internationales, 1942, Paris, 1968, p. 106.

[527] Leon Poliakov, *Histoire de l'antisémitisme, tome I*, Point Seuil, 1981, p. 212. Also read in *The Mirror of Judaism*.

[528] "Philip II, who died in September 1598, could still see how the two peoples he perhaps hated most, the inhabitants of the Netherlands and the Jews, lent each other mutual support to destroy the work he had relentlessly pursued. Holland, the enemy of intolerance and despotism, guaranteed the Portuguese Jews religious freedom. For their part, the Jews helped Holland to heal the ravages of its struggle against the King of Spain; they provided the capital that enabled it to wrest the Indies trade from Portugal,

In Amsterdam, the famous philosopher Spinoza (1632–1677), the scion of a Portuguese Marrano family, was in deep disagreement with his community, and was finally excommunicated in 1656[529]. But before him, Uriel da Costa (1594–1647), also of Portuguese origin and of a Jewish mother, had defied the rabbinical authorities in Amsterdam. When he came to the Netherlands to practise Judaism freely, his disappointment was immense. The Pentateuch, with its codex of six hundred and thirteen commandments, was only the visible part of a parasitic vegetation whose ramifications invaded all the innermost recesses of existence. Uriel da Costa attacked the extremely meticulous practices of Judaism and openly mocked the rabbis, whom he called *Pharisees*. For him, religions were mere human inventions. Threatened with excommunication, he nevertheless persevered in this way. The college of rabbis then excluded him from the community and his closest relatives and friends distanced themselves from him. Isolated from his co-religionists and close friends, still unable to relate to his fellow Christians because he did not know the language, Da Costa published in 1623 a work entitled *Examen de las tradiciones farisaicas*, in which he proclaimed his definitive break with Judaism[530].

Representatives of the Amsterdam Jewish community burned the book, following their custom, and accused da Costa of denying and rejecting not only Jewish doctrines, but also the teachings of Christianity[531]. He was imprisoned for several days and had to pay a heavy fine.

It took him fifteen years to reconcile with the Synagogue. But this reconciliation was rather short-lived. Once again he declared war on Judaism, and once again he was summoned to appear before the rabbinical college. His judges decided that he could only escape a second excommunication by submitting to a solemn penance, and at first, out of self-respect, he refused to yield. But shortly afterwards he decided to accept the sentence of the rabbis. He was led into a synagogue full of men and women, where he had to publicly proclaim his repentance. On a platform, he read a detailed confession of all his sins, accusing himself of having

---

Spain's ally, and to create the great companies across the seas that made it so rich. The secret links between the Portuguese Jews and the Marranos established in the Indies also favoured the Dutch enterprises". Heinrich Graetz, *Histoire des juifs V*, Éd. Durlacher, Paris, 1897, p. 135–136. (NdT).

[529] On Spinoza, see *Planetary Hopes* and *Psychoanalysis of Judaism*.

[530] On Uriel da Costa read *Jewish Fanaticism*.

[531] In the 12th century, in Paris and Montpellier, Maimonides' opponents burned his books. In the 18th century, the books of the Jewish philosopher Mendelssohn were anathematized and burned in several Polish cities. In Israel, Christian gospels were burned at the stake on 20 May 2008 by Yehuda's students. Read about it in *The Mirror of Judaism*.

transgressed the Sabbath rest and dietary laws, and of having denied various articles of faith. After solemnly promising never to repeat his mistakes, he vowed to live henceforth as a good Israelite. He retired to a corner of the synagogue, stripped to the waist and received thirty-nine lashes with a strap. Then he sat on the floor and the sentence of excommunication was lifted. Finally, he had to lie on the threshold of the Temple and let all present pass over his body.

The rage he felt at this humiliating treatment made him consider suicide, although the desire to take revenge on the person he considered the main instigator of this persecution, his brother or cousin, was even stronger. To shock his contemporaries and posterity about his unfortunate fate, Heinrich Graetz recounted, Uriel da Costa "wrote his autobiography and confession, which contained no new thoughts, but only bitterness and furious attacks against the Jews, interspersed with new slanders against them… This document, written in the midst of preparations for death, breathed nothing but vengeance against his enemies. After finishing his passionate testament, he loaded two pistols and fired one at his relative, who was passing by his house. He missed, so he closed the door of his room and killed himself with the other gun (April 1640). On entering his residence after the shot was fired, they found on the table his autobiography entitled "*An Example of Human Life*", in which he brought Jews and Judaism to the stand and attacked with pathetic sentences[532]…"

In 1623, the year in which Uriel da Costa had published his first book, another da Costa, Vicente da Costa, published in Lisbon a 428-page book against his former co-religionists: *"Breve discurso contra a herética perfidia do judaísmo"*. His work was immediately translated into Spanish under the title *Discurso contra los Judios*. The Jews were described as "greedy, rebellious and liars by nature…It would be impossible to enumerate all their vices: envy, pride, their noble pretensions, their ostentatious luxury which they display daily in Portugal and even more so in Madrid, as well as their insolence and their "*disrespect*". Sodomy (to which he devotes a separate chapter) stems from their natural lasciviousness and the idleness in which they indulge…In fact, the Jews of North Africa regularly sodomise their wives and children[533]!"

Daniel Tollet, who published the book in which we collected these testimonies, pretended not to take these at first sight grotesque accusations seriously. But we have seen, in *Psychoanalysis of Judaism, Jewish Fanaticism* and *The Mirror of Judaism*, that these practices were indeed

---

[532]Heinrich Graetz, *History of the Jews V*, Philadelphia, The Jewish Publication Society of America, 1895, p. 64–65.
[533]Daniel Tollet, *Les Textes judéophobes et judéophiles dans l'Europe chrétienne à l'époque moderne*, Presses Universitaires de France, 2000, p. 30, 34, 39.

encouraged by the Talmud and manifestly quite frequent within the community, judging by the invasive literary and cinematographic production of Judaism, as well as by the numerous problems of a psychopathological nature within the incestuous sect.

CI. Back in liberated Spain

Thanks to the Holy Inquisition, Spain, which had expelled the Jews in 1492, was able to rid itself of the deleterious influence of the Marranos, apparently good Catholics, but fifth columnists who tried to destroy the Church and the country from within[534].

---

[534] The first 50 years of the Inquisition were the harshest and most decisive. According to the English Hispanist Henry Kamen, the Spanish Inquisition executed some 2,000 people between 1480 and 1530, almost all of them Jewish converts accused of "Judaising". Historian Geoffrey Parker believes that, in its 350 years of existence, this tribunal caused some 5,000 deaths. When people speak of higher figures, it is usually because they tend to count all the people who were tried, and assume that they were all executed or died, when this is not the case. According to Jaime Contreras and Gustav Henningsen, who have studied the period between 1540 and 1700, when the Inquisition prosecuted 49,000 people, death sentences were passed in 3.5% of cases, according to Gustav Henningsen's calculations, but only 2% of those sentenced to death at the stake were actually executed. The rest had either died before the end of the trial, escaped or were never caught at all. In the latter two cases, wooden images were burned in their representation. For example, in the largest summary execution of the Inquisition, held in 1680, 61 people were condemned to die at the stake, of which 34 were statues representing the defendants. Those who "repented" were strangled before being burnt: few were burnt alive. The rest of those prosecuted in this period of 160 years (i.e. more than 96% of them) were punished with fines or years in the galleys. At that time in Spain, the prosecutions had the following causes: 27% for blasphemy, 24% for Mohammedanism, 10% for false Judaising converts, 8% for Lutheranism, 8% for witchcraft and superstition and 32% for sodomy, bigamy and sexual crimes of the clergy. We can find Marranos in different categories apart from the 10% of Judaisers, such as in cases of blasphemy, witchcraft or sexual offences, so perhaps the number of Marranos prosecuted was even higher. In any case, until 1700 it seems impossible that more than 4,000 Marranos were condemned by the Inquisition, either directly or indirectly. All these cases were considered crimes all over Europe, also in civil, municipal, regional courts, etc.... Even in Spain, some of these crimes could also be judged by the civil courts, which were more severe. So much so that some detainees in civil courts blasphemed in order to be tried by the Inquisition, which they considered to be more "benign". César Cervera points out that despite the image that has transpired, the Spanish Inquisition offered more extensive procedural guarantees than the ordinary courts and, in fact, executed less. To begin with, the Inquisition resorted to torture rarely, and always under the supervision of an inquisitor who was ordered to prevent permanent damage, often together with a doctor, in contrast to the savage tortures applied by civil authorities throughout Europe. The course of the torture was scrupulously recorded by the secretaries, including the groans and exclamations uttered

But the problem had not been completely solved, for in 1575 a Cordovan of noble family, Diego de Simancas (whose pseudonym was *Didacus Velasquez*), a famous jurist, published the *Defensio statuti toletani (Defence of the statute of purity of blood of the Church of Toledo)*, in which he insisted on revealing the "Jewish perfidy" and accused the converts of being false Christians. It acknowledged that there were sincere converts, but they had to agree to go through a social purgatory. By the middle of the 16th century, the blood purity statutes had acquired the force of law. The decisive episode was the purge of the Toledo chapter, in which the New Christians had entrenched themselves.

The man who declared war on them was Juan Martínez Siliceo (1485–1557), archbishop of Toledo, who came from a modest family of *old Christian* farmers in Extremadura. Trained in Paris, he was the preceptor of the young King Philip II, before being appointed archbishop of Toledo in 1544 and made a cardinal by Pope Paul IV in 1555. He ardently defended this concept of "purity of blood". Juan Martínez Siliceo was also the first to have thought that Christ was not of Jewish blood[535]. During the process of admission to an Order or College, an investigation was carried out at the expense of the candidate to establish his non-belonging to the "Jewish race".

It should be noted here that *limpieza de sangre* was specific to each institution and was never generalised throughout the Spanish state. A memoir written around 1600 stated that there were two types of nobility in Spain: a higher type, the hidalguía, and a lower type, *the limpieza*. A *clean* commoner was esteemed more highly than an *unclean* nobleman. Thus, all Spanish peasants proudly considered themselves to be legitimately of noble blood.

The Spanish "Estatuto de limpieza de sangre" had some influence in Europe. In France, Joachim de Bellay (1522–1560) advised the king to preserve the purity of his aristocracy:

"And let not the less bold blood allow a more generous blood to bastardise. For if we are so careful to preserve the breed of good horses and good hunting dogs, how much more should a King carefully provide for the breed, which is his chief power?"

But this idea of purity of blood would never achieve as much

---

by the victims. Confessions obtained during the torment were not valid in themselves and had to be ratified outside the torture within twenty-four hours. The Spanish black legend has survived to the present day, but fortunately many contemporary studies have completely demystified it. (NdT).

[535]Léon Poliakov, *Les Juifs dans notre histoire*, Science Flammarion, 1973, p. 57. In the 19th century, Houston Stewart Chamberlain took up this theme in his work *The Genesis of the 19th Century*.

importance in France, Germany and England as it did in Marrano-infiltrated Spain. The Jesuit order had taken measures to prevent the infiltration of crypto-Jews and the destruction of the Society from within. Only in the time of its founder, Ignatius of Loyola, was cleanliness of blood disregarded. From then on, the Society of Jesus considered Jewish converts to be somewhat impure, *maculated*, whose blood was stained (*macula*). It was therefore inappropriate for them to have access to Christian offices and public honours, especially the priesthood.

The fact is that many Marranos did not hesitate to declare themselves "more Christian than Christians", "more Spanish than Spaniards", but wished in their hearts the destruction of the Church and of Spain, praying for a Turkish or Protestant invasion. The Spaniards' mistrust was therefore legitimate, even if there were certainly, as we have seen, many Jews who had sincerely abandoned Judaism. But once again, as we have shown in our previous works, we must insist that the sincerity of a Jewish convert is only judged by the degree of his anti-Judaism.

Three dates marked the history of the Society of Jesus in this regard. First, in 1593, after the death of Ignatius of Loyola, the Convention of the Order ceased to admit into its midst "any Christian of Jewish descent"; in 1608, a decree stipulated that novices had to prove that they had no Jewish blood for five generations; in 1623, finally, an amendment to the previous decree reduced the requirement to four generations.

So that R.P. Koch, in his work *Jesuiten-Lexikon*, could write with satisfaction in 1934 (one year after the triumph of the National Socialist Party in Germany): "Of all the orders, the Society of Jesus has the rules which best protect it against Jewish influence".

CII. Bogdán Jmelnitski, 1648

In 1648, a general uprising against the Jews broke out in Eastern Europe during the wars waged by Bogdan Khmelnitsky's Cossacks against the Polish kingdom. The kabbalists of the time had predicted that the Messiah would appear that year, but once again it was not to be.

Catholic Poland dominated the entire region stretching from the Baltic to the Black Sea, and part of the Ukraine was under its rule. The Cossacks, of the Orthodox Christian religion, formed a kind of barrier against the Turks and Tartars in those lands. Many Jews served as administrators and tax collectors for the Polish aristocracy. They also acted as rulers of manor estates, while the Ukrainians remained in the status of practically enslaved peasants, living in very difficult conditions. In fact, in Ukraine, the Jews were the accomplices of the Polish nobility and oppressed the Cossacks and the Ukrainian peasants. In 1638, there was a first uprising of the Cossacks of Zaporiyia led by their leader *hetman* Pawliuk. Two hundred

Jews were annihilated and several synagogues razed to the ground.

After the death of the Polish King Ladislaus during the interregnum (May-October 1648), Poland fell into anarchy and a general uprising took place at that time led by Bogdán Jmelnitski. The Cossack leader was a brave warrior and a seasoned strategist who managed to defeat the Polish army for the first time. After this victory, the Cossacks invaded the towns east of the Dnieper River between Kiev and Poltava, plundering and massacring the Jews in their path. To escape death, four Jewish communities comprising three thousand souls were transferred to the Crimea and ransomed (bought) by their Turkish co-religionists. In order to raise the men necessary to buy the freedom of all the prisoners, the Constantinople community had sent a delegate to the Netherlands to collect aid and subsidies.

Jmelnitsky arranged for his lieutenants and troops to sweep through the Polish provinces, and they carried out large-scale massacres of Poles and Jews. Morosenko was one of the chiefs who led the revolt. Another leader, Ganja, marched against the fortress of Nemirov, where 6,000 Jews were sheltered. They were attacked by the Cossacks with the help of the Greek Catholics of the city who hated them even more. The Jews were all put to the sword, their throats slit.

In Tulezyn, there were 6,000 Christians and some 2,000 Jews willing to sell their lives at a high price. The hatred of the Catholic Poles for the Jews was undoubtedly as strong as that of the Cossacks, for the latter began negotiations by declaring to the Polish nobles that they were prepared to withdraw if their former oppressors were handed over to them. After an agreement was reached, the gates of the city were opened and the Jews had to fight for their lives alone against their enemies.

Other insurgents led by Hodki penetrated Little Russia and killed numerous Jews in Gomel, Starodub, Chernigoc and other towns west and north of Kiev. During ten years of war (1648–1658), more than 300 Jewish communities were destroyed in Poland and more than 250,000 Jews met their death[536]. The Jewish historian Poliakov estimated the number of dead at 100,000. But one thing seems clear: there were no longer any Jews on the left bank of the Dnieper.

Later, the rifts between the Cossacks and the peasants, on the one hand, and the Jews, on the other, grew even greater. The Jews continued to ruin

---

[536]The number of Jewish victims was estimated at 500,000, even divided by 10 by a contemporary Jewish researcher named Jonathan Israel (*European Jewry*, Oxford, 1985), in Israel Shamir, *L'autre Visage d'Israel*, Éditions Al Qalam, 2004. Shamir added: "The same decline already occurred at the time of the Chisinau pogrom [in 1903]. At first, Jewish organisations and witnesses claimed five hundred dead. The figure then plummeted to 48, i.e. ten times less".

the peasants with their usury and various practices, for they had now become sellers of alcohol. The naive peasant, who took a loan to have a good time in the village tavern, ended up ruined, forced to sell his land, his farm and his animals.

A further settling of scores took place with an uprising that broke out in the Ukraine against the Jews in 1734. In 1768, the massacre of Uman took place. The Jaidamakas (Ukrainian Cossacks and peasants), led by the *ataman* Ivan Gonta, slaughtered thousands of Jews in the city of Uman. The leader Basil Vochtchilo proclaimed himself as follows: "Ataman Vochtchilo, grandson of Jmelnitsky, great hetman of troops, charged with the extermination of Jewry and the defence of Christianity." He vehemently accused the Jews of murder, blasphemy, rape of Christians, etc.: "Driven by my love for the holy Christian faith, I decided, together with other good men, to exterminate the accursed Jewish people and, with God's help, I have already destroyed the Jews of the Kritshchev and Popoysk districts. Although the Jews armed the government troops against me, God's justice protected me at all times."

Jewish pimps and slavers were already making waves on both sides of the Black Sea. In the 17th century, Jews in the Ottoman Empire had specialised in the sale of slaves trained to all kinds of depravity and in the trade in women. Apparently, the brothels already belonged exclusively to them, for "there were in Constantinople Jews who had no other function than to verify the virginity of the young women sold as pleasure meat[537]."

CIII. William Prynne, 1656

The Jews, expelled from England in 1290 by King Edward, attempted to return to England in the wake of the political upheaval caused by the revolution of 1648, following the beheading of King Charles I. Menasseh ben Israel, a writer, scholar, diplomat and printer in Amsterdam, also came from a family of Portuguese converts who had openly returned to Judaism in the Netherlands. In the autumn of 1655, he travelled to London, accompanied by several co-religionists, in order to convince Cromwell to accept the Jews back. The regicide welcomed them with great cordiality: "He was received in a friendly manner by Cromwell and was granted a residence. Among his companions was Jacob Sasportas, a learned man, accustomed to socialising with people of high rank, who had been a rabbi in African cities. Other Jews accompanied him in the hope that the admission of the Jews would not encounter difficulties. Some secret Jews

---

[537] M. Yarden, in *Les Chrètiens devant le fait juif*, Éd. Beauchesne, Paris, 1929, p. 131, in Georges Valensin, *La Vie sexuelle juive*, p. 65, 66.

from Spain and Portugal were already domiciled in London, among them the wealthy and respected Fernández Carvajal [538]," Heinrich Graetz reported.

Menasseh ben Israel's plea made a favourable impression on Cromwell and some influential members of Puritan circles [539], so that in 1656 Cromwell decided to allow Jews to stay in England again. "Cromwell was decidedly in favour of the admission of Jews. It is possible that he had in mind the likelihood that the extensive trade and capital of Spanish and Portuguese Jews, those who professed Judaism openly and secretly, might be brought to England, which at that time could not yet compete with Holland... But what influenced him most was the religious desire to win the Jews to Christianity by friendly treatment. He thought that Christianity, as preached in England by the Independents, without idolatry and superstition, would captivate the Jews, hitherto deterred from Christianity. Cromwell and Manasseh ben Israel agreed on an unspoken, visionary, messianic reason for the admission of Jews into England. The Kabbalist rabbi believed that, as a result of Jewish settlement in the British Isles, the Messianic Redemption would begin, and the Puritan protector believed that Jews would accept Christianity in large numbers, and then the time would come for a shepherd and a flock[540]," Graetz explained. His decision was also preceded by an incident: a wealthy Portuguese merchant named Robles had been summoned to court accused of being a papist. Since England was at war with Portugal, his fortune was confiscated. But thanks to Cromwell's initiative, the Council of State lifted the seizure because the defendant was in fact a Jew, not a Catholic. This meant implicitly recognising that Jews already had a de facto right to remain in England.

The Marranos settled in London were quick to remove the mask of Christianity. In February 1657, they were even able to buy a special cemetery for the members of their community. They were also allowed to celebrate their feasts publicly and to worship in a private house. Cromwell could not have been more liberal at this time because the clergy and the people were unanimous in their refusal to admit Jews into the kingdom. They continued to be regarded as foreigners and therefore taxed more heavily.

The Jews' main adversary at the time was William Prynne, a very popular publicist in the mid-17th century. Prynne, who left behind nearly two hundred books and pamphlets, had raised his voice against the

---

[538] Heinrich Graetz, *History of the Jews V*, Philadelphia, The Jewish Publication Society of America, 1895, p. 38.
[539] Read again footnote 490.
[540] Heinrich Graetz, *History of the Jews V*, Philadelphia, The Jewish Publication Society of America, 1895, p. 43.

readmission of Jews into the country. In a 1656 pamphlet, *A Short Demurrer to the Jews...*, he took up the accusation against them of ritual murder and brought together all the decrees enacted against them in the Middle Ages. These were "a race of evil-doers, a generation of vipers that did evil greedily and with joined hands, according to all the nations around them, equal or worse than Sodom and Gomorrah[541]."

Thus, by the mid-18th century, England was home to some 22,000 Jews, of whom 20,000 were Ashkenazi. In 1753, the House of Commons voted the "Jewish Bull" which granted naturalisation facilities to Jews who had been settled in the country for three hundred years and whose children were born on English soil. But the law was rejected the following year by King George III, who had issued an edict stipulating that army officers, civil servants and members of parliament had to swear an oath: "On my Christian faith".

CIV. The expulsion of Austria, 1670

In Spain and Portugal, the problem of the Marranos had not yet been resolved by the middle of the century. In Lisbon, the Marrano Manuel Fernando da Villa-Real, who for a time headed the Portuguese consulate in Paris, was imprisoned on his return to Portugal, tortured and executed (1 December 1652). In Cuenca, on 29 June 1654, fifty-seven Judaising Christians were brought in a single day to the auto de fe and ten were burnt alive. "Among them was a distinguished man, Baltasar López de Valladolid, who had amassed a fortune of 100,000 ducats. He had emigrated to Bayonne, where a small community of former Marranos was tolerated, and had returned to Spain with the purpose of persuading a nephew to return to Judaism. He was seized by the Inquisition, tortured and condemned to death by the gallows and the stake. On his way to the gallows, Balthasar Lopez ridiculed the Inquisition and Christianity. He exclaimed to the executioner who was about to tie him up: "I do not believe in your Christ, even if you tie me up", and threw down the cross that had been imposed on him[542]."

Spain was ruled by Mariana of Austria, the widow of Philip IV (d. 1665), who had elevated her confessor, the German Jesuit Neidhard, to the rank of Inquisitor General and Prime Minister. In 1669, following several complaints from victims, the queen decided to expel the Jews living in

---

[541]Daniel Tollet, *Les Textes judéophobes et judéophiles dans l'Europe chrétienne à l'époque moderne*, Presses universitaires de France, 2000, p. 172.
[542]Heinrich Graetz, *History of the Jews V*, Philadelphia, The Jewish Publication Society of America, 1895, p. 91–92.

North Africa, in Oran and some other localities. The governor gave them a deadline of eight days, just before Passover (end of April 1669). The exiles had to sell their belongings and real estate at ridiculous prices. Most of them were able to settle on the other side of the Mediterranean, in Savoy, Nice and Villefranche.

Her daughter, Margaret Theresa, the Empress of Germany, soon followed her mother's example and decreed the expulsion of the Jews from Vienna and the Archduchy of Austria where they had been reintroduced. At that time, Vienna had become the residence of the Germanic emperors. In the Middle Ages, the Jews had been expelled, but in the course of the 16th century, a new community had been reconstituted there. The emperors had allowed the Jews to settle, "because among them," wrote the Jewish historian Simon Dubnow, "were many very rich men who had financed the government with money and credit". But their spirit of treachery in favour of foreign powers, especially the Ottoman Empire, was rightly feared.

After long resistance from Emperor Leopold I, the Jesuits finally succeeded in convincing him and, on 14 February 1670, an expulsion order was issued against the Jews, forcing them to leave Vienna and its environs. The Jews sought the intervention of one of their wealthiest and most influential co-religionists at the time, Manuel Teixeira, Queen Christina of Sweden's representative in Vienna. Teixeira contacted some of the Spanish grandees with whom he had relations to ask them to intercede on their behalf with the empress's confessor. He also approached the powerful and able Cardinal Azzolino in Rome, a friend of Queen Christina. The latter, since her conversion, enjoyed great credit in the Catholic world and had pledged her support to Teixeira. But her intervention was futile, and the Emperor, or rather the Empress, upheld the edict of expulsion. The Magistrate of Vienna bought the Jewish quarter for 100,000 guilders and renamed it *Leopolstadt*, in honour of the emperor. A church was built on the site of the synagogue, the foundation stone of which was laid by Leopold himself on 18 August 1670.

The exiles spread to Moravia, Bavaria—where they were allowed to settle temporarily—Prague and Berlin; Hungary vetoed them. But a few years later, the Jews managed to get themselves readmitted to Vienna in exchange for a large sum of gold.

That year a new case of ritual crime took place. It involved an animal trader from Boulay, in Lorraine, called Raphael Levy. On 5 September 1669, Rafel Levy had travelled to Metz to make some purchases to celebrate the Jewish New Year. That same day, in Glatigny, a village on the road from Boulay to Metz, a mother noticed that her son, the three-year-old Didier Le Moyne, was missing. Shortly afterwards, the child was found in a forest, horribly mutilated. A horseman later claimed to have seen the Jewish merchant carrying the child under his cloak. In 1670, Raphael Levy was sentenced by the parliament of Metz to be tortured and executed. On 17 January 1670, the Jew was burned alive in Glatigny for his horrible crime.

CV. Madrid, 30 June 1680

Spain, which had suffered so much from the presence of the Jews since the early Middle Ages, was determined to extirpate the marrano poison from its territory once and for all. In 1674, a Franciscan monk named Francisco de Torrejoncillo, prior of several convents of the order of St. Francis, published the book *Sentinela contra judíos (Sentinel against Jews)*. The work was divided into fourteen chapters and tried to show that the Jews were presumptuous and mendacious, that they had always been traitors, that those who favoured them ended badly, that they and their works were not to be believed in, that they were boisterous, vain and seditious, and that the Church was only preserving them so that they could beget the Antichrist, their messiah, who would finally be defeated at the end of time.

Torrejoncillo also noted that it was not necessary to have two Jewish parents in order to feel completely Jewish. The author spoke here of the deleterious influence of "Jewish blood", although in reality it was only the "Jewish spirit", which is transmitted from generation to generation, and which can even infect true gentiles through hysterical contagion[543]: "Denying the coming of the Messiah, they persecute the Christians with riots and raids[544]; and for this to come almost by generation, as if it were an original sin, to be enemies of Christians, of Christ and of his Divine Law, it is not necessary to be of Jewish father and mother, only one is enough: it does not matter if the father is not, the mother is enough, and not even the whole mother, for half is enough, and not even that much, a quarter is enough, and even an eighth. And the Holy Inquisition has discovered in our times that up to a distance of twenty-one degrees it has been known to judaise[545]". And it is "that the sin of the father is the death of the son; and as in the seed the whole tree is included and enclosed, so in the father and in his vices are deposited those which the children are to have. Consequently speaking, such properties, and such bad inclinations, as the Antichrist must have strength, is that they derive from Jewish and

---

[543] To understand the typically hysterical nature of Judaism it is necessary to read our earlier books, especially *Psychoanalysis of Judaism*.

[544] Deception, ambushes. NdT.

[545] In reality, Jewish identity is much more fragile and labile than Francisco de Torrejoncillo believed. For one only has to look at the number of Jews who turn against the sect. It is above all the rabbis who claim that a Jew can only remain a Jew.

converted parents, of base and base thoughts, in whose lineage are found many Judaisers, and burnt ones whom the Holy Tribunal of the Inquisition has penitentiated on different occasions." Francisco de Torrejoncillo even added: "And in the palaces of kings and of many princes, the mistresses who are chosen to bring up their children must be old Christians, because the children of princes it is not right that they should be brought up by Judaic vileness, because that milk, as from infected persons, it is impossible that it should engender anything but perverse inclinations[546]."

Spain was then ruled by the young King Charles II the "Bewitched",

---

[546]Francisco de Torrejoncillo, *Centinela contra Judíos, puesta en la Torre de la Iglesia de Dios* (1674), Josep Giralt Impresor, Barcelona year 1731, p. 60, 210, 206. Cases of Judaisers appeared even well into the 18th century, proof of the fanatical racial and spiritual atavism generated by Jewish supremacism. A recent university study gives an account of the last case recorded by the Tribunal of the Holy Inquisition in the 18th century. Here are some extracts from the study:

"The documentation shows how the defendants formed part of extended families with complex clientelistic relationships and linked to other family nuclei by kinship ties, consanguineous or fictitious, with common interests that were made stronger by sharing a secret, that of Judaism. The key element in this strategy was marriage, with the celebration of marriages in which even a triple endogamous level can be observed: territorial (although the territory was often distant), socio-economic and ethnic. We have been able to establish that this custom was widespread: they looked for those in Portugal who shared their secret, those of the "caste". Like the Jews, our protagonists avoided marriages with gentile or *goyoth* women: the men went to the *family plots* in search of the "primitive origin"... Alternatively—or perhaps in the first instance—they turned to acquaintances who acted as *procurers* to find a woman of the "caste" who was willing to marry...".

"In conclusion, we recognise among our protagonists individuals with different levels of income: itinerants, shopkeepers, artisans and even a doctor and a teacher. However, the most frequent occupation was that of shoemaker (and tanner), which identified half of those processed for whom we have data. Many of them also had, as a method of personal and family safeguarding, a double profile, that is, the exercise of a mechanical trade and the practice of commerce and the manipulation of money. They were, for the most part, independent producers who received a price for their products and who established in their commercial relations mechanisms of family dependence and clientelism, allowing trade to develop in a secure and firm manner. In addition, they took advantage of mobility: with the excuse of travelling, they strengthened ties and affirmed their solidarity, alerting each other to dangers and preparing to flee in case of need".

"It thus appears that there may indeed have been a deep-rooted survival of beliefs and practices of the Judaic faith among our defendants: rituals, ceremonies, religious criticism of Christianity, prayers, dietary practices, introduction to forbidden religious literature, escapes in search of lands of freedom... That is to say: beliefs that would have resisted and that were not able to erase the Christian indoctrination and the fear pedagogically administered by the Holy Office". *Serranía críptica: la última gran persecución contra judaizantes en la España del siglo XVIII*, José Luis Buitrago González, Universidad Autónoma de Madrid, p. 17-18, 22-23, 44.

the last king of the House of Austria. By his order, the Grand Inquisitor Diego Sarmiento de Valladares required all the courts of Spain to send all the condemned heretics to Madrid. A month before the appointed date, heralds solemnly announced the execution of the traitors to the inhabitants of the capital. For several weeks work was done on erecting platforms for the court, the nobility, the clergy and the common people.

On the expected day, 30 June 1680, one hundred and eighteen people of all ages, among them seventy Marranos, barefoot and dressed in St. Benedict's and holding a candle, were led early in the morning to the place of execution, flanked by clergy and knights in the midst of the crowd of the people. The king, the queen, the ladies of the court, the high dignitaries and all the nobility witnessed the spectacle from early morning until nightfall. After all they had suffered at the hands of the Jews, the Christians took their revenge.

CVI. Johann Andreas Eisenmenger

The Jewish question was on everyone's mind in Germany. A Protestant from Phrygia, Jacob Geusius, a churchman and physician, had published two booklets, *Anan and Caiaphas Fled from Hell* and *Human Sacrifices*, in which he had detailed all the crimes committed by Jews from the time of Apion and Tacitus to the testimonies recounted by Bernardinus of Feltre in the story of the martyrdom of the boy Simon of Trent.

Fifteen years later, in 1697, the preacher Paolo Medici, an apostate from Livorno, published a pamphlet in which he too denounced the ritual murders committed by Jews. For forty years, he travelled around Italy to alert and warn all the inhabitants against the incestuous sect[547].

Johann Christof Wagenseil, born in Nuremberg, a great scholar and professor of history and Hebrew at the University of Altdorf, undertook to collect all Jewish works containing attacks on Christianity. In order to collect as many of these anti-Christian documents as possible, Wagenseil travelled as far as Spain and Africa. In 1681, he published the fruit of his research in a work he entitled: *Tela Ignea Satanæ, sive Arcani et Horribiles Judæorum Adversus Christum, Deum, et Christianam Religionem Libri (Satan's Nets of Fire, sive Arcani et Horribiles Judæorum Adversus Christum, Deum, et Christianam Religionem Libri)*. Wagenseil simply wanted the Jews to be brought to Christianity by persuasion. In 1703, he published in Altdorf a book, *Denunciatio Christiana de Blasphemiis Judæorum in Jesum Christum*, which he dedicated to high personalities of the Empire, imploring them to stop the advance of Jewish power and pride.

---

[547] Jean Delumeau, *La Peur en Occident*, Fayard, 1978.

He had also published several other works on Judaism, including a Latin translation of the Talmudic tractate *Sotah* (Altdorf, 1674), and his *Disputatio Circularis de Judæis* (Altdorf, 1705).

At the beginning of the 18th century, a German bibliographer named J. C. Wolf listed in his *Bibliothecae Hebraeae* more than a thousand works of *Scriptores Anti-Judaici*. This list was undoubtedly incomplete, but it showed that the Jewish question seriously preoccupied the spirits in Germany. The pamphlets, whose prototype had been established by Luther, all had explicit titles: *The Enemy of the Jews, The Jewish Plague, Jewish Practices, Little Repertory of Horrible Jewish Blasphemies, Jewish Snake Bag*, etc.

Johann Andreas Eisenmenger was much more influential. A German Protestant Christian, he distinguished himself in his youth at the Heidelberg College by his zeal in the study of Hebrew and Semitic languages. He taught Oriental languages, Hebrew, Arabic and Aramaic at Heidelberg, and for twenty years he studied Talmudic literature. The Talmud of the rabbis had long been "the only recognised authority" in Judaism, to the extent that it had made "the Bible almost completely forgotten", Graetz wrote. For while "unprejudiced men were to be found, who felt and expressed doubts as to the truth of Judaism in its later rabbinical and Kabbalistic form...such investigators, of course, were not to be found among German and Polish Jews, nor among Asians; these regarded every letter of the Talmud and the Zohar, every law of the code (*Shulchan Aruch*) as the inviolable word of God[548]."

Eisenmenger collected all the quotations found in 193 works and used them to write his two-volume book *Entdecktes Judenthum (Judaism Unveiled)*, which was for a long time the source for all critics of the Talmud and Judaism. The book was also presented under a secondary title: *True and sincere report on the way in which hardened Jews utter atrocious blasphemies against the Trinity, insult the holy mother of Christ, the New Testament, the Evangelists and the Apostles, mock the Christian religion and show their contempt and horror for Christianity.*

In this 2000-page work, Eisenmenger referred to all the cases of ritual murder and all the misdeeds that had resulted from the countless expulsions of Jews. It should be noted that at no time did the author mention Luther's diatribes against the Jews, nor did he cite his name even once.

Here are two passages that demonstrate quite well the seriousness and quality of his work: "In the Talmudic tractate *Baba Metzia* (the middle gate) folio 61, 4, towards the end, in the *tosephot* (or commentary), it is written:

---

[548] Heinrich Graetz, *History of the Jews V*, Philadelphia, The Jewish Publication Society of America, 1895, p. 55.

'It is permitted to cheat a non-Jew and take usury on him', as it is written in Deuteronomy, 23, verse 20: 'To a foreigner you may lend with interest, but to your brother you shall not lend with interest'. Moreover, it is permitted to cheat him, as it is written in Leviticus 25, verse 14: "And when you sell something to your neighbour, or buy from your neighbour's hand, let no one cheat his brother". So it is permitted to cheat a goy, since in the law of Moses it is only forbidden to cheat his neighbour or brother[549]."

And this other passage: "The Jews understand by neighbour only themselves, and no one who is not a Jew. By neighbour, however, they include only one who participates in their religion, since in the book *Choschen Hammishpat* (folio 132, column 2), in the notes or observations, in number 95, paragraph 1 of the Amsterdam edition, we read: "In all places where in the law of Moses they speak of neighbour, they exclude the idolater[550]."

When, in 1700, the Jews of Frankfurt learned that Eisenmenger was having a work printed in their city that was hostile to them, they tried to prevent its publication. They contacted the palace Jews (*Hofjuden*) of Vienna, in particular the money changer Samuel Oppenheimer, who financed the emperor's wars.

Oppenheimer succeeded in duping Leopold II, who issued an edict prohibiting the sale of Eisenmenger's pamphlet. This ban ruined the author, who had devoted his entire fortune to the printing of his work, and whose seized copies amounted to 2,000. Eisenmenger sought the intervention of Frederick I, King of Prussia, to lift the imperial ban, but died in 1704 without seeing his request granted. The work did not see the light of day until 1711, thanks to King Frederick William I, who decided to publish it at his own expense in Berlin, ordering a print run of 3,000 copies.

Undoubtedly, Eisenmenger, by the strength of his work, the precision of his sources and the quality of his interpretations, had surpassed all his predecessors, marking a milestone in the history of anti-Semitism. *Judaism Unveiled* was from then on a major source of information for the anti-Semites of the following centuries[551].

---

[549] Johannes Eisenmenger in the second volume of his book *Judaism Unveiled*, Frankfurt-am-Main, 1700, chapter XI, p. 577

[550] Johannes Eisenmenger in the second volume of his book *Judaism Unveiled*, Frankfurt-am-Main, 1700, chapter XI, p. 578

[551] Johann Jakob Schudt, born in Frankfurt am Main in 1664, was also a prominent orientalist. His most important work was *Jüdische Merckwärdigkeiten*, published in three volumes in 1714. The book took up the themes outlined by Eisenmenger. It also recounted details and anecdotes about the life of Frankfurt's Jews.

CVII. Rome's Jews under surveillance

In Rome, the Jews were closely watched. In 1667, Clement IX hit them with new taxes and forced them to pay obeisance to the city's representatives in a humiliating way: the rabbi had to prostrate himself before the Conservator, begging for Christian commiseration towards the Jews. The Curator would put his foot on the back of his neck and allow him to stand.

However, in 1668, Clement IX abolished an ancient vexation, recounted by Michel de Montaigne in his *Journal of the Journey to Italy*, who, *despite* the Jewish ancestry attributed to him, did not seem to be too moved. They took seven or eight Jews, dressed them as rags, stuffed them with food and made them run for more than a kilometre between two rows of laughing Romans. The merriment reached its paroxysm in bad weather: "Last Monday, the Jews were favoured by a rain and a cold worthy of this perfidious people...". This detail, like the masquerades of the Roman Carnival, obligatorily opened by a band of Jews in burlesque costume, gives an idea of the esteem in which the ghetto people were held in the city of the popes.

At the beginning of the 18th century, the papacy had to take measures again. Innocent XIII, in his bull *Es injunctis* and Benedict XIII in his bull *Aliæ emanerunt*, forbade Jews to sell new objects. Benedict XIII (1724–1730) forbade Christians to eat, play or dance with Jews. Christians were warned that it was strictly forbidden to attend Jewish ceremonies. Two edicts (1704 and 1721) reminded the Jews of the County of Venesino of the obligation to wear the yellow hat, a measure which they would not cease to respect until 1789.

CVIII. The Jew Süss, 4 February 1738

Joseph Süss Oppenheimer (1698–1738) was a Jewish palace courtier, as the Jewish financiers who advised the princes of numerous principalities of the Germanic Empire were called. They administered the finances, supplied the armies, minted money, supplied the court with fabrics and precious stones, and leased the royalties from the sale of tobacco or salt.

Süss had enjoyed a meteoric rise through society. He first worked for Jewish trading houses in Frankfurt, Amsterdam and Vienna, enriching himself considerably, and then lent money to various German princes and prelates. As he had a manifest talent for business, he was appointed tax collector of the Rhine Palatinate, and finally, in 1733, he rose to the position of adviser to Charles Alexander, the Duke of Württemberg, who promptly handed over the management of the government to him. To bring more money into the coffers, Joseph Süss Oppenheimer introduced the ducal monopoly on the salt, leather, card-making, tobacco and liquor trades, and created new fines. He founded a bank and became even richer. He led a luxurious lifestyle and ostensibly kept a Christian mistress. He became known throughout Germany as an exceptional businessman. He also systematically favoured his fellow countrymen, for example by signing large contracts with Jewish merchants to supply the Württemberg army. Politically, he and the Duke, who had converted to Catholicism, prepared a conspiracy against the parliament to abolish privileges. Arrested after the sudden death of his sovereign in March 1737, Joseph Süss Oppenheimer was sentenced to death on 13 December for "high treason, theft, usurpation, fraud and infringement of the law". On 4 February 1738, he was hanged in front of 12,000 people on the highest gallows in Germany, in an iron cage. His last words were "*Shema Israel*[552]".

Süss remained in history as the emblematic figure representative of the ten or so "palace Jews" who, in the 18th century, had risen to the pinnacle of power in a number of large German states. From 1737 to 1739, many pamphlets were published against the Jew Süss. Wilhelm Hauff devoted a novel to the character in 1827, painting an unkind portrait of Joseph Süss Oppenheimer as a Jew of dissolute habits. But the character was identified above all through Veit Harlan's film, released in 1940.

At the beginning of his book *The Süss Jew*, published in 1925, the Jewish novelist Lion Feuchtwanger gave an astonishing portrait of the type of Jew of the Ancien Régime who reigned in the shadows thanks to money: "Isaak Landauer knew that there was only one reality in this world: money. War and peace, life and death, the virtue of women, the power of the Pope to bind and loose, the freedom of states, the purity of the Augsburg confession, the ships that plied the seas, the sovereignty of princes, love, piety, cowardice, pride, vice and virtue, all came from money and returned to it, and all could be expressed in figures. He, Isaak Landauer, knew it, he was next to the spring that let that immense power flow and he could contribute to direct its course, drying up or fertilising the land. But he considered it madness to flaunt his power and kept it secret, and a brief smile, strange and amused, was all that betrayed his knowledge and power. And one more thing: the rabbis and the sages of the Jewish quarters were perhaps right when they spoke accurately of God and the Talmud, describing the Garden of Paradise and the Valley of Tears down to the smallest detail, as if they were real things. He, for his part, did not have much time to devote to such discussions, and was rather inclined to follow the tendency of certain Frenchmen who treated such matters with elegant

---

[552] "*Hear O Israel*", beginning of Deuteronomy VI, 4.

irony. Nor did they trouble him in practice, and he ate what he liked and regarded Saturday as a working day. But outwardly he clung tenaciously to tradition and his kaftan was like a second skin to him. Dressed like this he entered the offices of the princes and the emperor. This was another sign of his power, deeper and more secret. He disdained gloves and wigs. They needed him, and that was his triumph, in spite of his caftan and his curls[553]."

Meanwhile on the Iberian peninsula, the Marranos were experiencing a much less enviable situation. In Lisbon, on 1 September 1739, an auto de fe was once again held. Four men and eight women were burned alive after refusing to repent of secretly Judaising, and thirty-five other defendants were sentenced to life imprisonment[554].

CIX. Frederick II and the Empress Maria Theresa

In the 18th century, the largest Jewish community in the Empire was located in Prague. Its ghetto was a real Jewish city of fifteen thousand inhabitants, with its own magistracy and all kinds of institutions. This community had long enjoyed a high reputation in the Jewish world, thanks to its rabbis, schools and printing presses. Other, less important communities had been established in various towns in Bohemia.

In order to curb their expansion, an edict was issued that only the eldest son of each Jewish family had the right to marry and set up a household. The other sons, if they married, could not remain in the country.

In 1740, on the death of Emperor Charles VI, his daughter Maria Theresa asserted her rights of succession. King Frederick II of Prussia seized the opportunity to attack and invade Silesia, a rich Habsburg territory, triggering the War of the Austrian Succession.

At that time, the Jews had acquired a certain power in Prussia. Among those who had been expelled from Vienna in 1670, some had been allowed to settle in Berlin and other Prussian cities by the Grand Duke of Brandenburg, Frederick William. Jewish merchants and bankers quickly became wealthy and occupied important positions at court. Their business prospered even more despite the fact that "the philosophical King Frederick sympathised with his illustrious enemy Maria Theresa's antipathy towards the Jews, and enacted anti-Jewish laws worthy of the Middle Ages rather than the 18th century... He wished the Jews in his dominions to decrease

---

[553] Lion Feuchtwanger, *El judío Süss*, Editorial Sudamericana pdf (Edhasa, Barcelona, 1990), p. 10-11. And in Léon de Poncins, *La mystèrieuse Internationale juive*, 1936, p. 188–189. On Lion Feuchtwanger's *Jew Süss* read also our book *The Millards of Israel* (2014).
[554] Read again footnote 546.

in number, rather than increase⁵⁵⁵". Nevertheless, the king allowed them to make their fortunes during the wars he fought against Austria and France. Indeed, a large number of Berlin Jews supplied the army and profited from hard times to enrich themselves considerably.

When the Prussian army entered Prague, the population was surprised to find that the Jews were openly sympathetic to the Protestant Prussia of the "enlightened" emperor, a friend of Voltaire and the philosophers, all of whom were devoted to the ideas of the "Enlightenment".

Maria Theresa, the mother of the future Queen of France Marie Antoinette, then took the decision to expel the Jews from Prague and the Empire's dependent kingdom of Bohemia. On 22 December 1744, the empress forced the Jews to sew a yellow piece of cloth on their sleeves and issued this edict:

"For various reasons, I have resolved not to tolerate Jews in my hereditary kingdom of Bohemia in the future. Therefore, I intend that on the last day of January 1745 no Jew shall be left in the city of Prague; if any should still be found, he shall be expelled by soldiers. However, in order that they may settle their affairs and dispose of their belongings which they cannot take with them, they will be allowed to remain for another month in the rest of the kingdom of Bohemia. Finally, this evacuation of the whole country will take place before the last day of June 1745".

The Jews then panicked and fled Prague to seek refuge in the surrounding villages. Many ended up wandering through the cold countryside in autumn and winter. For four years, hundreds of families were reduced to this extreme. Finally, by dint of insistence and the offer of large sums of money, the Jews managed to persuade Maria Theresa to allow them to return to Prague.

CX. Benedict XIV, 1751

Benedict XIV marked the 18th century with his long pontificate of 18 years (1740–1758). He was a pope with a passion for science: physics, chemistry and mathematics. He established a faculty of surgery and an anatomical museum in Rome. He also sought to appease religious questions and controversies, especially with Jansenism[556].

---

[555]Heinrich Graetz, *History of the Jews V*, Philadelphia, The Jewish Publication Society of America, 1895, p. 304.
[556]Jansenism was a theological doctrine that gave rise to a religious, then political and philosophical movement that developed in the 17th and 18th centuries, mainly in France, as a reaction to certain developments in the Catholic Church and royal

At the beginning of his reign, he was favourable to the Enlightenment and maintained good relations with Frederick II of Prussia through the scientist Maupertuis. Voltaire sincerely admired this erudite pope who was open to the ideas of his time. He even dedicated his tragedy *Mahomet* to him in 1745. The pope's letter of thanks to the philosopher testifies to their good relationship.

But legislation was still necessary to contain the aggressiveness of the Jews. A letter to the governor of Rome dated 28 February 1747, *De baptismo Judaeorum sive infantum, sive adultorum*, was in fact a long treatise—of outstanding precision and clarity—in which the pope recalled the provisions of the councils against the Jews, the ancient canons and all the coercive measures taken by his predecessors. This did not mean, however, that they could be stripped of everything, the pope specified (*Non ab iis expetendum esse quod iure non potest exigi...Quidquid iniuriam sapit Christianorum indignum est*).[557]

In 1751, Benedict XIV promulgated an ordinance updating the decisions of Paul IV. The Talmud was outlawed and was to be burned; Jews were forbidden to sell or bring their books into the Papal States; they could not have Christian servants; they could not move about without authorisation, own carts or horses. They had to transport their dead in silence to the cemetery; all this under penalty of beating and fines. The ordinance was confirmed in 1755 and later in January 1793 by Pius VI. At the same time, however, severe decrees punished Christians who unjustly disturbed Jews with the same penalties.

The Encyclical of 14 June 1751, entitled *A Quo primum*, addressed to the Polish bishops and people, contained a number of recriminations against the Jews. The pope's statement was a warning, an alarm signal to

---

absolutism. The definition of Jansenism is problematic, as Jansenists rarely assumed the name, considering themselves to be Catholics only. However, they had some characteristic features, such as the desire to adhere strictly to Augustine of Hippo's (St. Augustine's) doctrine of grace, conceived as the denial of human freedom to do good and obtain salvation. According to them, this was only possible through divine grace. Jansenists were also characterised by their moral rigorism and hostility towards the Society of Jesus (Jesuits) and its casuistry, as well as towards the excessive power of the Holy See. Thus, Jansenism, as a Puritan movement, emphasises original sin, human depravity, the necessity of divine grace that will save only those to whom it was granted from birth, and the belief in predestination without free will. Jansenism is generally regarded as synonymous with intransigence. From the late 17th century, this spiritual tendency was joined by a political aspect, with opponents of royal absolutism widely identified with the Jansenists. Jansenism was condemned as heretical by the Catholic Church.

[557] Charles Auzias-Turenne, *Revue Catholique des Institutions et du Droit*, October 1893.

the decadent Polish kingdom. Unfortunately, the appeal went unheeded and what the pope had foreseen happened: the collapse of the kingdom of Poland, completely eaten away and undermined by the Jews, was soon torn to pieces by the neighbouring states.

"To be brief: from responsible persons whose testimony deserves credit and who are well acquainted with the state of affairs in Poland, and from people living in the kingdom, who through their religious zeal have made their complaints known to Us and to the Holy See, we have learned the following facts. The number of Jews has greatly increased there. Thus, certain localities, villages and towns which were formerly surrounded by splendid walls (the ruins of which bear witness to the fact), and which were inhabited by a large number of Christians, as we see from the old lists and registers still extant, are now badly kept and dirty, populated by a large number of Jews and almost despoiled of Christians. Moreover, there are in the same kingdom a number of parishes in which the Catholic population has considerably diminished. The consequence is, that the income from such parishes has so greatly diminished, that they are in imminent danger of being without priests. Besides, the whole trade in articles of general use, such as liquors and even wine, are also in the hands of the Jews; they are allowed to take charge of the administration of the public funds; they have become lessees of inns and farms, and have acquired estates of land. By all these means, they have acquired proprietary rights over unfortunate cultivators of the soil, Christians, and not only use their power in an inhuman and heartless manner, imposing severe and painful labours on the Christians, compelling them to bear excessive burdens, but, in addition, inflicting on them corporal punishment such as blows and wounds. Hence these wretches are in the same state of subjection to a Jew as slaves are to the capricious authority of their master. It is true that, in inflicting punishment, the Jews are obliged to have recourse to a Christian official to whom this function is entrusted. But, as this official is obliged to obey the commands of the Jewish master, lest he himself should be deprived of his office, the tyrannical orders of the Jew must be carried out.

"We have said that the administration of public funds, and the leasing of inns, estates, and farms, have fallen into the hands of the Jews, to the great and various disadvantage of the Christians. But we must also allude to other monstrous anomalies, and we shall see, if we examine them carefully, that they are capable of originating still greater evils and more extensive ruin than those we have already mentioned. It is a matter fraught with very great and serious consequences that Jews are admitted into the houses of the nobility with a domestic and pecuniary ability to fill the office of steward. Thus, they live in conditions of family intimacy under the same roof with Christians, and treat them continually in a contemptuous manner, openly showing their contempt. In cities and other places Jews may be seen

everywhere in the midst of Christians; and what is still more regrettable, the Jews are not in the least afraid of having Christians of both sexes in their houses added to their service. Again, as the Jews are much occupied in commercial affairs, they amass enormous sums of money from these activities, and proceed systematically to rob the Christians of their goods and possessions by means of their usurious exactions. Although at the same time they borrow sums of money from Christians at an immoderately high level of interest, for the repayment of which their synagogues serve as collateral, nevertheless, their reasons for doing so are readily apparent. First of all, they obtain money from the Christians which they use in trade, thus making enough profit to pay the agreed interest, and at the same time increase their own power. Secondly, they gain as many protectors of their Synagogues and of their persons as they have creditors[558]."

CXI. The Jews in the "Age of Enlightenment[559]"

The emancipation of Jews from the centuries-old tutelage of the rabbis had begun during the century of the Enlightenment. In Judaism, this intellectual current, called *"Haskala"*, was led mainly by the German Jewish philosopher Moses Mendelssohn who advocated secular education, the use of the local language and the integration of Jews into gentile society. Mendelssohn believed that the Jews would improve their lot by drawing closer to Christians, making themselves better known to them and no longer entrenched in their narrow traditions and mysterious ghettos, but without abandoning their ancestral religion. It was with this in mind that he translated the Bible into classical German.

On the Christian side, the movement for Jewish emancipation was represented by Gotthold Ephraim Lessing and Wilhelm von Dohm. Other intellectuals vigorously opposed these ideas. A Frankfurt am Main writer, Johann-Balthasar Kolbele, denounced the vileness of the Jews and the harmfulness of Judaism, and was particularly offensive in his *Letter to Herr Mendelssohn* (March 1770). But everywhere in Europe, Enlightenment ideas were gaining ground. In 1714, the English freethinker John Toland

---

[558] https://www.geocities.ws/magisterio_iglesia/benedicto_14/a_quo_primum.html
[559] The "Age of Enlightenment" or Enlightenment was a bourgeois philosophical, literary and cultural movement that swept through Europe in the 18th century, especially in England, France and Germany. Its aim was to promote rationalism, individualism and liberalism against the "obscurantism" and superstition of the Catholic Church and the arbitrariness of royalty and nobility, using empirical philosophy, liberal economics and the English constitutional monarchy as models. During this era, ideals such as liberty, equality, progress, tolerance, fraternity, constitutional government, cosmopolitanism and Church-State Separation spread.

had published a pamphlet calling for the complete emancipation of the Jews. But some English deists, such as Tindal, Morgan and Lord Bolingbroke, denounced Christianity by attacking its Jewish roots. This argument was taken up in France by Voltaire in his *Dictionnaire philosophique* (1764), in which he ridiculed ignorant and fanatical Jews.

The ideas of the Enlightenment bore fruit. In 1781, Joseph II of Austria, an emperor imbued with the ideas of the *Encyclopaedia,* issued an edict of toleration that put Jews on an equal footing with other citizens. But at that time, neither the princes nor the people were yet prepared to grant Jews full equality of rights, which was tantamount to letting the fox into the henhouse. Even the Prussian King Frederick the Great, the royal philosopher, refused to improve their situation.

In the newly created kingdom of Saxony, Jews remained subject to the restrictive laws that had governed them in previous centuries. The Jews rightly dubbed this country "Protestant Spain". Legally, they had no right to remain there; only a few were tolerated in Dresden and Leipzig, but under the reservation that they could be expelled at any time. They could not have synagogues, and for prayer they met in simple rooms. Even Russian Jews under Alexander I were treated more liberally.

CXII. The Jews in France in the 18th century

For three centuries, from 1394, France was *judenrein,* purified of Jews, until the annexation of Alsace by Louis XIV. Some Jewish families from Germany had also been reincorporated into the city of Metz at the behest of Henry IV. By 1720, they formed a nucleus of about a hundred families and were subject to very strict regulations: always wearing black clothes, living in the ghetto with only one opening to the outside. Their services were sometimes required for the purchase of fodder and horses, particularly for the army.

In those years, it was reported that a score of Jews had managed to infiltrate Paris. Behind them, a small gang had attempted the same escape, but the capital's police pursued them, and the operation was no more important than any other pursuit of rogues or suspects. This was a mere anecdote, very typical of the mentality of the time, which showed that the presence of Jews remained deeply repulsive.

Since 1719, the police had been identifying vagrants and had issued a warrant for the arrest of some twenty-five individuals who did not have the obligatory passports and who "deserved to be expelled". A post of vigilant inspector of the Jews had been created in 1721. In 1725, M. Hérault, replacing M. d'Argenson, redoubled his severity and himself demanded the expulsion without further delay of all Jews whose papers were not impeccably in order, "because the people of this religion are very suspicious and there are many scoundrels among them".

Jews were once again forbidden to hire the services of a Christian servant, even on Sabbath days. This measure was in response to the recruitment of Christian women workers by Jews in Bordeaux, where officially there were only "new Christians" expelled from Spain and Portugal a few centuries earlier: "The Jews have beautiful peasant maids who they impregnate to serve as wet nurses for their children, and they then give up the offspring that the young peasant women give birth to in hospices for abandoned children" (Rapport de Monsieur de Boucher, 1733). (*Rapport de Monsieur de Boucher*, in 1733).

Sexual relations with Christians were ruthlessly persecuted by the authorities. As a matter of principle, a Jew accused of having seduced a Christian woman was liable to be burned at the stake, and the clergy denied him baptism if he made any sign of wanting to convert. In 1726, for example, an Aryan maid named Marie Becquart was imprisoned for having been the mistress of a certain Lévy.

Under Berryer's general lieutenancy, from 1747 onwards, Jewry encountered a formidable adversary in the person of the vigilant inspector M. Legrand, who, as soon as he took office, complained about the indulgences received by the Jews and the resulting invasion. The number of Jews in Paris at that time was about five hundred.[560]

In 1750, Louis XV himself wrote a letter to the lieutenant-general to ensure that all Jews had their papers in order, that he would keep an eye on them and that in case of refusal they would be imprisoned. Compared to this "wandering rabble", wrote Lucien Rebatet, "Bordeaux Jewry, settled in its business, endowed with bourgeois charters by Louis XIV, confirmed in its privileges by Louis XV, evidently represented Jewish society in good standing". But there, too, complaints were raised. As long as the colony did not exceed five hundred members (1718 figure), it had never been heard of. Fifteen years later, it had already reached four thousand souls.

In Alsace, annexed by France under Louis XIV, the Jewish problem was much more pressing than in the rest of the country. Louis XIV, true to his political principles, had authorised Alsace to retain its special regulations, including, of course, those concerning the Jews, so closely aligned with the convictions of the monarchy.

Since the mid-14th century, Strasbourg had forbidden Jews to have a home or property in its enclosure, however modest or temporary it might be. At nightfall, all Jews returned to the ghetto to the sound of the Jewish horn, the *Kraüselhorn*, which signalled their entry. During the day, only a few shops remained open, for example, the livery trade, and they could

---

[560] Lucien Rebatet, *Je Suis Partout*, special issue of 17 February 1939

only enter the city on payment of a special toll. Thus, between 1389 and 1681, no Jews stayed overnight in Strasbourg. A few Jews were occasionally authorised to stay for one night, in case of justified need, but always in the inns designated by the police. For the rest, the ordinances against Jews were renewed in 1708 and 1750, and even tightened. In 1708, in order to prevent fraud by Jews who set up shop at the gates of the city and disguised themselves, they were forbidden to enter without safe-conduct. Christian subjects within an eight-mile radius of Strasbourg were also forbidden to engage in any business or contract with Jews, with the exception of the horse and cattle trade and the sale of staples, foodstuffs and clothing. These rules were so strictly observed until the French Revolution that the first Jewish owner of a house in Strasbourg since the Middle Ages was a certain Cerfbeer in 1780. Even so, this important supplier to the armies had secretly acquired this house. When it was discovered, the affair sparked popular indignation throughout the city, which immediately filed a lawsuit against him, very famous at the time.

As for the Jews of the shire villages, scattered in the most remote places and frequenting the peasants, the social plague of usury they caused—which we see century after century wherever Israel plants its fangs—was much more difficult to monitor and conjure up. The Jews used to prey on large families in difficulty or those whose crops had failed, lending them at exorbitant rates of interest, or selling their flocks on credit, which the Jews then trafficked. Gradually, the entire peasantry of Alsace had fallen into their clutches.

CXIII. Louis XVI

Of all the monarchs who successively occupied the throne of France, Louis XVI was undoubtedly the most liberal, but also the most indecisive and faint-hearted. After scrupulously studying the case of the Jews of Alsace, this monarch settled the matter on 10 July 1784 by royal patent. Here are a few extracts from the authentic text which give a precise idea of his zeal.

"Article I—Jews without a domicile in Alsace must leave this province within three months. We wish that those Jews who—after the expiry of the period fixed by the present article—are found in the said province, shall be persecuted and treated as vagabonds and people without confession, and that the strictness of the ordinances shall be applied.

Article II—Most expressly forbidding all lords and all cities and communities enjoying the right of lordship to admit in future any foreign Jew until We order otherwise.

Article VI—All Jews residing in Alsace are expressly forbidden to marry without our permission, even outside the States of our domination, on pain of immediate expulsion from the said province.

Article VII—This article imposes a fine of £3,000 on rabbis who perform unauthorised marriages, and orders their expulsion in case of repeated offences. Rabbis are also forbidden to accommodate Jews without passports, as they are continually doing".

Article VIII prohibited Jews from hiring Christian servants to run farms, and Article IX forbade them from acquiring real estate.

Lucien Rebatet also recounted this anecdote "difficult to verify, but of great moral verisimilitude": In 1787, while hunting in the woods near Versailles, Louis XVI is said to have come across a miserable entourage of ragged, distressed and frightened German Jews carrying on their shoulders the corpse of one of their own. They explained that they were carrying it to Paris, to the Montrouge cemetery that had recently been granted to them. Until the previous year, they had only had a corner in the courtyard of an inn in the Vilette to bury their dead. Louis XVI was moved, and it is said that from this meeting the idea of a general statute for the Jews of France was born. "This is very much in keeping with his sentimental nature," noted Lucien Rebatet.

That same year, a special commission chaired by Malesherbes studied the statute. The complete dossier is no longer available, but what we know of it suffices to reveal its spirit. Louis XVI wished to improve the physical condition of the Jews in France and to guarantee them full freedom in their worship and customs. But his draft stipulated that the Jews, a separate and impregnable nation, could not be assimilated into his French subjects, that this would mean "introducing a nation within the nation, an armed nation into an unarmed and unsuspecting nation."

The King of France maintained all the prescriptions, removing them from public employment and reinforcing the measures against their financial abuses, whether small or large. The Revolution did not allow him to complete his work.

CXIV. *François Hell*

In the last third of the 18th century, the situation in Alsace was inextricable. Conflicts arose at every turn. Jews were beaten severely, but they retaliated and took revenge in legal proceedings. The Alsatians were overwhelmed by the excessive immigration of German Jews. The latest count brought the number of Jews in Alsace to 19,624, a figure that seemed exorbitant. The Jewish population had tripled in thirty years.

François Hell, an Alsatian court clerk, intelligent and cultured, was one of his fiercest adversaries. He even learnt Hebrew so that he could understand their trade books himself and penetrate the secret of their operations. Appointed bailee by some Alsatian nobles, he took advantage of his position to teach the Jews' debtors to fabricate false receipts which the latter then opposed the creditors' claims.

He also published in 1779 his *Observations of an Alsatian on Jewish affairs in Alsace,* a text in which he exhorted the population to revolt against Jewish tyranny[561]. Once he even sent them letters in Hebrew threatening to denounce them for swindling and usury if they did not pay a fixed amount. Here is a text by Louis de Bonald concerning this scandal of false receipts. Louis de Bonald, a nobleman from Rouergue, former mayor of Millau, had fled France in 1791, later ending his career as a writer and politician at the Académie française. In 1806 he narrated this story of François Hell:

"About 1777 or 1778, the peasants of Alsace, burdened then, as now, by the usurious exactions of the Jews, had in their desperation attempted an illegitimate means of getting rid of them, and a skilful forger, it seems, had gone through the province and furnished a large number of debtors with false discharges. Doubtless the Jews feared the courts of a country where they were abhorred; or perhaps the great number of cases of the same kind rendered recourse to ordinary justice too slow and costly. Be this as it may, the creditors preferred to carry their grievances to the higher authority; and it may also be believed that the irresistible arguments, as Figaro says, of which the Jews always have their pockets full, must have been listened to more favourably by the administration than by the magistrates."

After the publication of François Hell's pamphlet, the Jews, Bonald told us, "had enough credit to imprison the Hell dance". Indeed, in 1780, François Hell was arrested by order of Louis XVI and sentenced to a three-year exile. When he returned, he was received as a martyr by the Alsatian peasants.

At the beginning of 1788, new riots broke out in Lorraine because of the increase in the price of bread. The Jews were then accused of speculation, as they owned several wheat granaries throughout the region. In Lunéville, Pont-à-Mousson, Nancy, Lixheim and Sarreguemines, granaries were raided, synagogues shot at and Jews attacked in the streets. Troops were sent in to restore order, but the population's feelings of animosity did not diminish.

---

[561] "For the blood of the crucified Righteous One fell upon them and upon their children…There is no country or century whose history does not show us scenes of persecution which the righteous wrath of Heaven has brought down upon this criminal race. Everywhere the Jews attract to themselves the enemies which persecution arouses. The hardness of their hearts, the blindness of their minds, the spirit of rebellion, the inclination to usury, the character of cruelty have made them and will forever make them the object of the abhorrence of the peoples among whom they are scattered." In François Hell, *Observations of an Alsatian on Jewish affairs in Alsace.*

François Hell's book was not printed again until 1790 in Neuchâtel, when its author was elected to the National Assembly. Bonald, who was a moderate democrat, remarked that the Assembly had never debated this case and commented ironically: "While abolishing noble feudalism, we saw the same legislators cover up and protect this new feudalism of the Jews, the real high and mighty lords of Alsace, where they received both tithes and seignorial rights; and certainly, if in philosophical language the word feudal is synonymous with oppressive and odious, I know of nothing more feudal for a province than eleven million mortgages owed to usurers [562]." François Hell ended his days on the scaffold. He was guillotined in 1794 for being a royalist.

CXV. The Revolution and the Empire (1789–1815)

The notebooks of the Estates General contained countless complaints from the Alsatians and Lorraine about the Jews. Thionville, Pont-à-Mousson, Mirecourt, Sarrebourg, Nancy, Nomény, Sarreguemines, Bitche, Boulay, Bouzonville, Dreize, Fenestrange, Strasbourg, Vic and many other localities demanded that the legislation on the Jews be applied more strictly, that their number in trade, especially in fodder and grain, be limited. But from the first day, the Constituent Assembly, dragged along by a handful of orators and demagogues, was ready to let ideology take precedence over the interests of the nation.

The storming of the Bastille had inaugurated the fight against the "enemies of the people". In Alsace, the enemy of the people was embodied in Judaism. The day after 14 July 1789, the Alsatians attacked the Jews with armed force.

On 3 August 1789, Abbot Gregory, priest of Embermesnil in Lorraine, deputy of the bailiwick of Nancy, took this pretext to take the rostrum and make an impassioned speech. Some protests were raised. At the session of 23 December 1789, when the Assembly had put the question back on the agenda with the intervention of Monsieur de Clermont-Tonnerre, Abbé Maury replied in his turn to the pro-Jewish clan in the Chamber: "The word Jew is not the name of a sect, but of a nation which has its own laws, has always followed them and still wants to follow them. They have never been anything but money-handlers and will never be farmers, soldiers or craftsmen. The people feel for the Jews a hatred which their emancipation will not fail to explode. For their salvation, there must be no matter for deliberation. They must not be persecuted... Let them therefore be protected as individuals, but not as Frenchmen, since they cannot be

---

[562] Louis de Bonald, *Sur les Juifs*, Mercure de France, February 1806.

citizens".

Alsace, which supported more than half of France's Jewry, sounded all the alarm bells, the echo of which can be seen precisely in this unsigned report entitled *The Jews of Alsace*: "Let the Jew be a citizen in all respects in which he will not be a harmful citizen: very well (living everywhere, owning his own house, freedom of worship, admission to the guilds of the liberal and mechanical arts). But in no case should the Jew be eligible for political, administrative and judicial bodies. In other words, none of these important and delicate functions, which must always be governed by the principles of Christian morality, should be conferred upon him. Unlimited enjoyment of all the rights of citizenship would place the advantages of Jewish status above those of any other Frenchman. For, on the one hand, he would reap gold in abundance, and, on the other hand, this gold, by placing in his chains a great number of slaves, whose votes he would control in the assemblies, would serve him as an instrument to ascend to the chair of President of the Nation or to place himself under the fleurs-de-lis."

The Sephardic Jews of Bordeaux, more cautious and already fearing competition from their Ashkenazi brethren, claimed that they were very comfortable with their status and did not wish to change it.

But abruptly, on 28 January 1790, during a great debate, the Assembly proclaimed the Jews of Bordeaux, already in possession of their French naturalisation certificates, to be active citizens. The Assembly passed the measure with 374 votes in favour and 224 against. A motion by the Alsatian deputy Schwends, who wanted to make it clear that the law did not include the Jews of Alsace, whose number now stood at 26,000, was rejected.

As soon as the vote became known, anti-Jewish demonstrations were organised in Bordeaux. In Alsace, revolutionary revolts turned into furious attacks on Jews. Gunshots were fired at their synagogues, the roofs of their houses were blown off. Gibes and rumours flew everywhere, and the question was asked whether from now on one had to be a Jew to be a bishop.

The Jews of Paris demanded citizenship with all their might, but the Assembly, due to the tensions that the issue generated among its members, preferred to postpone the final law.

However, on 27 September 1791, Mr Duport demanded active citizenship with eligibility for all Jews, including those of the Venesine County recently annexed by France. The Alsatian deputy Rewbell, followed by numerous deputies, raised his voice, recalling that the Jews in Alsace had enormous debts because of the usury they practised and that the Assembly was therefore going to take sides against the victims. The extremists won despite these reasonable words and the law of emancipation of the Jews was promulgated on 27 September 1791. On 13 November, the law was officially registered by royal decree. Jews were henceforth citizens like everyone else. Soon, this measure would spread throughout Europe with the Napoleonic wars, and they were emancipated in almost all European states, at least provisionally. For the first time in the history of Europe, the henhouse doors had been thrown wide open.

Louis de Bonald ironised: "The assembly declared them active citizens: a title which, together with the declaration of the rights of man, just decreed, was then considered the highest degree of honour and beatitude to which a human creature could aspire". But he spoke out against the blaming of Christians: "The Jews," he said, "were rejected by our customs far more than they were oppressed by our laws. Consequently, the Assembly made the enormous and deliberate mistake of putting its laws in contradiction with morality. Bonald finally warned his contemporaries: "Take care that the emancipation of the Jews does not become the oppression of the Christians[563]!"

A large number of Jews immediately enlisted in the National Guard, where they could enjoy hunting down suspects. By contrast, they were few in number on the battlefields of the Republic. One of the few documents that recounts their presence is a decree of Laurent, commissary of the people in the Army of the North, on *16 Messidor II*, which reported the swarming of spies and plunderers of Jewish corpses: "Jews are strictly forbidden to follow the armies on pain of death. The generals, the commanders of army posts and the vigilance committee of the municipality of Mons will process complaints against offenders and arrest them immediately for execution within 24 hours".

In Alsace, since the decree of 1791, Jewish domination had become a real obsession. The Jews demanded 1.50 francs of interest per month for 24 francs borrowed, without leaving documented proof of these usurious rates. Every year in Alsace, forced sales worth 1,500,000 francs were executed, 85% of which were at the request of the Jews. From the year VII to January 1806 (1798–1806), their mortgage loans had risen to 21 million. Finally, they used to falsify their civil status, changing their name in each town to evade justice and above all military conscription. Of the 66 Moselle Jews who should have been part of the contingent, none had served in the army[564].

Bonaparte then decided to commission a study on the question from one of his most famous and objective jurisconsults, Jean-Etienne-Matie Portalis, who wrote a detailed memoir: "By assimilating the Jews without precaution with all the other French, a large number of foreign Jews were attracted and have infested our frontier departments, and the happy changes

---

[563] Louis de Bonald, *Sur les Juifs,* Mercure de France, February 1806.
[564] Lucien Rebatet, *Je Suis Partout,* special issue of 17 February 1939

promised by the system of naturalisation adopted did not come about in the mass of Jews who had been established in France for the longest time. In this respect, the present circumstances speak for themselves."

Napoleon Bonaparte himself declared: "I would like to point out once again that there are no complaints from Protestants or Catholics, in the same way that they complain about the Jews. This is because the harm caused by the Jews does not come from individuals, but from the very constitution of this people. They are caterpillars, locusts that plague France... The States General of the Jews must be assembled. I want there to be a general synagogue of the Jews. I am far from wanting to do anything against my glory and which may be disapproved of by posterity. It would be a weakness to expel the Jews, but it will be strength to correct them."

The emperor despised the Jews. But at the height of his power, defeating so many rulers, he felt strong enough to reduce them to his will. In order to integrate the Jews into French society, he felt it necessary first to obtain the alliance of the rabbis. Thus, on 30 May 1806, he decided to convene the "Jewish States General" that he desired, i.e. to constitute the majority of the Israelite notables gathered in an official body. The Grand Sanhedrin of France, composed of seventy members, was convened for the first time on 4 February 1807.

Unfortunately, by centralising and consecrating the religious organisation of the Jews, the Emperor reaped the opposite effect, for he had provided a powerful instrument of unity and national activity for the Jews.

The decree of 17 March 1808 established the legal organisation and protection of the Jewish cult. But one measure came to counteract the exactions and swindles of the Jews which had only multiplied in all the departments of Eastern France in recent months. Jews not domiciled in the Upper and Lower Rhine were henceforth forbidden to settle in these departments, and the courts were authorised to grant debtors extensions for all Jewish debts, including non-usurious ones. Magistrates could annul the Jewish debts of the incapacitated, minors and military personnel not authorised by their officers. Any bill of exchange, any promissory note, any bond or pledge subscribed by merchants in favour of a Jew would only be valid to the extent that the bearer proved that the value had been provided in full and without fraud. The courts were to reduce all debts with accrued interest in excess of 5% and annul those with interest in excess of 10%.

Furthermore, no Jew could engage in trade or business without having received a special patent from the prefect of the department attesting that the Jew had not practised usury; the consistory had to prove his good conduct and probity. Contracts or obligations entered into in favour of a Jew who lacked this patent could be reviewed and revoked. Finally, Jews could not be replaced in military service. These measures would be in force for ten years. The Jews of Bordeaux and the South-West were exempted on condition that they did not give rise to any complaint[565].

The Jews, who had already put down solid roots in France and did not intend to suffer any more obstacles, cried foul at the "infamy" of the decree, and the liberator of the chosen people was immediately vilified as an executioner "worthy of the Middle Ages".

Since they no longer had anything good to expect from the emperor, the Jews began to support England.

Bonaparte's Jewish policy had been both grandiose and imprecise. Thanks to his prestige, he would have better served the interests of the nation by restoring the essential principles of the policy of kings. But it is likely that, had fate granted him twenty more years of reign and peace in 1815, he would have re-examined the problem in the light of the experience he had gained.

CXVI. The Bourbon Restoration in France (1815–1830)

Catholic reaction to revolutionary ideas was represented under the Restoration by two prominent writers, Joseph de Maistre and Louis-Gabriel de Bonald, whose ideas were very similar. Indeed, Maistre wrote to Bonald before his death: "I have not written or thought anything that you have not written, I have not written anything that you have not thought." The two were the main representatives of the traditionalist Catholic current.

Joseph de Maistre (1753–1821), born in Chambéry in Savoy, the eldest son of ten children, had studied with the Jesuits and was deeply Catholic. When in 1792 Savoy was invaded by the revolutionary armies, he left for Lausanne, where he carried out various functions for the Duke of Savoy, who was also King of Sardinia. At the end of 1798, he emigrated to Venice, before being sent by King Charles Emmanuel IV to Sardinia, where he was regent of the Chancellery. Three years later, he was appointed ambassador to Russia.

Joseph de Maistre said little about Judaism. But according to him, Jewish hatred of Christianity was never to be forgotten or overlooked by the legislator, on pain of seeing Jewish actions disintegrate the social fabric and undermine the foundations of the state. In the face of such a threat, authority was to inspire fear and make the secret members of the Synagogue tremble. In his *Letters to a Russian Gentleman* of 1815, he praised the efforts of the Spanish Inquisition: "It was therefore necessary to daunt the imagination, by constantly showing the anathema which the

---

[565] Lucien Rebatet, *Je Suis Partout*, special issue of 17 February 1939

mere suspicion of Judaism entailed. It is a great mistake to believe that to defeat a powerful enemy it is enough to stop him: nothing has been done unless he is forced to retreat. The question was, then, whether a Spanish nation would continue to exist... whether superstition, despotism and barbarism would continue to win this dreadful victory over the human race".

Louis de Bonald (1754–1840) was born in Millau, in an old noble family of Rouergue. A politician, philosopher, monarchist and Catholic writer, he was a great opponent of the French Revolution. In his numerous works, he attacked the Declaration of the Rights of Man, Rousseau's Social Contract and the social and political innovations of the Revolution, advocating a return to the monarchy and the principles of the Catholic Church.

In 1785, he became mayor of Millau. Initially a supporter of the revolution in 1790, he was a member and president of the Assembly of his department. However, he disapproved of the Catholic Church's withdrawal (sale of the clergy's property, civil constitution) and, in January 1791, resigned from his posts as president and deputy of the departmental assembly. He emigrated with his two eldest sons to Heidelberg where Condé's army was stationed.

In Heidelberg, Bonald discovered his vocation as a writer. His first work, *The Theory of Political and Religious Power*, was printed in 1796 in Constance. In 1797, Bonald entered Paris clandestinely, but did not reappear officially until the coup d'état of 18 Brumaire[566]. He frequented Chateaubriand, published several political and legal essays before retiring to his own country, but continued to write for the newspapers *Mercure de France* and *Journal des débats*.

During the Restoration, his struggle in favour of the monarchy earned him official recognition and he was made a knight of Saint-Louis. In 1815, he was elected to the Chamber of Deputies. In 1816, he was appointed to the Académie française. Finally, he was elevated to the dignity of Peer of France in 1823.

In his essay entitled *On the Jews*, published in 1806, Louis de Bonald studied "the religion and customs of a people openly at war with the religion and customs of all peoples". He was forced to recognise that evil was deeply rooted in most Jews. Perhaps even an "enlightened and virtuous" Jew was not really so: "It is no more permissible, in good logic, to justify

---

[566] The coup d'état of the 18th of Brumaire in 18th century France refers to the coup d'état on that date in the French Republican calendar, corresponding to 9 November 1799 in the Gregorian calendar, which ended the Directory, the last form of government of the French Revolution, and initiated the Consulate with Bonaparte as its leader. (NdT)

a nation accused of a general disposition to baseness and bad faith, by pointing to a few educated and honest individuals, than to incriminate a virtuous nation, by the example of a few evildoers it has produced[567]", he wrote judiciously.

During the Restoration, in 1818, many deputies demanded the extension of the decree of 1808, which was about to expire, and even reinforced it with new precautions: suspension of all sales with the right of repurchase by Jews, prohibition for Jews to trade in real estate.

Some, like the Marquis de Lattier, deputy of the Drôme, proposed confining the Jews to the territories where they lived before the Revolution, limiting their numbers, forbidding women to marry before the age of 25, and even forbidding them to have recourse to justice. As always, his accusations referred to the systematic and continuous picaresque behaviour of the Jews of Alsace and Lorraine. But the Chamber of Peers rejected all his requests, as well as the extension of the decree.

In 1827, the celebrated Rabbi David Drach, who had sincerely converted to Catholicism, informed us of the hopes of the sect. In his *Second Letter to the Israelites from a converted rabbi* (Paris, 1827), he wrote: "The Messiah must be a great conqueror, who will make all the nations of the world slaves of the Jews. The Jews will return to the Holy Land, triumphant and laden with the riches taken from the infidels. The purpose of their mission will be to liberate scattered Israel, to return them to the Holy Land, to establish and consolidate a temporal kingship whose duration will be the duration of the world. All nations will then be subject to the Jews, and the Jews will reign freely over the individuals who compose them and over their property[568]."

Here is another passage from his book: "The Talmud expressly forbids to save a non-Jew from death... to return his lost belongings... to take pity on him, etc. According to the Talmud, the total number of precepts of God's law is not less than six hundred and thirteen, i.e. 248 affirmative precepts and 365 negative precepts. The affirmative precepts number 185 and 198 command, in the first case, that usury should be practised on non-Jews, and in the second, that idols and idolaters should be exterminated without mercy and contemplation[569]."

A few decades later, the Jewish Bolsheviks of 1917 Russia would be animated by this same Talmudic hatred. For thirty years, from 1917 to 1947, no less than thirty million Russians, Belarusians and Ukrainians perished, victims of Jewish fanaticism clinging to power.

---

[567]Louis de Bonald, *Sur les Juifs*, Mercure de France, February 1806.
[568]Quoted by Abbot Chabeauty, *Les Juifs, nos maîtres*, 1882.
[569]David Drach, *De l'harmonie entre l'Église et la Synagogue*, 1844, in Chabeauty, *Les Juifs, nos maîtres*, 1882, p. 167-170.

CXVII. Germany, 1814–1819

In most German principalities, Jews had acquired equal rights through the introduction of the Napoleonic Code. Numerous voices were raised against the admission of predators into German society. In 1793, the famous philosopher Johann Gottlieb Fichte was a Jacobin, but his republican ideals did not blind him to the danger posed by the admission of Jews into society. In his first major work on the revolution, he wrote: "To protect ourselves against them, I see only one way: to conquer for them their promised land and expel them all there".

In 1806, in *The Fundamental Features of the Present Age*, he expressed his vision of Christianity, which he saw in its purest form in the Apostle St John, even doubting the Jewish origins of Jesus. After what the Archbishop of Toledo, Juan Martínez Siliceo, had written, we see here how the idea of an Aryan Christ once again appeared. Following the example of Voltaire, Fichte railed against the Old Testament and criticised the New Testament, especially the epistles of St. Paul. In 1808, his famous *Addresses to the German Nation became* the Magna Carta of pan-Germanism.

In Berlin in 1803, Karl Grattenauer had published *Wider die Juden* (*Against the Jews*), with a circulation of 13,000 copies. Grattenauer regarded the Jews not from a religious point of view, but as a different race. In the same year, Christian Ludwig Paalzow's *Ueber des Bürgerrecht der Juden* (On the *Civil Rights of the Jews*) was published in Leipzig.

Numerous pamphlets transcribed the population's disgust with the Jews. In 1809, the novelist Achim von Arnim had founded a patriotic society in Berlin, the *Deutschechristliche Tischgesellschaft*, to which "Jews and Philistines" were barred: "Neither Jews, nor Jewish converts, nor descendants of Jews", he wrote. His brother-in-law Clemens von Brentano was famous for his tales of evil Jews.

Louis de Bonald, who had spent some time in exile in Heidelberg during the French Revolution, had had the opportunity to study closely the problems caused by the numerous Jews living in Germany. The country had not yet been completely disrupted by the Jewish spirit, as would be the case at the end of the century. The German people, wrote Bonald in his essay published in 1806 entitled *On the Jews*, are "tranquil in their tastes and moderate in their desires". In some regions, however, the people were starving. Bonald quoted an article from the *Publicist's Bulletin*, dated 11 Vendimary. The article, taken from a German gazette, revealed the "bad faith and trickery that the Jews are displaying at the Leipsick fair". The author added: "We know how the Jews of Alsace treat the farmers who can only borrow from them, and that in this province alone the farmers' lands are mortgaged with them to the value of eleven million. In fact, it was they who, in agreement with Christian third parties, organised the terrible famine in Moravia and Bohemia, in order to regain the privileges and monopolies of which they had been deprived. In the Bavarian States, old and new, they are daily gaining more and more influence as money men, and all things considered, it is not Christian, but Jewish bankers, who regulate the rate of exchange, not only at the Leipsick fair, but in Hamburg, Amsterdam, and London."

The author advocated the re-establishment of the rhodella as indispensable, and denounced the Jews as counterfeiters: "It is necessary to preserve a distinctive mark for these persons, who, in the present state of things, excluded from the full enjoyment of the rights of citizens, either by obstinacy or their wretched condition, are necessarily the enemies of the public good. It has been proved that no class of men have been so injurious as the Jews to the fertile provinces of the House of Austria, especially since 1796; who, by their counterfeit notes and counterfeit coin, and by making the numeraire disappear, were able to produce this horrible general dearth which could only benefit them."

Wealthy Jews were not the only ones alluded to: "Further on," wrote de Bonald, the same author: "There is no limit to the baseness of the Jewish beggars or pedlars, nor to the incredible multiplication of their families. The records of the Leipsick police courts during the fair show that, out of twelve robberies or swindles, eleven involved Jews." This is one of the few testimonies that have come down to us about Jewish criminality prior to 20th century studies.

A German author named A. F. Thiele, a senior official in the Prussian administration, had published in 1841 an important study entitled *Die jüdischen Gauner un Deutschland* (*The Jewish swindlers in Germany*), which we shall see in more detail in a later chapter. Thiele confirmed that the French occupation had been a golden age for them: "During the war years, he wrote, between 1806 and 1814, there were legions of the worst Jews in the French armies. They worked as spies and customs agents; others engaged in pillaging. These Jews committed many crimes. Most of the older Jewish criminals claim to have taken part in the later French campaigns. They certainly took part in them, but they were undesirable volunteers". (Volume I, page 73).

Indeed, many Jews followed the Napoleonic armies and pillaged wherever they went. Numerous Jews from Poland had come to Germany during the Napoleonic wars in the wake of the Russian armies. Since the French armies had opened the gates of the prisons and released the alienated from the asylums, and the German police were paralysed by the military occupation of the country, all the scum had a free hand to perpetrate their misdeeds and misdeeds.

The collapse of the Napoleonic empire marked the end of the process of Jewish penetration of German society. The reaction movement began in

Frankfurt. In January 1814, as soon as the French were leaving the city, the city council re-established the old legislation. Jews were excluded from meetings where the interests of the city were discussed. The city expelled them from the official jobs they held and banned them from numerous other professions. They were refused permission to marry and were once again segregated in a special quarter.

The Senate's struggle against the Frankfurt Jews lasted nine years (1815–1824). The Jews appealed to the highest authorities, but, in response to the detailed *report* submitted, the five jurists of the Berlin faculty gravely declared that by virtue of the regulation of 1616 the Jews of Frankfurt were to remain subordinate, almost as serfs, to the bourgeoisie of that city.

The example of Frankfurt was followed by the three main Hanseatic cities of Germany, which also decided to protect themselves from the Jews. In Hamburg, the Senate was favourable to them, but the people, as was usually the case everywhere, were hopelessly hostile to them.

In Lübeck and Bremen they were expelled outright. Hanover, Hidelsheim, Brunswick and Hesse withdrew their acquired rights. Only the states of Saxony-Weimar, Hesse-Cassel and Württemberg emancipated their Jews.

Germany was thus more prudent than the France of King Louis XVIII. In the Habsburg states, the liberal traditions of Joseph II were abandoned in favour of the reintroduction of some of the old restrictions dictated by Empress Maria-Theresa. New laws of exception were even added to them. The Jews were not expelled but isolated in their ghettos. They were denied access to the Tyrol, as were Protestants. In Bohemia, they were denied the right to settle in small towns and villages in the mountains; in Moravia, on the other hand, they were forbidden to settle in large cities such as Brno and Olomuc. Emperor Franz II did, however, ennoble some wealthy Jews.

Anti-Jewish literary agitation unleashed passions and caused unrest for several years. The Kantian Jakob Friedrich Fries (1773–1843), a pupil of Fichte, physician and professor of natural sciences in Heidelberg, published a book entitled *On the Danger of the Jews to the Prosperity and Character of the Germans*[570], in which he did not hesitate to advocate the annihilation of Judaism.

Among Fries's emulators, Professor Fredric Ruehs of the University of Berlin also knew how to interpret the feelings of the population. In January 1816, in his work entitled *Vindication of Civil Rights for the Jews of Germany,* he denied Jews citizenship and proposed subjecting them, as in the past, to the payment of a special tax and the wearing of a distinctive

---

[570] *Über die Gefährdung des Wohlstandes und Charakters der Deutschen durch die Juden* (1816):

sign.

Dr. Köppe, for his part, said in one of his pamphlets that the enlightened Jews were "cosmopolitan scoundrels" who had to be "pursued and hunted everywhere".

Unrest began in earnest in Wurtzburg in March 1819. The common people ransacked Jewish houses and shops, throwing goods out of the windows to the cry of *Hep, Hep* (initials of *Hierosolyma est perdita*). The Jews defended themselves vigorously and a real pitched battle broke out in the streets, with dead and wounded. Order could only be restored by the soldiers. The municipality then decided to expel the Jews and about four hundred families were forced to leave the city. The Jews temporarily camped on the outskirts, under tents and in neighbouring villages.

These scenes were repeated in Bamberg and in almost every town in Franconia. As soon as a Jew was in sight, he was chased away with the insulting cry *"Jude verreck" (Die Jew!)*. Such was the animosity and exasperation of the population.

On 9 and 10 August, in Frankfurt, Jews were insulted in public places and on the city's promenades, attacked with stones, their houses broken into and ransacked. The agitators vented their wrath above all on the mansion of the financier Rothschild. The Diet of the Confederation, whose headquarters were in Frankfurt, called in the troops from Mainz for help. But despite the presence of the soldiers, the riots continued for several days. Numerous Jews sold their property and left the city, but the blood hardly flowed.

In Darmstadt and Bayreuth, the people revolted against the Jews; Meiningen expelled them. In Karlsruhe, on the morning of August 18, the words *Death to the Jews!* appeared on the walls of the synagogue and the houses of Jewish notables. There were also scenes of disorder in Hamburg. In a small town in Bavaria, a synagogue was invaded and the scrolls of the Law were torn up.

It was also at this time that the ritual murder of Anderl von Rinn, committed by Jews many years earlier, became popular in Germany. Ritual crimes had stirred public opinion at regular intervals since the Middle Ages, with about one hundred and fifty recorded since the crime of Norwich in 1144. In 1816, the famous Brothers Grimm took up an old story in the first volume of their German fairy tales: little Anderl (Andreas) Oxner, a 3-year-old boy, had been murdered on 12 July 1462 by unknown Jews in his home village of Rinn in North Tyrol. It was in 1475 when, after the murder of Simon of Trent, the bones of little Anderl were transferred to the parish church of Rinn. The story did not become popular until 1620, when it was written down by Hippolyte Guarinoni, a physician from Halle in Saxony. In 1642, Guarinoni wrote a book about this crime entitled *Triumphal Crown of the Martyr and Epitaph of the Holy Innocent Child*. The place of the crime, Judenstein in Rinn, then became a place of pilgrimage. It was this story that was revived by the famous Brothers Grimm. In 1893, the book *Four Tyrolean Children, Victims of Hasidic Fanaticism*[571], by the Viennese priest Joseph Deckert, was published, which gave the little Anderl a new life. In 1953, after the Second World War, the feast of Anderl von Rinn was removed from the Tyrolean religious calendar by the Bishop of Innsbruck, Paul Rusch. In 1985, the bones of the martyr were even removed from the parish church, and in 1994, the worship of the child in Judenstein was banned by Bishop Reinhold Stecher. However, to no avail, as a pilgrimage to Judenstein near Rinn still takes place every year on the Sunday following 12 July.

CXVIII. The Rothschild era

At the time, the Rothschild brothers single-handedly epitomised the triumph of high finance in Europe. Moses Amschel, their father, born in 1743, was originally a clerk in the Oppenheim bank in Hanover. When he bought the old Red Shield shop in Frankfurt's *Judengasse* (Jewish Alley), he took that name and changed his surname to Rothschild (Red Shield).

From London, Nathan, one of the Rothschild sons, was a staunch opponent of Bonaparte's expansionism, which he opposed by extensively financing Wellington's actions. Wellington would have had the greatest difficulty in Spain in supplying his troops had he not received the decisive financial help he needed from the Rothschilds.

It is likely, as is commonly believed, that the Rothschild fortune was built on the defeat of the French armies at Waterloo in 1815. Informed in advance of the outcome of the battle, Nathan Rothschild would have come to the London stock exchange feigning despondency and disillusionment. This deception enabled him to buy back the securities that had been hastily sold[572]. This famous episode inspired a few verses by Victor Hugo, who

---

[571]Chassidism is the Kabbalistic and Gnostic stream of Judaism, a heretical form that has finally become normalised within present-day Judaism. Read more in detail in *Psychoanalysis of Judaism*.

[572]Some historians do indeed believe that Nathan Rothschild sold a large number of government shares, giving the impression that Britain had lost the war, causing a real panic in the stock market. So much so that, within hours, it is said that these public shares lost 98% of their value, allowing Rothschild to buy his competitors' shares at a very low price. One thing is certain: Nathan Rothschild was indeed the first to be informed in London of Wellington's victory. No one knows whether he learned of it from pigeons or spies. It also seems, although there is no trace of it, that he cautiously informed the Prime Minister, who refused to believe his information. For the latter, it was unthinkable that such news had not been communicated to him in the first place.

watched the financier pass in front of him:

> "Old man, I take off my hat! This one who passes/Made his fortune in the hour when you were shedding your blood/He was betting low and rising as we went/That our fall was deeper and surer/There had to be a vulture for our dead, he was."

On the death of the elder Amschel, his five sons divided up Europe. Nathan settled in London in 1804, James in Paris, Solomon in Vienna, Charles in Naples, while Amschel, the first-born son who bore his father's name, kept the mother house in Frankfurt. Five Rothschilds thus managed the main financial markets, keeping each other informed of what was happening here and there.

In every country in Europe, except Russia, the Rothschilds were lending money to the states, and Jewish financiers had a strong influence on the decisions of European governments. In Vienna, Salomon had become a personal friend of Metternich and had an intelligence agent working for him, one Gentz, as the Chancellor's right-hand man. The pope himself had contracted a loan with the Rothschilds. The bankers were guests in the salons of high society, and soon the families of the European aristocracy were consenting to intermarriage with these Hebrew careerists of high finance.

The Parisian revolution of 1830 catapulted the Orléans branch to the throne of France. "With the rule of Louis-Philippe, the reign of the Jew began," wrote Eduard Drumont. Rothschild placed the government loans (1830, 1831 and 1832), earning considerable sums from interest. The supreme leadership of French Judaism fell naturally to James de Rothschild, who, by the way, never became a naturalised Frenchman. The poet Alfred de Vigny wrote of the revolution of 1830: "The Jew has paid for the July revolution because he handles the bourgeois more easily than the nobles". In February 1831, the rabbis received a salary from the public purse for the first time, as did the Catholic clergy, by the way, although this was rather anecdotal in view of what was afoot behind the

---

Perhaps frustrated at not being believed, and being first and foremost a money man, Nathan Rothschild would have bought shares on the stock market, speculating on an inevitable rise as soon as the victory was announced. However, according to other historians who analysed trading volumes on the London Stock Exchange on 20 June 1815, few state funds were in circulation on that day. In reality, the growth of the Rothschild fortune had more to do with Britain's military campaigns on the Old Continent. But it would have had nothing to do with Waterloo or stock market speculation after the battle. In fact, between 1813 and 1815, the Rothschild family was responsible for half of all remittances sent from England to the rest of Europe. And its members, well spread across the continent, received a 2% commission for arranging all these transfers. This would have represented a gigantic sum for the time, given the magnitude of the funds transported to pay the armies. (NdT)

scenes.

In Spain, King Ferdinand VII had died, and since 1835 his brother Charles had opposed his widow Maria Christina, the regent of the kingdom. Spain was then torn by civil war and the government troops had difficulty resisting the Carlist assaults. Nathan de Rothschild, who feared for his lucrative mercury mines, knew that if the upright Charles came to power his concessions would be revoked. So he became the champion of Franco-British intervention. His brother James had travelled to London to see him and to organise together the British military preparations in favour of the regent and, by the way, to promote the rise of Spanish stocks. The Rothschild houses in London and Paris first speculated downwards on Spanish stocks. Within days, the Spanish share price plummeted from 70 to 37, after which the Rothschilds bought back at the lower price. Thousands of security holders lost two-thirds of their assets in the process. Loans to the Spanish government helped win the war against Don Carlos, who was forced to expatriate. The Rothschild house thus retained a world monopoly on mercury for decades[573].

After Nathan's death in July 1836, James inherited the management of the business, which he ran from his headquarters in rue Lafitte in Paris. In 1844, he negotiated a 200 million loan for the government, but this caused a great scandal. The Minister of Finance was publicly accused of sacrificing the country's interests to those of the Rothschild Bank. As the scandal continued, the banker decided to become a philanthropist. He deducted a few pesetas from the millions he had stolen from the taxpayer and ostensibly distributed them to charity.

The Chamber of Deputies then decided that the railways would be built and operated by private companies. The Northern Railways were awarded to Rothschild, which caused a new scandal as the award procedure had not been respected. But for the financiers it was another excellent deal. Everyone believed in a catastrophe when the British government suddenly sold all its shares, causing the stock to collapse. The small French shareholders sold in haste, but, forewarned by his brother in London, the Rothschilds of Paris snatched up all the shares. When calm returned, the shares returned to their normal price and the banker made a few million more[574].

The international crisis of 1840 revealed once again the influence of Jewish bankers on European governments. That year, on the fringes of the Turkish-Egyptian conflict, an incident occurred in Damascus, a partly Christian city, which caused a great stir. In 1840, a Capuchin monk, Father

---

[573] Henry Coston, *L'Europe des banquiers*, 1963
[574] Henry Coston, *Les Financiers qui mènent le monde*, 1955, 1989 edition, p. 69.

Thomas, mysteriously disappeared. His body was found in March (after the feast of Purim) in the sewers of the Jewish quarter. The French consul Ratti-Menton blamed his disappearance on members of the Jewish community and supported legal action against distinguished personalities accused of ritual murder. In Paris, Adolphe Thiers, who had just been appointed president of the Council by Louis-Philippe, expressed his solidarity with the French consul. But the financiers Fould and Rothschild intervened with all their might and promoted a press campaign against Thiers. The latter counterattacked from the rostrum of the Chamber, declaring: "You claim in the name of the Jews and I claim in the name of France!" Historian Leon Poliakov then gave us an idea of the power of the international Jewish community at the time: "The Rothschilds finally won the cause, threatening to profit from the fall in rent. Thiers had to resign. The Jews then took up the struggle for the rehabilitation of the victims of the medieval slander and obtained it thanks to British intervention. But the warning had been given, and this affair marks the origin of Jewish defence organisations, starting with the Universal Israelite Alliance[575]."

Napoleon III rather favoured the Rothschilds' competitors, the bankers Fould and Pereire, who were also Israelis. But the Rothschild bank was still in business. In 1870, when the Prussian armies invaded France, Wilhelm I, Bismarck and Moltke took up residence in Ferrières, in the Rothschild château, to receive Jules Favre and negotiate the compensation imposed on the vanquished. Their "accountant" was the Jewish financier Bleichroeder, Bismarck's right-hand man. On the French side, the negotiations were conducted by a friend of his, Alphonse Rothschild, and between them they agreed on the figure of 5 billion to be paid by France to Germany. The French Jew was strongly suspected of having suggested this amount to his German counterpart. Indeed, the benefits that the Parisian Rothschilds would receive from the French government's loan would be proportional to the size of the indemnity to be paid. Among the parliamentarians, no one dared to oppose this decision. The lead mines in Spain, nickel in New Caledonia and diamonds in South Africa remained in their hands. So the Rothschilds retained their hegemony until the end of the century. The only man to break their power in Europe would be Adolf Hitler—albeit temporarily.

---

[575] Léon Poliakov, *Los Samaritanos*, Anaya & Mario Muchnik, 1992, Madrid, p. 111. A book published on the subject in 2005, *La Sangre cristiana*, presented the confessions of a repentant former rabbi from Moldavia (*Refutación de la religión de los judíos*, 1803). He claimed that a few drops were enough. On the Damascus case, one can read that all the accused Jews confessed to the murder. Ten of them were sentenced to death, but finally pardoned thanks to the intervention of Adolphe Crémieux, Moïse Montefiore and international financiers.

CXIX. France: the anti-Semitic scare

All observers saw that Jewish financiers had acquired incredible power, but the inherent political project of Judaism was not yet understood at the time. The French were probably not sufficiently familiar with these upstarts. France counted some 70,000 Jews in 1840, two thirds of whom lived in Alsace and Lorraine. This community then grew from year to year, drawing in thousands of Jews from Germany and Austria, who were very numerous and even came from the large reservoir of the "Zone of Residence" in Russia. Jews flocked to the west of the continent, to this liberal paradise where at last everything was permitted to them. Liberalism, in politics as well as in economics, effectively favoured the Jews, who were better armed than anyone else for banking, speculation and international trade, and who had no scruples about the Goyim.

In France, as in Germany, the extreme socialist left was naturally imbued with anti-Semitism, for they saw clearly with their own eyes that gold and ducats passed mainly through Jewish hands. The very famous Charles Fourier[576] distinguished himself by writing a few pages on the subject[577]. But his disciple, the Lorraine-born Alphonse Toussenel (1803–1885), insisted even more on the question. He was the first to sound the alarm with his book *The Jews as Kings of the Age, a History of Financial Feudalism (1845)*. The work was undoubtedly successful, as it was published in a second edition in 1847. This was a fiery denunciation of the absolute domination of Jewish merchants and financiers over the economy. It must be said that the text has aged rather badly and is no longer of much interest, except for the introductory passage quoted above in the chapter on the *"conquest of Judea by the Romans"*, which ended as follows: "Ask these Jews, who earn a hundred millions a year from us, if they are so eager to see again the long-wept walls of Zion...Now, what people have been more bloodthirsty in their vengeance, more persevering in their hatred and contempt for the rest of mankind than the Jews? ... The religion of the Jewish people has inevitably made them the enemy of mankind, for the Bible is the catechism and the code of the executioner peoples[578]." And

---

[576]Charles Fourier (1772–1837) was a French utopian socialist of the first half of the 19th century and one of the fathers of cooperativism. Fourier was a critic of the economy and capitalism of his time. He was an opponent of industrialisation, urban civilisation, liberalism, the family based on marriage and monogamy, and a forerunner of feminism. The jovial character with which Fourier made some of his criticisms makes him one of the great satirists of all times. (NdT).

[577]See the book by Marc Crapez, *L'Antisémitisme de gauche au XIXe siècle*, Berg International, 124 pages, 2002.

[578]Alphonse Toussenel, *Les juifs rois de l'époque, histoire de la féodalité financière*,

Toussenel wisely concluded "that the Jews are never victims, but only as long as it takes for them to become persecutors. The state that unwisely grants them the right of citizenship creates for itself future masters, and that France, having yielded too soon to the impulses of its generous charity, is already their slave[579]."

In October 1847, the *Israelite Archives (Archives israélites)* published an article by a certain Cahen who wrote quite frankly: "The Messiah came for us on 28 February 1790, with the Declaration of the Rights of Man". In the same year, Pierre-Joseph Proudhon, the leading theoretician of socialism who opposed the Jew Karl Marx head-on, wrote in his *Notebooks*: "Rothschild, Crémieux, Marx and Fould are bad, bilious and envious people who hate us. By iron or by fire, or by expulsion, the Jew must disappear". Like Voltaire, Proudhon forgot his anti-clericalism when he came across a Jew: "The Jew is the enemy of the human race. This race must be sent back to Asia or exterminated".

Obviously, the third revolution of 1848 did not solve the problem. "France has only changed its Jews", wrote Proudhon. Indeed, James de Rothschild did not suffer much from the Parisian revolution. Only his villa in the Suresne was sacked and burned, but he received good compensation afterwards. On the other hand, he had the satisfaction of seeing two of his Jewish friends occupy ministerial portfolios in the Republican government: Crémieux in Justice and Goudchaux in Finance. The Alsatians, at least, took advantage of the occasion to raid the usurers and recover their pledges and debts with weapons in hand. They were acquitted in the city of Colmar amidst the applause of the crowd after the plea of Monsieur de Sèze, who delivered a relentless accusatory speech against the Jews. This was the last "pogrom" in France.

"In 1790," wrote Edouard Drumont in *The Jewish France*, "the Jew

---

(1845), Gabriel de Gonet Edit., Paris, 1847, Introduction, p. II, IV, IX. [I tell you that there are predatory peoples who live on the flesh of others, and that they are the merchant peoples, those who were once called Phoenicians and Carthaginians, and who are now called English, Dutch and Jews, and that the Bible is the religious code in which all these predators find justification for their tyrannies and their hoardings. The Englishman, whose main profession is to steal pieces of land in order to exploit those who cultivate it, never travels without his Bible. Cromwell, the Puritan executioner, is a biblical figure. So is Malthus, the philanthropist Malthus, who refused to give the children of the people a place at the banquet of life, who only wanted a place at this banquet for the rich, Malthus, I can assure you, was imbued with the spirit of the Bible to the marrow of his bones. In all the wars of fanaticism, it is in the name of the Bible [Old Testament, ndt] that people are slaughtered, not in the name of the Gospel of Christ". *Les juifs rois de l'époque*, p. VI. NdT]

[579]Alphonse Toussenel, *Les juifs rois de l'époque, histoire de la féodalité financière*, (1845), Gabriel de Gonet Edit., Paris, 1847, Introduction, p. IX.

arrives; under the First Republic and the First Empire, he enters, loiters, seeks his place; under the Restoration and the July Monarchy, he sits in the drawing-room; under the Second Empire, he lies in bed; under the Third Republic, he begins to drive the French out of their homes and forces them to work for him."

During the Second Empire (1852–1870), the Jews already had the power to censor or ban books or plays they did not like. Thus, in 1854, a drama entitled *The Jew of Venice,* an adaptation of Shakespeare's play, was to be performed at the *Ambigu-comique* theatre. But the horrible Jewish usurer had already been cancelled and turned into an ordinary Venetian usurer and the play was performed under the original title of *Shylock or the Merchant of Venice*[580].

In 1867, the journalist and politician Gustave Tridon, a loyal supporter of the famous Auguste Blanqui[581], wrote his book entitled *On Jewish Molochism,* which was not published until 1884 in Brussels. Gustave Tridon opposed the "Aryans" to the "Semites". He saw in Judaism a relic or survival of the bloodthirsty cult of Moloch, that bronze statue with fire inside in which the Phoenicians threw live children. Christianity was for him contrary to the Aryan tradition, so he professed atheism: "The Semites," he wrote, "are the shadow in the picture of civilisation, the evil genius of the earth. All their gifts are pests. To combat the Semitic spirit and ideas is the mission of the Indo-Aryan race".

On the side of the "conservatives", anti-Semitic resistance was then rather weak. Louis Rupert, in *The Church and the Synagogue* in 1859, accused Jews of being the main recipients of stolen goods:

"The Jew will never do business with Christians unless he is motivated by a desire to deceive them. Dreaming only of deceit against them, he receives with full and unscrupulous hands the fruit of sacrilegious robbery committed to their prejudice, and he himself teaches the malefactor to perfect his art. It would be in vain to look for a sect more dishonest, more dangerous and baneful to the Christian people than the filthy sect of the Jews. Night and day, these men do nothing but meditate upon the means of destroying and overthrowing the power of the Christians. They employ

---

[580] Édouard Drumont, *La France juive,* 1886, tome I, p. 195.

[581] Auguste Blanqui (1805– 1881) was a French revolutionary socialist, often wrongly associated with the utopian socialists. He defended essentially the same ideas as the nineteenth-century socialist movement and was one of the non-Marxist socialists. After 1830, while still a student, Blanqui realised that revolution could only express the will of the people through violence. His radicalism earned him imprisonment for most of his life. In 1880 he published the newspaper *Ni Dieu ni Maître (Neither God nor Master),* the title of which became a reference and a motto for the anarchist movement. Karl Marx considered Blanqui "the head and heart of the proletarian party in France". (NdT).

every possible kind of fraud, and insinuate themselves everywhere, with every apparent sign of the most attractive benevolence, friendship, or commerce[582]."

Father Ratisbonne, a former Jew of Alsatian origin who became a Catholic priest, wrote in 1868 in *The Jewish Question*: "Thanks to their know-how and possessed by the instinct of domination, the Jews have gradually invaded all the roads leading to wealth, dignity and power. They control the stock exchange, the press, the theatre, literature, the administration, the great means of communication by land and sea, and by the ascendancy of their fortune and their genius, they now hold Christian society as a whole in their grip, as in a net[583]."

But it was not until 1869 that a book finally informed the French in a clear way about the dreadful misdeeds of Jewish power. In his 550-page work entitled *The Jew, Judaism and the Judaisation of the Christian peoples*, Roger Gougenot des Mousseaux, Gentleman of the Chamber of King Charles X, analysed the Jewish problem in depth. This book contains many relevant elements that allow us to grasp the profound nature of Judaism, even if it is sometimes a little old-fashioned and tiresome to read. Gougenot, who observed the German and Italian unification, wrote with good sense: "And before our eyes, from one end of the earth to the other, the political world, the economic and commercial world, led or directed by the societies of the occult world whose princes are the Jews, were set in motion in unison by the great cosmopolitan unity[584]. This is the name, in modern parlance, for the system from which would come the abolition of all frontiers, of all homelands, or, if you will, the replacement of the particular homeland of each people by a great and universal homeland which would be the homeland of all men. Does not this unity, then, which claims a head, prepare, in its formation, the prodigious advent of a single supreme ruler in whom the Jews might see the Messiah[585]?"

---

[582]Louis Rupert, *L'Église et la Synagogue*, Paris, 1859, p. 208-2011, in Abbé Chabeauty.

[583]R.P. Ratisbonne, *La Question juive*, Paris, 1868, p. 9, in L'Abbé Chabeauty, *Les Juifs, nos maîtres*, 1882, p. 167, in Mgr Henri Delassus, *La Conjuration antichrétienne III*, Desclée De Brouwer, Lille, 1910, p. 1156.

[584] "May the whole of humanity, docile to the philosophy of the *universal Israelite Alliance,* unhesitatingly follow the Jew, a truly cosmopolitan people, the only one that can be so, and which from today governs the intelligence and the interests of the most progressive nations; may this humanity look towards the reconstituted metropolis of the world and may this metropolis be neither London, nor Paris, nor Rome, but Jerusalem, raised from the ruins, a new Jerusalem, "called to great destinies" and which is "at once the city of the past and the future"." Isidore, Grand Rabbi of France, *Archives israelites*, XI, p. 495; 1868, in Gougenot des Mousseaux. *The Jew, Judaism and the Judaisation of Christian peoples*, p. 336.

[585]Roger Gougenot des Mousseaux. *The Jew, Judaism and the Judaisation of Christian*

For the first time the Jewish project of world unification was pointed out—although perhaps still too concisely.

CXX. The policy of interference in Romania

The Jewish power, comfortably installed in Europe, especially in Austria, France and England, was working to destabilise the countries where the Jews did not yet enjoy "equal rights", i.e. the right for the predators to establish their ruthless rule. At that time, only Russia and Romania were still resisting.

The Crimean War (1854–1856) against Russia, waged by Victorian England and Napoleon III's France, had been a war for "democracy". The pretext had been the occupation of the Romanian provinces seized from the Ottoman Empire and the supposed threat of Russian control of the Straits. In reality, however, the aim was to weaken an authoritarian monarchy in the name of "human rights" and the "emancipation" of the Jews. According to Duke Ernest de Cobourg, who recounted it in his *Memoirs*, Rothschild would have told him that any sum would be available for a war against Tsarist Russia that resisted Jewish power.

After the Crimean War, the 1856 Treaty of Paris ended the Russian protectorate. The principalities of Moldavia and Wallachia were united in 1859, forming a provisional government that offered the crown of the new Romania to the young German prince Carol Hohenzollern Sugmaringen. This new state was home to a large number of Jews from the Ukraine and Galicia, who had no civic rights, as in neighbouring Russia, although this did not prevent them from exploiting, plundering and extorting money from the common people at will. But they also needed political domination. On the day in July 1866 when the question of Jewish emancipation was discussed in the Romanian Parliament, anti-Jewish riots broke out in Bucharest and the new synagogue was destroyed. The same happened in the city of Iasi, where a large Jewish community resided.

In the spring of 1867, Interior Minister Ion Bratianu signed a decree

---

peoples, pdf version. Translated into English by Professor Noemí Coronel and the invaluable collaboration of the team of Nacionalismo Católico Argentina, 2013, p. 500. ["Everything is ready for the great cosmopolitan unity of which this man must be the expression. — When the work of de-Christianising the world is finished, will it be able to accept as master a hypnotist of Jewish race? — Examples of dominators rejected and then unanimously accepted. — Examples of men who suddenly came out of nowhere to rise to the pinnacle in times of crisis. — With the speed of ideas and events, how can we be surprised that in the heart of Judea, the man who would realise the ideas of cosmopolitan sovereignty with Jews as his apostles should emerge?" *The Jew, Judaism and the Judaisation of Christian peoples,* p. 497].

prohibiting Jews from staying in rural villages, owning hotels or cabarets and renting property. Many Jews were expelled from villages, outside Romanian borders. These expulsions culminated in the drowning of two Jews in Galati on 30 June 1867.

This was intolerable to Adolphe Crémieux, then head of the French Jewish community. Adolphe Crémieux, whose real name was Isaac-Jacob Crémieux, had been Minister of Justice in 1848. A lawyer and president of the Consistoire Israelite de Paris, he was a Frenchman from the south of France, "perfectly integrated", as they say. In 1860, Crémieux and his friends founded the Alliance Israelite Universelle in Paris with the aim of helping Jews around the world obtain civil rights in all countries. Crémieux used his great influence in political and financial circles to defend the interests of his fellow Romanians. In 1866, he had already gone to Russia: "In Saratov, a group of Jews was accused of ritual murder. Adolphe Crémieux went there and got them acquitted[586]", wrote Leon Poliakov.

In 1870, Crémieux was appointed Minister of Justice of the new French Republic. His first measure was to automatically grant French nationality to his fellow Algerians, some 40,000 individuals, just when Prussian troops were still occupying the national territory. This decision aroused the Muslims' legitimate resentment against the French.

Crémieux then turned his attention to his compatriots in Romania. In Western Europe, the mainstream press, controlled by Jewish finance, was indignant, kicking and screaming ad infinitum. In Vienna, Paris and London, newspapers published the "atrocities" committed by the Romanians. There was a wave of articles defending these poor Jews persecuted for no reason. The Israelite Alliance organised meetings, contacted ministers and so on. It was absolutely essential to force the Romanian government to grant civil rights to the Jews.

Crémieux travelled to Bucharest, accompanied by another illustrious and indefatigable defender of the Jewish cause, 83-year-old "Sir" Moses Montefiore. This famous Jewish banker had been elected Mayor of London in 1837 and in the same year Queen Victoria, who had just ascended the English throne, elevated him to the rank of "Sir"; in 1846, he received the title of Baron from Her Majesty.

At the very moment when the new Romanian constitution was being discussed in Bucharest, Crémieux appeared there. He proposed to the government to grant civil and political equality to the Romanian Jews in exchange for a loan of 25 million at a preferential rate of interest. The offer was so attractive that the cabinet hesitated. Fortunately, that day the Romanian people, galvanised by the great anti-Semitic newspaper *Trumpet*

---

[586] Léon Poliakov, *Histoires des crises d'identités juives*, Austral, 1994, p. 67.

Carpatilor, invaded the Palace and razed the Jewish quarter to the ground, destroying the synagogue, thus forcing the withdrawal of the project at the last gasp. From now on, Romania would attract the vengeful hostility of the Jewish international, which would lie in wait for the first opportunity to strike again.

Crémieux and Montefiore listened to King Carol's promises, but the riots and expulsions continued. Several incidents, brutal beatings and expulsions *manu militari*—provoked by Jews stealing holy vessels from Orthodox churches and throwing them into cesspools—led Napoleon III, spurred on by the recriminations of the Israelite Alliance, to intervene directly and harshly in Romania. From then on, the Romanians also reproached the Jews for trying to drive a wedge between them and their best ally, France, even though the natural sympathies between the two nations were reciprocal. The trade treaty facilitating exports and imports with the European powers was not ratified by Austria. Just as France, England and Italy, managed by Jewish finance, had backed out of their respective agreements.

An anti-Jewish riot broke out again on 24 January 1872 in Isma'il, after a Jew robbed the cathedral. The scenes of looting spread to the town of Cahul on 30 January and lasted for several days. On 6 February 1872 and 4 April 1873, two new laws were passed: one concerning the sale of tobacco and the other concerning the sale of spirits. The fact is that these laws first affected the large Jewish wholesalers, just as the law of 1867 on hotels and cabarets had aimed to curb pimping and prostitution, largely carried out by Hebrew criminals. Leon Gambetta, who ruled republican France, told the Romanian delegate that France would not recognise Romania until that country granted civil rights to all Jews without distinction. In 1874, it turned out that England was ruled by a Jew, Benjamin Disraeli, who headed the English government until April 1880. Disraeli belonged to the Conservative Party and was one of Queen Victoria's close friends.

In 1878, Romania, which had participated in the Russo-Turkish war, gained complete freedom and became a kingdom. At the international congress in Berlin in the same year, the fate of the Romanian Jews was discussed at length. Recognition of the independence of Serbia, Bulgaria and Romania, freed from the Turkish yoke, was made conditional on the granting of "equality" to the Jews of these countries. The Western powers, which supported this liberation, demanded in return that the Jews be promoted to the status of citizens. But the Romanian minister Bratianu resisted, replying that it was out of the question to grant citizenship rights to Jews who ran brothels and cabarets where adulterated spirits were served. Finally, the Romanians signed, but with all possible amendments to get around this law, and, by dint of diplomacy, made their system of individual naturalisation prevail, which only benefited a thousand Jews for a period of ten years. It was not until 1923 that a new constitution extended Romanian citizenship to all Jewish residents.

But despite all these obstacles, Jews had some interest in living in Romania with the Romanians, for by the end of the 19th century the Jewish population had grown to 300,000. In Moldova, the trading houses were owned by Jews in a proportion of 70–94%, and most of the doctors in Iasi were Jewish. This led the government to take further measures, such as limiting the places granted to Jews in schools and universities.[587]

In retaliation, in 1885, the French-Jewish government countered with a 50% customs duty on all Romanian products. It was a veritable trade blockade.

On the other side of the strait, in the Ottoman Empire, influential Jews remained close to the Sultan, most of them acting in the shadows behind a Muslim mask[588].

A few years earlier, in 1862, a great popular novel written in Greek and entitled *The Devil in Turkey* was published in London. The action takes place in Constantinople under the reign of Sultan Mahmud in 1827. In Chapter XXVI entitled *The Communion of the Jews*, author Stephanos Xenos shows the Sultan and his Greek advisor, Daniel Kokkalas, lost in the narrow streets of the Jewish quarter of Balat. Suddenly, a group of enraged Greeks enter the scene in pursuit of Jews who have just abducted a young Greek girl and are holding her in a synagogue. The Sultan, eager to "see with his own eyes these abominable things that the Jews do", is encouraged to follow the Greeks who force their way into the synagogue. It is there that Sultan Mahmud finds out that the slanders circulating about the Jews are true:

"As soon as they separate a child from its parents, they feed it with pine nuts, walnuts and the like. When the unfortunate victim gets fat enough, they put it in a big barrel filled with nails inside. Then they roll the barrel to drain the child's blood. They bury the corpse in secret and share the blood in the synagogues for communion. There are two reasons why they do this horrible and abominable thing. They say: "If Jesus is really the expected messiah, we obey his command: 'Take and drink, this is my blood shed for you'. If not, we mock him as he deserves" (page 384).

In fact, the Sultan finally discovered the fake barrel with the body of a child in the cellar of Rabbi Benvista. Stephanos Xenos added the following dialogue between the sultan and the rabbi: "So you have had this horrible custom for centuries. —For centuries, Your Majesty, but not all Jews, only

---

[587] Lucien Rebatet, *Je Suis Partout*, 15 April 1938
[588] On the role of the Donmehs (crypto-Jews) in Turkey, see *Psychoanalysis of Judaism* and *The Mirror of Judaism*.

one heresy[589]."

CXXI. Jewish criminality in Germany

As in times past, Jews were vastly overrepresented among thugs and criminals. A.F. Thiele, a high official and royal commissioner of Prussia, published in 1841 in Berlin an extraordinary two-volume study entitled *Die jüdischen Gauner in Deutschland* (*The Jewish Criminals in Germany*), *ihre Taktik, ihre Eigentümlichkeit, ihre Sprache* (*Their Tactics, Their Peculiarity, Their Language*). Due to his duties, Thiele had noticed that the biggest crooks and the most dangerous criminals came from the Jewish community[590]. After consulting extensive documentation, police files and records, Thiele described the "atmosphere", the mentality of the criminals, the nomadism of the Jews, their identity theft and the extent of their criminal activities. His aim was to facilitate the work of German policemen, to show how organised gangs functioned and to provide investigators with a consistent working tool. The author denied being anti-Jewish: his work was simply that of a criminologist. The first edition of the book ("auf Kosten des Verfassers", published at the author's expense) sold out within two months[591].

In Germany, Thiele wrote at the beginning of his work, there are Jewish and Christian criminals, but there is "an over-representation of Jews among the criminals...Although fewer in number, the Jewish rogues are the most dangerous, both for their intelligence and skill and for their agility in carrying out their crimes". They also used a particular jargon, full of Hebrew expressions. In one chapter of the book (pages 195 to 328 of Volume I), the language used by these criminals to avoid being understood by Christians was analysed. The author referred to old books that discussed this language, in particular a small dictionary of the language of thieves from 1520, printed in Frankfurt, the *Liber vagatorum, which* contained 200

---

[589] This was confirmed in February 2007 by Professor Ariel Toaff. Excerpt from the Jewish review *Yod, Revue des études modernes et contemporaines hébraïques et juives*, issue 35, 1992, p. 79.
[590] Our 2008 book, *The Jewish Mafia*, is an eye-opener for even the most sceptical.
[591] We would like to thank here Marc, an Alsatian friend, for the French translation of the main passages of A. F. Thiele's book. Another important book on the Jewish criminal world is J. Keller and Hanns Andersen's *Der Jude als Verbrecher*, published in Berlin and Leipzig in 1937. The authors took up part of Thiele's book. They reported that the noun *Gauner* was not of German origin. Its origin would be *Jauner*, a transformation of the Hebrew word *Janah* (to deceive, to swindle). Andersen cited another German author, W. Giese, who had studied criminality in Prussia at the end of the 19th century.

words. Also the *Expertus in truphis*, from 1623; and *Die Rotwelsche Grammatic*, published in 1620, among others[592].

Jewish criminals, the author informed us, "had been there for centuries, probably as long as there had been Jews in Germany. The *Liber vagatorum* of 1520 already referred to their criminal activities. In the 18th century, two sources mentioned Jewish swindlers: Wherever they appeared, they were seen presenting themselves as rich bankers or merchants; dressed with refinement, fingers covered with gold rings, with gold watches in their pockets, this is how they appeared in the cities; and always with the best passports and documents". (t. I, p. 11.)

These ruffians always presented themselves as traders because in their language "*handeln*" (to trade) is synonymous with "to steal" (*stehlen*). Their main rendezvous were the fairs and markets of Leipzig and Frankfurt. "Much more than the Christian crooks, the Jewish crooks used to be in permanent contact with each other." They were a mafia, with their own principles and community ties. "When they met, even if they had never met before, they became *Chawern* (comrades) and robbed together." (p. 16). Throughout Germany, Jewish criminals knew each other by name or by sight.

The Jewish scoundrels were one big family. They married among themselves, and the wife of the Jewish criminal had her own role. When her husband was arrested, she would erase the evidence, go to the judge and make "a scene of weeping and wailing with her children, explaining to the judge that her husband was innocent and the victim of a miscarriage of justice".

"When they are arrested, Thiele wrote, they have one big rule they never break: always deny everything. They always deny inflexibly. The Jewish criminal is unsurpassed in skill and impudence and in the art of lying. "If you have done something, deny it!" is their cardinal rule." (p. 17). Jewish criminals call "*brav*" the one who always denies the facts to the authorities and never denounces his accomplices.

They constituted a closed society and were bitter enemies of laws and institutions. "The word "fellow-citizen" is unknown to them, for they have

---

[592] A study on the language and speech of criminals had been carried out by the Berlin police in 1831. A. F. Thiele seems to have been inspired by it. [Such communication between Jews and non-Jews in the cellars of society found expression in the fact that the jargon of the German underworld was essentially Yiddish, Jewish. The whole underworld made it its own, simply as a secret language, and precisely the Hebrew elements of Yiddish spoken by the Jews were accepted with special gusto as code words by the non-Jewish underworld, as those languages with which prisoners communicate among themselves." Gershom Scholem, *Everything is Kabbalah. Dialogue with Jorg Drews, followed by Ten ahistorical theses on Kabbalah*, Editorial Trotta, Madrid, 2001, p. 22].

only comrades. Their aim is to harm others, whether Jews or Christians; to achieve this aim is their whole reason for living[593]."

In the early 19th century, justice was manifestly lenient. Defendants were quickly released from prison, often pardoned or released for lack of evidence. Moreover, escapes were frequent. Sometimes, these criminals were deported to the border. They continued their activities elsewhere in Germany or returned to their favourite hunting ground. The courts hardly succeeded in curbing their criminal activities by imprisoning them for a few years. There was, therefore, no special severity towards Jewish malefactors.

In 1807, Reuben Abraham, who had been convicted several times, had committed two house raids with his gang in Wolfenbuttel, during which the owners had been mistreated and seriously injured. The leader of the gang, Rammelsberg, had been executed by decapitation in 1815 (p. 55 of volume II).

In 1818, Kirsh Abraham stole 1,500 silver thalers[594] from a shopkeeper. He was arrested and received 90 lashes and 10 strokes of the cane. Four years later, with his gang (Gutkind, Rosenthal, Schwerin, Reinhardt and Manheim), he reoffended by stealing 2,500 thalers from a landowner who was violently beaten; the victim died of his wounds. They were arrested and sentenced to 20 years in prison, but Kirsch Abraham managed to escape again.

One is struck by the number of these Jewish criminals and the scale of their activities: each had been arrested once, twice, three or even four times, convicted and imprisoned repeatedly; all were repeat offenders. The author gave the example of a Jew named Marcus Abraham, who preferred the life of a malefactor, or of a certain Jacob Herz, an equally hardened and recidivist Dutch Jew.

In 1810, Philipp Aron Anhalt took part in the armed robbery of a

---

[593] In connection with this behaviour you can read the chapter on the Sabbatean (Hasidic) Jews and the doctrine of evil in our book *Psychoanalysis of Judaism*.

[594] The thaler is an ancient silver coin that first appeared in the early 16th century and circulated first in Europe and then around the world for nearly four hundred years. Its relatively large size and weight varied somewhat over time, and its initial popularity was linked to the development of silver mines in the lands of the Holy Roman Empire and the power of the Spanish Empire. The Prussian taler (*Preussenthaler*) was first used as the currency of the Kingdom of Prussia in 1701, with its specific characteristics. After 1815, it was Prussia's economic and financial response to the Austrian Empire, which took the form of the Treaty of Monetary Union of the North German states signed in 1834 (Zollverein). In the mid-19th century, the thaler fell into disuse. The Austro-Hungarian Empire abandoned it in favour of the florin, while Germany adopted the mark, which followed the decimal system (3 marks to 1 thaler). It was demonetised in 1908. The word thaler was used in Germany until the late 1920s.

Magdeburg jeweller during the Leipzig Fair. His accomplices were two other Jews, Samuel Reiss and Magnus Aron Stein, and together they made off with a fortune in diamonds. In 1811, they stole 11,000 ducats at the Leipzig fair, after which they were arrested and sentenced to 4 years unconditional imprisonment (p. 82 of volume II).

In 1810, a trial took place in Mainz against a gang of Jewish malefactors. In 1815, another trial was held in Munster, but the Jews had fled.

Page 74 we read the case of Moses Levin Alyenburger: "He wears gold rings on his fingers. His face shows every conceivable sign of cunning, malice, lying and deceit... When we searched his body, we found several gold coins in his mouth." He had managed to steal a haul of 2500 thalers during a fair in Braunschweig in 1816. He was continually arrested, sentenced to light sentences or released for lack of evidence and kept reoffending elsewhere. He was constantly changing cities: Breslau, Berlin, Brauschweig, etc. He confessed to 48 robberies with violence.

The author then cited a study conducted in Kassel between 1816 and 1818, based on police investigations of 650 Jewish criminals. Many had fled to Austria and Bohemia after escaping from German prisons. From there, they went to commit their misdeeds in Prussia and Saxony. Many others went as far as Holland and Amsterdam.

The case of Moses Levin Löwenthal particularly attracted the attention of the Royal Commissioner (Volume I, pages 21 to 69): In Berlin, in 1830, numerous merchants had been robbed and the amounts stolen had been "enormous": 9000 talers stolen from one merchant, 2500 talers stolen from another, etc. The culprits were arrested. They were Jewish thieves: the Nelky brothers, who collaborated with an accomplice named Moses Levin Löwenthl, a merchant who was an expert in all kinds of swindles. The police found the loot hidden in flower pots and under the floor in their house. Several witnesses identified them positively, but this did not prevent them from firmly denying everything. Levin Löwenthal then proposed to "rat out" the names of the members of the Jewish criminal gang operating around Berlin in exchange for the promise of a pardon. The Jew accepted the deal and confessed to another 37 burglaries in 2 years in Berlin, 6 of which were committed without accomplices. In addition, he denounced some thirty Jewish criminals, fourteen of whom were immediately arrested. The Nelky brothers and another Jew named Samuel Moses Sachse managed to escape.

Among those arrested was a criminal named Samuel Jonas who had committed several crimes abroad and was hiding in Berlin in 1816. He had married a Jewish woman with whom he had eight children. Another was called Joseph Adolph Rosenthal, nicknamed "the fat man". He was a robber who had already been arrested and imprisoned in 1820 in Posen. He had worked for a police service before falling back into illegality. All these "good people" formed a gang called the *Chawrusse* or *Chäwre* (Berlin Jewish mafia). The *Chawrusse* was a criminal organisation, a mafia with its rules, its specific functioning, its financing and its solidarity pacts.

On 11 May 1831, Levin Löwenthal was released after posting bail. Before his release, he confessed to twenty-eight other violent robberies. Since he refused to denounce all his accomplices, he did not receive the agreed pardon. In June 1831, thirty-four Jews were behind bars. All of them denied the facts, which was a serious problem for the police, since in many cases no truly incriminating evidence had been discovered. One of them, Hirsh Salomon Wohlauer, had already been arrested and imprisoned for swindling in the autumn of 1830. Furious at having been betrayed by Löwenthal, he decided to tell the truth to the judge for the first time in his life. On 27 October 1831, he confessed to 54 violent robberies, incriminating his informer, who was arrested again.

But on the other hand, the testimonies were piling up against Rosenthal (the "fat man"), and he finally collapsed. In tears, he admitted to more than 200 robberies and burglaries, as well as 36 different robberies between 1799 and 1812 in Berlin, Magdeburg and Posen (the former Polish city of Poznan, recently annexed by Prussia). The number of robberies and crimes was so great that the Prussian Public Prosecutor's Office and the Ministry of the Interior decided to set up a commission of enquiry to collect and record all the criminal acts of this unprecedented mafia. They used Rosenthal, who agreed to infiltrate the Jewish milieu.

Joseph Adolph Rosenthal was born in 1778. He had begun his career as a petty chicken thief, frequently convicted and always a repeat offender (pages 123–131). His criminal record was impressive. Between two robberies and arrests, Rosenthal had married a Christian woman who had converted to Judaism.

In November 1813, Rosenthal and his accomplices robbed a priest by night, Abbot Friedrychowitsch in the Duchy of Posen. Rosenthal, Simon Reinhardt, Salomon Levin Alyenburger, etc., had entered the presbytery, but the abbot and his vicar were awakened by the noise of the thieves. Friedrychowitsch, still young and strong, managed to knock out the Jew Simon Reinhardt. The other robbers burst in and the two clergymen were beaten, tied up and tortured. The priest then revealed where the parish savings were to be found: behind the altar. But this booty seemed insufficient and they tortured the two victims again, although they were unable to extract any more confessions from them. The next day, the two clergymen were found bound "and close to death" (t. I, p. 134). The priest died of his wounds shortly afterwards.

In 1816, Rosenthal had been caught at night in Memel in flagrante delicto robbing a shop with several Jewish accomplices and was sentenced to 40 lashes and 6 months in prison. In November and December 1818, several robberies were reported in Silesia and Rosenthal was again implicated in the cases. He then left behind him a trail of looting, breaking into peasants' houses with or without violence. On the night of 31 March to 1 April 1823, the Gusow savings bank was robbed, during which Rosenthal and Wolff Strasburger stole 300 talers. There were many more crimes, but always from Jews to Christians: innkeepers, peasants, royal customs posts, craftsmen, priests, savings banks, merchants, stockbreeders, etc.

Thiele had this to say about Rosenthal: "He is the strangest man I have ever met. His appearance was not at all consistent with his criminal record. There was nothing false or twisted about his face. He looked good and flawless. Wherever he went he made a good impression because he was likeable." (t.I, p. 131).

The lair of this mafia was in the region of Posen (Poznan), which had been infested with Jews since ancient times when it was part of the kingdom of Poland: "Around 1800, an investigation had already been opened in Posen against a large gang of Jewish gangsters. At that time, the Prussian part of Poland, known as South Prussia, was full of Jews who, having neither homeland nor domicile, led a nomadic life, living together in the middle of the fields. Their activities escaped the control of the authorities" (p. 43). (p. 43).

The consequence of this situation had been the publication of a government decree forbidding all Jews to reside in the villages. So, for example, sixteen families of bandits living in a village called Grochnow had been forced into exile. The bandits had then settled in Betsche, a small town of 1200 inhabitants where police surveillance was less strict. In 1832, this small town of Betsche was known to the police in Berlin and throughout Germany as the haunt of Jewish bandits and their families.

Between 1806 and 1815, this region of Posen had been integrated into the new grand-duchy of Warsaw, created by Bonaparte, and criminal activities quickly exploded. The Jews feared Prussian rule far more than the Polish administration, which seemed less organised and less able to investigate and suppress their activities, so that an additional forty Jewish families ended up settling in Betsche. Jews then accounted for a quarter of the population of the municipality, which had acquired a terrible reputation: Betsche became "the capital, the focal point of criminal activities, not only of Prussia, but of the whole of Germany". Fugitives were taken in, hidden and protected.

It was not easy to clean up the site due to the lack of hard-to-gather irrefutable evidence and clan solidarity. But the Prussian police pulled out all the stops:

On 19 January 1832, the German commissars and policemen left Berlin with all the necessary judicial documents for the searches, and on 20

January 1832, at four o'clock in the morning—in the middle of the Sabbath (for on that day it was easier to locate the Jews in their homes)—the arrests began. The entire city had been cordoned off by the gendarmes, assisted by the local authorities in order to prevent the Jews from escaping; all the houses of the thugs were searched by the police, and the information gathered enabled many other arrests to be made, even in cities such as Frankfurt on the Oder.

In all, fifty-nine people were arrested in the Duchy of Posen; twenty-two in Frankfurt/Oder; all of them were sent to Berlin for questioning. In their homes, the policemen found large amounts of cash (12,000 talers, an astronomical sum) as well as countless valuables. Ten other Jewish criminals were arrested. They had stolen 11,000 talers in a robbery in Strehlen in 1830. The operation had been a resounding success.

In the same year, during the annual fair in Frankfurt on the Oder, there was—for once—not a single theft. (p. 49).

Other identical commissions were set up in Magdeburg and in Austria, because there, too, "a large number of Jews who had been sentenced to imprisonment were in hiding".

On 16 January 1833, the police launched a second raid on the instructions of the felon Rosenthal, who continued to inform on his comrades. The raid ended on 15 March and resulted in the recovery of a large number of stolen objects of great value. Twenty-three Jews ended up in prison.

Operations multiplied in Germany in an unprecedented way. More than five hundred people—almost exclusively Jews—were arrested. After each arrest and search, the police found new, unexplored leads that led to new networks. The number of police officers employed in the investigations then reached a proportion never before seen in the country. According to the police records of the investigations (p. 132–192), Löwenthal, Rosenthal and their accomplices admitted to having committed more than 800 robberies, break-ins, burglaries, thefts, robberies and various swindles during their criminal careers.

In total: 520 people were condemned, "the vast majority of whom were Jews" (p. 50). Michel David Cohn, Elias Dubsky, Engelmann, August Froehlich, Zaremba, Meyer Friedberg, Salomon Fürstenheim, Baruch Glanz, Christian Herbe, Julius Jacobi, Marcus Joel, Jette Klein, Loefer Meissner, etc. Twenty-nine had managed to flee to a foreign country. Among these 520 knaves, there were only nineteen Christians and three baptised Jews. These Jews must still have had a lot of gold and cash hidden somewhere, for they had been able to pay the large bonds required for their release.

The impudence of these Jews," wrote the author, speaking in their Hebrew language of knaves, "went very far. During interrogations, when they were in their cells, they did not hesitate to shout at each other to exchange information about the state of the investigation and to devise versions to tell the police. Right under the noses of the investigators". (p. 62). But many of them received harsh prison sentences.

The techniques employed by Jewish criminals were diverse and varied. There was breaking and entering, whether daily or at night, classical burglary, pickpocketing, theft during currency exchanges. This last type of crime was committed "almost exclusively by Jews". They used pickpocketing techniques to steal a few gold coins during the exchange, without the victim noticing. To do this, the Jewish crook would arrive in a town, go to a wealthy merchant, a bank or a bureau de change and ask to exchange gold for local currency. By sleight of hand, the Jew managed to recover some of these gold coins. He would then leave town and the offended party would not realise it until later. "They have a monopoly on these crimes," wrote Thiele, and "surpass the Christian rogues in skill" (p. 90). (p. 90).

Another quite typical type of Jewish crime consisted of going around the countryside and swindling the peasants, selling them objects far above their value, making them believe that a certain object was gold when in fact it was only gold; or selling fake silverware for real silverware, and so on.

Another classic technique: a Jewish man, elegantly dressed, would arrive in a village posing as a foreigner with a strong French or Italian accent. He would explain that he had lost all his money and was in a hurry to return to his distant place of origin. The rich traveller was therefore forced to sell one of his goods (a pot or a gold watch, in fact a trinket). The peasant then believed that he was making an excellent bargain by buying the item for a modest sum, and also felt that he was doing a good deed. The Jew would then continue on his way to another village where he would swindle another villager.

Jewish hoodlums were born that way: "Their parents are thieves or hoodlums, their grandparents were thieves or hoodlums, their great-grandparents were thieves or hoodlums, and so this characteristic is passed down from generation to generation. At the age of 14, the child leaves the family home, where he has only seen and learned bad things. He then begins his career as a delinquent. He will have to prove himself worthy of his teachers and his ancestors". (t. I, p. 99).

The problem was that all these Jewish criminals had children, so this criminal environment was naturally perpetuated. It was necessary, A. F. Thiele, to break the ties between parents and children, even if this seemed "humanly painful". The children of criminals were to be taken in by an institute set up by the government to re-educate them. The fact is that, as adults, they were "absolutely incorrigible". The sanctions of the law never changed them (p. 101). In fact, the repressive judicial system was powerless to neutralise them definitively. For this reason, in 1802, the Prussian government had made an agreement with Russia to deport these Jewish criminals to Siberia, where fifty-eight criminals were sentenced to life imprisonment.

Another way to alleviate the problem was to prevent Jews from trading, as had already been done in Saxony. Ninety out of 100 Jews are engaged in trade," explained Thiele, "and at least two-thirds of them are actually engaged in illegal activities.

For them, trade was a pretext, a cover, a legal façade to hide their trafficking. Hence the need to forbid them to trade and travel freely. "Any Jew who travels through Germany with his knapsack on his back, spending most of his time on the roads, in markets and inns, is more or less in contact with the rabble of crooks and thieves". (t. I, p. 103, 104). "They will only bend under the yoke of public authority: they should be breaking stones, chopping wood or working in the fields".

The Jewish evildoers were also "unbelievably pious". Some had been influenced by the atheistic movement of that century and considered that stealing on the Sabbath was not a sin, but those who thought so were very rare. Most were very orthodox and forbade themselves to steal on the Sabbath; but they stole unscrupulously six days a week. Theft and larceny were their trade. It was for them an activity like any other, and they could not even imagine living in any other way. On the other hand, they had great respect for the rabbi, the Sabbath and the synagogue. On the Sabbath they stayed at home and did not move. They went to the synagogue and "prayed to the god of Israel to bless their business". (t. I, p. 118).

Alsace was then one of the main bases of the Jewish mafia. In 1842, two individuals were investigated in Switzerland, in Frauenfeld, for a case of swindling. The Jewish mobsters had German and Swiss passports and used Alsace as a base to commit their acts in Switzerland and in several southern German states. The police report from the Swiss canton of *Thurgau zu Frauenfeld in Switzerland* had enabled A.F. Thiele to summarise the case (volume II, p. 1–19). He had made his debut with two Jews by swindling a Swiss innkeeper and robbing him of all his savings. After reporting them, the policemen had managed to identify the two thieves. They were Gabriel Leval (actually called David Meier), Heinrich Moritz and Abraham Gottschaur, who were known for their swindling in currency exchange operations and who were identified by the innkeeper. Gottschaur's French passport indicated that he was born in Toul, in the Meurthe department. They told the police that they were on a journey from Bavaria via Basel to Zurich, but their testimonies were contradictory. Finally, they denied everything "en bloc".

Imprisoned on remand, Gottschaur and Moritz revealed certain information to a 14-year-old Jewish boy who shared a cell with them: Jakob

Isak (his real name was Jakob Lazarus), a resident of Rixheim, near Mulhouse. The latter, interrogated later, divulged what the other two had recklessly confessed to him. The criminals then asked their wives to provide them with an alibi, claiming that they were both at home when the events took place. Six Jews from Altkirch (Alsace) came forward as witnesses. Nanette Levi from Hegenheim, Florette Mauss and Magdalena Joseph also came forward, all willing to testify falsely in order to clear Gottschaur and Moritz.

In April, Gottschaur finally confessed everything, revealing all the names he knew and recounting his entire life in the process. He was originally from Bade and was actually called Joseph Hirschberg. He had two illegitimate children by a Christian woman, Elisa Pikart from Zurich. He had wanted to marry her, but her family had objected. He was expelled from his home, but a rabbi in Bischofsheim agreed to marry them (despite the prohibition against marrying a Christian) in exchange for "a large sum of money" (p. 10). He subsequently persuaded a French Jew from Toul named Abraham Gottschaur to sell him his own passport for five francs. In Alsace, he met other Jews who formed a gang of gangsters. Joseph had decided to give away the whole scheme, but only as long as his family in Alsace was protected from the other criminals. It was in this way that Gottschaur confessed the swindle to the Swiss tavern keeper. A few days later, Moritz also confessed (his real name was Samuel Moses). These two Jews gave away no less than seventy names of Jews who were part of the same network of criminals.

They had had to leave Germany because they were being chased by the police and had taken refuge in Alsace. There they met and planned their activities. It was a community of about a hundred individuals who shared the proceeds of their thefts. There was no leader. In Alsace, on the other hand, these Jewish criminals did not commit crimes in order to avoid problems with the local authorities and to be able to continue their business in the neighbouring areas: Switzerland, Baden, Württemberg and Bavaria. They travelled in pairs or threes, with their families (wives and children), sleeping in inns. As soon as they felt in danger, they fled to Alsace to hide with their loot. The women helped them get out of prison by providing them with imaginary alibis.

We can see from A. F. Thiele's study that already at that time the ideology of human rights had become the orthodoxy of democratic society, and that any divergent thinking was considered morally monstrous: "I know of a fairground village," wrote Thiele, "where the police chased a Jew for a swindle, and called him a 'Jew' because they didn't know what other word to use. They called him 'Jew' because they didn't know what other word to use. And what happened? The police were flooded with protests against the use of the word "Jew", and there were threats to boycott the fair." (t. II, p. 43-55). "Civic equality is demanded, and anyone who opposes it is a barbarian, an obscurantist incapable of recognising and appreciating the sacred human rights, written in letters of gold in the book of history."

CXXII. Austria-Hungary under the Jewish Boot

Napoleon III's policy in favour of Italian unification had been to the detriment of Austria, defeating it at Magenta and Solferino (June 1859) and expelling it from northern Italy. Weakened, Catholic Austria was again defeated at the Battle of Sadová in 1866 by Protestant Prussia, which was to take control of the German Confederation. The following year, in 1867, Hungarian claims forced the Austrians to negotiate. From now on, the Hungarians would have their own constitution, parliament and government, while recognising the power of the emperor—in this case Emperor Franz Joseph who would reign until 1916.

An extraordinary account of Franz Joseph's Austria was left to us by a French journalist named François Trocase who lived in Vienna for 22 years. His book, *L'Autriche juive* (Jewish *Austria*)[595], published in 1899, deserves greater recognition.

Austria, excluded from the Germanies, was the most decayed and decaying state in Europe. There were at that time perhaps three million Jews in Austria-Hungary, eight or ten times as many as in France; in fifty years, they had become lords and masters. Three generations had been enough to annihilate patriotic sentiment, to lower public morality, to ruin the family ideal and the fragile peasant economy[596].

The liberal empire had been proclaimed by an imperial patent in February 1861, but as early as 1849 a new era of "progress and fraternity" had been opened for the peoples of the Empire: Germans, Slavs,

---

[595] François Trocase, *L'Autriche juive — L'Autriche contemporaine, telle qu'elle est: Politique, Économique, Militaire et Sociale*, P. Dupont & A. Pierret, Paris, 1899.

[596] "Many Jews living in the big cities have turned from Rabbinism to nihilism. The so-called Reformed Jews profess the most absolute atheism, freethinking, or rather the most complete negation of any religious confession. The last word in their theories is materialism, which manifests itself in the Austrian capital with unprecedented boldness, with a somewhat unconscious absence of all restraint and modesty. Under the pressure of these doctrines, all notions of right and wrong are erased from the souls; there is nothing left to dictate to the people a more austere morality, acts more in keeping with human dignity. It is not only in the religious sphere that this recent nihilism is wreaking havoc. In the sciences, in the arts, in politics and even in sentimental relationships, the degrading doctrines of denial and materialistic doubt are making their influence felt." François Trocase, *L'Autriche juive*, P. Dupont & A.Pierret, Paris, 1899,p. 128.

Hungarians, Jews, Serbs, Romanians and Poles, "without distinction of race or religion".

Here is how François Trocase described the situation: "The Jews were nothing in Austria before 1848. Today they play a dominant role in the Habsburg Empire. It is no exaggeration to say that they have conquered it. They were the only ones who benefited from the Revolution which shed so much blood in the streets of Vienna; it seems that only for them noble victims were sacrificed and human rights proclaimed...The Slavs, the Hungarians, the Romanians of Transylvania and the Germans of Austria have become their prey and bow down to their insolent domination. Half a century has been enough to destroy the very idea of the Austrian homeland[597]."

Jews had converged on Vienna from all over, and within a few years they had taken over industry and the finance companies: "The Jews already owned more than half of the houses in Vienna. If we look only at the title deeds, they own 40%. However, if we look at mortgage claims, which can easily lead to expropriation, 70% are Jewish".

They had also grabbed land and forests: "As for land ownership, until 1849 they were prohibited from acquiring it. Since then, they have made up for lost time. Baron de Rothschild alone owns about a quarter of the large estates in Bohemia (seven times more than the imperial family), not to mention what he also owns in the other provinces, in Lower Austria, Moravia, Silesia and Hungary.

"The ban on Jewish land ownership in Galicia (Austrian Poland) lasted until 1867, at least as far as arable land was concerned. In 1867, there were only 38 Jewish landowners in all of Galicia. However, three years after the ban was lifted, in 1870, there were already 68 Jewish landowners in the province with voting rights. By 1873, the number had quadrupled to 289, and in 1880, according to official information, there were 680 Jewish landowners out of a total of 3,700.

"Unfortunately, the figures for small property are even more significant. In the space of eighteen years, from 1874 to 1892, it has been calculated that 43,000 smallholdings passed into Jewish hands. They now possess the most fertile land in the country; and more than 2 million inhabitants who were formerly proprietors serve as servants to the Jews on the former estates of their fathers[598]."

In Hungary, the situation was identical: "Many Hungarian properties, in so far as they do not yet belong to the Jews, are leased by them, as is also the case in Galicia; Jewish peasants can be seen, whip in hand, watching

---

[597]François Trocase, *L'Autriche juive*, P. Dupont & A.Pierret, Paris, 1899, p. 124, 127
[598]François Trocase, *L'Autriche juive*, P. Dupont & A.Pierret, Paris, 1899, p. 134-135.

the ploughmen or reapers, keeping track of them as soon as they seem to take a minute's rest. Meanwhile, Jewish wives help their husbands by riding along the road in a two-horse cart to see if work is being done; and their sons, armed with long whips, trot along the roads on horseback. What a pitiful spectacle! You must have seen it in the Hungarian *puszta*; you must have seen the Polish peasant drooping with fatigue, with a piece of black bread in his hand, looking sadly at his sons who have only a shirt for clothes. Anyone who has seen these dreadful images, unworthy of a century that claims to be civilised, can understand the intensity of the hatred that gave rise to anti-Semitism[599]."

François Trocase then mentioned a problem that the Russians knew all too well: "In Galicia and in some Hungarian cantons, Jews run inns and liquor taverns; they also run small grocery and haberdashery businesses. For the lower classes, this is the most dangerous of all. These usurers, retail merchants, sell schnapps on credit to the peasants; they calculate in advance that they will be repaid the following year with the proceeds of agricultural labour. In this way, and in return for exceptionally high interest, they deprive the people of their last resources, drive them to madness by abusing liquor, and reduce women and children to begging. The ruined peasants gave themselves up to drink in order to be brutalised; and it is, as always, the Jew alone who triumphs amidst the universal disorder… The most heinous form of Jewish cruelty to date has been the exploitation of the human body. According to eyewitness accounts, the way Jews treat peasants in Galicia surpasses all imagination. It would seem incredible if it were not attested by reliable witnesses. Cases have been cited in which Polish peasants, as interest on a small debt, had to hand over their children to Jewish creditors, who had the right to keep them in their service without paying them any wages until the debt was paid off."

The variation in the price of wheat depended on speculation and not on the abundance of the harvest:

"It is not for nothing that they are also reproached for usury in foodstuffs. There are times when the price of wheat falls to half of what it was the year before; and yet the people do not pay less for bread, but pay more for it. The Jews gain on both sides. They seize all the available grain and, once they have almost all of it, they adjust the prices to their own interests. No one benefits apart from them… What they do to monopolise grain, they also do for all the necessities of life. Under the name of *Cartels*, they organise monopolies for oil, sugar, coal, etc. [600]."

In the big cities, the wholesale meat trade was already in the hands of

---

[599] François Trocase, *L'Autriche juive*, P. Dupont & A.Pierret, Paris, 1899, p. 144.
[600] François Trocase, *L'Autriche juive*, P. Dupont & A.Pierret, Paris, 1899, p. 143, 144, 145, 146, 148

Jews. Efrussi was the wheat king, Moses Ranger was the cotton king and Strousber was the railway king. In fact, the entire wholesale trade was in their hands. They had left the Viennese only a few small retail businesses.

In industry, laws had eased the condition of workers somewhat. But previously, the exploitation of children had reached intolerable extremes. In the textile industry, children had to work even at night. "These children, who belonged to peasant families, came every Monday from the most remote villages, bringing the week's food in a sack. They earned a maximum of 2 guilders (about 4 francs) a week; and when they succumbed to exhaustion or fell asleep, the Jewish boss would sprinkle them with cold water to get them up again."

In the Austrian capital there were numerous Jewish millionaires who had left their hometowns with less than the price of a bunch of onions in their pockets. Most of them came from Poland or Hungary. The three biggest fortunes—the "big Jews"—were the Rothschilds, the Gutmanns and the Reitzes: "Each of them alone owns more than the 1012 convents in Austria put together. Herr Gutmann has amassed his considerable fortune by monopolising the coal trade in the capital. As for the Jew Reitzes, he owes his fame exclusively to his stock-jobbing. A fourth Austrian Jew, who has also been described as "great", Baron Hirsch, is no longer with us. It was he who stripped Turkey of its last resources on the pretext of building the railways of the East. The Viennese have a sad memory of him, having suffered huge losses in the purchase of securities known as "Turkish lots[601]"."

Jewish speculators had also aroused the hatred of small savers: "What they are most reproached for, and rightly so, are the stock market crashes which periodically rob savers of the little they have managed to accumulate and preserve. More than a quarter of a century has passed since the terrible crash of 1873, and yet the appalling abuses of confidence that this catastrophe brought to light have not yet been forgotten. The crash of 1873, the work of the Jews, was undoubtedly one of the most dreadful economic disasters in history, and no one who witnessed it can ever forget it[602]." They collected the lion's share of the interest on public debt and private securities.

In Vienna and elsewhere, Jews lived in the most elegant quarters, rested in the most beautiful mansions and were at the centre of public life: "Worldly relations are everywhere dominated by Jews. Go to the city park, to the boulevards, to the *Prater*; most of them are Jews; open the newspapers to read the chronicles of festivals, announcements of weddings or births; Jews, always Jews. In the spa towns, in Karlsbad, Baden and

---

[601] François Trocase, *L'Autriche juive*, P. Dupont & A.Pierret, Paris, 1899, p. 167.
[602] François Trocase, *L'Autriche juive*, P. Dupont & A.Pierret, Paris, 1899, p. 146-147.

twenty other places, there are always Jews everywhere. The most beautiful spas around Vienna, in Semmering, Kahlenberg and Brühl, belong to them. The accumulation of wealth in their hands, the thirst for pleasure which consumes them, has produced a complete reversal of all social habits[603]."

Thanks to their gold, their political and media promotion was guaranteed: "At the same time as they amassed wealth, both movable and immovable, the Jews also aspired to positions and honours. They hold the highest public offices and enter parliament. They sit in provincial and communal assemblies. They participate in the making of laws."

The Jews had also thought of securing their security against the "reactionaries", the "faint-hearted", the "bitter" and the "envious of their success": "They took over everything. Public security in Vienna has been entrusted to Jewish policemen. No wonder, then, that things happen in the Austrian capital that would be absolutely impossible anywhere else. They also seem to be responsible for domestic and foreign policy. They are to be found in all public careers, and often at the top of them. The important place they occupy is absolutely disproportionate to their numbers."

Jews colonised professions such as law, journalism and medicine. These three liberal professions were almost their exclusive domain: "Literature, and especially journalism, are literally flooded with Jews. All the renowned political or literary editors of today's Vienna are of Jewish origin. Of the 16 leading daily newspapers published in Vienna, 10 are owned, edited and run by Jews. The others are party organs. They have also monopolised almost all the weekly press. And the Jewish doctors in Vienna? In 1893, there were 794 Christian and 763 Jewish doctors in the Austrian capital. The number of Jewish doctors is increasing every year and will soon surpass that of Christian doctors."

The Jewish press was dedicated to ridiculing the Christian faith, family values and patriotism. Jewish journalists poured out torrents of insults against Tsar Alexander III, sparing no false news and slanderous insinuations: "There is no nepotism comparable to that of the Jews; there is no closer solidarity. Everywhere the Jewish element asserts itself; everywhere it exploits the situation to its exclusive advantage…With the help of their newspapers, they make and unmake literary, artistic and all sorts of reputations[604]…"

---

[603]François Trocase, *L'Autriche juive*, P. Dupont & A.Pierret, Paris, 1899, p. 141-142.
[604]François Trocase, *L'Autriche juive*, P. Dupont & A.Pierret, Paris, 1899, p. 136, 137, 141, 142, 393. ["The Viennese Jewish press demonstrated its omnipotence over public opinion. It succeeded in creating such a current of animosity against Russia that no one dared to fight against these nefarious tendencies. For fifteen years, the Habsburg monarchy was in a state of latent hostility towards the Russian Empire, without even maintaining diplomatic decorum in the official organs. Until the death of Emperor

Indeed, the artists who received the praise of the press were almost exclusively Jewish: "In the arts, in music, in everything connected with the theatre, they occupy a dominant position. Since they monopolise criticism, no one can hope to capture the public's attention without their help, one might almost say without their consent. Men and women pay them the tribute they claim for themselves". Yet, noted François Trocase, "despite the bitter complaints poured out against them from all quarters, the Jews continue to present themselves as the defenders of all liberties."

In April 1882, a new case of ritual crime had broken out in Hungary, which François Trocase preferred to overlook, probably so as not to damage the credibility of his testimony, already astonishing enough for ordinary readers. A 14-year-old Christian girl, Eszter Solymosi, employed as a servant in the village of Tiszaeszlár, had been missing since 1 April. In May, the investigation pointed to Jews who had celebrated Passover. Excitement gripped the region and numerous acts of violence were committed. After placing the Jewish suspects under police surveillance, examining magistrate József Bary began by questioning Samuel, the five-year-old son of Jozsef Scharf, the synagogue's "chaplain". Samuel admitted that his father had taken Eszter home and that the *shohet* (ritual slaughterer) had slit her throat. According to the boy's account transcribed by Bary, the slaughterer, in the presence of his father and other men, had made an incision in the girl's neck, while he and his brother Moric had received the blood in a cup.

On 19 May 1882, Scharf and his wife were arrested, but denied any involvement. Moric eventually confessed that after Saturday morning prayer, her father had called Eszter to his house on the pretext of asking her to remove some candles (an act forbidden to pious Jews on the Sabbath), and that a Jewish beggar staying with them, Hermann Wollner, had taken the girl into the synagogue hallway and assaulted her. After stripping her naked, two slaughterers, Abraham Buxbaum and Leopold Braun, held her down, while another accomplice, Solomon Schwarz, cut her throat with a knife and emptied her blood into a bowl. These three men, candidates for the vacant positions of preceptor and *shohet* of the synagogue, had come to Tiszaeszlár to officiate on that particular Shabbat and had remained in the synagogue after the morning service. According to his confession, Moric had watched the whole scene, peeping through the door of the synagogue. During the 45 minutes he had been watching, he would have seen that after bleeding the young woman, Samuel Lustig, Abraham Braun, Lazar Weisstein and Adolf Júnger had put a handkerchief around her neck

---

Alexander III, no effort was made in Vienna's ruling circles to stop the torrents of insults directed against him by Jewish journalists." *L'Autriche juive*, p. 351-352. NdT.]

and dressed her again.

Despite the thorough searches organised by Bary, no bodies or traces of blood were found in the synagogue, in the houses of the Jewish suspects, or in the graves in the Jewish cemetery. However, twelve Jews were arrested, among them the young Moric Scharf. Exasperation against the Jews had reached paroxysm and the affair assumed international proportions. On 29 July, formal charges were brought against the following fifteen people: Salomon Schwarz, Abraham Buxbaum, Leopold Braun and Hermann Wollner for murder. Jozsef Scharf, Adolf Júnger, Abraham Braun, Samuel Lustig, Lazar Weisstein and Emanuel Taub for complicity and voluntary assistance in the crime; Anselm Vogel, Jankel Smilovics, David Hersko, Martin Gross and Ignác Klein for complicity in the crime and concealment of his corpse.

On 17 June 1883, the last act in this case took place before the Nyíreguháza court. Judge Ferenc Korniss presided over the court, with Eduard Szeyffert as state prosecutor. The court was to hold thirty sessions to examine the case in all its details and to hear the numerous witnesses.

Only the intervention of Jewish financiers and the corruption of the judges were able to exonerate these "victims of anti-Semitism" on 3 August. This scandalous acquittal immediately sparked riots in Pressburg (Bratislava), Budapest and other Hungarian cities. Géza Onody, Tiszaeszlár's representative in the Hungarian Parliament, expressed his indignation loud and clear when the Supreme Court rejected the appeal and upheld the verdict of the criminal court. Győző Istoczy, a member of Parliament, then founded the Anti-Semitic Party and demanded the expulsion of Jews from Hungary.

CXXIII. La Civiltá Cattolica, 1870–1903

After the unification of Northern Italy and the kingdom of the Two Sicilies, Victor Emmanuel II took the title of King of Italy in March 1861. All that remained was Rome and the Papal States to be annexed to the new kingdom, but French troops remained stationed there. Indeed, in order not to alienate France's ultramontane Catholics, Napoleon III had decided not to conclude his victorious campaign of 1859. By keeping French troops in Rome to protect the last vestiges of the Pope's temporal power, the French sovereign was preventing the new kingdom of Italy from completing its unity. Italian patriots took advantage of the Prussian invasion of France in 1870 to enter Rome with arms in hand and complete Italian unity.

The fall of the pope's temporal power was painfully felt by many Catholics. The revolution seemed to have triumphed, especially since during the captivity of Pope Pius IX in the Vatican, the Jews of Rome had given free rein to their hatred. The Lémann brothers, Jewish converts to

Catholicism, left some interesting pages on this episode:

"When, on 20 September 1870, the subalpine government forced the gates of Rome with cannon fire, the breach had not yet been completed and a troop of Jews had already passed through to congratulate General Cadorna. And the whole ghetto was decked out in Piedmontese colours... When the Zouaves[605] defending Pius IX were ordered not to continue their heroic defence, the Jews waited for them on the bridge of St. Angelo, hurling insults at them and even tearing off their clothes. During the days in which the usurper government was installed, they were seen running like jackals from one barracks to another to plunder them... On several occasions, they gathered at the doors of the churches to jeer and beat the Christians who came there to pray... Every time—added the Lémann abbots—that we asked for information about the despicable scenes that took place on the Corso, in front of the Quirinal and elsewhere, where the sacred was ridiculed, the priests insulted, the Madonnas profaned, the sacred images smashed, we were always told: the buzzuri and the Jews...".

The Zouaves who had defended Rome were leaving the walls and crossing the Porta Pia. Their sympathisers hurried to bring them civilian clothes, but at the end of the San Angelo bridge, "hordes of Jews, amidst the shouting, tore off their suitcases of clothes and everything they could and threw them into the river Tibre". "Down below were their sailors in their boats collecting everything they had thrown into the river."

The three ministerial dailies, *L'Opinione, La Liberia* and *La Nuova Roma* had then three Jewish editors: "Well! said Messrs. Lémann, they have not ceased a single day, since they became masters of Rome, to pour slander, insults and mud on the Catholic religion, its cult, its communities, its priests, on all that is most respectable and even on the august person of the Pope. His Holiness himself told us: "They direct all the revolutionary press against me and against the Church[606]"."

As happened at every triumph of the Jews somewhere, they then came from everywhere: "Jews from abroad, who flocked to the new capital, edited their newspapers and fed their attacks on the Church; Jews from Rome, who had betrayed their sovereign, who had gladly welcomed the Piedmontese, who frequented places previously forbidden to them. This is the real scandal: the Jews of Rome, the seat of Peter, the capital of

---

[605] The Zouaves were French light infantry units belonging to the Army of Africa. They were inspired by Algerian mercenaries recruited from the *Zouaoua* confederation, which supplied troops to the Regency of Algiers in its wars against European powers. Often associated with the image of the battles of the Second Empire and known for their distinctive uniform, these units existed from 1830 to 1962.

[606] Mgr Henri Delassus, *La Conjuration antichrétienne III*, Desclée De Brouwer, 1910, p. 1169.

Catholicism, supplant Christians, buy property and exercise functions of government[607]."

Nevertheless, the Lémann brothers acknowledged that the popes had "constantly protected the Israelites" of Rome. Pius IX had even been particularly benevolent towards them, since he had ordered the demolition of the gates and walls of the ghetto. For they recalled the substance of the Church's doctrine towards the members of the sect: "Because she is the repository of the sweetness of the Gospel, the Church defends the life of the Jews. Because she is the mother of the Christian nations, she preserves them from the Hebrew invasion which would be their death[608]."

But after the events of 1870, Pius IX finally uttered some unequivocal words: "Unfortunately, there are too many of them in Rome today, we hear them barking in every street, and they harass us everywhere... They write blasphemies and obscenities in the newspapers... but a day will come, a terrible day of divine vengeance, when they will have to give an account of the iniquities they have committed".

The Jewish question was then treated more rigorously by the Vatican. La *Civiltá Cattolica*, the newspaper of the Secretariat of State, launched the counter-offensive. In an article published in 1872, Father Francesco Berardinelli called the Vatican's persecutors: "Renegades and apostates... a pack of dogs... of the breed of the poisonous beasts of Golgotha".

Until the 1970s, the journal only dealt episodically with the Jewish question. But with Pope Leo XIII (1878–1903), the growing influence of Judaism in Europe came under close scrutiny[609]. Judaism was at last identified as the cradle of Freemasonry and secret societies and the driving force behind the forces that had sponsored the revolution in Europe.

The solution to the Jewish problem consisted, according to the *Civiltà Cattolica*, in bringing down the liberal state which had opened the door to

---

[607] G. Miccoli, *Santa Sede, questione ebraica e antisemitismo*, in *Storia d'Italia*, Annali vol. 11 bis, *Gli Ebrei in Italia*, Einaudi, Torino, 1997. In *Sodalitium* N°50, June-July 2000.

[608] A. and J. Lémann, *Lettre aux Israélite dispersés, sur la conduite de leurs coreligionnaires durant la captivité de Pie IX au Vatican (Letter to the dispersed Israelites, on the conduct of their coreligionists during the captivity of Pius IX in the Vatican)*, Rome, 1873, Libreria e Cartoleria romana, p. 5-14. In *Sodalitium* No. 50, June-July 2000. Joseph (1836–1915) and Augustin (1836–1909) Lévy were twin brothers from Lyon. They had sincerely converted to Catholicism in 1854 and became priests. Augustin was a professor at the Catholic University of Lyon. Joseph was consecrated bishop. They denounced Judaism in numerous books, such as *L'Entrée des juifs dans la Société française* (1886).

[609] R. Taradel— B. Raggi, *La Segregazione amichevole. La Civiltá Cattolica e la questione ebraica*, 1850-1945, Editori Riuniti, Roma, 2000, p. 27, in *Sodalitium* No. 50, June-July 2000.

the Jews. Jews were to be protected from the hostile popular reaction and Christians were to be preserved from the moral, political and commercial aggressiveness of the Jews.

In 1880, Jesuit Father Giuseppe Oreglia de San Stefano (1823–1895) wrote: "Catholics do not ask for the expulsion of the Jews, but only for restrictions on their activities insofar as they are harmful to the public. They want to preserve the Christian character of the State, legislation, teaching and social principles. They want the extirpation of the Jewish principles… made dominant by the liberal regime, but not the expulsion of a people who, after all, are of the blood of Abraham, and in whose bosom the Saviour was born. With a Christian organisation of the State, the Jews inspire no fear[610]."

Father Mario Barbera also promoted "charitable segregation". It was necessary to resort to the charitable segregation of Jews who had to live apart, like lepers in the leper colony, for their own health and that of other peoples.

But after 1903, the *Civiltà Cattolica* ceased to treat the Jewish problem with the same attention and turned its efforts to combating modernism within the Church, without changing its mind about the Jewish-Masonic danger.

After Pius X, Pius XI condemned Marxism and National Socialism. He died shortly before he could promulgate an encyclical in which he reaffirmed the traditional thesis of the Church. Here is part of the text: "The so-called Jewish question, in its essence, is a question neither of race, nor of nation, nor of territorial nationality, nor of the right of citizenship in the State. It is a religious question and, since the coming of Christ, a question of Christianity".

The priest Jules Meinvielle, whose 1936 book, *The Jew in the Mystery of History*, was widely circulated in the Catholic world, stated the following in the sixth point of his conclusion:

"Christians, who cannot hate the Jews, who cannot persecute them or prevent them from living, or disturb them in the observance of their laws and customs, must nevertheless guard against Jewish danger. They must guard against it as one guards against lepers. Lepers are not to be hated, persecuted or disturbed, but precautions must be taken against them so that they do not infest the social organism. It is a hard thing, no doubt; but it is irremediable. Thus Christians must not enter into commercial, social or political relations with that perverse caste which hypocritically seeks our ruin. The Jews must live separately from the Christians because that is what their Laws command them to do, as we shall see later on, and also because they are "infectious" to other peoples. If the other peoples reject these

---

[610] *Civiltá Cattolica* 35, (1884), III, p. 101 ff, in *Sodalitium* No. 50, June-July 2000.

precautions, they must abide by the consequences, that is to say, be lackeys and pariahs of this race, to which the superiority in the realm of the carnal belongs[611]."

CXXIV. German Anti-Judaism in the 19th Century

German anti-Judaism has played an important role in contemporary history. In 1840, there were about 350,000 Jews in Germany, 200,000 of whom lived in North Prussia. Jews, who represented 3% of Berlin's population, made up half of the industrialists. In 1807, they already owned 30 of the 52 banks in the capital, and by 1862, 550 of Prussia's 662 banks were in their hands[612]. The Dresdner Bank, the most powerful after the Deutsche Bank, had been founded by the Jew Eugen Guttman. When Chancellor Otto von Bismarck needed a banker in 1859, he turned to a Jewish banker named Gerson Bleichröder, who had been ennobled by Wilhelm II in 1872. In 1910, the Jewish population in Prussia then numbered 600,000. But the country was not as gangrenous as Austria and France, largely due to the severity of the recruitment of its officer corps and university professors.

Thanks to their extensive mastery of the country's finances, Jews invested in industry, particularly the railways. In 1835, Abraham Oppenheim of Cologne was vice-president of the Rhineland Railway Company; in 1869, Baron Maurice Hersch founded the Orient Express, which linked Berlin, Vienna and Constantinople.

The Hamburg-Amerika Line shipping company, which connected Germany to America, was owned by another Jew named Albert Ballin, a personal friend of Emperor Wilhelm II. The department stores were almost a Jewish monopoly. They sold more cheaply and ruined the small shopkeepers who ended up being taken over by Jewish entrepreneurs.

If the Jews had felt German, their successes would not have been a problem. But the very essence of Judaism is to destroy everything that is not Jewish, and not to integrate into the host countries. So, with their tireless newspaper propaganda, Jewish intellectuals managed to undermine and ridicule Christianity, to mock German customs. They surreptitiously instilled the ideas of "tolerance", "equality", exalted "universal brotherhood". The Jewish writers Ludwig Börne and Heinrich Heine, the leaders of the Young Germany movement, criticised "moral order",

---

[611] Julio Meinvielle, *El Judío en el misterio de la historia (1936)*, Cruz y Fierro Editores, Buenos Aires, 1982, p. 39.

[612] Ruth Gay, *Jews of Germany, a historical portrait*, in Gérard Messadié, *Histoire générale de l'antisémitisme*, Lattès, 1999, p. 353.

patriotism and family values. It is not without reason that German nationalists called this movement the "Young Palestine". In 1835, a censorship decree dealt a severe blow to these cosmopolitan writers. The German spirit was still strong and structured enough to effectively oppose Jewish propaganda.

The Prussian King Frederick William IV (1840–1861), trained by the historian Friedrich Carl de Savigny, had clearly understood the political project of the Jews. He had decided to exempt them from military service, to remove them from public service and to establish them as a "separate nation" under his special protection. In 1842, he wrote in a letter quoted by the historian Leon Poliakov: "The ignoble Jewish clique is daily, by its words and writings, taking the axe to the root of the German being: it does not wish (as I do) to ennoble and freely confront the states that make up the German people, it wants to mash and mix all the states together". As far as we know, this is the first mention that denotes some understanding of the Jewish project to destroy the states[613].

The most widely read author at the time was Gustav Freytag, whose masterpiece *Soll und Haben* (1855) went through 500 successive editions and was in every family library. His two main characters, the German Anton Wohlfart and the Jew Veitel Itzig, embodied virtue and vice respectively. The half-dozen Jews surrounding Itzig were equally repugnant.

It was at that time, around 1854, that the Brothers Grimm, whose fairy tales enchanted and taught German children, published their famous *German Dictionary*. On the word "*Jude*", the authors used these examples: "Dirty as an old Jew; stinks like a Jew; tastes like a Jew". Or: "You have to grease your gullet first, otherwise this manduca tastes like a dead Jew[614]."

But the anti-Jewish vigilance of some German intellectuals was not enough to preserve the government's egalitarian ideology. An 1864 law granting "civil equality to citizens of the Israelite religion" was ratified by the 1869 law on the equality of confessions in civil and civic matters. This law was extended throughout Germany after the proclamation of the German Empire in 1871. Bismarck, who had imposed a Judeo-Masonic republican regime on France after its defeat, thus contributed to making Germany a paradise for Jews.

The German mainstream press fell into the hands of Jewish businessmen. Leopold Sonnemann, the founder of the *Frankfurter Zeitung* in 1866, became the owner of a media empire. Rudolf Mosse founded the *Berliner Tageblatt* in 1871, Leopold Ullstein founded the *Berliner*

---

[613]It is true, however, that we do not know all the German anti-Semitic literature of the 19th century, which was never translated into French.
[614]Léon Poliakov, *Histoire de l'antisémitisme, Tome I*, Point Seuil, 1981, p. 383.

Abendpost in 1887 and the *Berliner Morgenpost* in 1898.

On the intellectual level, the anti-Semitic reaction in the German-speaking country was rather late in coming. In 1871, a book was published by a German Catholic priest, canon of Prague Cathedral and professor of theology and Hebrew antiquities at the University of Prague. August Rohling (1839–1931) had learned Hebrew in order to translate the Talmud. His book *Der Talmujude (The Jew of the Talmud)*, published in Münster in Westphalia, reinstated all the passages suppressed by the Talmud, based on the work of his illustrious predecessor, Einsenmenger. The work, which responded to public interest, was a resounding success, and a second edition was published in 1877[615].

The Jews, naturally, denounced the work and the quoted statements as "absurd anti-Semitic nonsense", "delusional assertions", and so on. The government, corrupted by Jewish gold, forbade Rohling to respond to the attacks. The Jews thus gagged their adversary, while shouting against bigotry and persecution and swearing that their throats were being slit. The case was widely publicised in Vienna and in Germany, and observers simply noted that the Jews did not want any light to be shed on the basis of their beliefs, morals and legislation.

In his book, *My Reply to the Rabbis or Five Letters on Talmudism and the Blood Ritual of the Jews*[616], published in 1883, August Rohling revealed the great interest in recognising the Jew behind his mask: "In the Middle Ages, Jews wore a yellow hat in order to be recognised. If the readers of the newspapers (in Vienna, for example, *Neue Freie Presse, Fremdenblatt, Tagblatt, Extrapost, Vorstadt-Zeitung, Wiener Allgemeine*, etc.) were to see every day on the front page a yellow stripe with the words "for Jewish interests", it would become clear what these feathered men were fighting for[617]."

After being singled out and rebuked by a Jewish polemicist named Bloch, Rholing defended himself by replying: "In the Talmudic tractate *Megillah*, the goyim are designated as dogs. In tractate *Aboda Zara (46a)* they refer to the face of a non-Jewish monarch as the 'face of a dog'. If Mr. Bloch thinks that I have copied this and other things and that I have not

---

[615] An edition of Eisenmenger's book had been published in England by J. P. Stekelin under the title *The Traditions of the Jews, with the Expositions and Doctrines of the Rabbins*, etc., 2 volumes, 1732–1734. A new edition of the *Entdecktes Judenthum* was published in Dresden in 1893 by F. X. Schieferl.

[616] *Meine Antworten an die Rabbiner oder fünf Briefe über den Talmudismus und das Blutritual der Juden*, Prague, 1883

[617] August Rohling, *Ma Réponse aux Rabbins, ou cinq lettres sur le Talmudisme et le rituel de sang chez les juifs, Quatrième lettre*, Prague, janvier 1883, voir édition allemande, Luhe-Verlag.

read it myself in the Talmud, I can inform him where to find it in the work cited, above in the seventh line (Venice printing). Rashi has explained it exactly as I have made it known, on the basis of the fifth book of Moses (XIV, 21): that a dog is better than a non-Jew; Bloch will know where to find it in the commentary on the Pentateuch; the Hebrew words are: *schehakkeleb nichbad mimmennu*[618]."

Priest Rohling also dealt with the question of ritual murder. Twelve such trials had taken place throughout the Germanic area between 1867 and 1914. Contrary to earlier times, Jews were almost systematically acquitted, although these acquittals merely reflected the power they had acquired over governments, as well as their capacity for corruption. All but a few of these trials ended in acquittals.

Rohling had a following throughout Catholic Europe, so much so that in France his book was translated by three different translators in 1889. A French edition enlarged by A. Pontigny was published under the title *Le Juif selon le Talmud (The Jew according to the Talmud)*, with a brilliant introduction by Edouard Drumont on 2 July 1889, which we summarise here:

"The general crisis in which the world is now struggling can be summed up in one word: the Talmud's revenge on the Gospel. The great phrases about philosophy, the rights of man, the regeneration of humanity, which, during the first years of this century, served as a screen for the Jew to act at his ease, no longer deceive anyone; they are an old paper scenery which is being torn to shreds... The Jew appears as master; he no longer even takes the trouble to disguise this domination; he has all the peoples in his power through finance, he modifies the labour laws according to the interests of his syndicates; he has bought all the statesmen who were for sale and has removed from all jobs those whom he could not corrupt. It is omnipresent and omnipotent wherever it is present, so powerful that people no longer even dare to attack it... What dominates these people is their hatred and contempt for the goy, their conviction that everything is legitimate against the goy, the foreigner, the non-Jew, the "cattle seed[619]", the certainty also that the Jew belongs to a privileged race destined to

---

[618] The Talmud is also a manual for everyday life: According to a decree of a chief rabbi of Israel, orthodox Jews (Jews who strictly observe the practices of the Law, ndt) may kill lice on the Sabbath without transgressing the holy day of rest, but only if the parasite is on a human being's head. However, combing one's hair to isolate lice is forbidden, as the law strictly forbids any work from Friday afternoon to Saturday night. On the other hand, if the louse is on the dress, it must be removed "without harming it". Likewise with rats, which the Torah expressly forbids killing on the Sabbath. They are to be seized by their tails "and thrown far away".

[619] Allusion to Talmud *Yevamot* (98a); Ezekiel (XXIII, 20). (NdT).

reduce all other peoples to servitude, to make them work for Israel. Thus armed, invested with a kind of mission, freed by the very prescriptions of his religion from all embarrassing scruples, the Jew sets out to conquer the capitals. He is the triumphant stockbroker, the influential journalist".

And to those Jews who replied that they had never read the Talmud, Drumond replied: "What need have the Jews of today to study the Talmud? It is imprinted in their brains by hereditary law, bequeathed to them by innumerable generations who have grown pale before its precepts, who have assimilated its doctrines. The Jews are saturated with this Talmud: they owe to it not only that idea of superiority over us which makes them so strong, but also that admirable subtlety, that absence of all moral sense, of all notion of Good and Evil which is almost disarming, for it is entirely native and spontaneous in the Hebrew[620]."

Drumond was already rebelling at the time against the incessant Jewish propaganda aimed at blaming the Europeans, at making them bow their heads and bring them to their knees to beg Israel's forgiveness: "Try to rectify some historical lie, risk, for example, a timid rehabilitation of your race and your fathers, insinuate that you are descended from men who were, perhaps, neither idiots, nor plunderers, nor murderers: then you make history lie, you lie to yourself with impudence, ignorance and fanaticism speak through your mouth. Dare to suspect the philanthropy of the Jews or the candour of the rabbis who created the Talmud and made their laws: you are a dark persecutor, an offender of innocent victims, an apostle of obscurantism, a dark and bloodthirsty man. Dare to point out that the Jews of today are, in fact, the heirs of the Jews of old, and that, consequently, certain security measures would not perhaps be an excess of prudence: it is vile envy that devours you, it is infamous greed that burns you; you are the shame of your time, the scum of humanity, the excrement of nature, and you receive on your head the dustbin that every polemicist of Israel always carries full in his hands."

Anyone can see that the Jews have not moved one iota at the beginning of the 21st century. Edouard Drumont also pointed out the attempts of the Jews to ban Rohling's book and many others before it: "While all other peoples march with their banners in the wind and open their gospels and their laws to the rays of the sun, only the Jew covers himself with darkness, only the Jew seeks mystery, only the Jew makes his civil and religious law a secret that must never leave the Israelite family, and makes it his sacred duty to lie eternally to all men of other races and other homelands[621]. For

---

[620] August Rohling, *Le Juif selon le Talmud*, Albert Savine Éd., Paris, 1889, p. II, III, IV, V, VI

[621] We wrote in our blog in 2009: "It takes a lot of films and documentaries to make an anti-racist and keep the pressure on the public all year round. But just one book is

the Talmud is the book par excellence of exclusivism, of separatism, of universal hatred, not only against all religions, but against all peoples of the human family, against their property, against their social and national existence, and we affirm, without fear, that not a single one of those who read this work will retain the slightest doubt in this respect[622]."

In 1873, the bankruptcy of the Jewish magnate Henry Strousberg, who had founded a railway company to connect Germany with Romania, had triggered a stock market crash that in turn triggered numerous bankruptcies and the ruin of small German investors. Anti-Semitism was reinvigorated, but it took a few more years for this underlying trend to be embodied in a political movement.

The nationalist Heinrich von Treitschke (1834–1896) embodied active anti-Semitic resistance. Originally from Dresden, he was a professor at the University of Berlin. From 1871 to 1884, he was a member of parliament who was very hostile to the British Empire. From 1878 onwards, he persistently denounced the power of the Jews and the waves of immigration from Poland and Russia. In November 1879, he published a relatively short text entitled *Our Perspectives*, in which he alluded to Jewish financial and cultural domination. His formula *The Jews are our disgrace!* (*Die Juden sind unser Unglück!*) was taken up by National Socialist militants during the Third Reich. His ideas were very successful and provoked countless university polemics.

By 1880, a wave of anti-Semitism swept through Germany. Wilhelm Marr, one of the leading thinkers of the resistance, had emerged from the ranks of the extreme left. Born in Magdeburg, he had been a journalist, a militant of the left wing of the radical-democratic party. In 1848, he was elected to parliament, opposing with all his might the granting of civic equality to German Jews. In 1879, he published in Berlin his book *Der Sieg des Judenthums über das Germanenthum (The Victory of Judaism over Germanness)*. Within a few years, his book went through a dozen editions. In the same year, he founded the *Anti-Jewish League* (*Antijüdischer Verein*), which was rather short-lived, although it published a newspaper for a year, *Die neue deutsche Wacht (The New German Guard)*, in which the term *anti-Semitism* appeared for the first time. Wilhelm Marr advocated the expulsion of all Jews to Palestine. However, it should be noted that Wilhelm Marr had three wives, all of them of Jewish origin...

The famous Berlin philosopher and economist Eugen Dühring (1833–1921) was a socialist and anti-Christian theorist. He also published many anti-Semitic tracts. In 1881, in his book entitled *Die Judenfrage als Frage*

---

enough to make a man an anti-Semite for the rest of his days".
[622] August Rohling, *Le Juif selon le Talmud*, Albert Savine Éd., Paris, 1889, p. 4, 5, 6, 7

der Racenschaedlichkeit (The *Jewish Question as a Question of Racial Risk*), he excluded the path of assimilation for Jews whom he regarded as a race distinct from that of the Germans.

The Berliner Paul de Lagarde (Paul Anton Bötticher) was also radically hostile to Judaism. A professor of oriental languages at the University of Göttingen, he had published several works on Semitic philology. He had a great influence through his nationalist and anti-Semitic writings, compiled in the *Deutche Schriften (German Writings, 1878–1881)*. Some of his ideas were taken up by the National Socialists, such as the idea of the living space to the East, or the aspiration for a "German Christianity" purged of its Jewish elements, which was to have a direct influence on Alfred Rosenberg and his famous book *The Myth of the 20th Century* (1930), to be hailed by the Nazi party as one of its great inspirers.

In 1880–1881, Berlin became the scene of violent actions. Non-Christian agitators such as Bernhard Förster, Nietzsche's brother-in-law, or the young Professor Henrici, were involved in these events. Organised gangs assaulted Jews in the streets, chased them out of cafés and smashed their shop windows.

Anti-Semitic resistance had been organised in the face of the Jewish subversive danger. In 1880, Bernhard Förster, inspired by a stay in Wagner's Bayreuth, launched the idea of an anti-Semitic petition addressed to Chancellor Bismarck calling for a census of Jews and their total exclusion from public service and education. Within a few weeks, nearly 225,000 signatures were collected, many of them from students. Soon, the teaching staff joined the movement, committing themselves to the struggle alongside the mentor of German nationalist youth, the historian Heinrich von Treitschke.

Chancellor Bismarck did not give an official response to the anti-Semitic petition, but the government took it into account. In fact, it was rare to see a state post conferred on a Jew in the universities or in the administration. Numerous student bodies did not admit them either. An international anti-Semitic congress took place in 1882 in Dresden, during which three hundred German, Austrian and Russian delegates met. Another congress took place in Chemnitz the following year.

A poster entitled *Eine deutsche Sieben (Seven Germans)* showed the portraits of seven pre-eminent German anti-Semitic activists of the period: Otto Galgau, Adolf König, Bernhard Förster, Max Liebermann von Sonnenberg, Theodor Fritsch, Paul Förster and Otto Böckel.

Max Liebermann von Sonnenberg, a former Prussian army officer, was the initiator of the petition. In 1881, together with Bernhard Förster, he had founded the *Deutschen Volksverein* and a strongly anti-Semitic newspaper, the *Deutsche Volkzeitung*. He was also a member of the Reichstag, and later, in 1894, he merged his organisation with that of Otto Böckel. His programme regarding Judaism was quite radical. Among his publications were *Die Judenfrage und der Synagogenbrand in Neustettin* (1883) and *Die Schädigung des deutschen Nationalgeistes durch die jüdische Nation* (1892).

In 1887, the young Otto Böckel, a native of Frankfurt and a fervent supporter of the small peasantry, was elected to the Reichstag. In the 1890 elections, his party, the *Antisemitische Volkspartei*, won four seats with 48,000 votes. But in 1893, Böckel won 260,000 votes and 16 seats.

As in France, due to the rise of international tensions, electoral anti-Semitism declined at the beginning of the 20th century. Radical anti-Semitic organisations crumbled into a multitude of small groups with esoteric or neo-pagan names.

The journalist Otto Glagau, originally from Königsberg, also contributed to the German anti-Semitic resistance with his journal *Der Kulturkämpfer* (1880–1888). In April 1883, he was the main organiser of the second international anti-Semitic congress in Chemnitz.

The Saxon Theodore Fritsch, a disciple of Wilhelm Marr, was probably the writer who had the greatest resonance in German society. He published several works on the Jewish question, the first of which was an 1887 book entitled *Antisemiten-Katechismus* (*The Catechism of the Anti-Semites*). From 1887 to 1944, the book was published forty-nine times in print runs of hundreds of thousands of copies. Fritsch was also the first German translator of *The Protocols of the Elders of Zion*. He wanted to unite all anti-Semitic organisations in Germany under one banner. But in 1890, there were almost two hundred organisations scattered all over the country. Theodore Fritsche had founded his newspaper, *Der Hammer*, in 1902. In 1912, his followers founded an anti-Jewish order, the *Reichshammerbund*, which in turn gave birth to the famous Thule Society (*Thule-Gesellschaft*), an organisation clandestinely linked to the Nazi party in its early days. His last work, *The True Nature of the Jews*, was published in 1926.

Pastor Adolf Stoecker, the son of a blacksmith, took over, putting anti-Semitism at the centre of his political programme. He contributed significantly to the spread of anti-Semitism within German Protestantism and the conservative parties. Stoecker, close to traditional Christian anti-Semitism, distanced himself, however, from the more radical racial anti-Semitism. After Bismarck's dismissal in 1890, he gained increasing influence within the conservative ranks. During the party congress, the *Tivoli-Parteitag* of 1892, he succeeded in firmly anchoring anti-Semitism in the programme of the *Deutschkonservative Partei* (*German Conservative Party*).

In 1899, Houston Stewart Chamberlain, son-in-law of the composer Richard Wagner, published his famous work *The Foundations of the 19th Century*, the French translation of which did not appear until 1913. In one of its chapters, entitled *The Advent of the Jews in Western History*, he attempted to prove that Jesus Christ was an Aryan. Chamberlain was also one of the leading theorists of pan-Germanism and biological racism. Emperor Wilhelm II paid him liberator's tributes and Adolf Hitler held him in high esteem, recognising him as an inspiration and attending his funeral in person.

Mention should also be made here of Richard Wagner, who, although not a professed anti-Semite, was at least as influential as some theorists on the subject, almost certainly read the books of Wilhelm Marr, Eugen Dühring, as well as Father Rohling's *The Jew according to the Talmud*.

In the 1830s–1840s, the Jewish composer Giacomo Meyerbeer was the "king" of opera. Wagner, who was twenty years older, was on friendly terms with him. But in 1850, Wagner published *Judaism in Music*, an essay in which he harshly criticised all the supposedly great Jewish geniuses fabricated by publicity. "The most urgent thing is to emancipate ourselves from Jewish oppression," he wrote. In his autobiography, Wagner claimed that this pamphlet had subsequently earned him the hostility of the entire European press: "This explains the unprecedented hostility that has been shown to me to date by the entire European press... The fury has taken the form of perfidy and calumny".

We know that Jewish intellectuals are in the habit of publicly insulting and slandering their opponents. The mainstream press, as we can see, was already in those years in the hands of big Jewish billionaire tycoons.

Although he denied them talent as composers, Wagner recognised the talents of Jewish performers. For example, he had forged a friendship with Joseph Rubinstein, a talented Ukrainian Jewish pianist who supported everything Wagner had written about Jews. On the maestro's death, Rubinstein, depressed, committed suicide over his grave. The fact is that Rubinstein had left Judaism behind and had long since ceased to be a Jew. At the height of his fame, Wagner had also entrusted the conducting of Parsifal, his German-Christian work, to the conductor Hermann-Levi. His anti-Semitism, however, had not diminished. In 1881, for example, he wrote to King Ludwig II of Bavaria: "I regard the Jewish race as the born enemy of humanity and all that is noble".

CXXV. *The anti-Jewish counter-offensive in France*

In Republican France at the end of the 19th century, the majority of ministers were Freemasons and Protestants, if not outright Jews. The new regime of the Third Republic began its work with the priority of priorities: the fight against Catholicism. In 1879 and 1880, Jules Ferry's school laws expelled the Church from primary education. The new offensive culminated at the beginning of the 20th century with the closure of numerous congregations and the adoption of the 1905 law on the separation of Church and State.

The republican system and universal suffrage would prove to be the ideal regime for the financial oligarchy. Indeed, it would be much easier to corrupt and manipulate parliamentarians and voters than to destabilise a hereditary monarchy of divine right, whose princes and notables do not need gold to attain power. On the other hand, it was demonstrated after a few decades of "democracy" that the electoral mass was easily manipulated, for people can be made to believe anything if they have all the loudspeakers of the media system at their disposal.

Dozens of works were published on the Jews at the time. In 1882, Abbot Chabeauty, honorary canon of Angoulême and Poitiers, published *Les Juifs, nos maîtres (The Jews, our masters)*:

"It is not possible for me to make my quotations with the actual text of the Talmud before my eyes: I do not have its enormous folios within my reach," he wrote; "but I shall rely on sources which, though secondary, are no less reliable: I shall take my first quotations from a thirteenth-century Latin manuscript entitled *Extracts from the Talmud* (*Extraits du Talmud*, No. 10, bis 8 of the Bibliothèque Nationale de Paris, fol. 231). I borrow all that I am about to say and quote from this manuscript from a very interesting work published by the *Revue des études juives*, 1880, no. 2, and 1881, nos. 4 and 5, entitled: *The 1240 controversy on the Talmud*, and signed by Isidore Loeb. This work was written in the wake of the Talmud controversy in Paris in 1240, by order of Eudes de Chateauroux, chancellor of the University, in order to enlighten theologians on the errors, obscenities and blasphemies of the Talmud, so that they would not consider, through ignorance, that the Talmud was a harmless book to be tolerated[623]."

At the end of the manuscript were, among other documents, thirty-five articles or charges that Pope Gregory IX had brought against the Talmud. In each article, the author (perhaps Nicolas Donin) indicated the places in the Talmud from which the charges were taken, as well as the words of the rabbis incriminated. "It is from this part of the manuscript, reproduced in full by the *Revue des études juives*, that I borrow my quotations", explained Abbot Chabeauty. The *Revue des études juives* stated that the translation of these passages from the Babylonian *Gemara* "was exact, precise and very scientific", and the meaning of these "generally well understood[624]".

Here are the kind of statements we can find in this code of life in Judaism: "Rabbi Simeon says: The best of Christians, kill him; the best of snakes, crush his head. Therefore, the best Christian can be killed as a

---

[623] Abbé Chabeauty, *Les Juifs, nos maîtres*, 1882, p. 192.
[624] Abbé Chabeauty, *Les Juifs, nos maîtres*, 1882, p. 193.

villain." And, further, "A Christian may be deceived, by trick or contrivance, without sin." This, Abbot Chabeauty reported, can be found in *Yeschuot*, treatise *Baba Kamma* (fol. 38A), chapter *Schor*[625].

These are other extracts from the Talmud referred to by Chabeauty, analysed and summarised by Sixtus of Siena, a 16th century Jewish convert, in his *Holy Library*. Sixtus of Siena carefully indicated the corresponding places in the Talmud[626]:

"We command that every Jew, three times a day, curse all Christians, and pray God to confound and exterminate them and their kings and princes. And let especially the priests of the Jews make this prayer three times a day, in the synagogue, in hatred of Jesus of Nazareth." (Babylonian Talmud, Ord I, tractate 1, Chapter 4).

"God commanded the Jews to seize the property of the Christians by any means, whether by trickery, violence, usury, or robbery." (Babylonian Talmud, Ord I, tractate 1, Chapter 4).

"All Jews are commanded to regard Christians as brute beasts, and to treat them exactly as brute beasts." (Babylonian Talmud, Ord IV, tractate 8).

"The Christian churches are houses of perdition and places of idolatry which the Jews must destroy". (Babylonian Talmud, Ord I, tractate 1, Chapter 2).

On the extreme political left, the anti-Semitism of the socialists was no less virulent at the time. In 1883, Auguste Chirac, a disciple of Proudhon and Toussenel, published *Les Rois de la République, Histoires des Juiveries (The Kings of the Republic, Histories of the Jewries)*. The first two volumes contained monographs on the great Jews of the time: Rothschild, Léon Say, Mallet, Camondo, Baron Hirsch, Jacques Stern, Cahen d'Anvers, Bischoffheim, Erlanger, etc. The third volume was published in 1885. In 1888, Auguste Chirac published *La haute Banque et les révolutions (High Banking and the Revolutions)*, which was partly based on an 1856 book entitled *Histoire des grandes opérations financières (History of the Great Financial Transactions)*, published by a Marseille journalist and legitimist called Jean-Baptiste Capefigue[627].

Edouard Drumont's *Jewish France* was, along with Ernest Renan's *Life of Jesus*, the French *best-seller* of the second half of the 19th century: 114 editions in one year, 200 editions in all, not counting a popular abridged edition. The very famous Edouard Drumont deserved his success. His book in two 600-page volumes contains many interesting statements. "One could make an admirable collection of his aphorisms", wrote Lucien Rebatet in

---

[625] Abbé Chabeauty, *Les Juifs, nos maîtres*, 1882, p. 196.
[626] On Sixtus of Siena read the end of the chapter on Paul IV.
[627] See Jean Drault, *Histoire de l'antisémitisme*, 1944.

the special edition on the Jews of the weekly *Je suis Partout* of 17 February 1939. Here is one, among many more: "Very wicked priests and friends of very greedy kings who amused themselves by persecuting the poor Jews because of their religion: that is the legend[628]." But Lucien Rebatet had his reservations and qualified his admiration for the great polemicist: "In 1939, a third of the text of *Jewish France,* while retaining its documentary value, had aged. It is the journalistic part, the part of immediate current affairs: portraits of characters and their associates that the future will not remember, news that inflamed one generation but left the next unmoved. It has to be said that Drumont was not very choosy in his choice of documents".

In 1889, Drumont published *La Fin d'un monde*. Then, in 1890, *La dernière Bastille,* and in 1891, *Le Testament d'un antisémite*. He then founded the newspaper *La Libre Parole,* the first copy of which went on sale on 20 April 1892, Charles Maurras' birthday, which was also Adolf Hitler's birthday. The paper's circulation reached 300,000 copies during the Panama scandal. At the time, *La Libre Parole* rivalled other newspapers and even set the general tone of the press. In May 1898, Drumont was elected deputy for Algiers with three political friends.

In its wake, numerous anti-Jewish books were published, both in Catholic and extreme left-wing circles; socialist anti-Semitism was more focused on "race" antagonism.

In 1889, the Breton socialist Augustin Hamon published *The Agony of a Society, a* book in which he attacked the Jews of high finance: "The Jews have invaded everything. Finance, like the press, belongs to them. In the administration of states and cities, especially in our country, the *Yiddish* occupy the highest offices, those which bring honour, money and prominence. In any ministry or prefecture you will see the May, Isaiah Levaillant, Kahn, Cohn, Cahen, Dreyfus, Mayer, Alphand[629]."

Albert Regnard, another radical socialist and atheist, was delighted with the success of Edouard Drumont's book. He published a dozen books at the same time, including one entitled *Aryens et Semites (Aryans and Semites)*.

The French National Anti-Semitic League was born in those years. Its vice-president, Jacques de Biez, also described himself as a "national socialist". He was also convinced of the "Aryanness" of Jesus the "Galilean", whom he affiliated with the Celtic race. Jacques de Biez used to ask the priests he met with some trepidation: "Are you sure that Jesus Christ was a Jew? Drumont is satisfied with that, but I am worried about it[630]." The League also had other prominent protagonists, such as the

---

[628] Édouard Drumont, *La France juive,* tome I, p. 145.
[629] Augutin Hamon, *L'Agonie d'une société,* Paris, 1889, in Marc Crapez, *L'Antisémitisme de gauche au XIXe siècle,* Berg International, 202, p. 74.
[630] Raphaël Viau, *Vingt ans d'antisémitisme, 1889-1909,* 1910, p. 14.

adventurous Marquis de Morès and his famous butchers de la Vilette.

As in Germany, a group was formed in the Chamber of Deputies. In November 1891, a bill calling for the expulsion of Jews received 32 votes in favour.

The financial scandals that regularly peppered politicians sparked a popular outcry. In 1892, Drumont accused in his diary some leading politicians of having used their influence and votes to fraudulently grant the Panama Canal Company the right to issue 700 million gold francs worth of bonds in a public loan, after receiving a favourable opinion in 1888. The Panama scandal broke: the Jewish banker and baron Jacques de Reinach was indicted. He was the distributor of funds that the Suez Company lavished on journalists, deputies and ministers. Cheques seized by the courts revealed that the baron had distributed four million gold francs. Most of the major republican newspapers had been corrupted. When he learned that he would be prosecuted, Baron Reinach committed suicide, but the financier's death did not put an end to the scandal.

The intermediaries in charge of contacting the politicians whose support the Company wished to win were two other Israelis, Emile Arton and Cornelius Herz. Emile Aaron, nicknamed Arton, had been charged with corrupting the deputies of the Bourbon Palace (National Assembly). As soon as he was discovered, he fled to England, taking with him his list of 104 "nominative cheques". His co-religionist, Cornelius Herz, was of a higher level. He came from a Jewish family in Besançon of Bavarian origin and was a Grand Officer of the Legion of Honour, a confidant of Presidents Grévy and Sadi Carnot, a friend of Freycinet and Clémenceau. When the case broke out, he also went into exile in England. Arton was arrested in London in 1897 and extradited. He appeared before the judges, but was acquitted. Cornelius Herz was convicted in absentia, as his extradition was never granted by England. Dozens of parliamentarians and journalists had been corrupted, but above all tens of thousands of small savers were ruined by the bankruptcy of the company. The historian Léon Poliakov tried to relativise the supposed importance of the Jews in France at the time: "Their total number was no more than eighty thousand (0.02 per 100 of the French population), of whom more than half were settled in Paris[631]." Léon Poliakov thus intended to discredit the madness of the anti-Semites of the time by recalling that there were only 80,000 Jews in France. But by giving this figure, the Jewish historian was merely demonstrating the extreme harmfulness of the Jews in relation to their proportion. So Jewish intellectuals also often point out that "anti-Semitic madness" sometimes goes so far as to create anti-Semitism where there are no Jews, as in Poland,

---

[631] Léon Poliakov, *Histoire de l'antisémitisme, tome II*, Point Seuil, 1981, p. 296.

for example. They pretend to wonder about this "inexplicable" phenomenon, when in fact the explanation is obvious: the Poles had an appalling memory of the presence of Jews on their territory and continue to hate them long after their departure[632].

In 1893, Mgr Meurin published his book *The Freemasonry Synagogue of Satan*. Mgr Meurin, archbishop of Port-Louis, near Lorient, was an expert in Hebrew and Sanskrit. We find in his work some passages that make direct reference to the Jews: "We believe that it would be enough to forbid Jews to be bankers, merchants, journalists, teachers, doctors and pharmacists. It does not seem unjust to declare the gigantic fortunes of certain bankers to be national property, because it is unacceptable that a man can, by financial manoeuvres, amass in a short time a more than real fortune and thus impoverish the country that gives him hospitality".

Undoubtedly, the Monsignor was quite right in rejecting the idea of expelling them: "The expulsion of Jews from a country is a lack of charity and justice towards the neighbouring countries on which these gnawing worms are dumped...".

But lo and behold, he naively expressed the idea that only a minority of Jews were dangerous, while the majority would be human beings like the others: "It is also too harsh a measure against those among the Jews who are not guilty of the crimes of the audacious handful who, through Freemasonry, exploit the nation".

Monsignor Meurin also quoted Abbot Kohn, the grandson of Jewish converts to Catholicism, a professor of theology who had been appointed Archbishop of Olmutz in Austria in 1892. In a passage from a course on canon law taught by him in 1891–1892, one could read: "The Christians of today would not be groaning under the oppression of the Jews if they had observed the prescriptions of the Church with regard to their relations with the Jews. The Church has always practised toleration towards them; she has even protected them; but she has never consented that Christians should live with them on a footing of perfect equality and absolute community[633]."

Monsignor Kohn, a professor of canon law, recalled that these prescriptions—in addition to the prohibition for Jews to exercise a public function that would give them any kind of authority over Christians—are all in the *corpus juris canonici* and were never abrogated.

Edouard Drumont had perfectly described the influence of the Jews and their role in the destruction of traditional society, but at no time, neither in his *Jewish France* (1886), nor in *The End of a World* (1889), had he sketched the slightest explanation of the universal "mission" of which

---

[632] Read about it in *Jewish Fanaticism*.
[633] Charles Auzias-Turenne, *Revue Catholique des Institutions et du Droit*, October 1893.

Jewish intellectuals boast. Later, in the 1930s, Lucien Rebatet, while analysing the Jewish question, also failed to set out clearly the aims of Judaism.

It was not until Monsignor Henri Delassus' book, *Americanism and the Anti-Christian Conspiracy*, published in 1899, that the motivations of the universal Jewish policy were clearly understood. Monsignor Henri Delassus, like Drumont, was originally from the North of France. He was born in Estaires in 1836. He was ordained a priest in Cambrai in 1862. A doctor of theology, he strongly denounced the French Revolution, Christian democracy, Americanism and Freemasonry. His main works on the Jewish-Masonic problem represent a veritable summation of counter-revolutionary thought. In 1904, Monsignor Delassus was appointed by Pius X as the pope's domestic prelate. In 1910, he published *The Anti-Christian Conjuration* in three volumes.

As far as we know, Monsignor Delassus was the first French author to have correctly explained the "planetary" project inherent in Judaism. The following are excerpts from his work that deal with this fundamental question:

"Indeed, the Jews—all, both those who hope for a personal Messiah and those who believe that this Messiah is born and grows and is none other than the idea of 1789—all hope to see realised, and soon—"*the times are near*"—the Messianic prophecies in the sense in which they have always understood them, that is to say, their kingdom over the whole world, the subjection of the whole human race to the race of Abraham and Judah. For this, they now say, two things are necessary: 1st, that the nations, renouncing all patriotism, should be founded in a universal republic; 2nd, that men should likewise renounce all religious particularity in order to merge also in a vague religiosity".

Mgr Delassus quoted one of his sources, an extract from the *Univers israélite* (VIII, p. 357, year 1867), which evoked the objectives of the universal Israelite Alliance founded by "Adolphe" Crémieux: "To bring down the barriers which separate what should be united. To unite all men, whatever their religion and region, in a common indifference. This is the aim which the founders and directors of the *Universal Israelite Alliance* set themselves... The programme of the *Alliance* does not consist of empty phrases. It is the great work of humanity..., the union of human society in a solid and faithful brotherhood[634]."

The *Israelite Archives* of 1886 gave an insight into the unifying project of the Jews through the words of an enlightened man named Hippolytus

---

[634] Monsignor Henri Delassus, *L'Américanisme et la conjuration antichrètienne (Americanism and the anti-Christian conspiracy)*, Société de Saint-Augustin, Desclée De Brouwer et Cie, Paris, 1899, p. 25-27.

Rodrigo (XIV, p. 628–629): "May temples be erected everywhere, welcoming into their precincts all men without distinction of religious origin! May all hearts, filled with the same sentiments of love, unburden themselves before the same God, the Father of all beings. Let all feed upon the same principles of virtue, morality and religion, and the hatreds of sects will disappear, and harmony will reign on earth, and the Messianic times, foretold by the prophets of Israel, will be realised[635]."

"Let us note in passing, wrote Monsignor Delassus pertinently, that Freemasonry has the same pretensions and expresses them in the same words. Nor does it fail to speak of humanitarian work and universal fraternity... Are these not the ideas which the Revolution has spread everywhere, the ideas which Freemasonry preaches without respite, the ideas of which liberalism prides itself?"

"Taking advantage of their dispersion and their presence on all points of the globe, the Jews want to be in humanity something like a leaven which will make of human society, at present divided into diverse nations and religions, a single and solid fraternity...All power must disappear to make room for the universal dominion of Judah, which will take the place of all powers existing at present, both in the spiritual and temporal order[636]."

In this totalitarian vision of the future of humanity, peoples and nations must unify to form a single, universal republic: "This universal republic will be infallibly governed by the Jewish people, the only truly cosmopolitan, universal people, the only people who at the same time happen to be the people who possess gold, the nerve of all power, the instrument of all dominion".

"To tear down all frontiers, to abolish all nationalities, beginning with the smallest, to make one State; to erase all idea of fatherland, to make common to all the whole earth, which belongs to all, to break, by cunning, by force, all treaties, to prepare everything for a vast democracy whose diverse races, brutalised by all kinds of immoralities, will be only of departments administered by the high ranks and by the Antichrist, supreme dictator who made himself their only god, such is the aim of the secret societies[637]."

Concerning "the mission that Israel claims to have received", Monsignor Delassus rightly wrote: "We know this mission, it is to prepare the way for the one they eagerly await, their messiah. The Talmudists are

---

[635] Henri Delassus, *L'Américanisme et la conjuration antichrètienne*, Société de Saint-Augustin, Desclée De Brouwer et Cie, Paris, 1899, p. 58.
[636] Henri Delassus, *L'Américanisme et la conjuration antichrètienne*, Société de Saint-Augustin, Desclée De Brouwer et Cie, Paris, 1899, p. 27-29.
[637] Henri Delassus, *L'Américanisme et la conjuration antichrètienne*, Société de Saint-Augustin, Desclée De Brouwer et Cie, Paris, 1899, p. 33-34, 42.

still waiting for a messiah in flesh and blood who will make them masters of the universe; the liberals say that there is no other messiah to wait for but the Revolution, whose 'principles' dissolve all societies and prepare their universal empire". "What they have in view is domination. To establish this dominion, it is not enough to annihilate patriotism in the hearts, it is also and above all necessary to extinguish religious faith, for nothing gives man so much dignity and independence as his union with God by faith and charity[638]."

Monsignor Delassus then quoted Monsignor Leon Meurin, who wrote in *Freemasonry, Synagogue of Satan*: "They believe themselves to be the people destined by Jehovah [Yahweh] to dominate over all nations. The riches of the earth belong to them, and the crowns of kings must be only emanations, dependencies of their *"Kether-Malkhuth"*. They imagined that the promised King would be an earthly king, his kingdom a kingdom of this world, and the *Kether-Malkhuth* a crown akin to that of the kings of human nations...For the Jews, the idea of universal dominion became something like their religion; it took root in their spirit, petrified in it as it were, and is indestructible [639]." Henri Delassus paid tribute to his predecessor who had understood that the attacks against the Catholic Church throughout the Middle Ages and up to contemporary times flowed from the source of the Judaic matrix: "It will be Monsignor Meurin's honour to have been the first to formulate, by emphasising on a serious examination of the documents, an answer that others had only glimpsed. For him, the agent of transmission of ancient errors down through the ages to the modern world, the true founder of heresies, their secret inspirer, then as now, from the Gnostics to the Freemasons, is the Jew[640]."

---

[638] Monsignor Henri Delassus, *L'Américanisme et la conjuration antichrètienne*, Société de Saint-Augustin, Desclée De Brouwer et Cie, Paris, 1899, p. 54, 56. ["It is necessary, however, to make oneself acceptable to the human groups with whom one wishes to exercise a "proselytism". What does this proselytism consist in, in inciting the faithful of the various religions to join Judaism? It never occurred to the Jews to do this kind of proselytising: they are a people, a race apart, "the first aristocracy of the world", the only true men; they never had the intention of elevating to them beings who are only human in appearance". Delassus, *L'Américanisme et la conjuration antichrètienne*, p. 54].

[639] Henri Delassus, *L'Américanisme et la conjuration antichrètienne*, Société de Saint-Augustin, Desclée De Brouwer et Cie, Paris, 1899, p. 19, 20.

[640] Henri Delassus, *L'Américanisme et la conjuration antichrètienne*, Société de Saint-Augustin, Desclée De Brouwer et Cie, Paris, 1899, p. 50. ["The historian who saw these various heresies constantly being born under his eyes, asked himself: Who then served as a link between all these sects? Who propagated these doctrines through the new peoples? How can we explain the sudden revivals of the pagan spirit, with the same ideas, the same symbols and the same practices within the Christian world, at such different times and in such different ways: with the Gnosis, in the first centuries; with

Delassus saw how the press at the end of the 19th century was already largely in the hands of Israel: "The opinion-makers today are above all Jews: they occupy the principal chairs of higher education and direct the press". "In France, in Europe, in all parts of the world, the Jews have created or acquired the most influential newspapers, they have men of their race in all the editorial offices; and by one means or another, directly or indirectly, they too often get into the Catholic newspapers facts, ideas and opinions which favour the execution of their plans". The Jews have "taken possession of the two most powerful organs of modern life-the bank and the press[641]"

So it was necessary to surrender to the evidence: "The Jews are now trapping the whole of Christian society as if in a net. One might almost say the whole world.

"Thanks above all to their action, which is as general as it is incessant, religious indifference is gaining ground every day and is advancing the "Jerusalem of the new order" which its followers are so eagerly awaiting. To reach this end, they work on the one hand to annihilate all patriotism and on the other hand to destroy all religious conviction. Under their direction, the press is employed in this work every day, all over the world, with indefatigable ardour, by sophistry, by the dissemination of facts which it judges favourable to its cause and the falsification of those which are contrary to it, and above all by the corruption of customs[642]."

In his 1910 work, *The Anti-Christian Conjuration*, Mgr Delassus

---

Manes, in the third century; in the eleventh century, with the Albigensians; in the thirteenth century, with the Templars; in the sixteenth century, with the Socinians; and today with the Masons? Was there between these heresies, diverse in name but identical in spirit, a living link, preserving, maintaining this spirit during their apparent periods of slumber?" Delassus, *L'Américanisme et la conjuration antichrètienne*, p. 49-50.

"The doctrines of the pagan Secret Societies were renewed in Gnosis by blending with Judaism, itself strongly blended with Paganism. Then, in Europe, the Gnostic, Manichaean, Albigensian and Templar sects succeeded one another, interpenetrating and inheriting each other's followers and doctrines. In turn, they were renewed in the powerful organisation of the Rosicrucians, where the ancient Gnosis was blended with the Jewish Kabbalah of the Talmud. And finally, it was Rosicrucian doctrine, both Gnostic and Kabbalistic, that Elias Ashmole introduced into the semi-professional groups of English Freemasons to form modern Freemasonry. In short, Freemasonry today is an extremely complex mixture of Eastern Paganism and Jewish Cabala. André Baron, *Secret Societies and their Crimes: from the Initiates of Isis to Modern Freemasons*, (*Les sociétés secrètes, leurs crimes — depuis les initiés d'Isis jusqu'aux francs-maçons modernes)*].

[641]Henri Delassus, *L'Américanisme et la conjuration antichrètienne*, Société de Saint-Augustin, Desclée De Brouwer et Cie, Paris, 1899, p. 69, 80, 21.

[642]Henri Delassus, *L'Américanisme et la conjuration antichrètienne*, Société de Saint-Augustin, Desclée De Brouwer et Cie, Paris, 1899, p. 212, 214.

already noted the growth of public debt in all States under Jewish rule, which was to rise exponentially throughout the 20th century: "Today, the Jews have succeeded in digging the abyss of debt in all States. It is a modern principle that States, Provinces, Cities, can tax the future for the benefit of the present. The Jewish capitalists provide the means. Senseless loans which will never be repaid, perpetually increase the crushing burden of taxation, and place all governments at the mercy of Jewry. Any "modern" government would be lost the moment it had the imprudence to antagonise the owners of big capital. How could it resist a coalition of Jews all at once closing their coffers[643]?"

"In the last century, with the help of the Revolution, the Jews have set out with a new ardour to pursue the ideal of their race, and to seize for this purpose all the living forces of the peoples who had the imprudence to admit them into their midst on an equal footing, using Christian morality towards them, whereas the Jews know only Talmudic morality. This is how they came to dominate us in France, or rather to tyrannise us from the point of view of political life and government, high banking and finance, industry and commerce, the press and public opinion[644]."

"The Jews, whose power has become so formidable in so short a time, will they see their hopes fulfilled, will they succeed in wrenching from the hearts what remains of patriotism, will they succeed, after rejecting religion in the temples, in depriving the souls of it, and then, when the ground has been thus prepared, will they see rise out of the midst of them the messiah whom they have for so many centuries longed for, to reduce the world to servitude? And then, when the ground has been thus prepared, will they see the messiah emerge from their midst whom they have been eagerly awaiting for so many centuries to reduce the world to servitude? It is certain that at no time in history have the times been more favourable to their domination. The political world, the economic and commercial world, the secret societies and the Jews work with indefatigable ardour for *cosmopolitan unity...Let there be* no mistake, the characters of the Talmudic messiah are the characters of the antichrist. The same sinister character is announced by both parties[645]."

However, according to Mgr Delassus, there should be no departure from the traditional doctrine and legislation of the Catholic Church. He recognised that the Church "had always protected the Jew against the

---

[643] Henri Delassus, *La Conjuration antichrétienne III*, Desclée De Brouwer, 1910, p. 1156.

[644] Henri Delassus, *La Conjuration antichrétienne III*, Desclée De Brouwer, 1910, p. 1124.

[645] Henri Delassus, *L'Américanisme et la conjuration antichrètienne*, Société de Saint-Augustin, Desclée De Brouwer et Cie, Paris, 1899, p. 214-218, 222.

legitimate but excessive indignation of the people whom he had exploited, deceived or betrayed". This was because he hoped for "the promised conversion of this people, in which he honours, in spite of everything, the remnants of what was the chosen nation, the people of God". "They must be guaranteed life and safety, but they must not be allowed to seize any power over Christians. If this legislation, so wise, had not been repudiated by modern governments, the Jewish question would not exist."

"In spite of their treachery and all their misdeeds, every good Christian must have for the Jews something of the feelings that were in the heart of St. Paul[646]."

Mgr Meurin had also noted the fabulous power acquired by the Jews since their emancipation: "Today it happens that these new citizens, after having monopolised most of the national wealth, tend to take over the government and to oppress those whom they have never ceased to consider as impure beings, gentiles, uncircumcised Philistines. All proposed measures, apart from those of the Church, will be futile, and those of the Church, to be effective, must be applied in concert with the State and by each of us personally, as is evident from the teachings of Bishop Kohn. As long as the Jews are Jews, that is, at least until the end of the world, the only policy to be pursued towards them will be to keep them at a distance, not by mistreating them, but also by relating to them as little as possible and by preventing them from doing any harm. *Iudaceos subiacere christianis oportet et ab eis pro sola humanitate foveri*".

Thus, for Monsignor Meurin, the Jewish question will not be resolved until "the end of time", when Jesus Christ triumphs over the Jewish messiah (the Antichrist). Catholics may therefore be encouraged to give their enemies a free hand, to let them work on the advent of their messiah, since they believe their final triumph is assured. But in reality, it is the Jew who triumphs in this present world. Christians are disarmed in the face of Jewish messianism, which constantly feeds the political activism of the sect members and strengthens their hope and will towards liberation and final triumph. But if we look at Jewish messianism with a mirror, a light appears, and the truth imposes itself naturally on all good men: The messiah will only come after the complete disappearance, after the apostasy of the last Jew.

Austria-Hungary at the end of the 19th century

---

[646]Mgr Henri Delassus, *La Conjuration antichrétienne III*, Desclée De Brouwer, 1910, p. 1119.

CXXVI.

In 1899, a ritual crime took place in Bohemia that sparked a new wave of anti-Semitism. Anezka Hruzová, a 19-year-old Czech Catholic girl, lived in Klein Veznic (now Veznicka), near Polná. She travelled there every day to work as a seamstress. On the evening of 29 March 1899, she left her workplace for the last time. Three days later, on 1 April, her body was found in a forest: her throat had been slit and her dress torn. The police's suspicions first focused on four vagrants who had been seen in the vicinity of the forest on the afternoon of the day the crime had been committed. Among them was Leopold Hilsner, a 23-year-old Jew. He claimed to have left the forest that afternoon long before the supposed time of the crime, but was unable to provide any verifiable alibi. Hilsner was arrested and tried in Kuttenberg (Kutná Hora) from 12 to 16 September. He denied any responsibility, despite the blood stains on his trousers and several witnesses who claimed to have seen him leaving the forest in a particularly disturbed state. His death sentence provoked cries of outrage from the international Jewish community.

Tomáš Masaryk, professor at the University of Prague and future president of Czechoslovakia, interceded by appealing to the Supreme Court, and a retrial took place in Pisek. Several anti-Jewish demonstrations, sometimes violent, took place in regions such as Holleschau and Nachod.

The leaders of Vienna's Jewish community intrigued the government and organised a major conference on 7 October. On 11 December, August Schreiber, one of the editors of the *Deutsches Volksblatt*, was sentenced to four months in prison for defamation of Jews, which only aggravated tensions. Two weeks later, Docgor Baxa, the family's lawyer, accused the government of bias in favour of the Jews in a speech to the Bohemian Diet.

Meanwhile, Hilsner was accused of another murder, that of Maria Klimova, a servant who had disappeared on 17 July 1898 and whose body was found on 27 October 1899 in the same forest as the body of Anezka Hruzová. Hilsner was tried for this second crime in Pisek between 25 October and 14 November 1900. On the last day, the court pronounced the verdict: Hilsner was found guilty of the two murders and sentenced to death. On 11 June 1901, however, the emperor pardoned the culprit and the sentence was commuted to life imprisonment.

At that time, in Vienna as in Berlin, London and Paris, the mainstream press was already largely in Israeli hands. The most popular artists, the ones who benefited most from laudatory articles in the newspapers, were mostly Jewish. In the Austrian capital at the end of the 19th century, the writers Stefan Zweig, Hugo von Hoffmanstahl, Arthur Schnitzler, the composers Guatav Mahler and Arnold Schönberg were the only ones to be mentioned. The cosmopolitan spirit triumphed everywhere. Catholicism, patriotism, family values were attacked and mocked almost everywhere. Pornography began to spread more and more, and soon, under the influence of Sigmund Freud working in the Viennese ghetto, homosexuality would be trivialised, as well as other genres of 'discovery'.

Adolf Hitler had noticed and written in some well-known pages of his *Mein Kampf* that pimping was particularly visible in the Austrian capital. Numerous women were literally kidnapped and sent abroad for prostitution.

The White slave trade scandalised European public opinion from the 1880s onwards. The journalist François Trocase, who lived in Austria, left some interesting notes on the subject: "In Austria, the Jews have instilled in young girls a dissolute morality, deplorable habits and an unheard-of demoralisation. The native baseness of their feelings, money and their utter lack of conscience predispose them singularly to the role of seducers. Prostitution is thus a constant menace at every door for the young girls who, in the big cities, become servants of the Jews in large numbers. It may be asserted that most of the unfortunate girls who become corrupt and prostitute themselves in the large Austrian cities owe their first downfall to the Jews. It must be remembered, indeed, that most of those who come from the provinces to work as servants in Vienna and Budapest are forced to enter the service of Jewish families, since many Christian families are no longer in a position to pay servants. It can be assumed that the two and a half million Jews living in Austria and Hungary have as many maids, if not more, as the 38 million Austrians and Hungarians belonging to the Christian denominations. Moreover, nine-tenths of the maids are Christian; there are very few Jewish maids. However, the constant and well-known customs of Israelite families towards their female servants too often exert a detrimental influence on the latter. It is not uncommon to see Jewish mothers taking charge of young girls who have the special task, in addition to their ordinary work, of satisfying the whims of the children of the house. The mother not only knows this and tolerates it, but often wants it to be so herself. In her mind, the aim is to prevent the young people from getting sick before they get married. Of course, we are only talking about Jewish mothers and families. Despite this special allowance, the maids' wages do not increase. It is usually 10 guilders (21 francs) per month. And all too often, when the young maid is dismissed to make way for another, she is forced by acquired habits to take refuge in one of the hospices, so numerous in the two capitals of the monarchy, run by the co-religionists of her former masters[647]."

François Trocase added: "The relationship between Jewish businessmen and Christian women workers is very similar to that between

---

[647] François Trocase, *L'Autriche juive*, P. Dupont & A.Pierret, Paris, 1899, p. 150-151.

young Jewish men and their mothers' maids. Unfortunately, they are tainted by the same character of immorality[648]."

An investigation into the working conditions of women workers had brought to light the behaviour of a large Jewish industrialist who employed in his workshops numerous apprentices aged fourteen to sixteen: "When they had completed their two years of apprenticeship without the slightest salary, they could only obtain from him the worker's certificate to which they were entitled, on condition that they sacrificed what Dumas called "their capital". The reported exploits of another Jew were no less typical. He alone operated 1400 looms in various parts of Austrian Silesia. He publicly boasted that over the years he had received intimate visits from more than a thousand of his workers, women and girls, married and unmarried, whom he had in turn invited to come and ask him for work. He shamelessly referred to these intimate visits as "commissions" which were deducted from wages."

"The deep poverty that reigns among the working classes, the lack of bread, in the full sense of the word, explains all too well these very common practices in Austria. As Mr. Gregorig, the Member of Parliament for Vienna, has said publicly, it has come to be accepted as a proven fact that workers in Austria generally only marry girls who have previously been deflowered by Jews. Mr. Gregorig uses an even stronger expression. He says: Girls discarded by the Jews as merchandise that no longer has any value (with *Juden abgelegle Waare*.) Marriage between Christians is by no means a guarantee against the sensual appetites of the Jews. Apparently, the Talmud only forbids adultery with a Jewish woman. The prohibition does not apply to the wife of a Christian, because one who is not a Jew, according to rabbinical doctrine, is not legally married. This is the living commentary on the Talmudic saying: "Only Jews are men; the rest, all those who are not Jews, are nothing but cattle seed[649]", explained Trocase. Thus, it is understood that for Jews, adultery with a goy woman is not a fault or offence.

In the rural world, the Jews exploited the misery of the people in the same way, especially in the poorer provinces, such as Bukovina and Galicia. When a ruined peasant could not pay the interest on his debt, his daughters offered their bodies to pay the debt. The forced surrender of her virginity had the unique power to prevent the father from being seized and thrown off his land.

Numerous young girls in Vienna and Budapest had disappeared; they had fallen into prostitution rings. The poorest Jews served as intermediaries.

---

[648] François Trocase, *L'Autriche juive*, P. Dupont & A.Pierret, Paris, 1899, p. 152.
[649] François Trocase, *L'Autriche juive*, P. Dupont & A.Pierret, Paris, 1899, p. 152-153.

They knew how to supply young women to Turkish harems and brothels all over the world. The Jewish gangsters had no scruples about sending the young Christian girls to prostitute themselves far from their homeland, to Istanbul or Buenos Aires: "This shameful speciality, which disgraces our century, belongs exclusively to the Jews. We must leave the infamy to them. For a long time we have ignored the details. Large numbers of young girls were seen to disappear mysteriously, without knowing what became of them[650]."

In 1892, the Lemberg (now Lvov, in Ukrainian Galicia) trial had been a high-profile affair. Twenty-eight Jews were accused of pimping. The network consisted of recruiters in Europe and local agents in Turkey. The girls were sent to Constantinople, Egypt, South Africa, India and America[651]: "These wretched men had tricked a large number of young Christian girls, most of whom were still at school, into a skilfully prepared trap. They had promised them the most advantageous working conditions in order to persuade them to go abroad. As soon as they crossed the border, they were treated as slaves and any attempt to escape was severely repressed. Once in Turkey, they were sold to brothels for an average of 1,000 marks each. Who are the owners of these houses in Turkey? Only Jews; no one else. The poor victims who wanted to resist were locked up in underground dungeons and subjected to ill-treatment. When the police finally decided to intervene, sixty of them were released. They were rescued from the clutches of these barbarians. But alas, they were lost in body and soul. The trial lasted ten days. It brought to light monstrous details. It was clearly established that hundreds of young girls had been driven by the Lemberg gang to shame, despair, disease and death. Due to loopholes in the law, the culprits were sentenced to insignificant penalties. The leader of the gang, Isaac Schifenstein, was sentenced to one year in prison. All the others served only a few months in prison and resumed their sinister trade, but with more cunning and mystery[652]."

In 1918, anti-Jewish riots broke out in the city, as the trafficking of women had not yet been stopped. Meanwhile, the Austrian parliament was still debating the disappearance of Christian maids sent to foreign brothels.

The Lemberg trial was naturally exploited by the anti-Semitic resistance. Predictably, the abuses committed by Jews against Christian women contributed to the population's deep animosity towards them. "Sensual misdeeds, which the law apparently could not punish, and, in general, abuses committed by Jews against women contributed greatly to the explosion of anger that gave rise to Austrian anti-Semitism. When these

---

[650] François Trocase, *L'Autriche juive*, P. Dupont & A.Pierret, Paris, 1899, p. 154.
[651] Read the long chapter on this subject in our book *The Jewish Mafia* (2008).
[652] François Trocase, *L'Autriche juive*, P. Dupont & A.Pierret, Paris, 1899, p. 154-155.

facts are mentioned in Vienna, people's looks take on an expression of unspeakable hatred[653]," Trocase observed.

The demoralisation of the masses gave way to hatred; the legitimate hatred of the victim against his oppressor. The resistance was organised under the leadership of Dr. Karl Lueger and his Christian Socialist party, which attacked above all the big Jewish capitalists. All kinds of anti-Semitic writings were circulating in the capital at the time. In Vienna, the anti-Semites gained ground, and in 1897 Lueger was elected mayor of Vienna, remaining in office until 1910.

The leading figures in Austrian anti-Semitism at the time were Prince Alois of Lichtenstein, Dr. Pattaï (deputy for Stiria), Dr. Gessman and Dr. Psenner. Vergani, a member of parliament from Lower Austria, had founded in 1881 the *Deutsches Volsblatt*, an anti-Semitic newspaper that published two editions a day. The paper was the target of the basest attacks by Jewish journalists. Figures such as Canon Scheiber and the intellectual Deckert also distinguished themselves. For his part, MP Schneider even considered using more radical means to put an end to the Jewish question.

CXXVII. The Fall of Tsarist Russia

Russia, which had administered most of the former Polish territory since the late 18th century, had inherited the large Jewish population that had settled there throughout the Middle Ages. Previously, the country had been *"judenrein"*, purified of the presence of Jews, since Ivan the Terrible had decreed that no Jew would set foot on Russian soil. After him, all tsars had remained faithful to this principle, including Peter the Great.

Jews in the annexed territories were to remain in the "Zone of Residence[654]", which stretched from the Baltic Sea to the Black Sea. Evidently, anti-Semitism was just as virulent as in other parts of Europe. Under Nicholas I (1825–1855), Jews in the Zone of Residence, suspected of spying for Germany, had to evacuate villages within 50 kilometres of the Russian border.

In his well-documented book *Two Hundred Years Together (1795–1995)*, published in 2002, the great writer Aleksandr Solzhenitsyn provided, for example, the valuable testimony of Senator Gabriel Romanovitch Derjavine, who had been sent by the Tsar at the end of the 19th century to investigate the causes of the famines ravaging Belarus. This statesman, who later became Minister of Justice under Alexander I, reported in his report that in the Belarusian countryside the Jews were mainly engaged in

---

[653] François Trocase, *L'Autriche juive*, P. Dupont & A.Pierret, Paris, 1899, p. 157.
[654] On the Zone of Residence read *The Jewish Fanaticism* (2007).

the production of firewater, going through the villages, especially in autumn, at harvest time: "They give the peasants and their relatives to drink, collect their debts and deprive them of their last subsistence...They cheat the drunks and rob them from head to foot, leaving them in complete destitution". It is true that the peasants, "when the harvests are over, sin by their excessive spending; they drink, eat, feast, pay the Jews their old debts, and then, to pay their drunkenness, all that the latter demand of them; so that when winter comes they are in want". These excesses were encouraged by the presence of numerous taverns: "In every village," wrote Derjavine, "there is one or sometimes several taverns built by the owners, in which vodka is sold day and night for the greater profit of the Jewish distillers...In this way, the Jews manage to extort from them not only their daily bread, but also their agricultural tools, their goods, their time, their health, their very life". They make use of "all sorts of tricks and subterfuges" which "reduce the poor and stupid villagers to hunger[655]".

This situation explained why the regulations of 1804 and 1835 forbade Belarusian Jews to reside in the countryside. In Ukraine they could live anywhere except Kiev and some villages; nowhere in Russia were ghettos within cities mandatory. In the second half of the century, under Alexander II, the limitations imposed on Jews fell one after the other, so that they could distil and sell alcohol in their places of residence. In 1872 they "owned 89% of the distilleries[656]" in the Southwest.

The mass of Jews certainly lived miserably, like the Russians, but some were immensely rich. The famous Israel Brodski owned seventeen sugar factories. Many great Jewish fortunes had also been built on the exploitation of Russian natural resources, especially the export of timber abroad and the extraction of gold. They also played a leading role in the export of agricultural products: "From 1878, 60% of grain exports passed through Jewish hands; soon it would be 100%". The Guinzbourg family was particularly prominent. Others, such as Samuel Poliakov, invested in railways, becoming known in the 1880s as the "railway king", although the Russian state would later become the main builder. Banking was naturally his favourite sector: "More than half of the credit, savings and loan institutions were located in the Zone of residence", and "in 1911, 86% of their members were Jews[657]". By the beginning of the 20th century, Jews had gained strong positions in vital sectors of the Russian economy and

---

[655] Alexandre Soljenitsyne, *Deux siècles ensemble, Tome I*, Fayard, 2002, p. 51-54.
[656] Alexandre Soljenitsyne, *Deux siècles ensemble, Tome I*, Fayard, 2002, p. 153, 175.
[657] Alexandre Soljenitsyne, *Deux Siècles ensemble, Tome I*, Fayard, 2002, p. 175, 333-335. This was confirmed by the Sephardic sociologist Edgar Morin: 'Seventeen Polish banks out of twenty were Jewish Gentiles in the mid-19th century' (*Le monde moderne et la queston juive*, Seuil, 2006, p.117).

had settled in the capitals despite regulations forbidding them to do so: 16,000 in Moscow in 1880, 30–40,000 in St. Petersburg in 1900, 81,000 in Kiev in 1913, and the number of Jews settled outside the Zone of Residence was increasing year by year. Tsar Alexander II had authorised young Jewish university graduates to settle throughout Russia. The same measure was approved in 1879 for pharmacists, nurses and dentists.

With the arrival of Alexander II in 1855, the regime was effectively liberalised and a policy of assimilation was to prepare Jews for full citizenship. Jews were thus able to enrol in high schools and universities. From 1874 onwards, they flocked to general education establishments, which was a privilege since only 55% of Russians were enrolled in school until 1914. In 1881, Jews accounted for about 9% of students, in 1887 this figure grew to 14.5%, but in some universities this percentage was much higher: the medical faculty in Kharkov had 42% Jews and the law faculty in Odessa 41%[658]. In the last decades of the 19th century, this Russian-speaking Jewish *intelligentsia was to play* a key role in the intellectual and political movements that were to undermine traditional Russian society. Tsarist power had itself helped to train in its universities those who were to be the main promoters of its downfall.

At the beginning of the 19th century, anti-Jewish vigilance was carried out by an Italian priest from Tuscany who had obtained the chair of Oriental languages at the University of Warsaw, then under Russian rule. Luigi Chiarini (1789–1832), an orientalist and well-versed in Hebrew, had obtained this post thanks to the protection of Potocki, the Minister of Education. In 1830, Chiarini published his two-volume *Theory of Judaism*, in which he demonstrated that the evils of Judaism were mainly rooted in the teachings of the Talmud. The Jews, he argued, should return to the simple Mosaic faith and the state should help them to free themselves by establishing schools where the Bible would be taught and the Hebrew language would be studied. Luigi Chiarini also worked on the French translation of the Babylonian Talmud, with notes of explanation and refutation. Encouraged by Tsar Nicolas I himself, he published this study the following year, but only the first two volumes saw the light of day. Chiarini was forced to abandon his project because of the Polish insurrection of 1830[659].

The ideologist Ivan Aksakov, the tireless animator of the Slavophile movement, had also risen up against Jewish power. In 1867, he paraphrased Karl Marx: "The real question is not to emancipate the Jews, but to

---

[658] Alexandre Soljenitsyne, *Deux siècles ensemble*, p. 180, 231

[659] *Encyclopedia Judaica*, Gerusalemme s. d. vol 5, p. 409-410. The Jewish Encyclopedia, New York-London 1905–1912, IV vol., p. 21–22. In Curzio Nitoglia, *Contre-révolution et judéo-maçonnerie, Sodalitium N°50*, juin-juillet 2000.

emancipate the Russian population from the Jews, to free the Russian men of the South-West from the Jewish yoke".

Aksakov found a valuable ally in Jacob Brafman. This convert, a professor of Hebrew at the Orthodox seminary in Minsk, was the Holy Synod's expert on the problems of the mission to the Jews. From 1867 onwards, he began to publish articles in the *Vilna Courier* on Jewish communal life and customs, which he then used to write two major works with their respective explanatory appendices: *The Book of the Kahal*[660] and *The Local and Universal Jewish Brotherhoods*, both published in 1869. These books were distributed by the government to all administrative services. In *The Book of the Kahal*, Jacob Brafman drew on the archives of the Minsk community to denounce the means employed by the Jews to expel the Goyim from trade and industry and to concentrate capital and real estate in their hands. All the *Kahal* ordinances published by Jacob Brafman in his book were from the period 1794–1833. Their authenticity, the author said, was proven by the age of the paper. The *Kahal* was officially abolished in 1844, but the Jewish communities nevertheless remained highly structured and cohesive. Be that as it may, this publication greatly annoyed the Jews, who rushed to buy and burn or hide as many copies as they could scavenge[661].

In 1837, Dostoyevsky, in his *Diary of a Writer*, lambasted the *"Jids"* and criticised financiers. Later, he would accuse the Jew Disraeli, England's lord and master, of using the Turks against Russia. In 1877, Prime Minister Disraeli actually sent the British fleet to the Sea of Marmara to protect Istanbul, threatened by the Russian army. Dostoyevsky, for his part, preached the crusade to liberate Constantinople. In 1880, shortly before his death, the great Russian genius even praised the "great Aryan race".

As for Tolstoy, while not clearly anti-Semitic, he defended the Aryanness of Christ: "I would like to write something to show how the teaching of Christ, who was not a Jew, has been substituted for that of the Jewish apostle Paul; but I doubt if I can do it. I lack the necessary time and I have other more pressing tasks to attend to. But it is an important and admirable subject[662]."

In 1879, in Kutais in the Caucasus, a ritual murder took place. At the same time, the former Polish priest Hippolytus Lutostansky, who had

---

[660] The *Kahal* was the institution that governed the Jewish community in Eastern Europe.
[661] An Argentinian writer, Hugo Wast, wrote in 1935 a strongly anti-Semitic novel entitled *El Kahal*, well known in Latin America (available from Omniaveritas, ndt). On Jacob Brafman and the kidnappers, read *The Mirror of Judaism*.
[662] Léon Poliakov, *Histoire de l'antisémitisme I*, 1981, Points Seuil, 1990, p. 318.

converted to Orthodox Christianity, had written a long treatise on the subject (*The Christian Blood for the Jews*, 1876), which gave rise to a lively public discussion. The first Russian newspaper, the *Novoïe Vrémia*, in turn published extensive passages from Wilhelm Marr's book, *The Victory of Semitism over Germanism*. Also reread was the book by Michael Neophyte, a former rabbi who had converted and taken vows, and who had published in 1803, in Iasi (Moldavia), a study dealing with cases of ritual crimes entitled *Refutation of the Religion of the Jews*. The book was published under the patronage of Metropolitan Iacov Stamati[663]. Michael Neophyte swore on a crucifix that these crimes had taken place and that he himself had been a former beheader. Encouraged by its success, Hippolytus Lutostanski published in 1879 another work entitled *The Talmud and the Jews*.[664]

The assassination of Alexander II on 1 March 1881 had the effect of interrupting the process of liberalisation of the regime, provoking repression and further radicalising the revolutionary groups. The attack, which culminated a series of failed attempts by *Narodnaïa* (The People's Will), confirmed all fears about the Jews. In Russia, as elsewhere, the Marxist socialist movement was widely promoted by Jewish doctrinaires, who were immediately the target of all accusations.

The Jewish historian Leon Poliakov tried to dismantle the 'myth' of the Jewish revolutionary movement in his pages: 'The bomber, Ignatius Grinevitzki, was described in the official report as a fairly typical Russian, "with a round, plump face and a broad nose", but the day after the bombing, the *Novoïe Vrémia* described an "Eastern-type individual with an aquiline nose"'. As for the *Narodnaïa*, Poliakof pointed out, it was an organisation "composed almost exclusively—it is worth specifying—of real Russians". The Jewish historian was thus making his contribution to the work of destroying the "legend".

Solzhenitsyn noted however in his work that the Tsar had been assassinated on the eve of Purim, an annual Jewish holiday during which Jews celebrate their victory over their enemies, and that the attack had been prepared at the home of one Hessia Helfman[665]. The information was

---

[663]This book was republished in 2005 by the *Librairie du Savoir*, under the title *Le Sang chrétien* (*The Christian Blood*).

[664]Recall that in February 2007, Professor Ariel Toaff, son of the former Chief Rabbi of Rome, published a 400-page book entitled *Pasque di sangue* (*Passover of Blood, the Jews of Europe and the Accusations of Ritual Murder*), in which he acknowledged that ritual murder was practised by some Ashkenazi Jews in the Middle Ages. Read about it in *Jewish Fanaticism* (2007).

[665]Frank L. Britton, *Behind communism*. On the festival of Purim read *The Mirror of Judaism*.

corroborated by another Jewish historian, Henri Minczeles: "Among the revolutionaries arrested was Hessia Helfman, a young Jewish girl who had stored dynamite in her garret[666]."

The assassination of the Tsar set off the powder keg and numerous anti-Jewish pogroms broke out, mainly in the Ukraine. Shortly afterwards, during Holy Week, on 24 April 1881—a week traditionally conducive to all anti-Jewish outbursts—a pogrom broke out in Elisabetgrad, followed by larger ones in Kiev and Odessa, and in dozens of other localities. The pogroms always took place exclusively in south-west Russia, Solzhenitsyn pointed out. The destruction was impressive, but no deaths were reported at the time.

The laws of May 1882 restricted the Jews' zone of economic influence. They were forbidden to settle in the countryside, near the peasants they used to exploit, as well as in some cities such as Kiev and Yalta, the imperial residence in the Crimea. Acquisition of land and real estate was forbidden. Outside the Zone of Residence, especially in the two capitals, Moscow and St. Petersburg, the few tens of thousands of privileged Jewish individuals who had been able to settle there were invited to leave those cities. Jews were forbidden to give their names and surnames in Russian, and their passports had to bear their true nationality written in red ink. But these measures were cushioned by the corruption of Russian officials who often allowed themselves to be bribed by the Jews.

In July 1887, a measure limited Jewish access to secondary schools: 10% in the Zone of Residence, 3% in the capitals, and 5% elsewhere. In 1901, these quotas were reduced to 7, 2 and 3%. The civil service, the teaching profession, the judiciary and many other careers were barred.

In 1891, 20,000 Jews were expelled from Moscow to the Residence Zone and more than 2,000 from St. Petersburg. Residence permits were only granted to a small privileged group of businessmen, graduates and master craftsmen.

On the other hand, the regime encouraged conversions: a married convert was thus cut off from the ties that bound him to his partner and children, and received a sum of fifteen to thirty roubles after his abjuration. In addition, the number of synagogues was severely restricted. The Moscow synagogue was closed in 1892 for *"indecency"*.

In 1892, the St Petersburg Academy of Sciences published the best and most careful anthology of Talmudic maxims concerning the figure of Jesus Christ and Christians in general: *Christianus in Talmude Judaeorum, sive rabbinicae doctrinae de christianis secreta* (*The Christian in the Talmud of the Jews, or the secrets of rabbinic teaching about Christians*), published

---

[666]Henri Minczeles, *Histoire générale du Bund*, 1995, Denoël, 1999, p. 31.

by the printing house of the Metropolitan Archbishop of Mogilev. Its author, Father Justin Bonaventure Pranaitis, was a Catholic priest of Lithuanian origin, holder of the chair of Hebrew at the Imperial Ecclesiastical Academy of the Catholic Church in Old St. Petersburg. The book reproduced the Hebrew text of the rabbinical prescriptions with its Latin translation. But the copies almost completely disappeared and only a small number were saved from the Bolshevik purge. An edition of one of the valuable copies, with the corresponding Italian translation, was published in Milan in 1939; the Argentine priest Julio Meinvielle used it to complete the successive editions of his book[667]. Later, the work was translated into English, French, Spanish, etc., under the title *The Talmud Unmasked*:

"Since the word Jeschua means "Saviour", the name of Jesus rarely appears in Jewish books. It almost always appears under the abbreviation Jeschu, mischievously composed of the initial letters of three words: *Immach SCHemo Vezikro*—'Let his name and memory be blotted out'".

"The book of Zohar III (282) relates that Jesus died like a beast and that he was buried "in a dung heap where the carrion of dogs and donkeys is thrown... and where the sons of Esau [the Christians] and Ishmael [the Turks], that is Jesus and Muhammad, the uncircumcised and impure are buried like dead dogs"[668]."

Meinvielle referred to the teachings of the Talmud unveiled by Bishop Pranaitis: "About Christ: He is called with contempt "this man", "a chidam", "the carpenter's son", or the "hanged one". It is taught that he is the spurious son of a menstruous woman. That he had in him the soul of Esau, that he was a fool, a conjuror, a seducer, an idolater, that he was crucified, buried in hell, and that he is to this day an idol to his followers. As a seducer or idolater, he could teach nothing but error and heresy, and this is irrational and impossible to fulfil... The most abominable thing imaginable is said of Christians. That they are idolaters, wicked men, worse than the Turks, murderers, libertines, unclean animals, unworthy to be called men, beasts in human form, pollutants like dung, oxen and asses, swine, dogs, worse than dogs; that they propagate after the manner of beasts, that they are of diabolical origin; that their souls proceed from the devil and are to return to the devil in hell after death; that the corpse of a dead Christian is indistinguishable from the remains of an extinct beast[669]."

---

[667] Julio Meinvielle, *El Judío*, First Edition, Editorial Antídoto, 1936—*El judío en el misterio de la historia*, Sixth Edition, Cruz y Fierro Editores, Buenos Aires, 1982, p. 48.

[668] These are the insults contained in the *Toledot Jeshu* (*The Life of Jesus*), a work from the second century AD.

[669] Julio Meinvielle, *El judío en el misterio de la historia*, Sixth Edition, Cruz y Fierro Editores, Buenos Aires, 1982, p. 48-49. [The Christians are called *Notsrim*, Nazarenes,

Pranaitis died in 1917, during the "Russian" revolution, probably tortured by Jewish militants who represented the spearhead of Bolshevism. Let us note in passing that the Russian Orthodox clergy did not then produce any champions of anti-Semitism, as did the Protestant pastor Stoecker in Germany or the Jesuits of the Civilta Cattolica in Rome.

After the creation of the S.R. (Socialist-Revolutionary) party, Jews constituted a solid majority within the leadership of the movement. The members of the small circle of leaders were Jews: Mendel, Wittenberg, Levine, Levite and Azev. The party decided early on to take up armed struggle to bring about the overthrow of the Tsarist regime and a Combat Organisation was immediately set up to spread terror. This organisation was led by an individual named Guerchuni (from 1901 to 1903). Of Jewish origin, a former trainer in a pharmacy, he was about thirty years old when he drew up the statutes of the Organisation. Under his leadership, the O.C. men assassinated Interior Minister Sipriaguine, shot Prince Obolinsky and killed Governor Bogdanovitch in 1903. Sipriaguine's successor, Plehve, was appointed Minister of the Interior in 1902.

When Guerchuni fell at the hands of the police in Kiev, he was replaced by one of his congeners, the engineer Evno Azev, who led the organisation until 1906. On 15 July 1904, a bomb put an end to Plehve's days. Grand Duke Sergius was also killed in another bomb attack. After Evno Azev, another Jewish terrorist took over: Zilberberg.

The Combat Organisation then suffered heavy casualties and was disbanded after several disagreements within the Central Committee. A new terrorist group was then formed by Zilberberg under the name of the Combat Detachment. But Zilberberg died in February 1907. A little later, on 2 September 1911, Stolypine, the Tsar's Minister of the Interior who had launched a major land reform between 1906 and 1910, was assassinated in Kiev by the Jewish extremist Bogrov, during the ceremonies marking the anniversary of the 300th anniversary of the dynasty[670].

After 1881, the most important pogrom took place in Kichiniev, the capital of Bessarabia, during the Passover holidays of 1903. The city was 45% populated by Jews. Paul Kruchevane, owner of the local newspaper and later editor of *The Protocols of the Elders of Zion*, had been denouncing Judaism for several years. But it was the murder of a teenager that lit the

---

and all the names by which non-Jews are called are applied to them. *Aboda zara*, **that** is, cultivators of idolatry; *Acum,* worshippers of the stars and planets; *Obde Elilim,* servants of idols; *Minim,* heretics; *Edom,* idumeans; *Goim,* gentiles; *Nokhrim,* foreigners, strangers; *Amme Aarez,* people of the earth, ignorant; *Apichorosim,* epicureans; *Cutim,* Samaritans. *The Jew in the Mystery of History,* p. 48].

[670]Roland Gaucher, *Les Terroristes,* Editions Albin Michel, 1965; and in *Planetary Hopes.*

powder keg. On the eve of Passover, everyone knew something was going to happen. On Palm Sunday, 6 April, the pogrom broke out. The mob attacked the Jews and set fire to their houses. Two people were killed on the first day, but on the second day, 47 were killed and half a thousand wounded. The army did not intervene until Monday evening to restore calm. Nearly a third of the houses in the town had been destroyed or damaged. Once again, the "International (Jewish) Community" was up in arms. The entire foreign press cried out against the Russian barbarity and expressed the need to establish a real democracy in the country, to give equal rights to the poor Jews and to enforce the rights of "man[671]".

In 1904 there was no recurrence, but in 1905, during the Sino-Russian war, a great wave of pogroms again swept through Jewish communities that made no secret of their pro-Japanese stance[672]. In Kiev, Odessa and several other Ukrainian cities, fierce clashes took place between the Ukrainians and the Jews. The Jews, for their part, had formed paramilitary groups of several thousand fighters. Violence broke out in hundreds of localities, probably encouraged by the authorities themselves. There were then some fifty large pogroms over the last decade until October 1905 and about six hundred smaller ones, causing a total of 810 dead and 1770 wounded. The international (Jewish) community, again outraged, and the Rothschild family refused to underwrite the Russian government's loans. In 1906, two major pogroms broke out again in Bialistock and Siedlce (110 dead in total).

From 1880 to 1910 more than 2.5 million Jews left Russia. Jewish historians always omit to explain the causes of this exodus, confining themselves to denouncing "persecutions" and unjustified pogroms. In reality, the emigration of Jews was mainly motivated by the establishment, in 1896, of the state monopoly on spirits and the suppression of all private distilleries. This measure aimed at protecting the peasantry and forcing Jews to leave the countryside, explained Aleksandr Solzhenitsyn, "had dealt a severe blow to the economic activity of Jews in Russia". It was therefore from that time onwards that Jewish emigration out of Russia increased markedly[673].

Anti-Semitic pamphlets flourished everywhere. As many as 2837 were

---

[671] A very serious historian such as Arkadi Vaksberg wrote: In April 1903, "a pogrom decimated the Jewish population of Kichiniev". (*Staline et les juifs*, Robert Laffont, 2003, p. 17). Jewish organisations and witnesses had first claimed five hundred dead; the number was later revised downwards.

[672] The New York Jewish banker Jacob Schiff supported Japan's foreign policy, see *Planetary Hopes*.

[673] Alexandre Soljénitsyne, *Deux siècles ensemble*, tome I, Fayard, 2002, p. 326. Read in *Jewish Fanaticism*.

counted in the decade 1906–1916. The writings of the German Eugen Dühring were well known in Russia in those years. In St. Petersburg, Peter Ivanovitch Ratchkovsky, appointed deputy director of the police department, was officially in charge of anti-Semitic propaganda.

In 1905, Sergei Nilus, a Russian magistrate of Swiss origin, procurator of the provincial court of the Caucasus, published the first edition of *The Protocols of the Elders of Zion*, acquired in 1901. The document was presented as the exposition of a supposed Sage of Israel speaking to his peers about a plan for world domination. It was the minutes of conversation during secret sessions, some twenty-four according to Sergei Alexandrovitch Nilus' version, and twenty-seven according to George Vassilievitch Butmi's version, published the following year. A world government, a universal super-government would reign Peace on the planet, a peace that would be universal and definitive after a world war, as revealed in these Protocols[674]. Here are some extracts from *The Protocols of the Elders of Zion*:

Session X: *"When we have made our coup d'état, we shall say to the peoples: everything was going frightfully wrong, you have all suffered more than can be borne. We have come to tear in pieces the causes of your torments: nationalities, frontiers and the diversity of currencies... To obtain this result, it is necessary to lead all to universal suffrage, without distinction of class or fortune. Our aim is to establish the despotism of the majority, something unattainable with the exclusive voting of the most enlightened and wealthy classes"*.

This idea was repeated later in the same session: *"The recognition of our world sovereign can be effected even before all constitutions are finally abolished. The most propitious moment for this will have come when the peoples, tormented by upheavals and disorders in view of the impotence of their rulers—provoked by us—will have lost all confidence in them and will*

---

[674]Protocol V: *"We shall so fatigue the Christians that they will be compelled to offer us an international power which will be able to monopolise the governmental powers of all and form a supreme universal government"*. Protocol VII: *"We must be prepared to deal with those who oppose our projects. If necessary, let the neighbouring country declare war on the nation that seeks to hinder us. But if both should unite against us, then we will unleash a world war... Already the world project is approaching the ends set out above. To achieve its complete success, we need to convince the governments of the gentiles through what is vulgarly called public opinion. Popular judgement has been predisposed by us through the press: this great power is almost entirely in our hands. The time will come when we shall prove that all the European governments of the goyim are enslaved. We will subject one of them to the great test of our great power. We will use outrages and crimes, using Terror. Should the others, outraged, turn against us, we will answer them with American, Chinese or Japanese war powers."* Sergei Nilus, *The Protocols of the Elders of Zion*.

have cried out: "Drive them away and give us one world sovereign, one King of the Universe, be he of the blood of Zion, who shall unite us all and drive away the causes of eternal discords—national boundaries, religions, national debts and conflicts between states—a king who shall at last bring us peace and tranquillity which we had futilely expected from our rulers..." The Xth protocol concluded: *"You know very well that, in order to make such aspirations possible, it is necessary to constantly disturb, in all countries, the relations of peoples with their governments. The aim of this project is to weary them all with disunity, enmity, hatred, martyrdom itself, hunger, the inoculation of disease and misery; thus the Christians will find no other remedy for their ills than our full sovereignty. I might add that, if we were to grant the least respite to the peoples, there might never be an occasion to subjugate them*[675].*"*

In 1911 another case of ritual crime was highly publicised. On 12 March, a thirteen-year-old Ukrainian boy, Andrei Yushchinsky, disappeared on his way to school. Eight days later, on 20 March, his mutilated body was found in a cave near a brick factory. A Jewish factory worker named Menahem Beilis was arrested on 21 July after a witness claimed to have seen him abduct the boy. Menahem Beilis spent more than two years in prison awaiting his trial, which finally took place in Kiev from 25 September to 28 October 1913. One of the witnesses for the prosecution, an expert in Jewish rituals, was the Catholic priest Justinas Pranaitis, who had come especially from the distant city of Tashkent. Pranaitis spoke for eleven hours straight, arguing that the murder of little Yushchinsky was a sacrifice, a religious ritual. Another expert, Professor Silorski, a medical psychologist at the University of Kiev, also considered it to be a ritual murder. The Russian intellectual Vladimir Dahl, a doctor by training, famous for having accompanied Puchkin in his long agony, was the author of a study on ritual crimes entitled *Investigation of the Murders committed by Jews on Christian neo-Nazis and the Use of their Blood*. This work, published in 1884 in St. Petersburg, was used as evidence in the Beilis case.

The trial was no longer presented as the trial of a single Jew, but as a general battle between world Jewry and the Russian government. Prosecutor General Vipper described the situation of Jews in Russia as follows: "The Russian press is only Russian in appearance; in reality, almost all our publications are in the hands of Jews...Legally, the Jews live under our laws of exception, but in fact, they are the masters of our world, and, in a certain sense, we see the biblical promises being fulfilled before our eyes[676]."

---

[675] Sergei Nilus, *The Protocols of the Elders of Zion*, (allcollection.net/archive.org).
[676] Leon Poliakov, *Histoire de l'antisémitisme*, 1955, Points Histoire, 1991, Tome II, p. 352.

The foreign press harassed the Russian government in an unprecedented way. In December 1911, the United States unilaterally annulled the Russian-American trade treaty. Beilis was defended by the best and most famous lawyers in Moscow, St. Petersburg and Kiev. For them, the accused was undoubtedly innocent. In fact, accusations of ritual crimes against Jews, as is well known to all, are nothing but "ridiculous legends" drawn from the stupid anti-Semitic brains or straight out of the retrograde spirit of obscurantist monks straight out of the Middle Ages. The Beilis trial was followed all over the world and in all the major Western newspapers the indignation and insults against the Tsarist regime and the Tsarist police were general and unanimous. It was in this context that Beilis was acquitted.

The Beilis case is often compared to the Leo Frank case. Originally from Brooklyn, Leo Frank ran a small pencil factory in Atlanta. In 1915, he was charged with the rape and murder of a young employee, Mary Phagan, then only 12 years old. During the trial, he was convicted and sentenced to death, but the governor of the State of Georgia commuted his sentence to life imprisonment. But the people of Atlanta did not take kindly to this clemency and proceeded to lynch him; Leo Frank was hanged from a tree. The Jews, as always, shouted throughout the press that Leo Frank was innocent. Indeed, the Jew is always "accused", but never guilty.

We know, however, that such cases are very frequent within the "incestuous sect"; paedophilia is part of the various psychic disorders generated by traumatic sexual abuse, which are frequent in Jewish families and are passed on from generation to generation. Psychiatrists speak here of "incestuous generations[677]".

CXXVIII. Jewish Messianism

The revolution that broke out in Russia in February 1917 aroused great hopes in Jews all over the world. From New York to Paris, from London to Buenos Aires, from Istanbul to Vilnius, Jews were celebrating, popping champagne corks and embracing. The Tsar had at last been overthrown and the Jews of Russia had at last gained access to the highest echelons of power. In October, thanks to the Bolshevik coup d'état, the long-awaited triumph would be complete.

From the outset, it was not just a question of "liberating the proletariat",

---

[677] At the end of 2009, the case of film director Roman Polanski was in the news again after his arrest in Switzerland for the rape of a thirteen-year-old girl in the US thirty years earlier. There is a disproportionate number of such cases in the target community. See *Psychoanalysis of Judaism* (2006), *Jewish Fanaticism* (2007) and *The Mirror of Judaism* (2009).

but of building a perfect world, a world without frontiers, where equality and harmony would reign. The past had to be "wiped out" to make way for a "new man".

In reality, the egalitarian fanaticism of communism immediately gave free rein to horrific massacres. In all, in the first thirty years of the new regime, more than 30 million Russians and Ukrainians perished, liquidated by the criminal madness of the new masters. After the Maoist experience in China, the Russian revolution was probably the second greatest tragedy in human history.

While it is permitted, at the beginning of this century, to denounce the horrors of communism, it is still totally forbidden in democratic countries to insist on the identity of its main doctrinaires and instigators. Despite this, it is common knowledge that communism was essentially a Jewish creation: Karl Marx was the grandson of a rabbi; Lenin had Jewish origins on his mother's side; Trotsky, the head of the Red Army, was actually called Bronstein; Kamenev, the president of the Moscow Soviet, had the surname Rosenfeld; Zinoviev, the master of Leningrad, Apfelbaum; Lenin's chief collaborator and the first president of the Soviet Union was a Jew called Sverdlov, etc., etc.

The list of Jewish Bolshevik dignitaries is truly endless. The revolution that broke out in Berlin in 1918 was led by other Jews: Karl Liebknecht and Rosa Luxemburg. In Hungary, at the same time, Bela Kun had taken the head of a revolutionary government almost exclusively composed of Jews, and we know that after 1945 many Jews were put at the head of the country, as in Poland, Czechoslovakia and Romania. The famous writer Aleksandr Solzhenitsyn, after many others, demonstrated the involvement of numerous Jewish leaders in this tragic history. Indeed, Jewish doctrinaires, officials and torturers bore overwhelming responsibility for the atrocities committed in the period 1917–1947 in the name of this bloody utopia[678].

After the collapse of the Soviet Union in 1991, Jewish intellectuals all over the world, in their entirety, transferred their planetary hopes to the Western democracies and encouraged with all their might the advent of the multicultural society, becoming the most ardent apologists and advocates of immigration and miscegenation in all countries. Obviously, it is the same project: to build a world of "peace" (*shalom*) and without borders, in which people are free and equal and in which all identities have definitively disappeared—except their own. Thus the Jews firmly believe that the messiah will come and that they will finally be recognised by all as God's

---

[678] See the chapters on this subject in *Planetary Hopes* (Russia, 1917) and *Jewish Fanaticism* (1930s USSR and Central Europe in 1945).

chosen people.

In 1999, the great rabbi of France, Joseph Sittruk, shared with us his vision of the Hebrew hopes. As of 10 September 1999, the Jews were facing the year 5760 of their calendar. Read this carefully:

"The Talmud, the rabbi wrote, speaks of the Messianic times, which will extend over a period of two thousand years, between the year 4000 and the year 6000 of the Hebrew calendar, beyond which the world as we know it cannot endure. We are approaching the expiration date...We are, so to speak, in the approach phase. Some signs of the coming of the Messiah have been noted by all rabbinical authorities, such as the return of the Jews to the land of Israel or the Gulf War, which could be interpreted as one of the phases of the famous war between Gog and Magog[679]."

The Talmud symbolically compares the six thousand years of the world to a week, which consists of six days plus the Sabbath:

If we follow the metaphor to the end," continued the Chief Rabbi of France, "we are today in the second half of Friday afternoon, and the Sabbath is approaching. This time corresponds to the moment when all

---

[679] "The war of Gog and Magog that will accompany the process of messianic liberation of the Jewish people will take place around Jerusalem, with Jerusalem as a pretext, and with the aim of destroying the Jewish presence in Jerusalem. Furthermore, Maimonides (Law of Kings, 12) insists that the precise development of this final phase will not be known until it has taken place. In this matter, we have only the teachings of the Sages who repeat that the pre-Messianic phase will be characterised by great world disorder and a confusion of values from which only those who devote themselves to Torah study and acts of goodness will be saved (*Sanhedrin* 97, 98; *Sota* 49). This war, mentioned in chapter 38 of the book of Ezekiel, will be preceded by a confrontation between the world of Edom, i.e. Rome and by extension the West, and the world of Ychmael, i.e. the Islamic world. These two entities will clash and seek to harm the Jewish people, and then, in the final phase of this conflict, 70 nations will come to make war in Jerusalem on *Mashiach* (the Messiah) and attempt to destroy the Jewish people." At https://www.torah-box.com/. Today, this popular prophecy gives rise to much speculation (or *midrash*) *by* rabbis who often conveniently involve, in addition to the West, countries such as Iran and Russia. On this great general *armageddon* expected by rabbis (and evangelical Protestant Christians), we invite readers to discover for themselves the *comments* (wishes) of some contemporary rabbis on digital platforms (Youtube, Bitchute, Odysee, XTwitter). For example: Rabbi Yosef Mizrachi, Rabbi Alon Anava, Rabbi Abraham Benhaim, Rabbi Yekutiel Fish, Rabbi Cahn, Rabbanit Kineret Sarah Cohen, Rabbi Rav Zamir Cohen, Rabbi Rod Reuven Bryant, Rabbi Rav Ron Chaya, Rabbi Rav Avidgor Miller, Rabbi Yaron Reuven, Rabbi Michael Laitman, Rabbi Michael Danielov, Rebbetzin Tziporah Heller, Rabbi Mendel Sasonkin, Rabbi Rav Touitou, Rabbi Rav Raphael Pinto, Rabbi Lawrence Hajioff, Rabbi Tovia Singer, etc. We also recommend the outreach work of the American publicist Adam Green on his social networks and his online information channel *KnowMoreNews.org*, which includes these comments and warns about Jewish messianism from the United States. (NdT).

Jewish families become busy and the pace of activity quickens. They close their tents, pack up their things, run to wash[680]."

In the October 2001 issue of *Israël Magazine*, Rav Haim Dinovicz wrote: "The countdown to liberation has already begun". And in the December issue: "Soon, we will have no other option for survival but to assume our role in history and become once again that beacon of the peoples that the nations so desperately need".

There is this conviction in Judaism that the coming of the messiah—"the birth of the messiah", Jewish intellectuals always write—will take place in the midst of horrible suffering. Dreadful catastrophes, epidemics and terrible wars will destroy a large part of humanity.

Isaac Abravanel, the leader of the Spanish Jewish community at the time of the expulsion from Spain in 1492, wrote in turn: "The times of the Messiah will be preceded by a great war, in which two thirds of mankind will perish" (*Masmia Jesua, 49a*)[681].

It is then that the messiah "son of David" will appear: when the world is fully pacified. In our previous books we have set out in detail with numerous quotations the characteristics of Jewish messianism[682].

As for the identity or provenance of the Messiah, the "son of David", Rabbi Sittruk explained: "The Messiah is a descendant of the tribe of Yehuda on the paternal side and of the tribe of Dan on the maternal side. Tradition further adds that he is a descendant of King David, himself the son of Ruth, who had converted to Judaism. In a way, the messianic story integrates all of humanity[683]."

After the great war against the last enemies of Israel, the Messianic times will be for the Jews a blessed time, a golden age without parallel. The whole land will be unified and the Jews will be recognised by all as "the chosen people". The tractates Pesachim and Sanhedrin of the Babylonian Talmud further assert that in the time of the Messiah the treasures of the Jews will be so immense that *"it will take 300 donkeys to carry the keys to every vault[684]."*

We see, then, that the Jews really do have a plan for the whole of humanity, a plan which they have been pursuing for centuries against all odds. In the introduction to his monumental *History of the Jews*, the Jewish

---

[680] Grand Rabbin Joseph Sittruk, *Chemin faisant*, Flammarion, 1999, p. 374, 376.
[681] On Abravanel read *Psychoanalysis of Judaism*.
[682] *Planetary Hopes* (2005), *Psychoanalysis of Judaism* (2006), *Jewish Fanaticism* (2007), The *Mirror of Judaism* (2009).
[683] Grand Rabbin Joseph Sittruk, *Chemin faisant*, Flammarion, 1999, p. 375.
[684] *Pesachim* 118b and 119, and *Sanhedrin* 110b. On eschatology, i.e. the view of the end times in the great religions, read *The Eschatological War* (2013). And on the fabulous fortunes of the Jews, see *The Millards of Israel* (2014).

historian Heinrich Gratez, whom we have quoted at length, confirmed this idea that the Jewish sect follows a very special plan:

"Why did the Greeks, who, along with their martial art, also lived for ideas, succumb? It was because they had not given their lives a goal, a determined and meditated purpose. The Hebrew people had this goal, this vital task! It is what has held them together and kept them strong and resilient in the face of appalling odds. A people who know their mission are strong, because their lives are not spent dreaming and groping[685]."

To achieve this universal peace (the *pax Judaica*) and "hasten the coming of the Messiah", as they put it, the Jews must work relentlessly to destroy all differences among men: nations, races, religions and all local particularisms must be eradicated. It is this messianic tension that motivates their actions and multiplies their energy. They must work, as Heinrich Graetz wrote, to "overthrow and pulverise the pompous divinities of paganism". At the end of his introduction, the Jewish historian expressed in his own way this characteristic Jewish fanaticism which ""does not bow to fatigue and does not aspire to the rest of the grave"".

The longed-for world government will rise above the ruins of the nations, and it will impose a great and final peace.

All borders must disappear. And clearly, the liberal model has achieved better results than communism, which failed miserably in the 20th century. Every effort must therefore be made to establish democratic regimes throughout the world and to impose on all peoples the model of a cosmopolitan, open and multicultural market society that will make it possible to eradicate feelings of national and religious belonging. In 1977, the famous Jewish philosopher Emmanuel Levinas already spoke explicitly of the "necessity of a planetary West for the coming of the Messiah[686]."

We see then how frantically Judaism is working towards the destruction of peoples and nations. All civilisations must be shredded, all must be razed to the ground, leaving only the human dust which can then be coagulated into a new great planetary mould. So the very essence of Judaism is to destroy all that is not Jewish. Its project naturally turns the Jews into "enemies of humanity", as the Greek and Roman thinkers of antiquity already pointed out. After them, all the great thinkers of the Church throughout history have warned Christians against the *detested sect*—the abhorred sect.

The famous and acclaimed Elie Wiesel had admitted that Judaism lived in frontal opposition to the rest of humanity: "Rooted in suffering, but

---

[685]Heinrich Graetz, *Histoire des Juifs, Tome I*, Introduction, A. Lévy Librairie Éditeur, Paris, 1882, p. 3.
[686]Emmanuel Levinas, *L'Au-delà du verset, Lectures et discours talmudiques*, Les Editions de Minuit, 1982, p. 84-86.

anchored in defiance, Jewish history describes a permanent conflict between us and others. Since Abraham, we have been on one side and the rest of the world on the other[687]."

In the April 2003 issue of *Israël Magazine*, Dr Itzhak Attia, director of the International School of the Yad Vashem Institute [688], spoke very explicitly and with a clarity unusual for Jewish intellectuals, probably because he was speaking in a publication reserved for the community: "Despite the fact that reason cries out to us with all its might the absurdity of this confrontation between a small insignificant people like Israel and the rest of humanity, we are indeed engaged in an intimate combat between Israel and the Nations which can only be genocidal and total...however absurd, incoherent and monstrous it may seem, we are indeed engaged in an intimate combat between Israel and the Nations that can only be genocidal and total, for our respective identities depend on it". You read correctly: between the Jewish people and the rest of humanity, the combat can only be "genocidal and total".

The point is clear: Judaism is a war machine against humanity. Seen in this light, anti-Semitism is humanism: fighting Jewish nihilism is a duty for every human being in order to free humanity from destruction.

Anti-Semitism, said Chief Rabbi Joseph Sittruk, "is inherent in the foundation of the Jewish people itself. The fundamental text on this subject is found in the Talmud (*Sabbath*, page 89), and he stresses that the word Sinai means "hatred". The Jews wondered why the Torah was given at Mount Sinai and the sages answered: "From the moment the Jews received the Torah, the world hated them". And like all good Jewish intellectuals, Rabbi Sittruk loves to handle paradoxes, a very useful intellectual procedure to avoid facing reality: "It is a law of love that arouses hatred! Paradoxical, isn't it[689]?"

For him, as for all other Jewish intellectuals trained in the same school (*yeshiva*), anti-Semitism is simply inexplicable. It is an "irrational hatred[690]", he wrote. The words of Jewish intellectuals on this point are exactly the same in every age and in every latitude.

André Neher, for example, confirmed that Jews were innocent by nature: "Innocent of all guilt except that of being born Jews[691]". "Why is God so angry with the innocent [692] ?", wondered the psychoanalyst Rudolph Lowenstein. Or the "new French philosopher" André Glucksmann when he

---

[687] Elie Wiesel, *Mémoires*, tome I, Seuil, 1994, p. 30-32.
[688] The cave where the Holocaust is worshipped (NdT).
[689] Grand Rabbin Joseph Sittruk, *Chemin faisant*, Flammarion, 1999, p. 300.
[690] Grand Rabbin Joseph Sittruk, *Chemin faisant*, Flammarion, 1999, p. 341.
[691] André Neher, *Le dur Bonheur d'être juif*, Le Centurion, 1978, p. 33.
[692] Rudolph Loewenstein, *Psychanlyse de l'antisémitisme*, p. 234.

declared: "Hatred of Jews is the enigma among all enigmas... The Jew is by no means the cause of anti-Semitism; one must analyse this passion by and for itself, as if this Jew who persecutes without knowing him did not exist[693]." Stéphane Zagdanski went even further and wrote: "It is precisely because they are not the cause of anything of which they are accused that Jews have been so hated in so many places throughout time[694]". Statements of this kind are innumerable and we refer our readers to our previous books.

Jewish intellectuals are thus compelled to tell anything to try to justify their law and the acts of the members of their sect. In the course of our research, we have seen how the criminals and delinquents of this community were in the habit of systematically denying their crimes, even in the face of evidence, with total brazenness[695]. We have also seen how the intellectuals denied the dreadful crimes of their fellows during the Bolshevik revolution. In truth, this is because reality is unimportant in their eyes compared to the fabulous destiny of the "Jewish people", chosen by God to run the world. What really counts for them is the myth that corresponds to their idea of their role and historical mission on earth. They only write and interpret history in the interests of Judaism. Indeed, their great medieval thinker Maimonides considered the study of history a waste of time. Later, in the 16th century, Joseph Caro, author of the Jewish life manual *Shulchan Aruch* (The Served Table), the great codifier of rabbinic law, expressly forbade the reading of history, and not only on the Sabbath but all week long[696].

In a letter to his co-religionist James Darmesteter at the end of the 19th century, Theodor Reinach wrote pertinently: "To tell the truth, the Talmud does not know history; for it, reality and reverie mingle in a kind of ethereal cloud, it does not seem to discern or have a clear idea of time.Edom, Nebuchadnezzar, Vespasian, Titus and Hadrian, all the enemies of the Jewish race are confounded in one and the same individuality, and their figures substitute for one another in this long martyrology which is History".

The six hundred thousand Hebrews who crossed the Red Sea without getting their feet wet are thus confused with the six thousand years of the Jewish calendar or the six million dead of the Second World War. Their entire history is trafficked to correspond to the myth they have imagined and the destiny they have fabricated for themselves. It is futile to try to prove to them that they are not the descendants of the ancient Hebrews, but

---

[693] André Glucksmann, *Le Discours de la haine*, Plon, 2004, p. 73, 86
[694] Stéphane Zagdanski, *De l'Antisémitisme*, Climats, 1995, 2006, p. 10.
[695] Read *The Jewish Mafia* (2008).
[696] Esther Benbassa, *La Souffrance comme identité*, Fayard, 2007, p. 77, read in *The Mirror of Judaism*.

of the Khazars of Eastern Europe, a tribe converted to Judaism in the ninth century; just as it is futile to try to prove to them that they never migrated to the "Promised Land" from Egypt, since no archaeological trace has been found of their passage through Sinai or of their (bloody) conquest of the land of Canaan; it is in turn futile to try to prove scientifically the non-existence of the gas chambers, or that the figure of six million is completely exaggerated and implausible, for this new collective tragedy corresponds to a new chapter in their way of interpreting their unique destiny in this world.

In everyday life, Jewish intellectuals also know how to defend their ideas and argue for them using more prosaic tactics. The Talmud and rabbinic teachings thus inculcate in Jews the handling of "projection" and "accusatory inversion", procedures that we have studied in detail in *The Mirror of Judaism*. Rabbi Sittruk knew how to use them perfectly. In this way he projected the guilt of the Jews onto the rest of humanity, simply by inverting reality: "The relationship of the nations to the Jews is far from serene," wrote the rabbi. There is, in my opinion, a feeling of guilt towards the Jews[697]."

Emmanuel Levinas himself went so far as to classically project the Jewish problem on a universal plane, in order to get rid of it and foist it on the rest of humanity: "Israel's impasse," wrote the thinker, "is probably the human impasse. All men are of Israel. I would say, in my own way, that "We are all Israeli Jews". We, all men. This interiority is Israel's suffering as universal suffering[698]."

In the November 2004 *Israël Magazine* (pages 33–37), Illan Saada also typically used the accusatory inversion to exorcise anti-Semitism: "Anti-Semitism is a plague on all humanity, he wrote. The world should no longer mire itself in this ignoble sentiment, pursue this enterprise of destruction of the Jewish people because its own religious conscience would be affected and would disappear, buried under rubble of shame and dishonour". It is enough here simply to reverse the terms "Jew" and "anti-Semite" to understand the crux of the problem, of "his" problem.

See another example in *Israël Magazine* in October 2001, written by Leon Rozenbaum: "The madness of anti-Jewish hatred obscures the most elementary reason of a growing number of people in the world". The very famous Jewish historian Simon Dubnov had in turn evoked "the chronic disease of anti-Semitism". And the no less famous Hannah Arendt, in her study *On Anti-Semitism* (1951), also wrote that anti-Semitism was a "prerogative of fanatics in general and lunatics in particular", an "insult to

---

[697] Grand Rabbin Joseph Sittruk, *Chemin faisant*, Flammarion, 1999, p. 302.
[698] Emmanuel Levinas, *Du Sacré au saint. Cinq nouvelles lectures talmudiques*, Les Éditions de Minuit, 1977, p. 171.

common sense", an idea of "crackpots".

In November 2008, Claude Barouch, the distinguished President of the Union of Jewish Businessmen of France, speaking at a symposium organised on the theme of "democracies facing anti-Semitism", pointed out the "sickness of the soul and spirit that anti-Semitism represents", which was quite revealing of that mentality that tends to accuse others of its own faults. Readers of our books know that the statements on this subject are innumerable.

This "sickness of the soul" has been well known to us since the work of Sigmund Freud: it is hysteria, a pathology that is very present in Judaism, simply because its origin is incest, a practice that seems to be much more widespread in this community than in any other. It is no mere coincidence if psychoanalysis and the supposed "Oedipus complex" (or rather the "Moses complex") came from the brains of a son of Israel.

Moses himself was the fruit of incest. He was the son of Jochebed, the daughter of Levi. Jochebed, who had had incestuous relations with her father, was also the mother of his father's children. Moreover, she married Amram, being his grandmother, thus committing incest with her grandson, who was also her nephew. Moses was thus the son of Jochebed, his great-nephew and great-grandson; and Moses' mother was both his great-grandmother, as the wife of Levi, and his grandmother, as the daughter of Levi. Moses was therefore the offspring of a double incest: that committed by his mother with his own father and that committed by her with his grandfather, Moses' great-grandfather[699].

The very idea of the coming of the Messiah among the Jewish "people" is typically hysterical in nature: it corresponds, according to psychoanalysts, to the nervous and imaginary pregnancy of the hysterical woman, who so desires to have a child—from her psychiatrist or her father—that she comes to exhibit all the symptoms of pregnancy[700].

Jewish intellectuals always use the same terms: "bringing forth the Messiah", they say, as if "the community" was giving birth to the Messiah.

Jewish tradition, confirmed the Chief Rabbi of France Joseph Sittruck, presents the arrival of the Messiah as a birth: "At the moment of childbirth," wrote the rabbi, "the contractions accelerate. The pains increase, the Talmud assures us, and at the moment when they become more unbearable, the child comes out into the world[701]."

---

[699] Gilles Dorival, *Moïse est-il le fruit d'un inceste?* A propos de Nombres, 26, 59, *Interpreting Translation. Studies on the LXX and Ezekiel in Honour of Johan Lust*, F. García Martínez, M. Verenne, Leuven, Peeters, 2005, p. 97–108.

[700] Read the corresponding chapters of our previous books: *Psychoanalysis of Judaism* and *The Mirror of Judaism*.

[701] Grand Rabbi Joseph Sittruk, *Chemin faisant*, Flammarion, 1999, p. 374. Rabbi

"The Messiah will come in a desperate and desolate world", wrote the philosopher Emmanuel Levinas, who again used a metaphor taken from the Talmud: "...During the nine months of gestation of the one who is to give birth, our texts say, these may be nine months or nine years, or nine centuries of preparation for the coming of the Messiah. A great world with a new future[702]!"

Let us recall here what we have already seen in *Psychoanalysis of Judaism*: every misfortune that strikes the community, every catastrophe and cataclysm brings with it new and great hopes and is assimilated by the rabbis and Jewish intellectuals to the "birth pangs" of the Messiah—the "*Hevlei Mashiah*" in Hebrew.

In one of his books, Elie Wiesel had a Hasidic Jew from Poland living at the time of the French Revolution say: "Why not take the initiative and hasten liberation? ... Jews need the Messiah more than ever. Since he is so near, why wait passively for him, why not go out to meet him? Undoubtedly, the times are ripe and the time is ripe. These wars, these convulsions are the *Hevlei Mashiah, the* torments and anxieties of messianic liberation. All the symptoms, all the signs are here[703]."

The famous Rabbi Yosef Yitzchak Schneerson analysed the situation since the end of the Second World War: "The sufferings of Israel have now reached a terrifying level; the people of Israel are overwhelmed by the pangs of childbirth. The time of imminent deliverance has come. It is the only true answer to the destruction of the world and to the sufferings that have befallen our people... Prepare for the redemption that is soon to come!... The deliverer of righteousness is behind our walls, and the time to prepare to receive Him is very short[704]!"

You have understood, we are on the eve of terrible changes: "It is impossible, Rabbi Schneerson continued, that consolation will not come, for the pains are unbearable[705]."

The "new French philosopher" Alain Finkielkraut, who celebrated the triumph of his fellows throughout the Western world at the end of the 20th century, used this metaphor to describe the contemporary world: "We were pregnant with the new world: and it was this happy pregnancy that we call

---

Sittruk, like Elie Wiesel and a few others, does not capitalise the word "Jew". Fortunately.

[702] Emmanuel Levinas, *L'Au-delà du verset, Lectures et discours talmudiques*, Les Editions de Minuit, 1982, p. 84-86.

[703] Elie Wiesel, *Célébration hassidique II*, 1981, p. 124, 125. Read in *The Mirror of Judaism*.

[704] David Banon, *Le Messianisme*, Presses Universitaires de France, 1998, p. 120. On Hasidic Jews (Kabbalistic mystics) see *Psychoanalysis of Judaism (*2006) and *Jewish Fanaticism (*2007).

[705] It is clear that the Jews will not be able to make it on their own.

modernity[706]."

The journalist François Trocase, whom we have quoted in our chapter on the situation in Austria-Hungary in the 19th century, had perfectly observed and identified that the Jews of Central Europe had very specific defects:

"The Jewish race, which has outlived so many peoples who have disappeared from the face of the earth without a trace, is now composed almost entirely of degenerates who are at heart sick people. Their moral state is characterised in particular by a feeling of exclusion of all others, by a way of thinking which constantly tends towards the same preoccupations. The spirit of profit, the desire for domination drives out of their minds any other thought, any other affection, which is, as we know, the characteristic sign of an obsessive idea. The secondary disorders that arise, such as obscene passion for young Christian girls, cruelty towards the poor, and a vindictive spirit, are episodic symptoms of this unhealthy state. His efforts to seize control of the whole world, to make himself master of Europe, come likewise from this background, and complete the manifestations of his moral degeneration[707]."

In an article in the newspaper *L'Univers, dated* 27 January 1881, entitled *Mental Alienation in Italy*, we find the following reflections: "Strange thing, the Jews count five times more alienated than the other social classes. The predisposition of the Jews to insanity is not a particular case in Italy; exactly the same thing is observed in other countries[708]."

At that time, the French nationalist Edouard Drumond had also realised that the frenetic and permanent agitation of the Jews was above all the manifestation of a neurosis; this very specific neurosis corresponded precisely to the hysterical pathology that Dr. Charcot had studied and that Freud discovered and studied after him. Indeed, the famous Professor Charcot had observed that hysteria affected Jews in particular[709].

Zionism, the Jewish political movement born at the Basel Congress in 1897 under the impetus of Theodor Herzl, was essentially an attempt to cure the neurosis of the Jewish people. This is what we have tried to demonstrate at the end of the *Mirror of Judaism*. The *Israël Magazine* of October 2001 revealed another interesting testimony on the subject. This is what a certain David Cativaras wrote: "Zionism brings to the alienated Jew the possibility of being an authentic Jew...Zionism constitutes a desire for normalisation...Zionism rehabilitates the Jewish people by making them a normal people, with their land, their language and living according to their

---

[706] Alain Finkielkraut, *Le Juif imaginaire*, 1980, Points Seuil, 1983, p. 169.
[707] François Trocase, *L'Autriche juive*, P. Dupont & A.Pierret, Paris, 1899, p. 192.
[708] Abbé Chabeauty, *Les Juifs, nos maîtres*, 1882, p. 155.
[709] Read in *The Mirror of Judaism*.

law...Zionism enables Jews to be normal. In Israel, being a Jew is normal. In the rest of the world, it is normal not to be." And David Catarivas added: "Zionism is a psychoanalysis session on a national scale[710]."

Religious faith, which has sublimated this neurosis, seems also to sanctify this obvious secular disposition to masochism. Isaac Cardoso, an Italian Jew who lived in the 17th century, wrote a plea in favour of his co-religionists which he modestly entitled *Superiority of the Hebrews*, and in which he expounded the greatness of the mission of the Jews. He was quoted by Heinrich Graetz in his work: "The people of Israel," he said, "loved by God and hated by men, have been scattered among the nations for two thousand years, in atonement for their sins and those of their forefathers. Oppressed by some, beaten by others, despised by all, it has been mistreated and persecuted in every land. But—Cardoso added—if Israel has undergone all these sufferings, it is because it is the chosen people, whose mission is to spread the knowledge of the One God".

Another more contemporary Jewish intellectual, Manès Sperber, formulated this same idea in a way that allows us to better understand the very particular mental universe of the Jews: "God was just, for he condemned his enemies to become murderers, and to them [the Jews] he granted the grace of being the victims who in death would sanctify the Almighty. From John Chrysostom to the last pogromist mujik, the persecutors did not suspect the extent to which their momentary triumph reinforced the conviction of the persecuted that they were the chosen people[711]."

Heinrich Gretz did not say otherwise, as we have already seen, about the expulsion of the Jews from Spain: "... They, whom the hand of God had struck so hard, so persistently, and who had suffered such unspeakable pain, must occupy a peculiar position and belong to the specially chosen. This was the thought or feeling that existed more or less clearly in the hearts of the survivors. They regarded their banishment from Spain as a third exile, and themselves as favourites of God, whom, because of His greater love for them, He had punished with greater severity[712]."

So we must deduce that the persecutions they endured throughout their history have been fully integrated into the process of messianic redemption. "The Jews only become good if they are beaten well[713]", one can read in the Talmud.

We now understand better why the Jews, who have always aroused the

---

[710] *Israël Magazine,* October 2001, p. 30, 31
[711] Manès Sperber, Être *juif,* Éd. Odile Jacob, 1994, p. 60.
[712] Heinrich Graetz, *History of the Jews IV,* Philadelphia, The Jewish Publication Society of America, 1894, p. 383, 386–387.
[713] Treatise XXIX, *Menachot 53b.*

hatred and contempt of men everywhere, have throughout history been regarded as poor sick people, inspiring both disgust and pity, but also mockery, jokes and derision. Indeed, the history of this obstinate "people" is at least as ludicrous as it is tragic, if one judges it with a certain amount of foresight.

"When the pains are most unbearable, the child comes out into the world", Rabbi Sittruk assured us. But after so many centuries, it has become abundantly clear that the Jews will never succeed in bringing him forth on their own: once again, it will have to be the goyim who take matters into their own hands and bring about the longed-for messiah. When the hour of liberation comes, humanity will finally be relieved of the endless jeremiads and deafening cries of "the chosen community".

It would be a great peace that would reign in the world.

Paris, April 2010.

ANNEX I

MESSIANISM AND POLITICS IN JUDEA IN THE TIME OF THE ROMAN GOVERNORS

Prophets and royal suitors in the 1st century

The only source of information we have about the political movements that stirred Judaism during the first century in reaction to the Roman occupation is Flavius Josephus.

Josephus, of priestly origin but a member of the Pharisee party, had been given command of the troops of Galilee at the beginning of the Jewish war (66). Defeated and imprisoned, he joined the victor's cause without much reluctance. Transferred to Rome, he made a career in the service of the house of the Flavian emperors (Vespasian and then Titus). After the ruin of Jerusalem (70) and the suppression of the last strongholds of resistance (73), some pacifist Pharisees obtained from the Roman government the reconstitution of a Jewish academy in Yavne under the direction of Yohanan Ben Zakai. From Rome, Josephus gave this academy all the support he could in view of the salvation of his homeland. It was with this aim in mind that Josephus undertook the writing of his history *The Jewish War*, an indirect apologia for the Jewish people in which he attempted to hold uncontrolled groups of activists responsible for the recent conflict, systematically assimilating them to "robbers" (or bandits/bandits). Josephus continued in the same vein by exalting the *Jewish Antiquities*, in order to acquaint the public in Rome and Hellenistic cities with the history of their nation by presenting it in a favourable light.

Within this framework, Josephus devoted some succinct notes to the prophets and royal pretenders who, during the first century, made Palestine one of the most agitated provinces of the Roman Empire. Here are five examples in chronological order.

- *Judas, son of Hezekiah*

The capture and execution of a robber-chief named Hezekiah, who ravaged the Syrian frontier districts, is due to Herod the Great before his accession to power (*War of the Jews I, 204*). A generation later, Josephus mentions the subversive actions of his son Judas (*Jewish Antiquities, XVII, 271–272*). It cannot be entirely ruled out that this is the same Judas the Galilean (or the Gaulanite) to whom Josephus devotes another special note below.

"On the other hand, there was a certain Judas, son of the bandit chief Hezekiah, who had once attained great power and had been taken prisoner

by Herod at the cost of great hardship. Well, this Judas, having gathered in the area of Sephoris of Galilee a crowd of mad men, carried out a raid against the royal palace of the place, and, seizing the weapons deposited there, he armed all his men, without leaving a single one, while at the same time making off with the money that had been left there. And he was fearful to all, for he robbed and plundered all who fell into his hands. But he longed for a higher position and aspired to the rank of king, an honour he hoped to attain not by honest behaviour, but by an excess of insolence. "Jewish Antiquities, XVII, 271–272, Akal Classical, Volume II, p. 1061

While Josephus denounces this "thief", he highlights his real ambition, hardly understandable without the background of religious hopes that could mobilise the Jews against the hated and illegitimate dynasty of Herod.

- **The Atronges revolt**

The situation is even clearer for the pretender Attronges, whose activity developed after Herod's death.

"Stronges himself, though a man not illustrious either by the rank of his ancestors or by the excellence of his worth, or by the abundance of his possessions, but a shepherd and an obscure personage in everything and for everything, and only marred by his enormous physical frame and the strength of his arms, had the audacity to aspire to become king, and to attach no great importance to the fact of dying and losing his life for the pleasure of committing the greatest outrages. He, too, had four brothers, equally stoutly built and convinced that they excelled in the power of their arms, who thought they should aim for the throne. Each of them commanded a company, for they had been joined by an enormous multitude. These were generals but subordinate to Atronges, though they entered the fray with independence of their own. Attronges, who wore the royal crown, held councils to discuss the operations to be carried out, though any decision depended on his determination alone. This man's freedom of action lasted for a long time, during which time he received the title of king and no one deprived him of doing as he pleased. And both he and his brethren were greatly inclined to the annihilation not only of the Romans, but also of the king's soldiers, acting with equal hatred against one and the other, against the latter for the inconsideration with which they had treated them during Herod's rule, and against the Romans for the iniquities which, in their judgment, they had recently committed." Jewish Antiquities, XVII, 271–272, Akal Classical, Vol. II, p. 1062–1063

The continuation of the story, whose chronology is uncertain, however, mentions the tetrarchy of Archelaus, refers to an ambush of Roman soldiers at Emmaus and the final triumph of Roman power over these "robbers". The royal claim of the leader of the band is striking. While it is true that the example of Herod may have stimulated the ambition of many adventurers and impostors, the explicit mention of the struggle against Rome may perhaps imply a religious motivation which Josephus was careful not to reveal to his readers.

- ## *Judas the Gaullonite and his party*

A second wave of subversive movements is evoked by Josephus in the time of the first Roman governors. After the ruin of Archelaus, his tetrarchy (Judea and Samaria) was given by the emperor Augustus as a province to the procurator Coponius, with full powers, including the power to condemn to death.

"During his rule a Galilean, named Judas, incited the inhabitants of the place to revolt, for he reproached them for putting up with paying tribute to the Romans, and for submitting to other mortal lords besides God. This individual was a doctor of a sect of his own which had nothing to do with the others." War of the Jews, II, 118, Clásica Gredos 247, Madrid, 1997, p. 278–279.

The activity of this Judas is specified and partly rectified in *Jewish Antiquities, XVII, 4–10 and 23*. It would have taken place in the time of the Syrian governor Quirinius, when he came to Judea to carry out the census of the Jewish properties (year 6 AD).

"But a man, namely Judas, belonging to the region of Gaulanitide and a native of the city of the name of Gamala, with the co-operation of the Pharisee Sadducee, incited them to revolt, on the one hand by telling them that the census involved nothing more than an obvious slavery, and on the other hand by inviting the Jewish nation to defend their freedom, since, they told the Jews, if success accompanied them, the possession of freedom would offer them happiness, and if, on the contrary, they failed in their endeavour to achieve the good inherent in their own freedom, they would gain honour and fame for their magnanimity, while the Divinity would be inclined to help them to achieve the good inherent in their own freedom, they would gain honour and fame for their magnanimity, on the contrary, if they failed in their endeavour to achieve the good inherent in freedom itself, they would gain honour and fame for their magnanimity, while the Divine would be inclined to help them to succeed in this enterprise in no other case than when they collaborated in making these plans effective and, in a more concrete way, if they were enamoured of great ideas and spared no effort to attain them... Indeed, in these circumstances the Jews could not but suffer incessant violence on account of the continual wars provoked by these individuals, which caused them to lose the loved ones, who had contributed to alleviate their hardships, and on account equally of the attacks carried out against them by large groups of brigands, who produced the death of the principal males, ostensibly for the sake of the common good but in reality because those criminals believed themselves to

be gaining thereby for themselves." Jewish Antiquities, XVIII, 4–5, Akal Classical, Vol. II, p. 1079

The story of his party is then told in the context of the Jewish war, without the term "zealots" appearing in the text. For Josephus, Judas founded a "school of philosophy" parallel to that of the Essenes, Sadducees and Pharisees (*Jewish Antiquities, XVIII, 6–10).*

"Jude of Galilee, for his part, set himself up as the head of a fourth philosophical school. Those who hold the ideas taught by this school agree with the views of the Pharisees in all matters, with the only difference that their love of liberty is unshaken, for they accept no other ruler and sovereign but God alone. They consider it a small thing to suffer the most different kinds of death for opposing to give any man the title of sovereign" Jewish Antiquities, XVIII, 23, Akal Classical, Vol. II, p. 1082.

This last feature prepares the presentation of the role played by this same religious party at the time of the great Jewish revolt (66–70). Only at that time does Josephus mention the name "Zealots" (*War of the Jews, II, 651*). The apostle Luke also speaks of Judas the Galilean in Acts *V, 37*: "Then Judas the Galilean arose in the days of the census, and took many people after him. But he also perished, and all who obeyed him were scattered." Although the initial movement founded by Judas cannot properly be called messianic, it is at least a religious nationalism that brings a strong political character to the hope of Israel.

- ### *An impostor in the time of the Roman procurators*

Roman governors had to deal with these revolts with an iron fist. Pontius Pilate (26–36) was noted for his harshness. Luke mentions the adventure of some Galileans: "On that occasion some were present who told him about certain Galileans whose blood Pilate had mingled with the blood of their sacrifices" (Luke XIII, 1). (Luke XIII, 1): it is possible that his ritual piety was accompanied by an attitude of political resistance analogous to that of his compatriot Judas the Galilean. Luke himself knows that Barabbas was detained during the trial of Jesus; "then Pilate decided that what they asked should be done. He released to them the one whom they had put in prison for sedition and murder, whom they had asked for, and delivered Jesus to their will." (Luke XXIII, 24–25). Mark specifies: "And there was one called Barabbas, a prisoner with the rebels who had committed murder in the insurrection" (Mark XV, 7). John describes him as a "bandit" (John, XVIII, 40), an epithet reserved by Josephus for political activists who fought against Rome. So we see that the background of Jesus' life is full of revolt movements. But we see later, with the procurator Phadotus (44–46), how Josephus mentions the revolt of Theudas, whom he presents as a false prophet:

"On the *other hand, at the time when Pharez was procurator of Judea, a magician, by name Theudas, tried to persuade an infinite mass of people to gather their belongings and follow him to the river Jordan, for he told them that he was a prophet, and assured them that at his command the waters of the river would be opened and that in this way he would make it easy for them to cross. And with these words he deceived many. Fado, however, did not let them enjoy their folly, but sent a squadron of cavalry which fell upon them in an unexpected manner, annihilated many and made prisoners of others. And Theudas himself, whom they took alive, they cut off his head and carried it to Jerusalem."* Jewish Antiquities, XX, 97–98, Akal Classical, Vol. II, p. 1218.

It is noteworthy here that Theudas undertakes to repeat the miracles of the Exodus and the entry into the Promised Land as signs of his prophetic mission. His mission is manifestly consistent with a project of revolt.

- ### The Egyptian false prophet

A final series of movements of the same kind occurred in the time of the last procurators. In fact, in the Acts of the Apostles, when St. Paul is arrested in Jerusalem, we see the Roman official ask him: "Then are you not that Egyptian who provoked a sedition before these days, and brought out four thousand men of the murderers into the wilderness" (Acts XXI, 38). The episode, which occurred under the rule of Antony Felix (52–58), is narrated by Josephus who sees banditry on the increase and the Jewish war against Rome approaching.

"Thus it came to pass that the misdeeds committed by the bandits filled the city with such sacrileges, while the sorcerers and falsifiers endeavoured to persuade the masses to follow them into the wilderness, as, they assured them, they would show them prodigies and clear signs which were to be produced by divine prescription. And there were many who, allowing themselves to be persuaded, suffered the punishment inherent in their folly, since Felix executed them, after they had been referred to him. On the other hand, about this time there came to Jerusalem from Egypt an individual, who claimed to be a prophet and who advised the masses of the people to go with him to the so-called Mount of Olives, which is on the other side of the city and at a distance of five furlongs, since, he insisted on assuring them, he wanted to show them from there how, at his command, the walls of Jerusalem would crumble, through which, he promised them, he would offer them the possibility of entering the city. But Felix, hearing of this, commanded the soldiers to take up arms, and, rushing from Jerusalem accompanied by numerous forces of cavalry and infantry, charged upon the people accompanying the Egyptian. In doing so, he killed four hundred of them and also took two hundred prisoners. As for the Egyptian, he disappeared after escaping from the fray. But the bandits again incited the people to war against the Romans, telling them that they should refuse to

obey them, and they plundered the villages of those who would not listen to them by setting them on fire." Jewish Antiquities, XX, 168–171, Akal Classical, Vol. II, p. 1229–1230.

Again, although the real claim is not clear here, the political intention of the action gives the promise of the miracle something more value than the daydreaming of a simple enlightened man[714]. In the same way, we can ask ourselves what significance Jesus' entry into Jerusalem a few decades earlier had had for the Temple authorities and the Roman power (*Matthew, XXI, 1–17*).

Messianism and politics: Jewish parties in the face of the Roman occupation

"The events narrated by Josephus raise the question of the attitude adopted by the major Jewish parties to the Roman occupation.

"The Sadducees accommodated themselves to this all the better because the governors of Judea, having all the power for direct administration, continued and accentuated the policy of Herod in the appointment of the high priests. The latter, chosen from a few families of the priestly aristocracy, were appointed directly by them and sometimes remained in office only a short time. As creatures of the occupying power, they cooperated actively with it to ensure public order, as long as the normal functioning of the cult was guaranteed. In return for this submissive attitude, Rome respected the traditional freedoms of the Jews, not only in Palestine but in all the communities of the Diaspora. Under these conditions, the

---

[714]"Besides these, another group of bandits appeared, whose hands were purer, but whose intentions were also more unholy. This band destroyed the welfare of the city to no lesser extent than the assassins. They were liars and deceivers who, under the pretext of being inspired by God, sought innovations and changes. They incited the crowd to act as if they were possessed by divinity and led them into the desert with the idea that there God would show them the signs of their deliverance. As this seemed to be the beginning of a revolt, Felix sent armed troops of cavalry and infantry who killed many of them. However, the Egyptian false prophet caused the Jews greater evils than these. A charlatan appeared in the country and gained the reputation of a prophet. He gathered together about thirty thousand people deceived by him, and led them from the wilderness to the so-called Mount of Olives, whence it was possible to penetrate by force into Jerusalem, and, after imposing himself upon the Roman garrison, to reign over the people as a tyrant, for which purpose he would take as his personal guard those who entered with him. Felix, however, anticipated his attack and met him with Roman troops. The whole town took part in the defence of the city, so that when the clash between the two occurred, the Egyptian fled with a few, while most of his men were killed or captured. The rest of the band dispersed and each hid in his own house." *War of the Jews* II, 258–263, *Gredos Classics 247*, p. 311–312. (NdT).

messianic hope based on the prophetic texts took a back seat: Rome had no need to fear any seditious movement from the priestly circles that had embraced Sadducean ideas.

"The position of the Pharisees was very different. In regard to the Law, they held to the tradition of the Ancients and probably organised themselves into "purity groups" whose observances they followed. But as for hope, they attached equal importance to the tradition of the prophets, to which they linked the book of Daniel. Consequently, their hope in the Davidic Messiah and their faith in the resurrection of the dead radically differentiated them from their Sadducean opponents. In this sense, the doctrine represented by the Psalms of Solomon could be considered a "common doctrine" in the two schools between which they were divided: that of Hillel and that of Shammai. At the same time, any recognition of the Roman power as a legitimate authority was out of place for them; if they had broken with the Hasmoneans out of loyalty to the Davidic kingship, if they had then distanced themselves from Herod the Great for the same reason, it was impossible for them to deny themselves by officially recognising the empire occupying the land of Israel. However, they were hostile to violent resistance, which could only harm the nation by endangering its status of religious and legal autonomy. They counted on the faithful observance of the Law to obtain from God the sending of the liberating Messiah. In their eyes, this obviously had a political dimension, but they did not intend to hasten his arrival by reckless activism. This is why, during the revolt of 66–70, they gradually dissociated themselves from military action: tradition has it that Yohanan Ben Zakai left besieged Jerusalem to go to the occupied territory and prepare the reorganisation of the national institutions. However, it is not certain that this moderate attitude found favour everywhere among the population of the country. The Roman occupation, with the presence of pagan soldiers and the financial burdens it entailed, was considered odious and contrary to the legitimate rights of the nation. Consequently, *the resistance groups* described by Josephus easily found support and complicity among the people. Where Josephus, anxious to exonerate his compatriots, saw only armed bands of bandits, the public could easily see "zealots of the Law" and heroes. Josephus, who links all the troubles fomented by false prophets and leaders of armed bands to people he calls "brigands" or "sicarii" (= dagger-bearers: cf. *Jewish Antiquities XX, 186–187; War of the Jews II, 254–257*[715]), he

---

[715] Sicarii: Latin for assassins, the first terrorists in history? "After this cleansing *of the region*, there arose in Jerusalem another kind of evildoers, called hired assassins, who killed people in broad daylight in the middle of the city. This took place on the mud on feast days, for they mingled with the crowds. With small daggers that they carried hidden under their clothes, they wounded their enemies. Then, when their victims fell

points out that they only took the name of zealots under the high priest Ananus, deposed in 63, because of their claim to zeal for virtue (*War of the Jews* IV, 160–161)⁷¹⁶, i.e. for the practice of the Law (*War of the Jews* VII, 269–272). Now, in reproaching them for their policy of violence, Josephus also clearly states that the ideas of this fourth party—founded by Judas the Galilean (or the Gaullonite) towards the beginning of our era—"agree with the views of the Pharisees in all matters, with the only difference that their love of liberty is unshakable, since they accept no other chief and sovereign but God alone" (*Jewish Antiquities, XVIII, 23*)⁷¹⁷. The dividing line between the Pharisees and the activist groups was thus difficult to draw: it related essentially to practical attitudes, not to the more fundamental religious conceptions of Jewish messianism. It is therefore understandable that a sage like Hillel, a contemporary of Judas the Galilean, was very reserved in the face of this messianic agitation: "The children of Israel will have no more Messiah, for they wasted him in the days of Hezekiah" (Talmud, Sanhedrin 99a).

---

to the ground, the murderers joined the indignant crowd, so that they could not be discovered because of the confidence they inspired…The fear was more unbearable than the misfortune itself, for everyone, as if in a war, expected death at any moment. People spied their enemies from afar, and did not trust even their friends, when they came near. Nevertheless, they were killed in the midst of these suspicions and precautions, for so great was the swiftness and skill of such malefactors to pass unnoticed." *War of the Jews* II, 254–257, Classical Gredos 247, p. 311.

⁷¹⁶ "Josephus focuses on the term "zeal", which the Zealots apply to themselves because of their zeal for God and the Temple, as the basic notion for understanding the religious and social significance of the movement (cf. also VII 269–270). It is not easy to distinguish all the groups of the anti-Roman resistance that fall under this name: sicarii, supporters of John of Gischala, henchmen of Simon son of Giora, the companions of Eleazar and the followers of Judas the Galilean. Our author sometimes confuses the Zealots with the Sicarii, although he also distinguishes the latter from those whom he generically calls "rebels" or "factious" (cf. II 650–651). The common denominator of these revolutionary elements, however, was their passion for freedom, whose doctrine seems to have been inspired by what Josephus calls the fourth philosophy or sect, after the Pharisees, Sadducees and Essenes." *War of the Jews* IV, note 87, Classical Gredos 267, p. 40.

⁷¹⁷ Read Eleazar's harangue to the besieged of Masadah, which has become the quintessential Jewish nationalist myth: "My brave ones, we have long since made up our minds that we will not be slaves either to the Romans or to anyone else, but to God, for he alone is the true and just lord of men…". This was the basic doctrinal principle of the Zealots and the Sicarii. The Jewish rebels thought that with the expulsion of the Romans the coming of the kingdom of God would be more immediate. Rome symbolised evil, which according to the book of *Daniel* (11 and 12) would be the end of earthly history and the beginning of the messianic age." *War of the Jews* VII, 323 and note 151, Classical Gredos 264, p. 379.

"Finally, there are the Essenes. Analysis of the Qumran texts[718] has revealed in them an apocalyptic fervour that easily turned to violent action, as their *Rule of War* (1 QM) shows. Their particular messianism was spontaneously oriented in this direction, insofar as the "Prince of the Congregation" (or "Seed of David" or "Messiah of Israel") had first and foremost, in their eyes, a military function to lead the liberating war. In this respect, their mentality was very similar to that of the future zealots. Moreover, the place they accorded to the eschatological Prophet could contribute to maintaining excitement in the minds of the people whenever a supposedly inspired person appeared to announce the approach of the Great Day. This is the contrasting background against which the anecdotes related by Josephus must be set. It also sheds light on the Gospel episodes in which we see popular beliefs manifested at the time of Jesus."

Exposition by Pierre Grelot in his work *"L'Espérance juive à l'heure de Jésus"* ("Jewish *Hope at the time of Jesus"*), Désclée/Groupe Mane, Paris, 1994, p. 168–179.

---

[718] The Dead Sea Scrolls, so called because they were found in caves in Qumran, West Bank, on the shores of the Dead Sea, are a collection of 972 manuscripts. Most date from 250 BC to AD 66, years before the destruction of the Second Temple in Jerusalem. The first manuscripts were found in 1947. This is a major discovery in the world of archaeology and biblical studies. (NdT).

ANNEX II

FLORENCE: HUMANISM AND RENAISSANCE

After the fall of Constantinople in 1453, the most important humanists lived in Florence, the true symbol of the Italian Renaissance. They gravitated around Cosimo the Ancient (1389–1464) and his successor and grandson Lorenzo the Magnificent (1449–1492). Cosimo and Lorenzo were bloodthirsty despots who corrupted the Florentine city with their money, but also embellished it like no other. Official history tends to turn a blind eye to the politics of the financial dynasty of the Medici in order to avoid drawing attention to the imposture of "Florentine democracy" and to better extol its cultural and artistic legacy. Certainly, the famous Florence Academy played a crucial cultural and historical role in Europe, for Renaissance Humanism was truly born in Florence under the Medici[719].

Founded and financed by Cosimo da Medeci in 1459, the Florentine Academy was a major centre of anti-Christian subversion and the spread of Judeo-Eastern ideas, especially from 1462 with Marsilio Ficino (1433–1499) at its head. In fact, the Academy, directed by Ficino and Cosimo, was philosophically hermetic[720] and Plotinian, i.e. Neoplatonic, therefore under the influence of Gnosticism[721] and the Hebrew Kabbalah. In 1460, Cosimo acquired a copy of the *Corpus hermeticum and* commissioned Marsilio

---

[719] The Renaissance Humanism of letters and philosophy is to be distinguished from the Christian artistic renaissance (painting, sculpture, frescoes). After 1492, the Christian renaissance was mainly artistic and Roman, directly financed by the papacy.

[720] Hermeticism is an Alexandrian philosophical and religious tradition based primarily on pseudepigraphic texts, the *Hermetica*, attributed to Hermes Trismegistus, a legendary Hellenistic combination of the Greek god Hermes and the Egyptian god Thoth. The word "Hermeticism" can also be used to designate the broader set of doctrines, beliefs and practices, the nature of which became clearer during the Renaissance. They do not necessarily depend on the Alexandrian Hermetic tradition, but include the Kabbalah, Rosicrucianism, Paracelsianism and, in general, most forms of modern Western esotericism. (wikipedia, ndt).

[721] Gnosticism (from Ancient Greek: γνωστικός gnōstikós, "to have knowledge") is a set of ancient religious ideas and systems that originated in the 1st century among ancient Jewish and Christian sects. These various groups emphasised spiritual knowledge (gnosis) over orthodox teachings and traditions and the authority of the Church. Viewing material existence as flawed and malevolent, Gnostic cosmogony generally presents a distinction between a supreme, unseen God and a lesser, malevolent deity (a demiurge, sometimes associated with Yahweh of the Old Testament) who is responsible for creating the material universe. Gnostics considered the main element of salvation to be direct knowledge of the supreme divinity in the form of mystical or esoteric intuitions. Many Gnostic texts discuss not the concepts of sin and repentance, but those of illusion and enlightenment (wikipedia, ndt).

Ficino to translate it. According to Ficino, the *Corpus hermeticum* represented the most ancient Revelation and Hermeticism was the primordial tradition that had originated all esotericism and also philosophy. Ficino also worked within the Academy to edit the *Enneads* of Plotinus, whose metaphysics is irreconcilable with Christianity. Indeed, Plotinus' Neoplatonism descended from Jewish Hellenism, a pagan-Jewish syncretism created by the schools of Alexandria from Philo the Jew (20 BC - 45 AD). By linking Plato with Hermes and Plotinus, Ficino confirmed the submission of the Greek heritage to Egyptian esotericism by the Jews of Alexandria. Like the Alexandrian Gnostics of the early centuries, Ficino was a Neoplatonist and not a Platonist in the Christian sense (as the Christian tradition since Augustine), since he translated Plato by associating him with Plotinus and Origen, the latter being a Gnostic heretical monk of the 3rd century. With this translation, Ficino made Neoplatonism triumph in Florence, arousing passionate interest in Hermeticism throughout Europe. Through the *Corpus hermeticum*, gnosis penetrated Renaissance humanism and the whole of Europe.

The creation of this neoplatonic and hermetic fashion was not innocent, for it participated directly in the war of the Gnosis and the Cabala against the doctrine of the Church. It is no exaggeration to say that the Academy of Florence drove the Neoplatonic Humanists out of their minds, alienating them from Thomistic scholasticism (Aristotelian Christianity [722]) and bringing about the cultural downfall of the Christian West. The Plotinian metaphysics that Ficino took up and updated was monistic. His Being is One like the pagan Being, but also like the Gnostic and Kabbalistic Being (let us remember that Christian metaphysics is dualistic; God and Creation are not One, but two distinct beings, since God created the Universe out of

---

[722] In reality, they were not against Aristotle, but against the Aristotle of St Thomas, to which they counterposed the pagan Aristotle interpreted in a pantheistic way by Averroes. The first task of the Academy of Florence was to overthrow Aristotle, that colossus standing on the pedestal of the *Summa Theologica*, for St Thomas had achieved the feat of contradicting Averroes by Christianising Aristotle. For St. Thomas it was necessary to free Aristotle from Averroes, his doctrine from Arab pantheism and immanentism, but also his scientific realism from Neoplatonic idealism, and this was his work. In other words, it is not Plato who is responsible for the imposture of modern rationalism, but Neoplatonic idealism. It is not Platonism that is Gnostic, but Neoplatonism, the interpretation of both Plato and Aristotle that we owe to Philo the Jew and Plotinus. Renaissance humanism obviously raises the great question of Platonism, but even more so that of paganism and the interpretation of Greek philosophy. The big question is whether or not a Christian philosophy is possible, since Ficino is a transmission belt between Neoplatonism, Humanism and modern "rationalism". Ficino was anti-Christian, as were the humanist Erasmus and the idealist Descartes. They were not Christian philosophers because they did not respect the dualistic metaphysics of Christianity.

nothing and his Being is not confused with the Being of the created Being). Moreover, Ficino's initiation was hermetic and revived the magic of pagan antiquity that had been abolished by Christianity, though secretly perpetuated by the Gnostics, the Hermeticists and the Kabbalists down through the centuries. It is therefore wrong to link Renaissance humanism with ancient Greek humanism. It is not Plato (classical Greek Hellenism) that is reborn, but Plotinus (Eastern Hellenistic Alexandria). The Renaissance thus represents a return through the back door of the Judeo-Egyptian gnosis via the Jewish cabala.

A worthy successor to his grandfather, Lorenzo the Magnificent continued to promote the Renaissance and the cultural struggle against Christianity. He supported Ficino when the latter wrote his *Platonic Theology* in 1482, tolerated by the Church thanks to Lorenzo's influence, for Lorenzo had become the papacy's chief banker under Innocent III. Lorenzo learned philosophy from Ficino and wrote poems that were Gnostic and pantheistic odes to Nature. He was also a great hedonist and organised great neo-pagan festivals in Florence. Lorenzo frequented the literary Angelo Poliziano, a poet and great scholar who wrote in Latin and Greek, and whose works were inspired by pagan initiation. He is indebted to him for a remarkable *Fabula of Orpheus* and several translations of ancient authors (Homer, Epictetus, Herodotus). Poliziano taught classical literature at the Academy and his classes were so outstanding that they attracted students from all over Europe. His pupils included Christian humanists such as Thomas Linacre and William Grocyn, but above all more controversial figures such as Pico della Mirandola and Johannes Reuchlin, both of whom were outstanding students of the Florentine school. The last humanists of the Italian Renaissance, the Florentines trained by Ficino, would go to the end of hermetic and neo-Platonic reasoning, entering into kabbalistic initiation.

Pico della Mirandola (1464–1494) studied literature with Poliziano, but it was the lessons of Ficino that most impressed him. Pico is officially considered a "Christian Kabbalist", but in reality the Kabbalah is exclusively Jewish and has nothing to do with Christianity. He was a young student endowed with great curiosity and an exceptional form of genius; he had an uncommon memory and erudition. But his main defect, stemming from his youth, was that he had no judgement. Pico was open to all philosophies, to all faiths, so that he could not decide in favour of any system. He first studied at the Universities of Ferrara and Padua. In Padua, he studied Hebrew and Arabic with Elie del Medigo, a Jewish Averroist, who also taught him to read Aramaic manuscripts. Del Medigo also translated Jewish manuscripts from Hebrew into Latin for Pico, as he continued to do for several years. He came into contact with Yohanan Alemanno, an Italian Jewish Kabbalist who introduced him to the methods of Kabbalistic exegesis. This meeting between the two would lead to the creation of his Christian Kabbalah[723]. He spent the following years visiting the humanist centres of Italy. He hired translators, first Pablo de Heredia and then Samuel ben Nissim Abulfaraj, a Sicilian Jew who had converted to Christianity under the name of Flavius Mithridate, to obtain Latin translations of the main texts of the Kabbalah. Later, at the Academy in Florence, Pico imbibed Ficino's teachings and, like him, was initiated into Hermeticism. But Ficino's pupil was not very reasonable, for he mixed everything: mysticism with astrology and magic, the Cabala with Plato, Hermes with Jesus. Among the many heresies proposed by Pico della Mirandola, one statement was extremely important. Like Ficino, Pico claimed to trace the primordial tradition back to a single source prior to the Bible: the Cabala. Pico thus placed the Cabala before and not after the Bible. In order to remain Christian, Pico then invented a new Christianity which he linked to the Kabbalah. Evidently, Pico della Mirandola was already at that time a falsely Christian heretic, along the lines of Jewish Gnosticism. Having learned his lesson well from his Florentine and Jewish teachers and friends, the young Pico (he was 24 years old) went to Rome in 1486 to propose a philosophical challenge to the astonished and stupefied religious. Pico defended no less than 900 propositions, each one more extravagant than the last, in his famous *Discourse on the Dignity of Man (Oratio de hominis dignitae,* in Latin). His *Oratio* of 1486 was a veritable sum of ravings. In order to continue to call himself a Christian, Pico declared that the "Revelations" of Egypt and Asia were all supportive of Christianity since they all traced back to the one source, the Cabala, concluding that magic and the Cabala confirmed the divinity of Christ rather than refuted it. For Pico, no science provided more proof of Christ's divinity than magic and the Kabbalah...No one deigned to answer Pico's provocations and Pope Innocent III merely condemned thirteen of his propositions as heresy and dismissed him out of hand. Pico must have felt threatened in spite of everything, for he went into exile in the Low Countries before returning to Florence at the invitation of Lorenzo de' Medici. His last work, the *Heptatus,* was published in 1489. The spirit and direct influence of the *Zohar is* already directly perceptible in it. Surprisingly, at the end of his life, Pico della Mirandola distanced himself from the Medici and Ficino, publishing a treatise against astrology which was one of the foundations of his former master's cosmology. To make matters worse, Pico joined the Circle of San Marco which gathered all the dissidents of the Florentine Academy around the figure of the Dominican Savonarole, a real betrayal of his former teachers and friends. At the end of his young life, Pico

---

[723] The "Christian" Kabbalah = The philosophical Kabbalah of the Renaissance.

changed, became a disciple of Savonarole, burned his books of poetry, donated his possessions to the poor and even considered joining the Dominican order. He died suddenly before he could make up his mind, probably poisoned by arsenic on the orders of his former "masters and friends", the Medici[724].

In conclusion, the Humanists of the Italian Renaissance were hermetic initiates, strongly influenced by Gnosticism and the Kabbalah. They opposed the exoteric Christian dogma[725] and dualistic Christian dogma, constantly referring to a single, esoteric source, the supposed "primordial tradition". The spirit of the Florentine Renaissance is that of the Gnostics, of those nostalgic for Egyptian paganism coupled with Jewish esotericism. Mircea Eliade wrote: *"The Kabbalah has a nostalgia for a religious universe where the Old Testament and the Talmud coexist with cosmic religiosity, Gnosticism and mysticism... An analogous phenomenon appears in the "universalist" ideal of some Hermetic philosophers of the Italian Renaissance"*. Humanism thus broke with Christianity, which was centred on God, and gradually drifted towards a secular and individualistic morality, derived from Stoicism and hedonism (Epicureanism), and an anthropocentric vision of the world, an evolution that culminated with Erasmus (1466–1536). The Humanists had a profound influence on the future of Europe, as they were the initiators who inspired the Protestant Reformation, modern "rationalist" philosophy and cosmopolitan utopias, right up to the Masonic lodges and the Revolution of the Rights of Man.

Alain Pascal's exposition in his work *La Renaissance, cette imposture (2006), La Guerre des Gnoses III*, Éditions des Cimes, Paris, 2021. (*The imposture of the Renaissance, The War of the Gnoses III*).

---

[724] His assassination highlights the betrayal of the group of initiates and their pacts.
[725] Common, accessible to the vulgar, as opposed to esoteric, elitist.

Other titles

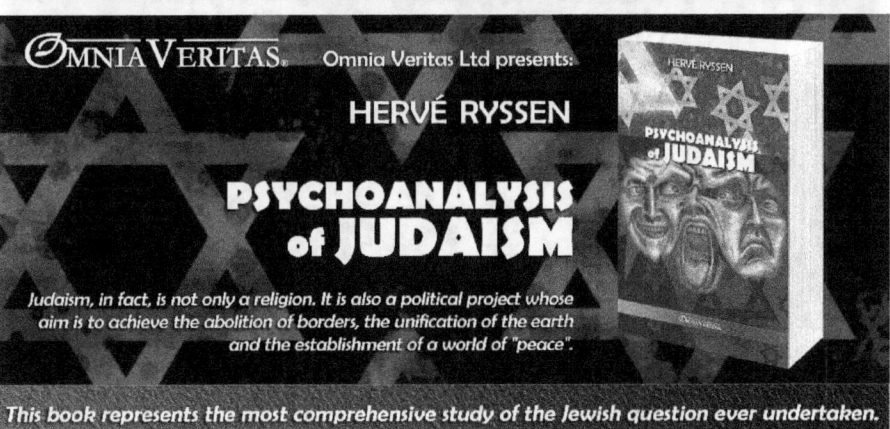

HISTORY OF ANTI-SEMITISM

OMNIA VERITAS

OMNIA VERITAS LTD PRESENTS:

SCARLET AND THE BEAST
ENGLISH FREEMASONRY, BANKS, AND THE ILLEGAL DRUG TRADE

English Freemasonry is wealthy and capitalistic, controlling the money and rulers of the world through banking and commerce. French Freemasonry, on the other hand, is poor and communistic, attempting to control state finances through an all-powerful socialistic government.

The Harlot's abominable cup is in the hands of English Freemasonry

OMNIA VERITAS® Omnia Veritas Ltd presents:

ARCHIBALD RAMSAY

THE NAMELESS WAR
THE JEWISH POWER AGAINST THE NATIONS

The author describes the anatomy of the machine of the Revolutionary International which today pursues the project of supranational world power, the age-old messianic dream of international Jewry...

Evidence of a centuries-old conspiracy against Europe and the whole of Christendom...

OMNIA VERITAS   Omnia Veritas Ltd presents:

"KILL THE BEST GENTILES!"
"Tob Shebbe Goyim Harog!"
(THE TALMUD: Sanhedrin 59)

JAMES VON BRUNN

WE ARE WITNESSING today on the world stage a tragedy of enormous proportions: the calculated destruction of the White Race and the incomparable culture it represents

The most concentrated attacks on the White Race are occurring in the United States of America

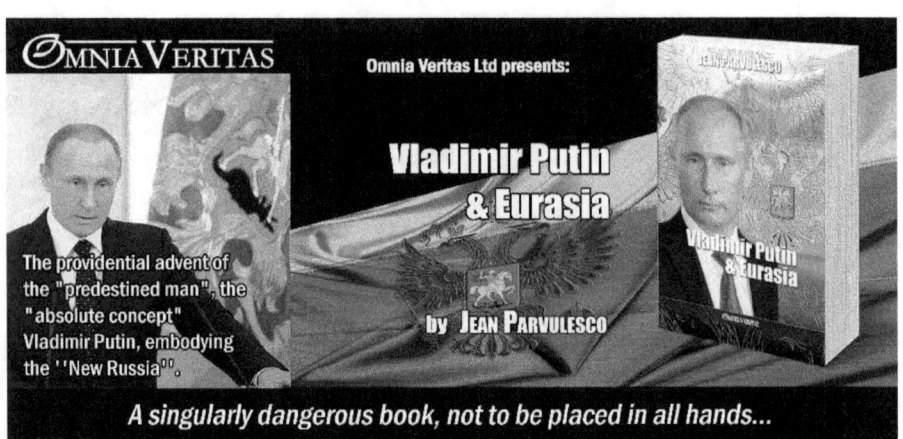
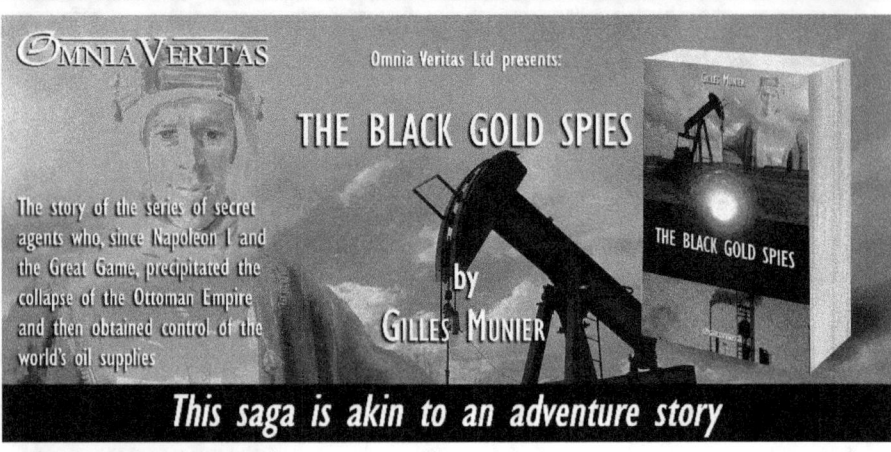
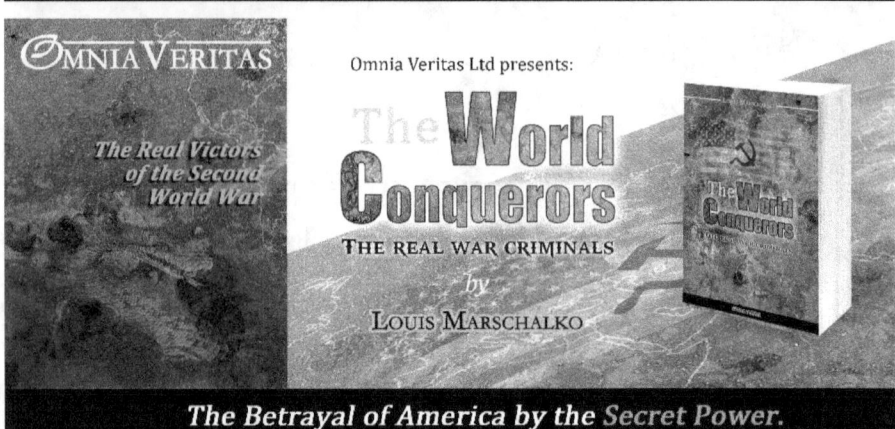

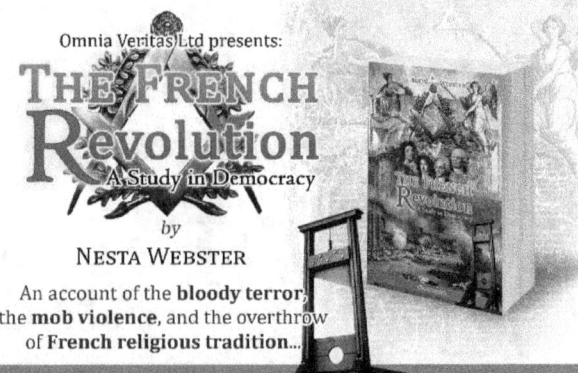

HISTORY OF ANTI-SEMITISM

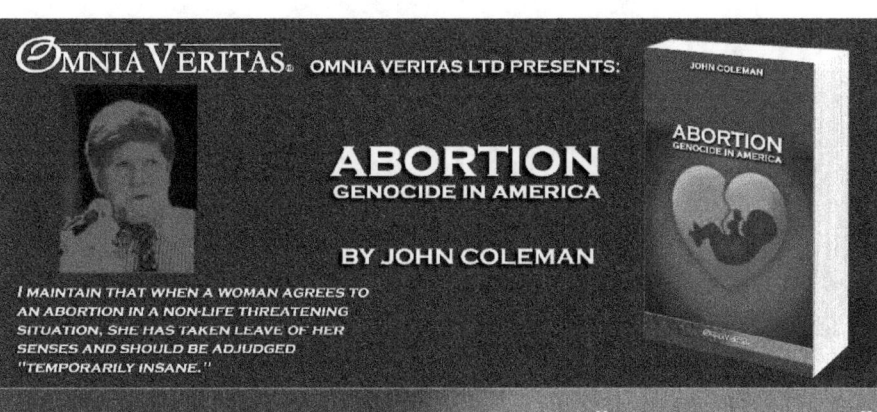

HISTORY OF ANTI-SEMITISM

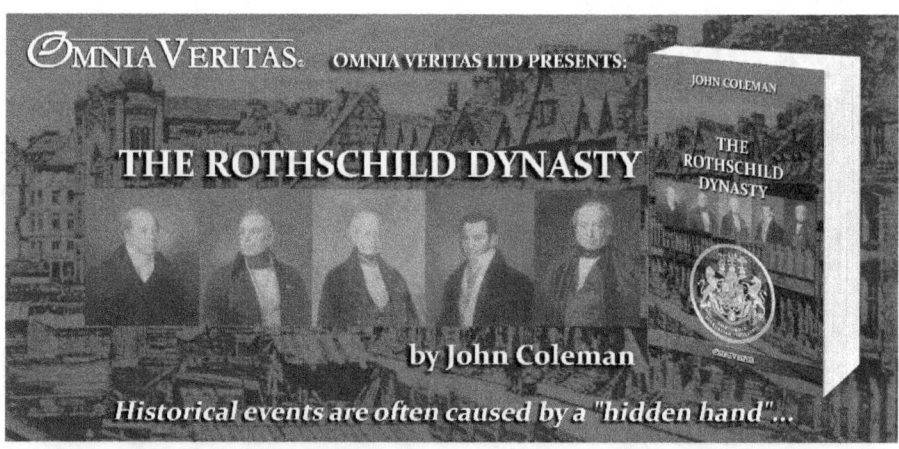

www.ingramcontent.com/pod-product-compliance
Lightning Source LLC
Chambersburg PA
CBHW050324230426
43663CB00010B/1735